Whitney Biennial 2019

WHITNEY MUSEUM OF AMERICAN ART
NEW YORK

DISTRIBUTED BY YALE UNIVERSITY PRESS
NEW HAVEN AND LONDON

Works

2019

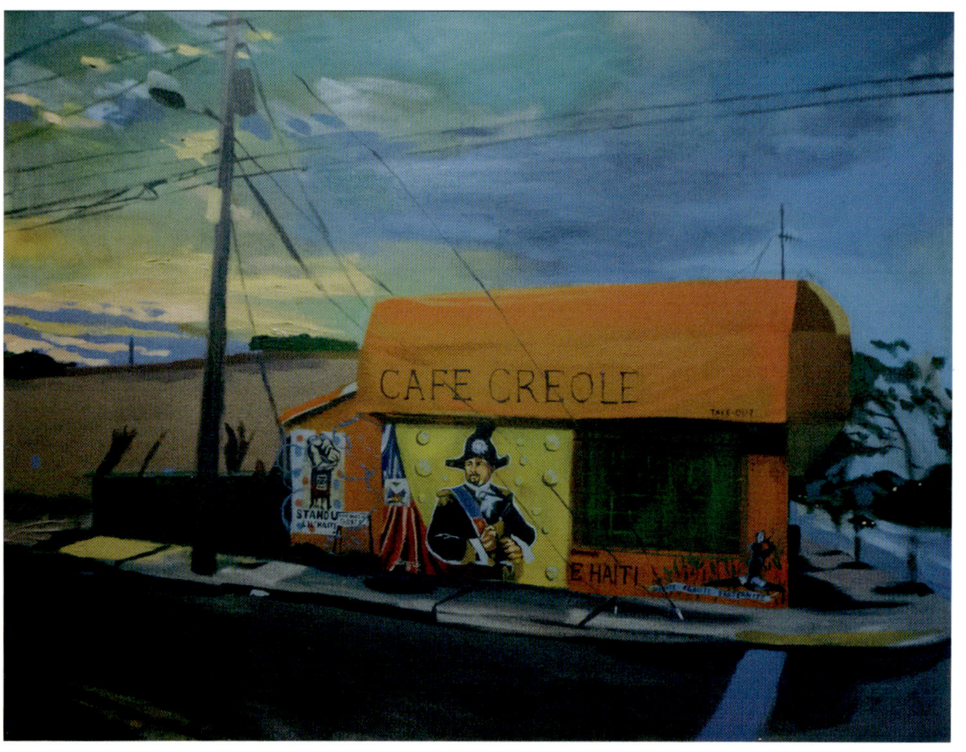

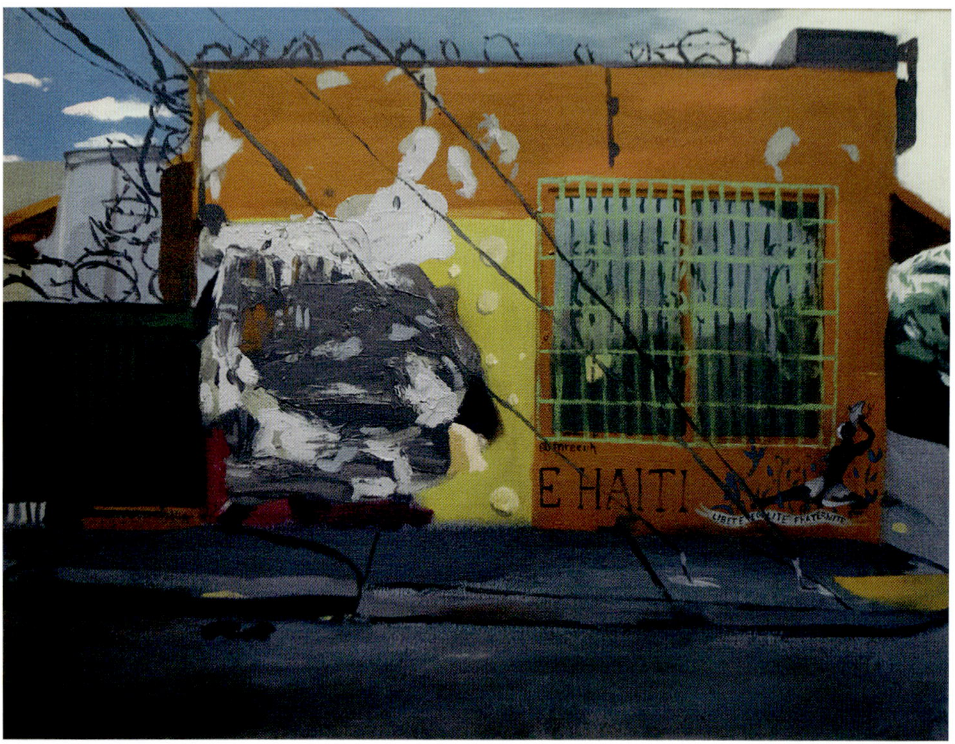

Eddie Arroyo, *5825 NE 2nd Ave., Miami, FL 33137,* 2016. Acrylic on canvas, 36 × 48 in. (91.4 × 121.9 cm). *5825 NE 2nd Ave., Miami, FL 33137,* 2017. Acrylic on canvas, 28 × 36 in. (71.1 × 91.4 cm).

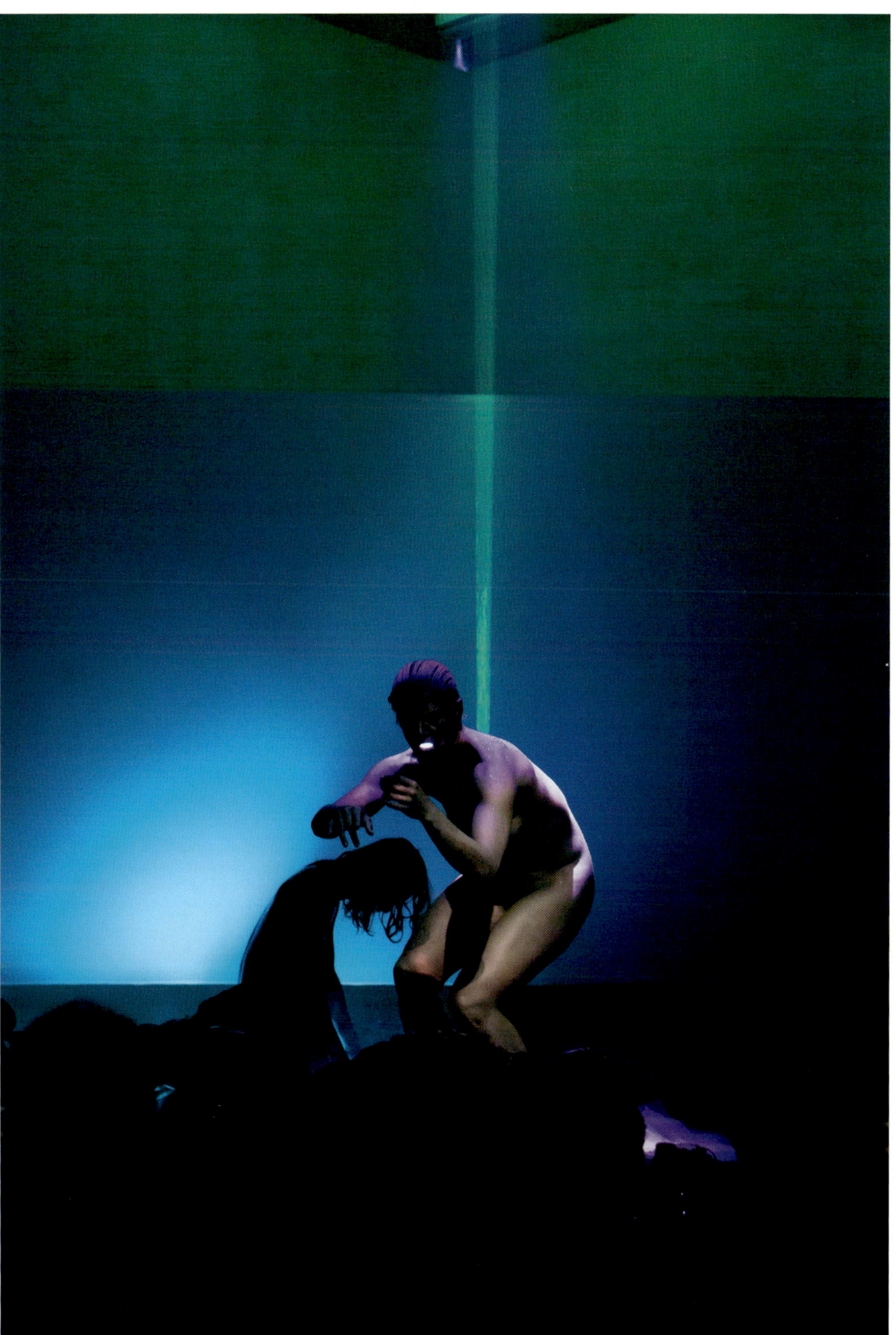

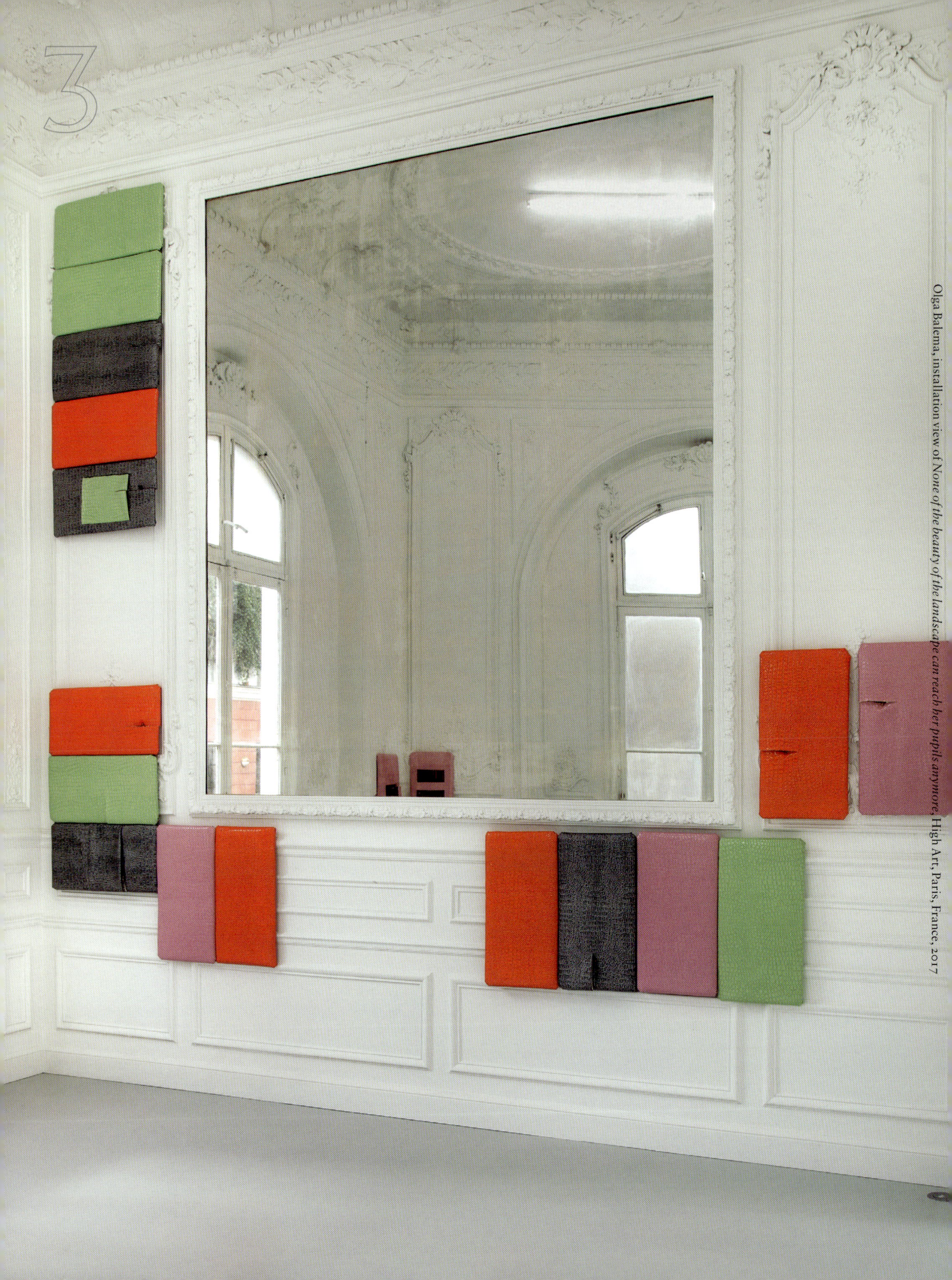

Olga Balema, installation view of *None of the beauty of the landscape can reach her pupils anymore*, High Art, Paris, France, 2017

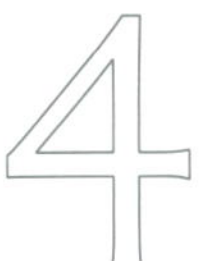

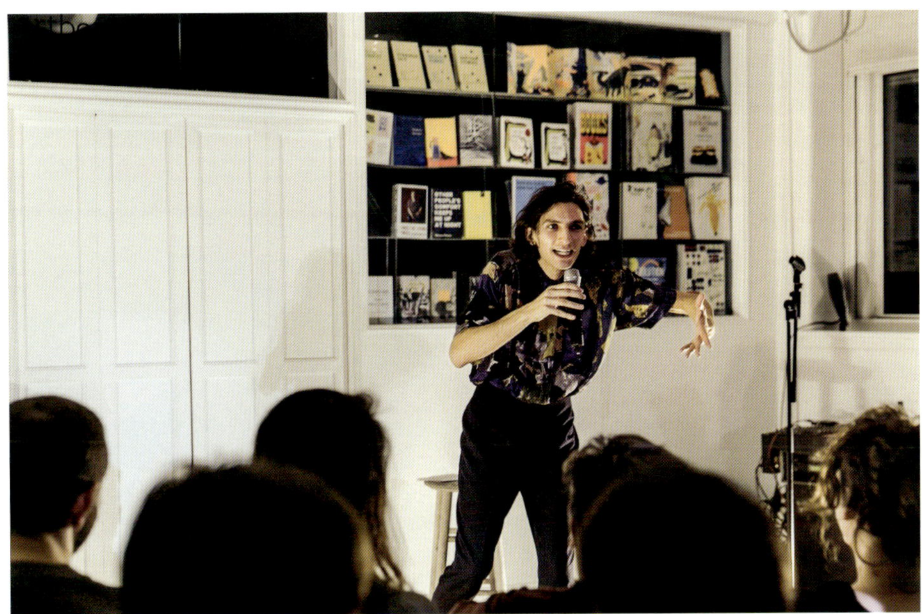

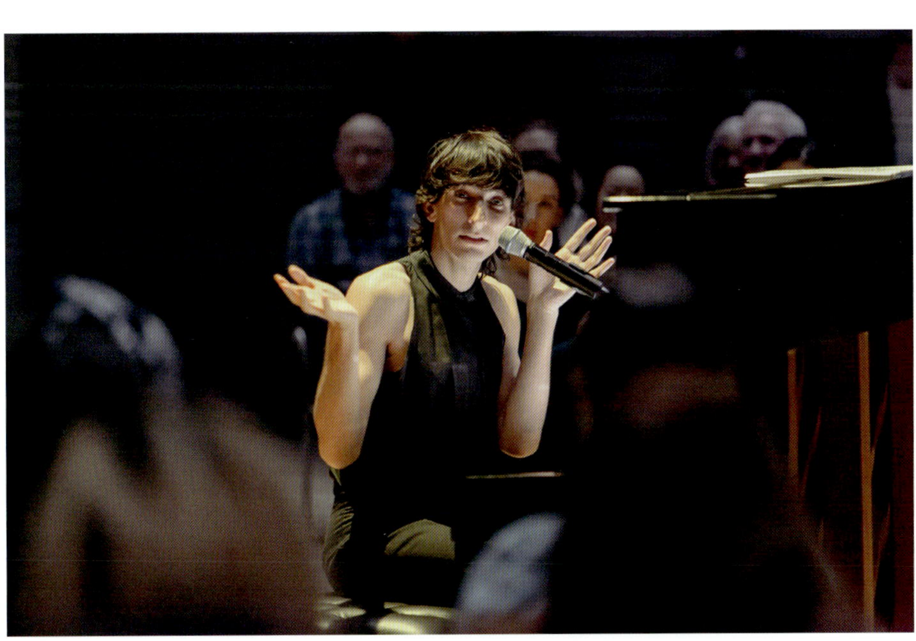

Morgan Bassichis, *Me, but Also Everybody! (Part II)*, 2017. Performance view, *Greater New York*, MoMA PS1, Queens, NY, 2015. Study Sessions: Morgan Bassichis, 2018. Performance view, Whitney Museum of American Art, New York, NY, 2018

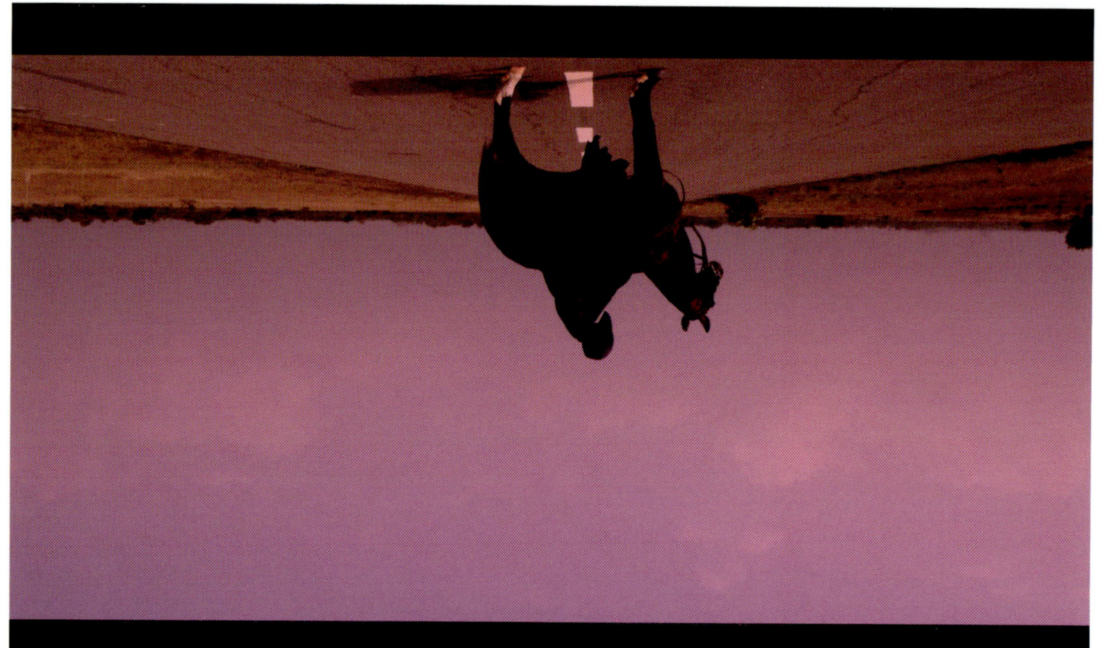

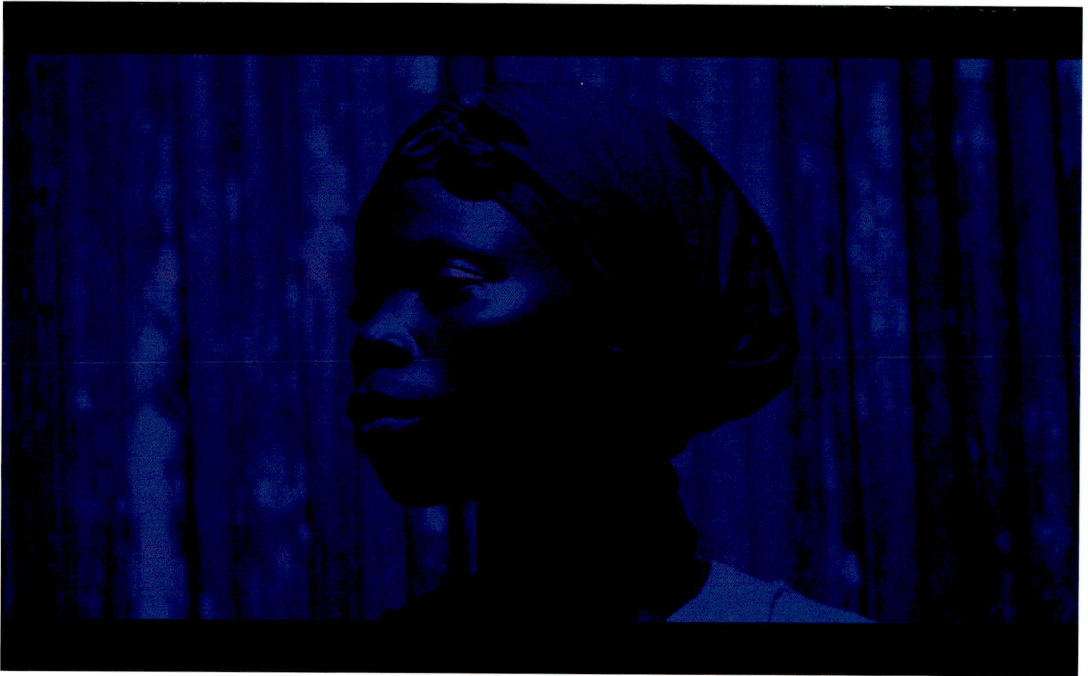

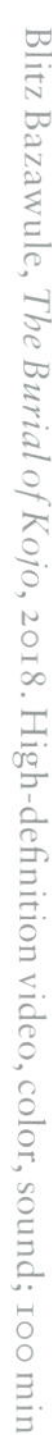
Blitz Bazawule, *The Burial of Kojo*, 2018. High-definition video, color, sound; 100 min.

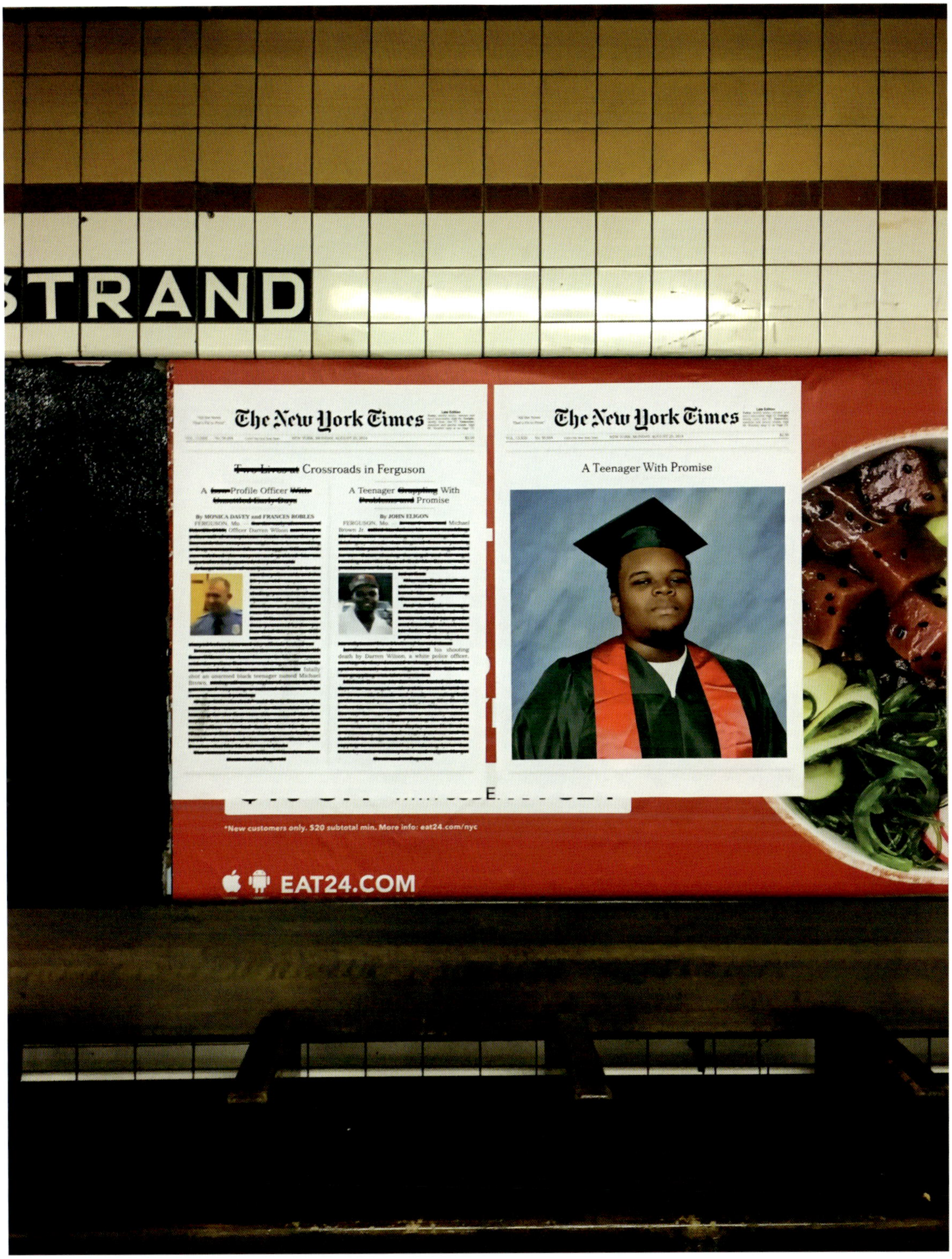

Alexandra Bell, *A Teenager With Promise*, 2017. Two inkjet prints on vinyl, 24 × 32 in. (61 × 81.3 cm) each

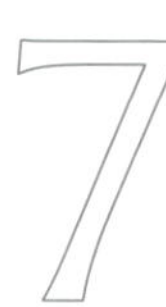

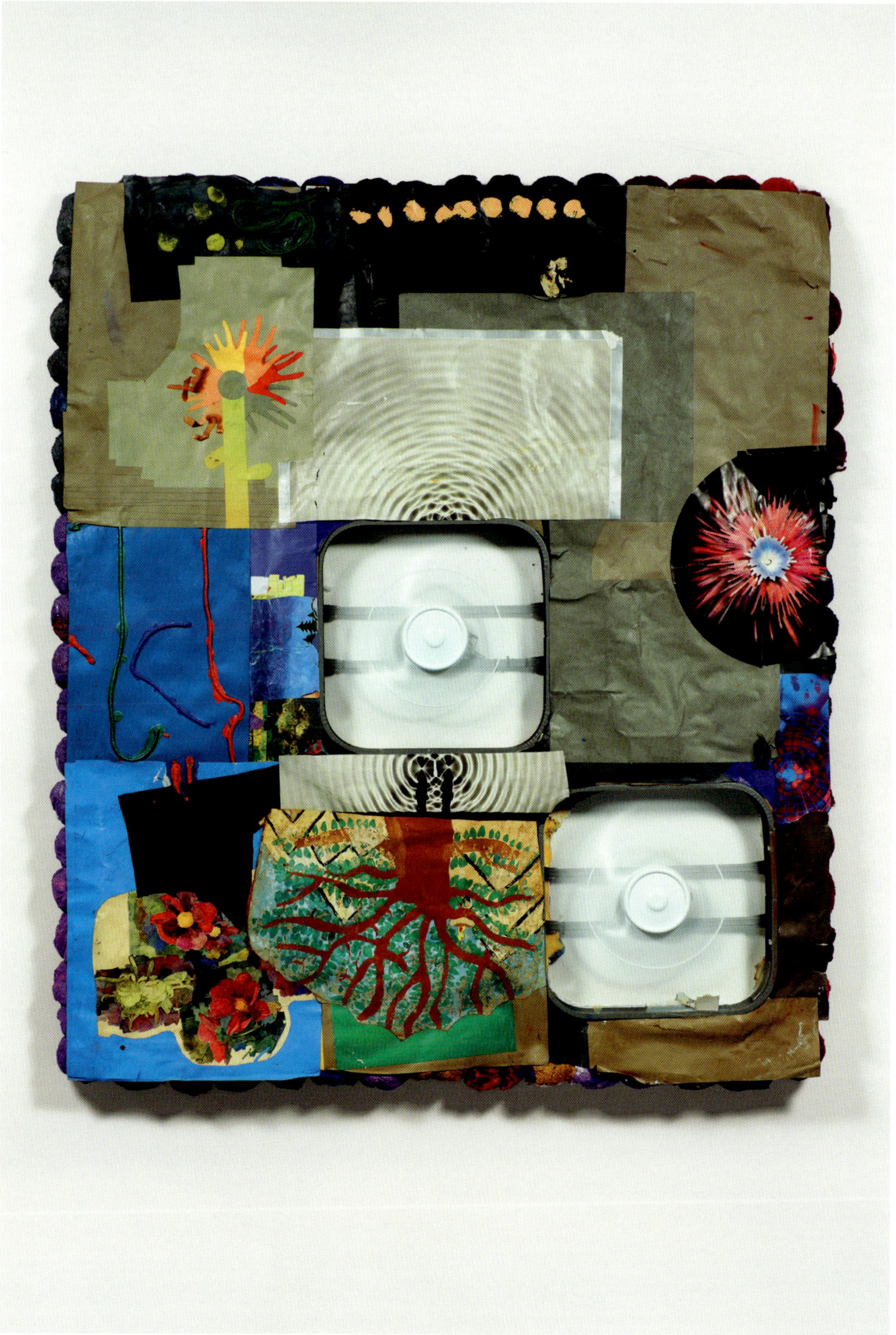

Brian Belott, *Untitled*, 2016. Paper, cotton batting, box fans, acrylic paint, rope, found children's mural, and pop-up book elements, 80 × 70 × 4 in. (203.2 × 177.8 × 10.2 cm)

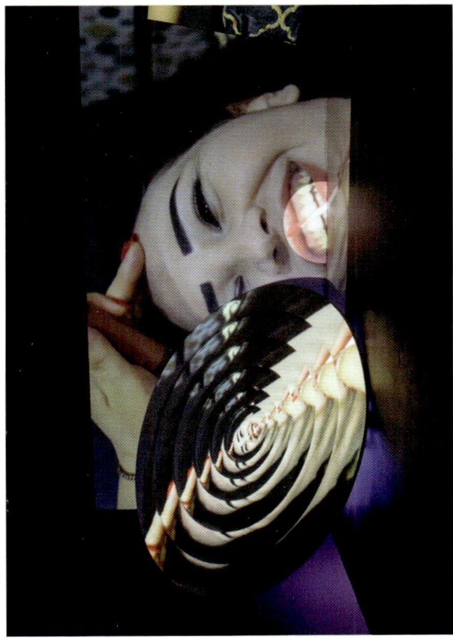

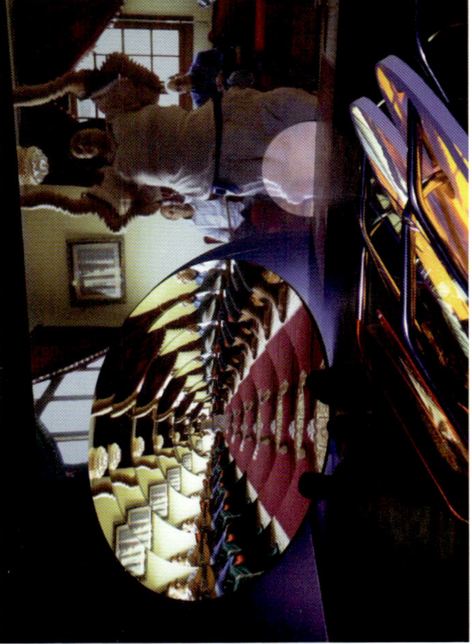

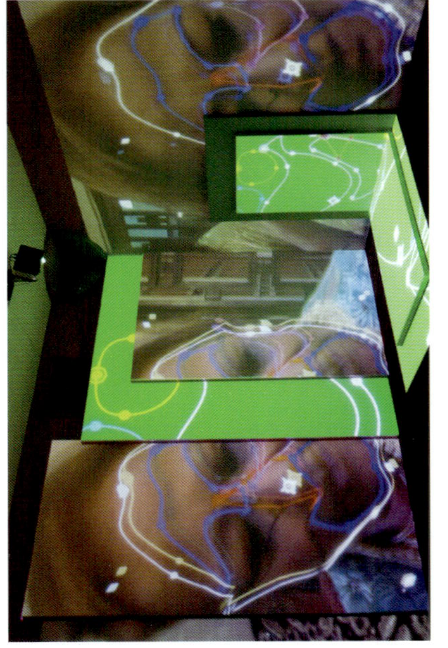

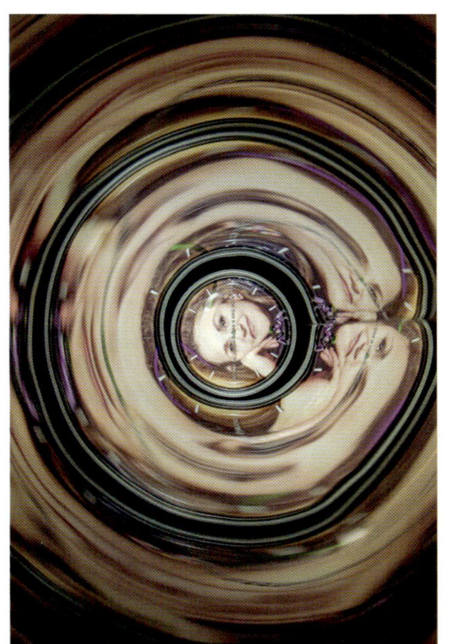

Works by Meriem Bennani. Top row: *Siham & Hafida*, 2017. Six-channel digital video installation, color, sound; 30 min. (looped). Installation view, The Kitchen, New York, NY, 2017.
Bottom left: *FLY*, 2016. Twelve-channel digital video installation, color, sound; 17:33 min. (looped). Installation view, MoMA PS1, Queens, NY, 2016.
Bottom right: *Ghariba (Stranger)*, 2017. Four-channel digital video installation, color, sound; 22:47 min. (looped); and custom sculptures. Installation view, Art Dubai, United Arab Emirates, 2017

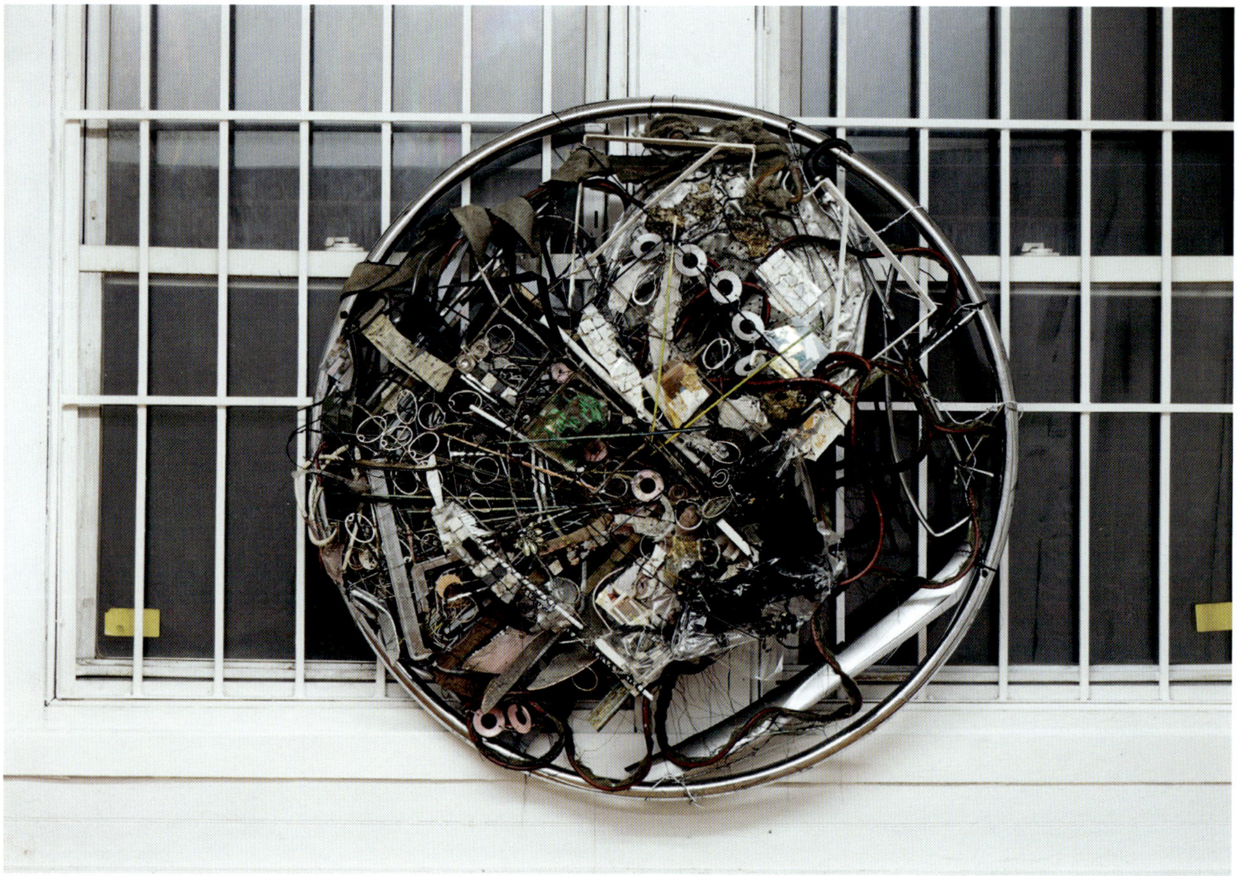

Robert Bittenbender, *Soulful Gardener*, 2016. Aluminum, plastic, wood, glass, and dry gourds, 46 × 46 × 15 in. (116.8 × 116.8 × 38.1 cm). Private collection

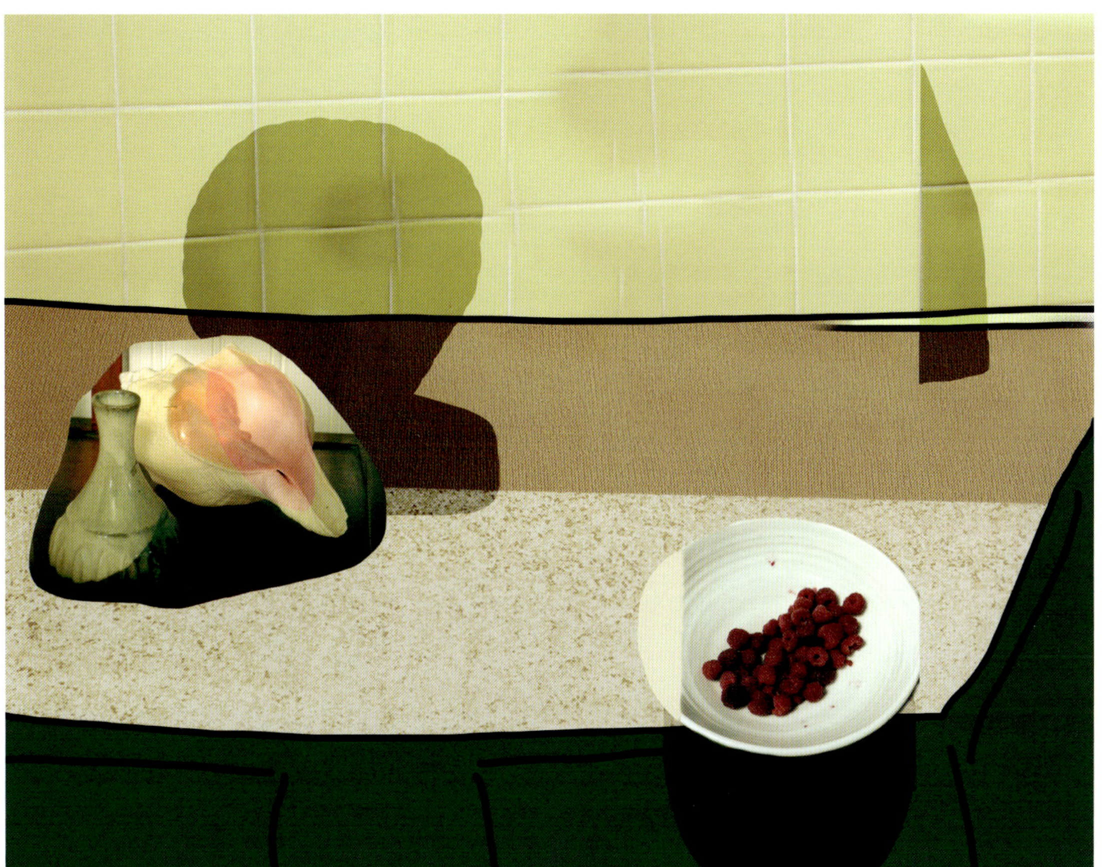

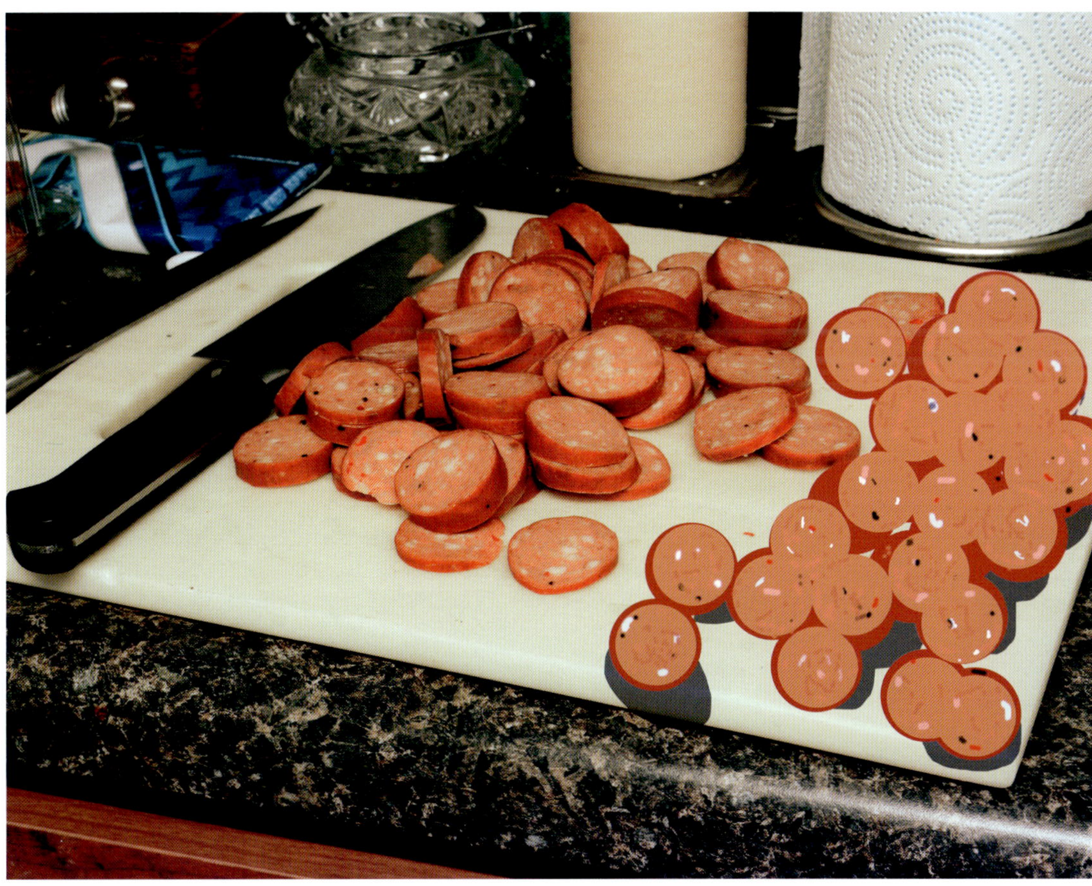

Lucas Blalock, *Conch and berries and*, 2015–17. Inkjet print, 32½ × 40½ in. (82.6 × 102.9 cm). *Double Recipe*, 2015–16. Inkjet print, 20½ × 25¼ in. (52.1 × 64.1 cm)

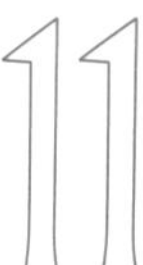

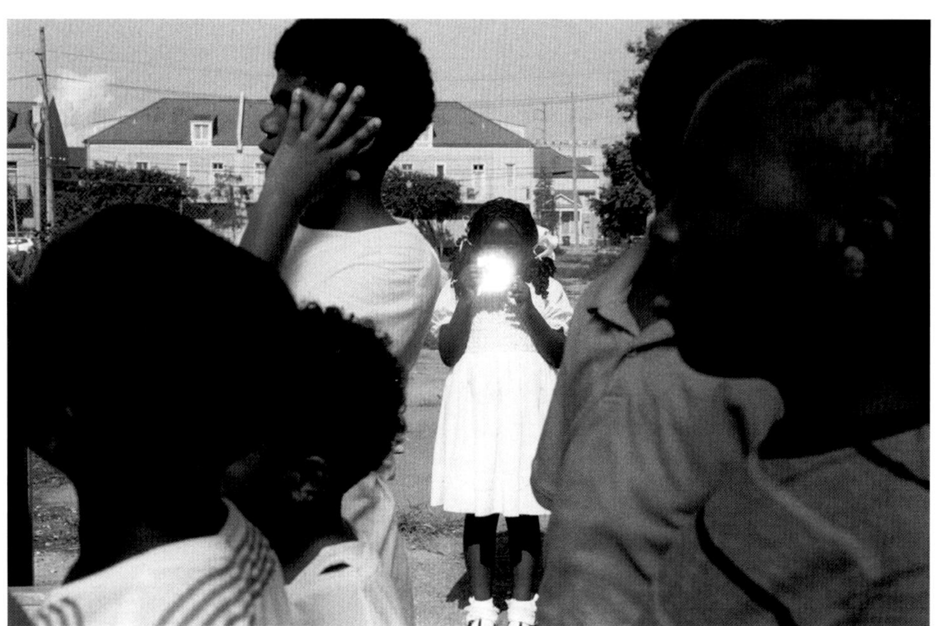

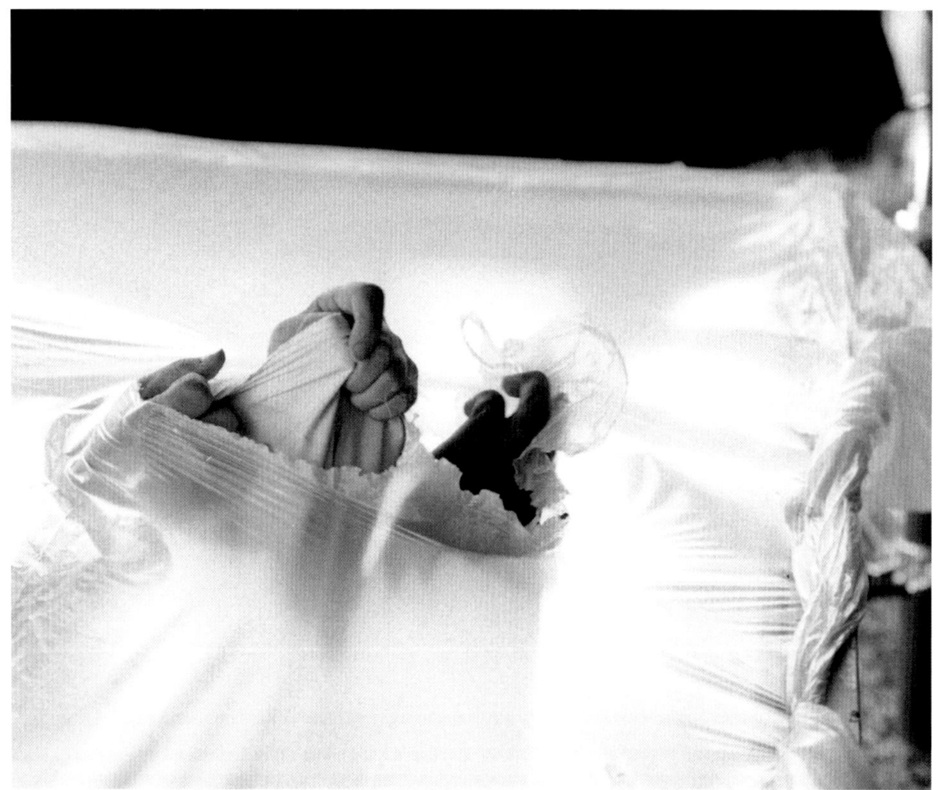

Garrett Bradley, *1928: Ball*, 2018. 35mm film transferred to high-definition video, black-and-white, sound; 2 min.
1915: The White Sheet (Hands), 2018. 35mm film transferred to high-definition video, black-and-white, sound; 2 min.

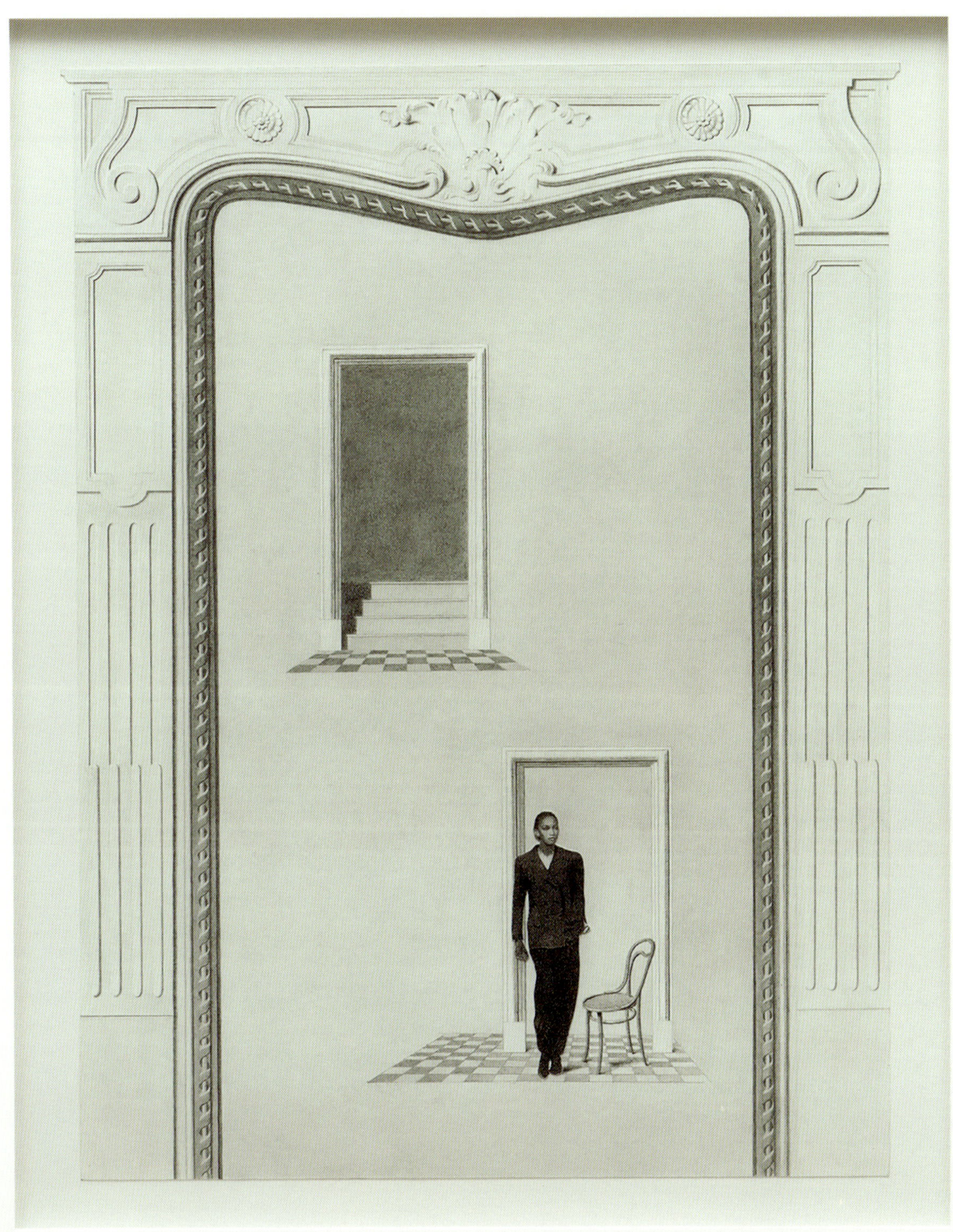

Milano Chow, *Entryway (Opening, Ground)*, 2018. Graphite, ink, vinyl paint, and photo transfer on paper, 20 × 15 in. (50.8 × 38.1 cm). Private collection

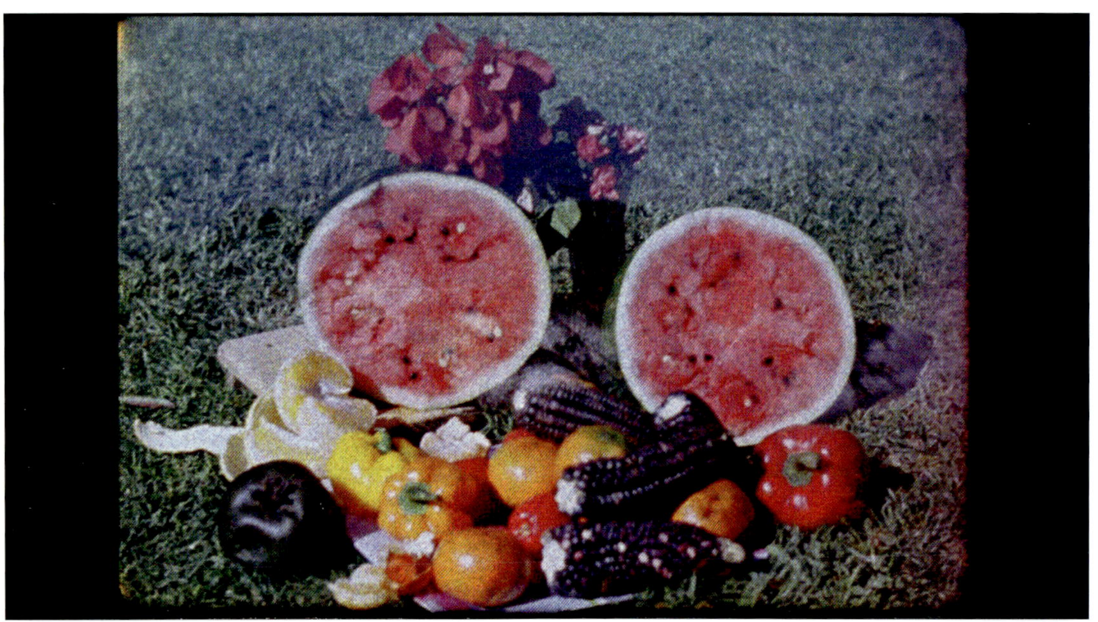

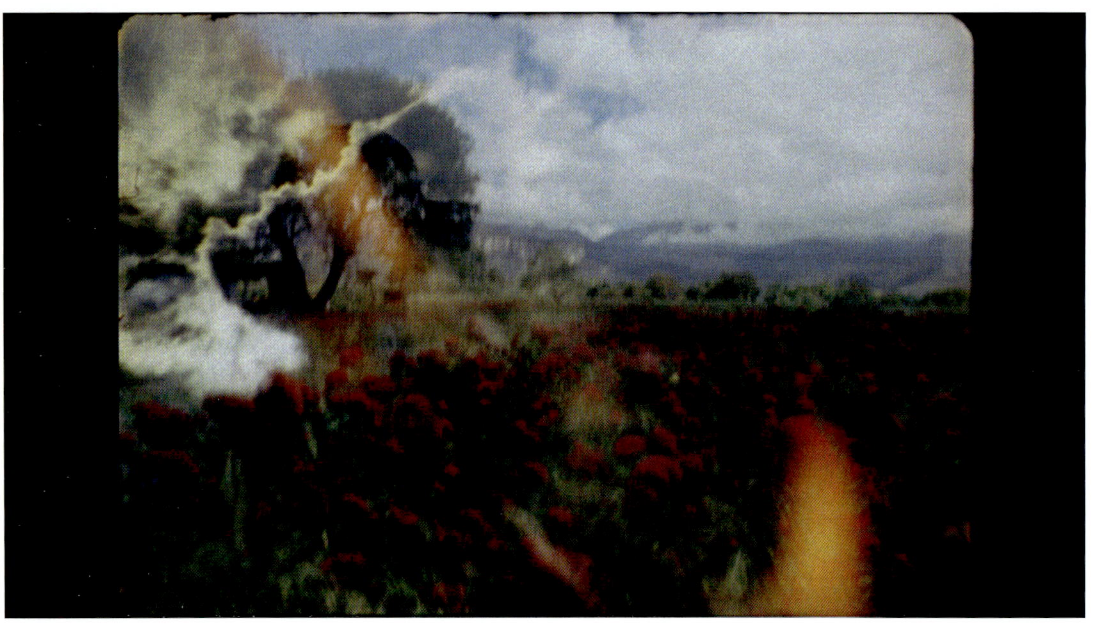

Colectivo Los Ingrávidos, *The Sun Quartet, Part 1: Sun Stone*, 2017. 16mm film, color, sound; 8:24 min. *The Sun Quartet, Part 4: Far from Ayotzinapa*, 2017. 16mm film, color, sound; 22:35 min.

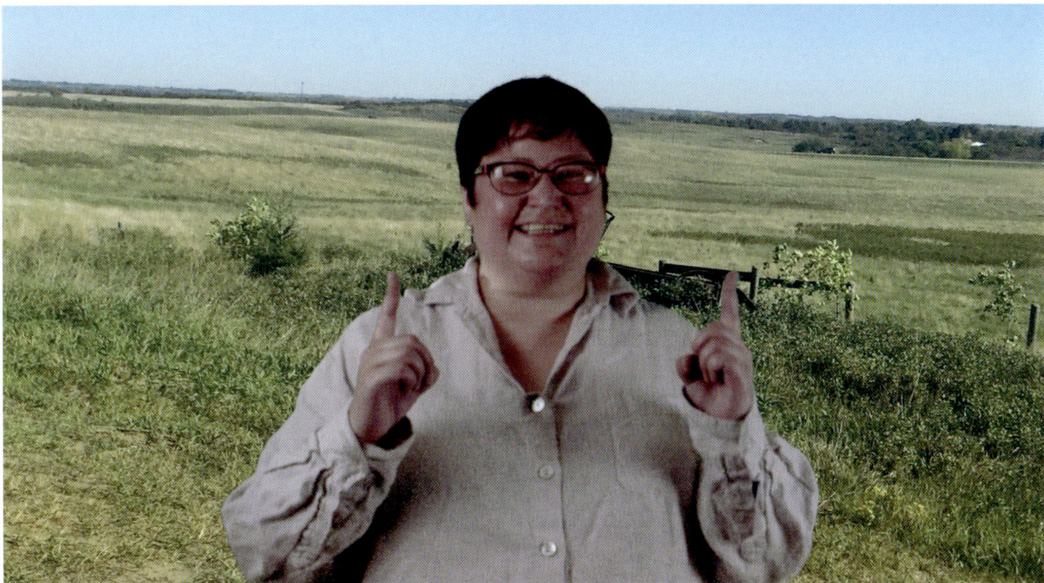

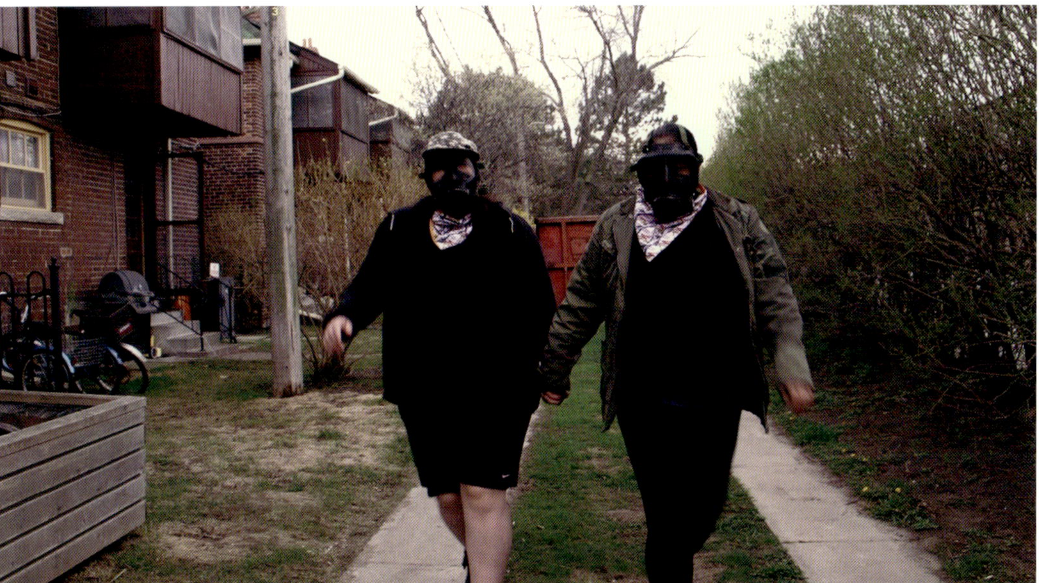

Thirza Cuthand. 2 *Spirit Introductory Special $19.99*, 2015. High-definition video, color, sound; 4:27 min. *Reclamation*, 2018. High-definition video, color, sound; 13:11 min.

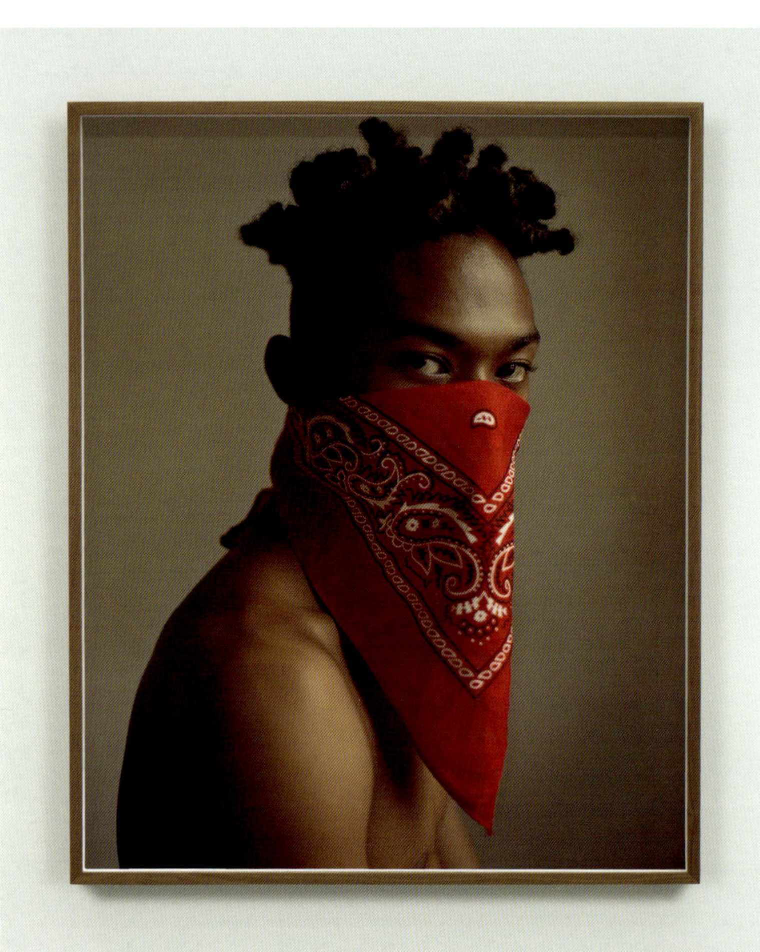

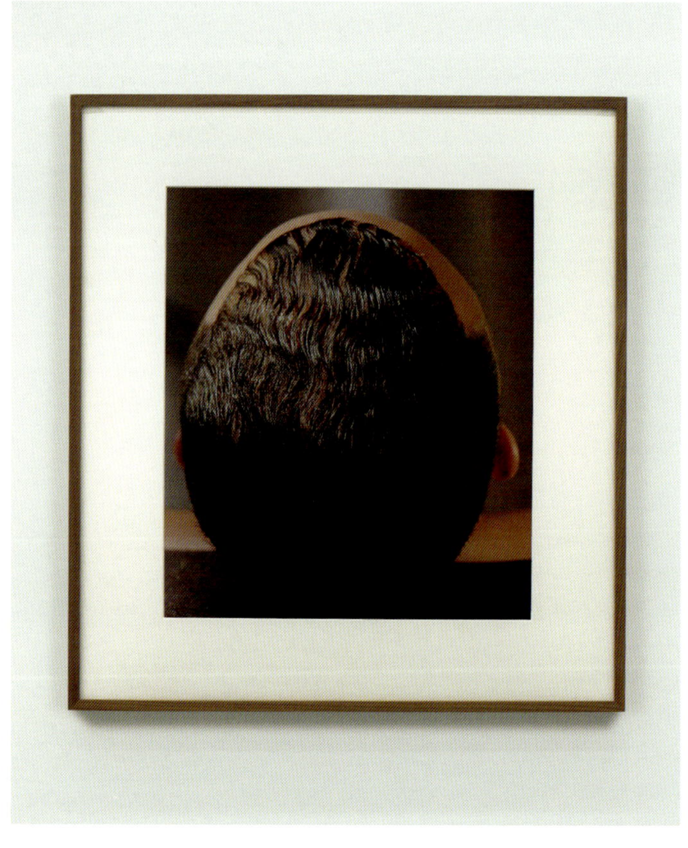

John Edmonds, *The Villain*, 2018. Inkjet print, 30 × 24 in. (76.2 × 61 cm). *Untitled (Head I)*, 2018. Inkjet print, 20 × 16 in. (50.8 × 40.6 cm)

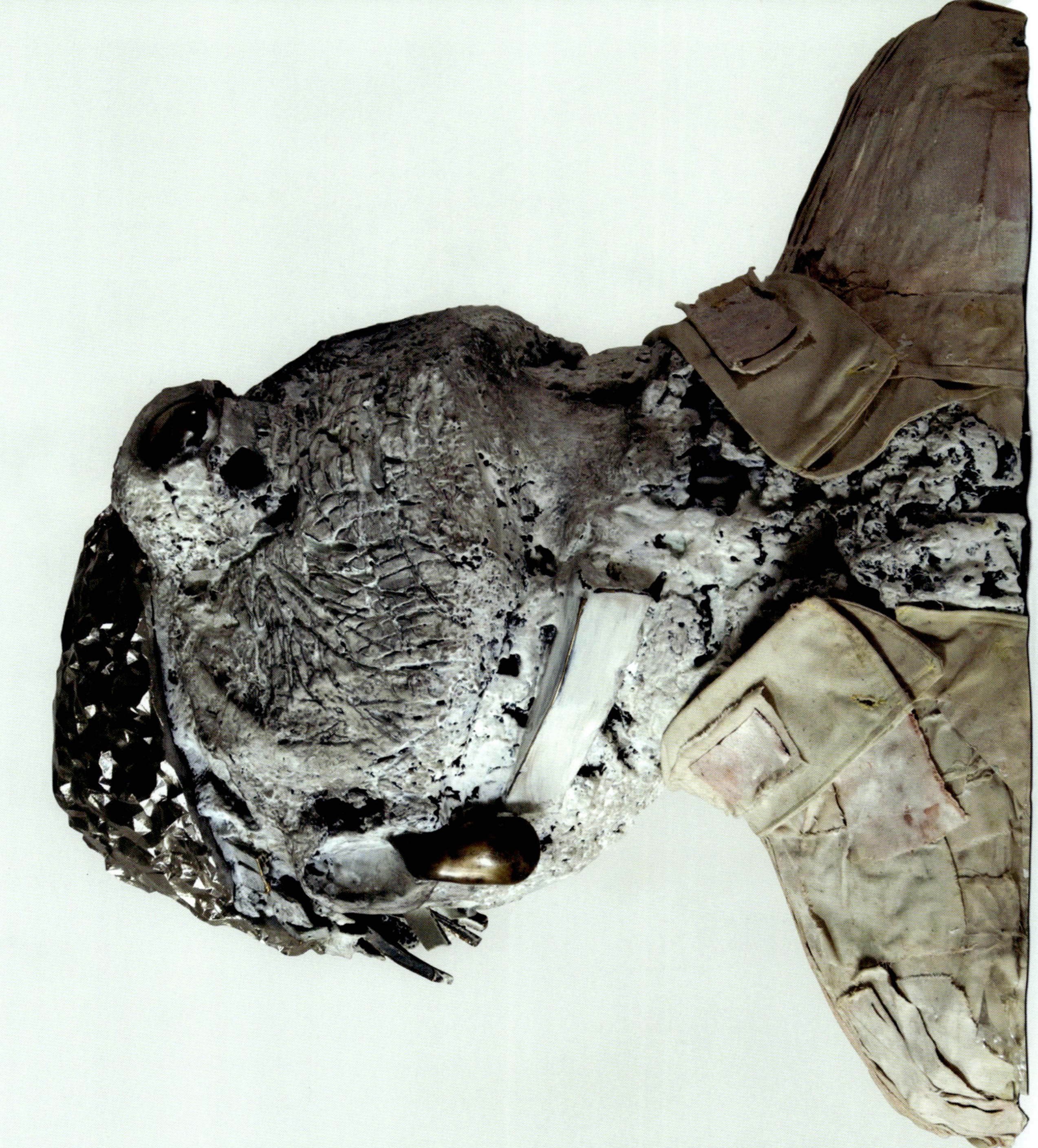

Nicole Eisenman, *The General*, 2018. Bronze, stainless steel, paint, and fabric, 30 × 33 × 19 in. (76.2 × 83.8 × 48.3 cm). Collection of Eric Green

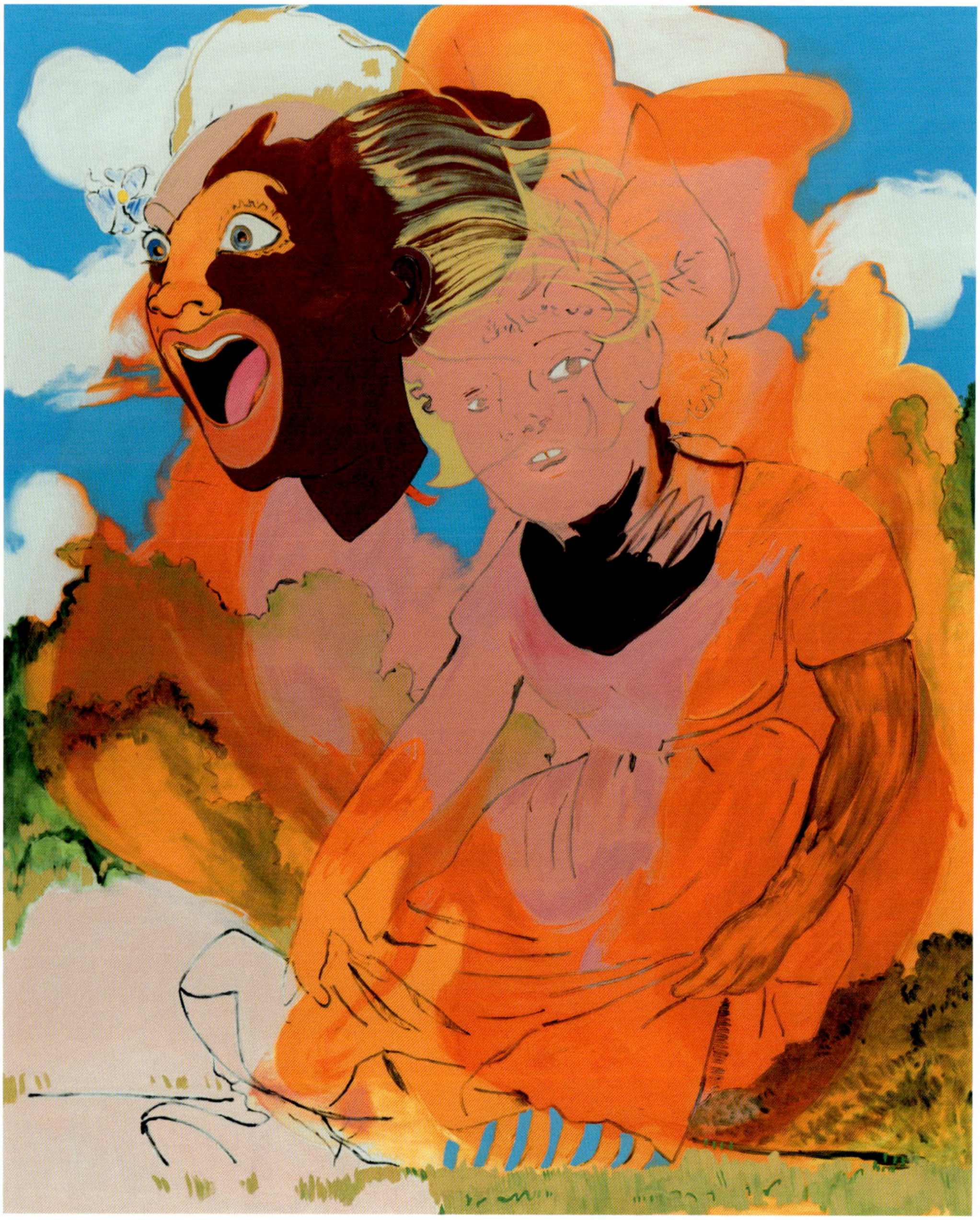

Janiva Ellis, *Thrill Issues*, 2017. Oil on canvas, 95 × 77 in. (241.3 × 195.6 cm). Rubell Family Collection, Miami

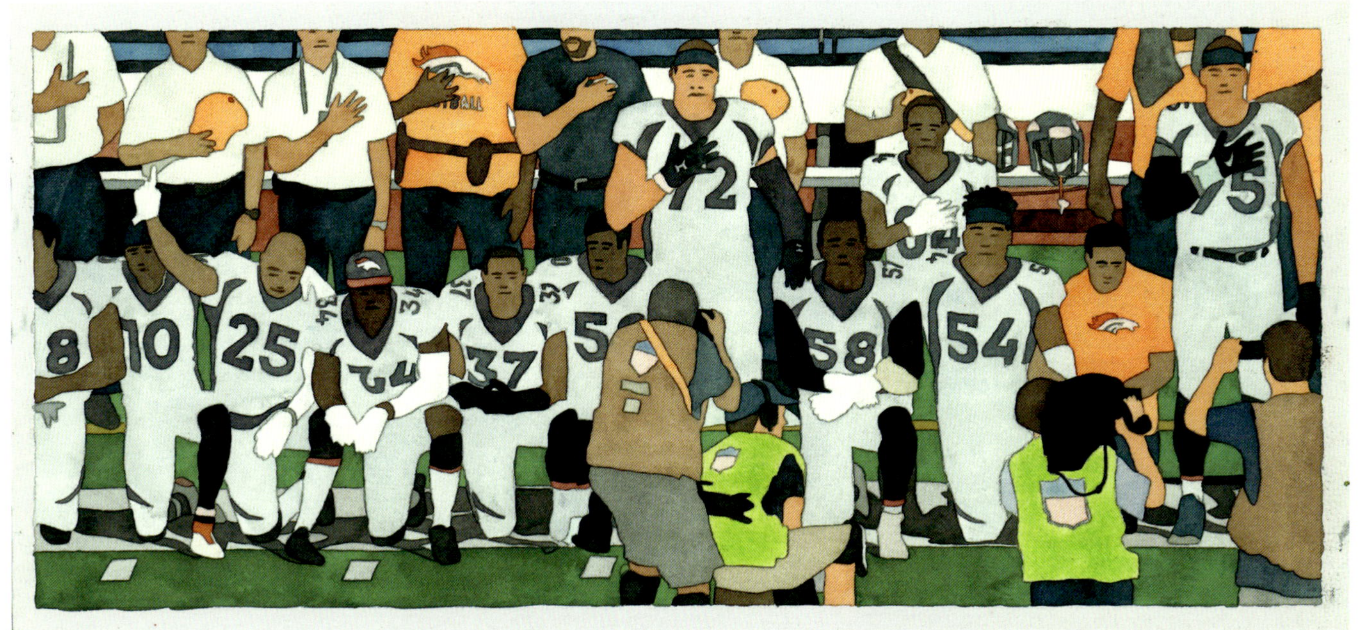

Kota Ezawa, *National Anthem (Denver Broncos)*, 2018. Watercolor on paper, 9 × 19 in. (22.9 × 48.3 cm)

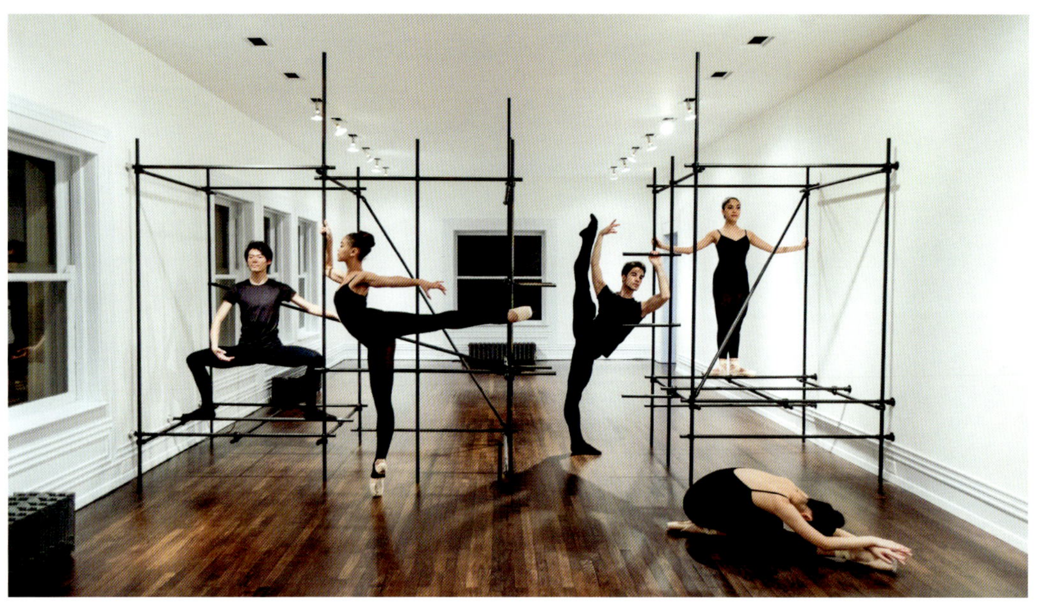

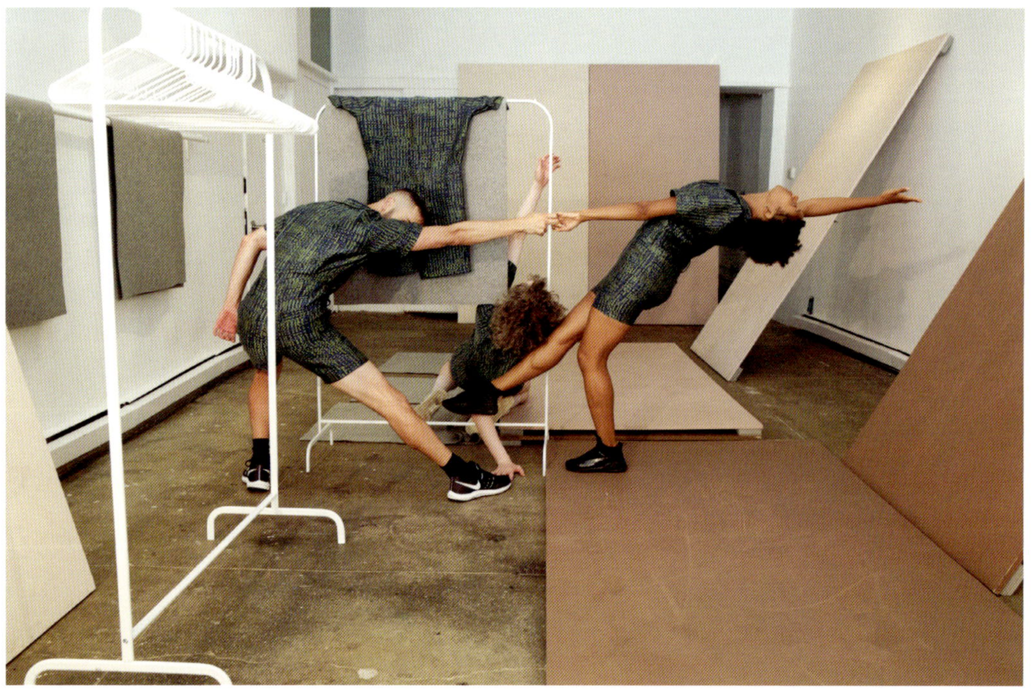

Brendan Fernandes, *The Master and Form*, 2018. Performance view, Graham Foundation, Chicago, IL, 2018. *Hit Back*, 2017. Performance view, Recess, New York, NY, 2017

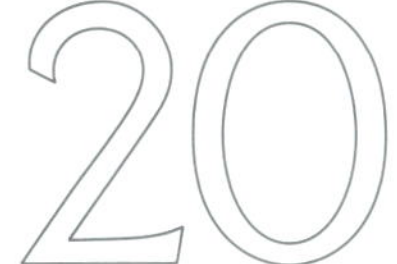

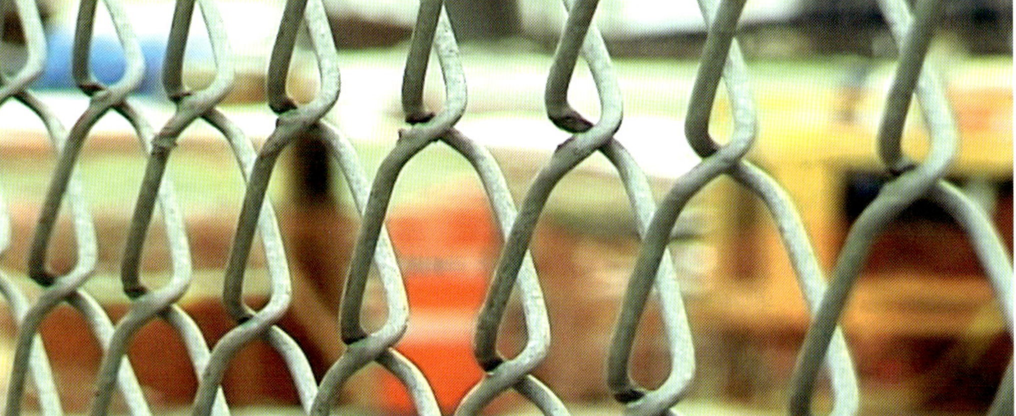

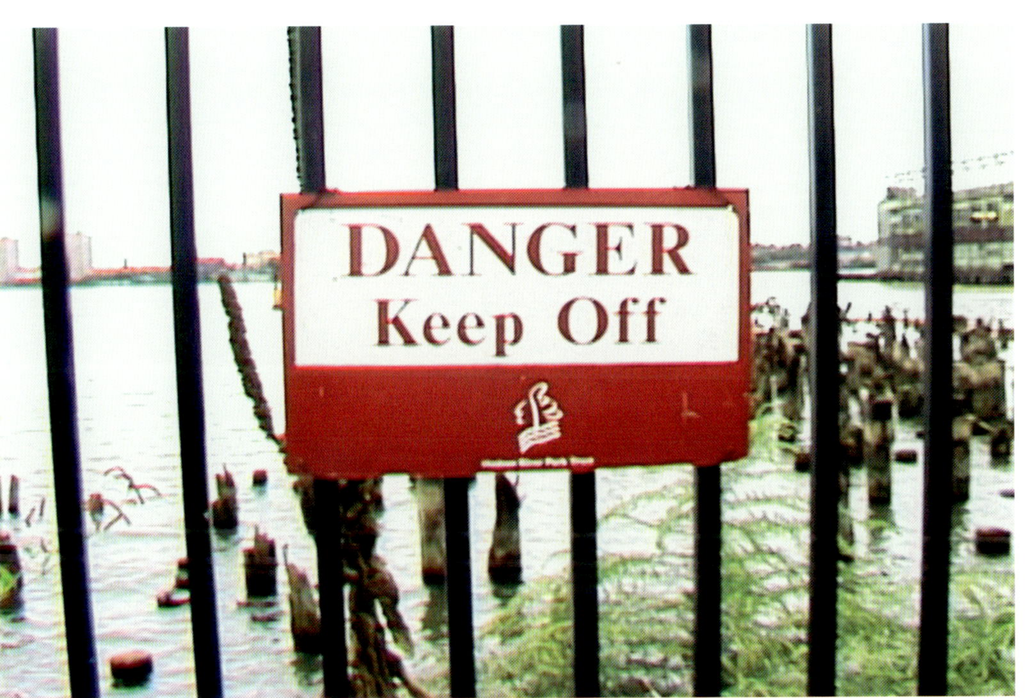

FIERCE and Paper Tiger Television, *Fenced Out*, 2001. Video, color, sound; 20:24 min.

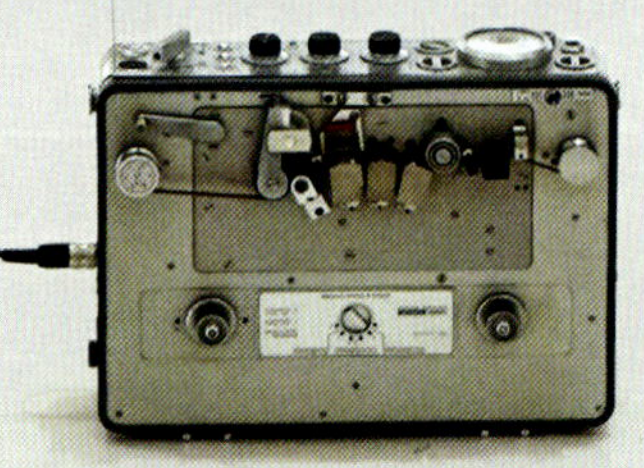

Marcus Fischer, *Untitled (Words of Concern)*, 2017. Tape recorder, tape loop, spindle, and sound; 3 min., overall dimensions variable

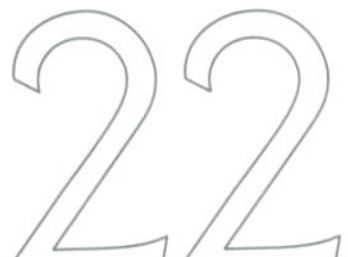

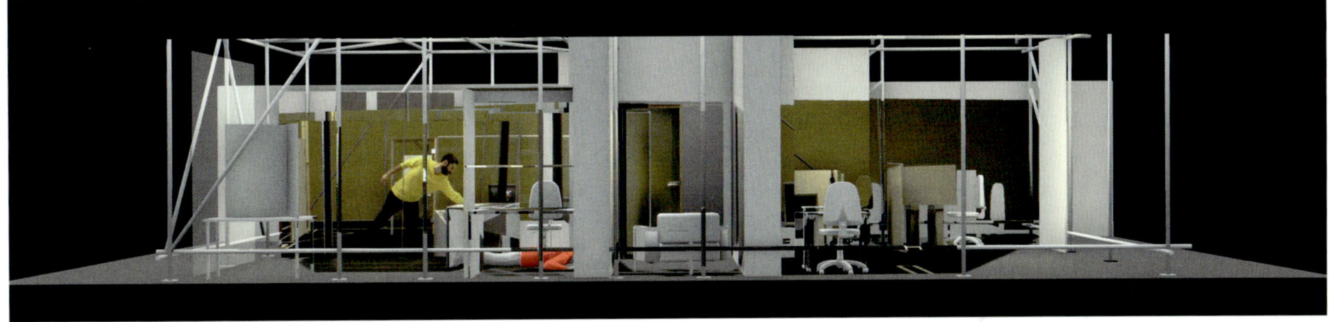

Forensic Architecture, *77sqm_9:26min* (detail), 2017. Three-channel high-definition video, color, sound; 28:55 min.

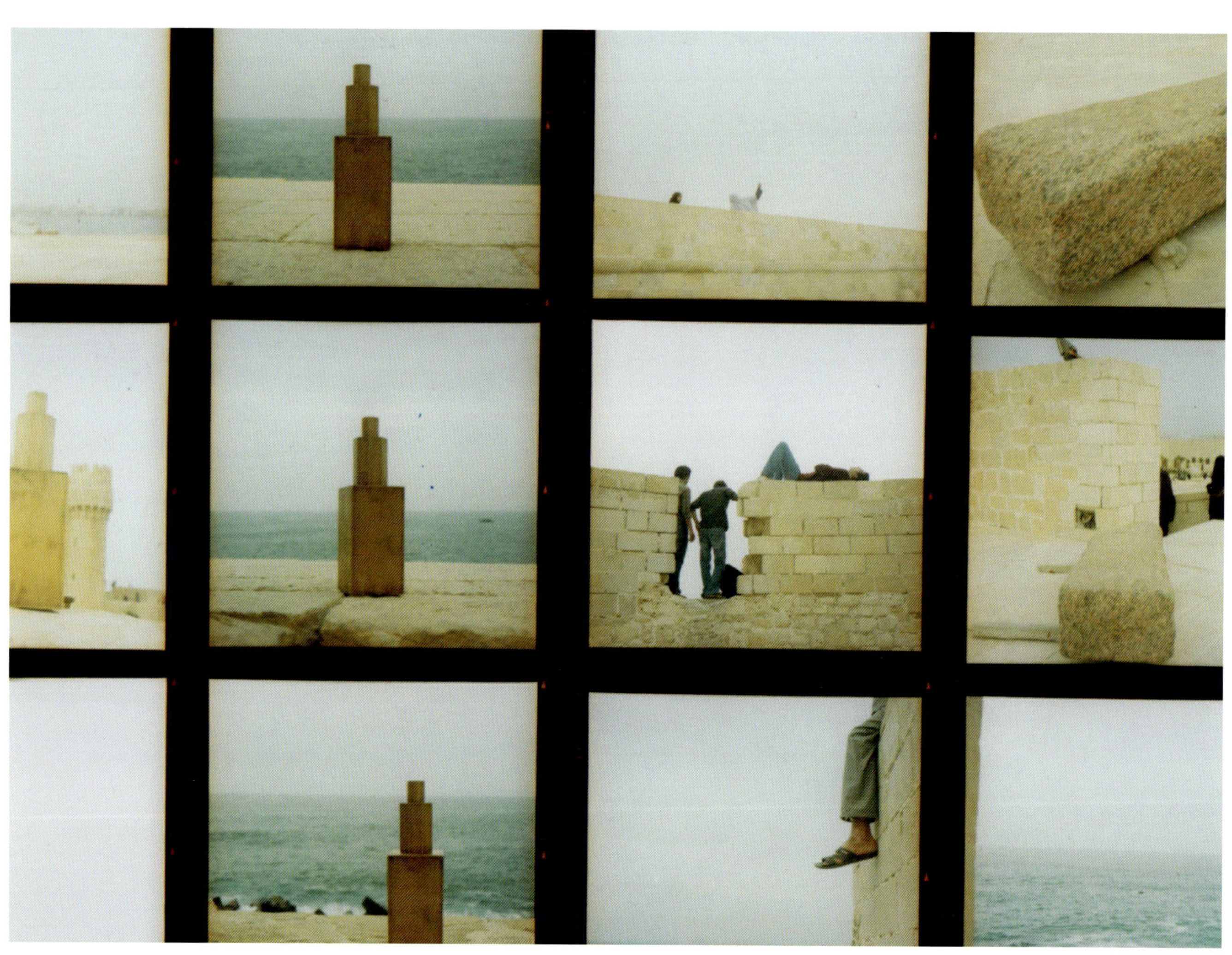

Ellie Ga, *Eureka, a Lighthouse Play* (detail), 2014. Contact sheet, 8 × 10 in. (20.3 × 25.4 cm)

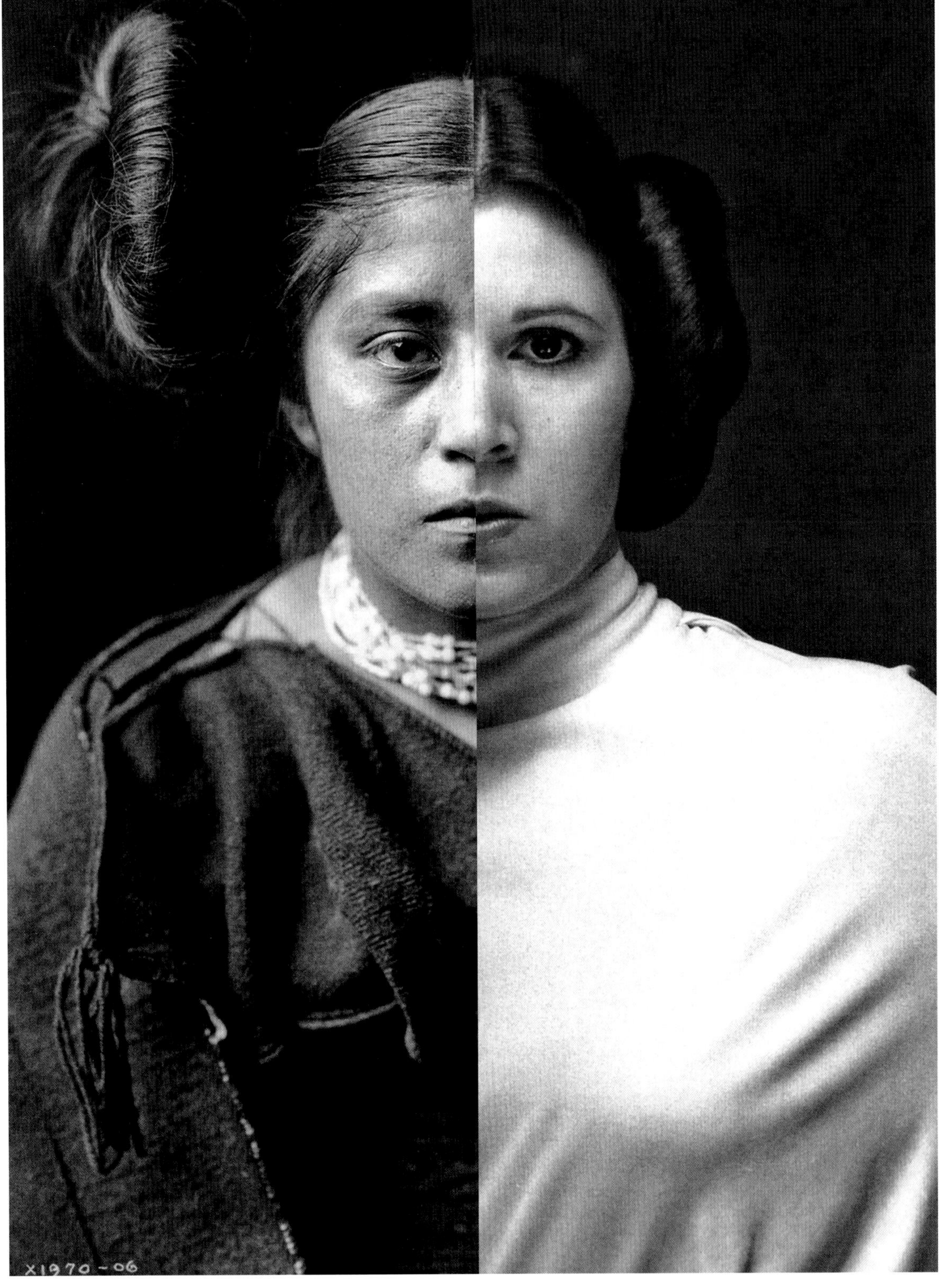

Nicholas Galanin, *Things Are Looking Native, Native's Looking Whiter*, 2012. Inkjet print, 15 ½ × 20 ¼ in. (39.4 × 51.4 cm)

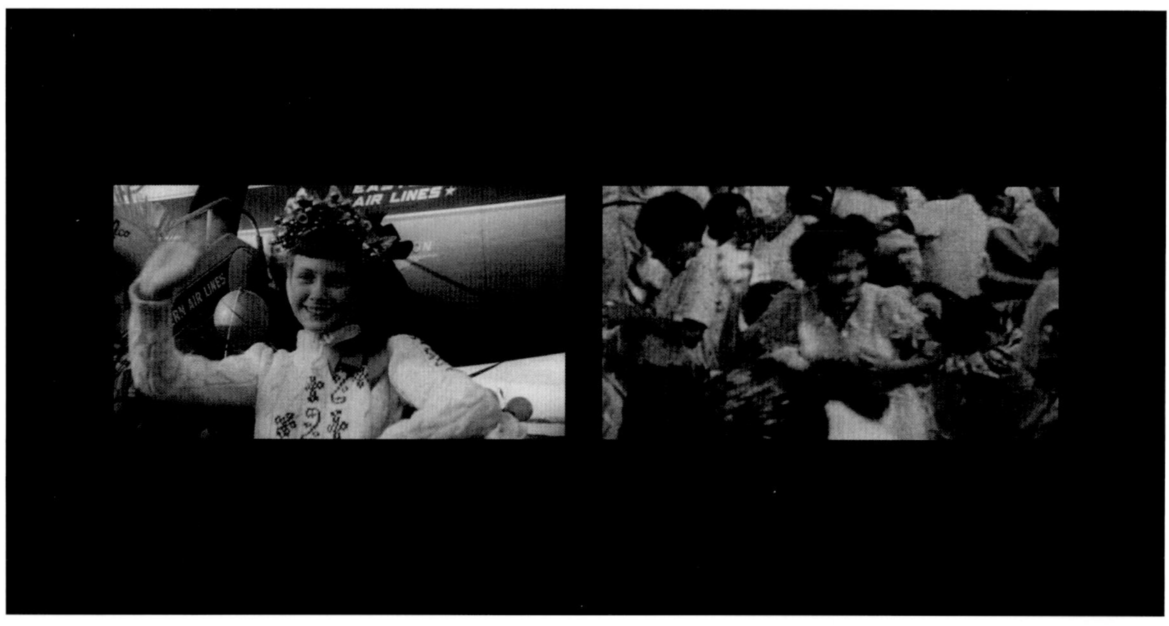

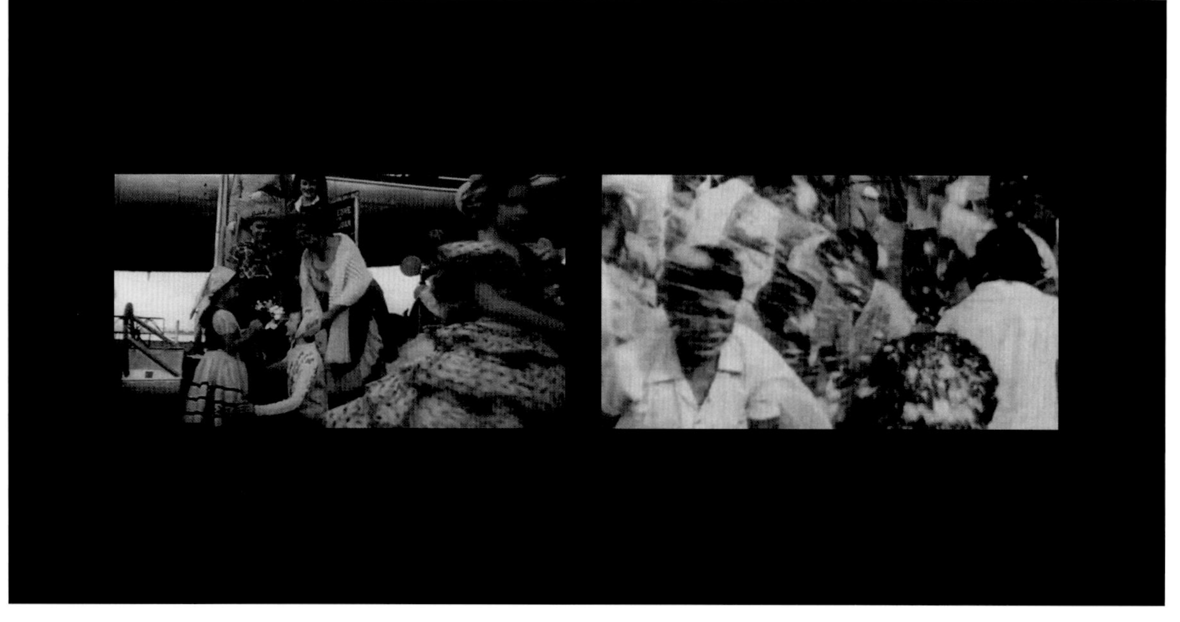

Sofía Gallisá Muriente, *Lluvia con nieve* (*Rain with Snow*), 2014. Two-channel video, black-and-white, sound, 13:32 min.

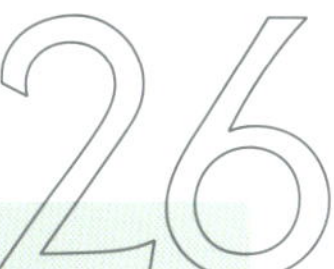

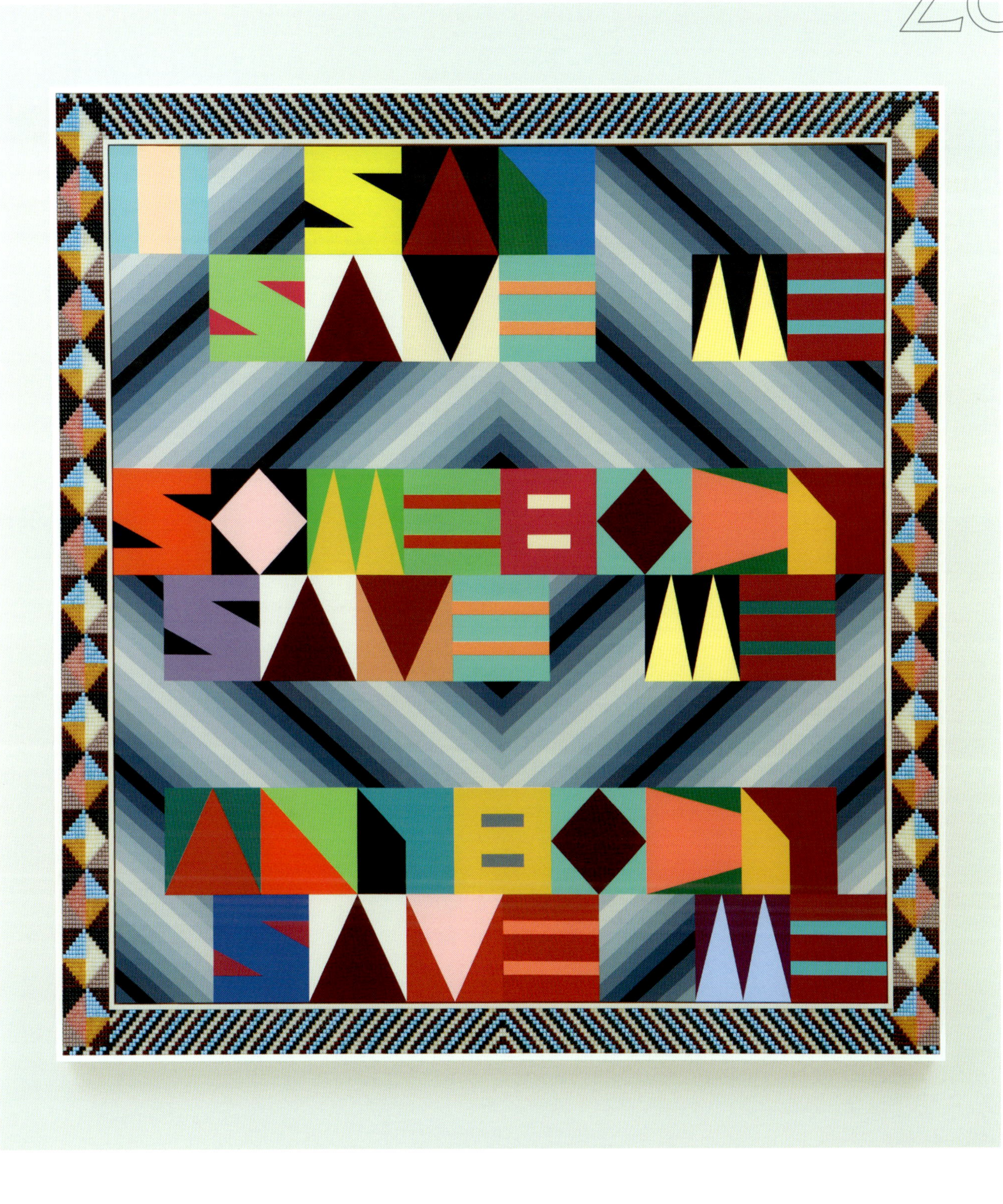

Jeffrey Gibson, *SAVE ME*, 2018. Acrylic on canvas and glass beads and artificial sinew on wood frame, 82 × 74 × 2½ in. (208.3 × 188 × 6.4 cm)

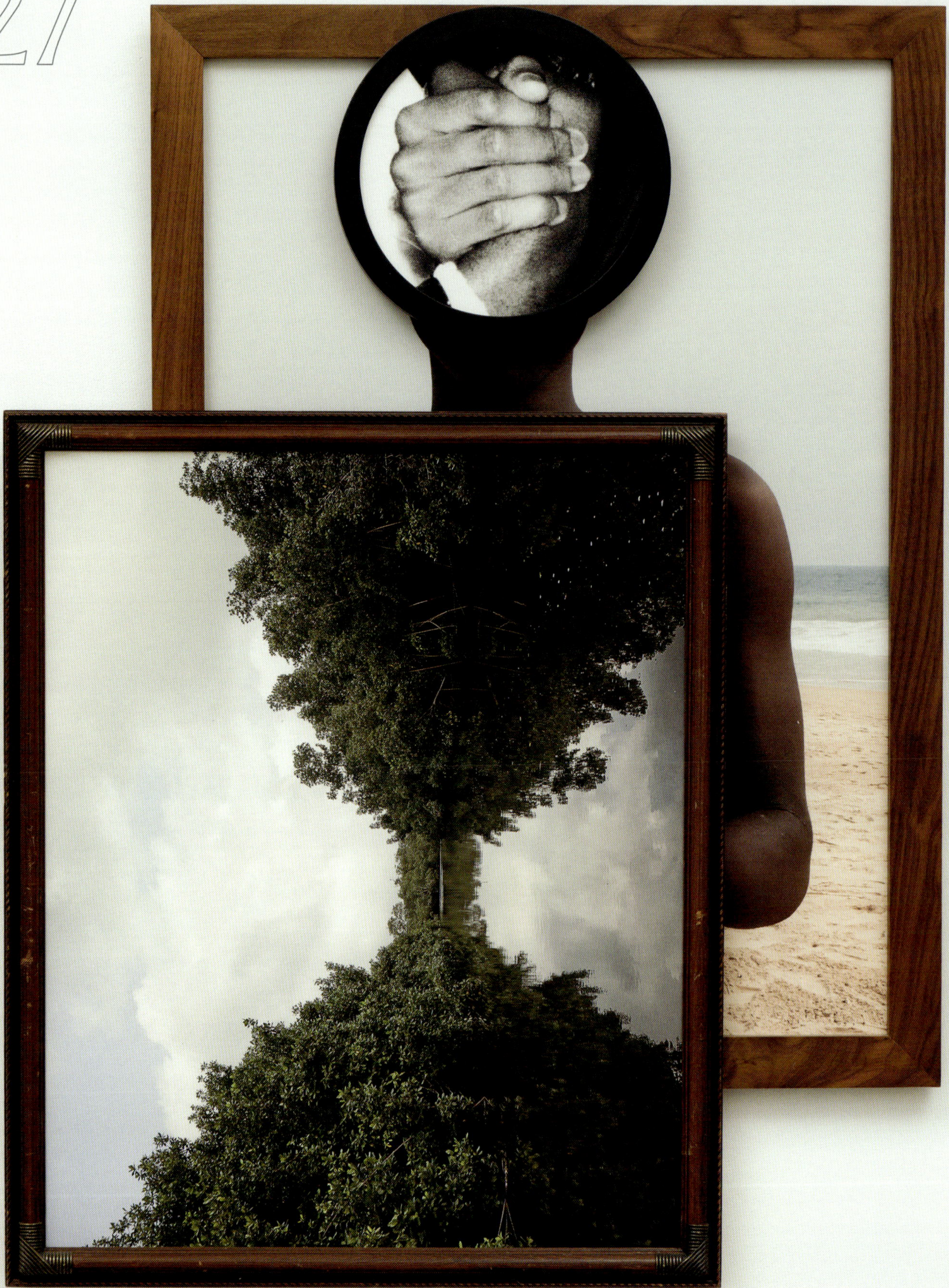

Todd Gray, *Maya Venus*, 2018. Three inkjet prints in artist's frames and found frames, 47¼ × 34¾ × 2 in. (120 × 88.3 × 5.1 cm). Collection of John Morace and Tom Kennedy

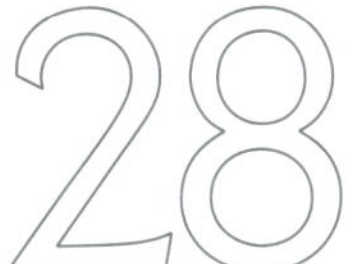

28

Sam Green and Kronos Quartet, *A Thousand Thoughts*, 2018. Performance view, Theatre at Ace Hotel, Los Angeles, CA, 2018

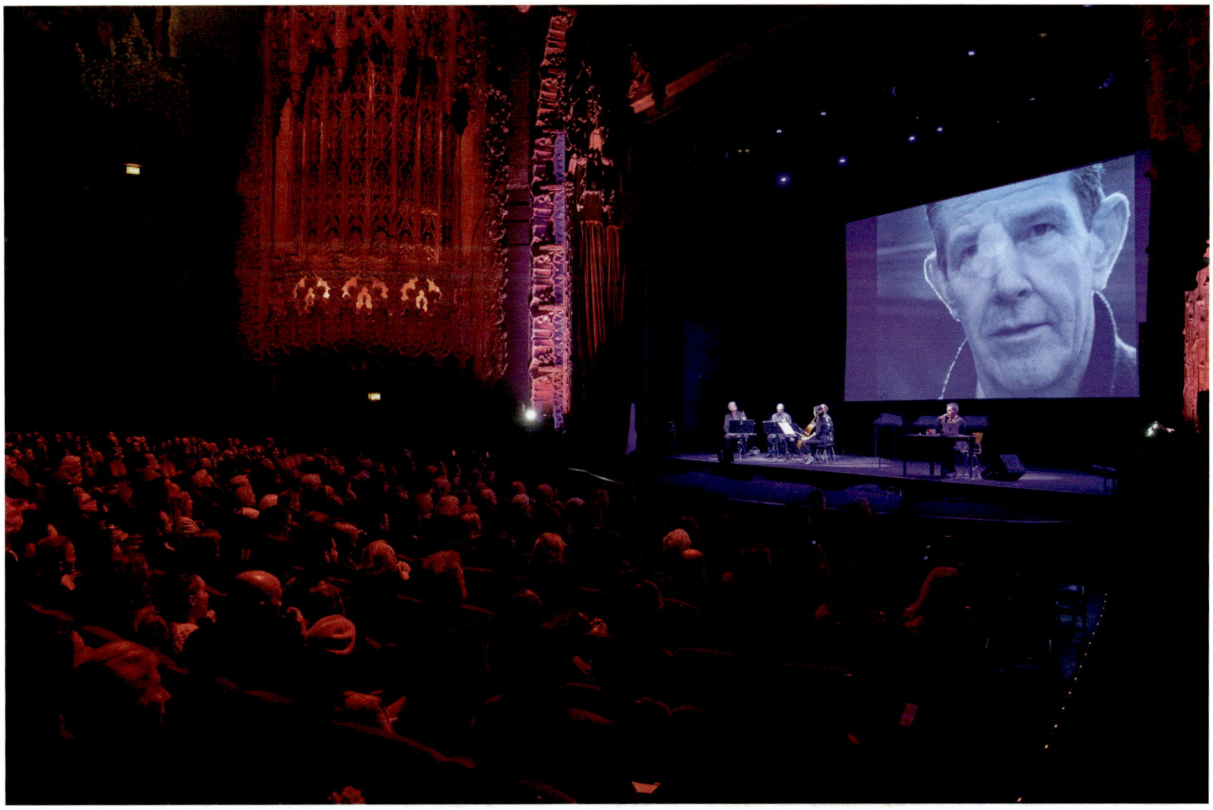

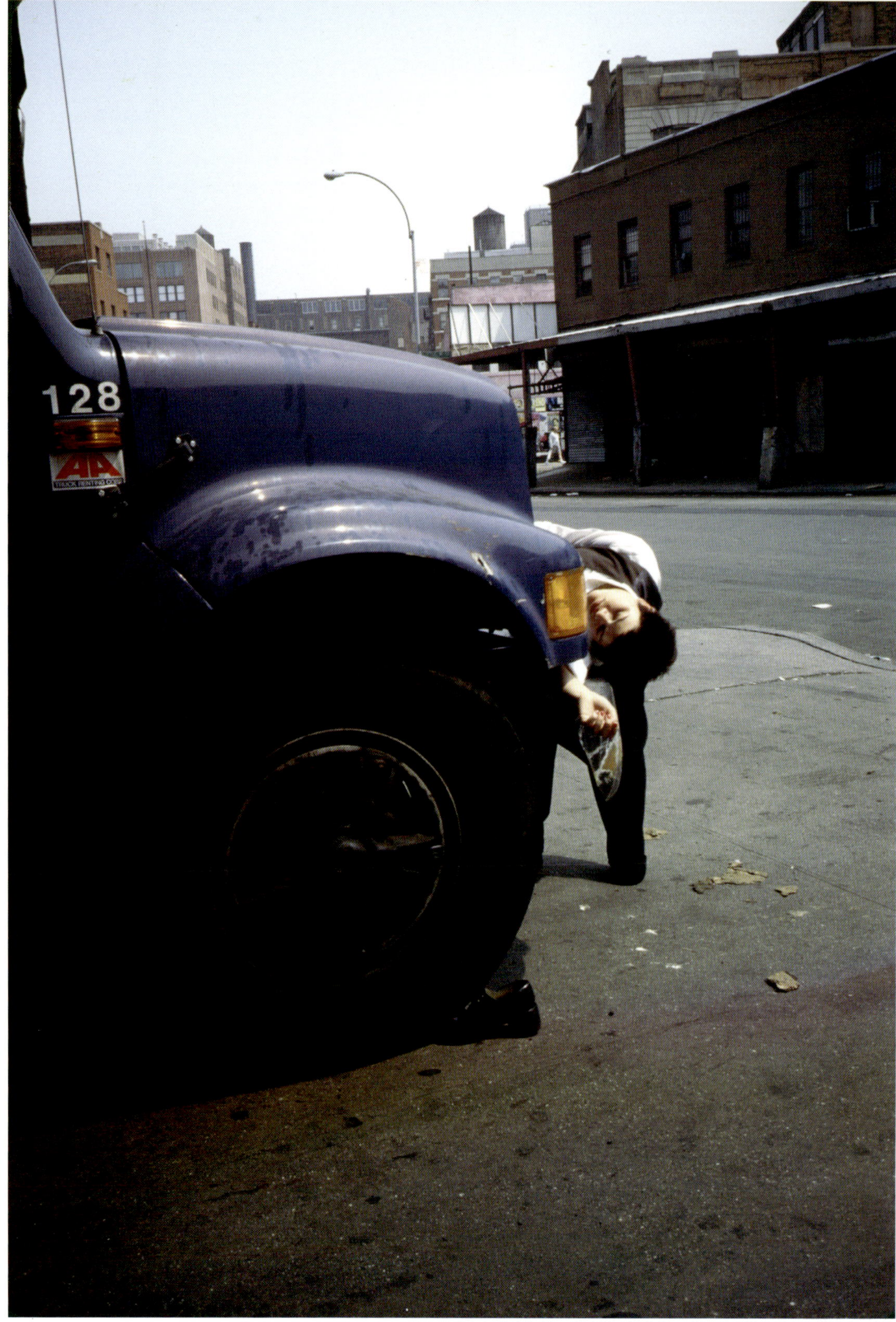

Barbara Hammer, *History Lessons*, 2000. 16mm film, color, sound; 66:51 min.

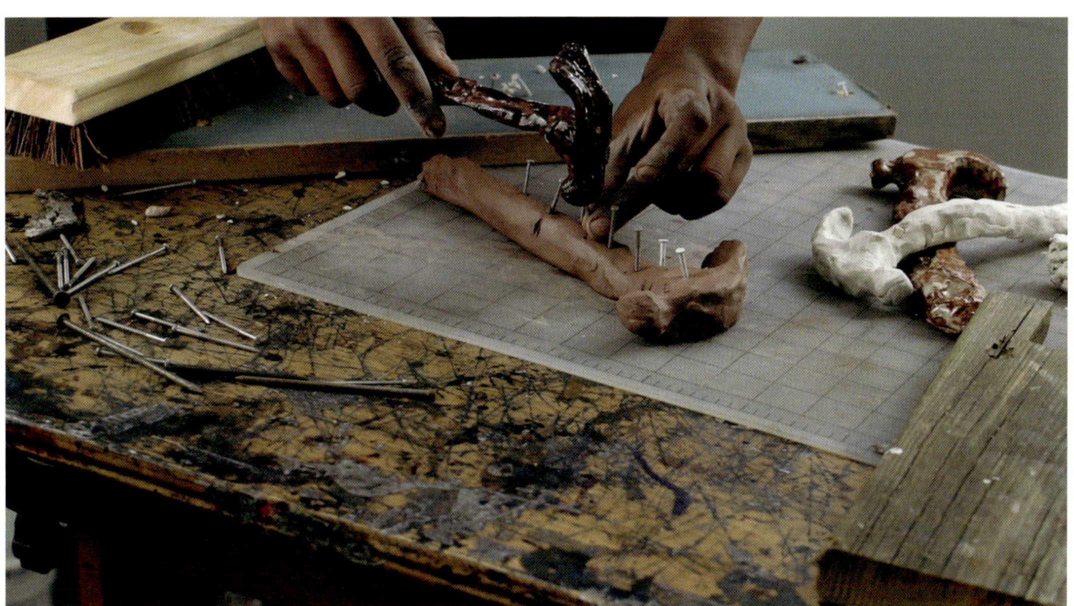

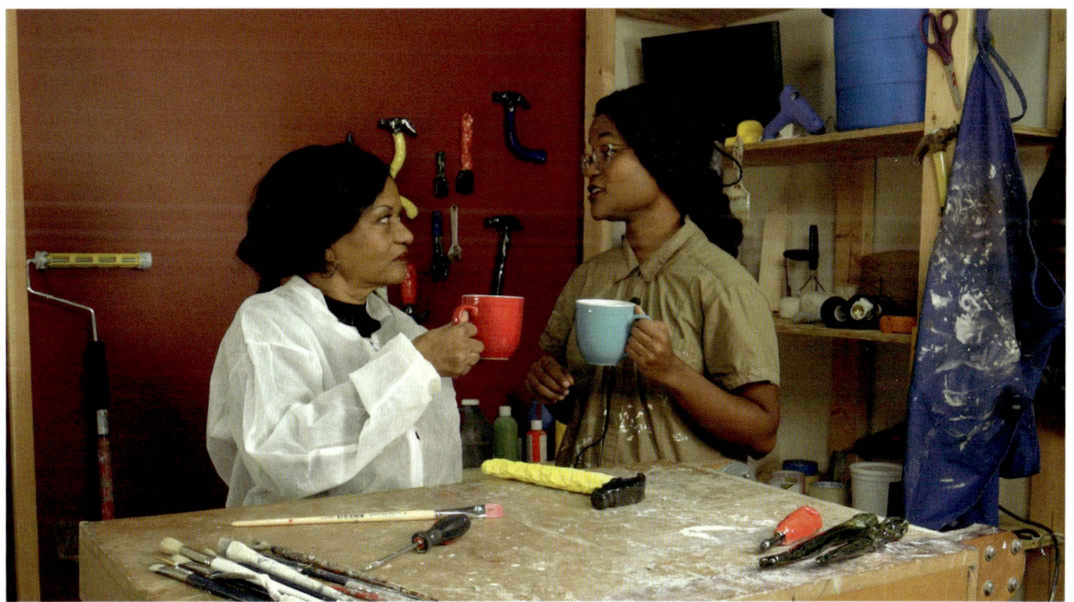

Ilana Harris-Babou, *Reparation Hardware*, 2018. High-definition video, color, sound; 4:05 min. *Finishing a Raw Basement*, 2017. Ultra-high-definition video, color, sound; 6:41 min.

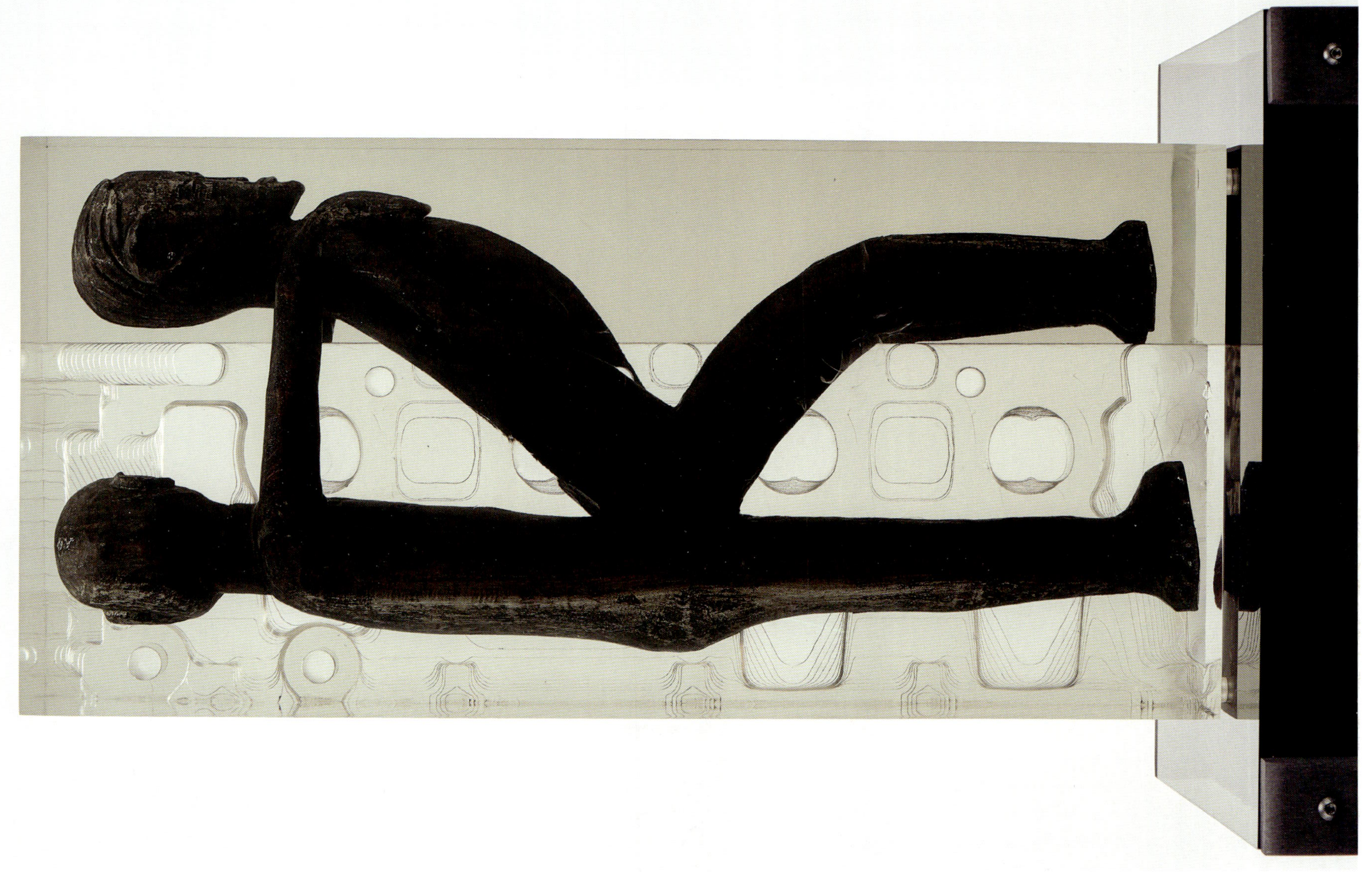

Matthew Angelo Harrison, *Dark Silhouette: Standing Couple*, 2018. Wooden sculpture from West Africa, polyurethane resin, anodized aluminum, and acrylic, 67⅜ × 13 × 13 in. (171.1 × 33 × 33 cm). Joyner/Giuffrida Collection, San Francisco

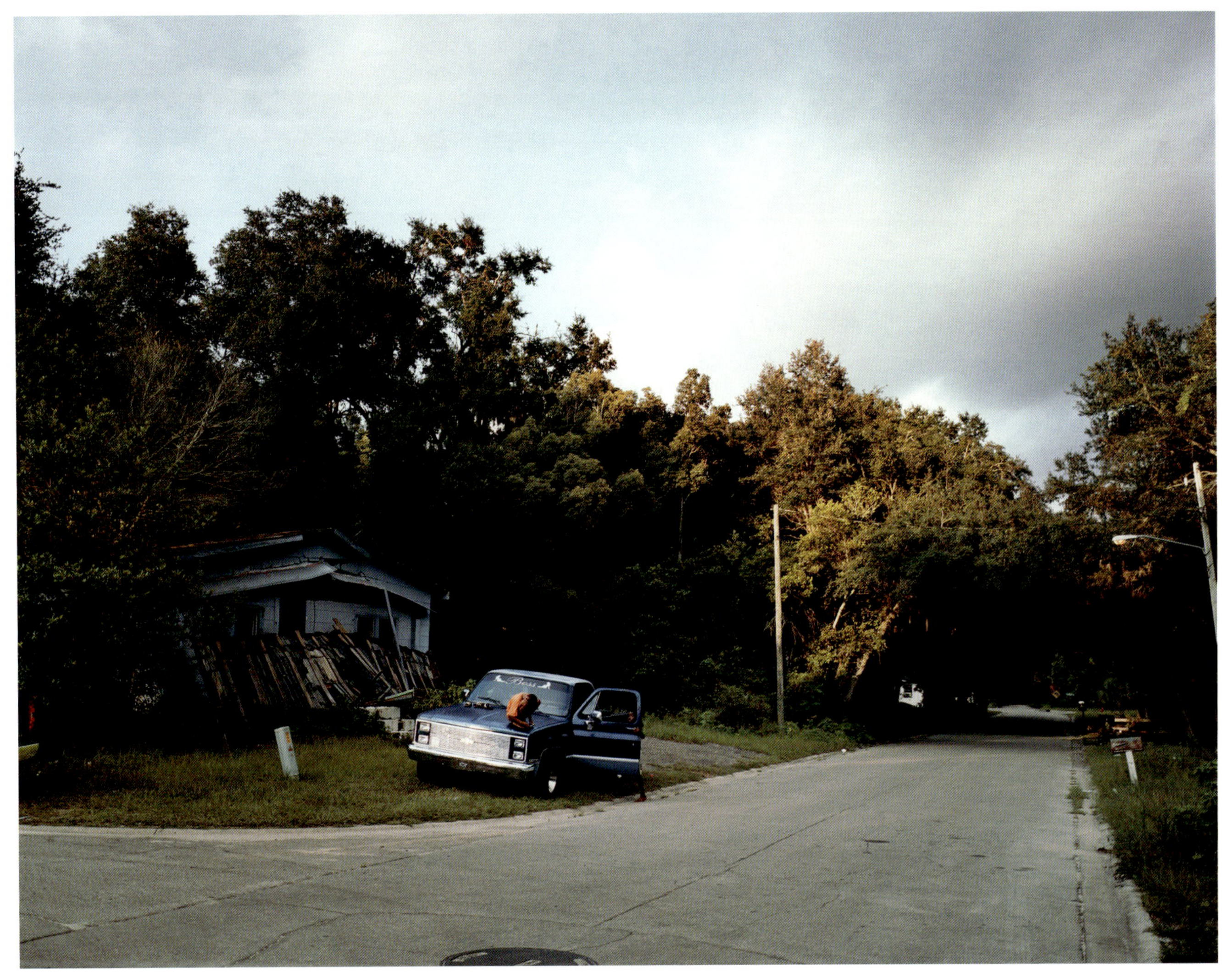

Curran Hatleberg, *Untitled (Blue Truck)*, 2016. Inkjet print, 26 × 32½ in. (66 × 82.6 cm)

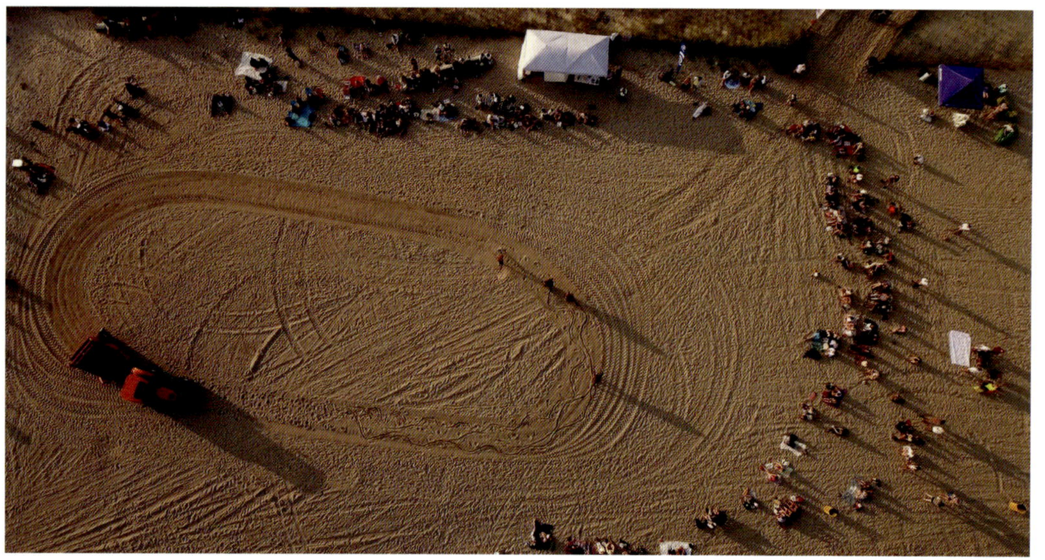

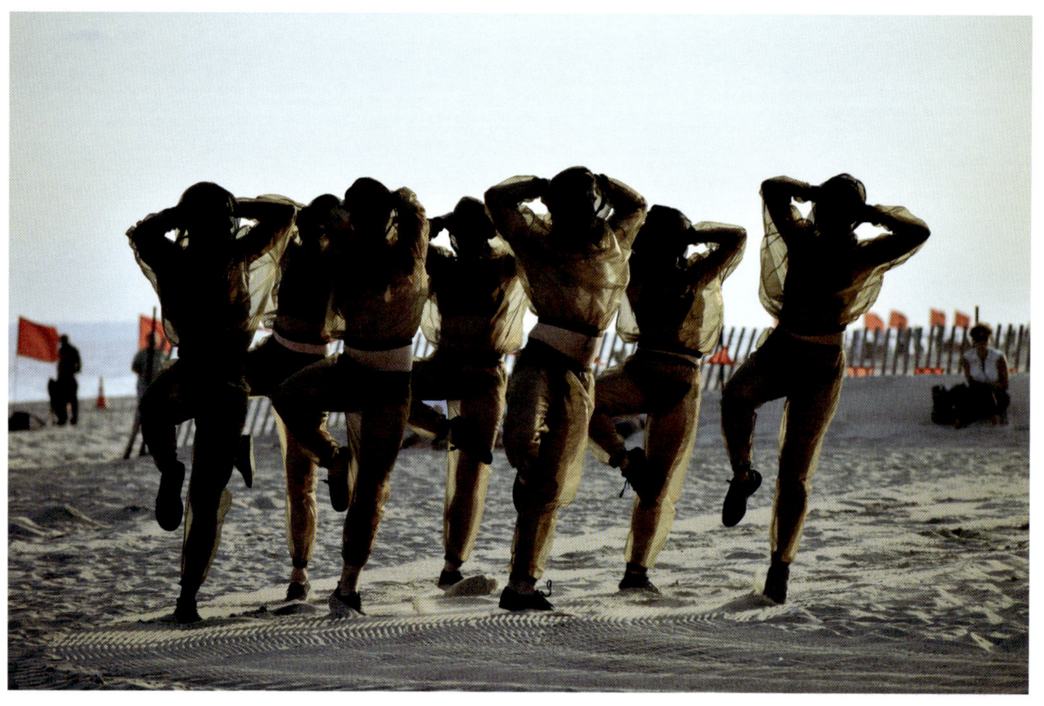

Madeline Hollander, ARENA, 2017. Performance view, Beach Sessions Dance Series, Rockaway Beach, NY, 2017

Iman Issa, *Heritage Studies #20* (detail), 2016. Aluminum, bronze, painted wood, and vinyl text, 49¼ × 9⅛ × 15 in. (125 × 23 × 38 cm)

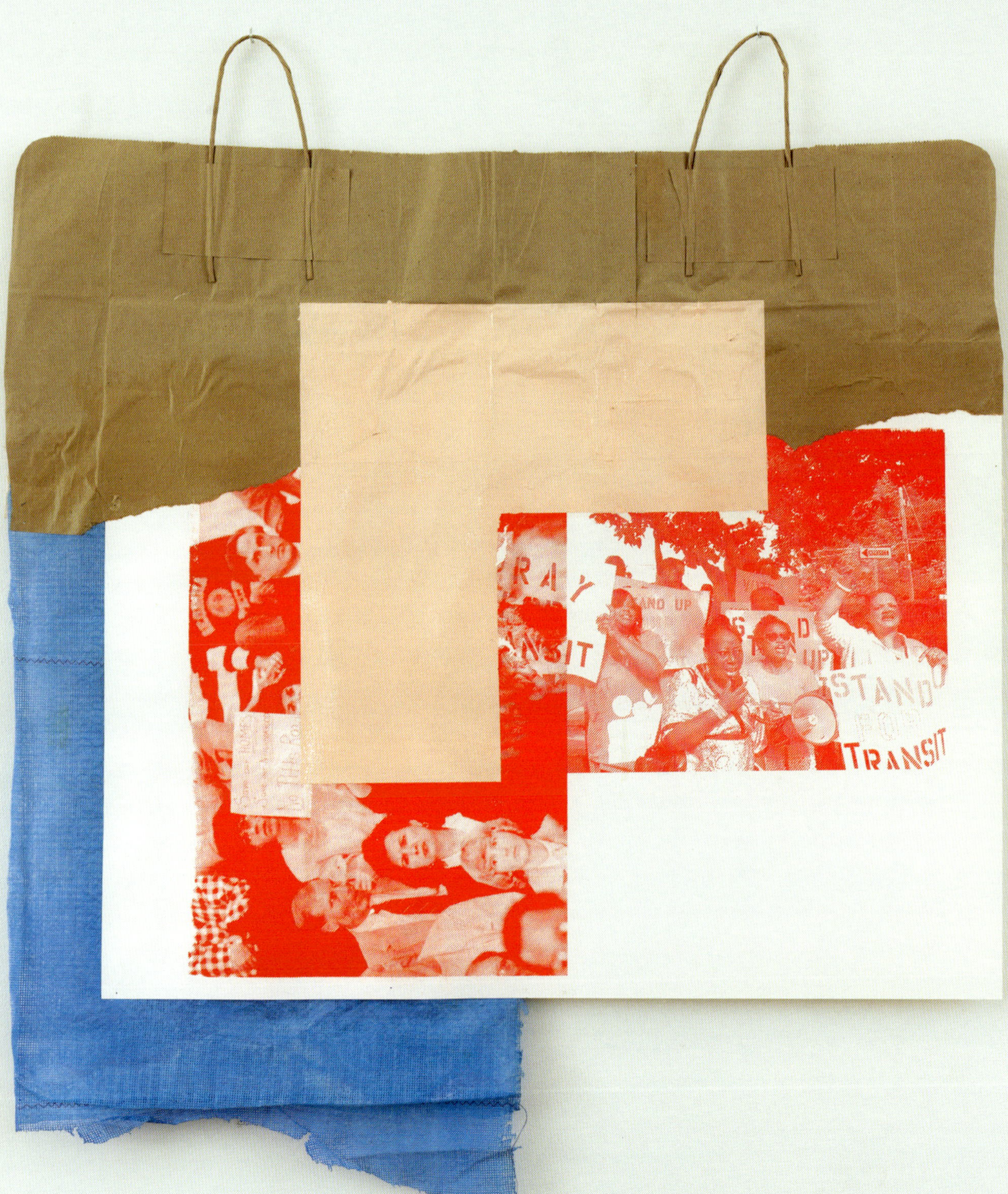

Tomashi Jackson, *Sideways / Side Eye (Peach Shape)*, 2018. Silkscreen ink, oil, and acrylic on gauze, canvas, and paper, 39 × 32 in. (99.1 × 81.3 cm), Schwartz Art Collection, Harvard Business School, Cambridge, MA

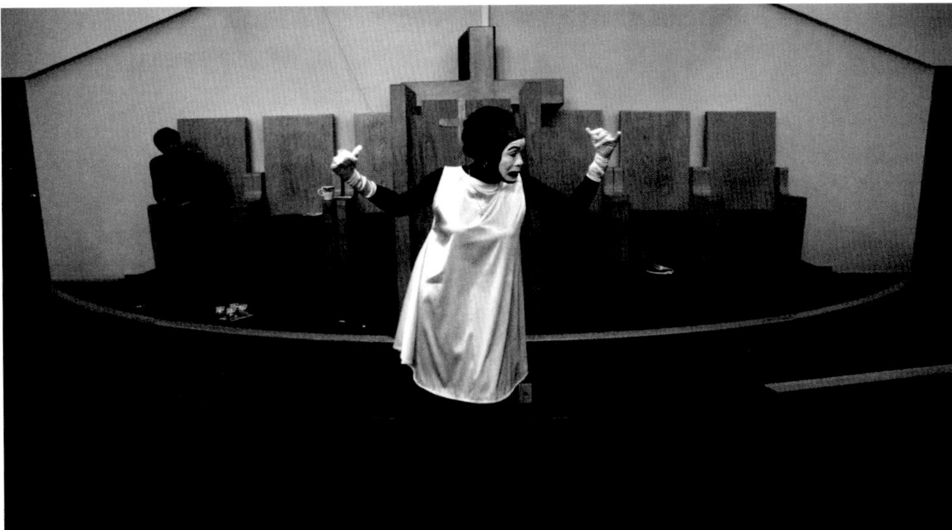

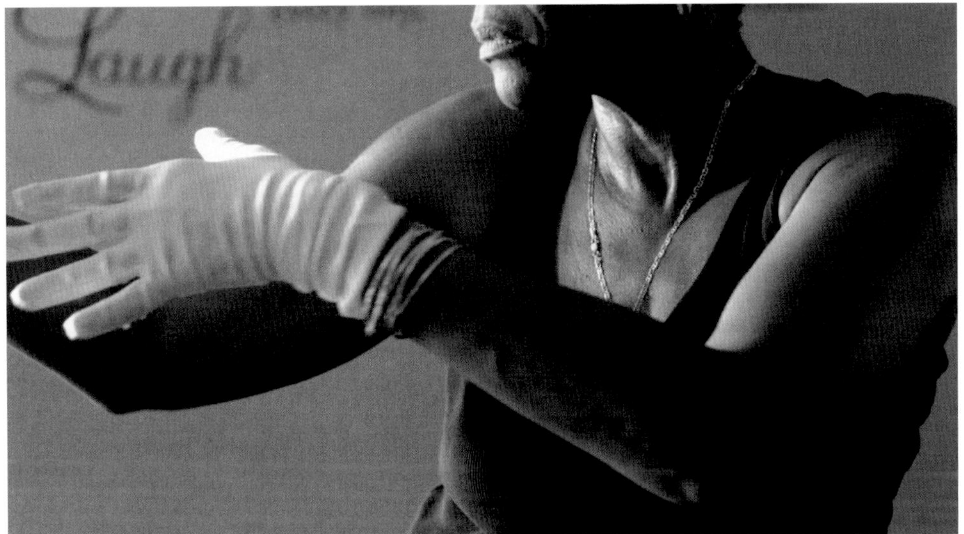

Steffani Jemison, *Sensus Plenior*, 2017. High-definition video, black-and-white, sound; 34:36 min.

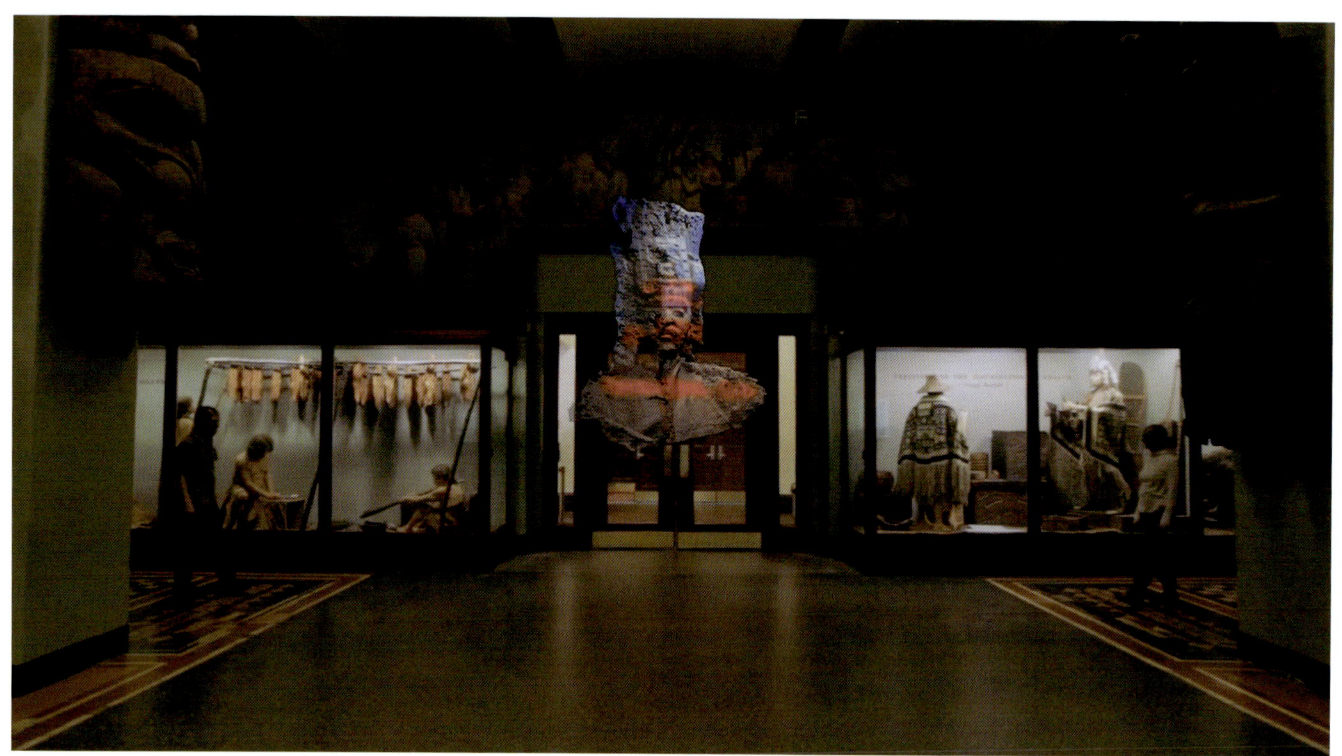

Adam Khalil, Zack Khalil, and Jackson Polys, *Culture Capture 001*, 2017. High-definition video, color, sound; 4:34 min.

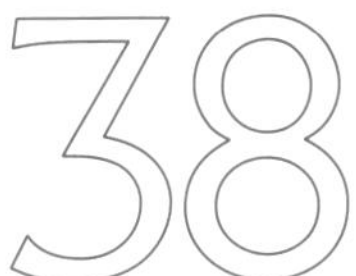

Christine Sun Kim, *Suggested Amount of Talking on Phone in the Presence of a Deaf Person*, 2018. Charcoal on paper, 11 ¾ × 16 ½ in. (29.7 × 42 cm). *Suggested Amount of Allowing Friends to Sing Songs to a Baby*, 2018. Charcoal on paper, 49 ½ × 49 ½ in. (125 × 125 cm).

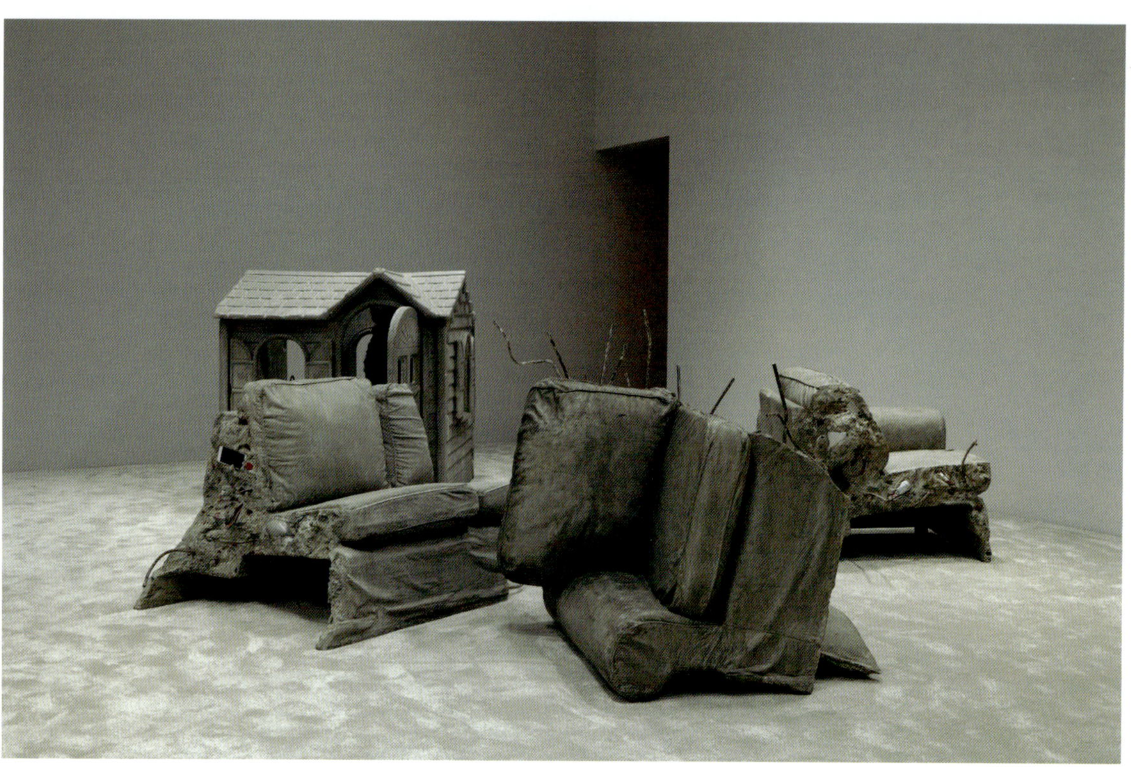

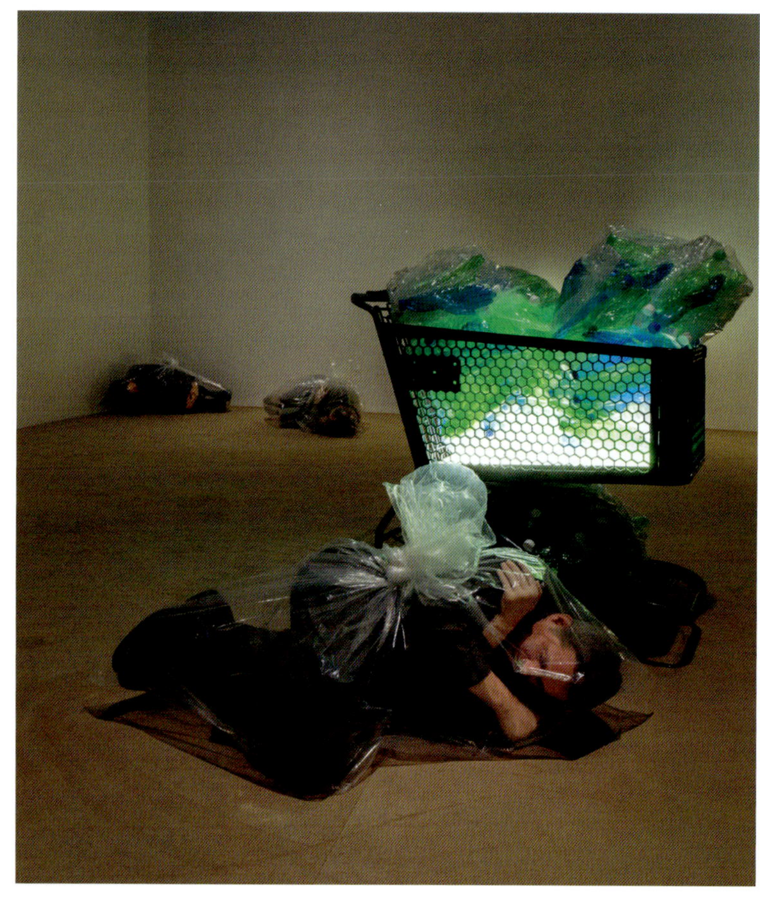

Josh Kline, installation view of *Civil War*, Modern Art, London, United Kingdom, 2017. Installation view of *Unemployment*, Fondazione Sandretto Re Rebaudengo, Turin, Italy, 2016

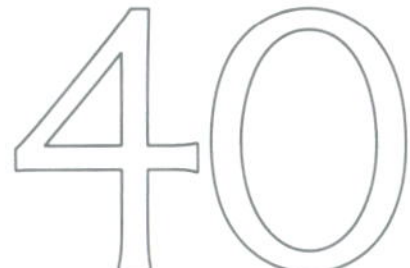

Autumn Knight and Chelsea Knight, *Manifest*, 2018. Performance view, Pioneer Works, Brooklyn, NY, 2018

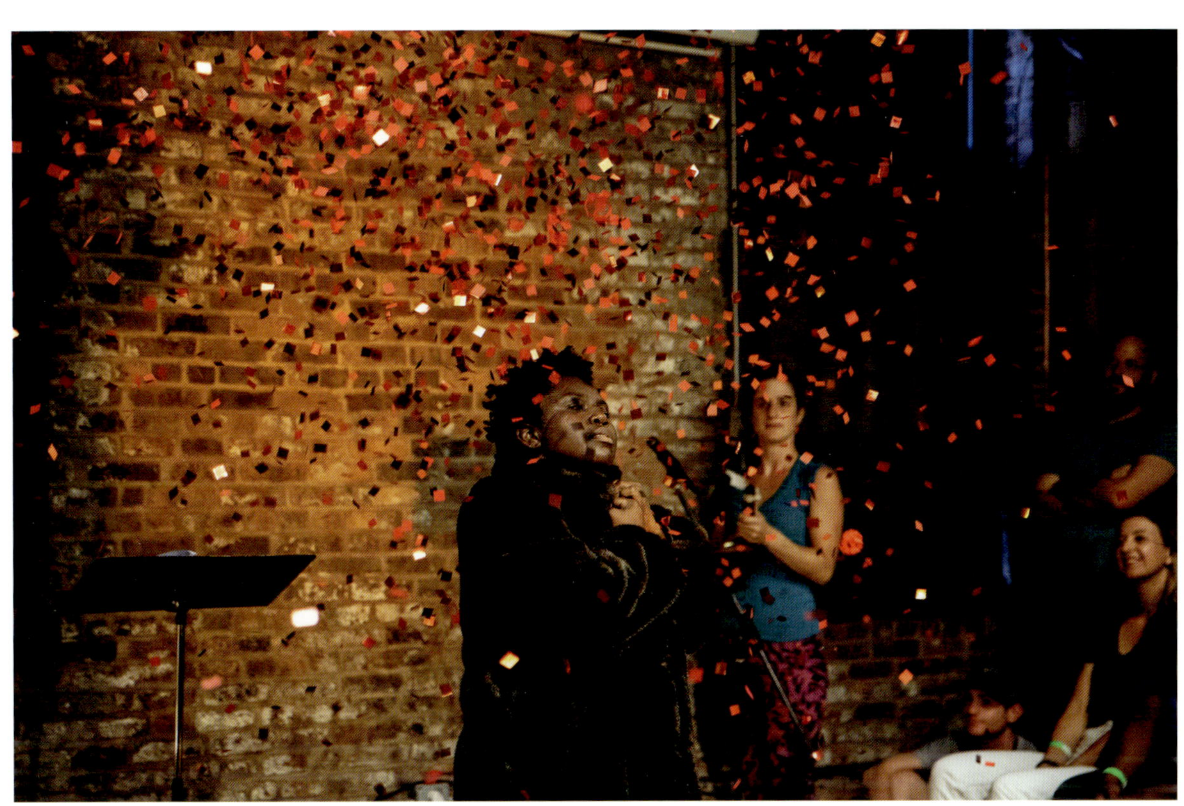

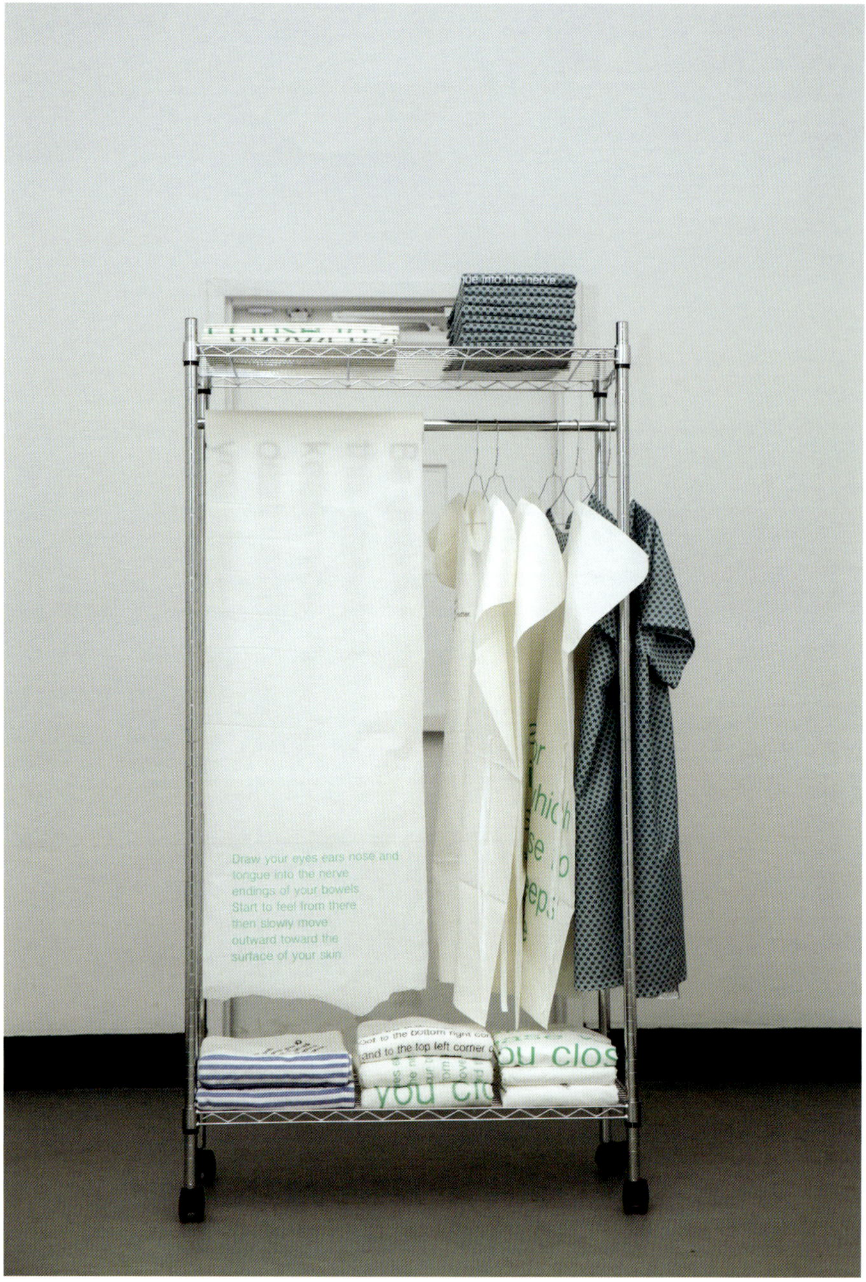

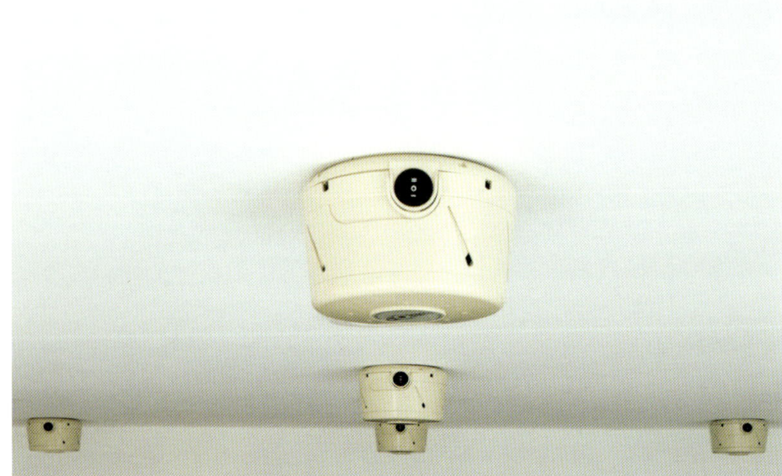

Carolyn Lazard, *Scores for Convalescing*, 2017. Clothing rack and screenprinted hospital gowns, hospital blankets, sheets, and towels, 35 × 17⅜ × 70½ in. (88.9 × 44.1 × 179.1 cm). *A Conspiracy*, 2017. Sound installation with white-noise machines, dimensions variable

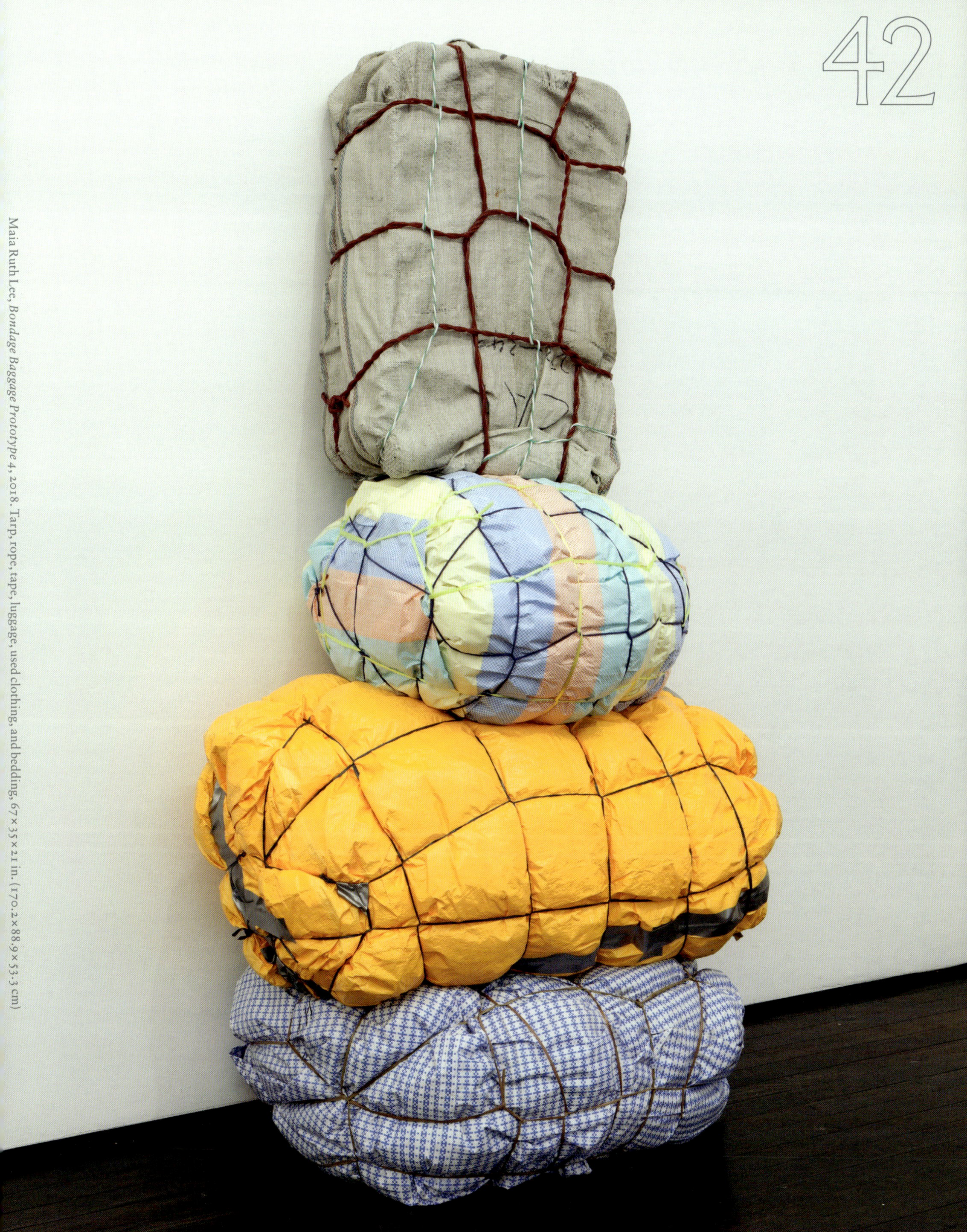

Maia Ruth Lee, *Bondage Baggage Prototype 4*, 2018. Tarp, rope, tape, luggage, used clothing, and bedding, 67 × 35 × 21 in. (170.2 × 88.9 × 53.3 cm)

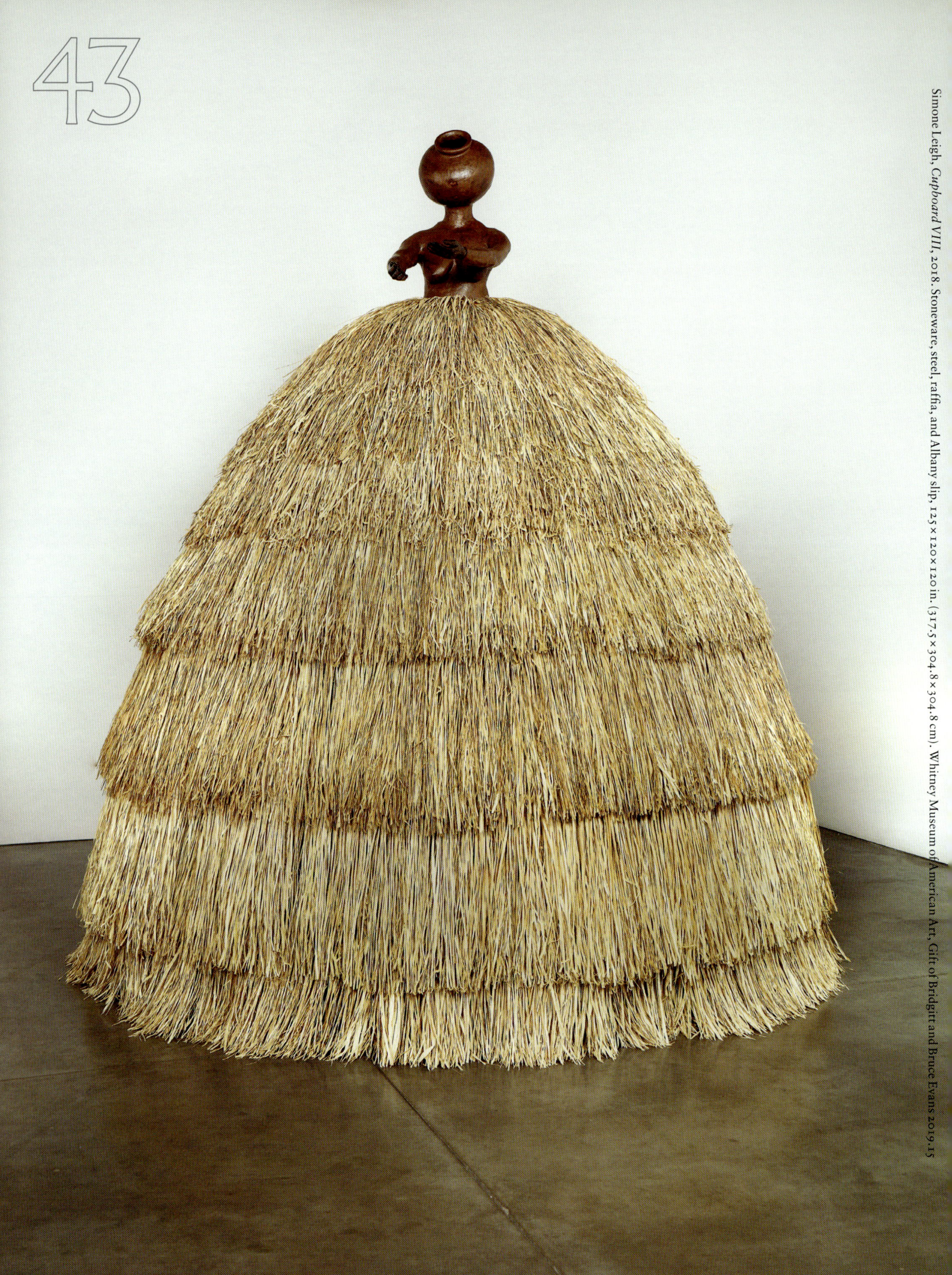

Simone Leigh, *Cupboard VIII*, 2018. Stoneware, steel, raffia, and Albany slip, 125 × 120 × 120 in. (317.5 × 304.8 × 304.8 cm). Whitney Museum of American Art, Gift of Bridgitt and Bruce Evans 2019.15

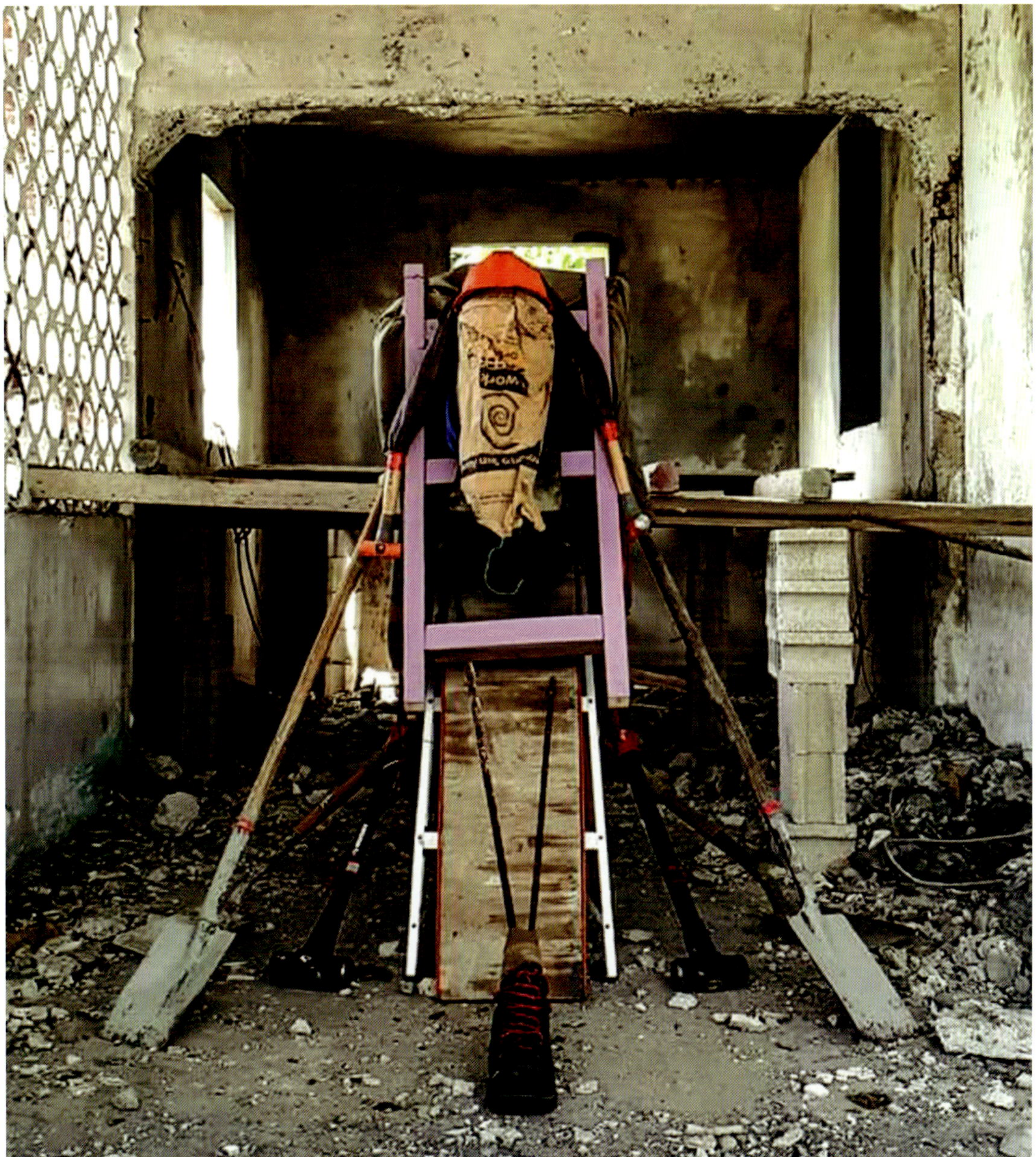

Daniel Lind-Ramos, *El viejo (Contratista)* (*The Old Man [Contractor]*), 2016. Carpenter's tools, wood, steel bars, stones, cement blocks, portable stairs, coat, helmet, gloves, concrete blocks, wood panels, wood beams, sifters, boots, wire, cement bag, plywood panels, and rope, dimensions variable

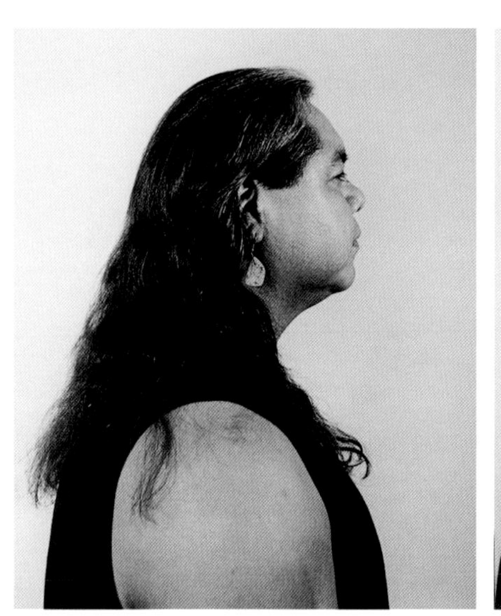 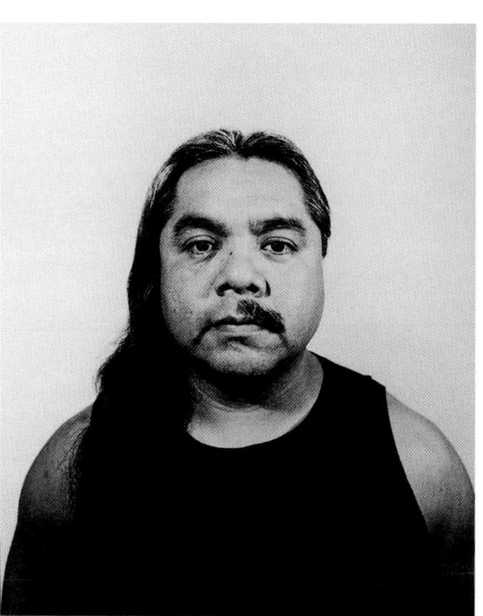 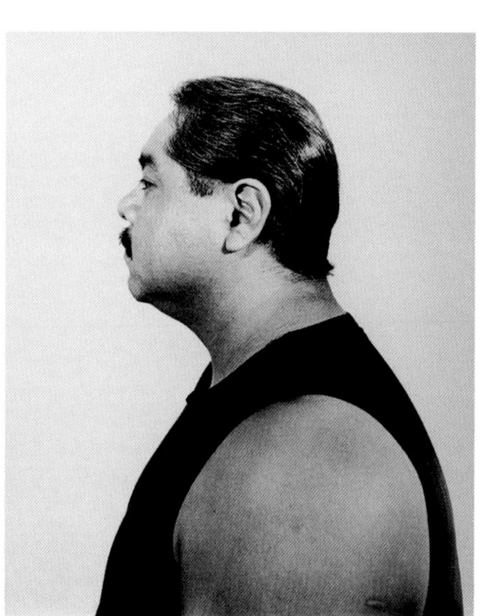

James Luna, *Half Indian/Half Mexican*, 1991. Inkjet prints, 30 × 72 ⅛ in. (76.4 × 183.4 cm) overall. Denver Art Museum

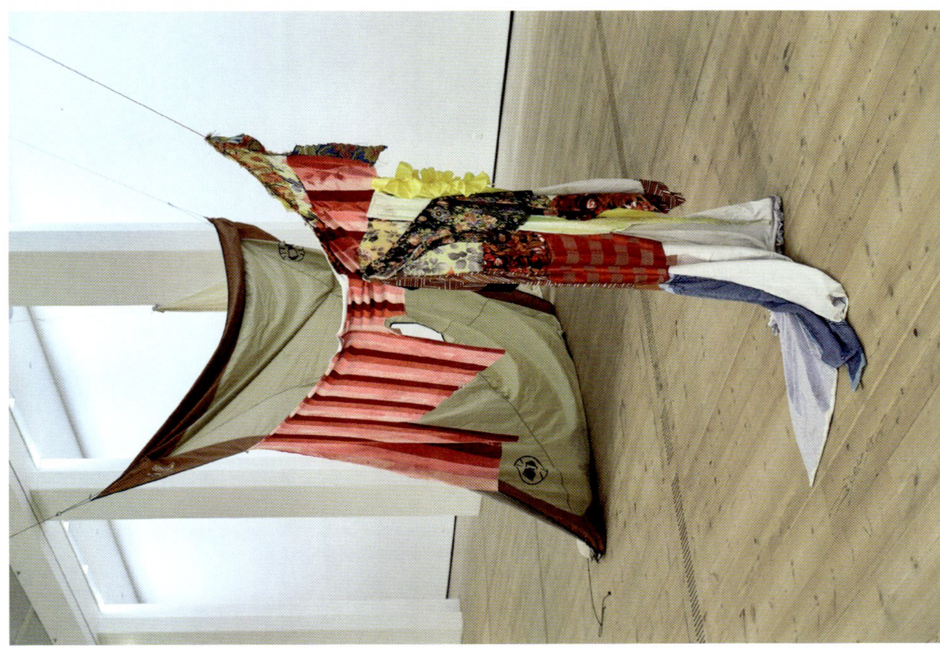

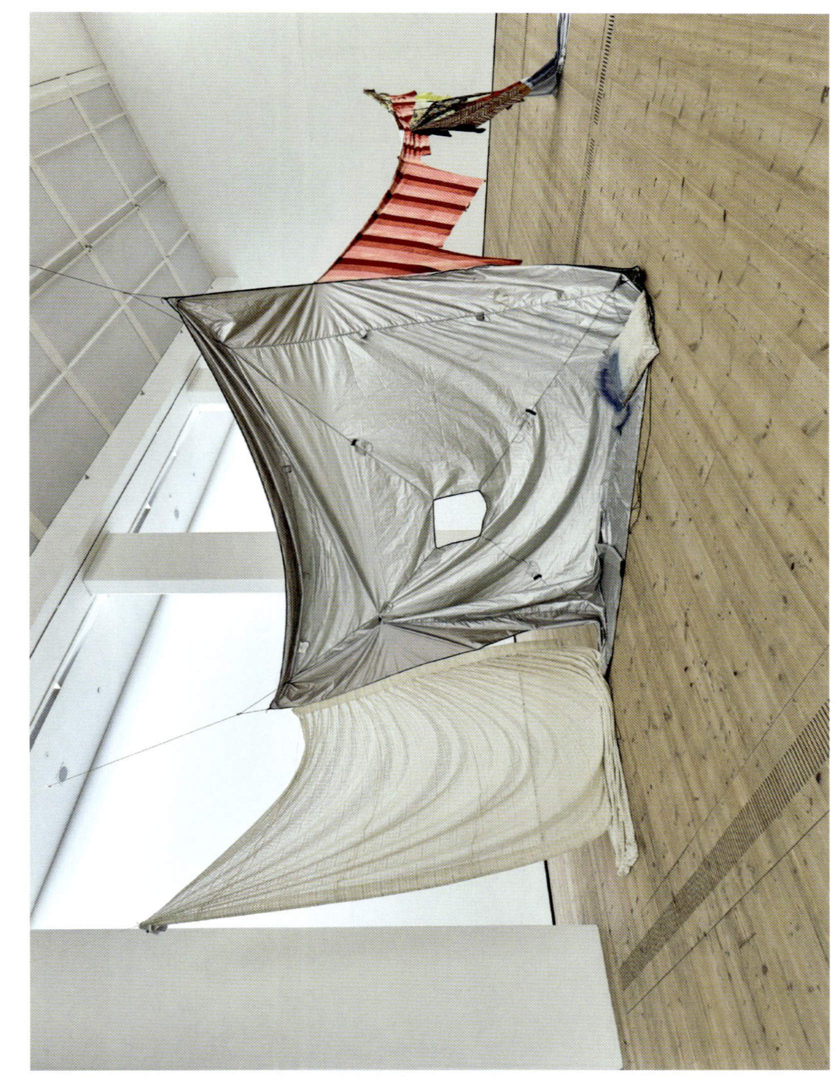

Eric N. Mack, *A Lesson in Perspective*, 2017. Wool curtain, tent cover, acrylic, linen, silk, polyester, and velour, panel 1: 124×71 in. (315×180.3 cm); panel 2: 127×43×148 in. (322.6×109.2×375.9 cm); panel 3: 85×192 in. (215.9×487.7 cm)

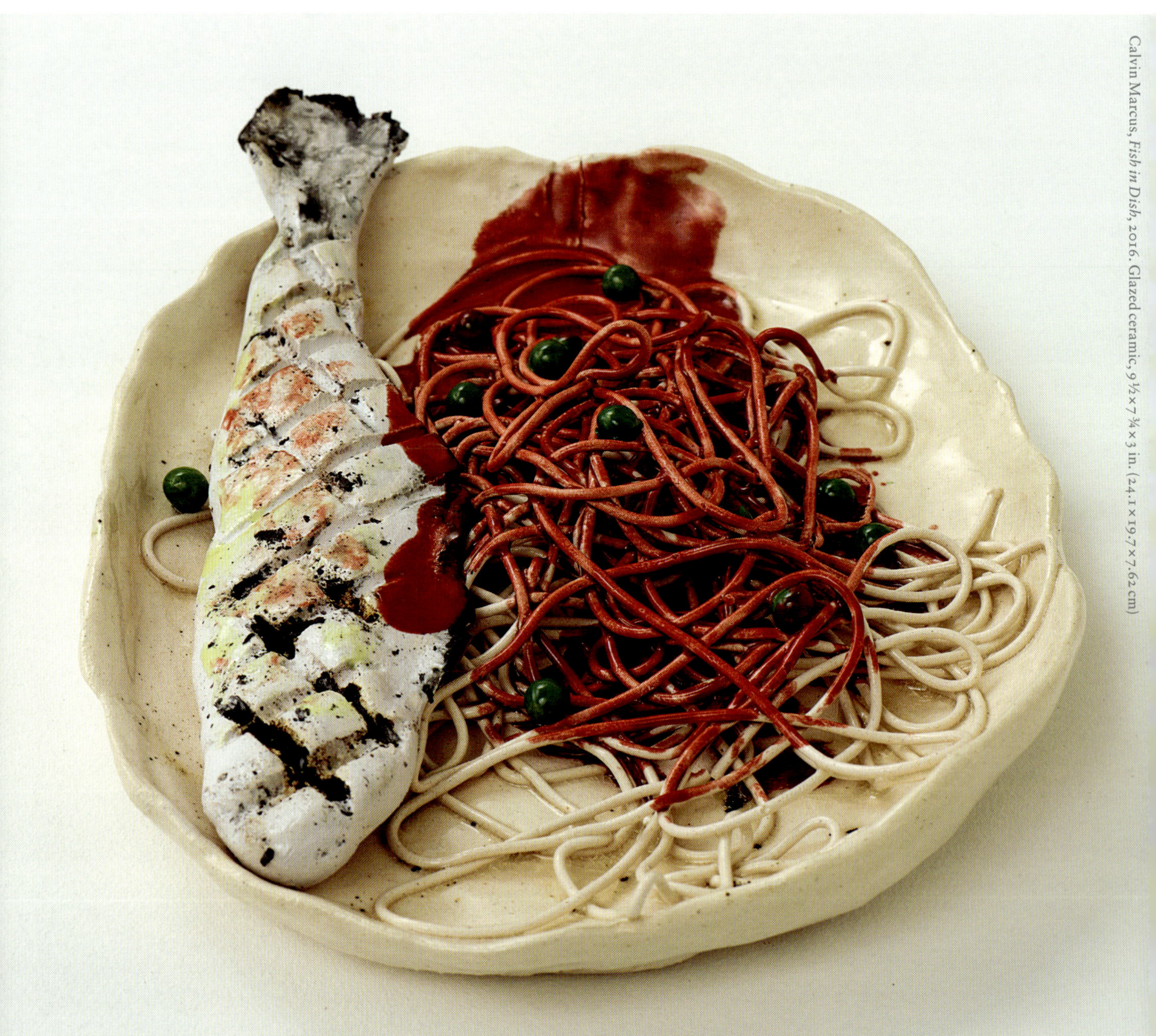

Calvin Marcus, *Fish in Dish*, 2016. Glazed ceramic, 9½ × 7¾ × 3 in. (24.1 × 19.7 × 7.62 cm)

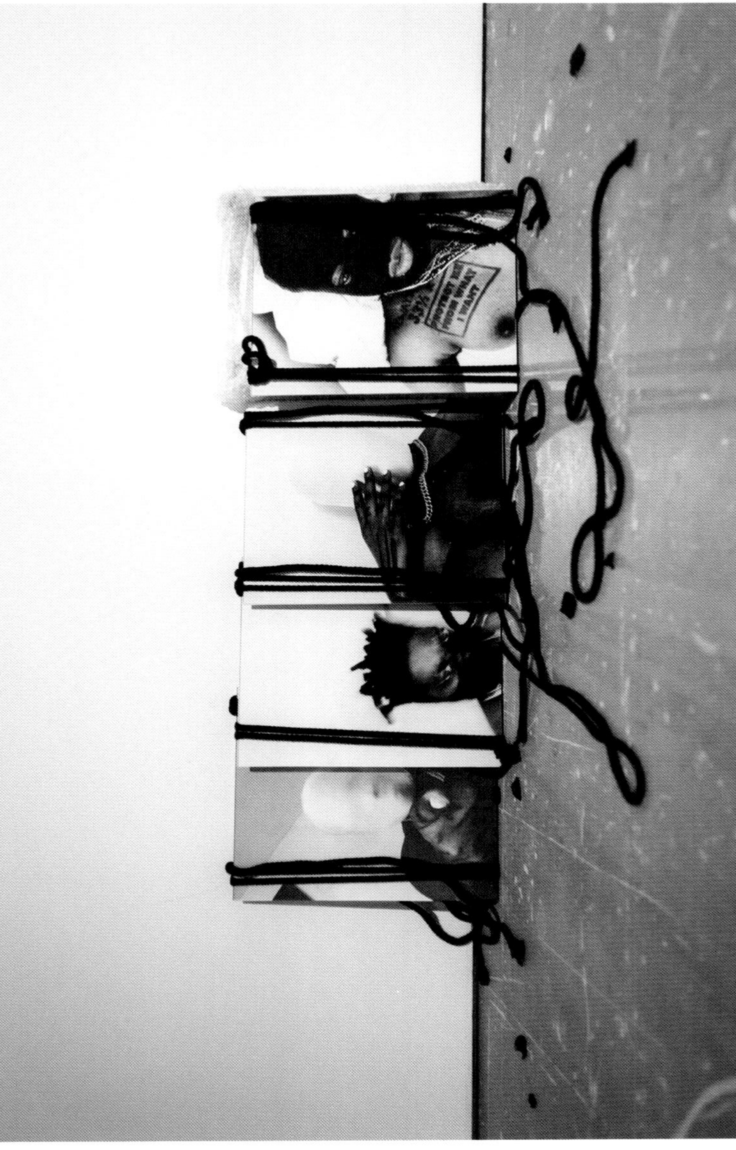

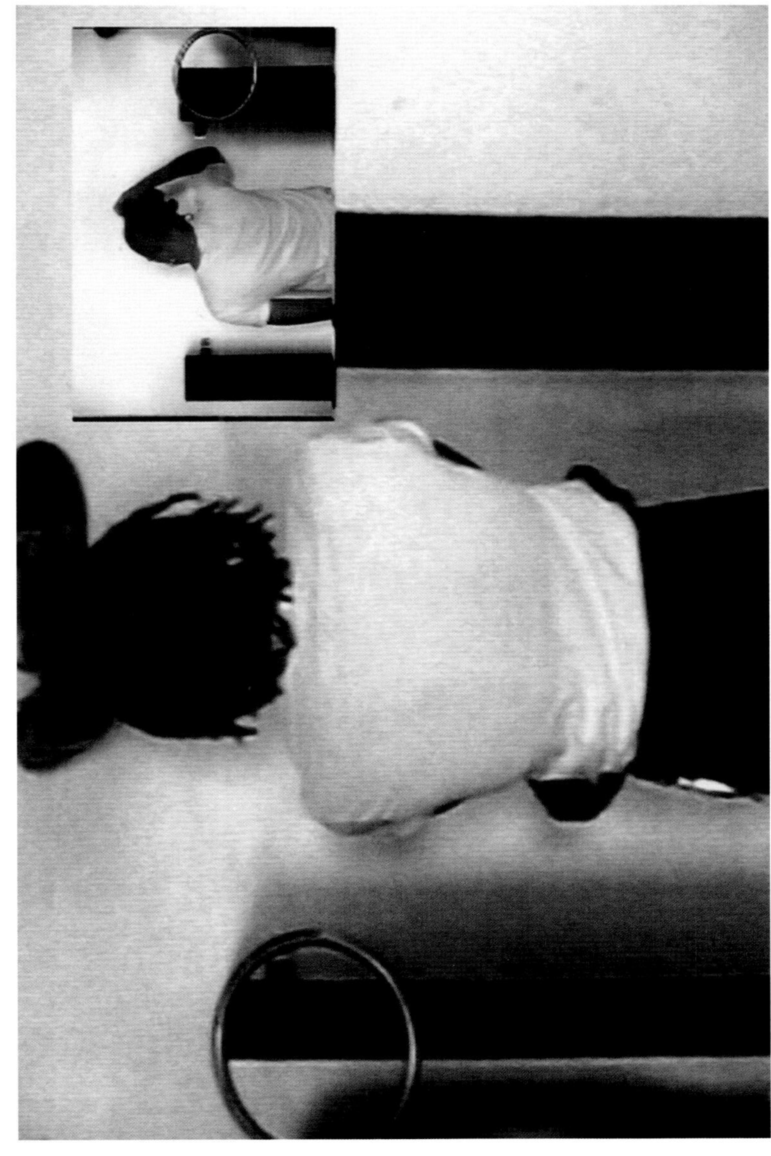

Tiona Nekkia McClodden, *The Brad Johnson Tape, X—On Subjugation* (detail), 2017. Installation view, *Speech/Acts*, Institute of Contemporary Art, Philadelphia, PA, 2017. *The Labyrinth 1.0*, 2017. Video, black-and-white, sound; 6 min.

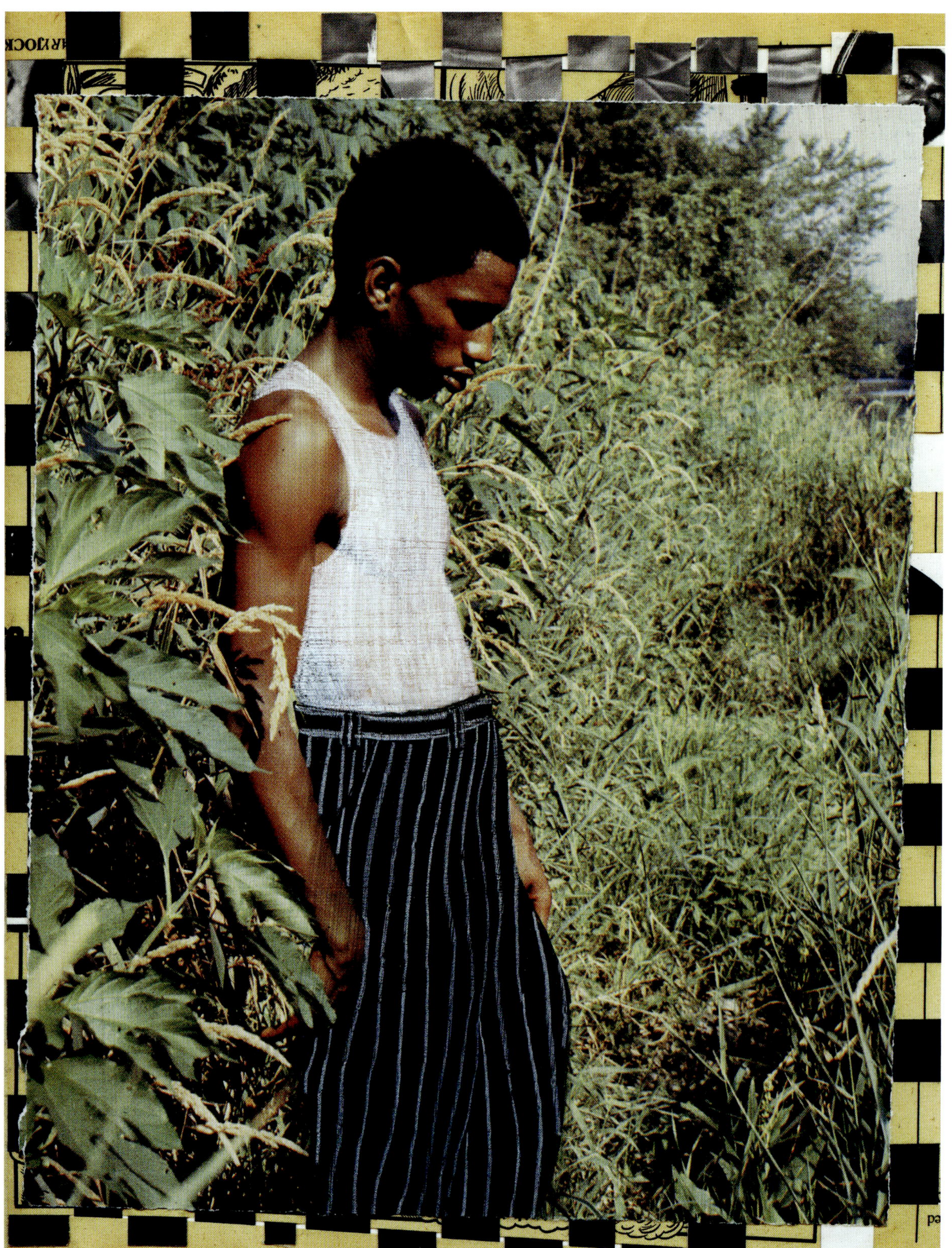

Troy Michie, *Untitled*, 2018. Ink, colored pencil, and graphite on magazine page, 11 × 8½ in. (27.9 × 21.6 cm)

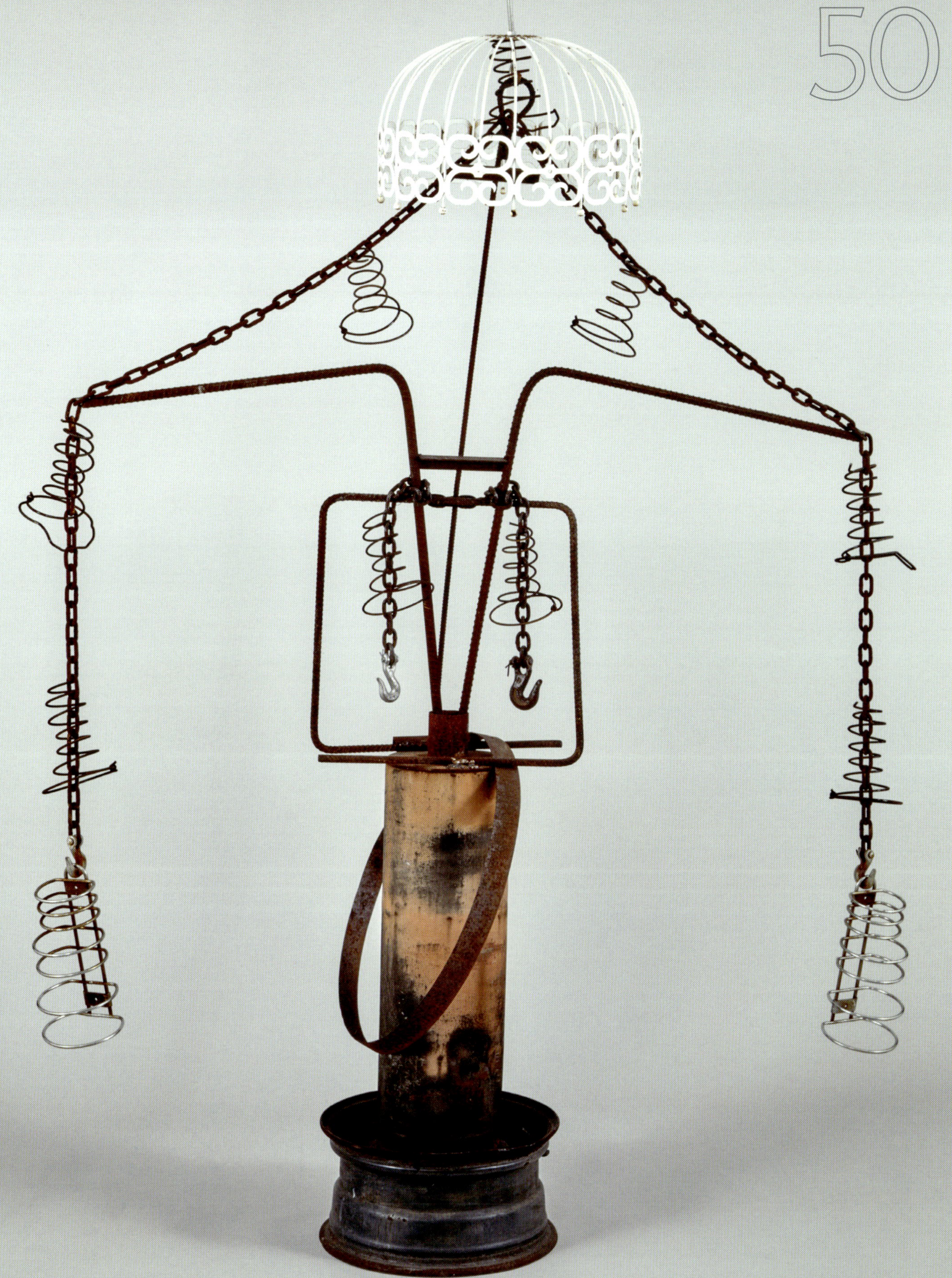

Joe Minter, *How Do I Look?*, 1997. Found metal, 85 × 58 × 24 ½ in. (215.9 × 147.3 × 62.2 cm). Collection of the Souls Grown Deep Foundation

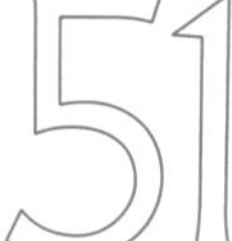

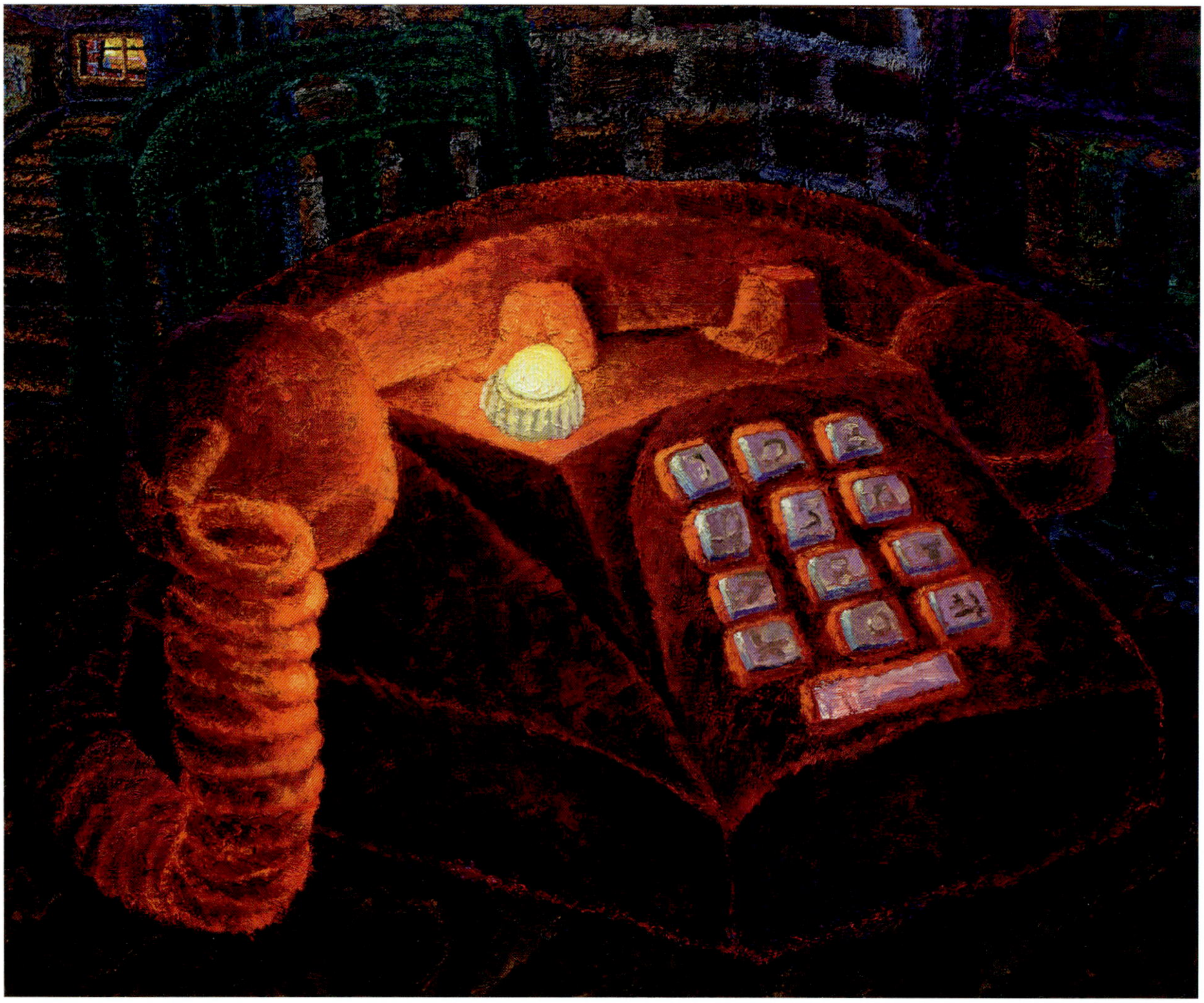

Keegan Monaghan, *Incoming*, 2016–17. Oil on canvas, 60⅜ × 72 in. (153.4 × 182.9 cm). Collection of Ninah and Michael Lynne

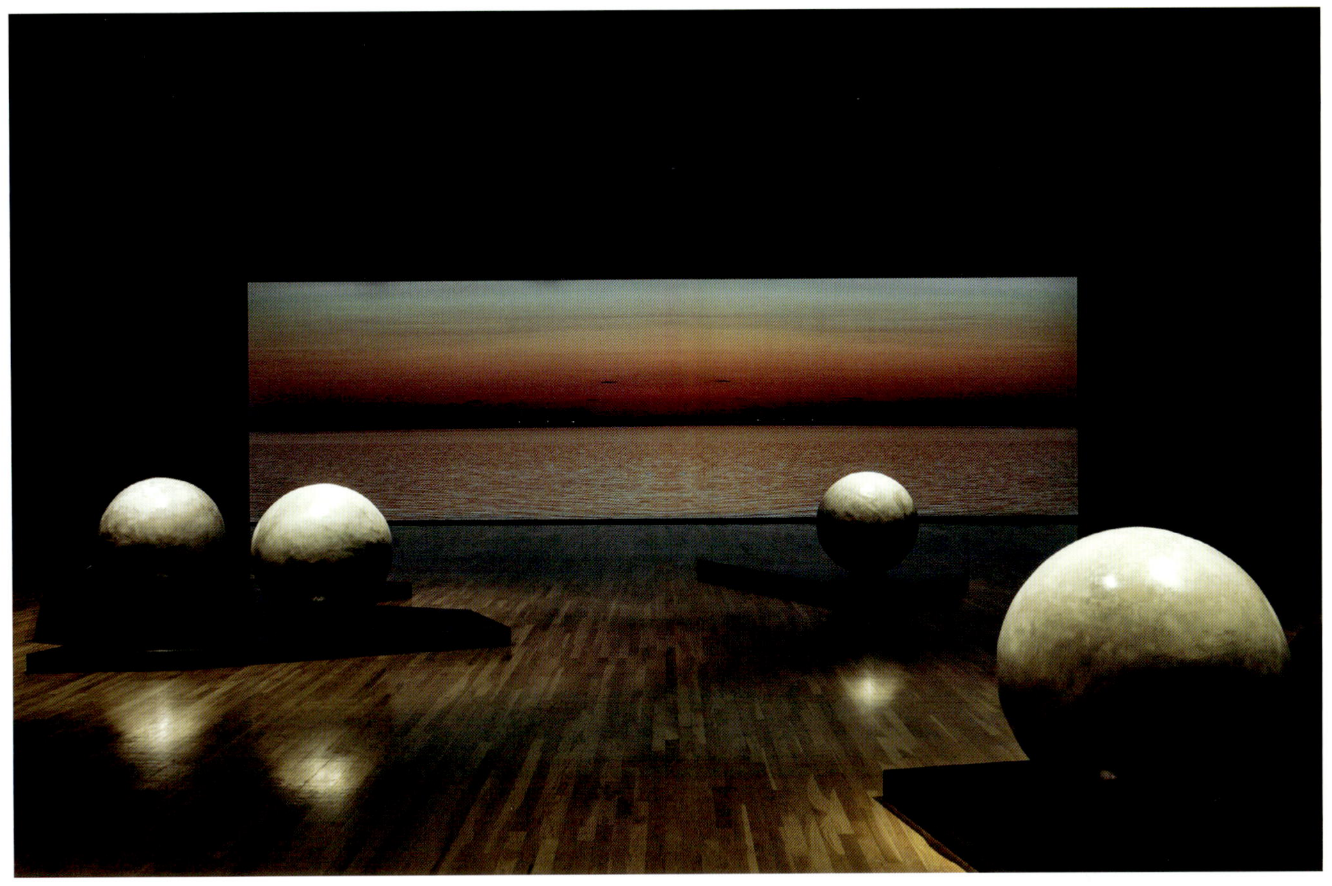

Caroline Monnet, installation view of *Like ships in the night*, Walter Phillips Gallery, Banff, Alberta, 2018

53

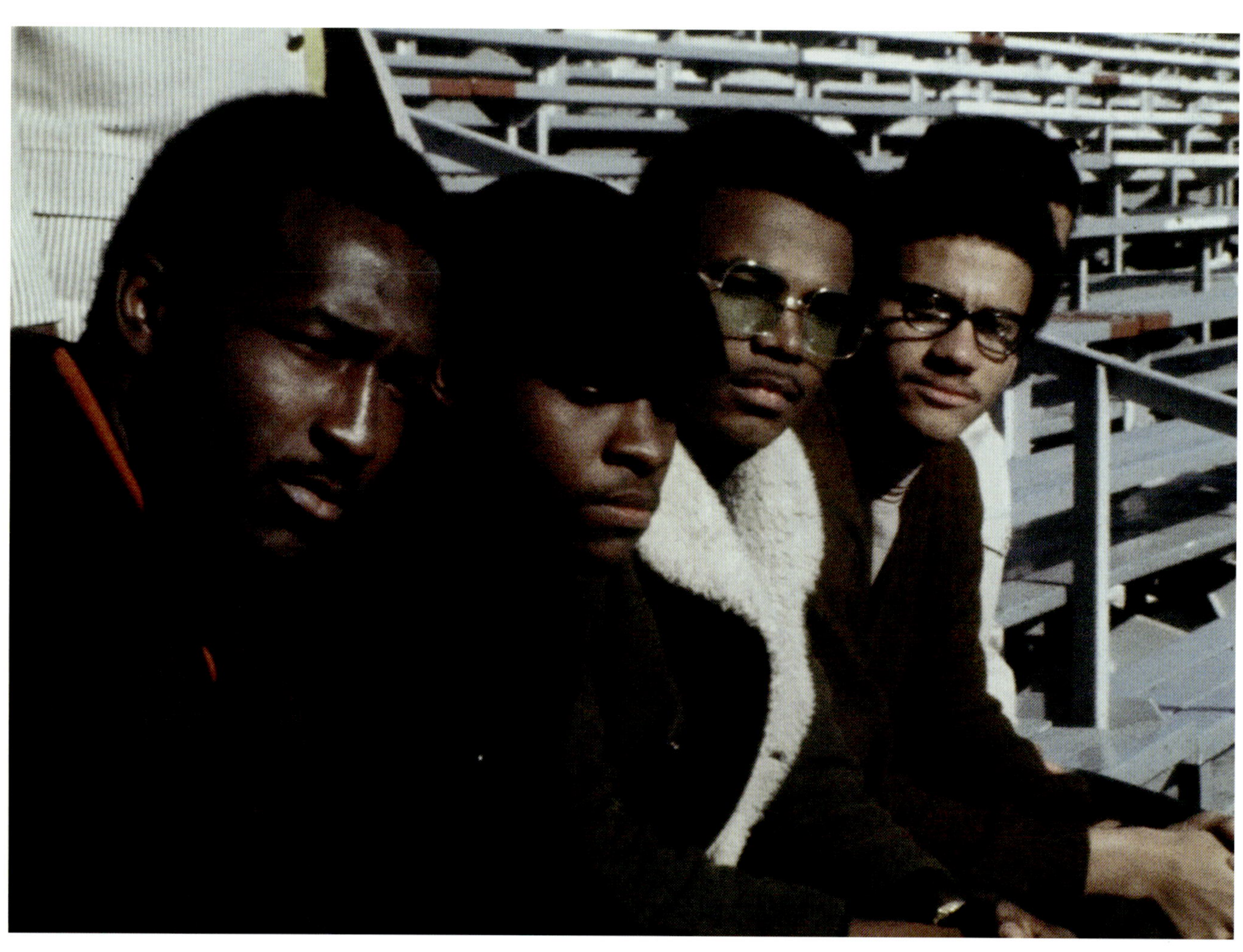

Darius Clark Monroe, *Black 14*, 2018. High-definition video, color, sound; 15 min.

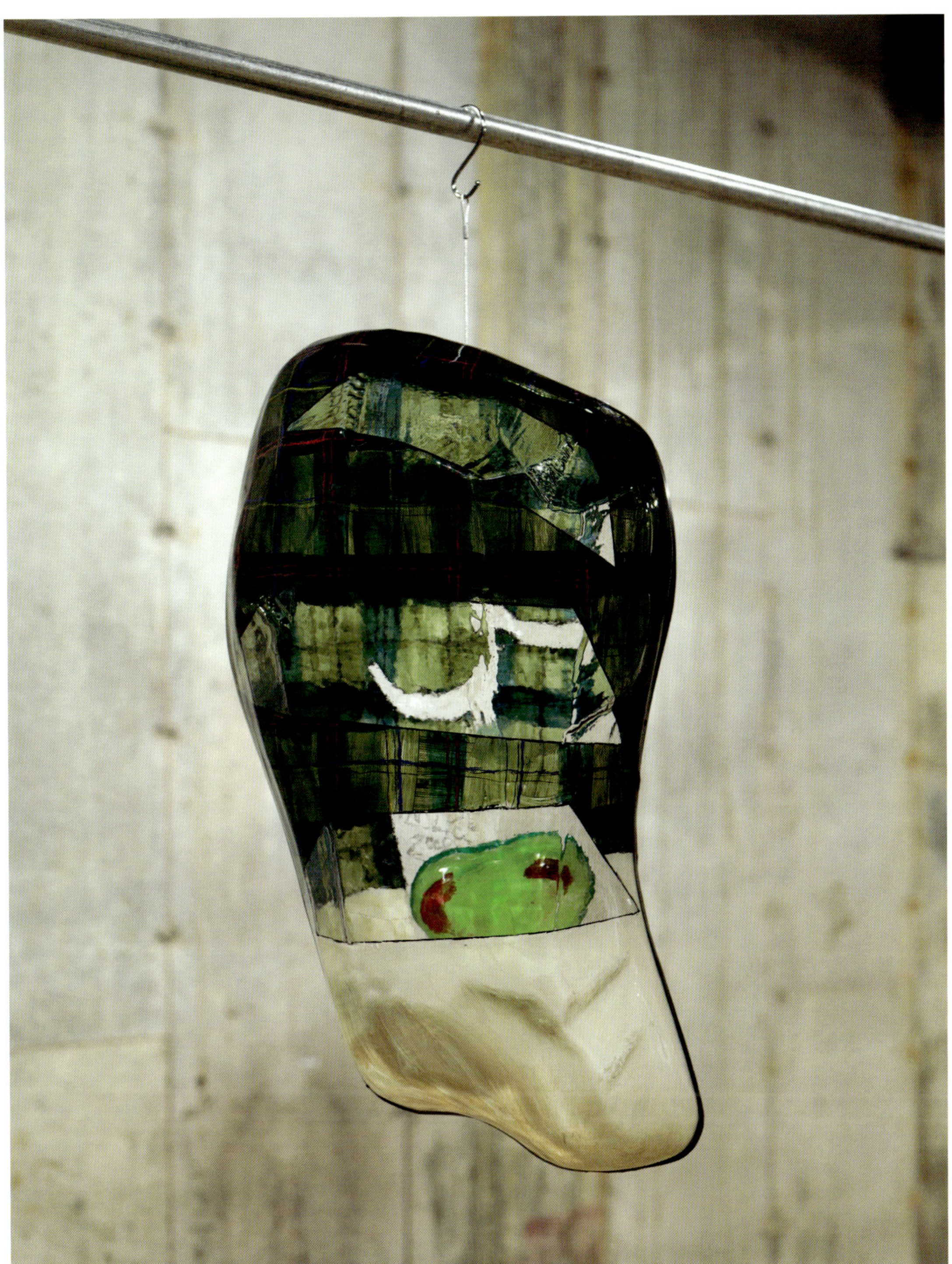

Ragen Moss, *Consumptive Reader, 2nd degree (with Apple)*, 2017. Polyethylene and acrylic paint, 31 × 16 × 9 in. (78.7 × 40.6 × 22.9 cm)

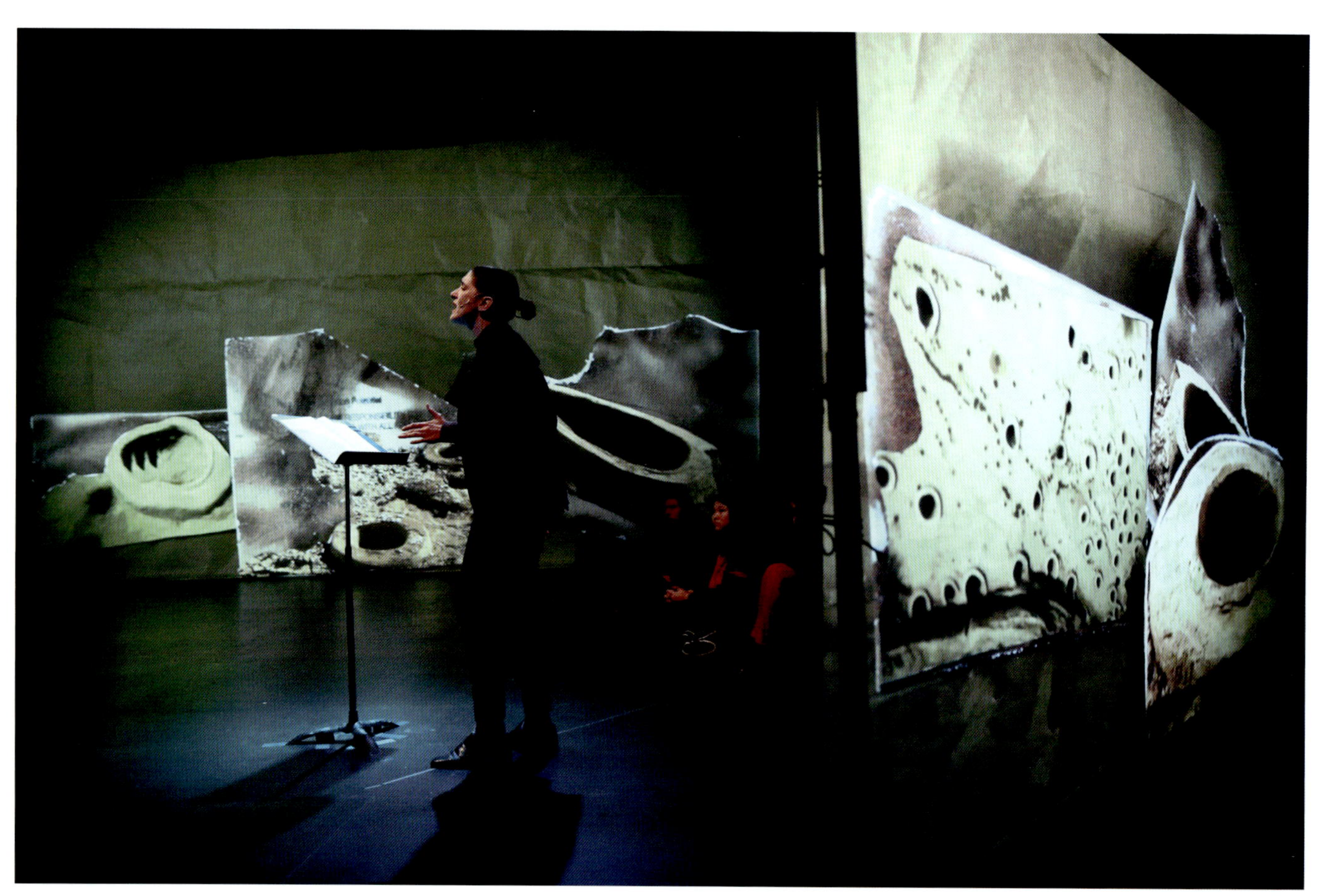

Sahra Motalebi, *Directory of Portrayals*, 2017. Performance view, The Kitchen, New York, NY, 2017

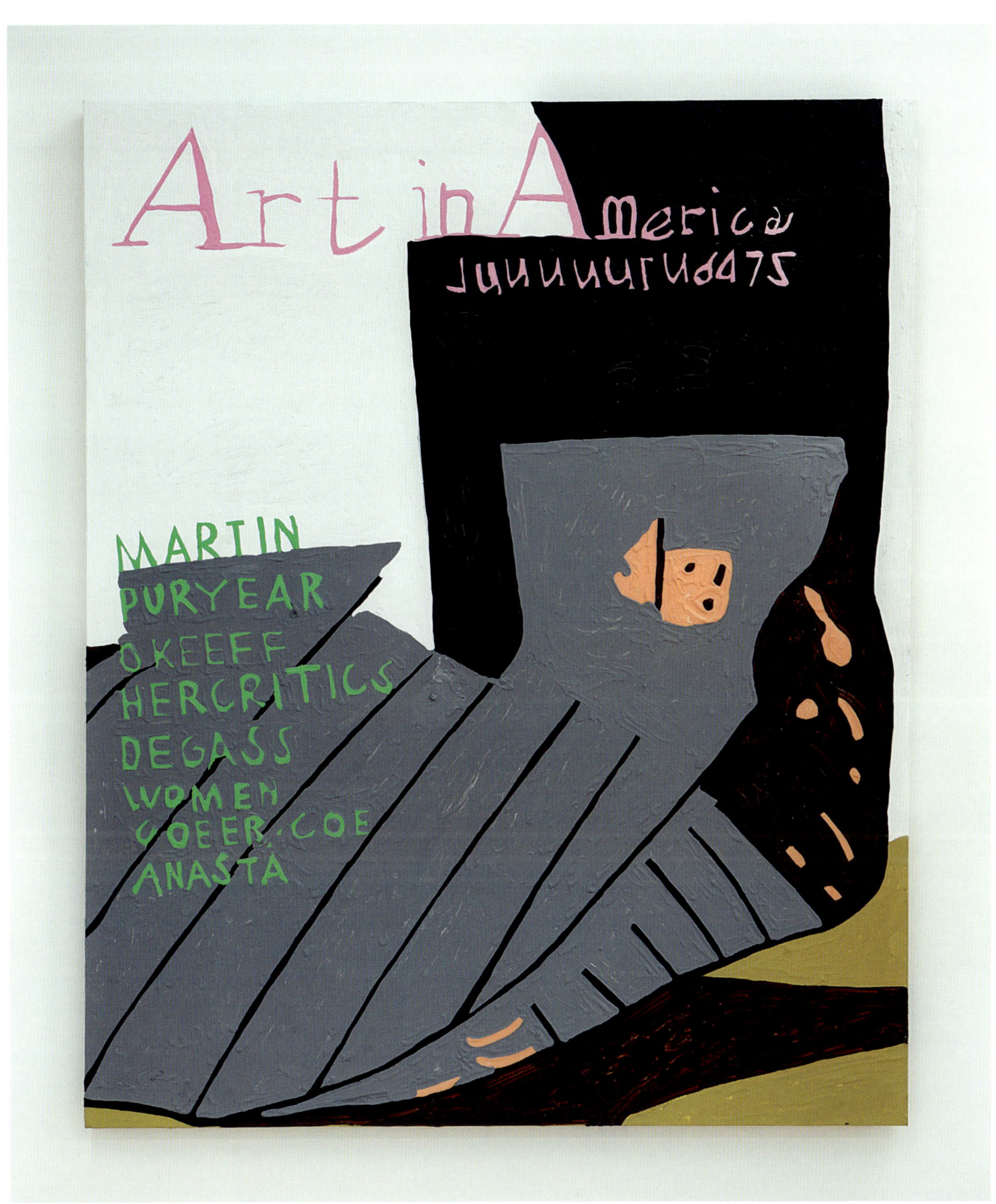

Marlon Mullen, *untitled*, 2018. Acrylic on linen, 40×32 in. (101.6×81.3 cm)

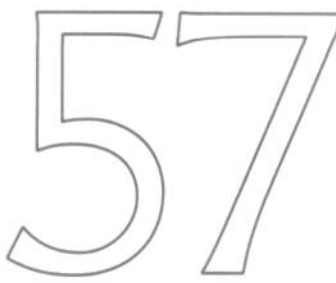

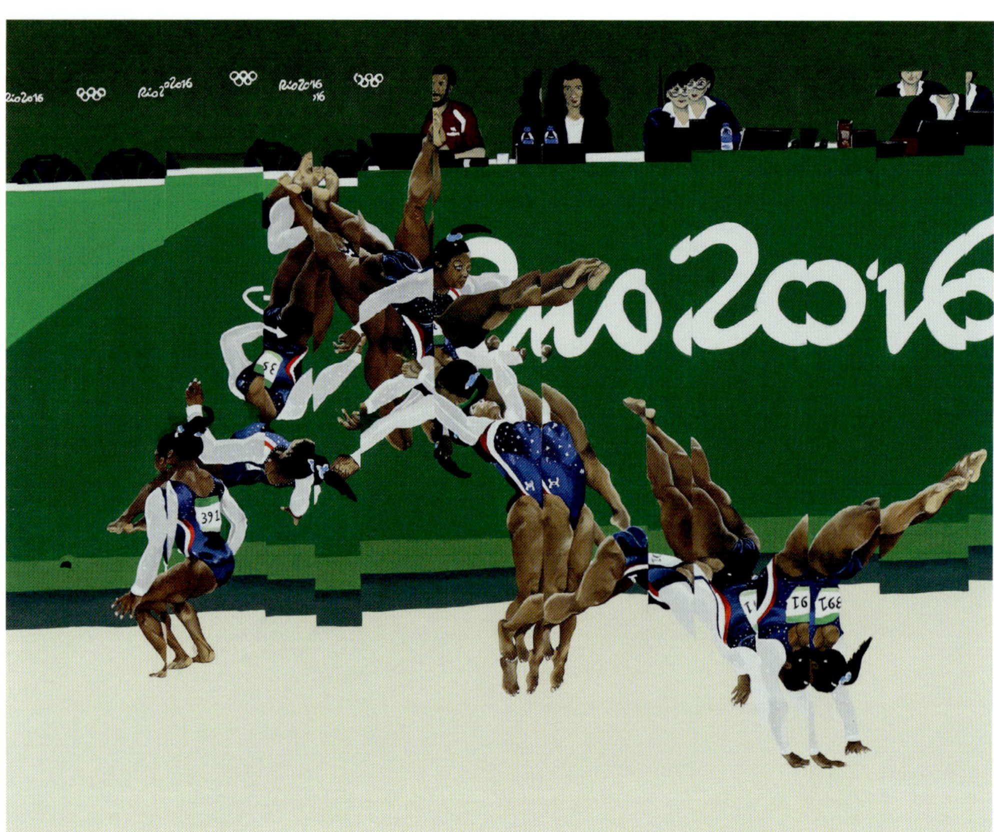

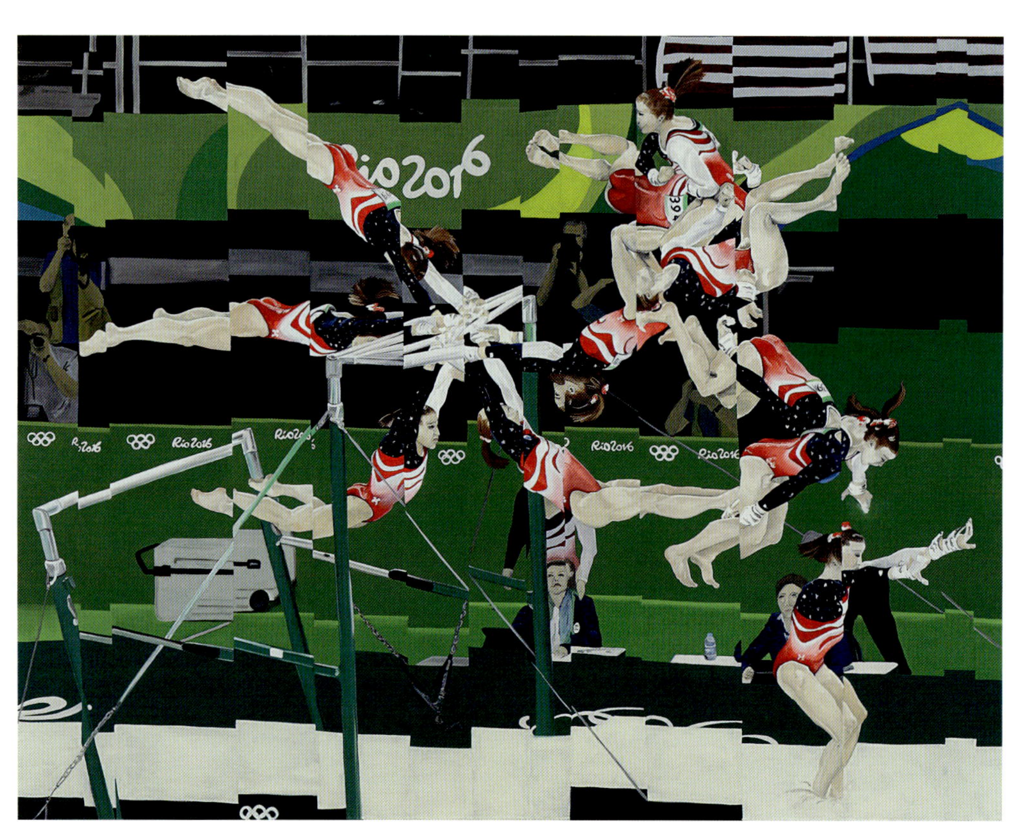

Jeanette Mundt, *Born Athlete American: Simone Biles II*, 2017. Oil and glitter on canvas, 42 × 50 in. (106.7 × 127 cm). *Born Athlete American: Madison Kocian I*, 2018. Oil and glitter on canvas, 48 × 60 in. (121.9 × 152.4 cm). Collection of Manny Kadre

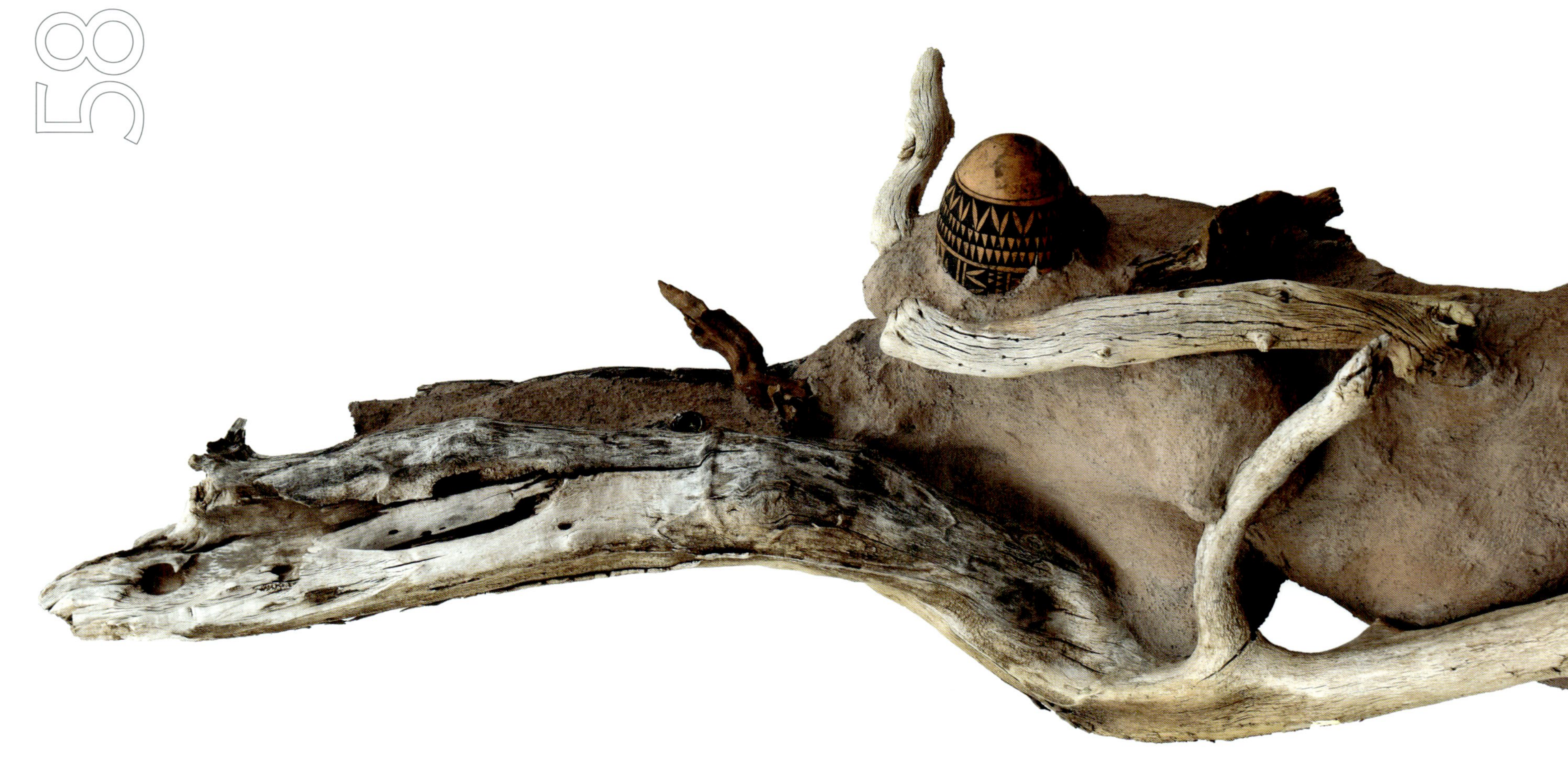

Wangechi Mutu, *Sentinel I*, 2018. Paper pulp, wood glue, concrete, wood, glass beads, stone, rose quartz, gourd, and jewelry, 87 ¾ × 17 ¾ × 22 in. (221 × 43.2 × 55.9 cm)

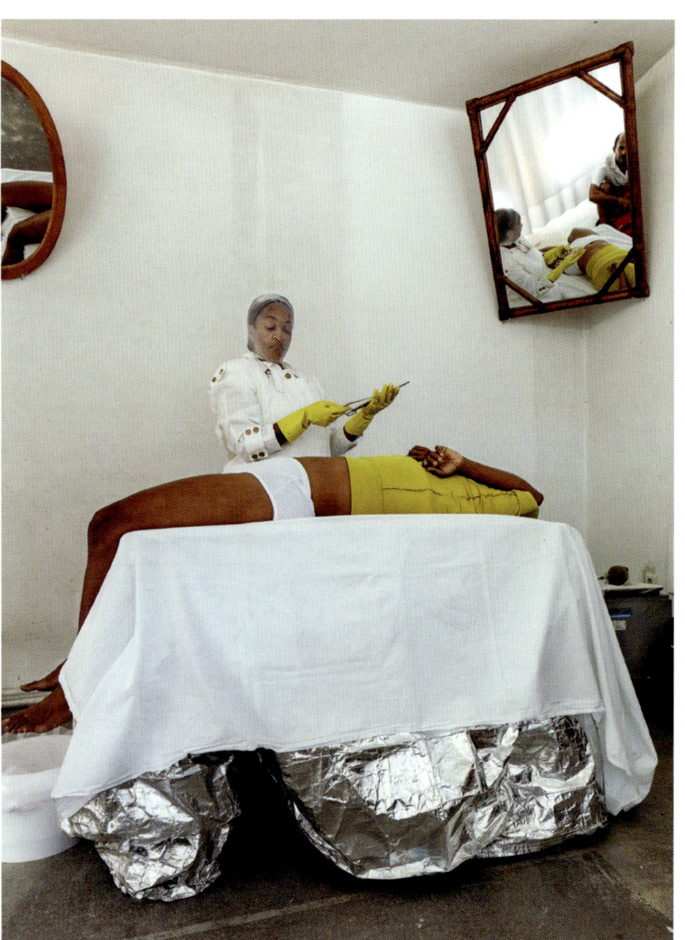
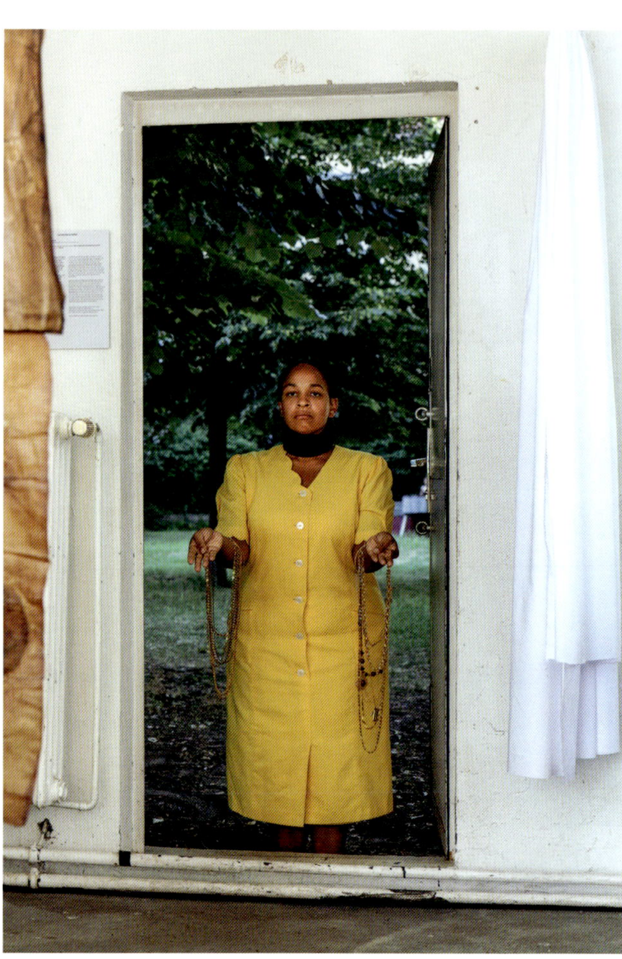

Las Nietas de Nonó, *Ilustraciones de la mecánica (Illustrations of the Mechanical)*, 2016–18. Performance view, 10th Berlin Biennale for Contemporary Art, Berlin, Germany, 2018

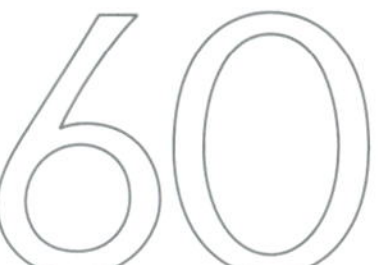

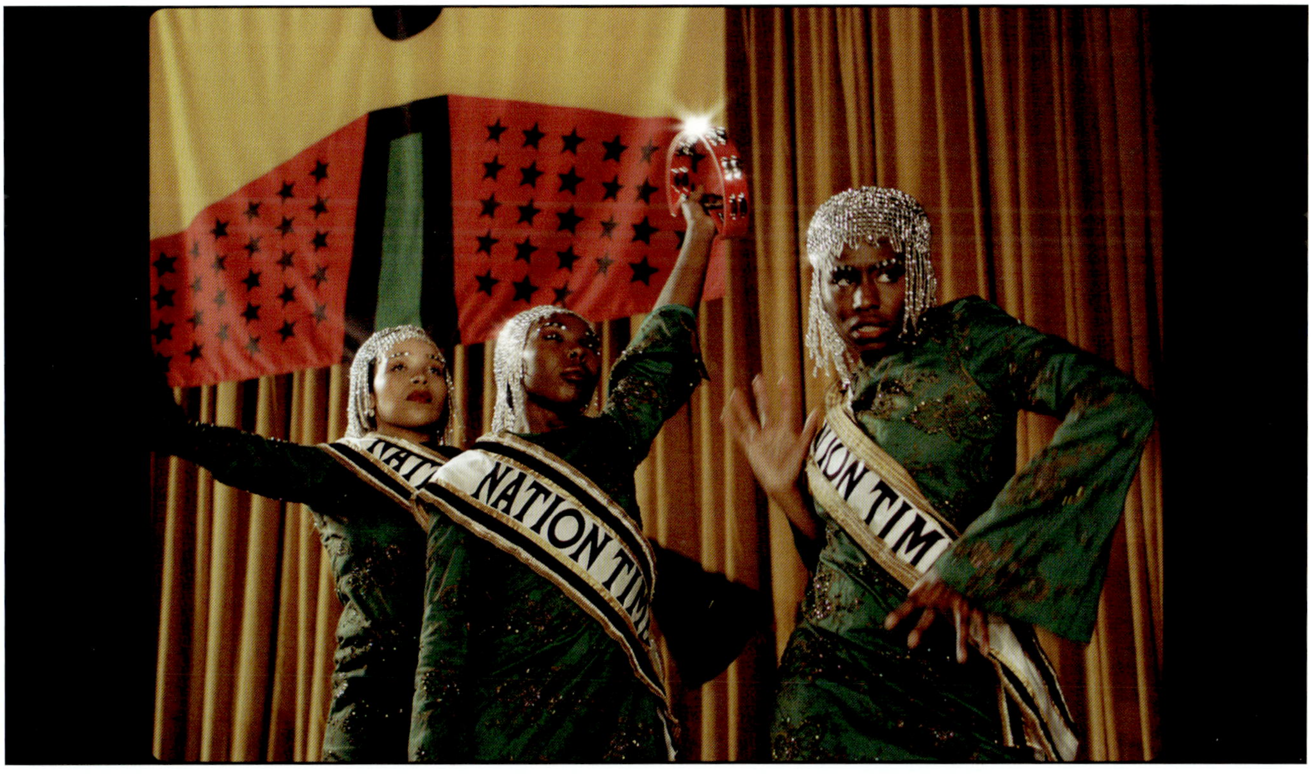

Jenn Nkiru, *Hub-Tones*, video for Kamasi Washington, 2018. High-definition video, color, sound; 9:27 min.

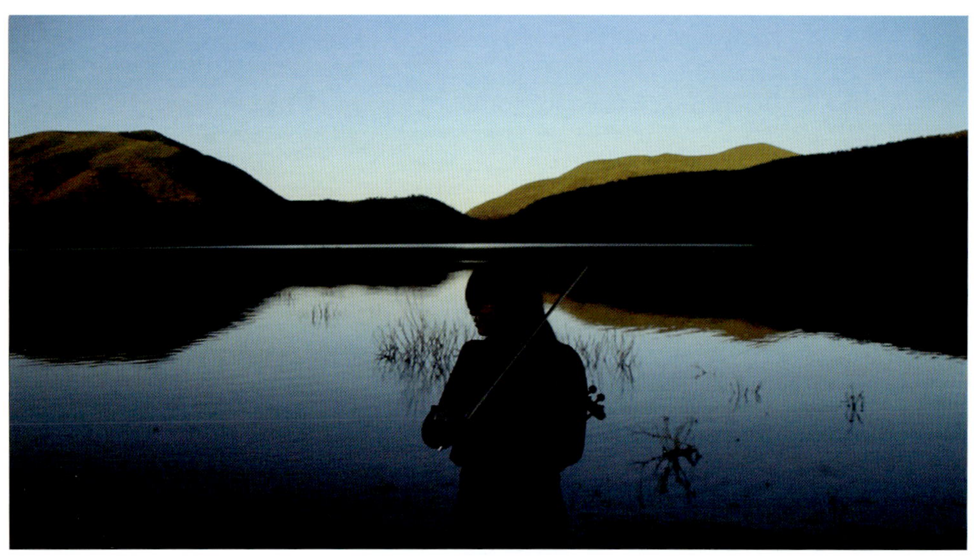

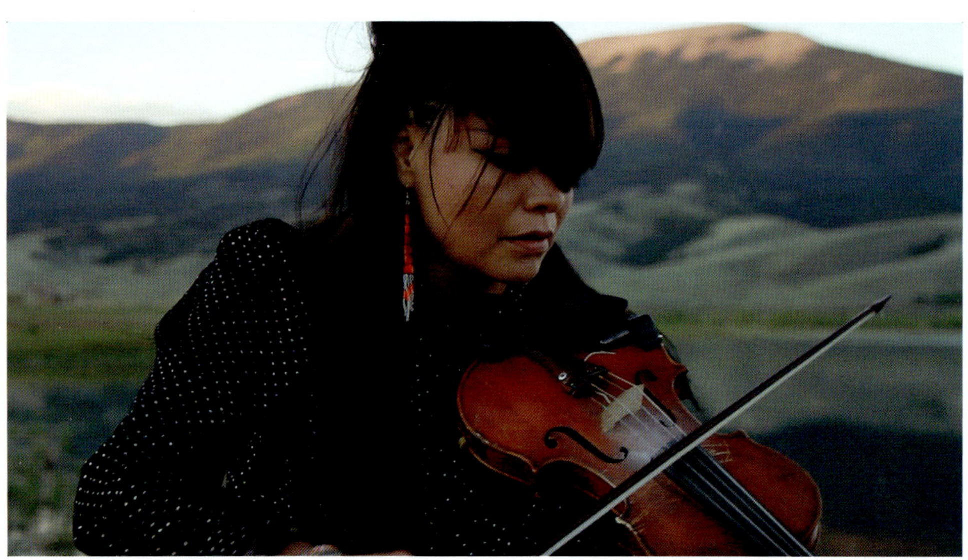

Laura Ortman, *My Soul Remainer*, 2017. High-definition video, color, sound; 5:44 min.

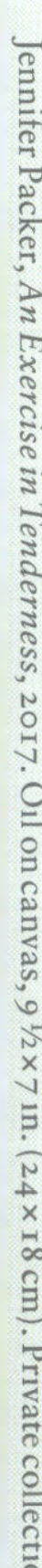

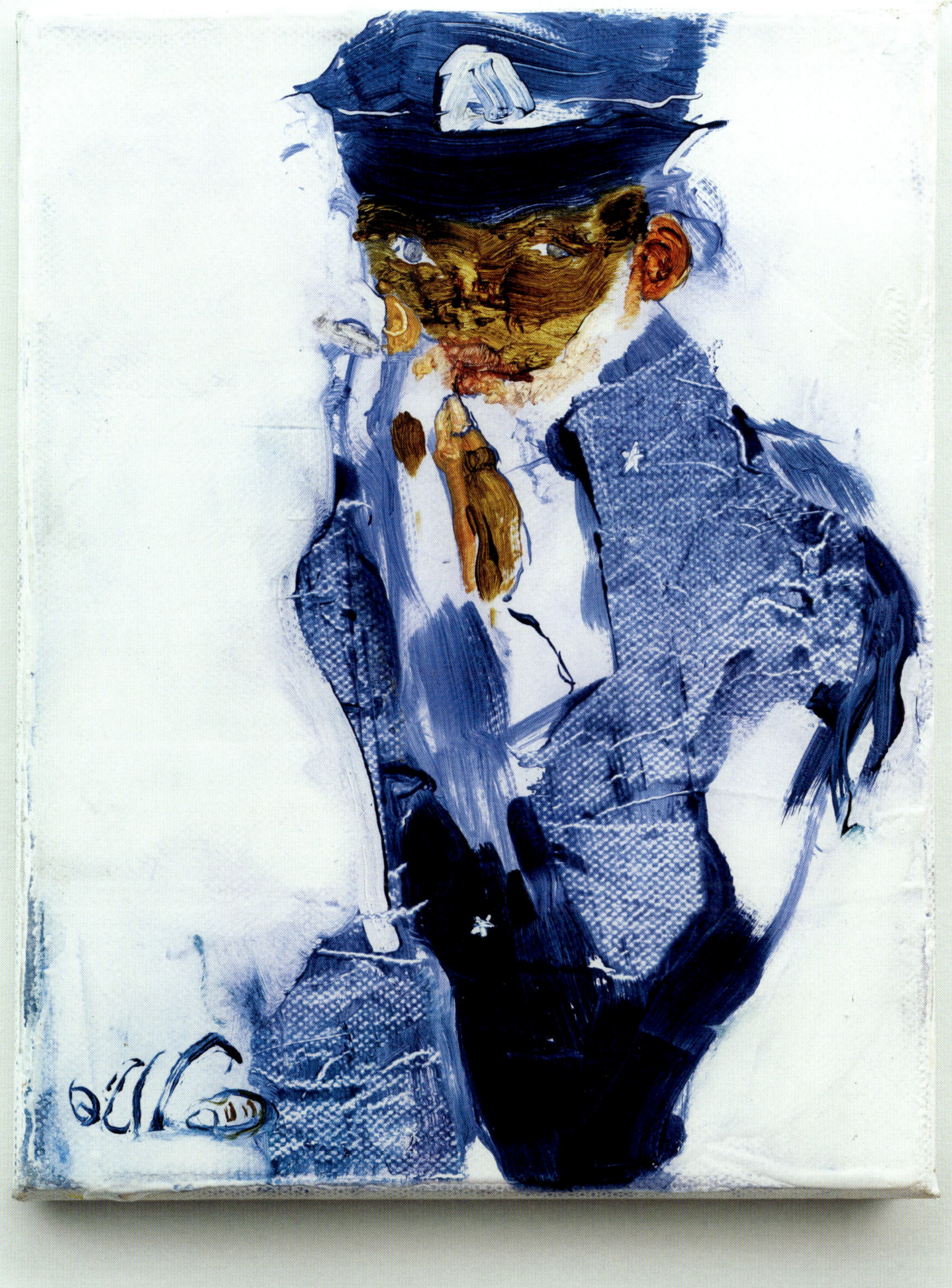

Jennifer Packer, *An Exercise in Tenderness*, 2017, Oil on canvas, 9½ × 7 in. (24 × 18 cm), Private collection

nibia pastrana santiago, condiciones materiales para la ficción y la fatiga (material conditions for fiction and fatigue), 2018. Performance view, Casa de los Contrafuertes, San Juan, PR, 2018

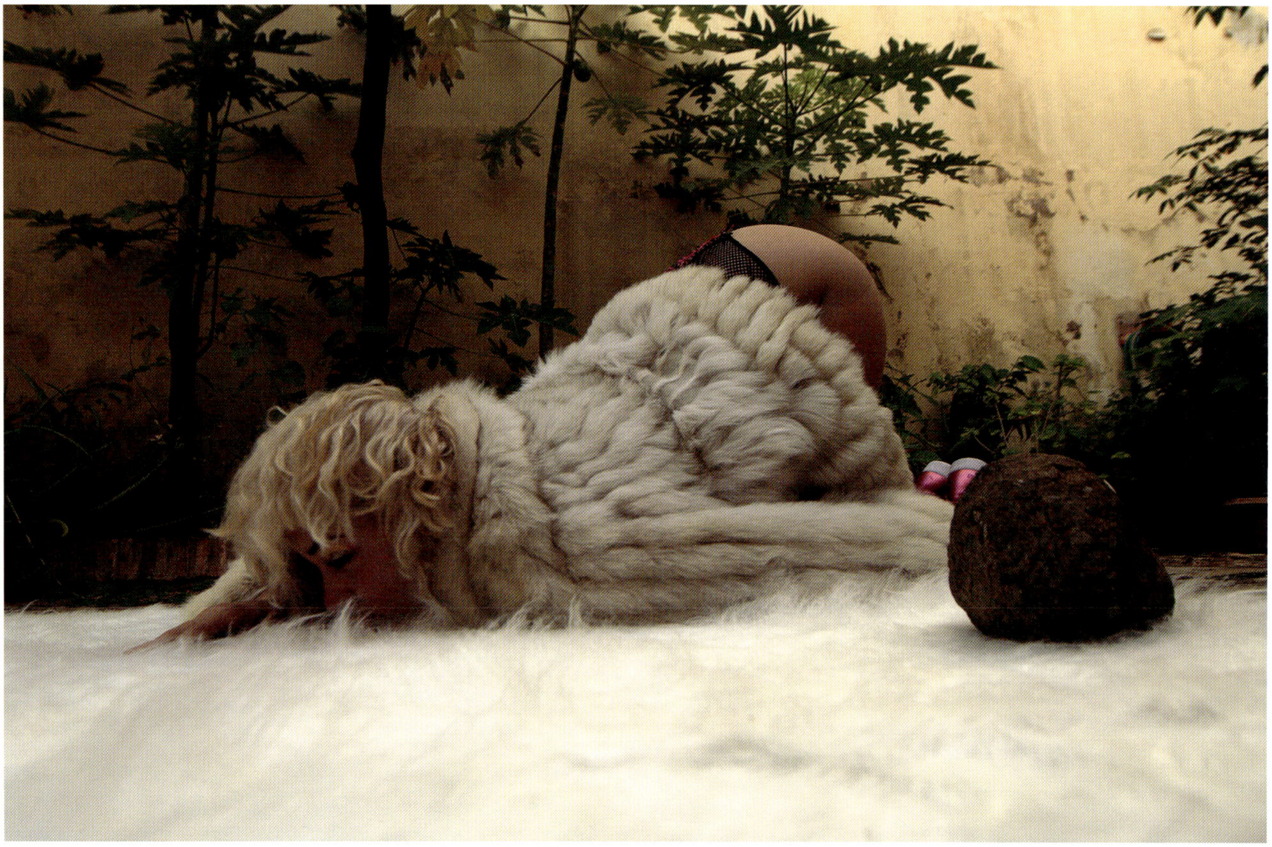

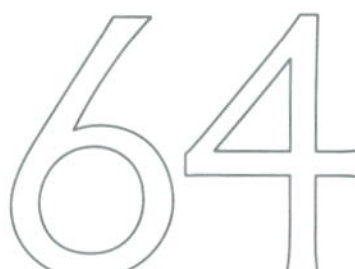

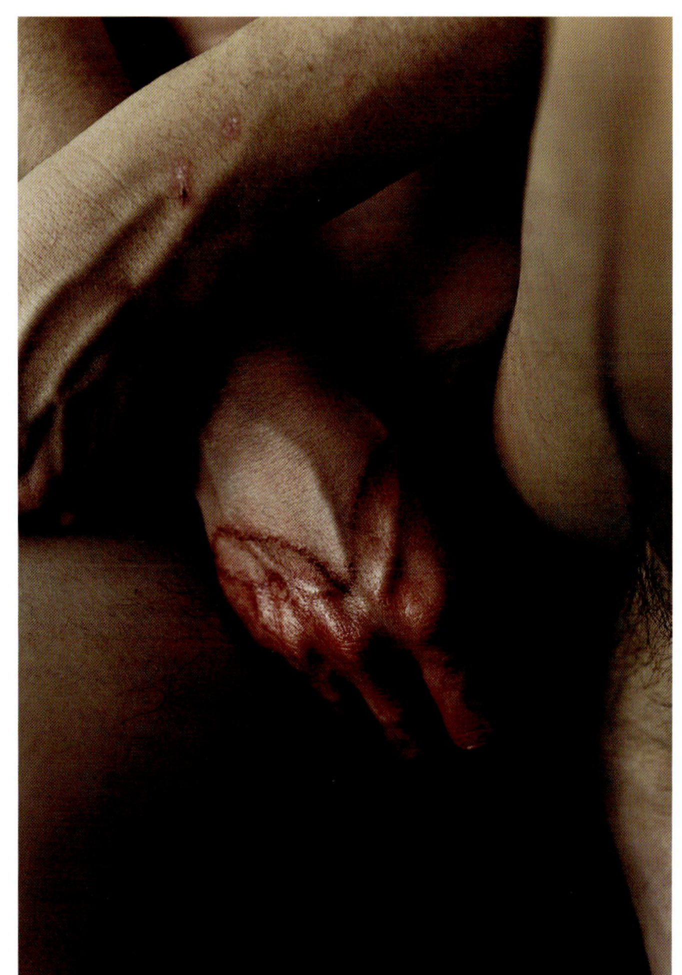

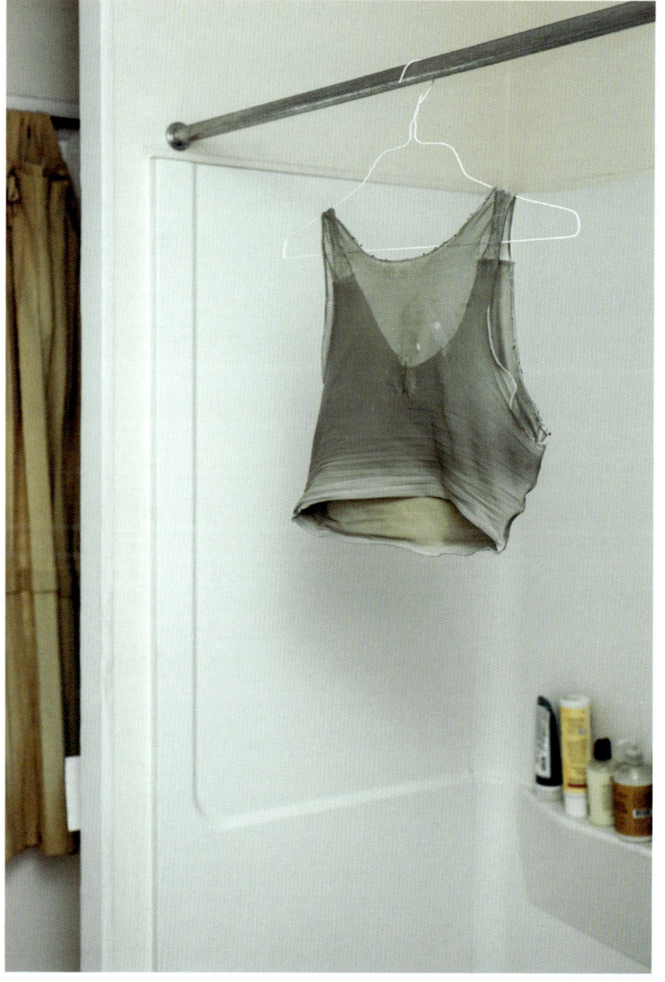

Elle Pérez, *Dick*, 2018. Inkjet print, 44⅜ × 31 in. (112.7 × 78.7 cm). *Binder*, 2015/2018. Inkjet print, 44⅜ × 31 in. (112.7 × 78.7 cm)

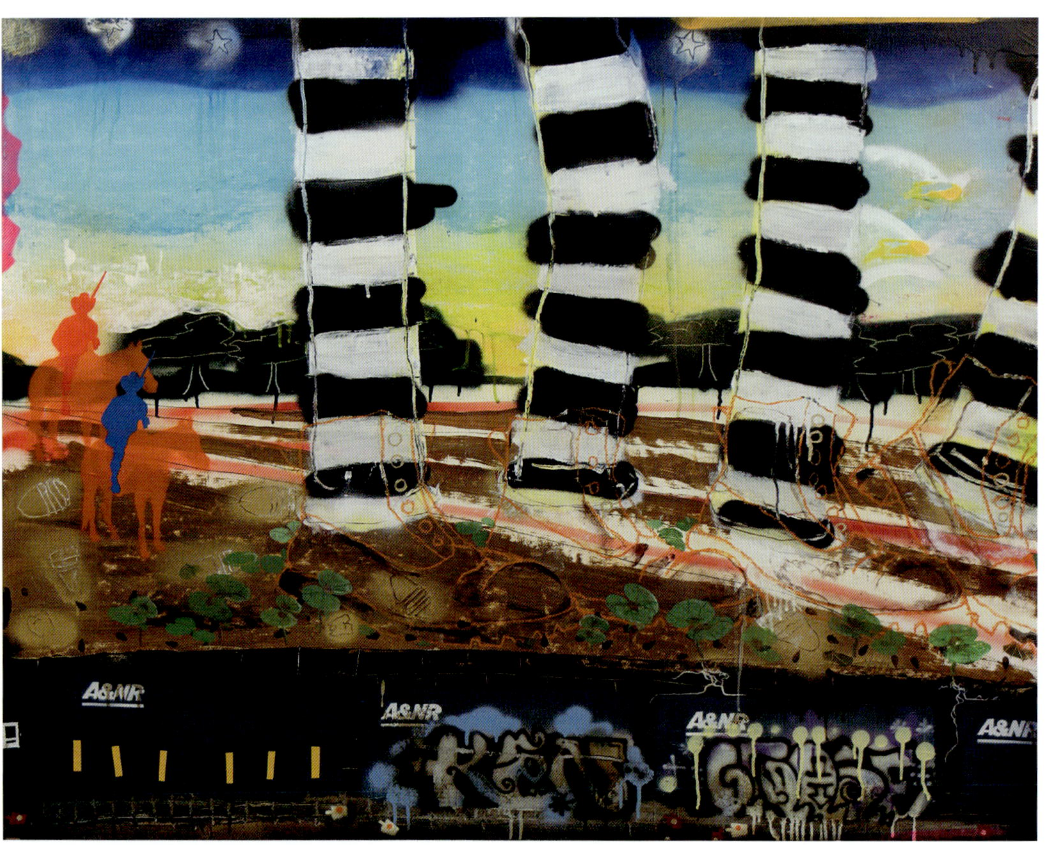

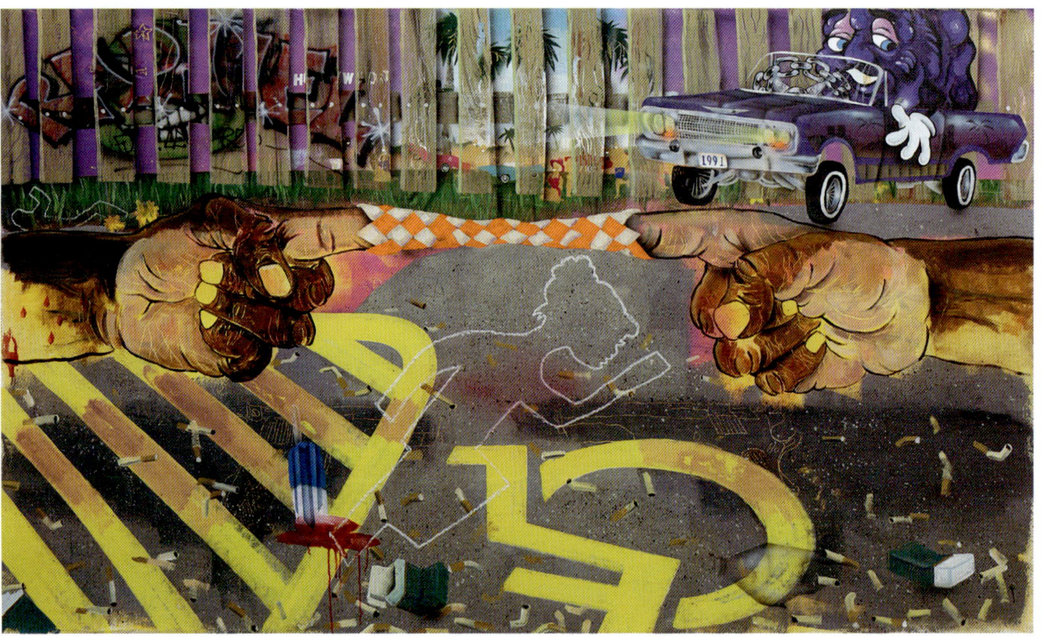

Pat Phillips, *Underground Railroad / Chain Gang*, 2016. Acrylic, oil pastel, airbrush, and aerosol paint on canvas, 40 × 49 in. (101.6 × 124.5 cm). Collection of Nathaniel Bohrer.

Korean Finger Trap, 2018. Acrylic, oil pastel, airbrush, and aerosol paint on canvas, 52 × 88 in. (132.1 × 223.5 cm)

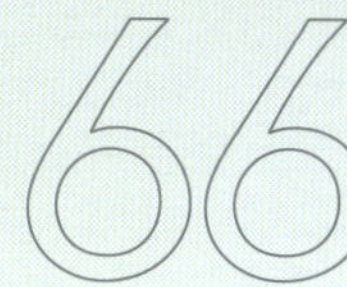

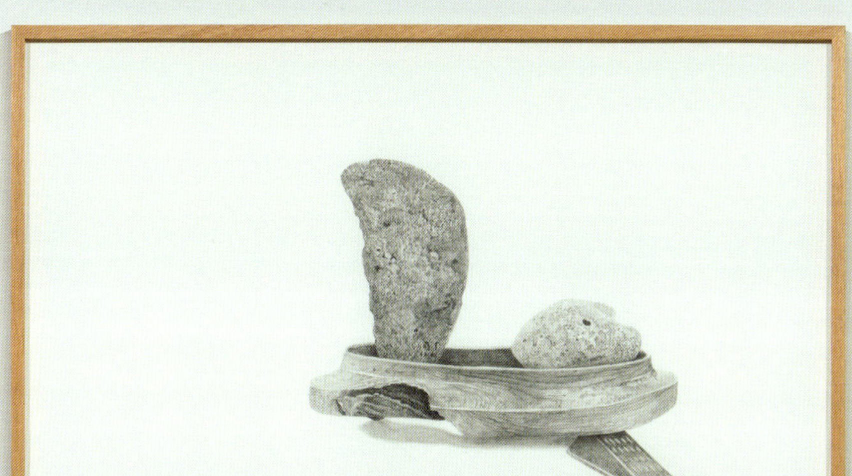

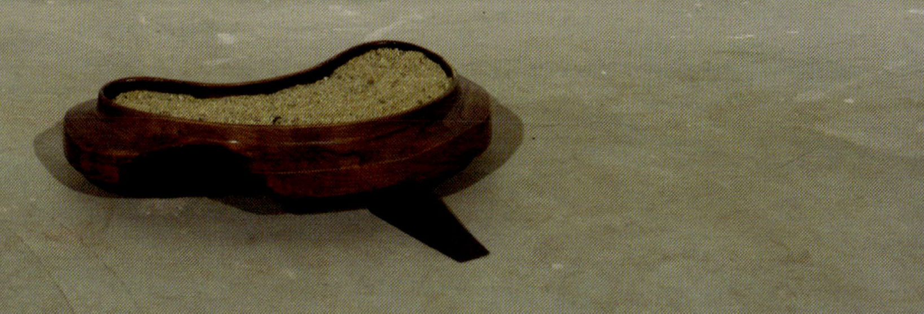

Gala Porras-Kim, *Two rocks, one pumice split in half, one generic rock, n.d. reconstruction (doorstop)*, 2018. Graphite on paper in artist's frame, doorstop, mahogany, and sand, 63 × 94 × 4 in. (160 × 238.8 × 10.2 cm)

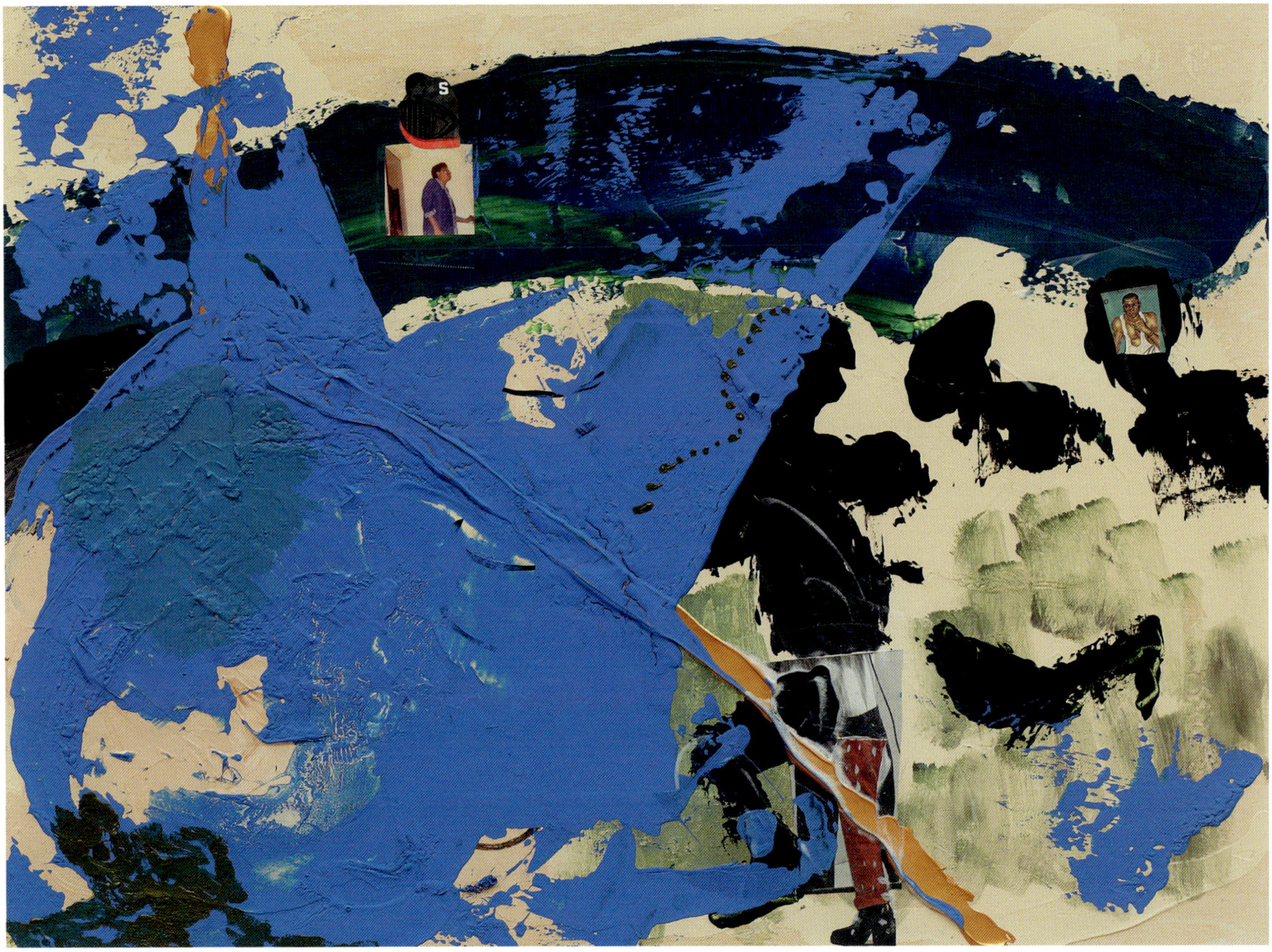

Walter Price, *POWER OF PRIDE #1*, 2017. Acrylic, paper, glue, strapping tape, and vinyl paint on wood, 19 × 25 in. (48.3 × 63.5 cm). Collection of Michael Ringier

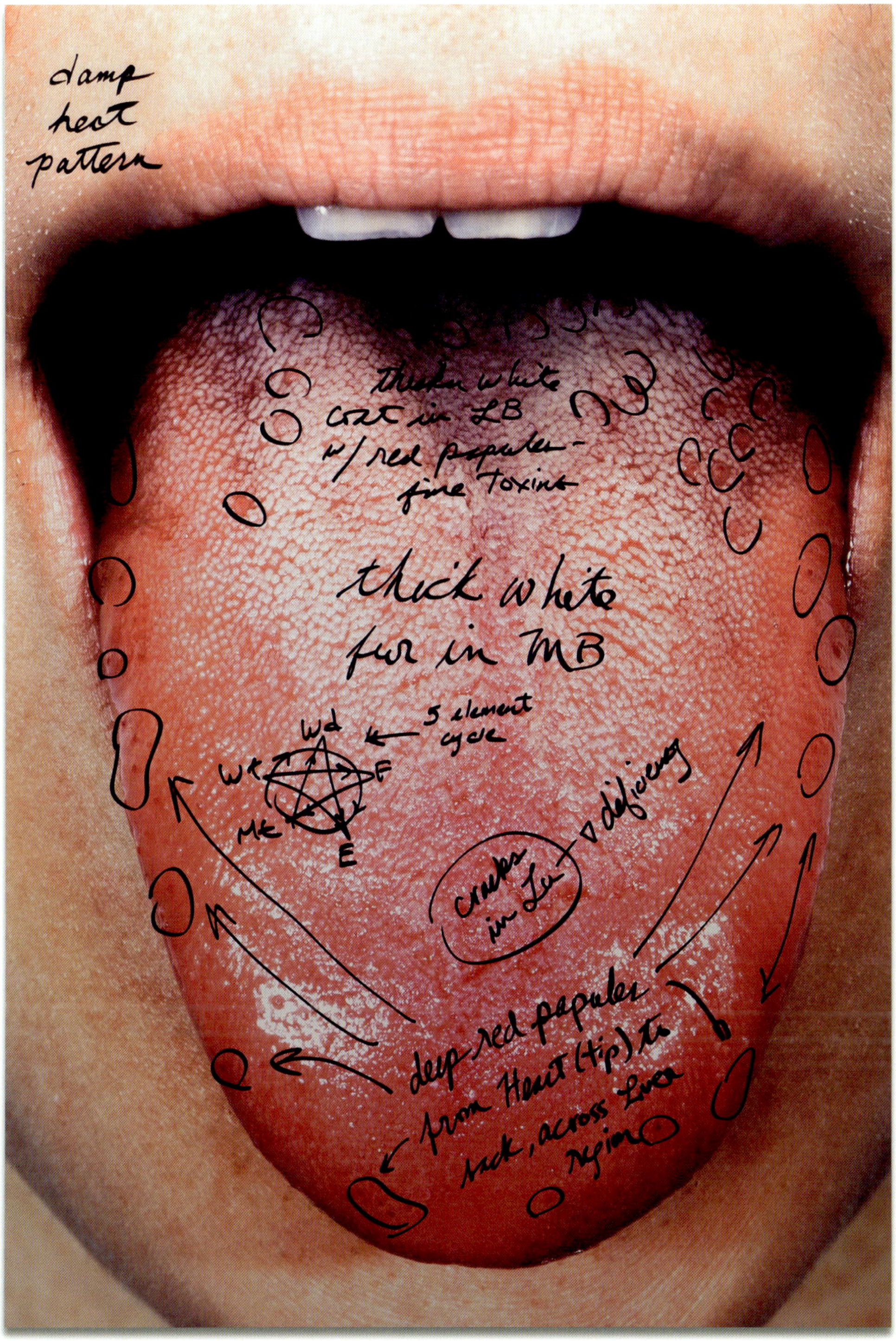

Carissa Rodriguez, *It's Symptomatic/What Would Edith Say?*, 2015. Digital chromogenic print with ink mounted on aluminum, 60 × 40 in. (152.4 × 101.6 cm)

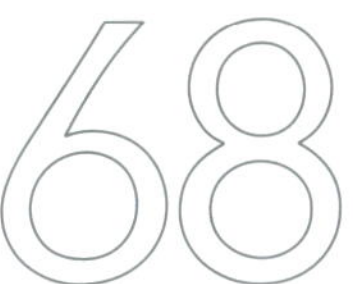

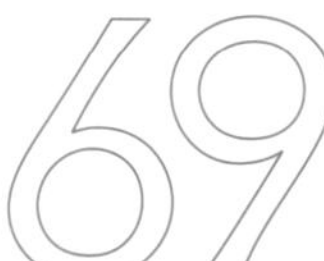

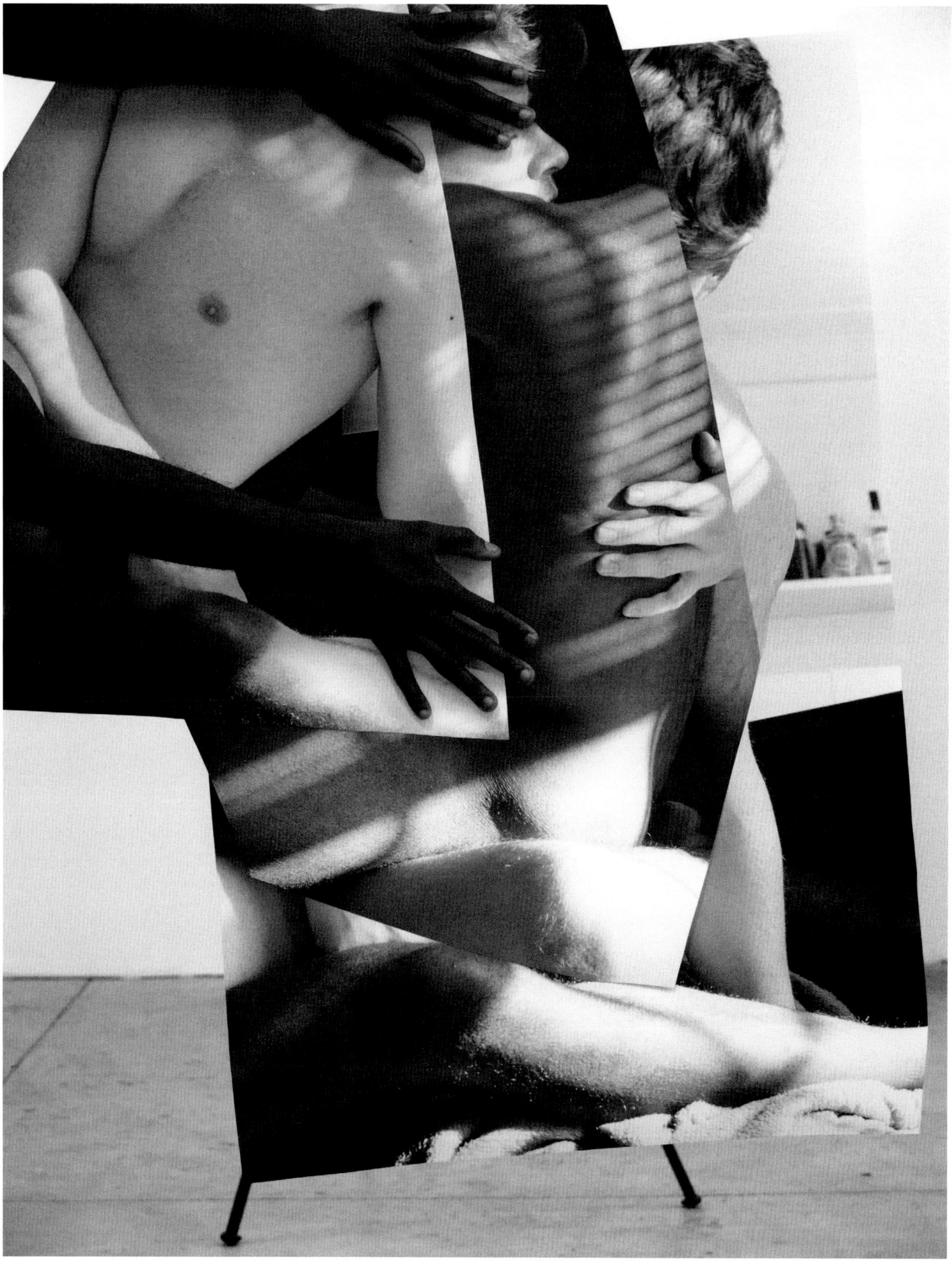

Paul Mpagi Sepuya, *Mirror Study for Joe (_2010980_)*, 2017. Inkjet print, 48 × 34 in. (121.9 × 86.4 cm)

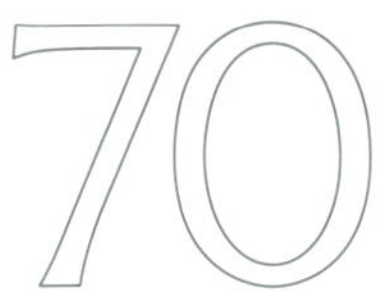

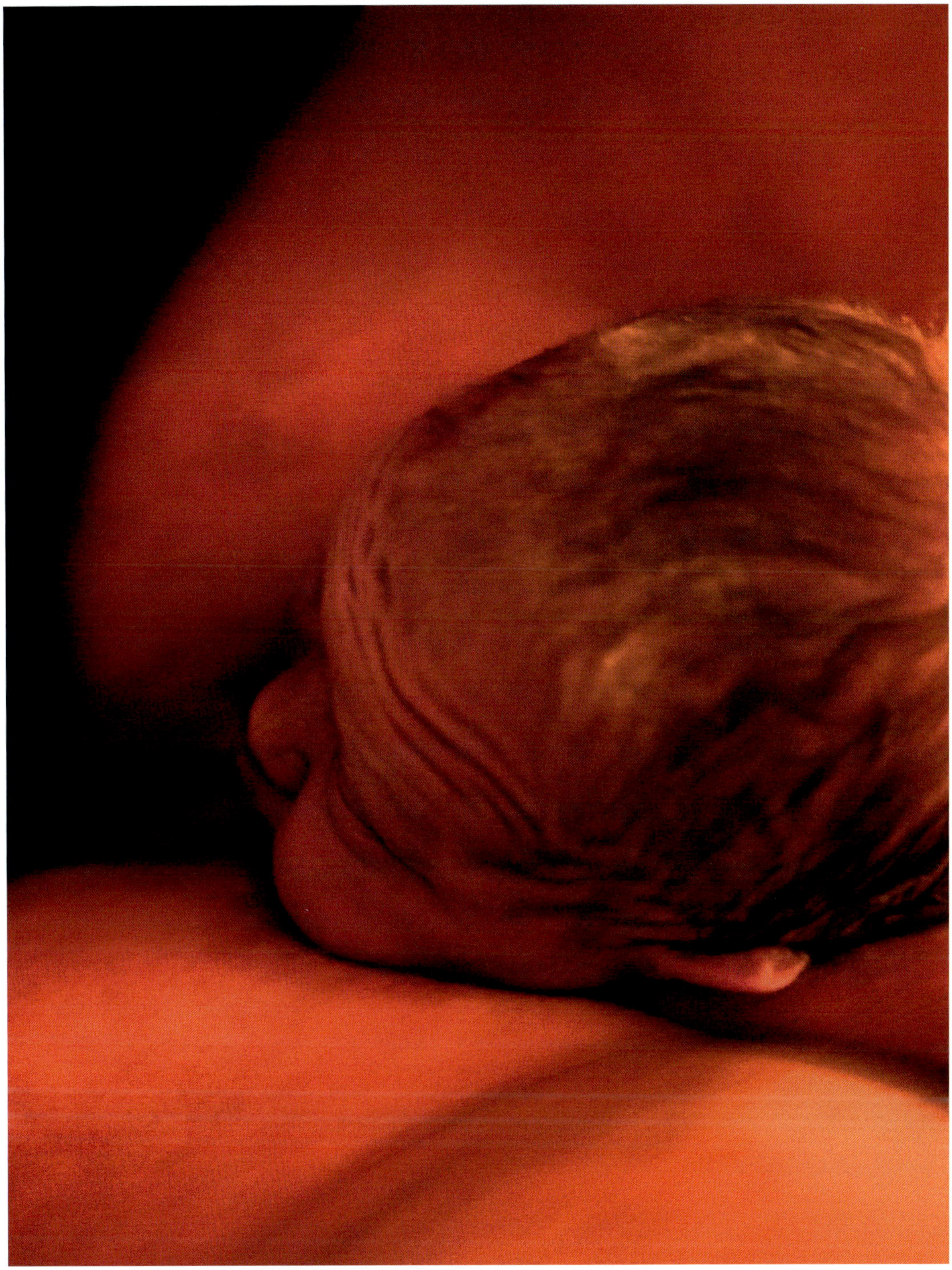

Heji Shin, *Baby 6*, 2016. Inkjet print, 30 × 23 in. (76.2 × 58.4 cm). Collection of Guy Bennett

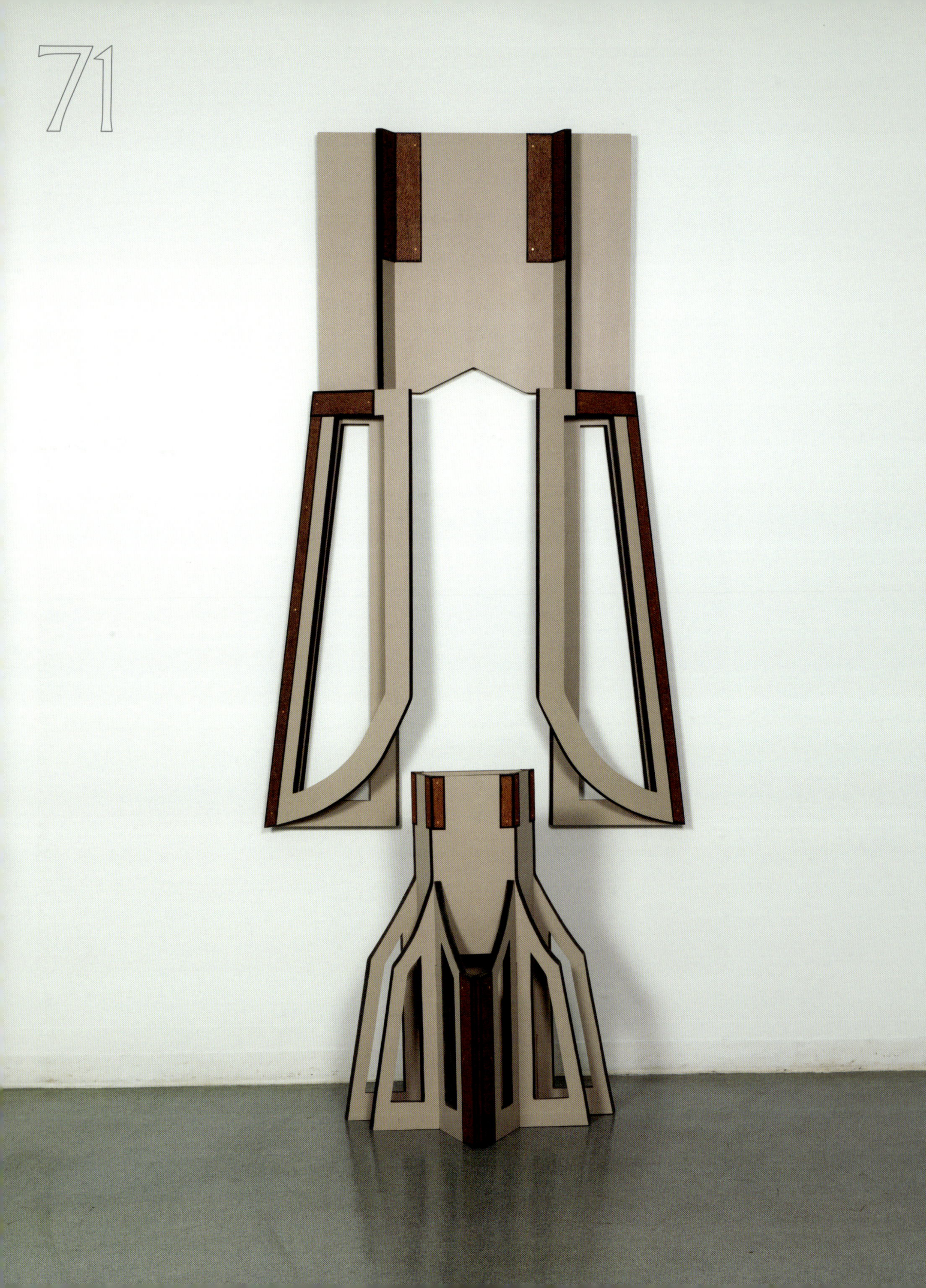

Diane Simpson, *Lambrequin and Peplum*, 2017. Painted fiberboard, crayon on polyester, and copper tacks, 109×50×31 in. (276.9×127×78.7 cm)

Martine Syms, *Misdirected Kiss*, 2016, *Lessons I—CLXXX*, 2014–18, and *Lightly, Slightly, Politely*, 2016. Installation view, *Martine Syms: Fact & Trouble*, Institute of Contemporary Arts, London, United Kingdom, 2016. *Is You Is or Is You Ain't*, 2016, and *SHE MAD: Laughing Gas*, 2016. Installation view, *Made in L.A. 2016: a, the, though, only*, Hammer Museum, Los Angeles, CA, 2016

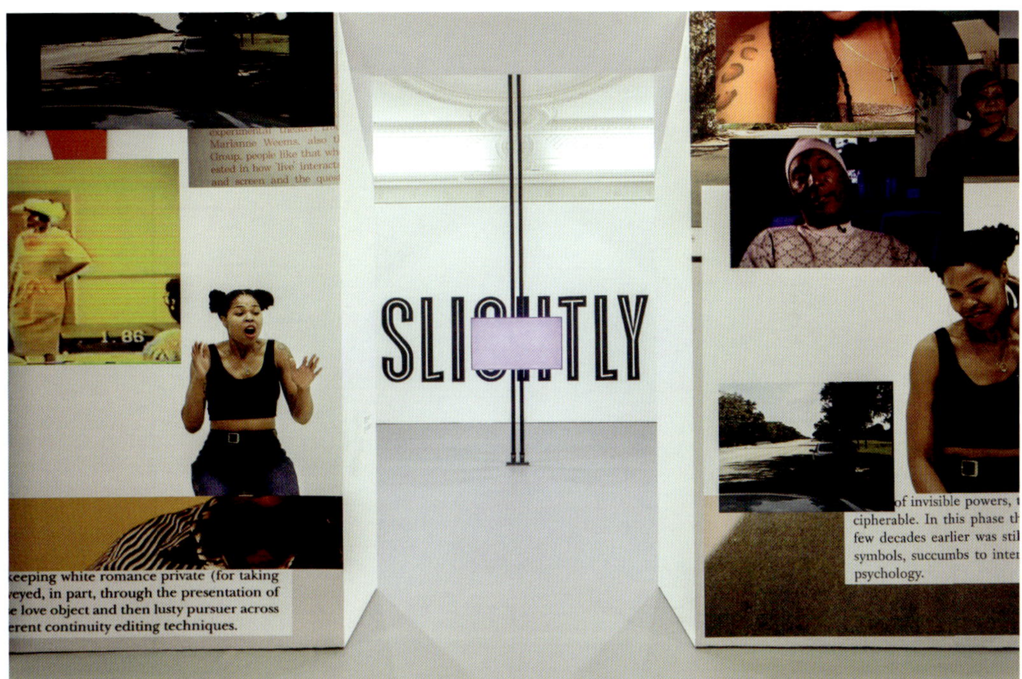

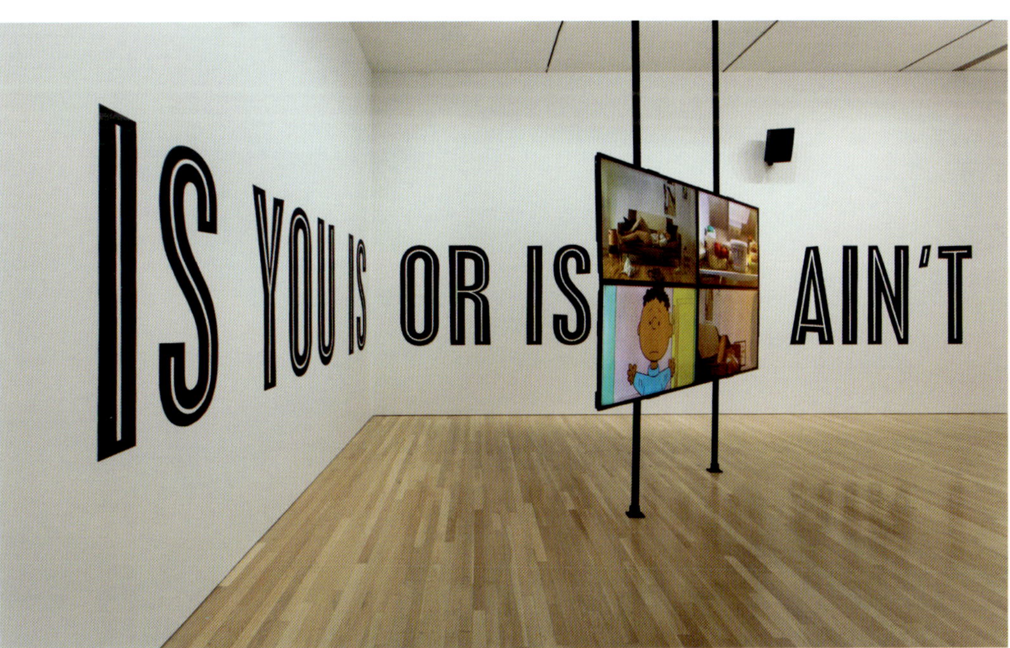

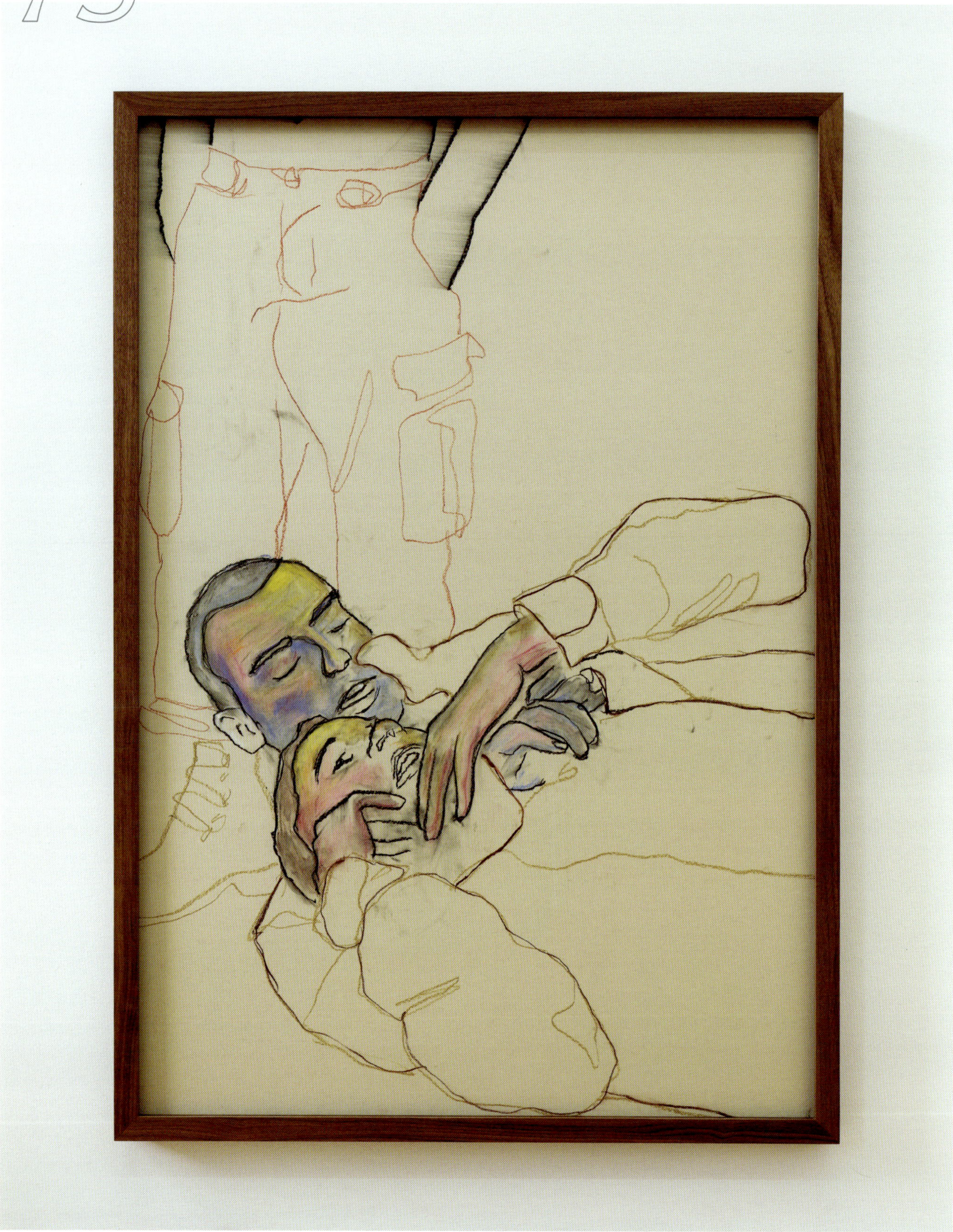

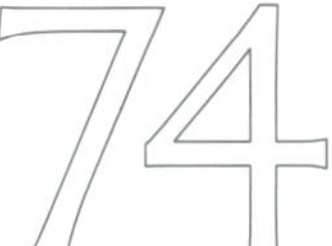

Mariana Valencia, *Yugoslavia*, 2017. Performance view, Danspace Project, New York, NY, 2017. *ALBUM*, 2017. Performance view, Hirshhorn Museum and Sculpture Garden, Washington, DC, 2018

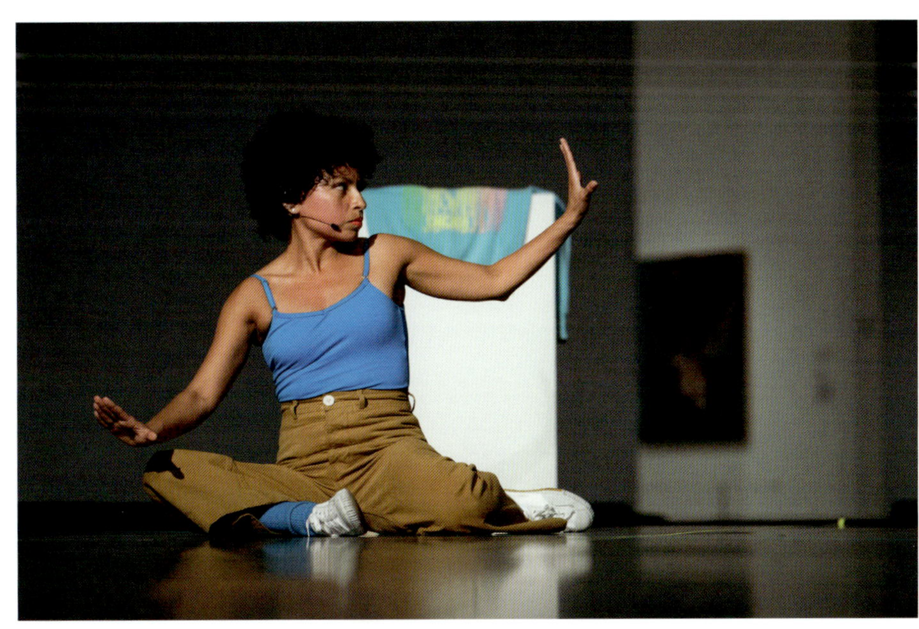

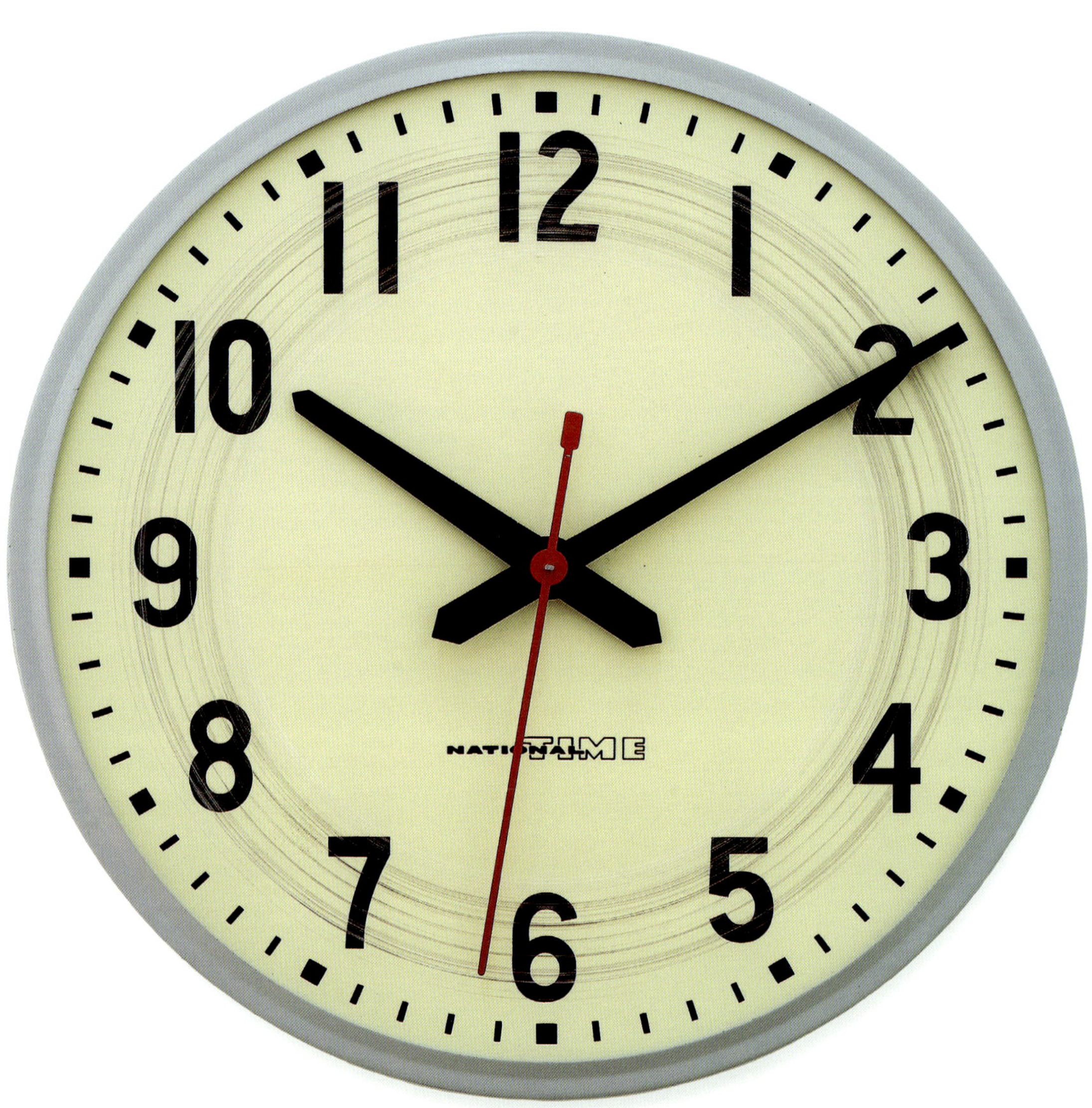

Agustina Woodgate, *National Times* (detail), 2016. Clocks, hardware, and sanding twigs, dimensions variable

Whitney Biennial

2019

Contents

		WORKS	PROCESS	ENTRIES
1	EDDIE ARROYO Born 1976 in Miami, FL; lives in Miami, FL	2	114	266
2	KORAKRIT ARUNANONDCHAI Born 1986 in Bangkok, Thailand; lives in New York, NY, and Bangkok, Thailand	3	116	266
3	OLGA BALEMA Born 1984 in Lviv, Ukraine; lives in New York, NY	4	118	266
4	MORGAN BASSICHIS Born 1983 in Newton, MA; lives in Brooklyn, NY	5	120	267
5	BLITZ BAZAWULE Born 1982 in Accra, Ghana; lives in New York, NY	6	122	267
6	ALEXANDRA BELL Born 1983 in Chicago, IL; lives in Brooklyn, NY	7	124	268
7	BRIAN BELOTT Born 1973 in East Orange, NJ; lives in Brooklyn, NY	8	126	268
8	MERIEM BENNANI Born 1988 in Rabat, Morocco; lives in Brooklyn, NY	9	128	269
9	ROBERT BITTENBENDER Born 1987 in Washington, DC; lives in Brooklyn, NY	10	130	269
10	LUCAS BLALOCK Born 1978 in Asheville, NC; lives in Brooklyn, NY	11	132	270
11	GARRETT BRADLEY Born 1986 in New York, NY; lives in New Orleans, LA	12	134	270
12	MILANO CHOW Born 1987 in Los Angeles, CA; lives in Los Angeles, CA	13	136	270
13	COLECTIVO LOS INGRÁVIDOS Founded 2011 in Tehuacán, Mexico	14	138	271

	WORKS	PROCESS	ENTRIES
39 JOSH KLINE Born 1979 in Philadelphia, PA; lives in Brooklyn, NY	40	190	283
40 AUTUMN KNIGHT Born 1980 in Houston, TX; lives in New York, NY	41	192	283
41 CAROLYN LAZARD Born 1987 in Upland, CA; lives in Philadelphia, PA	42	194	284
42 MAIA RUTH LEE Born 1983 in Busan, South Korea; lives in New York, NY	43	196	284
43 SIMONE LEIGH Born 1967 in Chicago, IL; lives in Brooklyn, NY	44	198	284
44 DANIEL LIND-RAMOS Born 1953 in Loíza, PR; lives in Loíza, PR	45	200	285
45 JAMES LUNA Born 1950 in Orange, CA; died 2018. Payómkawichum, Ipi, and Mexican American	46	202	285
46 ERIC N. MACK Born 1987 in Columbia, MD; lives in New York, NY	47	204	286
47 CALVIN MARCUS Born 1988 in San Francisco, CA; lives in Los Angeles, CA	48	206	286
48 TIONA NEKKIA McCLODDEN Born 1981 in Blytheville, AR; lives in Philadelphia, PA	49	208	287
49 TROY MICHIE Born 1985 in El Paso, TX; lives in Brooklyn, NY	50	210	287
50 JOE MINTER Born 1943 in Birmingham, AL; lives in Birmingham, AL	51	212	287
51 KEEGAN MONAGHAN Born 1986 in Evanston, IL; lives in Brooklyn, NY	52	214	288

	WORKS	PROCESS	ENTRIES
52 CAROLINE MONNET Born 1985 in Ottawa, Ontario; lives in Montreal, Quebec. Algonquin/French	53	216	288
53 DARIUS CLARK MONROE Born 1980 in Houston, TX; lives in Brooklyn, NY	54	218	289
54 RAGEN MOSS Born 1978 in New York, NY; lives in Los Angeles, CA	55	220	289
55 SAHRA MOTALEBI Born 1979 in Birmingham, AL; lives in New York, NY, and Delaware County, NY	56	222	290
56 MARLON MULLEN Born 1963 in Richmond, CA; lives in Rodeo, CA	57	224	290
57 JEANETTE MUNDT Born 1982 in Princeton, NJ; lives in Somerset, NJ	58	226	290
58 WANGECHI MUTU Born 1972 in Nairobi, Kenya; lives in Brooklyn, NY, and Nairobi, Kenya	59	228	291
59 LAS NIETAS DE NONÓ Lydela Nonó: Born 1979 in San Juan, PR; lives in Carolina, PR Michel Nonó: Born 1982 in San Juan, PR; lives in Carolina, PR	60	230	291
60 JENN NKIRU Born 1987 in London, United Kingdom; lives in London, United Kingdom	61	232	292
61 LAURA ORTMAN Born 1973 in Whiteriver, AZ; lives in Brooklyn, NY. White Mountain Apache	62	234	292
62 JENNIFER PACKER Born 1984 in Philadelphia, PA; lives in New York, NY	63	236	293
63 NIBIA PASTRANA SANTIAGO Born 1987 in Caguas, PR; lives in San Juan, PR	64	238	293

		WORKS	PROCESS	ENTRIES
64	ELLE PÉREZ Born 1989 in the Bronx, NY; lives in Brooklyn, NY	65	240	294
65	PAT PHILLIPS Born 1987 in Lakenheath, United Kingdom; lives in Pineville, LA	66	242	294
66	GALA PORRAS-KIM Born 1984 in Bogotá, Colombia; lives in Los Angeles, CA	67	244	295
67	WALTER PRICE Born 1989 in Macon, GA; lives in Brooklyn, NY	68	246	295
68	CARISSA RODRIGUEZ Born 1970 in New York, NY; lives in New York, NY	69	248	295
69	PAUL MPAGI SEPUYA Born 1982 in San Bernardino, CA; lives in Los Angeles, CA	70	250	296
70	HEJI SHIN Born 1983 in Seoul, South Korea; lives in New York, NY	71	252	296
71	DIANE SIMPSON Born 1935 in Joliet, IL; lives in Wilmette, IL	72	254	297
72	MARTINE SYMS Born 1988 in Los Angeles, CA; lives in Los Angeles, CA	73	256	297
73	KYLE THURMAN Born 1986 in West Chester, PA; lives in Brooklyn, NY	74	258	298
74	MARIANA VALENCIA Born 1984 in Chicago, IL; lives in Brooklyn, NY	75	260	298
75	AGUSTINA WOODGATE Born 1981 in Buenos Aires, Argentina; lives in Miami, FL, and Amsterdam, the Netherlands	76	262	299

The Whitney Biennial is anything but a systematic overview of art of the last couple of years. Since its inception in 1932, it has never been and never could be based on numbers and statistics. There is no set formula or manual for creating this exhibition. Instead, it is accomplished with as few pre-conceived notions as possible and is deeply inflected by the curators responsible for organizing the exhibition. The 2019 Biennial, co-curated by Rujeko Hockley and Jane Panetta, both members of the Whitney's curatorial department, began with instincts, experiences, curiosities, knowledge, and histories. The curators visited some three hundred artists working in the United States and abroad. Everywhere they went they engaged in careful and thoughtful looking and listening, which led them to discover networks, connections, and patterns of approach and production. They sought to reach beyond the domination of the art market, not so much to develop a counter narrative but in a search of authenticity, an unadulterated but not uncomplicated heartbeat of art making at this moment. Theirs is a desire to grasp the impulses of creation and to grapple with what makes America tick at this extremely difficult and tumultuous period. Their efforts raised essential questions: How do artists continue to work in the face of mass dislocation and migration, racism and xenophobia, the crisis of neoliberal capitalism, the rise of fascism, and the rapidly deteriorating environment? How do artists, particularly younger ones, survive when success is often measured by salability and financial gain rather than the quality of ideas? How do emerging artists with little means of support—often with considerable debt and no gallery representation—get a foothold? What are the conceptual, material, and formal strategies that all artists employ in a visual environment driven by commerce and algorithmic measures of quality? How do they embrace complexity, subtlety, ambiguity, and poetry in a world that is increasingly binary and polarized and wants simplistic answers to overwhelmingly complex problems?

At the time of this writing, well before the Biennial itself is open, I have heard the curators' observations and discussion of concepts, seen numerous images, read many texts, and studied the layouts for this catalogue. I am struck by how this Biennial, perhaps more than most, is an invitation to firsthand experience and learning. Just as the curators entered the process of curating the Biennial with openness, we too are encouraged to enter into conversations in which the curators themselves are participants and interlocutors as much as experts. It is as if they are saying that we are all in this together. The work and the conditions of society are for all of us to grapple with. We are not and cannot be bystanders. The works in the Biennial, as the curators point out, are generally hopeful, yet they have an urgency and suggest that we, as individuals, have agency and the ability to act. Many objects have handmade qualities that can be viewed as individual actions against a society dominated by electronic media. And, although the works in this Biennial are replete with indirect and direct sociopolitical concerns, this is not an exhibition made up of one-liners that are hectoring or finger wagging. The artists present us with works that are nuanced and complex, striving for new definitions of beauty through the consideration of fresh truths. In the words of the curators, the seventy-five artists in this Biennial allow us "to reenvision the way we see the U.S. and the world."

Like the honest and forthright discourse into which the curators have invited us, the works themselves are utterly lacking in pretension; they reckon with the real and the authentic in a world marked by the fake, the simulated, and the fraudulent. Many of the artists seem to subject themselves to a kind of self-analysis through their work—sometimes deconstructing the body as well as examining gender and race in a manner that emphasizes the importance of exploration and introspection. Similarly, this catalogue includes an extensive selection of images supplied by the artists that lay bare the procedures, means, inspirations, motivations, systems, and progressions of their works. It is in effect a statement that working process is inherently a search for authenticity and is as important as the destination. In addition, the inclusion of a substantial number of performances and performance-based works in this Biennial further underscores the curators' emphasis on process, ephemerality, and veracity.

When I was reading the individual artist entries in this volume, it was immediately clear that many of the artists work across a wide variety of media. Even those artists who could be described, for example, as painters, photographers, or sculptors take an uninhibited approach to materials, exemplifying the complexity of the 2019 Biennial artists' practices. I was equally struck by the phrases that describe the artists' work because they variously suggest resistance to simplification and by implication resistance to art historical and political categorization. A quick scan of such descriptions reveals the use of words such as: "confound," "disrupt," "interrogate," and "complicate," as well as phrases including "a penchant for heterogeneity," "polymorphous nature of identity," "exist in the margins of popular imagination," and "the possibilities of what has been overlooked"—all of which speak to the inadequacy of singular identities while simultaneously revealing a desire to be identified and identifiable.

We live in polarized, desperate times fomented by the speed and lack of accountability of social media. Paradoxically, the more people seek to be individuated and have a voice, the more difficult it seems to have one. In a 1966 interview with the art critic Dore Ashton, Marcel Duchamp prophetically said: "Technology will surely drown us. The individual is disappearing rapidly. We'll eventually be nothing but numbered ants. The group thing grows. You can already feel the tendency in the arts today. Speed, money, interest." Ashton retorted: "You've suggested . . . that artists today are corruptible and too much involved in commercialization to amount to much. In that case, why do you continue to say you are interested in artists, not art?" And Duchamp answered: "Because artists are the only people who have a chance to become citizens of the world, to make a good world to live in. They are disengaged and ready for freedom."[1] The artists in this exhibition, I believe, hope and work for that good world. And, while they must have a level of detachment to do what they do, unlike what Duchamp posits, these artists are fully engaged.

• • •

I would like to congratulate and extend my deepest thanks to Rujeko Hockley and Jane Panetta for their devotion in creating this Biennial and their commitment to each other in shared spirit and ideas. Through their intrepidness and deep engagement with artists, they have achieved a grounded and vociferous yet poetic exhibition. Their approach acknowledges the complexities and contradictions as well as the frustrations and anger of our times. My great thanks also go to Scott Rothkopf, Senior Deputy Director and Nancy and Steve Crown Family Chief Curator, who served as a wise sounding board through a very challenging process. I am also grateful to Maori Karmael Holmes, Sky Hopinka, and Matt Wolf for organizing the film program for this Biennial and to Greta Hartenstein for collaborating with Rujeko and Jane on the performance program.

The Whitney Biennial is always an ambitious undertaking and this year is no exception. I am extremely appreciative of Tiffany & Co.'s ongoing commitment to the Museum's signature exhibition. The Rosenkranz Foundation and the Whitney's National Committee provided support that was essential to the realization of the curators' ambitions. My sincere gratitude also goes to Lise and Michael Evans and the John R. Eckel, Jr. Foundation for their generous contributions. My great

1
Dore Ashton, "An Interview with Marcel Duchamp," *Studio International* 171, no. 878 (June 1966): 244–46.

appreciation also goes to Biennial Committee Co-Chairs Beth Rudin DeWoody, Bob Gersh, Miyoung Lee, and Fred Wilson; Biennial Committee members Ashley Leeds and Christopher Harland, Diane and Adam E. Max, Annette and Paul Smith, Bill Block, the Debra and Jeffrey Geller Family Foundation, Rebecca and Martin Eisenberg, Amanda and Glenn Fuhrman, Barbara and Michael Gamson, Marjorie and James D. Kuhn, Kourosh Larizadeh and Luis Pardo, Melanie Shorin and Greg S. Feldman, and Dora and Cranford Stoudemire. Additional essential funding came from the Further Forward Foundation, the Kapadia Equity Fund, The Keith Haring Foundation Exhibition Fund, Katie and Amnon Rodan, and Sotheby's. We also benefited from additional support from the Consulate General of the Federal Republic of Germany and the Consulate General of Sweden in New York. I am deeply grateful for the foresight of Melva Bucksbaum, Emily Fisher Landau, Leonard A. Lauder, and Fern and Lenard Tessler for creating generous endowments that support this exhibition and emerging artists. I am also appreciative of the endowment established by Rosina Lee Yue and Bert A. Lies, Jr., for curatorial travel and research.

Above all, I thank the artists for their participation in the exhibition and for leading the way forward.

Adam D. Weinberg
Alice Pratt Brown Director

Organizing the Whitney Biennial has been an incredible experience and a privilege. For both of us, particularly in our roles as full-time curators at the Whitney, it has been especially meaningful to spend a concentrated period of nearly two years in a deep and sustained dialogue with so many artists across the United States and across generations, including those new to us and ones we've followed for many years. The Biennial has afforded us a unique opportunity to think hard about art making in this country in its varied forms and communities, a project that has felt especially critical in the troubled environment of the United States in 2018–19. Our reflections and research led us to deeply consider how current art production relates to both the broader sociopolitical context and to the history of this long-standing survey of American art at the Whitney. We are honored to have been asked to organize this exhibition and grateful for the chance to have done so, especially at this historic moment.

The 2019 Biennial includes work by seventy-five artists and collectives, and our heartfelt thanks go to them above all others. This exhibition is a direct outgrowth of their powerful work, and we feel personally honored to have worked alongside each of them throughout this process.

We deeply appreciate Adam D. Weinberg, the Whitney's Alice Pratt Brown Director, for supporting this project from start to finish. We are also extremely thankful to Scott Rothkopf, Senior Deputy Director for Programs and Nancy and Steve Crown Family Chief Curator, for inviting us to organize the Biennial and for providing essential guidance throughout. We further acknowledge Greta Hartenstein, who coorganized the Biennial performance program, and Maori Karmael Holmes, Sky Hopinka, and Matt Wolf, who coorganized the Biennial film program. We express our gratitude to the Whitney's trustees as well as to the members of the 2019 Biennial Committee, cochaired by Beth Rudin DeWoody, Bob Gersh, Miyoung Lee, and Fred Wilson.

This enormous undertaking would have been impossible without our tireless, talented Biennial team. We gratefully acknowledge Ramsay Kolber, curatorial project assistant; Carly Fischer, curatorial research assistant; Maura Heffner, assistant director of exhibitions; Lindsey O'Connor, Biennial co-coordinator; Amanda Davis, former performance coordinator; and Danielle Levy, assistant performance coordinator. We are also grateful to curatorial interns Jun Mabuchi, Olivia Porte, and Grace Rogers.

We extend deep thanks to our colleagues in the Whitney's curatorial department. David Breslin, DeMartini Family Curator and Director of the Collection; Christopher Y. Lew, Nancy and Fred Poses Curator; Chrissie Iles, Anne and Joel Ehrenkranz Curator; Barbara Haskell, curator; Elisabeth Sussman, Sondra Gilman Curator of Photography; Adrienne Edwards, Engell Speyer Family Curator and Curator of Performance; Jennie Goldstein, assistant curator; Marcela Guerrero, assistant curator; and Greta Hartenstein, former senior curatorial assistant, in particular, shared their indispensable knowledge, insight, and essential guidance. Additionally, Emily Russell, director of curatorial affairs, was a tireless and steadfast ally and advocate throughout this process. For their collegial support, we also extend our thanks to Donna De Salvo, deputy director for international initiatives and senior curator; Kim Conaty, Steven and Ann Ames Curator of Drawings and Prints; Claire Henry, assistant curator, Warhol Film Project; David Kiehl, curator emeritus; Christiane Paul, adjunct curator of digital art; Carrie Springer, assistant curator; and Joanna Epstein, assistant to the chief curator. We also acknowledge the emerging artists working group for its invaluable input: Christopher Y. Lew; Elisabeth Sherman, assistant curator; Marcela Guerrero; Laura Phipps, assistant curator; Melinda Lang, curatorial assistant; Ambika

Trasi, curatorial assistant; Margaret Kross, curatorial assistant; and Megan Heuer, director of public programs and public engagement.

The volume you hold in your hands is a key element of the Biennial, reflecting some of the essential thinking and organizing principles that went into the show more broadly, and will live on long after the exhibition itself is over. We thank Beth Huseman, director of publications; Elizabeth Levy, project manager; Lindsey O'Connor; Domenick Ammirati, editor; and Nerissa Dominguez Vales and Sue Medlicott, production, for their exceptionally conscientious and thoughtful guidance of this project. We also thank its dedicated and insightful designers, Yoonjai Choi and Ken Meier of Common Name, New York, for their refined aesthetic. Additionally, we extend our deep thanks to those who wrote the artist entries: Erika Balsom, Jessica Bell Brown, Andrianna Campbell, Dessane Lopez Cassell, Ashton Cooper, Ayanna Dozier, Julia Pelta Feldman, Alex Fialho, Carly Fischer, Leo Goldsmith, Marcela Guerrero, Greta Hartenstein, Carmen Hermo, Megan Heuer, Frances Jacobus-Parker, Eunsong Kim, Daniella Rose King, Ramsay Kolber, Lola Kramer, Margaret Kross, Christopher Y. Lew, Jessica Lynne, Lindsey O'Connor, Laura Phipps, Allie Rickard, and Elisabeth Sherman.

Staging an exhibition as large and multifarious as a Biennial depends on the support and attention of every department at the Museum. We thank the Whitney's extraordinary staff in its entirety, especially the following members: Jehad Abu-Hamda, projectionist; Stephanie Adams, director of individual and planned giving; Justin Allen, assistant to access and community programs; Marilou Aquino, director of philanthropy; Morgan Arenson, director of foundation and government relations; I. D. Aruede, co-chief operating officer and chief financial officer; Wendy Barbee-Lowell, manager of visitor services; Bernadette Beauchamp, telecommunications administrator; Jeffrey Bergstrom, projectionist; Danielle Bias, senior communications manager; Richard Bloes, senior AV technician; Veronica Brown, communications associate; Ron Burrell, network administrator; Anne Byrd, director of interpretation and research; Elizabeth Cabot, major gifts coordinator; Jane Carey, community affairs manager; Sunil Chaddha, finance and treasury manager; Max Chester, theater manager; Brenna Cothran, assistant registrar, exhibitions; Kim Craig, major gifts officer; Margo Delidow, assistant conservator; Isabelle Dow, assistant to public programs; Anita Duquette, senior visual resources manager; Reid Farrington, audio visual manager; Lauri Freedman, product development manager; Hilary Greenbaum, director of graphic design; Peter Guss, director of information technology; Adrian Hardwicke, director of visitor experience; Andrew Hawkes, coordinator of public programs; Jennifer Heslin, director of retail operations; Albert Hicks, graphic designer; Ann Holcomb, senior officer, foundation and government relations; Nicholas S. Holmes, general counsel; Jacob Horn, editorial coordinator; Gina Im, senior coordinator of special events; Zoe Jackson, director of marketing; Rory Keely, administrative assistant to the CFO and general counsel; Eunice Lee, director of corporate partnerships; Sang Lee, manager of information technology; Jen Leventhal, chief of staff; Brianna O'Brien Lowndes, director of membership and annual fund; Claire Malloy, membership coordinator, Whitney Contemporaries; Carol Mancusi-Ungaro, Melva Bucksbaum Associate Director for Conservation and Research; Rachel Marino, senior marketing coordinator; Anna Martin, exhibition designer and production coordinator; Madison Martin, major gifts coordinator; Heather Maxson, director of school, youth, and family programs; Graham Miles, assistant head preparator; Zabie Mustafa, associate exhibition designer; Lindsay Pollock, chief communications and content officer; Kathryn Potts, associate director, Helena Rubinstein Chair of Education; Eric Pullett, benefits manager; Christy Putnam, associate director for exhibitions and collections management; Emma Quaytman, assistant to interpretation and research; Gregory Reynolds, art handler, supervisor; Gina Rogak, director of special events; Justin Romeo, executive coordinator, director's office; Joshua Rosenblatt, director, exhibition and collection preparation; Amy Roth, co-chief operating officer; Peter Scott, director of facilities; David Selimoski, engineering manager; Dyeemah Simmons, coordinator of teen programs; Matthew Skopek, associate conservator; Joel Snyder, senior manager of membership; Michele Snyder, assistant director of leadership gifts; Stephen Soba, director of communications; Barbi Spieler, head registrar, permanent collection; John S. Stanley, former chief operating officer; Mark Steigelman, director, exhibition design production; Betty Stolpen, associate major gifts officer; Emilie Sullivan, registrar, exhibitions; Jocelyn Tarbox, manager of corporate sponsorships; Melanie Taylor, director, exhibition design; Alexandra Wheeler, former deputy director and chief advancement officer; Sasha Wortzel, director of access and community programs; Madison Zalopany, coordinator of access and community programs; and Jessica Zhao, director of strategy and planning.

At every stage of the exhibition we have relied on the wisdom and generosity of wonderful friends and colleagues who have supported us in many ways. In this regard, we acknowledge and thank Taylor Aldridge, Andrea Andersson, Naomi Beckwith, Fred Bidwell, Luke Boehnke, Graham Boettcher, Tim Buckwalter, Erin Christovale, Kristen Conover, Ursula Davila-Villa, Jill Dawsey, Ryan Dennis, Carter Foster, Daniel Fuller, Alex Freedman, Jeffrey Gibson, Allison Glenn, Thelma Golden, Cat Gund, Gia Hamilton, Deana Haggag, John Hanhardt, Lauren Haynes, Andria Hickey, Candice Hopkins, Eleonore Hugendubel, Amanda Hunt, Jamillah James, Nina Johnson, Tilane Jones, Naima Keith, Kristan Kennedy, Christine Y. Kim, Amanda King, Nora Lawrence, Thomas Lax, Justin Leroy, Melissa Levin, Michel Linares, Glenn Ligon, Mia Locks, Lauren Mackler, Micky Marxuach, Manuel Mendoza, René Morales, Matt Moravec, Christopher Myers, Diana Nawi, Erin Jane Nelson, María Elena Ortiz, Paulina Pobocha, Laura Raicovich, Larry Rinder, Hallie Ringle, Veronica Roberts, Walter Robinson, Jay Sanders, Trevor Schoonmaker, Cauleen Smith, Catherine Taft, Jenenne Whitfield, Wendy Yao, Kibra A. Yohannes, and Lynn Zelevansky. We also acknowledge the following nonprofit organizations for their time and thoughtful discussions, which helped us to better understand the many communities from which they are working that we visited: AFRICA'SOUT!; Beta-Local, San Juan; Core Program, Houston; Creative Growth, Oakland; Graham Foundation, Chicago; Heidelberg Project, Detroit; Joan Mitchell Center, New Orleans; National Memorial for Peace and Justice and the Legacy Museum, Montgomery, Alabama; NIAD Art Center, Richmond, California; NXTHVN, New Haven, Connecticut; Portland Institute for Contemporary Art, Oregon; Power House Productions, Detroit; Project Row Houses, Houston; Stony Island Arts Bank and Rebuild Foundation, Chicago; 356 Mission Road, Los Angeles; and Underground Museum, Los Angeles.

We extend a special thank-you to the following galleries for their support and kindness: Adams and Ollman, Portland, Oregon; Anton Kern Gallery, New York; Barbara Wien, Berlin; Barro Arte Contemporáneo, Buenos Aires; Bridget Donahue, New York; Bureau, New York; Carlier | Gebauer, Berlin; Chapter NY, New York; Clearing, Brussels and New York; Company Gallery, New York; Corbett vs. Dempsey, Chicago; Corvi-Mora, London; Croy Nielsen, Vienna; David Kordansky Gallery, Los Angeles; Document, Chicago; 47 Canal, New York; Galerie Eva Presenhuber, Zurich; Gavin Brown's enterprise, New York; Gladstone Gallery, New York; Haines Gallery, San Francisco; Hannah Hoffman, Los Angeles; Herald St, London; High Art, Paris; Higher Pictures, New York; James Fuentes, New York; Jane Lombard Gallery, New York; Jessica Silverman Gallery, San Francisco; JTT, New York; Karma, New York; Lomex, New York; ltd los angeles; Luhring Augustine, New York; Mary Mary, Glasgow; Meliksetian | Briggs, Los Angeles; Modern Art, London; Monique Meloche Gallery, Chicago; Morán Morán, Los Angeles; Roberts Projects, Los Angeles; Rodeo, London; Sadie Coles HQ, London; Sikkema Jenkins & Co., New York; Simon Lee, London;

Société, Berlin; Spinello Projects, Miami; Susanne Vielmetter Los Angeles Projects; Team Gallery, New York; Tilton Gallery, New York; Victoria Miro, London; and White Space Beijing. Our thanks extend as well to the film production and distribution companies Array, Iconoclast, and Video Data Bank at the School for the Art Institute of Chicago.

Our sincere gratitude goes to the lenders to the exhibition, who include the Arnett Collection, Sascha S. Bauer, the Birmingham Museum of Art, Andrew Black, Du Yan, Dr. Ernesto and Malena Erdmann, Eric Green, the Jansen Collection, the Joyner/Giuffrida Collection, Miyoung Lee and Neil Simpkins, Ninah and Michael Lynne, and the Rennie Collection, as well as those who wish to remain anonymous.

Lastly, we want to extend a heartfelt thanks to Jan Postma and Hank Willis Thomas for their exceptional guidance and patience with this project. They both provided a critical and loving foundation of support from which we were able to venture out into this complex and exhilarating endeavor.

Jane Panetta and Rujeko Hockley

A conceptually sprawling survey meant to address the art made across a broad, complex geography over a roughly two-year period, the Whitney Biennial presents a daunting challenge to its organizers. Mounting such an exhibition when there are more artists and art worlds than ever, and the number of biennials and biennial-like exhibitions seems to increase daily, makes the process even more difficult. But the Whitney's Biennials and Annuals have faced a landscape of comparable shows since they began.[1] As the Museum's founding director, Juliana Force, explained in the catalogue for the inaugural edition in 1932, "In presenting the First Biennial Exhibition of Contemporary American Painting the Whitney Museum of American Art is following a precedent established by almost every important art museum in the United States."[2] Facing a dilemma not unlike our contemporary one, Force responded by highlighting the focus on American artists, seeing it, as we have, as a strength of the concept.

The attempt to take a snapshot of contemporary art making in the United States is in keeping with a central tenet of the Whitney's institutional mission—no matter how ambiguous or fluid the category of "American art" may be. When the Museum opened its building downtown in 2015, Dana Miller, then curator of the permanent collection, pointed out that the very definitions of American art and an American artist have long been contested. Highlighting questions at the core of the Whitney's mission, Miller wrote: "Can only American artists make American art?" and "By what criteria is an artist even considered American?"[3] The answers to these questions have evolved throughout the Museum's history. The Whitney's newest chapter has seen ongoing adjustments to its priorities. These changes have resulted in its embracing a much more expansive view of American art and its bringing visibility to lesser-known works and artists rarely or never before seen at the institution.

Such shifts informed our thinking about the 2019 Whitney Biennial—where we traveled, with whom we met, the art and artists that we ultimately selected. The question of America more broadly has loomed over the organization of this Biennial in ways far beyond the province of the art historical. We have worked during a particularly tumultuous two years at the Whitney, during which the Museum has engaged with conversations vital to the United States' overall wrangling with its present and its history, including issues of representation, gentrification, transparency, and the historicizing of the AIDS epidemic. On occasion, the Museum itself has become the site and subject of protest. We strive to be a space for open dialogue, a role that is fundamental to our institutional identity.

Rather than existing in isolation, museums are part of the country and the world around them, and expectations around what institutions can or should be have changed. The complicated and essential conversations that have emerged at the Whitney over the past two years have tangibly affected the breadth of the collection, the exhibitions we present, the ways we discuss the work in our galleries, how we engage with both visitors and colleagues, and much more. Inevitably this shifting landscape has inflected our process for the 2019 Biennial in conscious and subconscious ways. We brought a self-questioning approach to bear in conceptualizing the exhibition, asking how the challenges of the past few years could become a productive lens through which to do our own looking.

Much of the art that we selected for the 2019 Biennial is steeped in sociopolitical concerns—an engagement important to us as curators—while at the same time remaining open ended and hopeful. In the nearly three hundred studio visits we conducted across the country, the acute anger that we might have expected to find in this polarized era seemed at times sublimated, present but directed toward thoughtful experimentation, the reenvisioning of self and society, and honing

---

1
After presenting Biennials from 1932 to 1936, the Whitney began to organize Annuals starting in 1937. The practice continued until 1973, when the Biennial format that continues through the present was reinstituted.

2
Juliana Force, foreword, in *First Annual Exhibition of Contemporary American Painting*, exh. cat. (New York: Whitney Museum of American Art, 1933), p. 5.

3
Dana Miller, "Defining 'American,'" in *Whitney Museum of American Art: Handbook of the Collection*, ed. Miller with introduction by Adam D. Weinberg (New York: Whitney Museum of American Art, 2015), p. 24. As Miller points out, "Questioning and interpreting the term 'American' is part of our institutional DNA." Ibid., p. 31.

political and aesthetic strategies for survival. The resulting exhibition includes an array of artists working across a diversity of ideas, materials, and approaches with work that feels optimistic, generative, and forward thinking. The connective tissue that runs through the exhibition frequently involves certain key issues or approaches, including the mining of history as a means to reimagine the present or future; a sustained consideration of questions of race, gender, and equity; explorations of the body and its vulnerabilities; and concerns for community, both in the content and engagement of the work and in the ways that these artists navigate the world. We were struck by many artists' use of materials in prominent ways—sculptures assembled out of found materials and objects, heavily worked paintings, painstaking drawings, elaborate and multilayered collages, and the use of Photoshop and other digital tools in unexpected ways. A related emphasis on the artist's hand seemed to reflect a turning away from the ubiquity of digital space and the packaged presentation of the self common to it, as well as an impetus to make work that is less slick and more idiosyncratic. These artists stake their claim to the current moment, as if to say *I am here, making this now, with my own two hands.* Curatorially, we also gravitated toward geographically and aesthetically diverse work that was seemingly made without the market as touchstone. Accordingly, we have included a robust performance and film program in the exhibition, given that artists in those areas often struggle even more than their peers with object-based practices.

Though in past Whitney Biennials, and in the many similar exhibitions we visited during our research, artists are often presented in monographic rooms, we felt strongly about privileging an intermingled and overlapping installation. Taking a cue from our own experience working on thematic and collection-based exhibitions, which often foreground the relationships between different artists and ideas, we've pursued this approach for this Biennial. The impetus extends to the catalogue, where each artist is represented in three distinct ways: images of finished work, a short essay, and a spread of "process" images of their choosing—notes, drawings, sources, archival research, and other relevant materials fundamental to their thinking and making. Taken together, we hope these perspectives create a more expansive understanding of each artist than might otherwise be available.

In this hyperbolic, bombastic era in the United States, marked by anger and frustration over the machinations of our elected officials and political system, the depredation of our environment, and the exploitation of the disempowered, emotions run high. We've also recently experienced more optimistic events—the election of a record number of women to the House of Representatives in 2018, for example, and the ongoing national removal of monuments to Confederates and other dubious "heroes." Though our national temperature seems to be at a boiling point, the artists in this exhibition seem less inclined toward pure agitprop, instead making work that leans into the subjective, the poetic, and even the opaque. While the work often acknowledges our frightening reality, it offers alternative visions for what our world could be and what the future might hold. In organizing the 2019 Whitney Biennial, we have attempted to synthesize what we have seen, read, and learned over the course of the undertaking. We have had the great privilege of working with some of the most visionary, empathetic, and thoughtful artists of our time and hope that the exhibition we have made demonstrates the same texture and ambition as their work.

Jane Panetta and Rujeko Hockley

Civic Lessons: Notable Characteristics of America

Jane Panetta

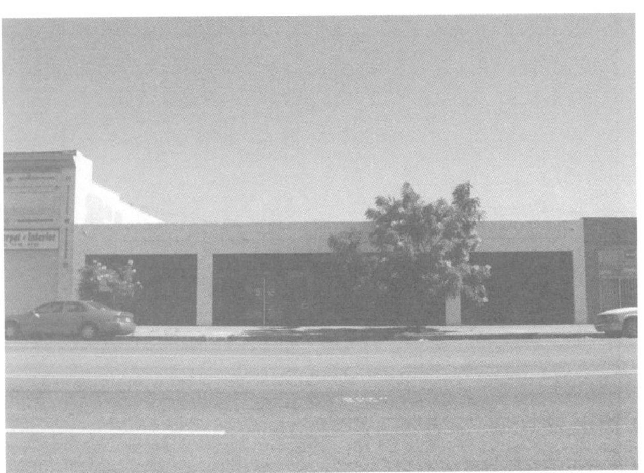

Fig.1 Underground Museum, Los Angeles, California. Image courtesy *Los Angeles Times*, photo by Carolina Miranda

Founded by the late artist Noah Davis and his wife, artist Karon Davis, the Underground Museum is located in the Arlington Heights neighborhood of Central Los Angeles. It occupies an important place in the city both physically and figuratively. Located in a predominantly Black and Latinx neighborhood—and one that is notably underserved in terms of art and community resources—the space provides both an environment in which to gather and a mechanism for bringing the high level of art present in Los Angeles to a location outside affluent pockets like Brentwood or now-tony sections of Downtown. The museum functions equally as exhibition and community space, presenting shows often focused around Black artists while also offering programming such as yoga classes and film screenings. Such events implicitly reinforce the institution's hoped-for accessibility by bringing individuals through its doors for a broad range of reasons. Amid the city's hypergentrification, entities such as the Underground Museum seem more important than ever.[1]

On our first trip to Los Angeles as the curatorial team responsible for the 2019 Whitney Biennial, Rujeko Hockley and I visited the Underground Museum (fig. 1)— it was high on our list of priorities for the city. The building itself is modest, with pleasingly scaled galleries and an inviting bookstore at the front of the complex. In the back, beyond the exhibition area, are an exquisite outdoor area and garden that host events and are open to the public during museum hours, offering an important green space within Central LA. Our guide for the visit was Justin Leroy, public programs manager at the museum, who walked us through the exhibition *Artists of Color*, which examined questions around the power of color, largely through abstraction; included artists ranged from Michael Asher to Jennie C. Jones and EJ Hill. The show had come together through a partnership with the Museum of Contemporary Art, Los Angeles, that allows the Underground Museum to borrow works from its collection for exhibitions. It felt fresh and compelling, both in its unique use of the space itself and its mixture of historical and contemporary figures and artists of color within narratives that have too often been dominated by white male figures. (Other exhibitions at the site have included 2016–17's *Non-Fiction*, which looked at the Black body and its relationship to history, and 2013's inaugural presentation, *Imitation of Wealth*, which interrogated concepts of truth, authenticity, and high culture.) *Artists of Color* was thoroughly in keeping with Davis's initial impulse to create a space where he could "bring what he called 'museum-quality art' to a traditionally African-American and Latino working-class neighborhood," which the institution has successfully done for more than five years.[2]

Of course venues such as the Underground Museum are nothing new. Artist-run alternative spaces have existed for decades in American cities and have long been essential to artists' ability to experiment and create dialogues with and for their communities. In the Whitney Museum's hometown of New York, one thinks immediately of pioneering, still-essential nonprofits such as Artists Space and White Columns, and newer ones such as the Laundromat Project, that have offered some of the city's most progressive and ambitious programming. What struck us in our travels around the country while conducting research for the Biennial was the essential nature of so many of these spaces. No longer "alternative," an implicitly disparaging characterization that suggests they exist external to more essential critical dialogue, they are instead vital epicenters for art and the conversations around it in the United States.

The subtitle of this essay, "Notable Characteristics of America," borrows a phrase from the foreword to the catalogue for the first Whitney Biennial, from 1932–33. See Juliana Force, Foreword, in *First Annual Exhibition of Contemporary American Painting*, exh. cat. (New York: Whitney Museum of American Art, 1933), n.p.

1
The need for entities such as the Underground Museum seems increasingly acute given the struggle for many nonprofits to exist as brick-and-mortar spaces in Los Angeles given the city's rising rents, a complaint we encountered regularly during our visits there.

2
"Imitation of Wealth," Underground Museum, accessed December 2, 2018, https://theunderground-museum.org/Imitation-of-Wealth.

• • •

Based in New York and with strong historical ties to Europe, the Whitney has undeniably manifested certain biases over the years in its exhibitions and its collecting practices. Despite a mandate to focus on American art overall, the Whitney's Annuals and Biennials tended to have a strong emphasis on artists from the Museum's immediate environs, even into the 1980s.[3] The Annuals of the 1930s went so far as to list only street addresses for New York City residents, with the assumption that any participant not otherwise identified would be, naturally, from New York.[4] Given the city's status throughout the twentieth century and into the twenty-first as the single most important art center in the United States, and one of its key nodes internationally, a persistent geographic focus on New York in Biennials is perhaps understandable, if not always healthy or representative. Rectifying this provincialism has required a conscious effort for decades now, and one that requires constant reaffirmation.

With this mandate to account for American art in a reasonably fulsome way, we found our challenge for 2019 to be how to focus this long-running survey of the art of the United States against the stark backdrop of intense national political discord, harrowingly heightened with the 2016 election and its aftermath. These events shined an alarming light on the problematic disconnect across geography throughout the country, a result of profound economic disparity and an increased sense of disenfranchisement, particularly outside coastal, urban centers.[5] At the time of the swearing-in of the forty-fifth president in January 2017, which saw the largest Inauguration Day protest in American history, the country seemed more fragmented than ever (at least when compared generationally). Further inflaming the social climate were the escalated racial strife and outright violence of the past several years, particularly since 2014.[6] (This violence has continued throughout the U.S., even as it has recently and problematically fallen out of the daily news cycle.[7]) Over the past year and a half, tensions have swirled around concerns about sexual violence against women and the ensuing #MeToo movement, arguably culminating (for now) in the contested appointment of Judge Brett Kavanaugh to the Supreme Court in fall 2018. Immigrants were aggressively and increasingly made vulnerable as actions were taken to deny their legal status, including previously unthinkable, unprecedentedly harsh actions against children. We have all received the message loud and clear that whatever America is, it is less and less even *aspirationally* a unified entity with shared interests and goals. To the contrary, it seems rife with diametrically opposed positions, emotions, and candidates for office.

Of course, dealing with social and political issues and their acute presence on the national stage is, like the Biennial's core difficulty (or impossibility) of representing the entire country, by no means a new problem either. A scan of Biennial publications over the past few decades underscores as much. The press release from the 2017 edition, which took form during the run-up to the 2016 election and the subsequent installation of President Donald Trump, made explicit reference in its very first sentence to the exhibition's relationship to our "turbulent" society.[8] In the preface to the 2006 Biennial catalogue, cocurators Chrissie Iles and Philippe Vergne, writing at the height of the Iraq War, referred to the show's occurring at "a moment when world opinion of the United States [was] at its lowest ebb."[9] And the introductory text for the now-infamous 1993 Biennial by then-director David Ross cited a "deepening crisis of belief and a profound sense of displacement experienced almost universally as the end of this troubled century draws near."[10] The postwar United States has been constantly in and out of traumatic political periods, from the civil-rights movement and the seemingly endless Vietnam War during the 1960s and '70s to the crisis related to the Reagan administration's

3
See, as examples of this phenomenon spanning a nearly fifty-year period, *1937 Annual Exhibition of Contemporary American Painting*, exh. cat. (New York: Plandome Press, 1937), and *1985 Biennial Exhibition*, exh. cat. (New York: Whitney Museum of American Art, 1985). In both shows, nearly three-quarters of the participating artists hailed from New York.

4
1937 Annual Exhibition of Contemporary American Painting, pp. 75–79.

5
Matthew Bloch, Larry Buchanan, Josh Katz, and Kevin Quealy, "An Extremely Detailed Map of the 2016 Election," *New York Times*, July 25, 2018, https://www.nytimes.com/interactive/2018/upshot/election-2016-voting-precinct-maps.html.

6
I am thinking in particular of events involving racially motivated police bias and violence in 2014 and 2015 that became polarizing on a national scale—the shooting of Michael Brown in Ferguson, Missouri; the arrest and subsequent death of Sandra Bland in Waller County, Texas; and the "McKinney pool incident," also in Texas, among other incidents.

7
Wesley Lowery, "Police Are Still Killing Black People. Why Isn't It News Anymore?" *Washington Post*, March 16, 2018, https://www.washingtonpost.com/outlook/police-are-still-killing-black-people-why-isnt-it-news-anymore/2018/03/12/df004124-22ef-11e8-badd-7c9f29a55815_story.html.

8
"2017 Whitney Biennial, the First to Take Place in the Museum's Downtown Building, to Open March 17," Whitney Museum website, exhibition press release, https://whitney.org/uploads/generic_file/file/502/2017_biennial_artist_list_pr._with_image.pdf.

9
Chrissie Iles and Philippe Vergne, preface, in *Whitney Biennial 2006: Day for Night*, exh. cat. (New York: Whitney Museum of American Art, 2006), p. 20.

10
David Ross, "Know Thy Self (Know Your Place)," in *1993 Biennial Exhibition*, exh. cat. (New York: Whitney Museum of American Art in association with Harry N. Abrams, Inc., 1993), p. 8.

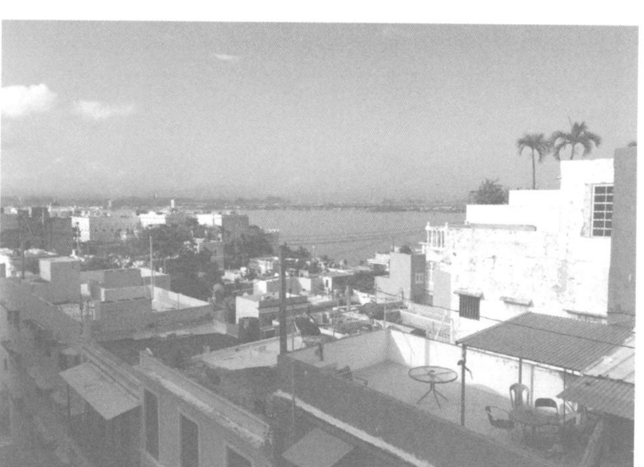

Fig. 2 San Juan, Puerto Rico. Photograph by the author

neglect of the AIDS outbreak in the 1980s to the acute flaring-up of racial tensions in the early 1990s, notably in Los Angeles and New York. But in 2019, mix together ongoing conflict over race and gender with the hyper-gentrification raging across American cities, continued fallout from the 2008 financial crisis, and an unprecedentedly volatile president, and we find ourselves at a uniquely trying moment for young Americans—and for young artists.

With all this history and context in mind as we prepared for the 2019 Biennial, we decided early on that we would make a concerted effort to venture extensively to areas beyond the East and West Coast corridors in our research for the exhibition (something our colleagues and 2017 Biennial cocurators Christopher Y. Lew and Mia Locks also did). We decided that we needed to do what we could, however modest our efforts might be, to work our way out of familiar zones, doing our best to encounter art and artists in varied locations across the United States. During this experience, we quickly grasped firsthand the extent to which the national sociopolitical situation is making it extremely difficult for artists to live and work, both psychically and in practical terms; our trips were both eye opening and essential. Unsurprisingly, the work we encountered was politically and socially minded, but it was equally committed to what is possible formally. Perhaps as anger has settled, any initial impulse to make more vitriolic work has felt unproductive.

In addition to making myriad trips to artists' studios, we felt it was important to visit nonprofit artist spaces around the country, especially those that function in ways beyond simply mounting exhibitions—providing residencies and educational programming, serving as important sites for community activity. The Underground Museum in Los Angeles is just one example. These visits fit into our overall desire to gain a clearer understanding of the sociopolitical landscape and art communities in places less familiar to us. (Perhaps uncoincidentally, a number of artists who themselves lead nonprofits or work as community organizers—Eddie Arroyo, Sofía Gallisá Muriente, Carolyn Lazard, and Maia Ruth Lee, for example—are among those we selected to appear in the 2019 Biennial itself.) In many instances, we were able to spend significant chunks of time meeting people at these organizations, resulting in a narrative parallel to that which our conversations with artists produced. While such modestly scaled, often artist-run nonprofits in underserved neighborhoods are thankfully not a new phenomenon, and with nearly all of them operating in direct relation to the neighborhoods they inhabit, we found a high number of them fulfilling an essential civic role. As we've witnessed the rise of megagalleries and often-private museum-building projects across the United States in recent years, it felt heartening to see a range of nonprofit, art-affiliated organizations thriving—with new ones set to open soon in many places—as they perform important work and cater to underserved communities.

The critical social positioning of such groups was perhaps most evident in Puerto Rico. In September 2017, Hurricane Maria struck the island with sustained wind speeds of 155 miles per hour, producing enormous rainfall and widespread damage.[11] The results would have been catastrophic anywhere in the United States, but Puerto Rico's infrastructure had already suffered years of neglect from the federal government, and the island's long-standing debt crisis had already caused schools and hospitals to shutter and other services to be cut—all of which was

11
"Major Hurricane Maria— September 20, 2017," National Weather Service, accessed December 2, 2018, https://www.weather.gov/sju/maria2017.

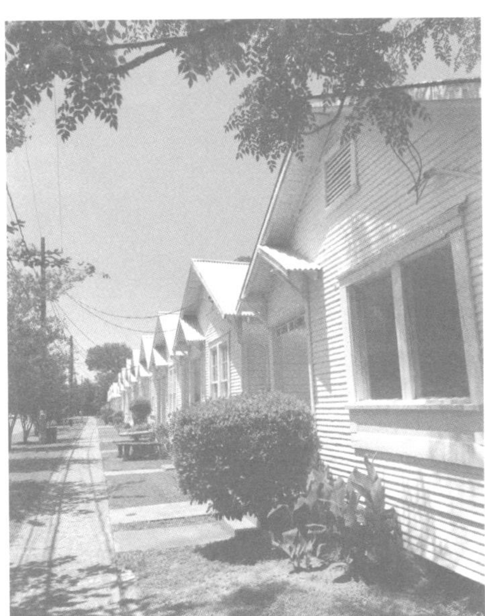

Fig. 3 Project Row Houses, Houston, Texas. Photograph by the author

only exacerbated by the storm.[12] And the response by the United States government, led by a president who barely seemed to understand that Puerto Rico is part of the U.S. and its people American citizens, verged on the obscene, especially compared with the attention paid to victims of hurricanes that hit Texas and Florida around the same time.[13] For Puerto Rico, Hurricane Maria came as a devastating blow in an already unstable and deeply unsupported situation.

During our visit to San Juan (fig. 2), we spent considerable time at the art space Beta-Local. Founded in 2009 and run by a group of artists (including the aforementioned Gallisá Muriente), Beta-Local provides residencies to artists and thinkers of Puerto Rican descent, recently awarding as much as $350,000 in annual grants. It also hosts exhibitions and public programming, providing a space for dialogue and community action. Additionally, the organization has established several important programs and residencies, including Sesiones and La Práctica, designed to foster the growth of the artist community in Puerto Rico, develop discussions around the island's politics and geography, and bring international thinkers and practitioners to a place that has often been neglected by the international art circuit. In a city otherwise highly limited in terms of analogous spaces and lacking a significant market around contemporary art, Beta-Local is in many ways similar to the Underground Museum. Its physical presence, in a welcoming building in Old San Juan, marks its engagement with the community and provides a place for artists to convene and do important thinking. Beta-Local has become an incubator for talent in Puerto Rico, helping artists gain traction and experience, enabling them to become part of a larger, networked art world, and bolstering their ability to realize projects locally and beyond. Immediately following Hurricane Maria, with the island profoundly crippled and artists without necessary aid, Beta-Local established El Serrucho (The Handsaw), a fund designed to help artists and their families with issues such as damaged studio spaces and to provide needed supplies. During our visit to Puerto Rico, we also met with eventual Biennial artists Las Nietas de Nonó and Daniel Lind-Ramos, both of whom work outside San Juan and are grappling with the lasting infrastructural impact of Maria, in the content of their work as well as in the raw terms of their daily existences and fundamental struggles to make art.

Of all the places we visited in preparing for the Biennial, Puerto Rico faced perhaps the most dire circumstances. But in fact a large number of our visits with nonprofits (and artists) happened against a broadly difficult backdrop, and more so in particular cities: Project Row Houses in Houston (fig. 3) and Power House Productions in Detroit both come to mind. In New Orleans, while Hurricane Katrina devastated the city in 2005 in ways from which it still has yet to recover, the city's problems also have very deep roots related the legacies of racial politics in the South. During our curatorial research in New Orleans, a recent book by historian Walter C. Stern, *Race and Education in New Orleans: Creating the Segregated City, 1764–1960* (2018), kept coming up in conversation or appearing in places we visited. It outlines the long deterioration of the city's educational system largely due to racial stratification, reinforcing the fact that the historical racial politics of a place like New Orleans persist and yield problematic present-day realities, a message reinforced for us by the artists we visited there.

Among the resources New Orleans has struggled to secure is adequate support for contemporary art and for local and regional artists.[14] The Joan Mitchell Center (fig. 4), which opened in 2015, provides a much-needed platform for art in the city

12
See Nelson A. Denis, *War against All Puerto Ricans: Revolution and Terror in America's Colony* (New York: Nation Books, 2015), pp. 259–61. Denis outlines the dire situation for Puerto Rico directly leading up to Hurricane Maria, with the territory rife with unemployment and poverty (Puerto Rico is poorer than the poorest state in the union) and burdened with crippling public debt in the vicinity of $70 billion.

13
Matthew Norman, "Does Donald Trump Even Know That He's Responsible for Puerto Rico?" *Independent*, September 26, 2017, https://www.independent.co.uk/voices/donald-trump-puerto-rico-wall-street-email-servers-lock-her-up-dependency-a7968056.html.

14
One should note that the now nearly ten-year-old Prospect New Orleans triennial has been a game-changing presence in the contemporary art scene in the city, engaging it both physically and in terms of local artists and art communities.

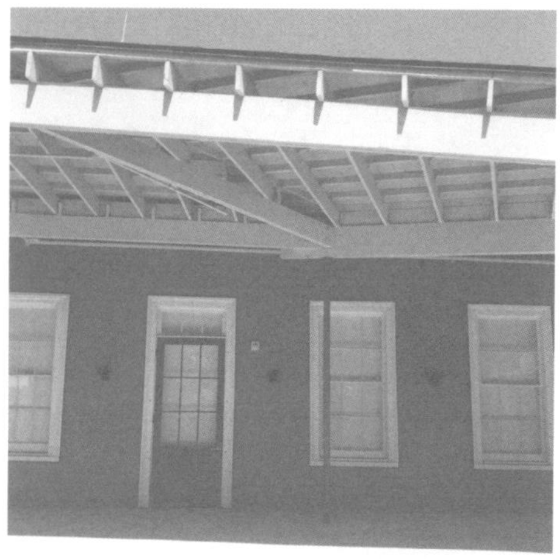
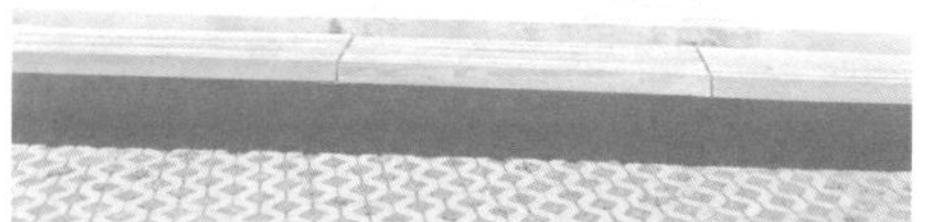

Fig.4 Joan Mitchell
Center, New Orleans,
Louisiana. Photograph
by the author

and its surrounding area. The center was established by the Joan Mitchell Foundation (based in New York) partly in hopes of bringing more attention to artists from the region, who frequently go underrecognized. Offering ten artist's studios and more than eight thousand square feet of studio space, the institution has looked to help emerging artists from Louisiana specifically, refocusing attention on what is happening locally while also providing important funding and fostering a sense of community around contemporary art more generally. (This effort's primary manifestation is a residency for artists and thinkers from the region or with a particular connection to New Orleans; it was during our visit to the center that we encountered the work of Pat Phillips, a painter who lives and works in Louisiana whom we decided to include in the Biennial.) The center has been a significant addition to both the national art landscape and to New Orleans, as well as a real contribution to a city with one of the richest cultural heritages in the country.

Like Beta-Local and the Underground Museum, the Joan Mitchell Center occupies a space that neither traditional museums nor the marketplace is filling, supporting a neighborhood and city that already possess great legacies and active artist communities that can deeply benefit from improved cultural infrastructure. For us, organizations such as these, as well as others we visited, including Project Row Houses; NXTHVN in New Haven, Connecticut; Power House Productions; NIAD in Richmond, California; and Creative Growth in Oakland became critical sites for dialogue during our research and for obtaining a better understanding of their various milieus from the vantage point of artists and art workers.

For all our travels, we inevitably encountered the reality that New York retains a significant place in American art making, with an exceptionally high number of artists living, working, and exhibiting here. Thus the 2019 Biennial is no exception to the event's long history of engaging its own local community, with a substantial dose of participants currently living and working in New York. But the difficulties of trying to get by as an artist came up frequently in our talks with practitioners living in the country's art capital as well. Conditions in the New York area are in their own ways fierce, particularly vis-à-vis studio space and the overall cost of living. In selecting artists from New York, community also became a notable structuring device, even if it was less often expressed through art organizations. This iteration of the Biennial features various communities of New York artists—artists who have at various points worked together, studied together, or made use of shared studios. Something we saw in a concentrated way in New York as well as in the rest of the country was that community has become an important mechanism for artists to cope with the difficulty of surviving professionally. These alliances can be creatively generative while also providing a means of finding support, dialogue, and working space amid a system that seems to favor giant galleries, megacollectors, and more established artists. In many ways, it was this dynamic that often led us away from work that felt more market friendly and instead toward artists with limited gallery and collector support, with many of them working outside the contemporary art system.

Throughout our research, we encountered a seemingly endless number of interesting voices, ideas, and practices. Ultimately only a fraction of these form a tangible part of the final exhibition. But working on this show offered us the opportunity to push for a better understanding of the larger cultural landscape and the ways in which many broader civic and sociopolitical concerns dovetail with artists' work, especially work that *did* end up in the 2019 Biennial. Along the way, we learned, in this moment of national struggle and intensely felt disenfranchisement, how modestly scaled organizations have been able to foster necessary local spaces for community building and for communities of artists. While the Biennial will live most distinctly in the exhibition itself and this accompanying catalogue, there will be more to the story, thanks to the time we spent outside New York and in conversation with so many thoughtful art workers, artists, thinkers, and leaders. This text hopefully provides a small window into our process and the thinking and discussions that influenced us. We hope this spirit of supporting both artists and much-needed experimental thinking and doing is palpable in the show itself.

The End of the World or the Beginning of the Next

Rujeko Hockley

As I sit down to write, eleven people have been murdered in Pittsburgh at the Tree of Life synagogue. They range in age from fifty-four to ninety-seven; they were targeted because of their faith. Though this attack is among the deadliest against a specific religious group and house of worship in the United States to date, and certainly among the deadliest against its Jewish communities, it is not a surprise—not really.[1] I don't check—I can't quite bear to—but I am positive that this massacre is not the only disaster to have occurred or been reported this week, not to mention those that have unfolded more quietly and gone unremarked. It takes a lot to make the news cycle these days, and it takes even more to stay there; which is to say that almost nothing does. A week later, the Tree of Life massacre is still on the front page of the *New York Times*, but barely.[2]

This is how we live today in these deeply divided United States, lurching from one previously unimaginable horror to the next, steeped in vitriol and bile, hyperbole and confusion. There has always been an element of this poison lurking in the dark—unity without caveat or exception has not been our national strength—but it has come roaring to the fore in 2018. It feels increasingly difficult to distinguish hypochondria from true threat, friend from foe—until it doesn't, and then the difference becomes crystal clear. On some level, it is as it is meant to be; there is nothing accidental about our heightened states of fear, mistrust, and anxiety. Unease is what we are meant to feel, what the stimuli we receive from our president, our media outlets, our twenty-first-century world are meant to engender. It seems that, truly, nothing is OK.[3]

But was it ever?

What has it meant to organize a Whitney Biennial in these harsh and harrowing times? Almost every edition of the exhibition from at least 1993 onward has framed itself in relation to its uniquely turbulent moment; almost every one of them seems to have felt some certainty in asserting that its time has been the most unsettling, the most exceptional. From my perspective in 2018, looking to 2019 and beyond, all we can know is that we don't know, and that state of not knowing is itself deeply unsettling. We don't know what trauma awaits in the wings, what the future will bring, what the consequences will be, what our children or their children will say—or if there will be a world left for them at all. We have a hunch (nothing good), but often it seems as if uncertainty, and maybe some measure of denial, are the only certainties.

In this year of our travels, this year of talking and looking and listening and learning, my cocurator Jane Panetta and I have seen much that confirms this dyspeptic view but also much that defies it. Times are dark and dire, but people are kind and life prevails. Both things are true, and hasn't it always been so? Visiting Puerto Rico only six months after Hurricane Maria made landfall on September 20, 2017, we saw wooden houses slumped down into themselves, sliding off their foundations. We saw ubiquitous blue tarps dotting the flat roofs of San Juan. We saw mangled street signs piled on the sides of highways and electrical wire dangling in the breeze, and we were told about the closing of almost two hundred public schools (which happened well before Maria—more collateral damage of the island's debt crisis[4]). But we also walked with Daniel Lind-Ramos through the streets of his native Loíza, admiring clusters of moriviví, the "shy plant" that closes its delicate leaves at the slightest touch, and greeting members of his family. We learned how local history, like Great Britain's unsuccessful 1797 invasion of Puerto Rico—rebuffed by Afro–Puerto Rican residents of Loíza and neighboring towns—informs his life and work. In Carolina, we were welcomed with homemade kombucha and lemon tart by Lydela and Michel Nonó (known collectively as Las Nietas de Nonó) to Patio Taller, the community space/garden/theater/kitchen/workshop/artist residency/day care that they created for themselves and their

Thank you to artist and designer Jon Santos for the loan of this title, at the time of this writing emblazoned on a billboard in Flint, Michigan. It is one of almost two hundred unique billboards that were installed by For Freedoms, an artist-founded platform for creative civic engagement, discourse, and direct action, across the United States in the run-up to the 2018 midterm elections. See https://forfreedoms.org.

1
Campbell Robertson, Christopher Mele, and Sabrina Tavernise, "11 Killed in Synagogue Massacre; Suspect Charged with 29 Counts," *New York Times*, October 27, 2018, https://www.nytimes.com/2018/10/27/us/active-shooter-pittsburgh-synagogue-shooting.html.

2
The article appearing on the front page that day reported on a meeting between Rabbi Jeffrey Myers of Tree of Life and Rev. Eric S. C. Manning of the Emmanuel African Methodist Episcopal Church in Charleston, South Carolina, where nine parishioners were shot and killed in a similarly bigoted attack in June 2015. Kevin Sack, "Anguished by 'Spiral of Hate,' Rabbi and Pastor Grieve as One," *New York Times*, November 4, 2018, p. 1, available online at https://www.nytimes.com/2018/11/03/us/pittsburgh-synagogue-charleston-emanuel.html.

3
I draw inspiration here from Sadie Barnette's artist's book and video both titled *NOTHING* (2013/2018).

4
Frances Robles, "Puerto Rico's Debt Crisis Claims Another Casualty: Its Schools," *New York Times*, May 10, 2017, https://www.nytimes.com/2017/05/10/us/puerto-rico-debt-schools-close.html.

neighbors out of their grandparents' home in the working-class neighborhood of Barrio San Antón. We observed firsthand what artists, and the arts, can do, particularly where government and other institutions or formalized avenues have failed. Led by local arts organization Beta-Local, a tight-knit community of artists and culture workers fanned out across the island to ask people what they needed in the wake of the storm (and the ensuing storm of official neglect and mismanagement) in order to recover their homes, lives, and careers—be it a grant to pay for medical expenses or studio/home repairs or a literal hand in replacing still-disconnected water pipes in a remote part of the island.[5]

In Detroit, we saw the destruction wrought on a place and populace by a similarly manufactured debt crisis, a city left to fend for itself for decades and now facing inattention and a lack of resources once unthinkable in the "developed" world. (Almost five years after Flint, Michigan's drinking water was contaminated with lead in an effort to save money, its residents still do not have clean water.[6]) We saw the long-term corrosive force of clear-eyed racialized violence, literal and figurative, in Grosse Pointe, a once-upon-a-time "sundown" town that abuts the city limits of Detroit.[7] With its perfectly manicured lawns, perfectly maintained streets, and perfectly coiffed, upwardly mobile residents (entirely white in my brief observation), complete with sidewalk cafés and specialized boutiques and glossy dogs promenading, the municipality stands in stark contrast to Black Detroit, with its relentless potholes and shuttered homes and storefronts, some of which are occupied by people with nowhere else to go—all less than a hundred yards away. What a difference a tax base, and hundreds of years of preferential treatment and access to everything, can make.

But visiting Matthew Angelo Harrison, we also saw how materials and technologies innate to Detroit's historical role as a hub for innovation in automotive manufacturing and design might take on productive new forms and unexpected new life, even if that industry itself may be comparatively much reduced in this century. Before becoming a full-time artist, Harrison worked at Ford Motor Company as a clay sculptor, performing a job still essential to their design process even in 2018. To create his artwork, he uses resin casting and 3-D scanning, printing, and modeling—all methods used in automotive and other manufacturing. Harrison makes his own custom 3-D printers, which generate sculptures of thinly layered coils of extruded clay based on his scans of sculptures from various regions of Africa. Such repurposing of these industrial technologies will not bring back the jobs and resulting security once provided by Ford and other automotive companies, but if we can envision new uses for old technology on even a small scale, perhaps we can do more, envision more? It's an exercise worth attempting at least, and admiring.

In Berlin, we walked, increasingly unnerved and confused, as street after street appeared inexplicably blocked off. The gruff police officers in riot gear whom we tentatively approached were less than forthcoming. We entered a café, where a barista calmly told us, almost as an aside, that there was a march that day by Alternative for Germany, the country's growing far-right political party. The streets had been barricaded to keep the demonstrators away from counterprotesters, with the goal of keeping everyone safe. From the woman's demeanor, it was a wholly unremarkable event. "They're just down the street," she said casually. "You can see them." We could. She was unruffled; I was undone. The fear—and consequences—of being other, of being marked unavoidably as different by virtue of culture or genetics, is visceral. It can rise in your throat at a moment's notice, causing your heart to race and your palms to sweat—fight or flight. As I experienced in Berlin, it rises in direct proportion to the presence of waves of people you've been told see that difference, and thus your existence, as a threat, particularly when they are marching past, chanting slogans with flags held high.

Here again, though, there was more. Christine Sun Kim, an American artist living in Berlin and a new parent, detailed the incredible benefits offered by the

5

This is exactly what Michy Marxuach, curator and cofounder of Beta-Local, was doing the day we were meant to meet in San Juan.

6

For a comprehensive overview of the crisis, including its roots in Flint's history of redlining and segregation, see Anna Clark, *The Poisoned City: Flint's Water and the American Urban Tragedy* (New York: Metropolitan Books, 2018).

7

See James W. Loewen, *Sundown Towns: A Hidden Dimension of American Racism* (New York: New Press, 2005).

German state to families, especially in the early years of a child's life. Her, and our, incredulity were only in relation to the obscenely paltry offerings of our own nation during this singular and critical time of life. She showed us a series of charcoal drawings questioning the appropriate amount of sound her infant daughter, the hearing child of a culturally Deaf mother, should be intentionally exposed to by the world and its inhabitants—for example, how much should she play with noise-producing toys? How much should hearing visitors (such as ourselves) speak or sing aloud to the child, when her mother communicates with her in American Sign Language and she is also learning German Sign Language and being raised in a multilingual and multicultural household? As a mother, as a person, how best to navigate these questions, at once both deeply personal and deeply political? As an artist, how best to represent them?

Everywhere that we traveled, we saw this dichotomy between disillusionment, devastation even, and hope—so much so that we thought perhaps it was not a dichotomy but the way forward. These reflections on a very few of the places we touched down and a very few of the artists we ultimately included in this Biennial highlight the ideas and approaches that ultimately became our guiding principles. In studio after studio, we saw artists grappling with the legacies of the past, reframing them in order to both complicate the present and reimagine our future. Much of this unpacking and reconceiving hinges around making central, and even foregrounding, race, gender, disability, and access—the myriad ways a body can exist in this world and the potential beauty and pain extracted thereby. Medium specificity rarely seemed of primary concern; even within an individual practice, experimentation is the norm, with a range of media often used—whatever works for the situation and gets the message across. We also saw a turn away from the slick and hyperfinished. In its place, we found an interest in and commitment to the work of one's own hand, the process of making, and the provisional. Community in all senses also seemed critical—community among artists, constituents, likeminded (or not) people. We have known that another world is possible, but it is in the hard work of collectively envisioning, and then the even harder work of enacting, that we often falter. This is not to say that the artists in this exhibition, or any one group of people, have all the answers, but perhaps they have some. Neither sticking their heads in the sand to avoid the painful realities of our times, nor throwing up their hands in despair and dwelling exclusively in negativity and muck, these artists, the majority of them under forty and first-time Biennial participants, strike the balance that we need, one of equity, of fortitude, of curiosity, of compassion for the self and others, of productive confrontation—of possibility.

In Montgomery, Alabama, we attended the opening of the Equal Justice Initiative's National Memorial for Peace and Justice.[8] It is the first national memorial in the United States dedicated to the legacy of enslaved Black people and their descendants and the almost five thousand African American men, women, and children who were brutally murdered across this country between 1877 and 1950 by their fellow Americans, victims of racial terrorism. (There are almost five thousand who have been counted through EJI's research; it is likely that many more remain unknown.[9]) Set on a grassy hill overlooking a Black working-class neighborhood where modern civil-rights activism began in the U.S., the memorial consists of eight hundred steel columns, one for each county where an act of racial violence occurred. Each column lists the names of the victims in that county and the date of their murder. Some list only a very few names. Some, like that representing Lafourche Parish, located in south Louisiana, list an unthinkable many—fifty-two to be exact, the majority of victims indicated as "Unknown," and all except two murdered on the same day: November 23, 1887. I wonder what happened that day; I am grateful to be spared that knowledge.[10] I am grateful for my life, for the lives of my loved ones.

8
The Equal Justice Initiative is a private nonprofit organization that works to end mass incarceration, excessive punishment, and unequal treatment within the American criminal-justice system. The organization, founded in 1994 in Montgomery by Bryan Stevenson, is committed to challenging racial and economic injustice and protecting the basic human rights of the most vulnerable and marginalized in our society. See https://eji.org and Bryan Stevenson, *Just Mercy: A Story of Justice and Redemption* (New York: Spiegel and Grau, 2014).

9
In 2015, EJI produced *Lynching in America: Confronting the Legacy of Racial Terror*, which documented the thousands of racial-terror lynchings they uncovered in their research, which initially focused on the Deep South but was subsequently expanded to include states outside the region. See https://lynchinginamerica.eji.org/report.

10
But in revisiting our time in Montgomery, I did need to know. I searched for "Lafourche Parish" and very quickly came to the Thibodaux Massacre. It was a state-sanctioned attack by white paramilitary groups in Louisiana on Black sugarcane workers—one of the most violent labor disputes in United States history. On November 1, 1887, at the start of the harvest season, ten thousand cane workers across four parishes went on strike to protest the exploitative and slavery-like conditions under which they were forced to work. On November 23, with the strike unabated, Black workers and their families were attacked in their homes and on the streets of the town of Thibodaux, with at least fifty people shot and killed and many more injured or missing. In addition to cane workers thought to be part of the strike, victims included the elderly, women, and children. They were buried in a mass grave in Thibodaux that remains unmarked and unexcavated, though plans are reportedly underway for the Louisiana Public Archaeology Lab to do so. See John DeSantis, *The Thibodaux Massacre: Racial Violence and the 1887 Sugar Cane Labor Strike* (Charleston, SC: History Press, 2016), and DeSantis, "Tracing an Atrocity: How an Obscure Affidavit in the National Archives Unraveled a Historical Mystery,"

At the exit of the memorial, an excerpt from Toni Morrison's *Beloved* is inscribed on a marble wall. It is pulled from one of the loveliest and most important passages in that novel, and indeed, anywhere in twentieth-century letters. The day that we were there, the Alabama sun shone over it, and the letters glowed and dazzled in the light. The passage is one worth reading in full, and often:

Here, in this here place, we flesh; flesh that weeps, laughs; flesh that dances on bare feet in grass. Love it. Love it hard. Yonder they do not love your flesh. They despise it. They don't love your eyes; they'd just as soon pick em out. No more do they love the skin on your back. Yonder they flay it. And O my people they do not love your hands. Those they only use, tie, bind, chop off and leave empty. Love your hands! Love them. Raise them up and kiss them. Touch others with them, pat them together, stroke them on your face 'cause they don't love that either. *You* got to love it, *you*! And no, they ain't in love with your mouth. Yonder, out there, they will see it broken and break it again. What you say out of it they will not heed. What you scream from it they do not hear. What you put into it to nourish your body they will snatch away and give you leavins instead. No, they don't love your mouth. *You* got to love it. This is flesh I'm talking about here. Flesh that needs to be loved. Feet that need to rest and to dance; backs that need support; shoulders that need arms, strong arms I'm telling you. And O my people, out yonder, hear me, they do not love your neck unnoosed and straight. So love your neck; put a hand on it, grace it, stroke it and hold it up. And all your inside parts that they'd just as soon slop for hogs, you got to love them. The dark, dark liver—love it, love it, and the beat and beating heart, love that too. More than eyes or feet. More than lungs that have yet to draw free air. More than your life-holding womb and your life-giving private parts, hear me now, love your heart. For this is the prize.[11]

Baby Suggs's sermon, delivered to her community at an open space in the woods known as the Clearing, reminds me that however bad we think things are in 2018, however desperate, disastrous, or truly horrific the world seems, it has been worse—and it can get better. It has before, and will again. It is Morrison's reminder that we ourselves are the prize, and the resultant almost obstinate optimism that it engenders, that keep us going and that animate this exhibition.

Prologue Magazine 49, no. 2 (Summer 2017), https://www.archives.gov/publications/prologue/2017/summer/thibodaux.

11
Toni Morrison, *Beloved* (New York: Plume, 1987), p. 88.

National Memorial for Peace and Justice, Montgomery, Alabama. Photograph by the author

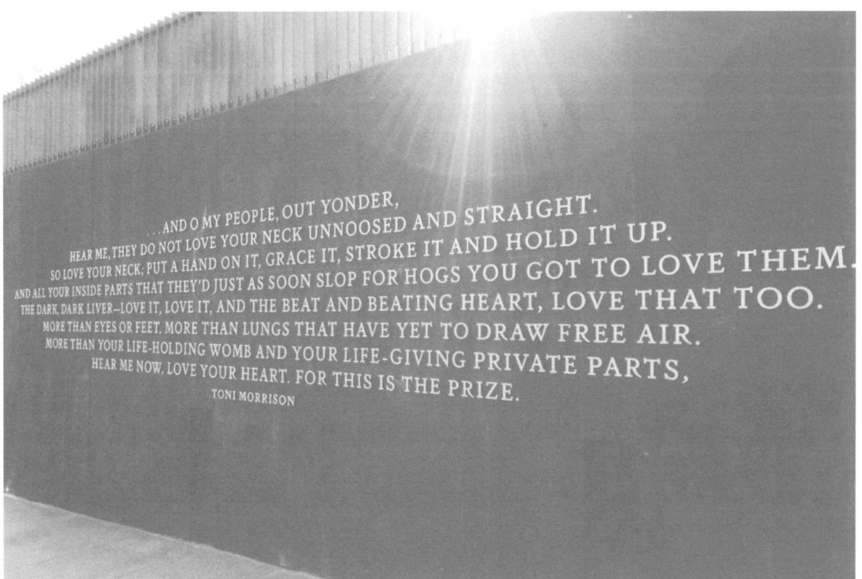

Process

2019

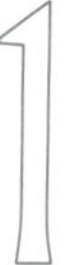

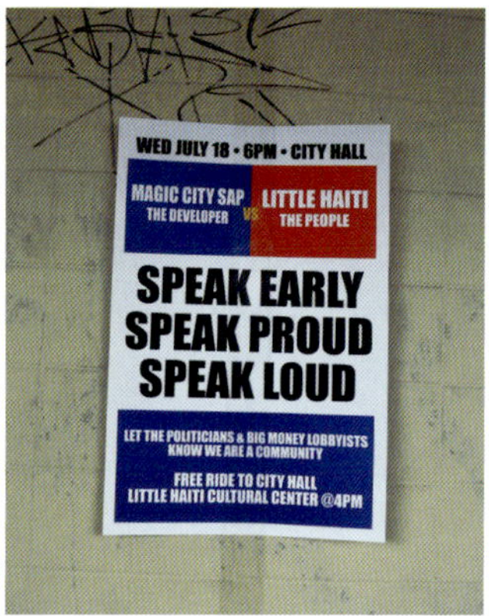
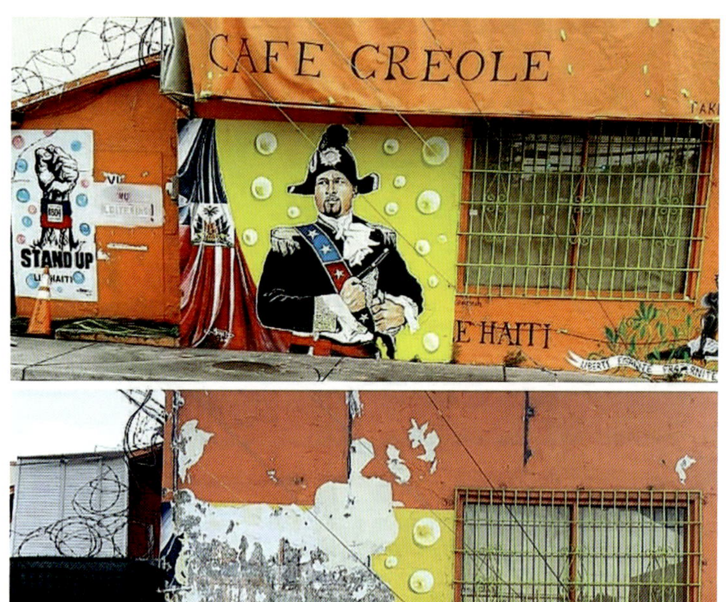

Source image for *Speak
Early, Speak Proud, Speak
Loud*, 2018

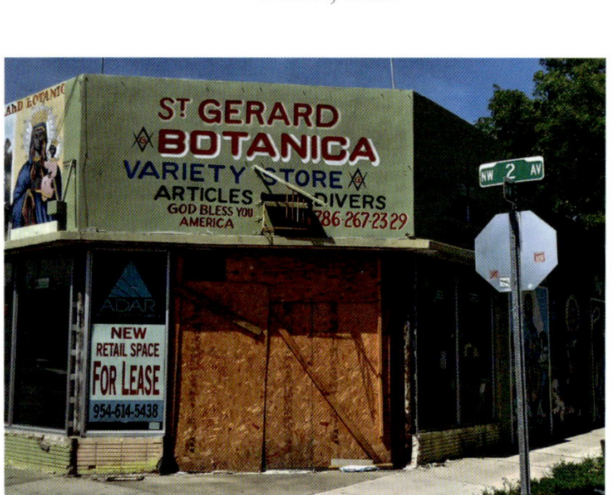

Source image for *5825 NE 2nd Ave.,
Miami, FL 33137*, 2016

Source image for *5901 NW 2nd Ave.,
Miami, FL 33127*, 2018

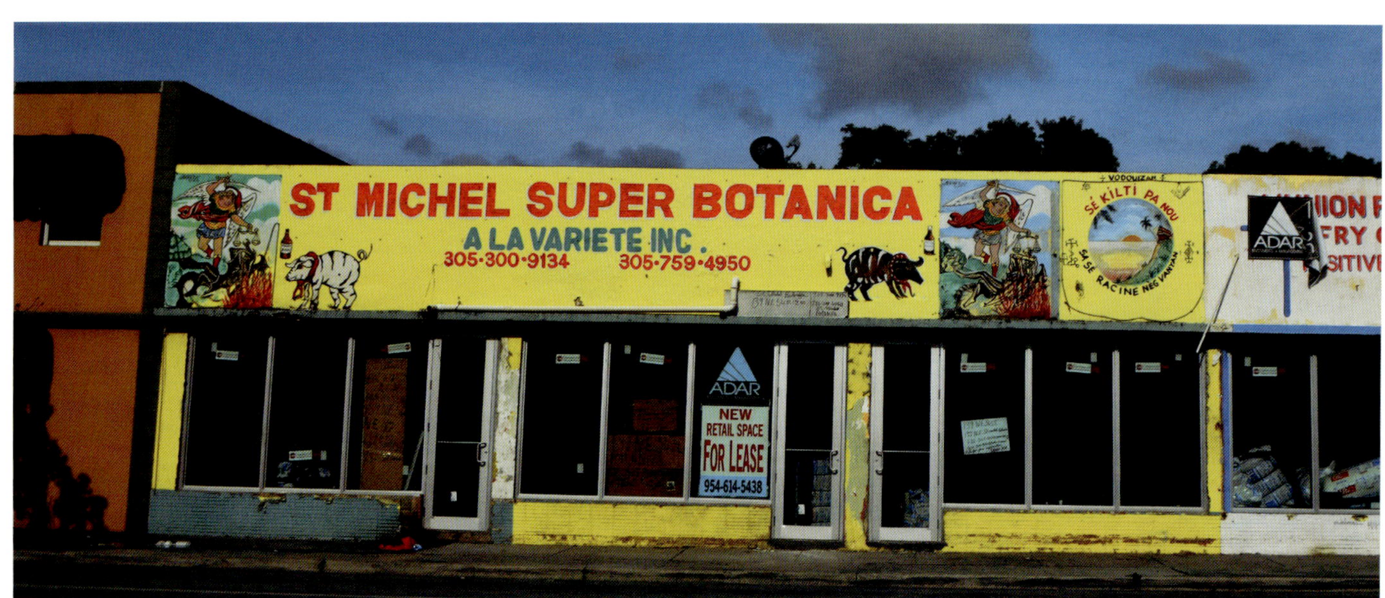

Source image for *5901 NW 2nd Ave., Miami, FL 33127*, 2016

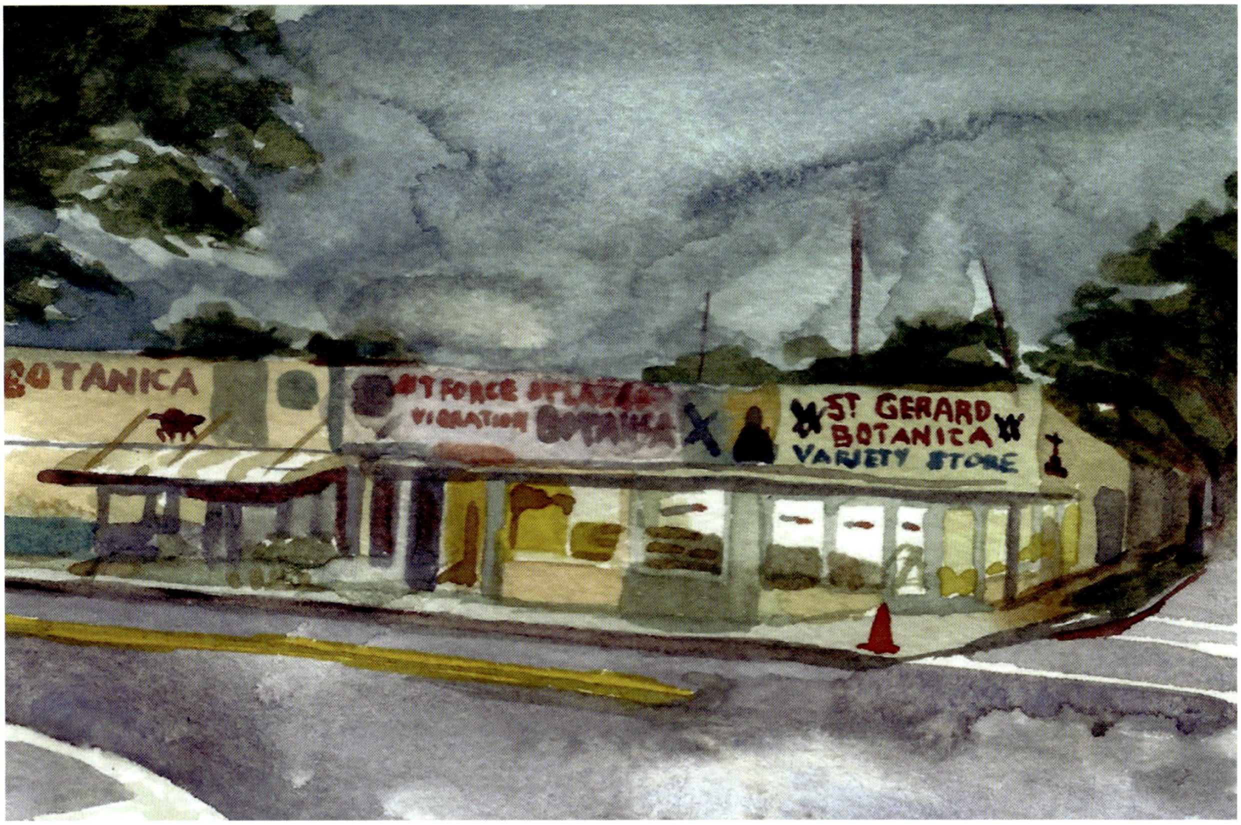

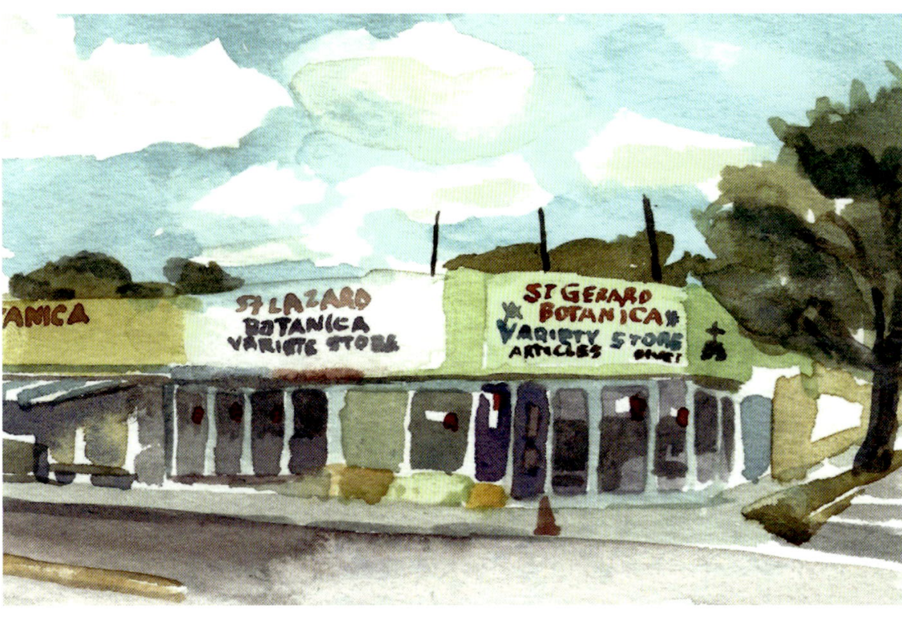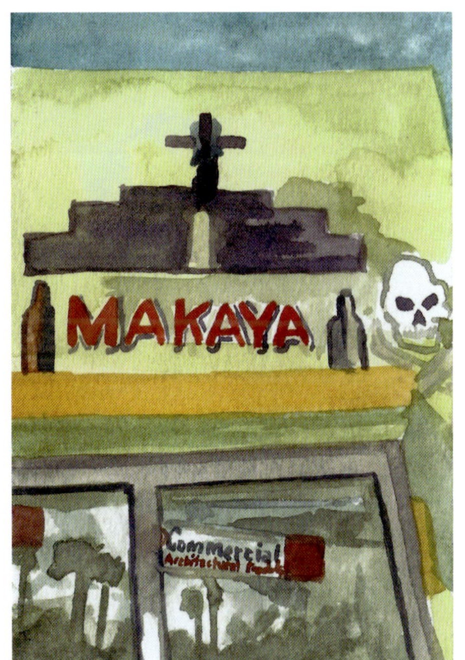

5901 NW 2nd Ave., Miami, FL 33127 Night, 2018

5901 NW 2nd Ave., Miami, FL 33127 Day, 2018

5901 NW 2nd Ave., Miami,
FL 33127 Makaya, 2018

EDDIE ARROYO

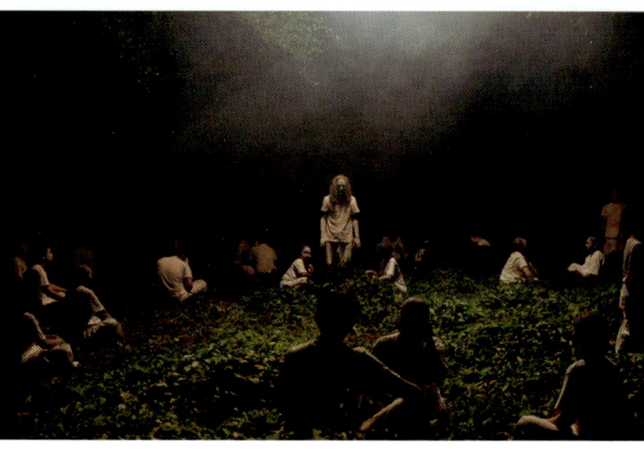

2

Production still from *No history in a room filled with people with funny names 5*, 2018

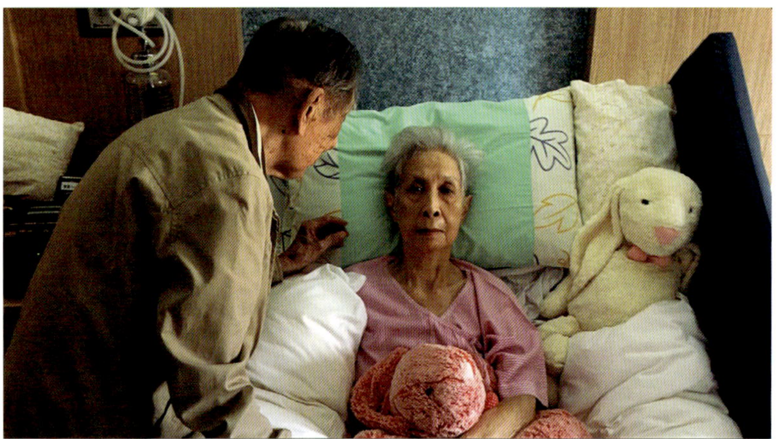

Process image of the artist's grandparents for *No history in a room filled with people with funny names 5*, 2018

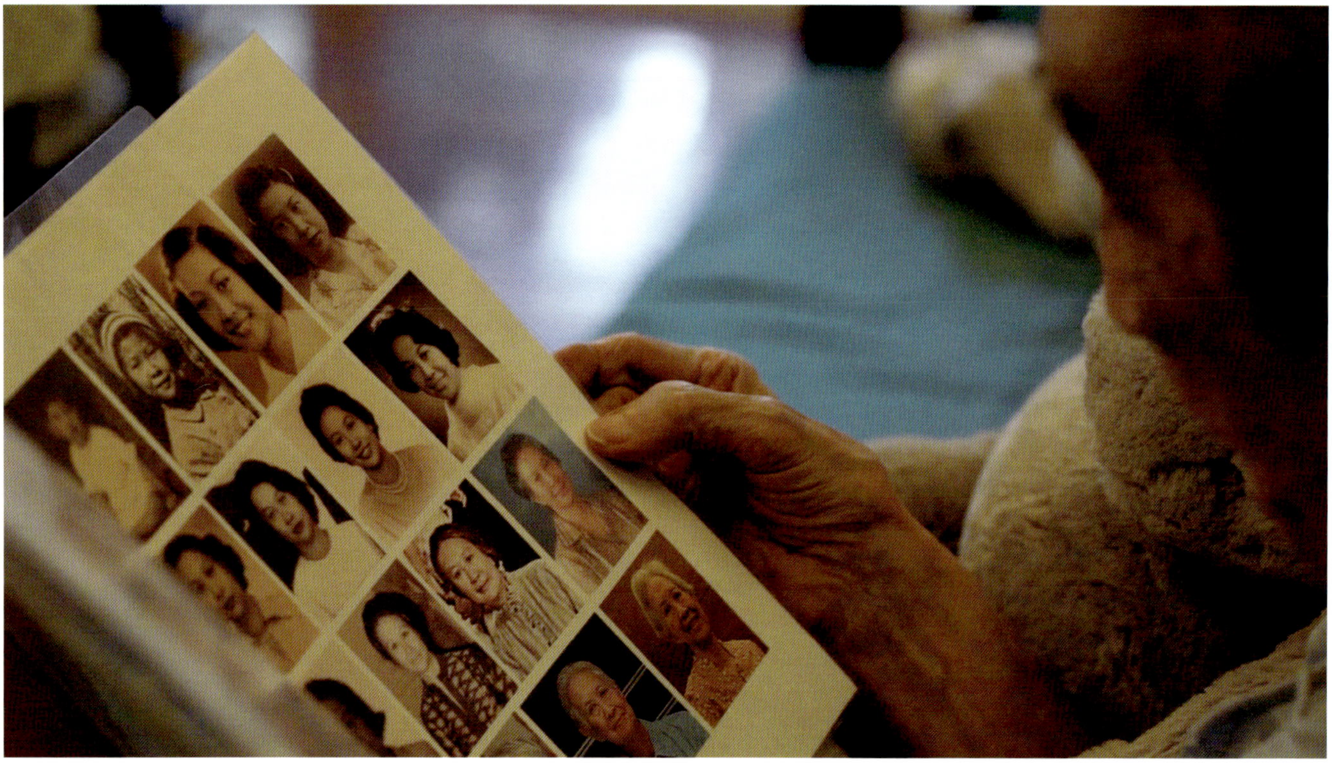

Process image for *No history in a room filled with people with funny names 5*, 2018

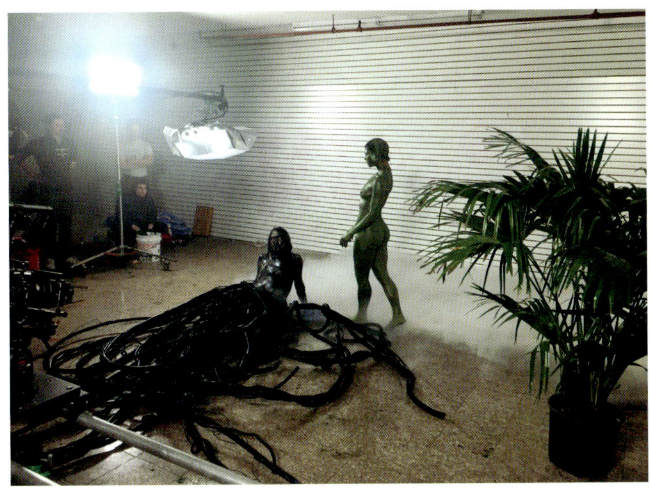

Production still from *with history in a room filled with people with funny names 4*, 2017

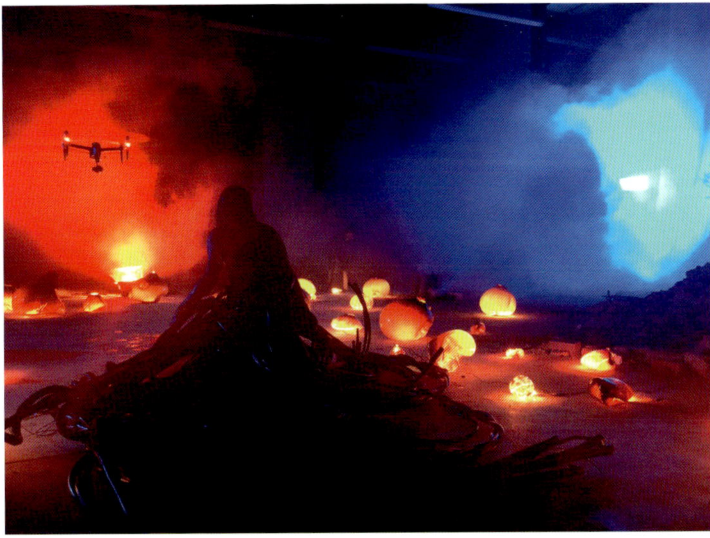

Production still from *with history in a room filled with people with funny names 4*, 2017

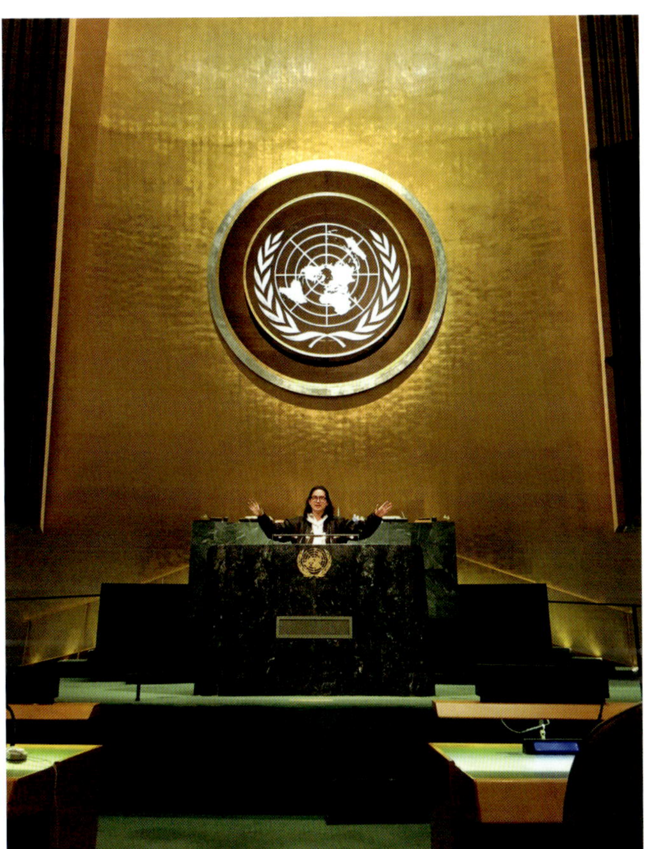

Process image of the United Nations Headquarters for *with history in a room filled with people with funny names 4*, 2017

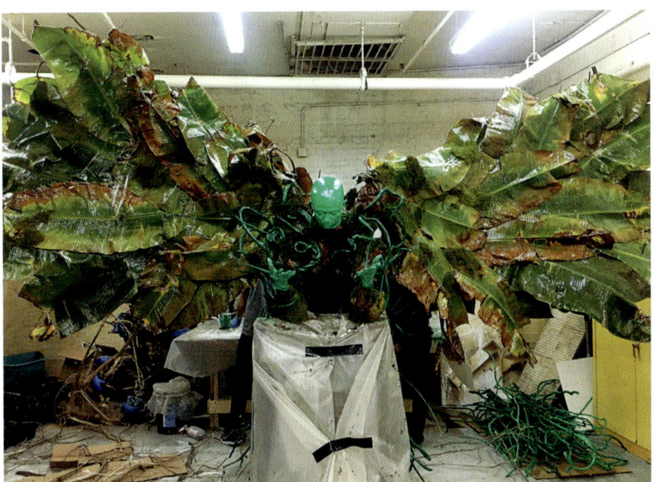

Process image for *Workshop for Peace, from a place/ not so familiar/ but relatable/ through the sound/ of its breath*, 2018

KORAKRIT ARUNANONDCHAI

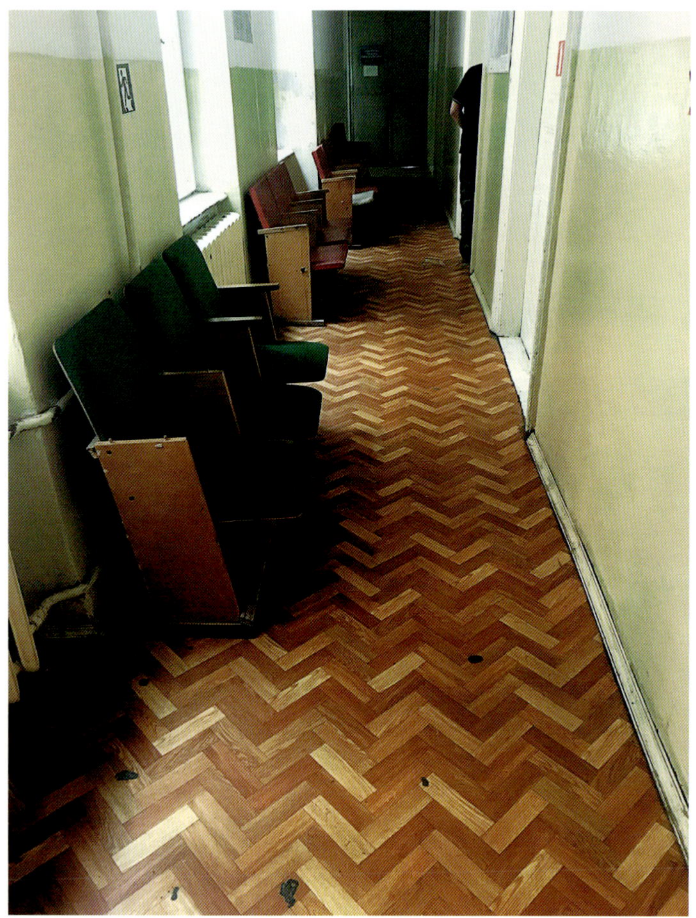

3

Waiting room, Lviv, Ukraine, 2018

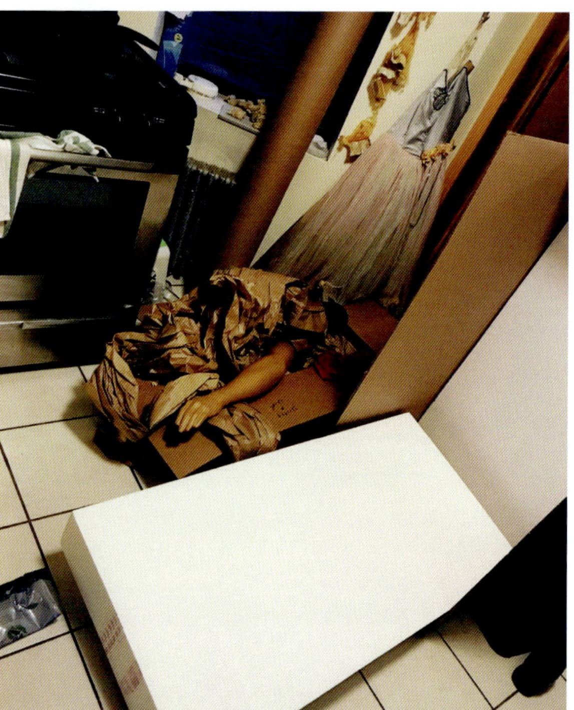

Materials stored in the artist's apartment, 2018

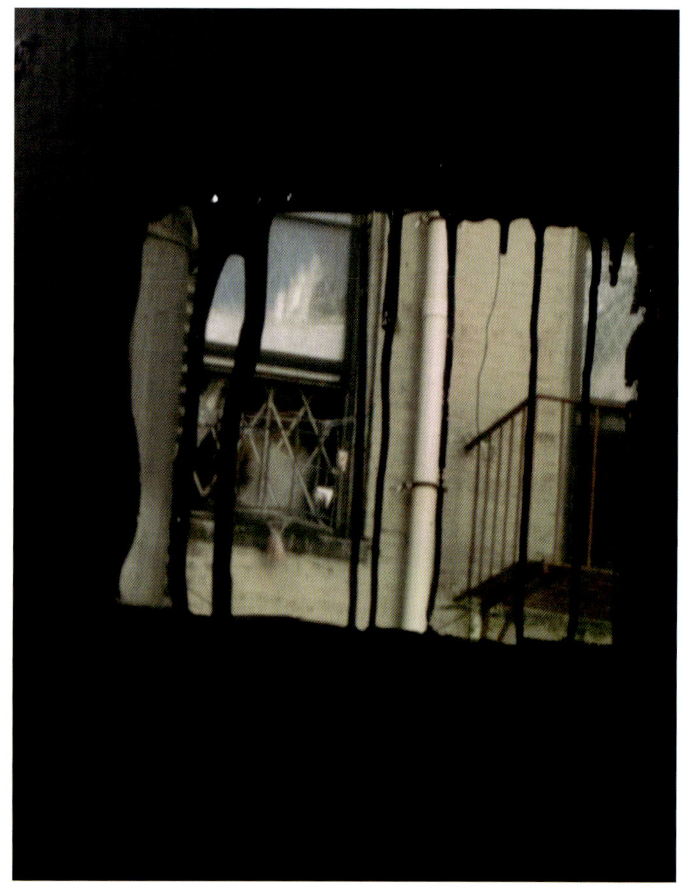

Process image, 2017

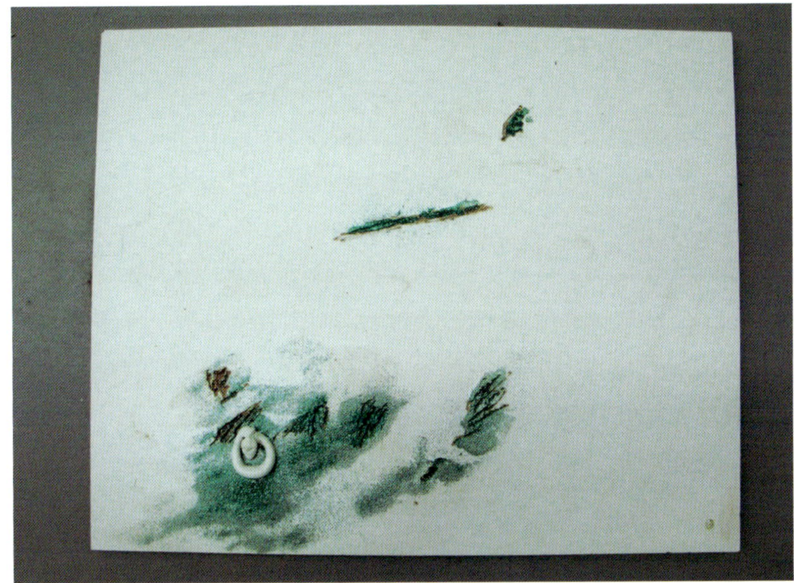

Untitled work in progress, 2010

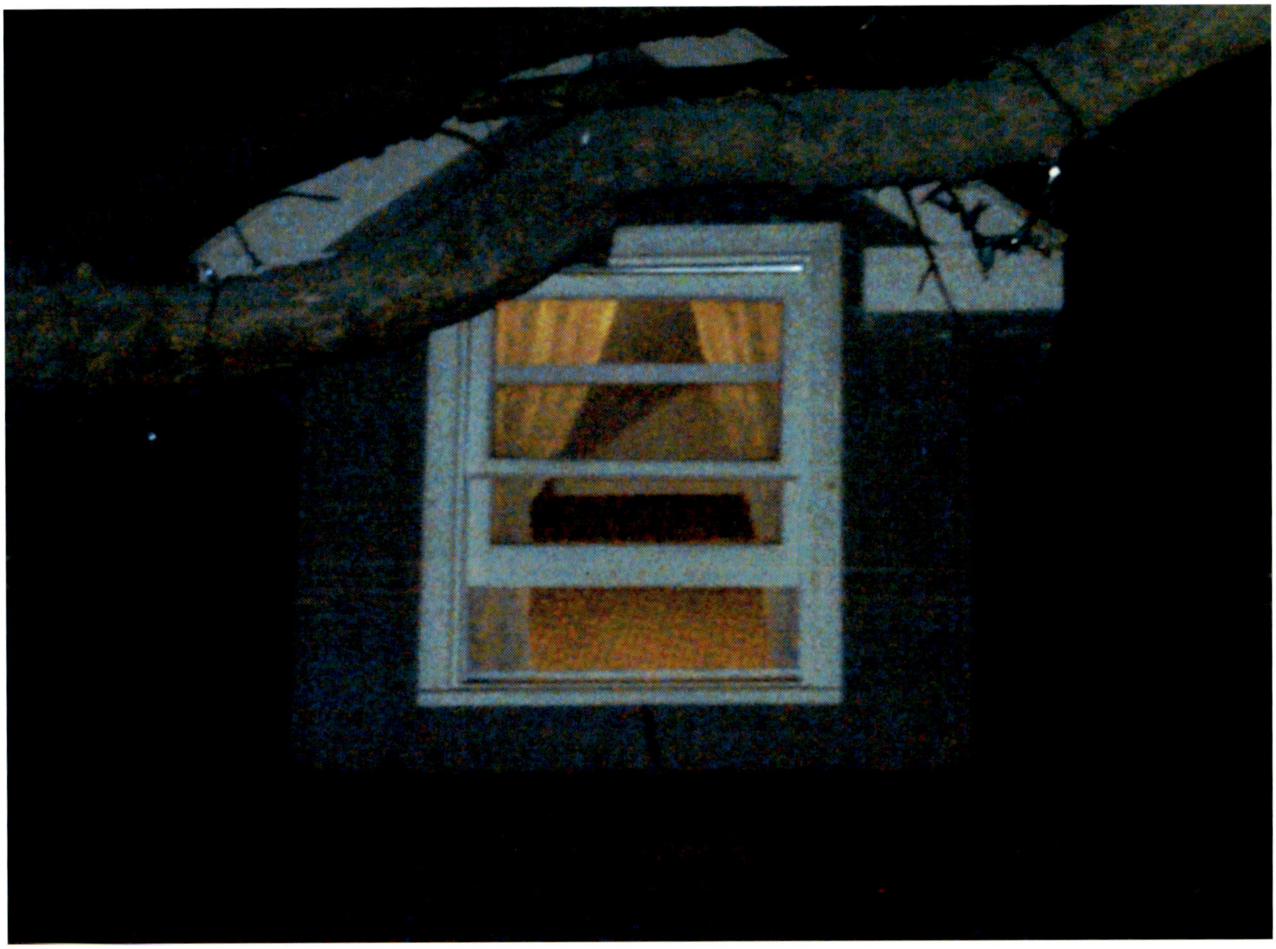

House on the Rock, Iowa County, WI, 2009

OLGA BALEMA

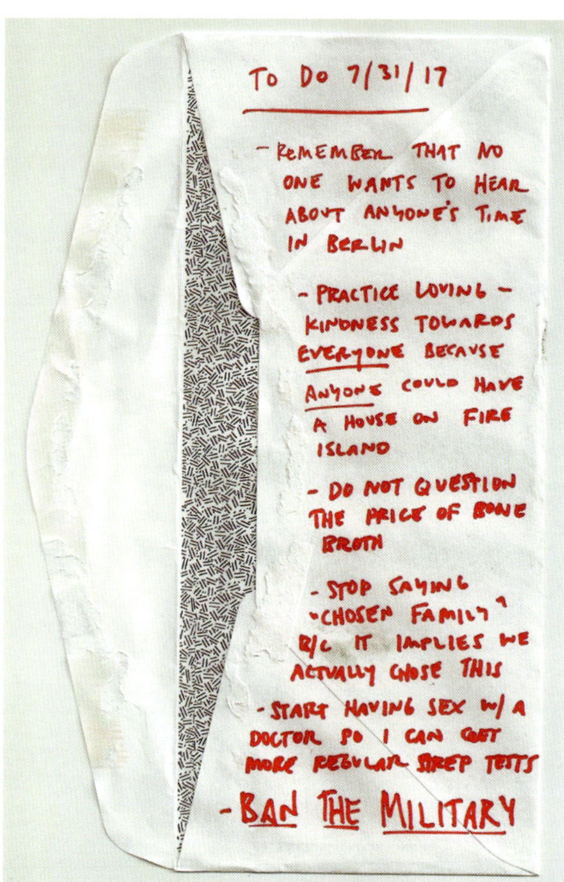

4

To Do 7/31/17, 2017

THE MUSICAL EXPERIENCE

TO DO 5/29/17
- STOP TALKING ABOUT THE FUCKING RICE COOKER
- FIND OUT IF STEALING FROM DEAN + DELUCA IS ACTIVISM
- KEEP IT COLD SO WE DON'T HAVE TO GO TO THE NUDE BEACH
- DON'T BE ASHAMED OF HOW I ACTED AT STAPLES
- WWW.ASK8BALL.NET

To Do 5/29/17, 2017

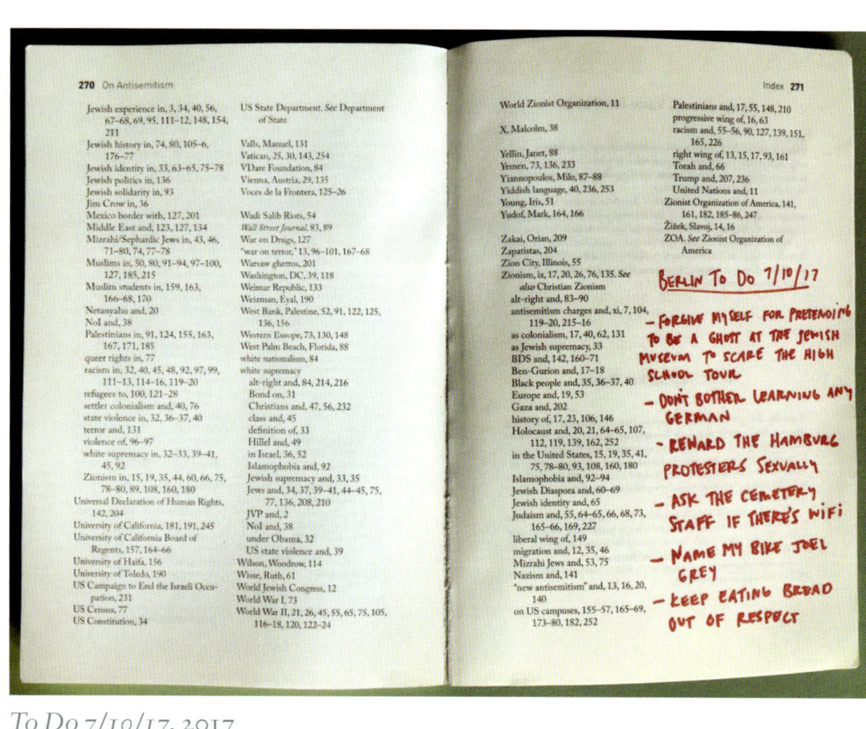

To Do 7/10/17, 2017

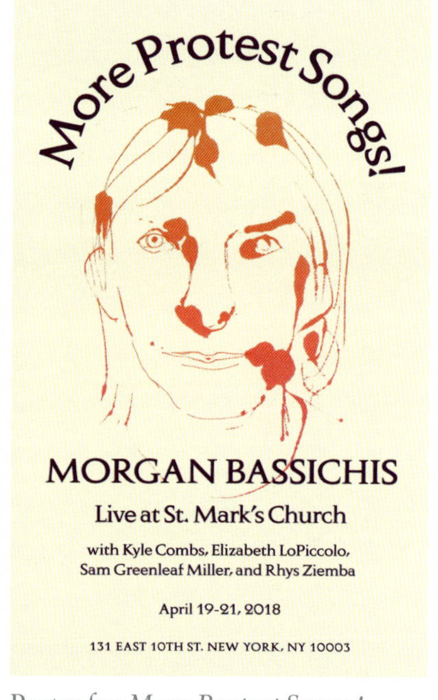

Poster for *More Protest Songs!*, 2018. Danspace Project, New York, NY, 2018. Artwork by Nicole Eisenman, design by Carl Williamson

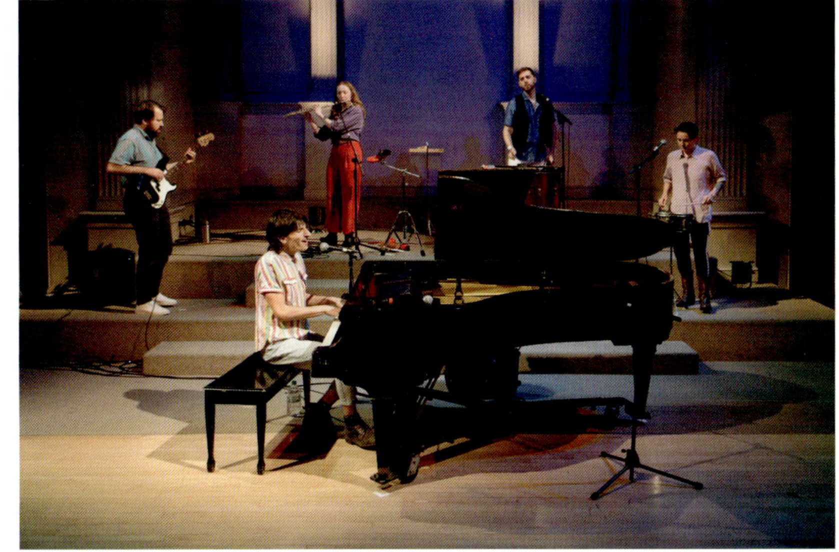

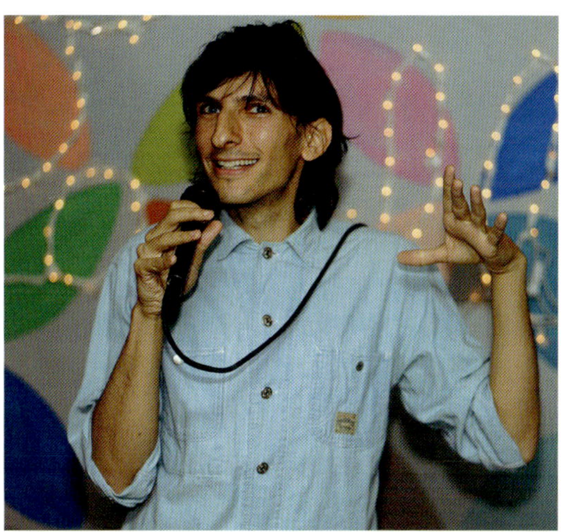

Performance view, Max Fish, New York, NY, 2018

More Protest Songs!, 2018. Performance view, Danspace Project, New York, NY, 2018

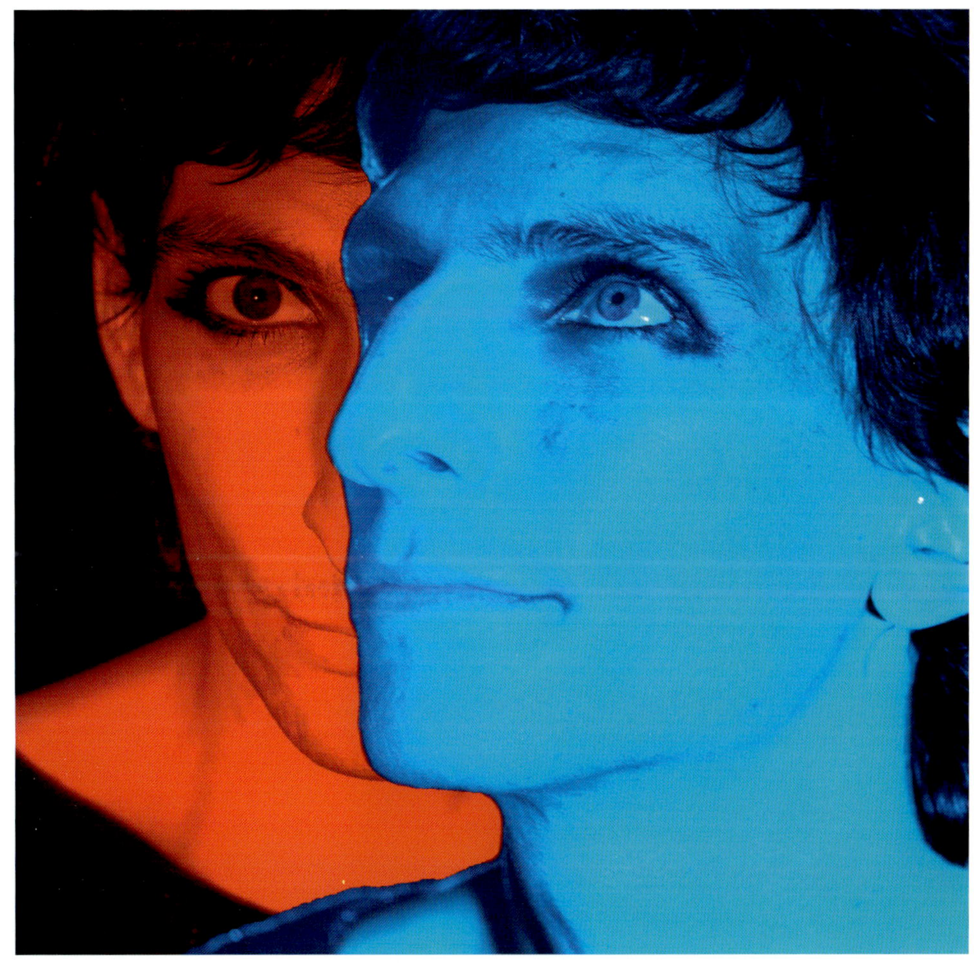

Publicity image for *Damned if You Duet*, 2018. The Kitchen, New York, NY, 2018

MORGAN BASSICHIS

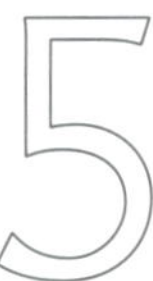

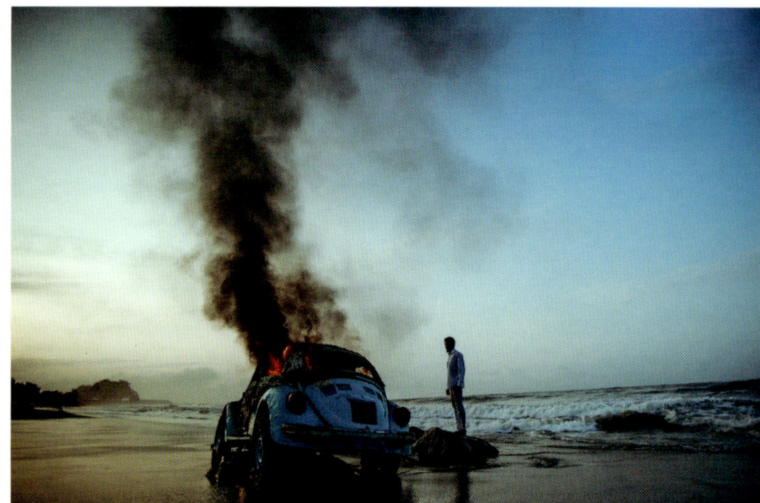

The Burial of Kojo, 2018

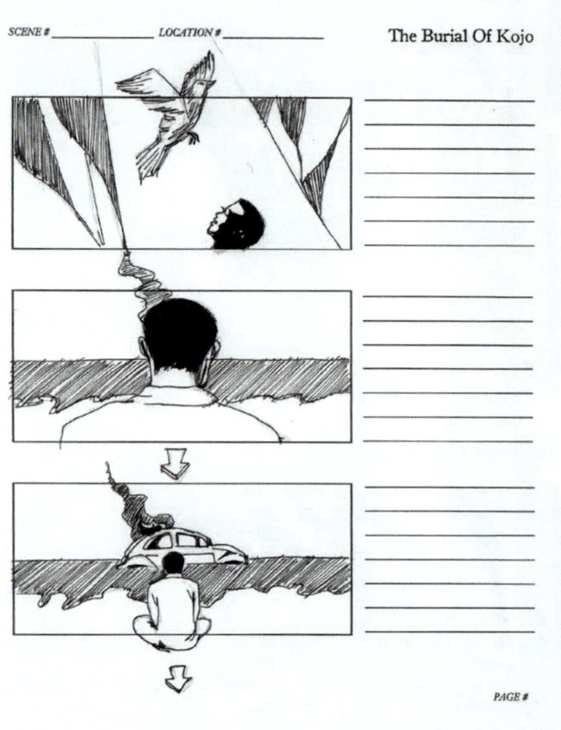

Storyboard for *The Burial of Kojo*, 2018

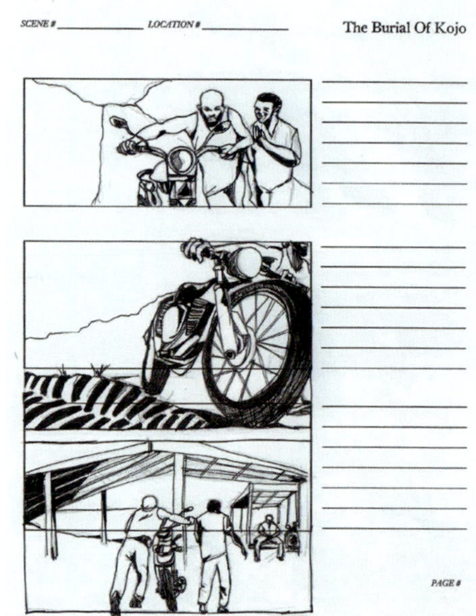

Storyboard for *The Burial of Kojo*, 2018

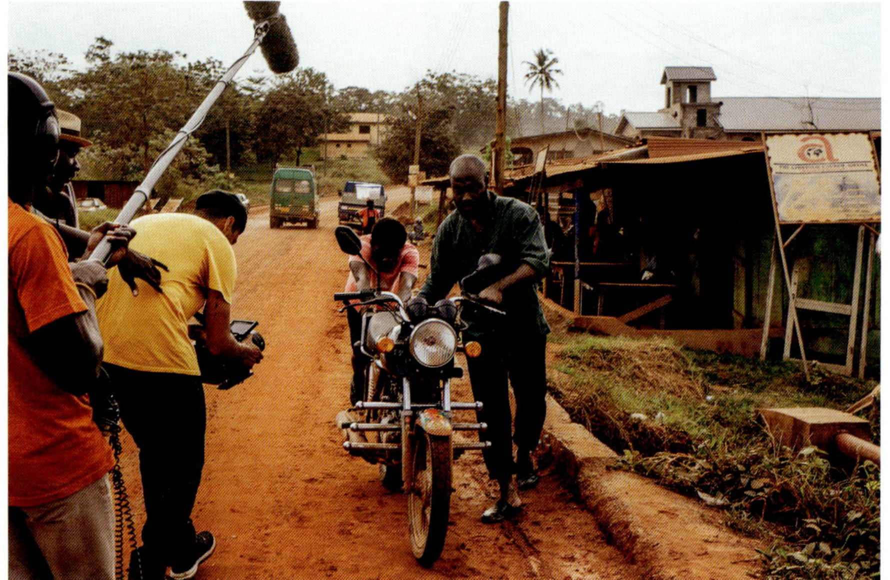

Production still from *The Burial of Kojo*, 2018

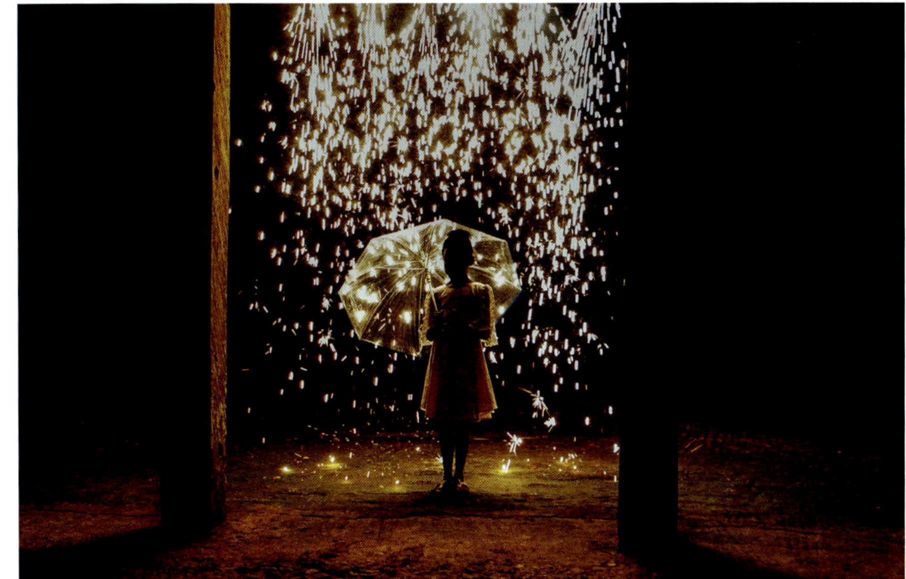

The Burial of Kojo, 2018

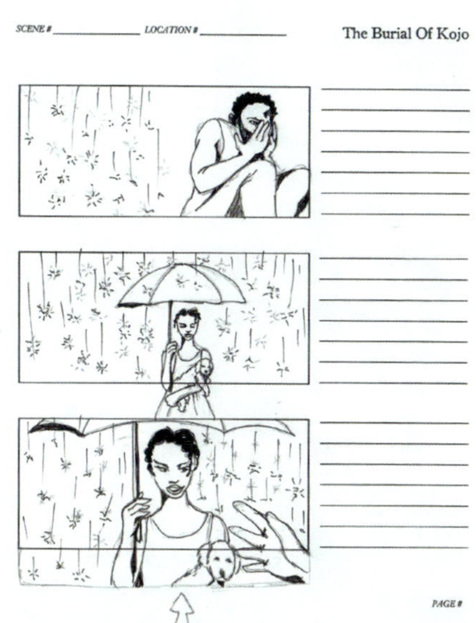

Storyboard for *The Burial of Kojo*, 2018

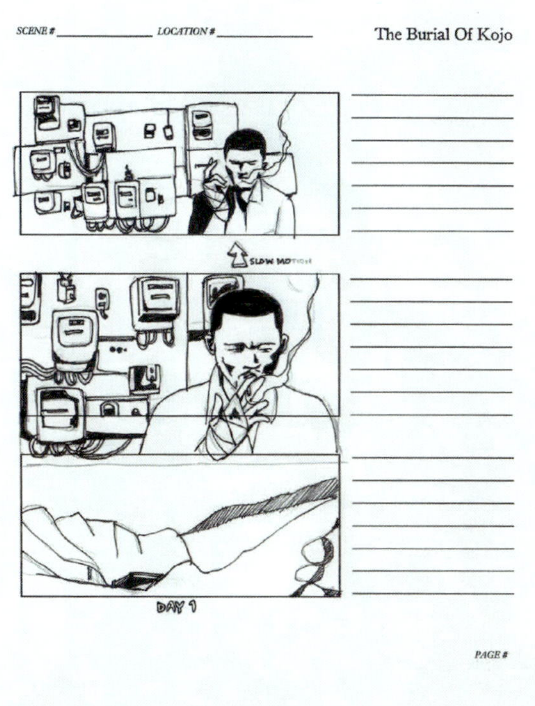

Storyboard for *The Burial of Kojo*, 2018

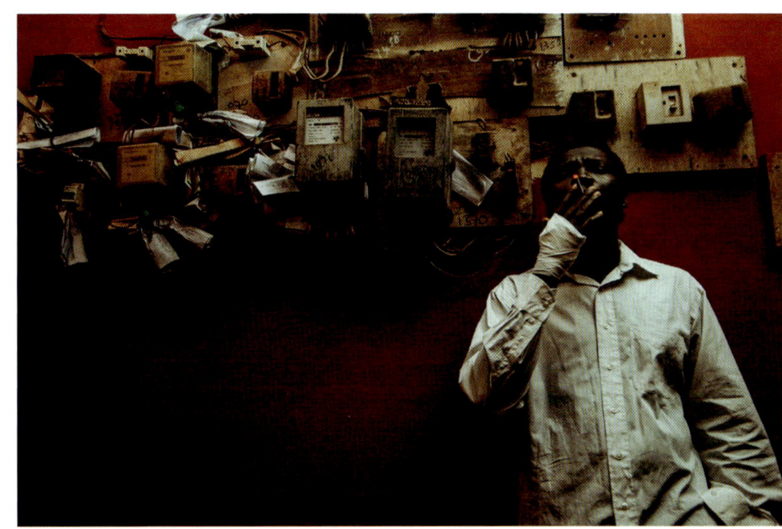

The Burial of Kojo, 2018

BLITZ BAZAWULE

123

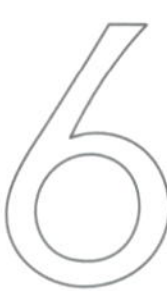

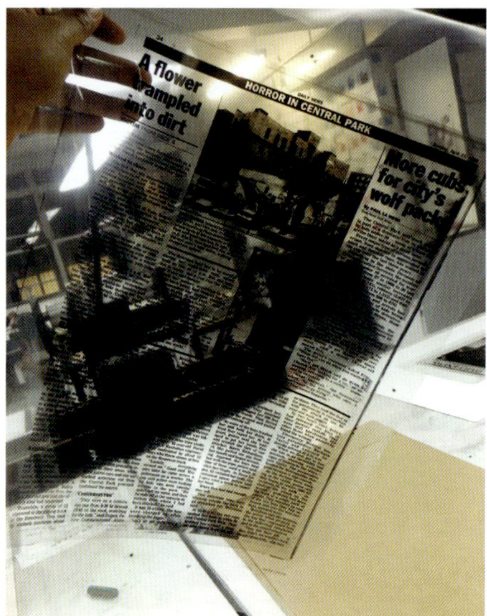

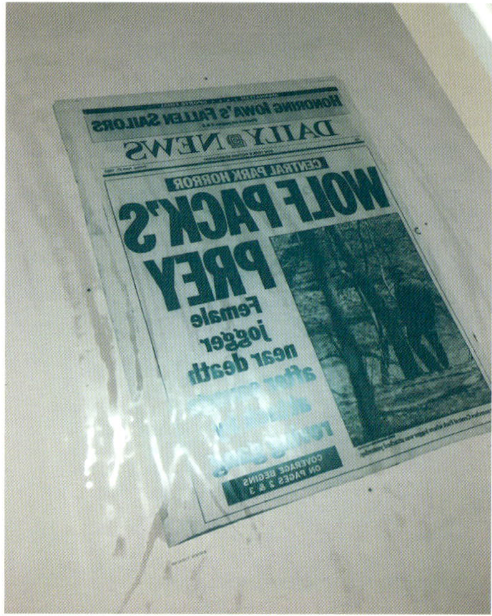

Positive film, 2018

Photolitography plate, 2018

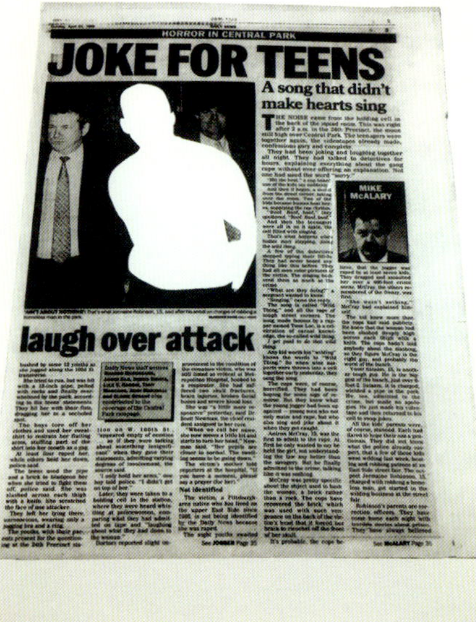

Process image, 2018

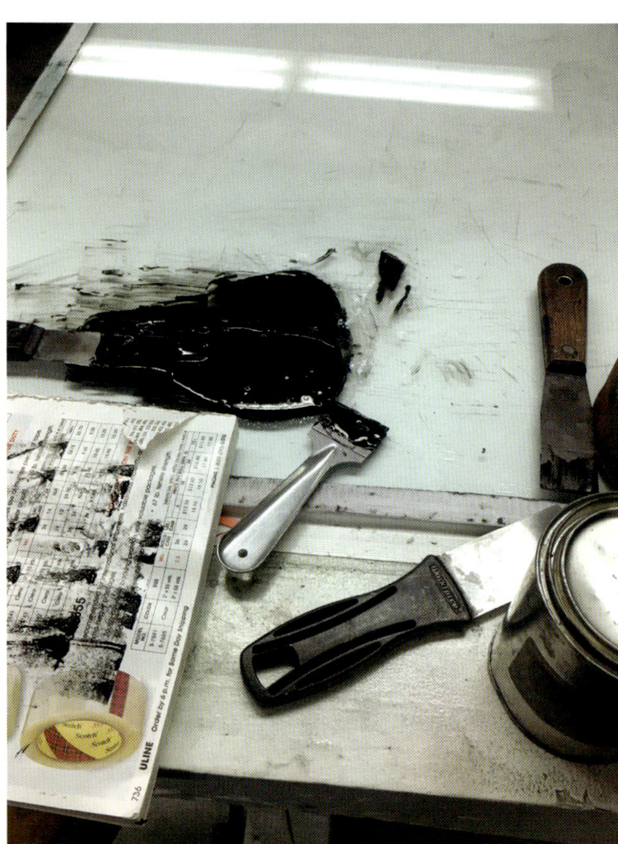

Mixing ink, 2018

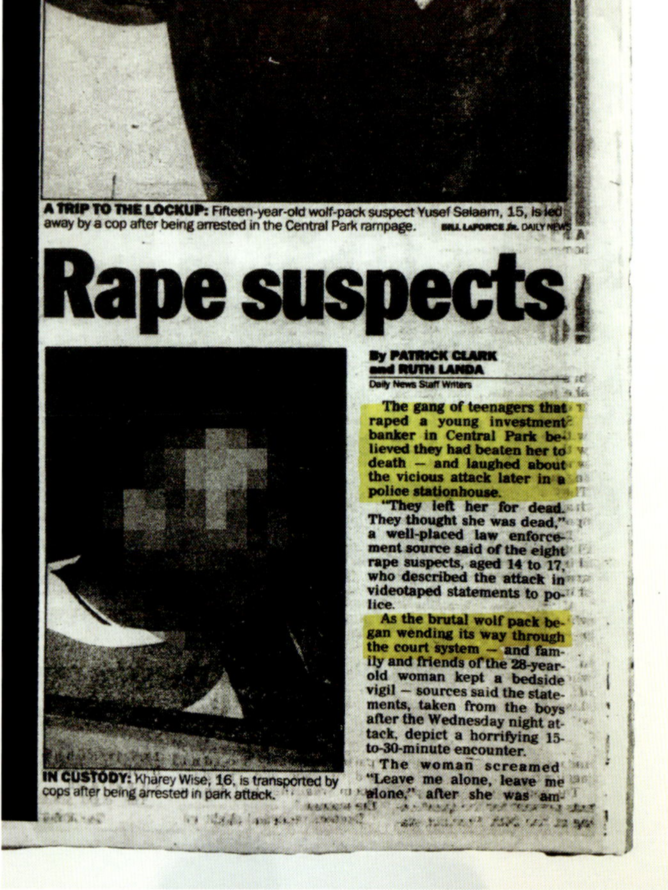

Detail of *No Humans Involved: After Sylvia Wynter*, 2018

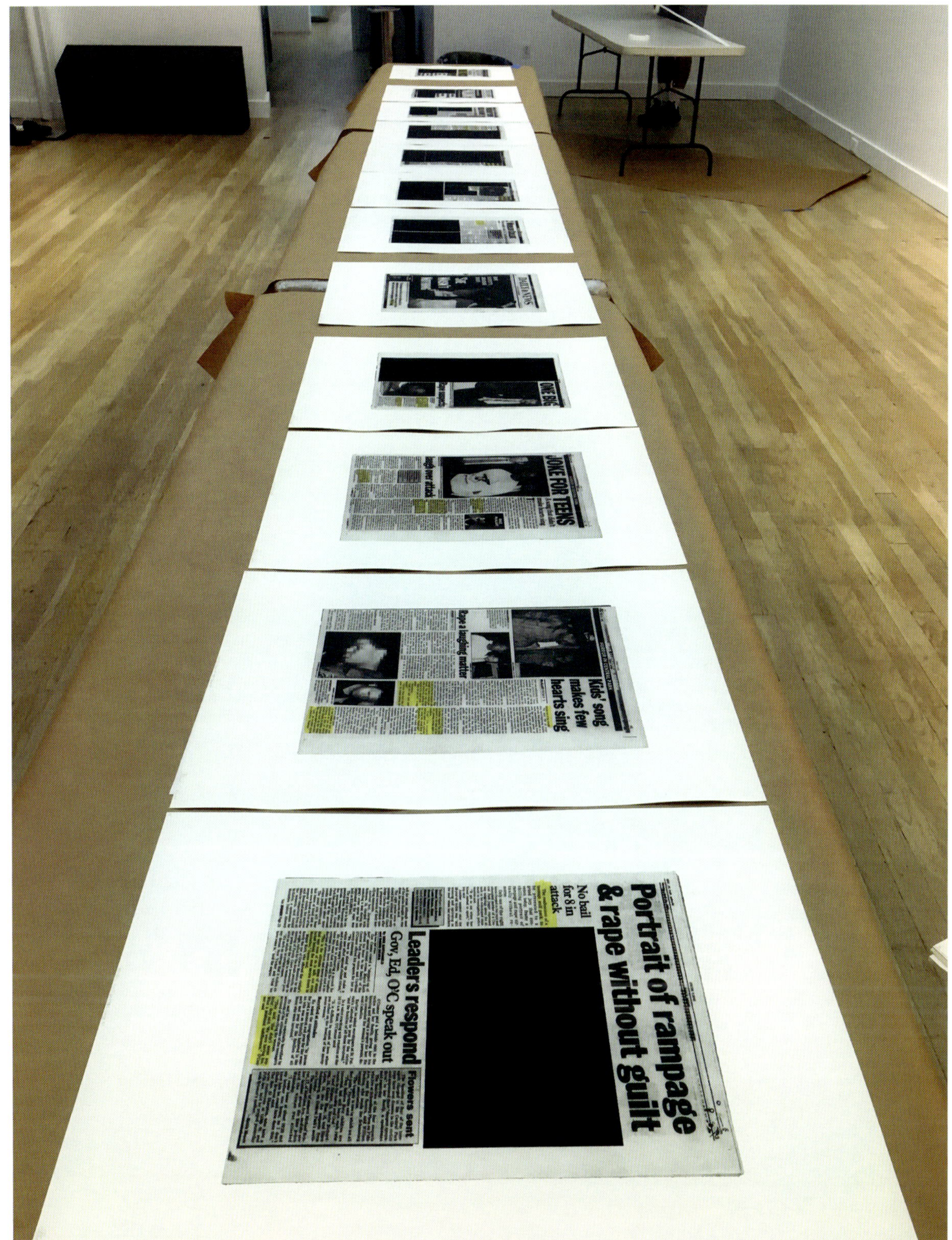

Test prints for *No Humans Involved: After Sylvia Wynter*, 2018

ALEXANDRA BELL

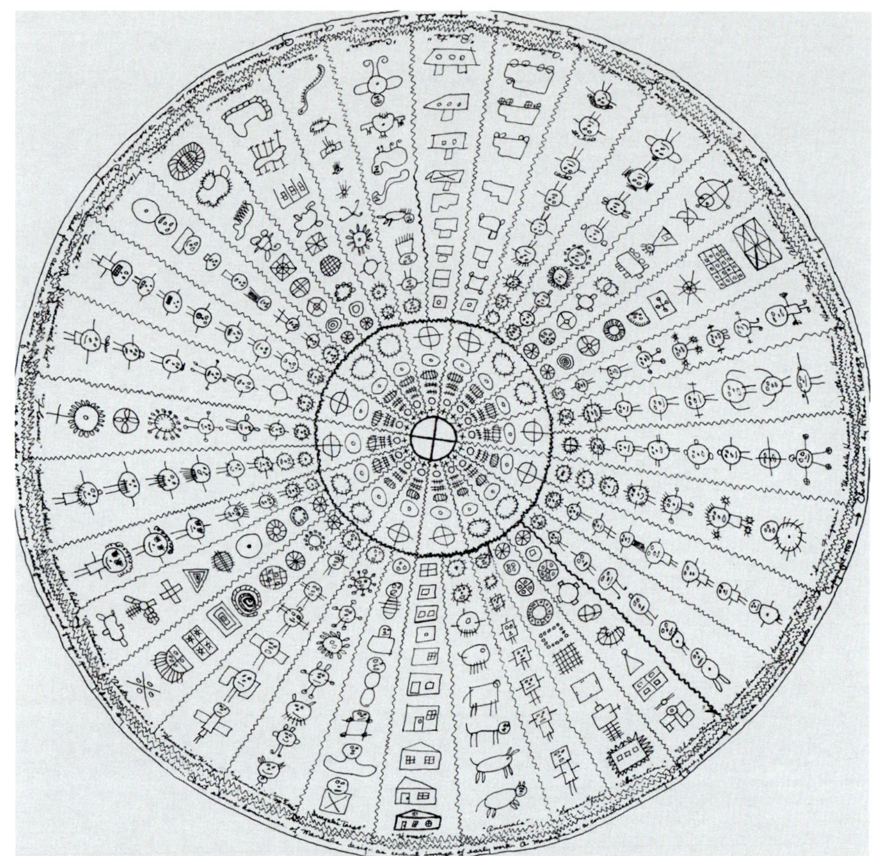

Rhoda Kellogg, mandala with traced children's art depicting the evolution
from scribbles to pictorialism, 1954

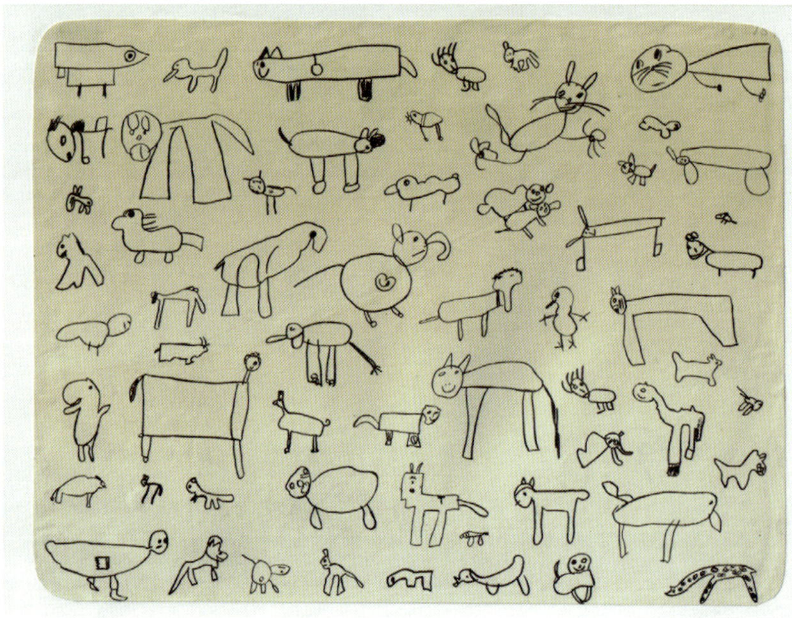

Rhoda Kellogg, traced taxonomy of children's art with animals, 1950s

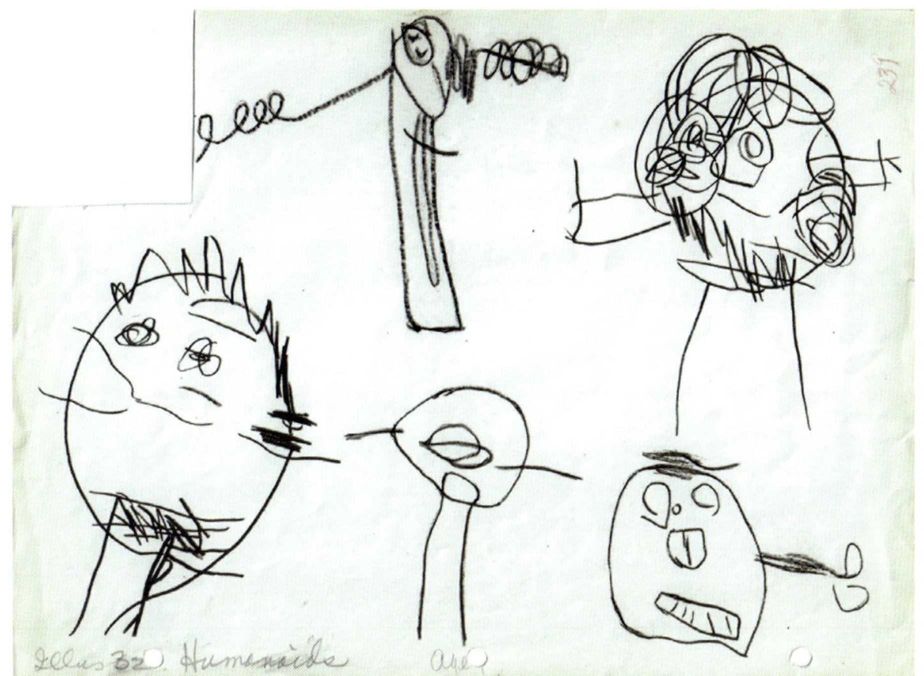

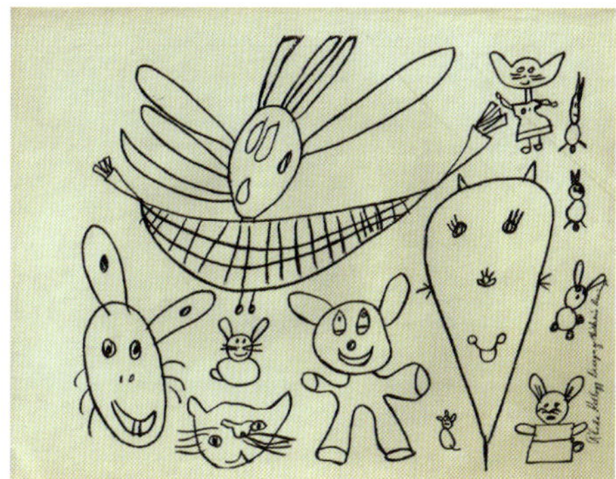

Rhoda Kellogg, traced taxonomy
of children's art with bunnies and
kittens, 1950s

Rhoda Kellogg, traced taxonomy of children's art with humanoid
forms and faces, 1950s

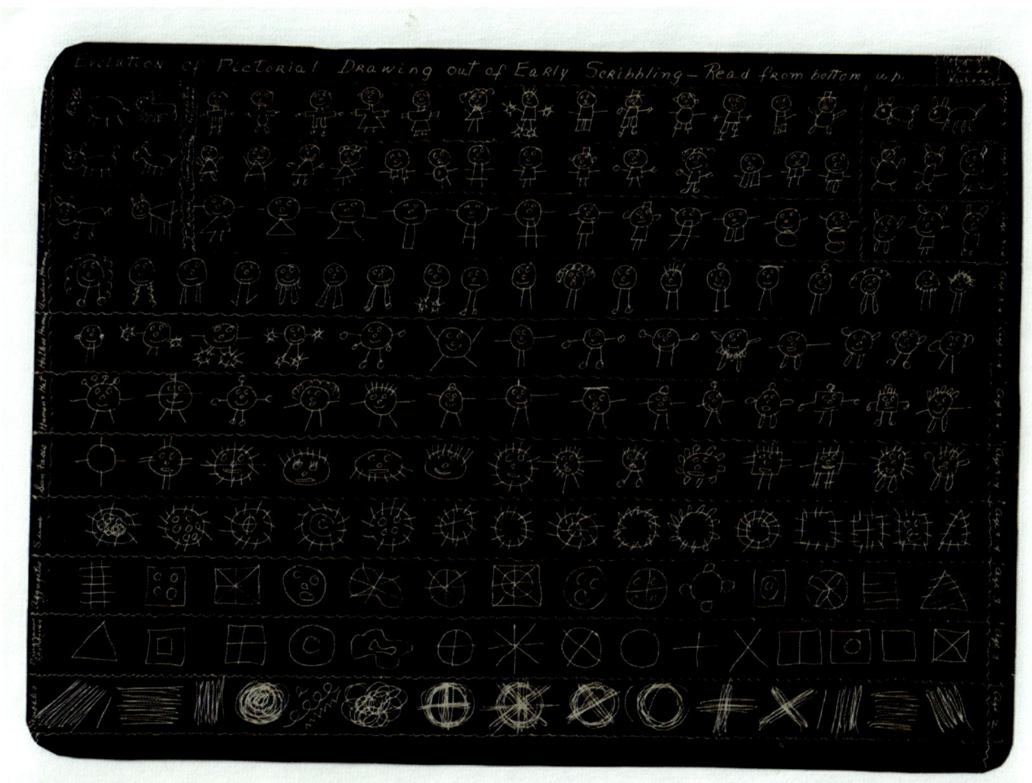

Rhoda Kellogg, traced taxonomy of children's art depicting the evolution from
scribbles to pictorialism, 1954

BRIAN BELOTT

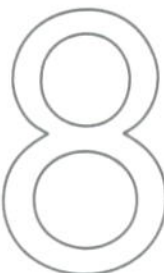

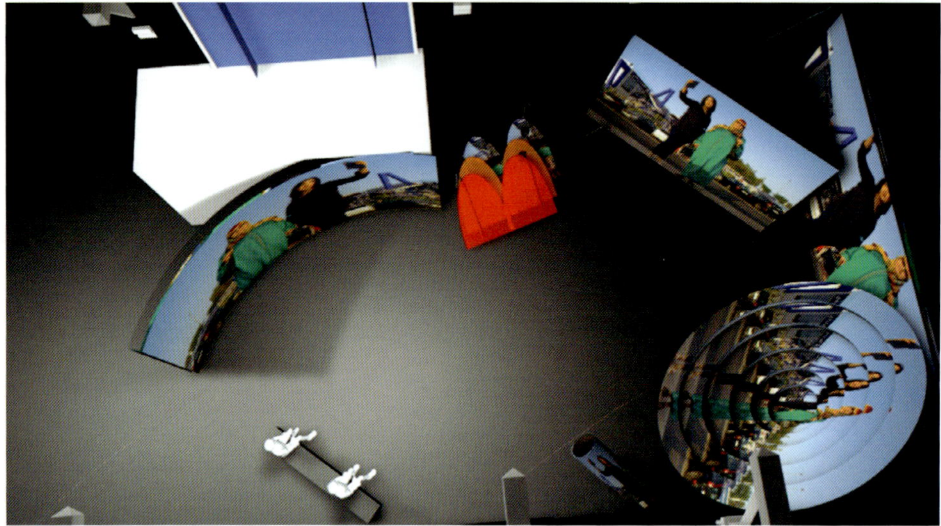

Rendering for installation of *Siham & Hafida*, 2017

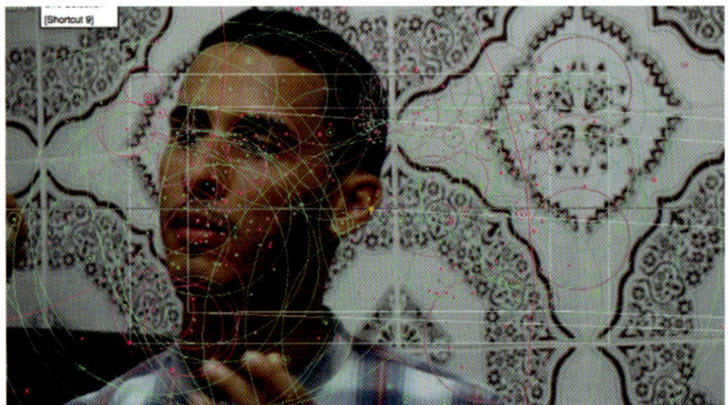

Process image for *Siham & Hafida*, 2017

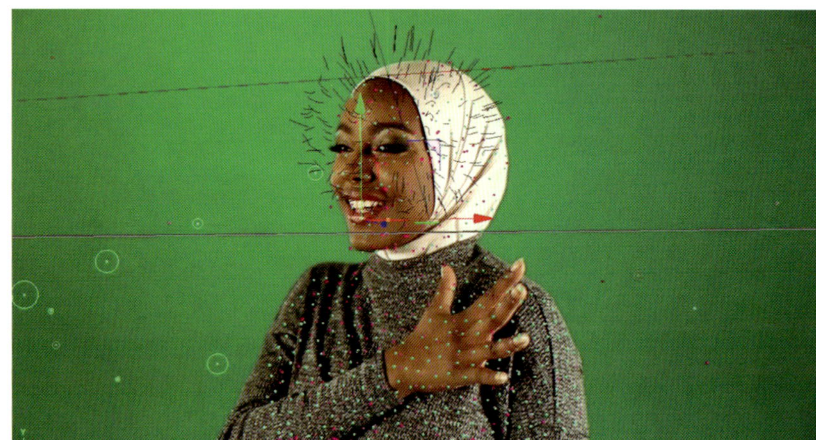

Process image for *Your Year by Fardaous Funjab*, 2017

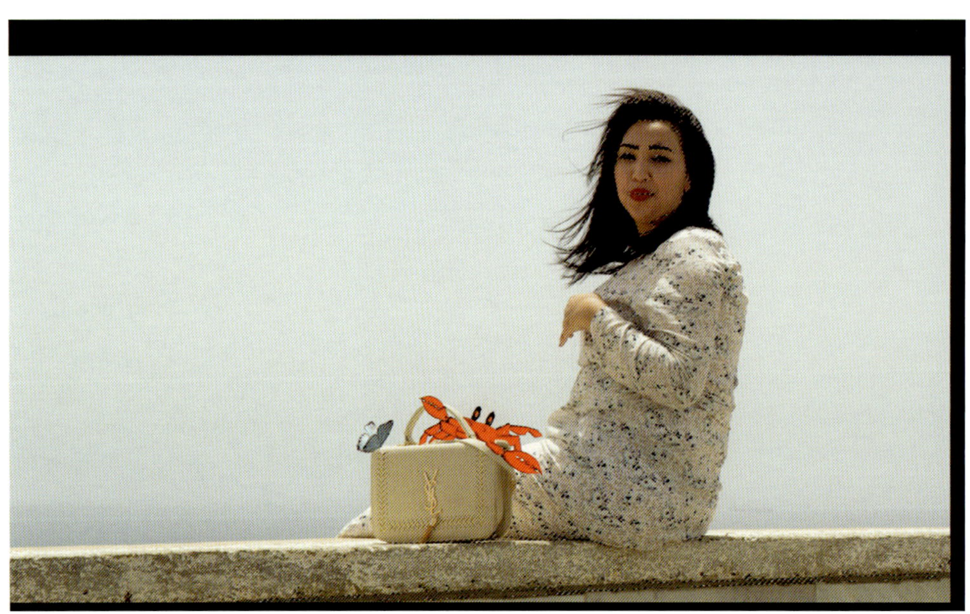

Process image for *Siham & Hafida*, 2017

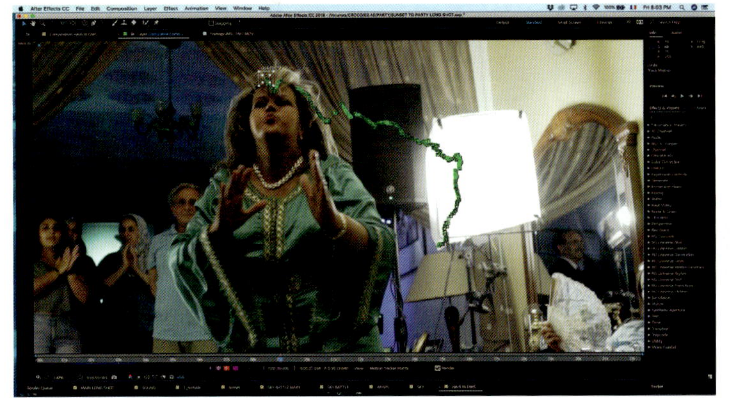

Process image for *PARTY ON THE CAPS*, 2018

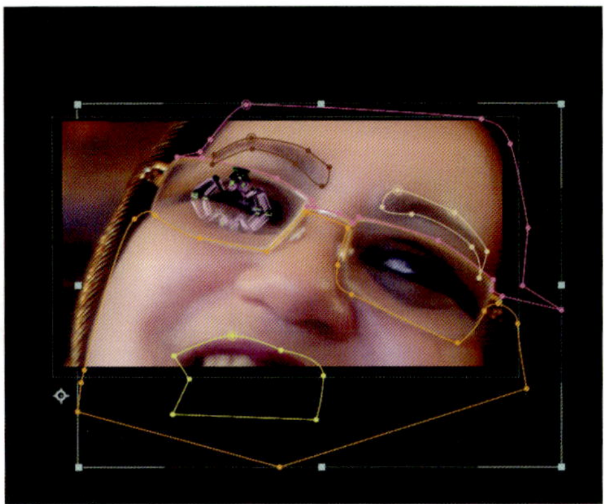

Process image for *Ghariba (Stranger)*, 2017

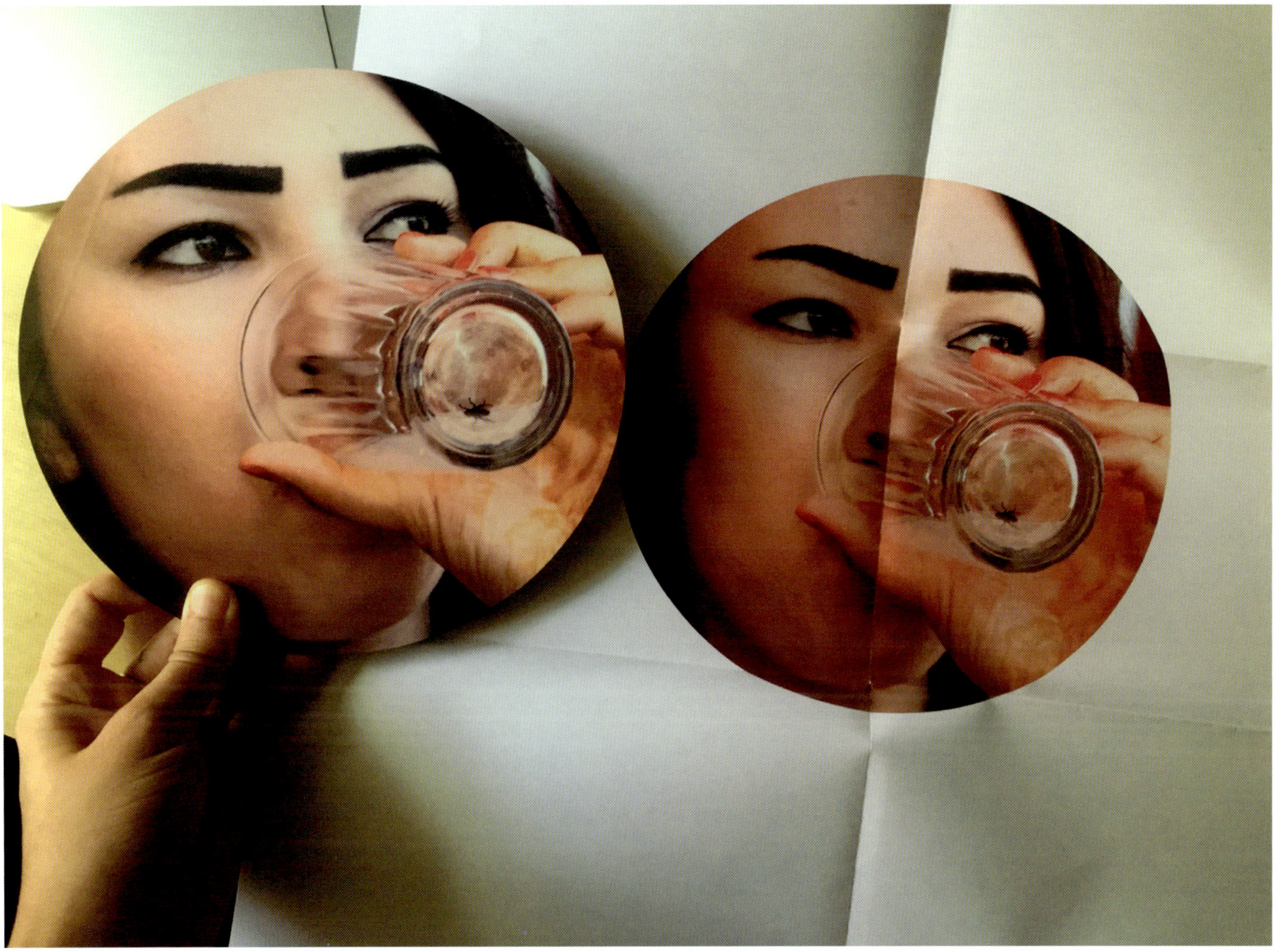

Test prints for *Siham & Hafida* at the Kitchen, New York, NY, 2017

MERIEM BENNANI

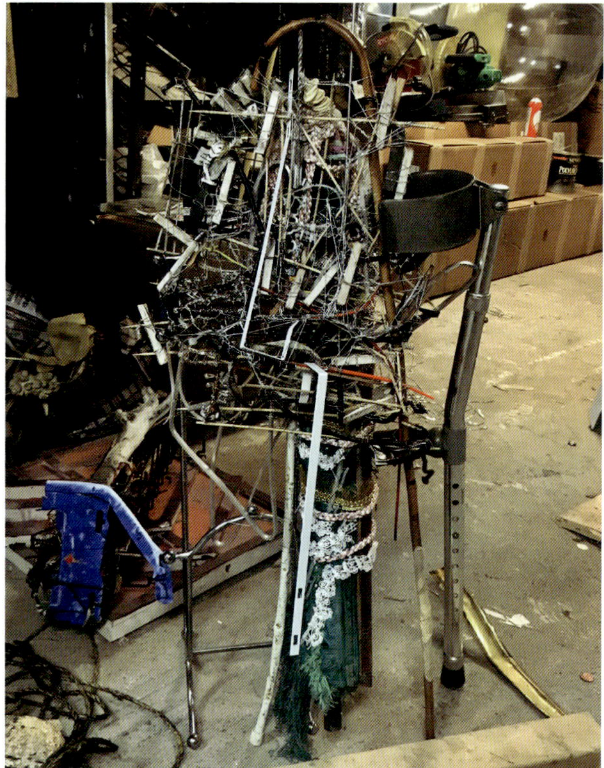

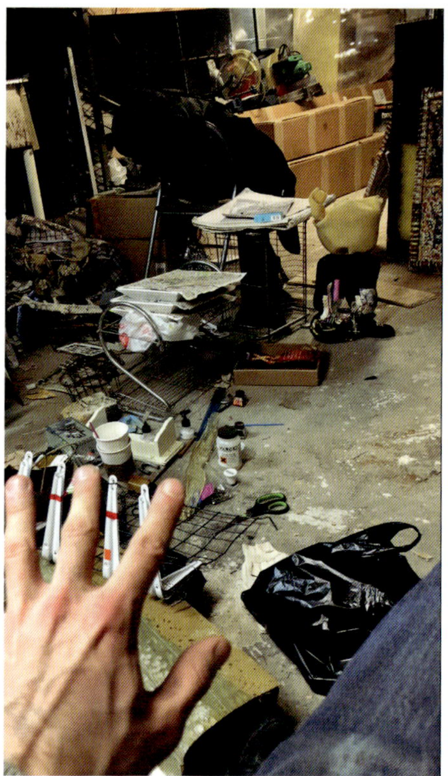

Studio, Brooklyn, NY, 2018

Studio, Brooklyn, NY, 2018

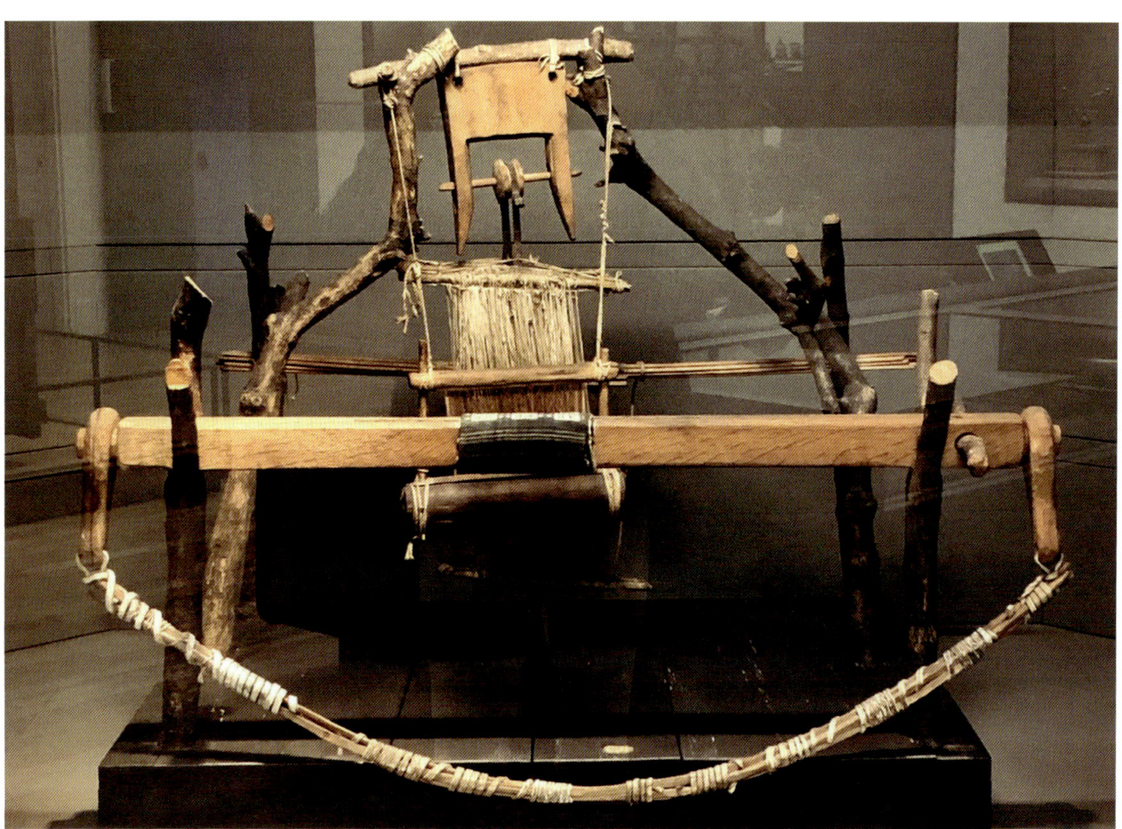

Photograph of a loom, Musée des Arts et Métiers, Paris, France, 2018

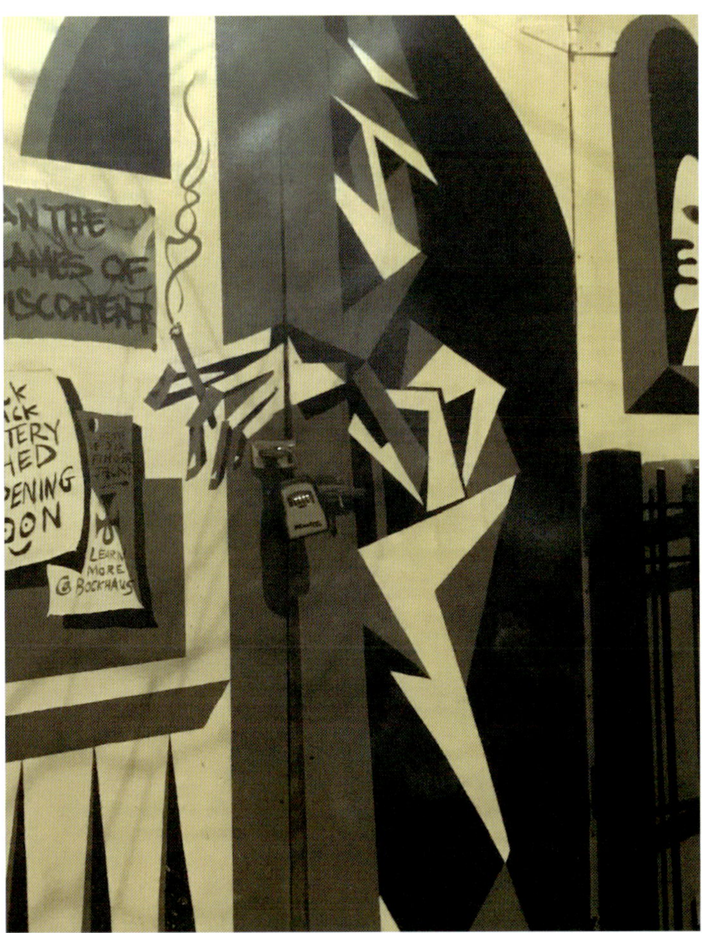

Detail of mural outside the artist's apartment,
Brooklyn, NY, 2018

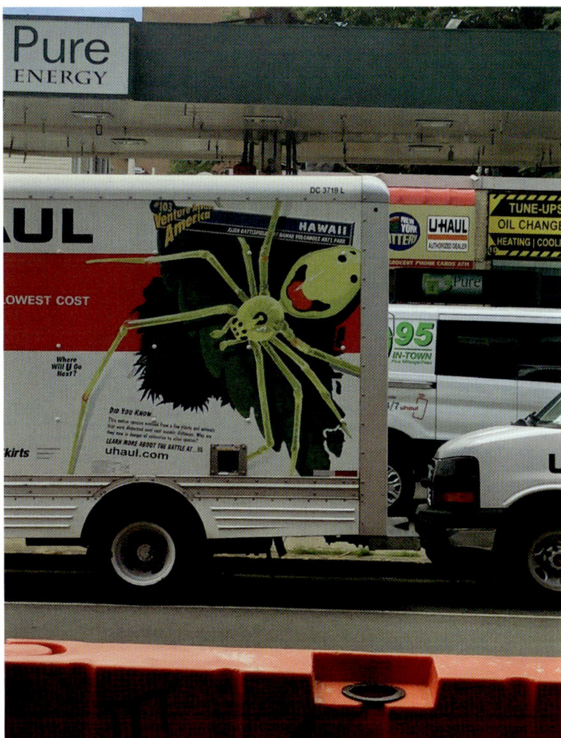

"Hawaii" U-Haul outside the artist's studio,
Brooklyn, NY, 2018

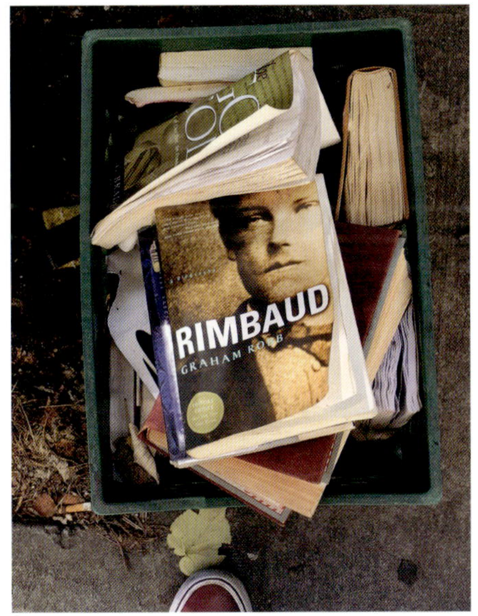

Found books outside the artist's
apartment, Brooklyn, NY, 2018

ROBERT BITTENBENDER

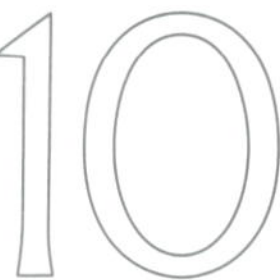

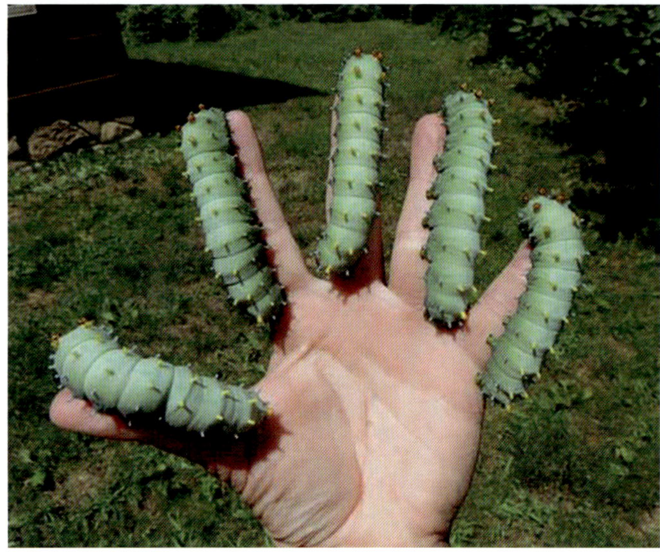

Internet source image

Internet source image

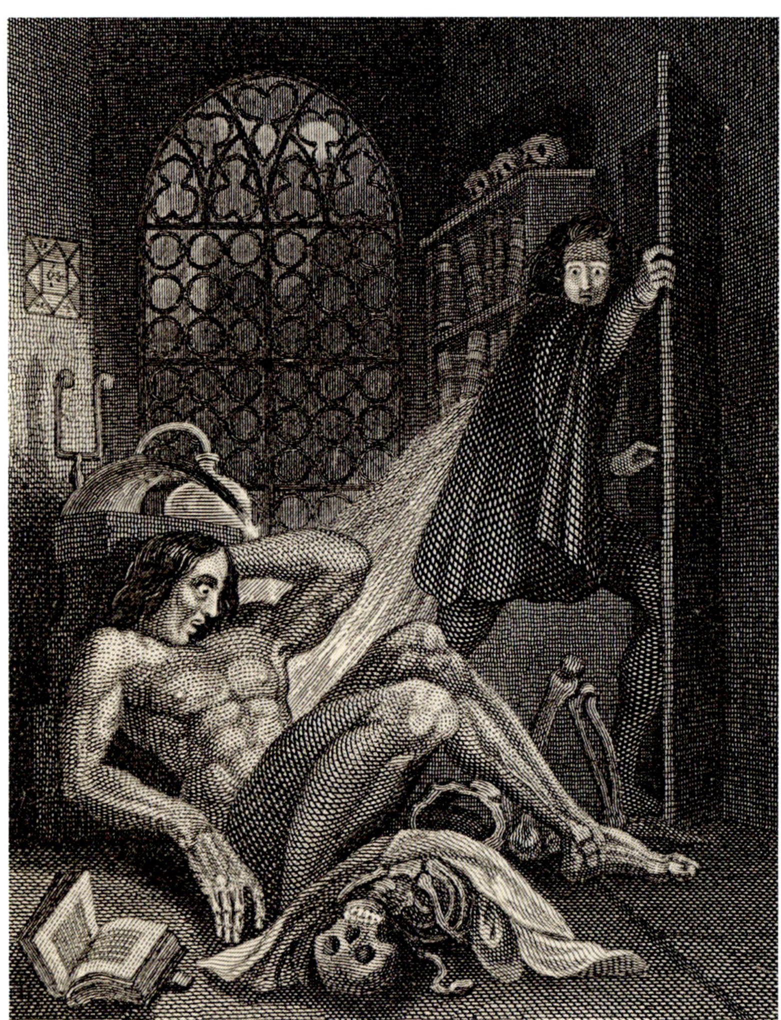

Frontispiece of Mary Shelley, *Frankenstein*, 1831

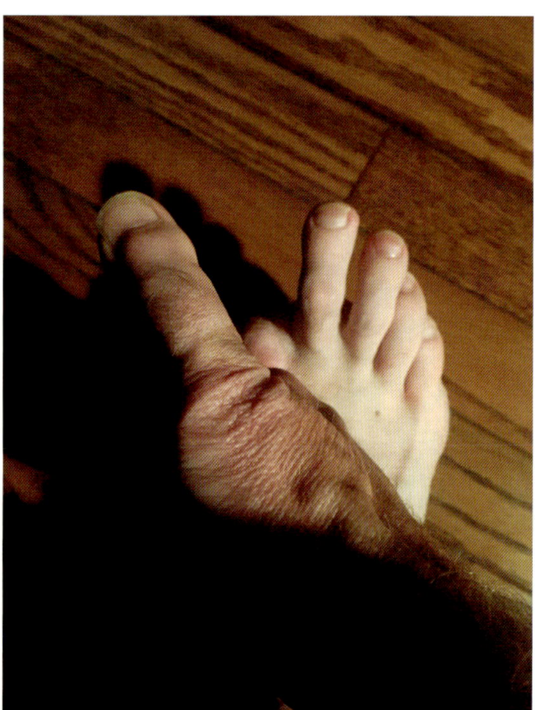

The artist's hand and foot, 2018

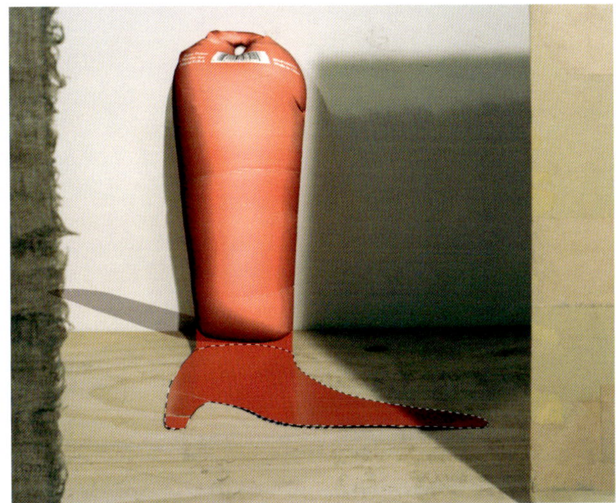

Screenshot of *Parts* (work in progress), 2018

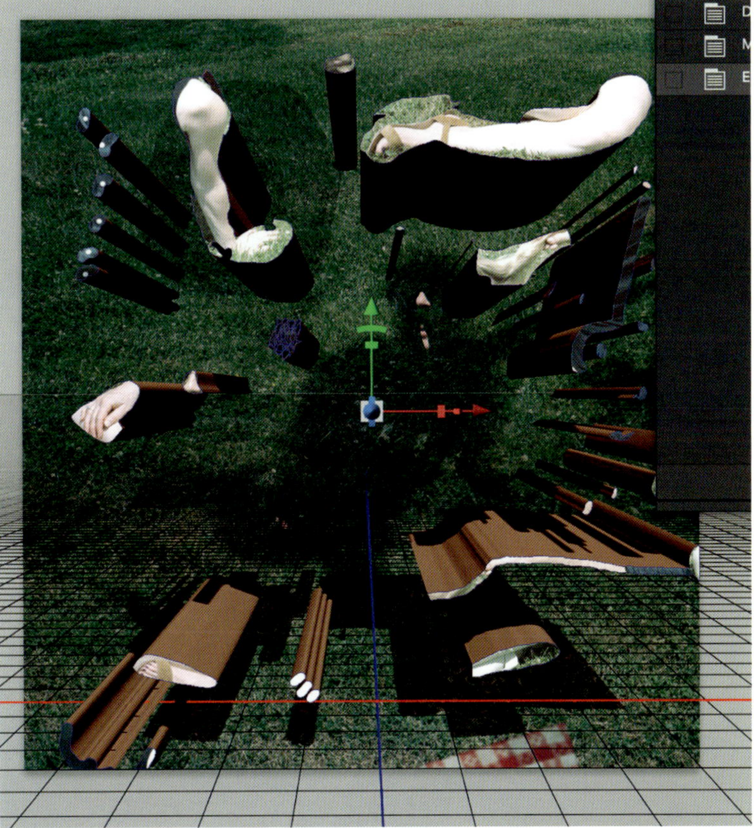

Screenshot of *In the Grass* (work in progress), 2018

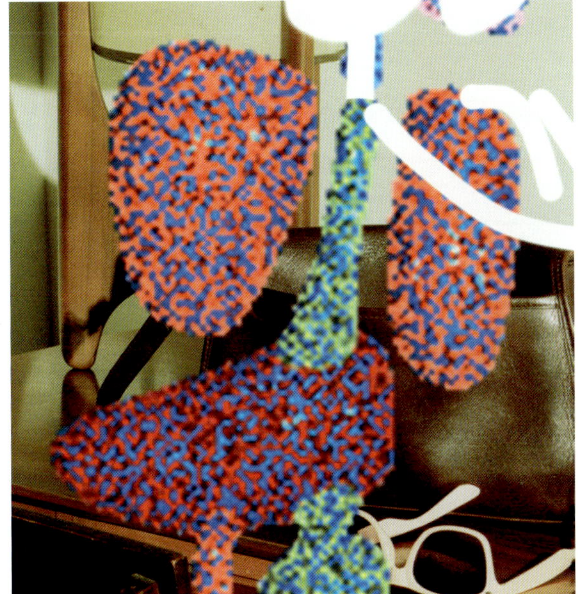

Detail of *Who Is at the Country House?*
(work in progress), 2018

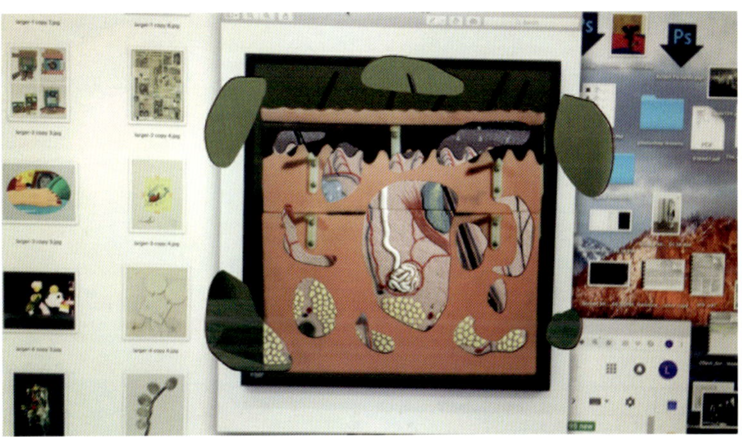

Process image of photograph using *Making Memeries* app, 2018

LUCAS BLALOCK

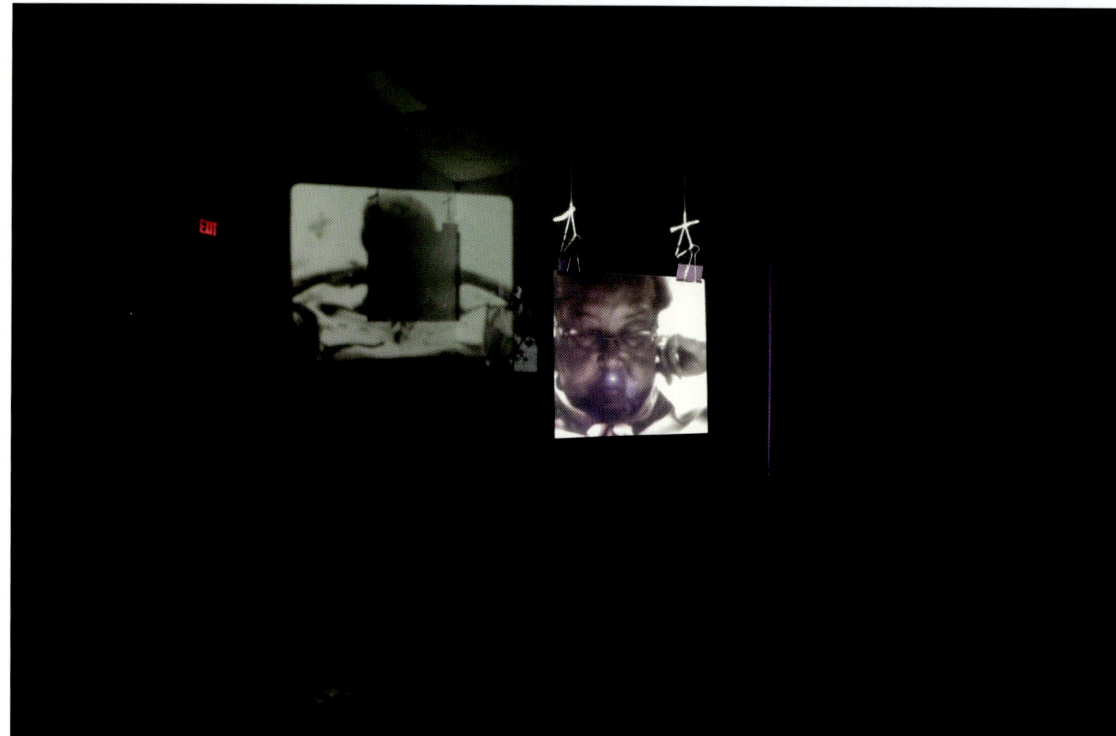

11

Projection test for *America*, 2018

FILMS REQUEST, AVAILABLE AND PULLED FOR VIEW:
A PICTORIAL VIEW OF IDLEWILD
VERDICT NOT GUILTY
HELL BOUND TRAIN (1929/30)
SCAR OF SHAME (1927)
WITHIN OUR GATES (Oscar Micheaux)
COMMANDMENT KEEPER CHURCH (Zora Neale Hurston)
ELEVEN P.M. (Maurice Film Company of Detroit - Richard D. Maurice)
THE FLYING ACE (The Norman Studios)
THE LOVE BUG (fragment, The Norman Studios) with BULL DOGGER

Abbie Mitchell
Big Timers
Bipp Bang Boogie
Birth of a Race
Black Sherlock Holmes
By Right of Birth [fragments]
Colored Quartet and Piano
Comeback of Barnacle Bill
Dark and Cloudy
Eddie Green and Company, Sending a Wire
Escapades of Estelle
Eubie Black at the Piano and Sissle and Blake
Hazel Green and Company, Foremost Female
Hid De Ho Trailer
Low Down: A Bird's Eye View of Harlem
Mercy the Mummy Mumbled
A Night in Dixie – silent and sound versions
Norman Thomas Quintette, Harlem Mania
Of One Blood
Reckless Rover
Revival Day
Shake it Up
Spying the Spy
Two Knights of Vaudeville
Unidentified Tayler Nol. 8: The Beautiful Davis and Her Three Little Negroes
Willie and Eugene Howard, Music Makers
Yamekraw
FLA 5222 THE STREETS OF NEW YORK
FLA 4947 WHAT HAPPENED ON TWENTY-THIRD STREET, NEW YORK CITY
FLA 5812 WHEN A MAN LOVES
FLA 5482 THE INDIAN (Bert Williams)
FLA 3774 GOLD DUST TWINS
FLA 5026 EVERYBODY WORKS BUT FATHER (Blackface)
FLA 3647 THE GATER AND THE PICKANINNY
FLA 3307 A HARD WASH

FLA 3608 HOW CHARLIE LOST THE HEIRESS
FLA 3663 A KISS IN THE DARK
FLA 3194 LAUGHING BEN
FLA 4725 THE MIS-DIRECTED KISS
FLA 4428 NELLIE THE BEAUTIFUL HOUSEMAID
FLA 3820 POMPEY'S HONEY GIRL
FLA 4394 THE SEERESS
FLA 5725 THE SUBPOENA SERVER
FLA 5741 THE THIRTEEN CLUB
FLA 5780 UNDER THE OLD APPLE TREE
FLA 3660 WHAT HAPPENED IN THE TUNNEL
FLA 3445 THE AMERICAN SOLDIER IN LOVE AND WAR, NO. 3
FLA 5301 A CLOSE CALL
FLA 5380 THE FEUD AND THE TURKEY
FLA 5422 THE GUERRILLA
FLA 5445 HIS TRUST
FLA 5446 HIS TRUST FULFILLED
FLA 5913 UNCLE TOM'S CABIN (1903)
FLA 5837 THE ZULU'S HEART
FLA 4301 COLORED TROOPS DISEMBARKING (Spanish-American War)
FLA 5335 DIXON-CHESTER LEON CONTEST
FLA 3021 DANCING DARKEY BOY
FLA 5874 JACK JOHNSON VS. JIM FLYNN FOR THE HEAVYWEIGHT CHAMPIONSHIP OF THE WORLD, LAS VEGAS, N.M., JULY 4, 1912
FLA 4741 NATIVE WOMEN COALING A SHIP AND SCRAMBLING FOR MONEY
FLA 4742 NATIVE WOMAN COALING A SHIP AT ST. THOMAS, D.W.I.
FLA 3635 NATIVE WOMAN WASHING A NEGRO BABY IN NASSAU, B.I.
FLA 3651 NATIVE WOMAN WASHING CLOTHES AT ST. VINCENT. D.W.I.
FLA 5919-21 PAUL J. RAINEY'S AFRICAN HUNT
FLA 4856 A SCRAP IN BLACK AND WHITE
FLA 4940 A WATERMELON CONTEST
FLA 4943 WEST INDIAN BOYS DIVING FOR MONEY
FLA 3379 WEST INDIAN GIRLS IN NATIVE DANCE
FLA 3607 WHARF SCENES AND NATIVES SWIMMING AT ST. THOMAS, D.W.I.
FLA 3381 CAKE WALK

UNAVAILABLE THROUGH LOC (From Book tour screened at MoMA and Harvard)
Happy Though Married – British Film Institute
The Symbol of the Unconquered – Museum of Modern Art
Body and Soul – George Eastman House
Ten Nights in a Barroom – George Eastman House

Library of Congress film request with notes, 2015

Library of Congress film request with notes, 2015

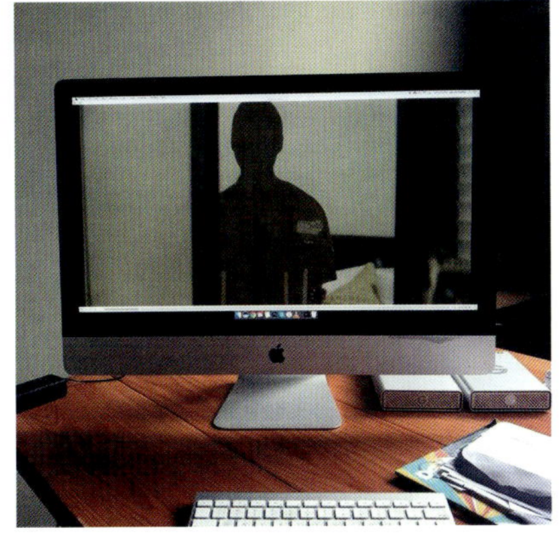

Process image for *Power*, 2018

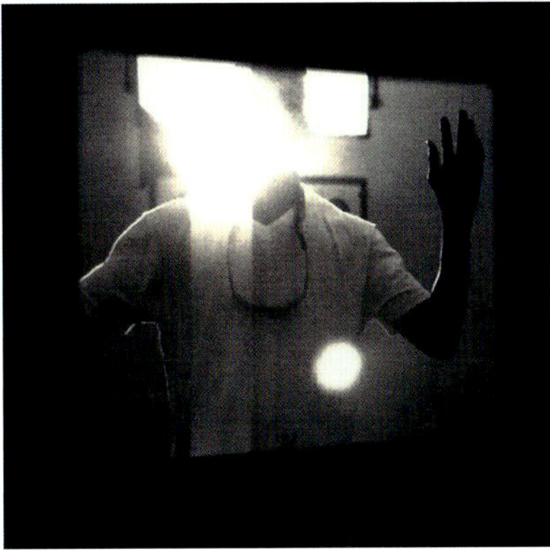

Light test for untitled video, 2018

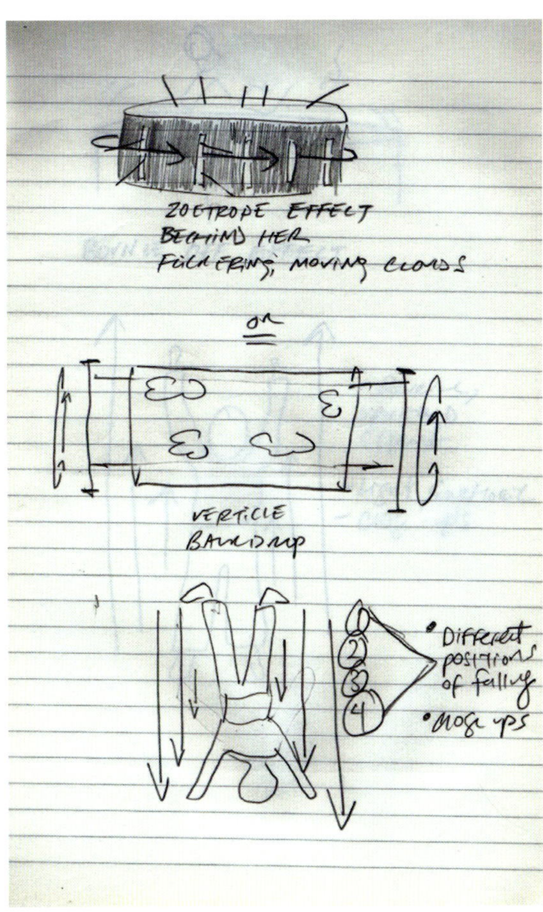

Movement test for untitled video, 2018

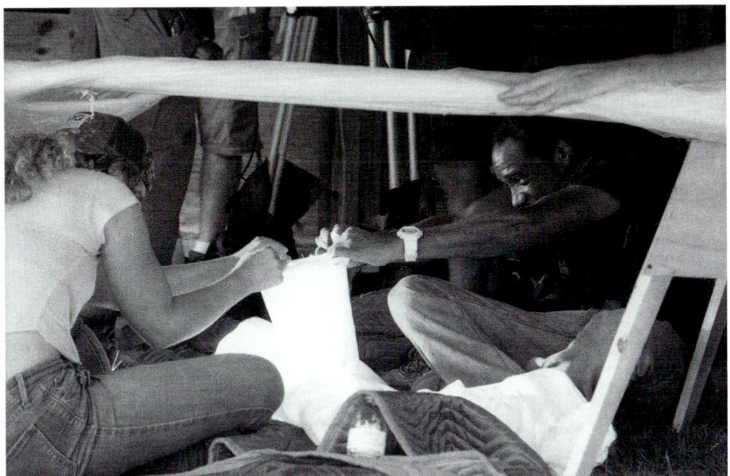

Production still from *1915: The White Sheet*, 2018

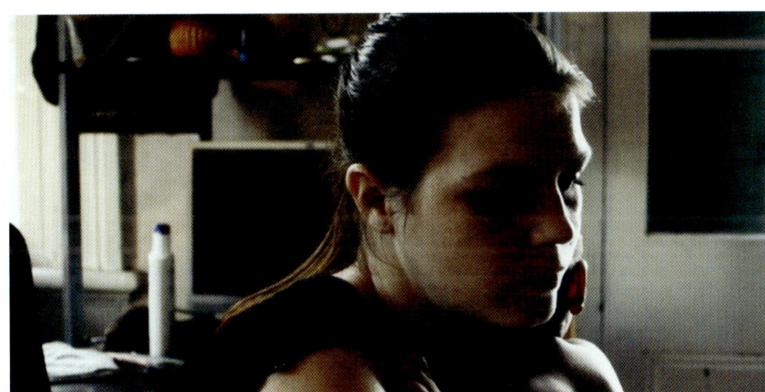

Production still from *Below Dreams*, 2014

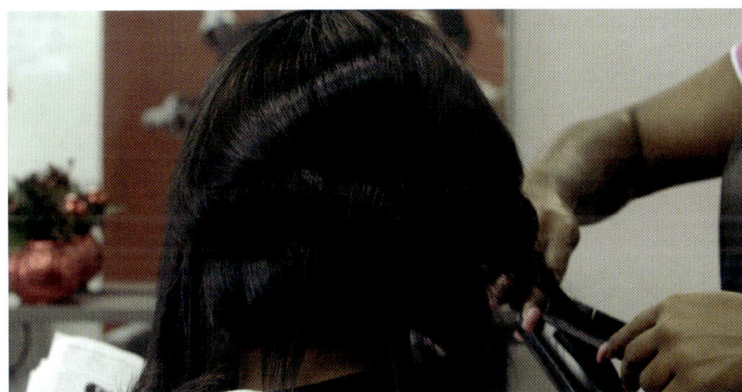

Production still from *Power*, 2018

GARRETT BRADLEY

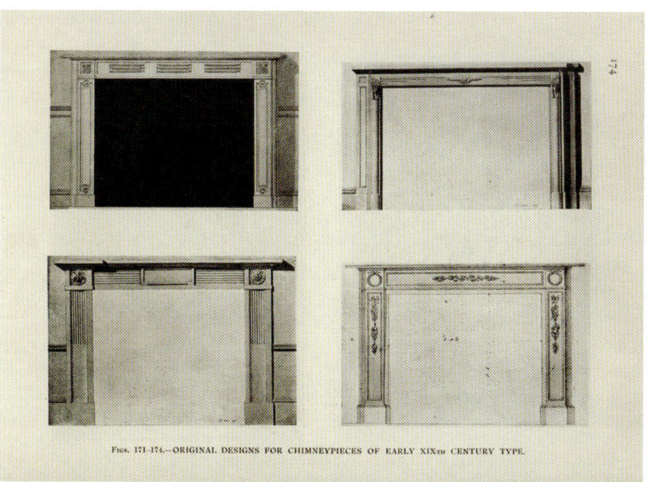

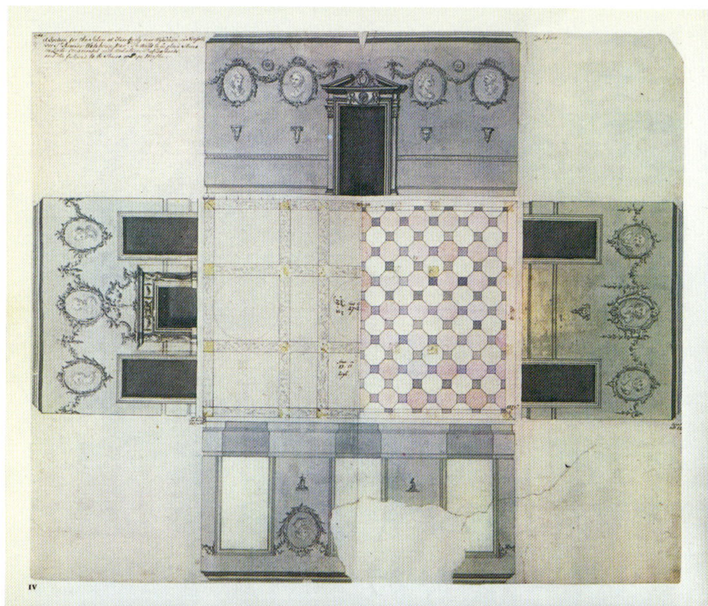

12

John Sanderson, wall plan design, 1761. From John Harris, *The Palladians*, 1981

Page from of M. Jourdain, *English Interiors in Smaller Houses: From the Restoration to the Regency, 1660–1830*, 1923

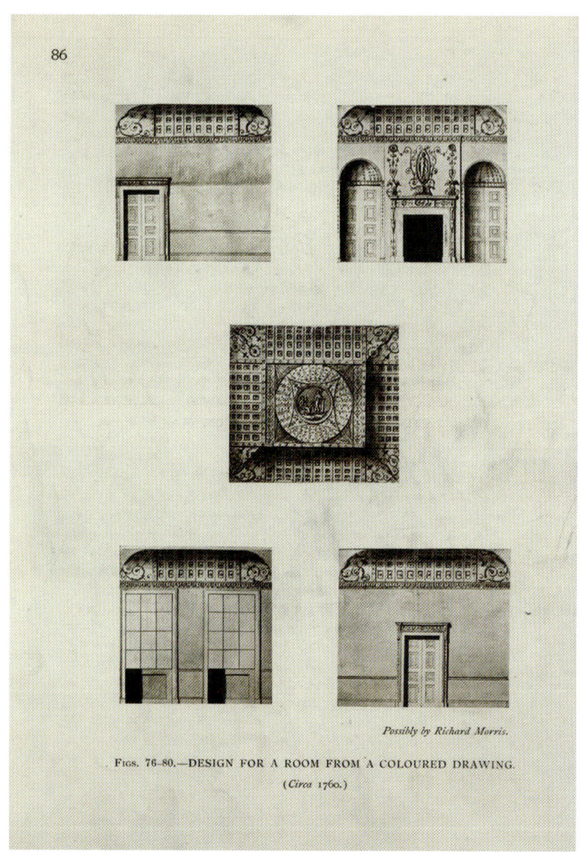

Page from of M. Jourdain, *English Interiors in Smaller Houses: From the Restoration to the Regency, 1660–1830*, 1923

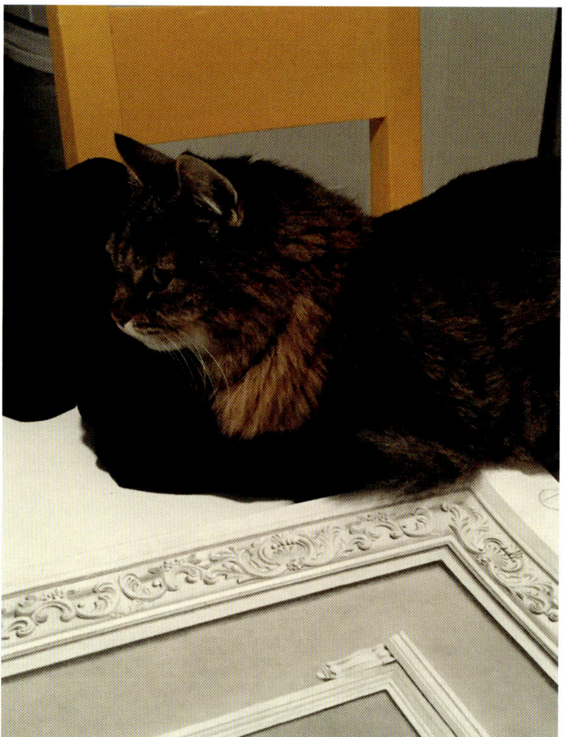

Lulu with untitled work in progress, studio, Los Angeles, CA, 2016

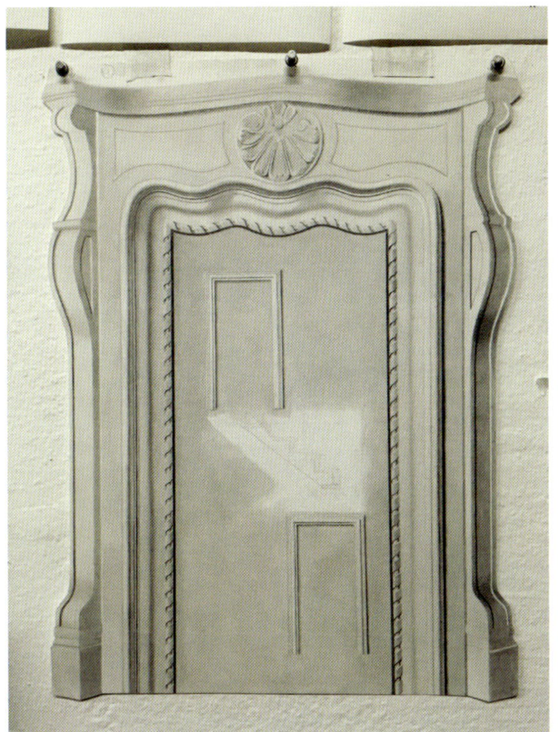

Untitled work in progress, 2017

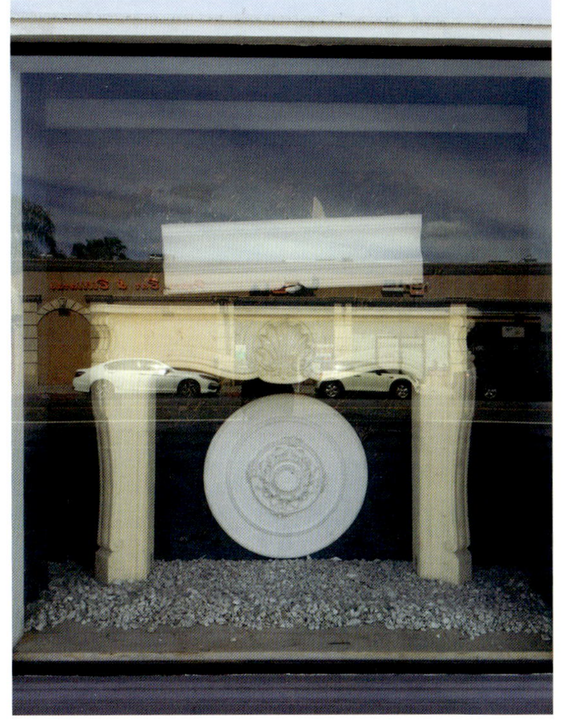

Storefront, Los Angeles, CA, 2018

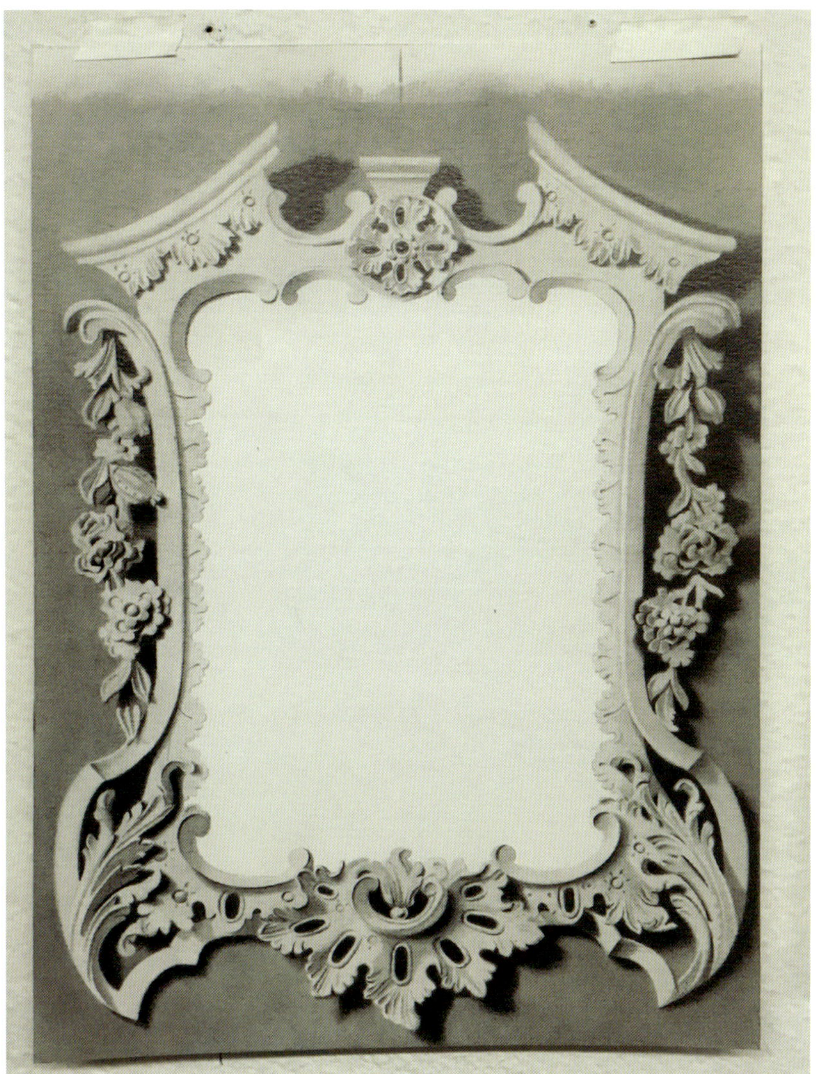

Untitled work in progress, 2017

MILANO CHOW

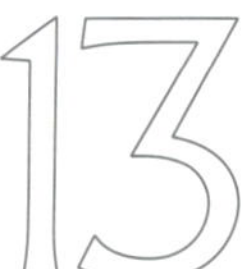

13

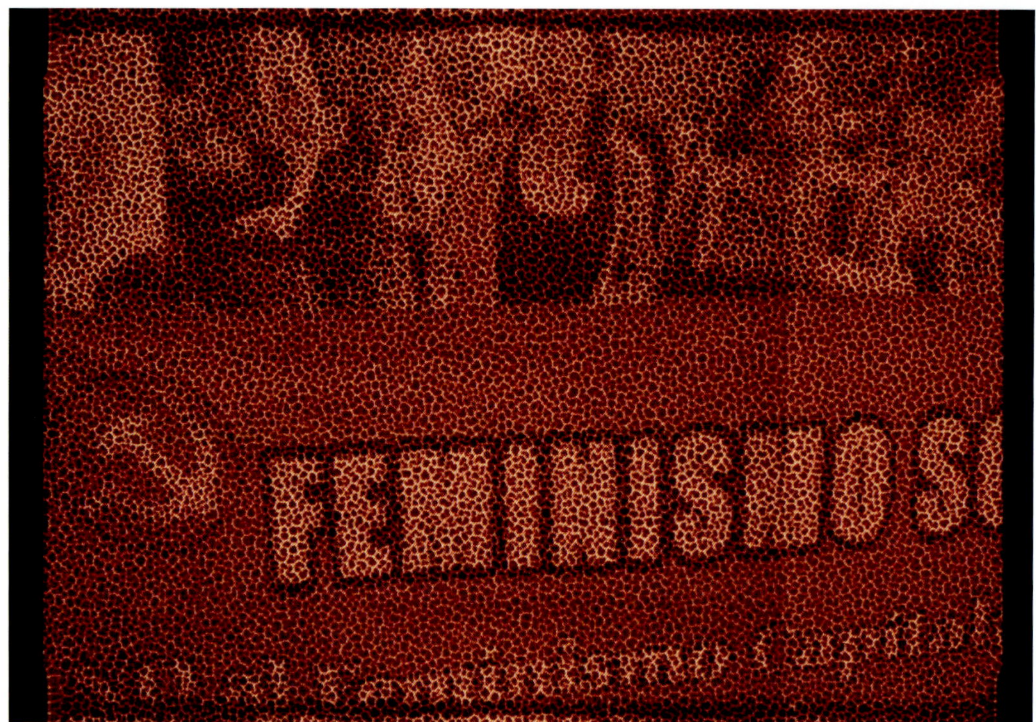

Sangre seca (Dried Blood), 2018

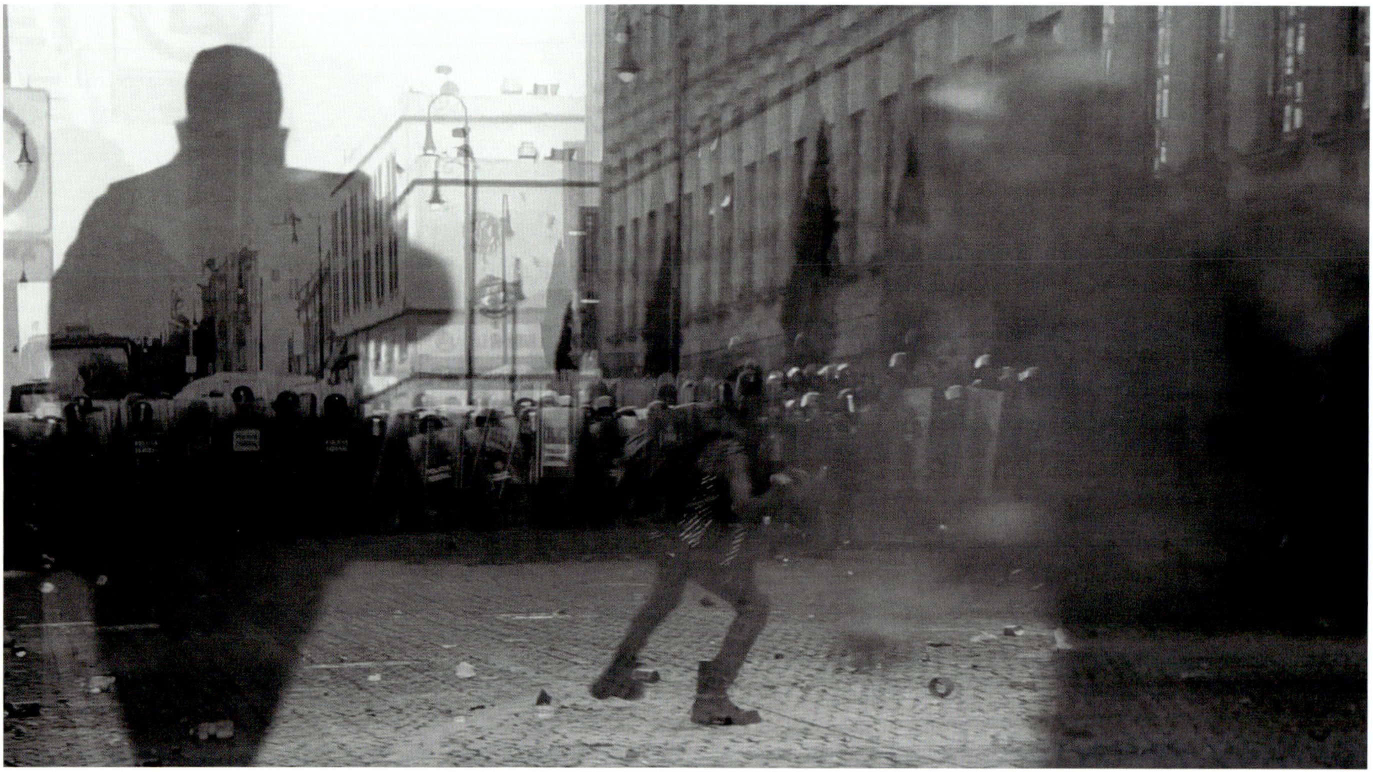

Templo Mayor (The Greater Temple), 2016

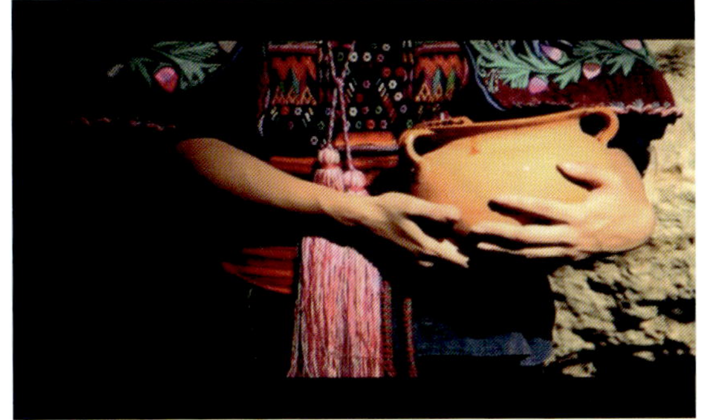

Zapatista, 2013

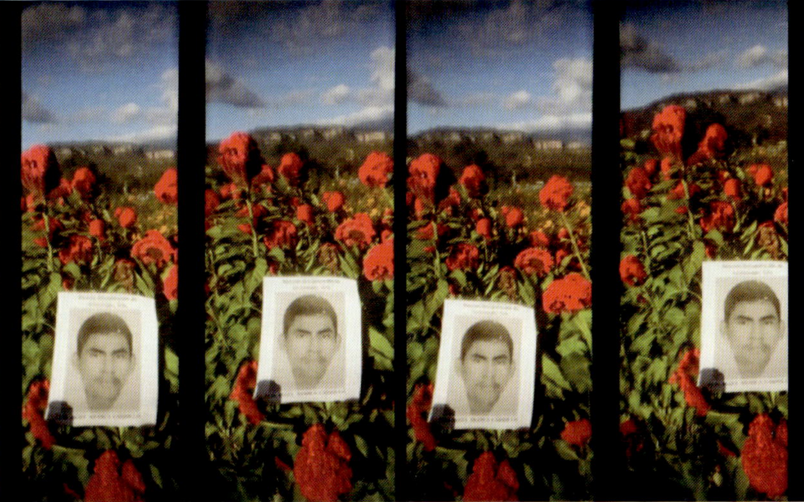

Triptych, 2015

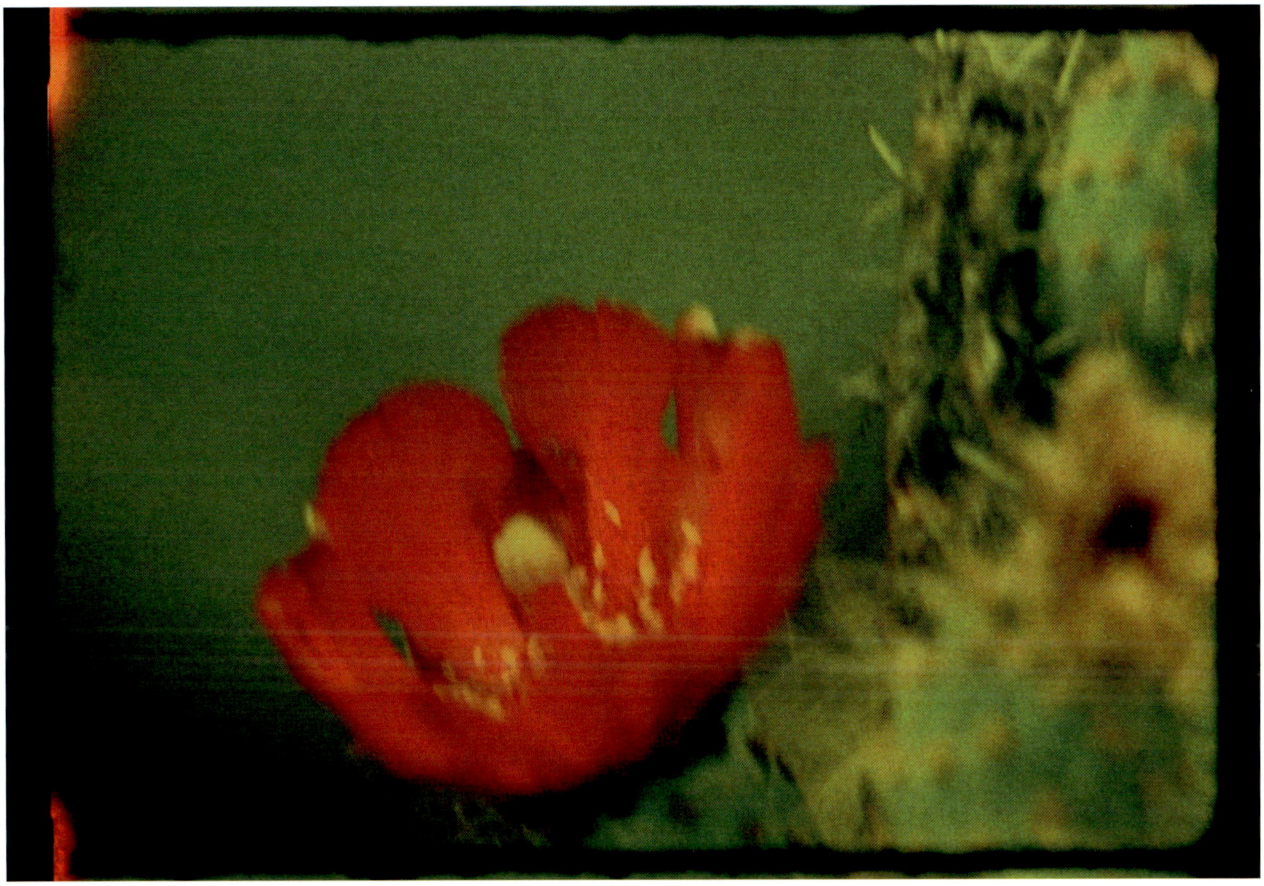

Pirámide erosionada (Eroded Pyramid), 2018

COLECTIVO LOS INGRÁVIDOS

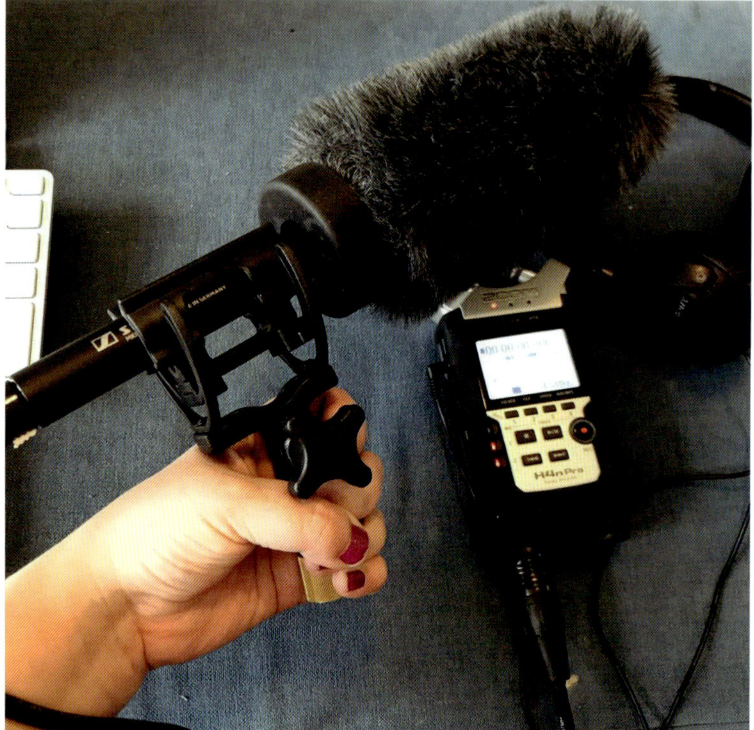

Production still from *Reclamation*, 2018

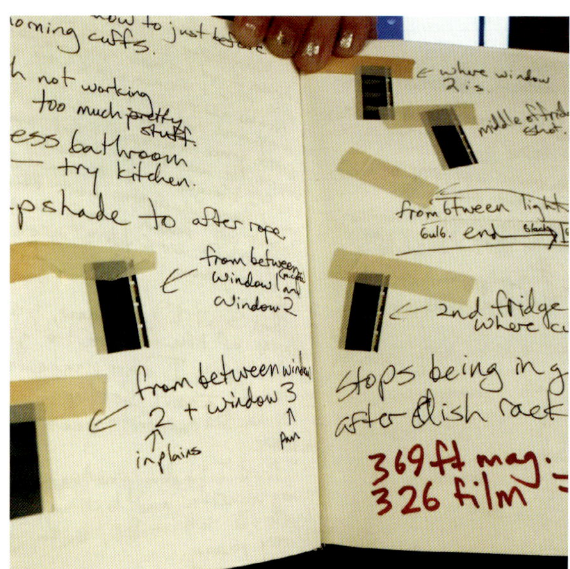

Sketchbook page for untitled film, 2000

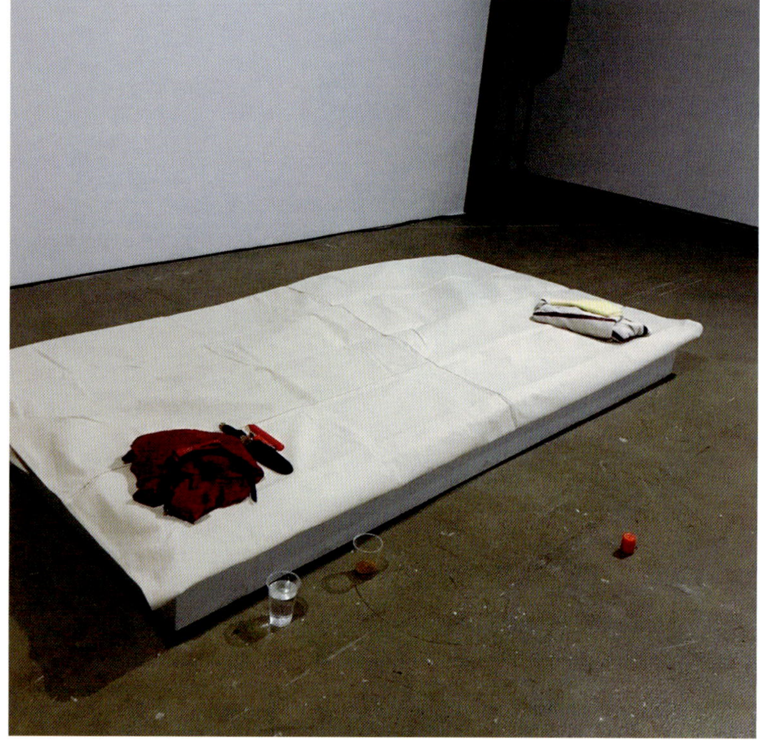

Process image for *Love Is the Only Acceptable Psychosis*, 2018

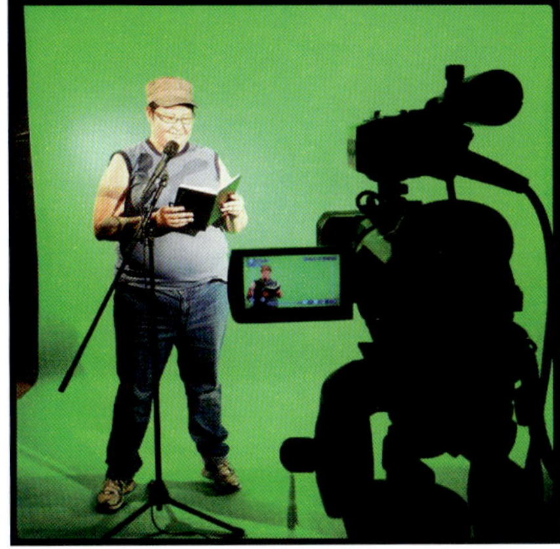

Production still from *Just Dandy*, 2013

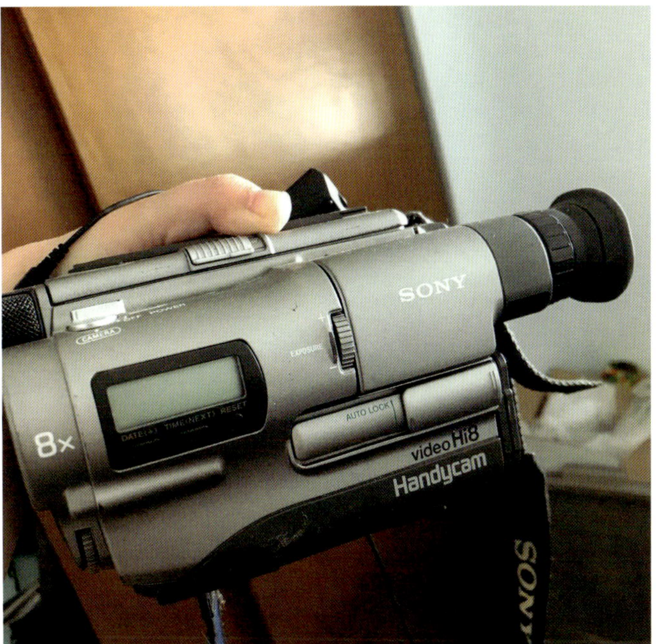

The artist's first camcorder, 1995

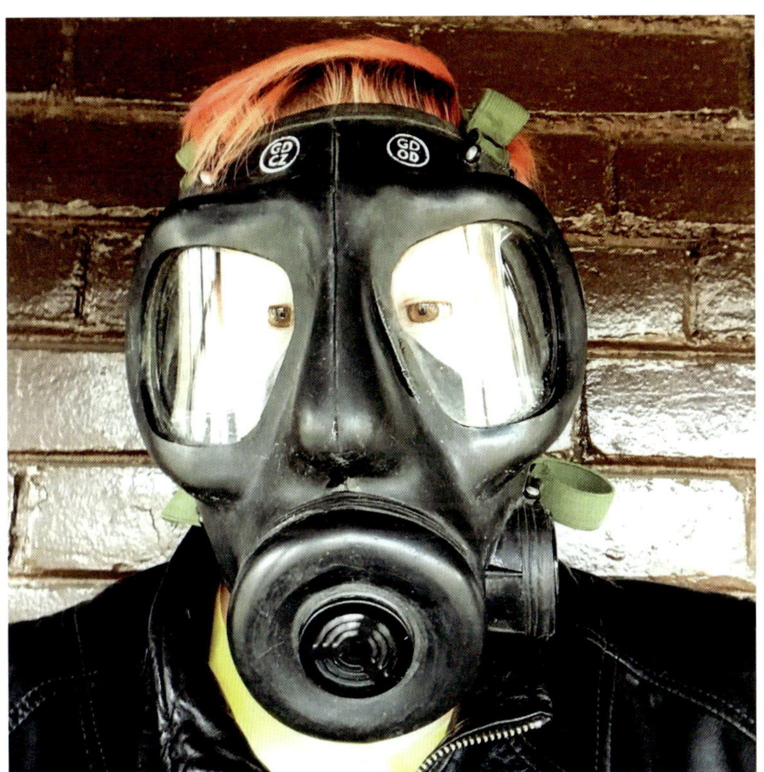

Prop for *Reclamation*, 2018

THIRZA CUTHAND

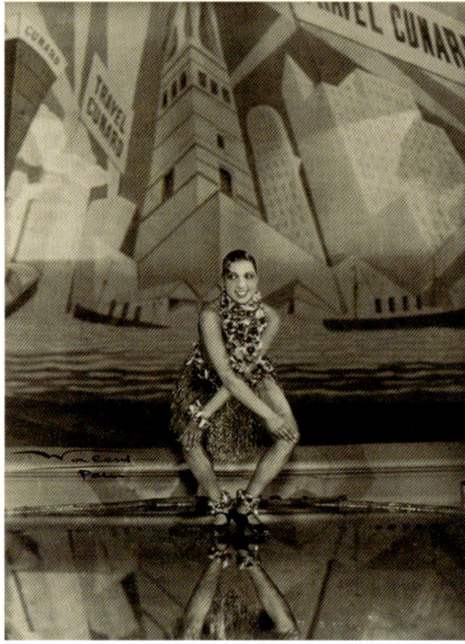

15

Stanislaus Julian Walery, *Josephine Baker*, 1926

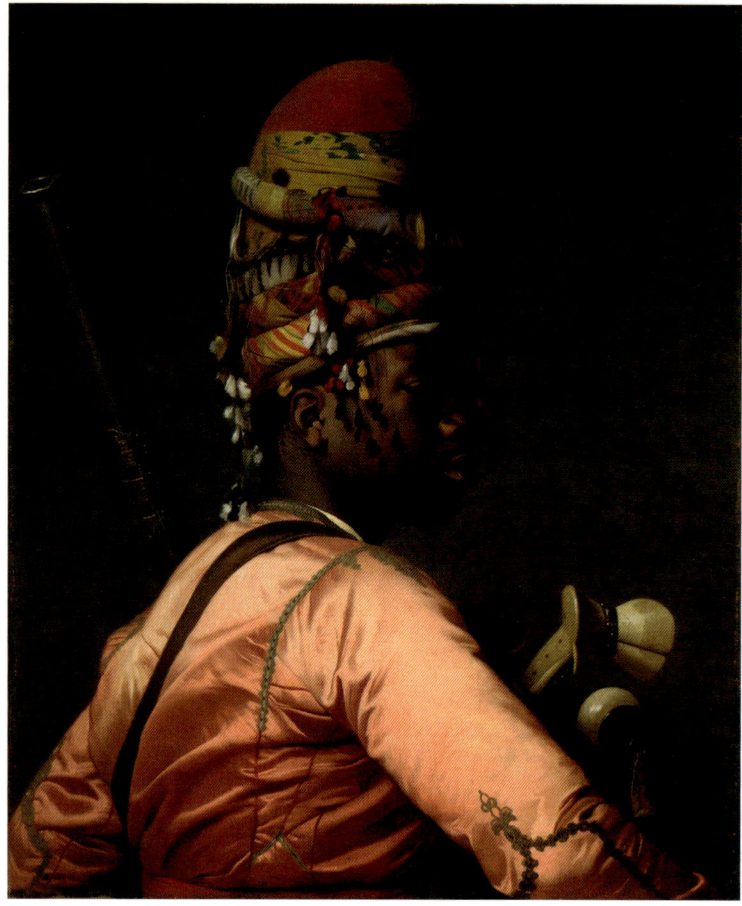

Jean-Léon Gérôme, *Bashi-Bazouk*, 1868–69

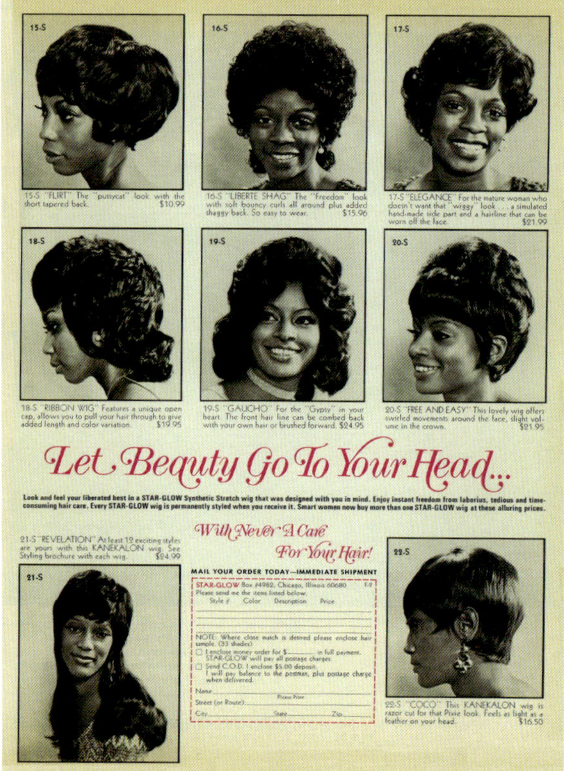

Star-Glow ad, *Ebony*, 1972

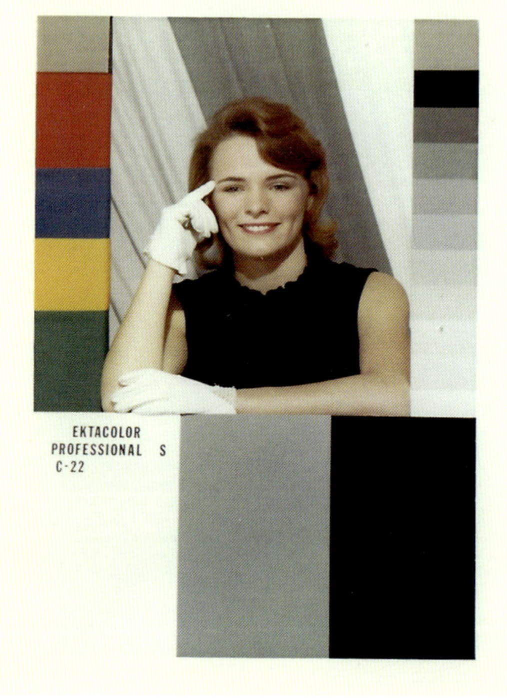

Kodak "Shirley card," 1966

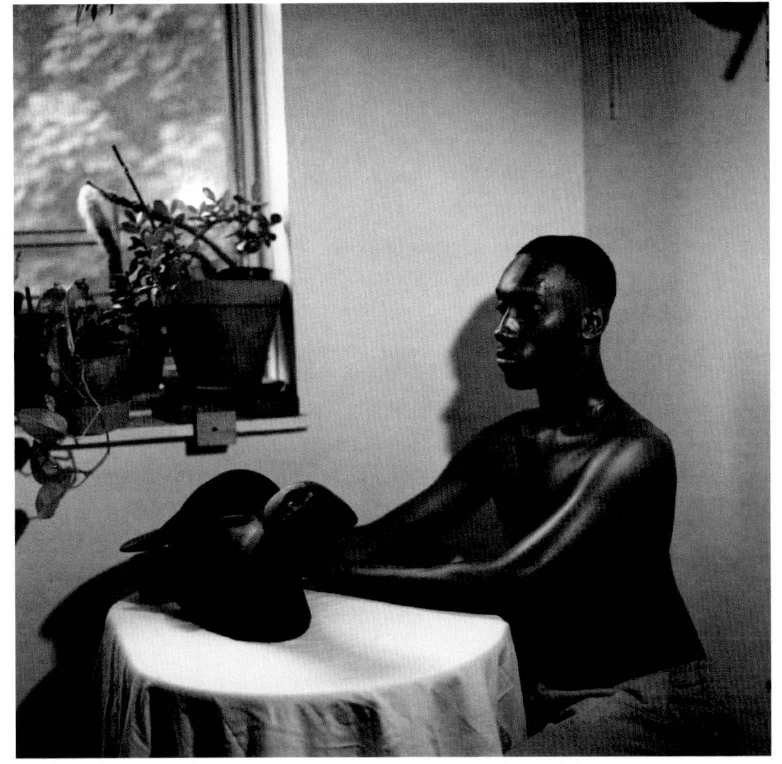

Model with bull mask from the Ivory Coast, 2018

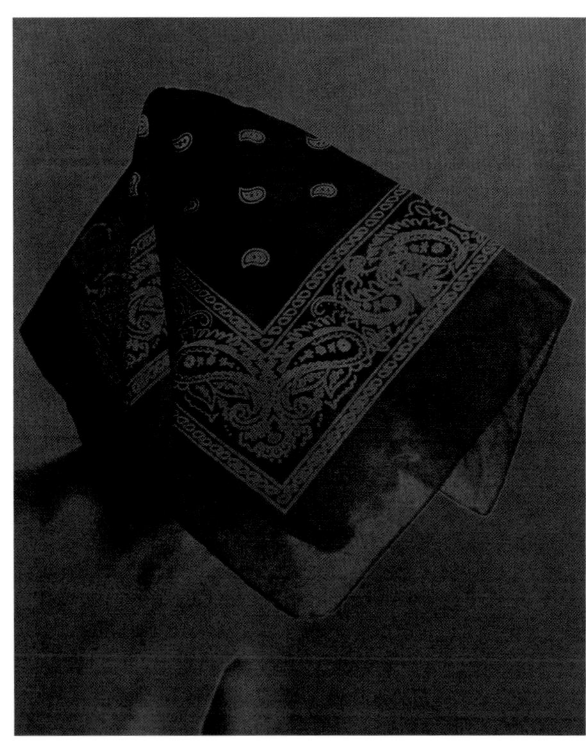

Untitled 2 (Tylan Wearing Bandana), 2018

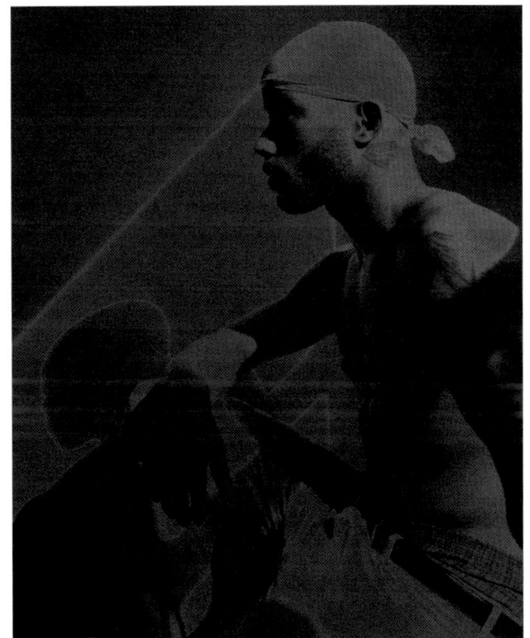

Untitled 1 (Light passing over Victor seated profile), 2018

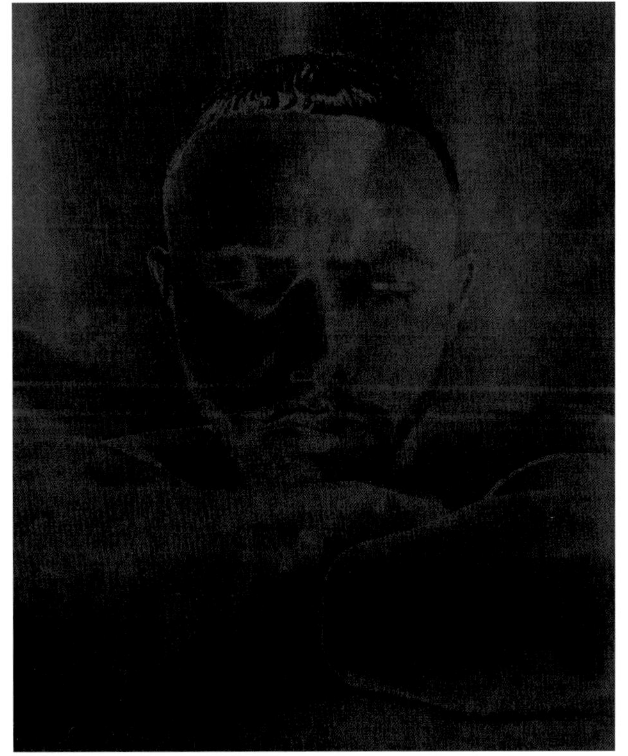

Untitled 4 (Facial Expression), 2018

JOHN EDMONDS

16

Human Proportions for Artists

ADULT FEMALE METRIC MEASUREMENTS

LOWER EXTREMITY MEASUREMENTS

3/8 Life (cm.)	1/3 Life (cm.)	1/4 Life (cm.)			1/6 Life (cm.)	1/8 Life (cm.)	1/12 Life (cm.)
38.7	34.4	25.8	L1 V	Crest of Ilium to Sole	17.2	12.9	8.6
36.2	32.2	24.1	L2 V	Ant. Sup. Spine of Ilium to Sole	16.1	12.1	8
32.1	28.6	21.4	L3 V	Greater Trochanter Femur-Sole	14.3	10.7	7.1
28.6	25.4	19.1	L4 V	(Crotch to Sole)	12.7	9.5	6.4
29.6	26.3	19.7	L5 V	Gluteal Furrow-Sole	13.1	9.9	6.6
16.2	14.4	10.8	L6 V	Posterior Knee Crease to Sole	7.2	5.4	
18.1	16.1	12.1	L7 V	Ant. Sup. Spine of Ilium to Knee	8		
14.5	12.9	9.7	L8 V	Pubis to Knee	6.4		
18.3	16.3	12.2	L9 V	Knee at Patella			4.1
16.2	14.4	10.8	L10 V	Tibia to Sole			3.6
3.4	3	2.3	L11 V				0.8
2.4	2.1	1.6	L12			0.8	0.5
9.5	8.5	6.4	L13 T	Inter Bou...		3.2	2.1
7.9	7	5.3	L15 T	Breadth E...			1.8
9		6	L15 T	Breadth Bo...			2
2.1		1.4	L16 T	Breadth ...			0.5
5.7	5		L17 D	...rior-Posterior			
4.3	3.8		L18 D	Knee, ... Posterior.	1.9		
4.3	3.8		L19 D	Mid Calf, Anterior-Posterior	1.9	1.4	
7	2.4		L20 D	Ankle, Anterior-Posterior	1.2	0.9	0.6
	3		L21 D	Ankle at Maleoli, Anterior-Post	1.5	1.1	0.7
				Length of Foot	4.1	3.1	2
				Heel to 5th Toe	3.4	2.6	1.7
				Breadth Foot at Rest	1.5	1.1	0.8
				Breadth Foot Standing	1.7	1.3	0.8
				Width of Heel	0.9	0.6	0.4

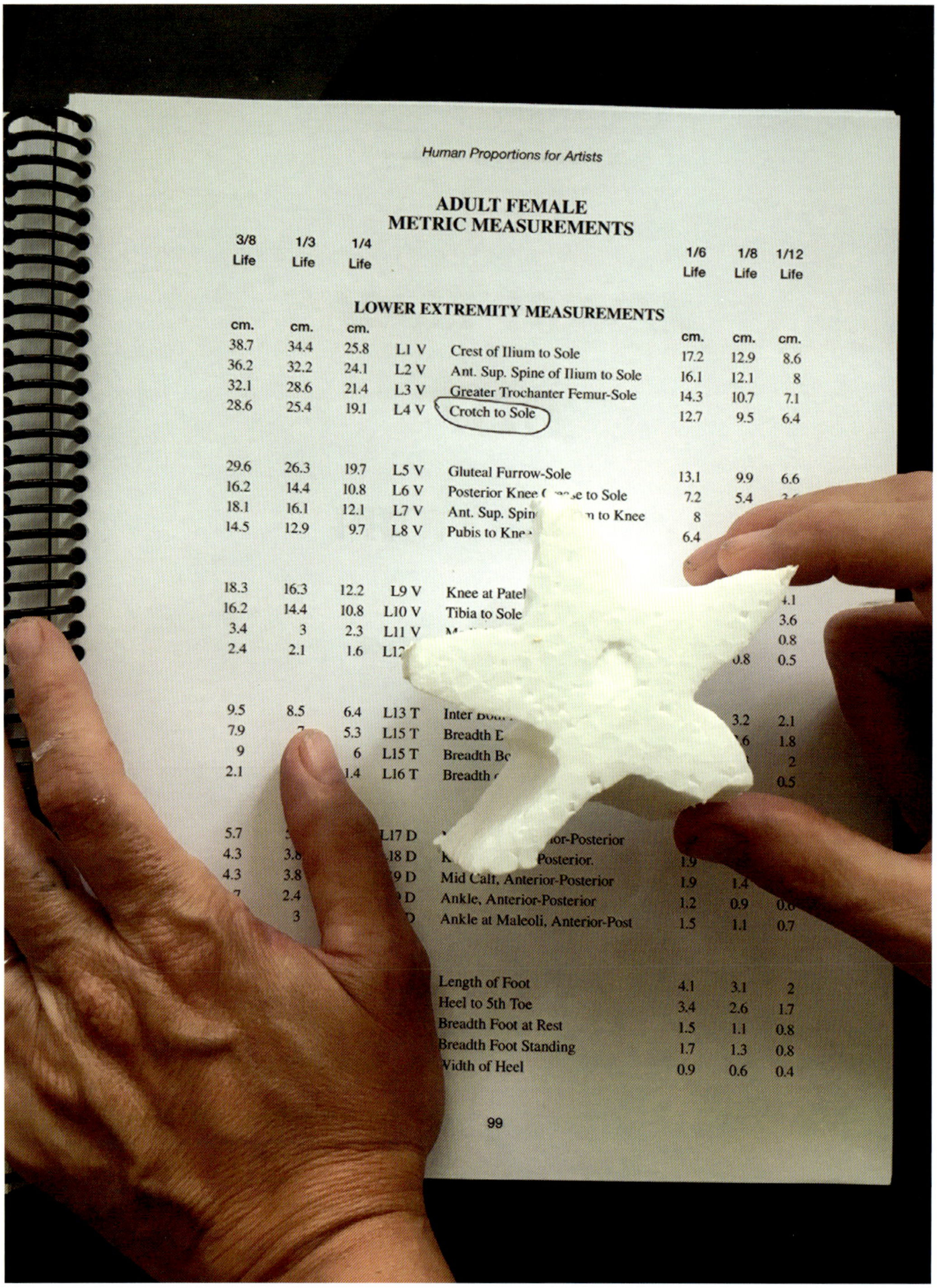

Chart for adult female metric measurements, 2018

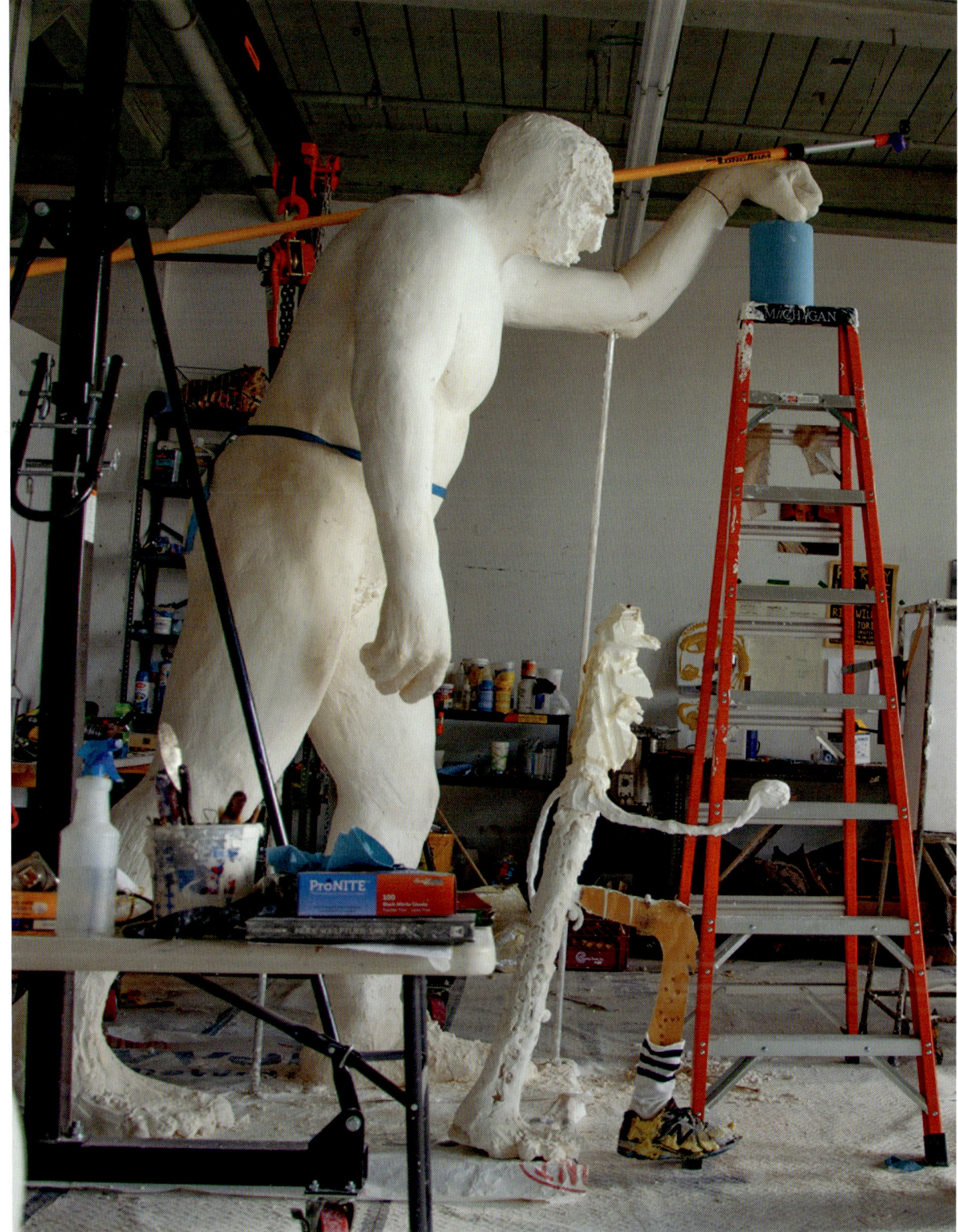

Studio, Brooklyn, NY, 2018

NICOLE EISENMAN

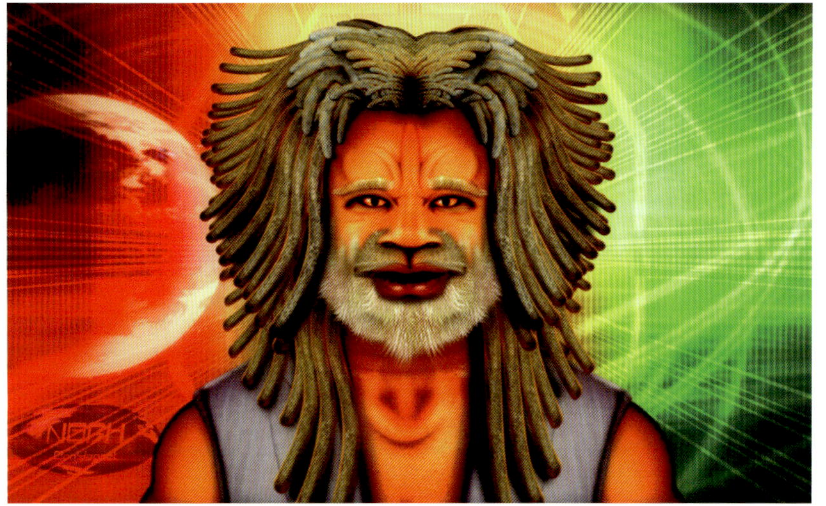

17

Shelley Doty and G. B. Hajim, *Strange Frame: Love & Sax*, 2012

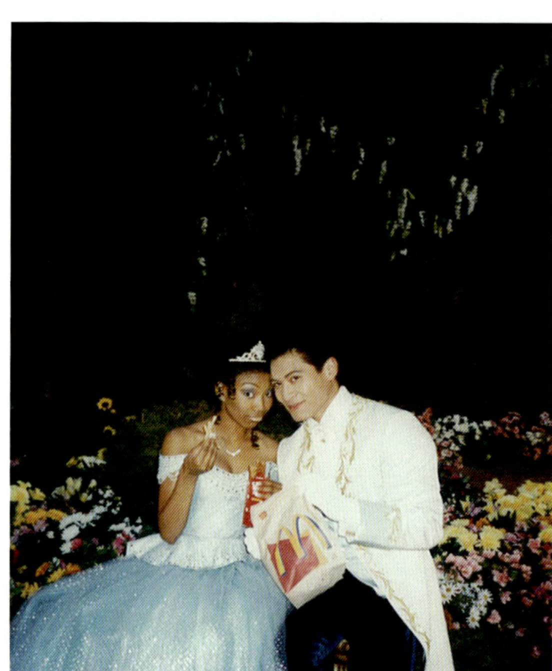

Brandy Norwood and Paolo Montalbán
on the set of Rodgers and Hammerstein's
Cinderella, 1997

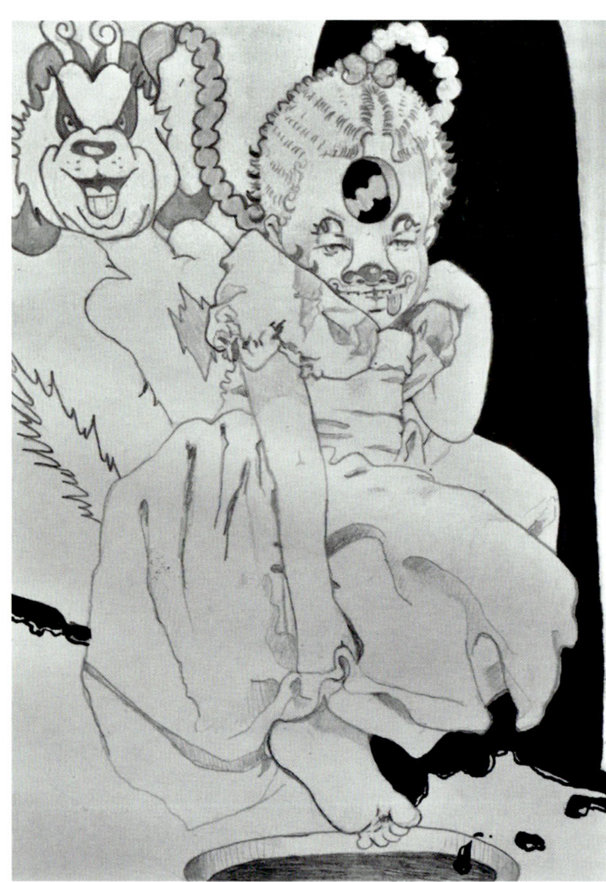

Untitled drawing, 2018

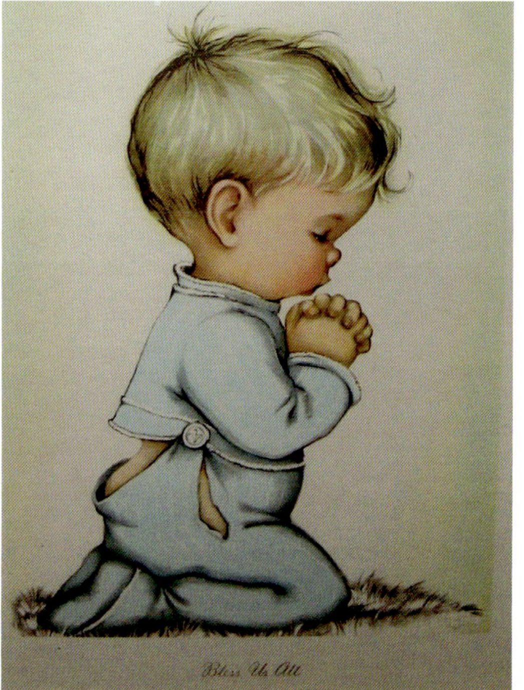

Charlot Byj, *A Child's Prayer*, 1957

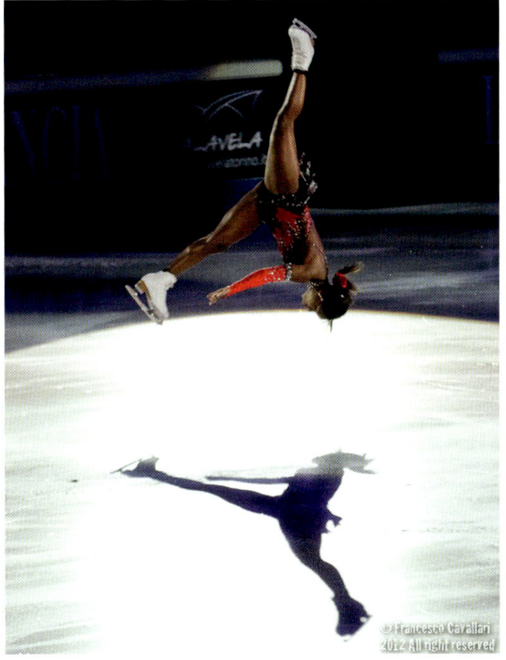

Surya Bonaly in *Capodanno on Ice*, 2012

Untitled work in progress, 2018

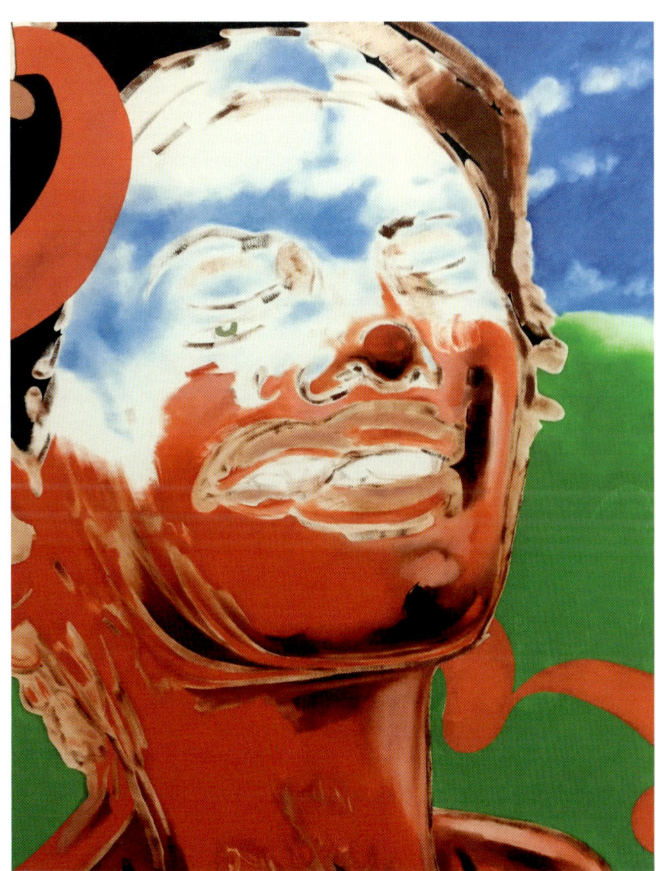

Untitled work in progress, 2018

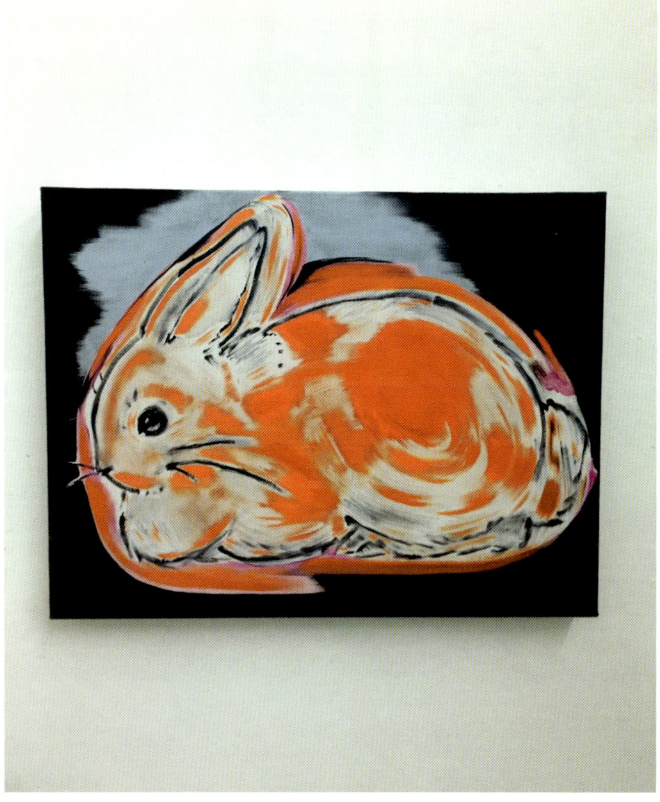

Untitled work in progress, 2018

JANIVA ELLIS

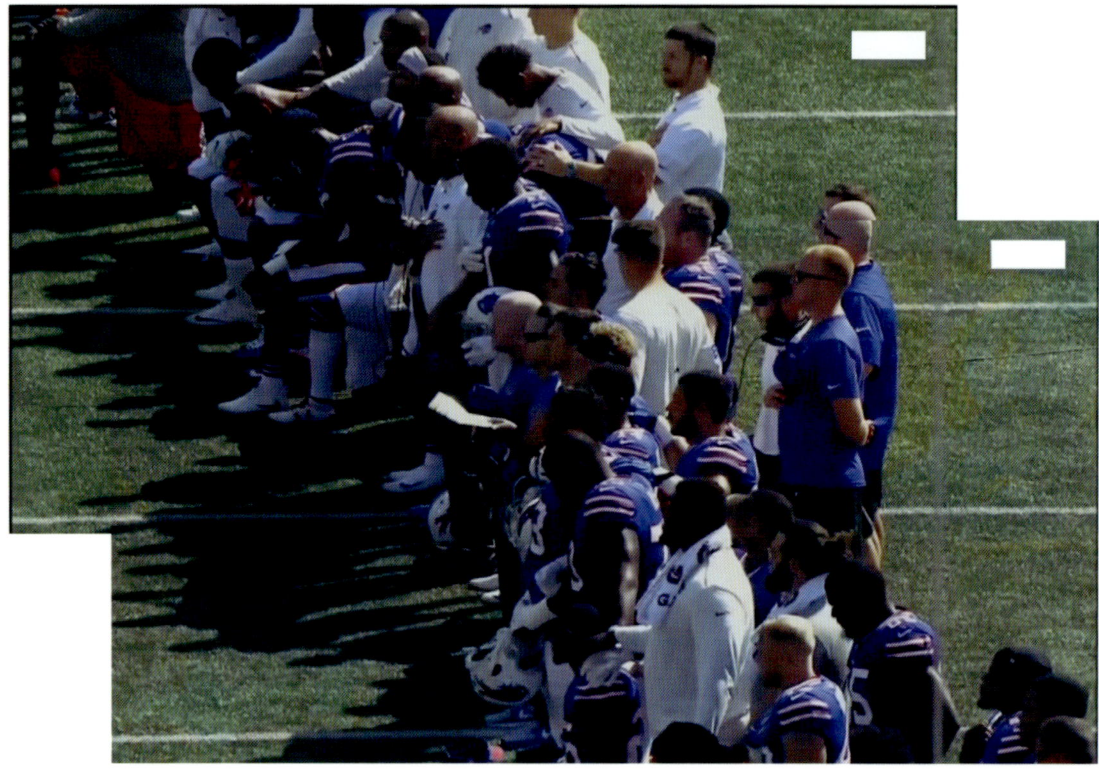

18

Source image for *National Anthem*, 2018

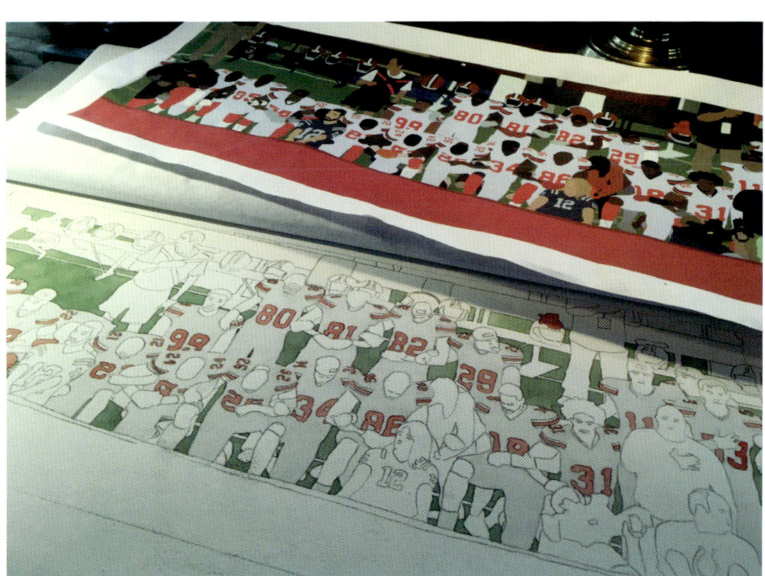

Watercolor for *National Anthem*, 2018

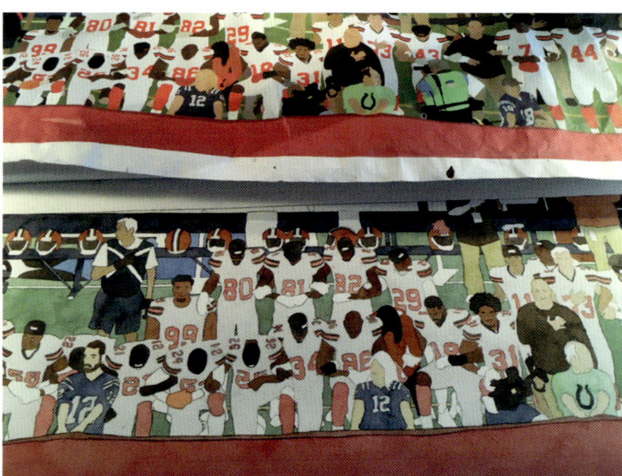

Watercolor for *National Anthem*, 2018

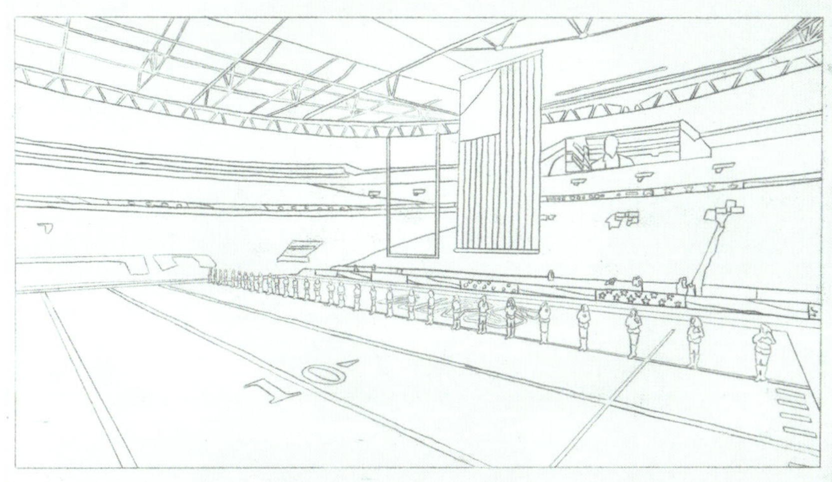

Sketch for *National Anthem*, 2018

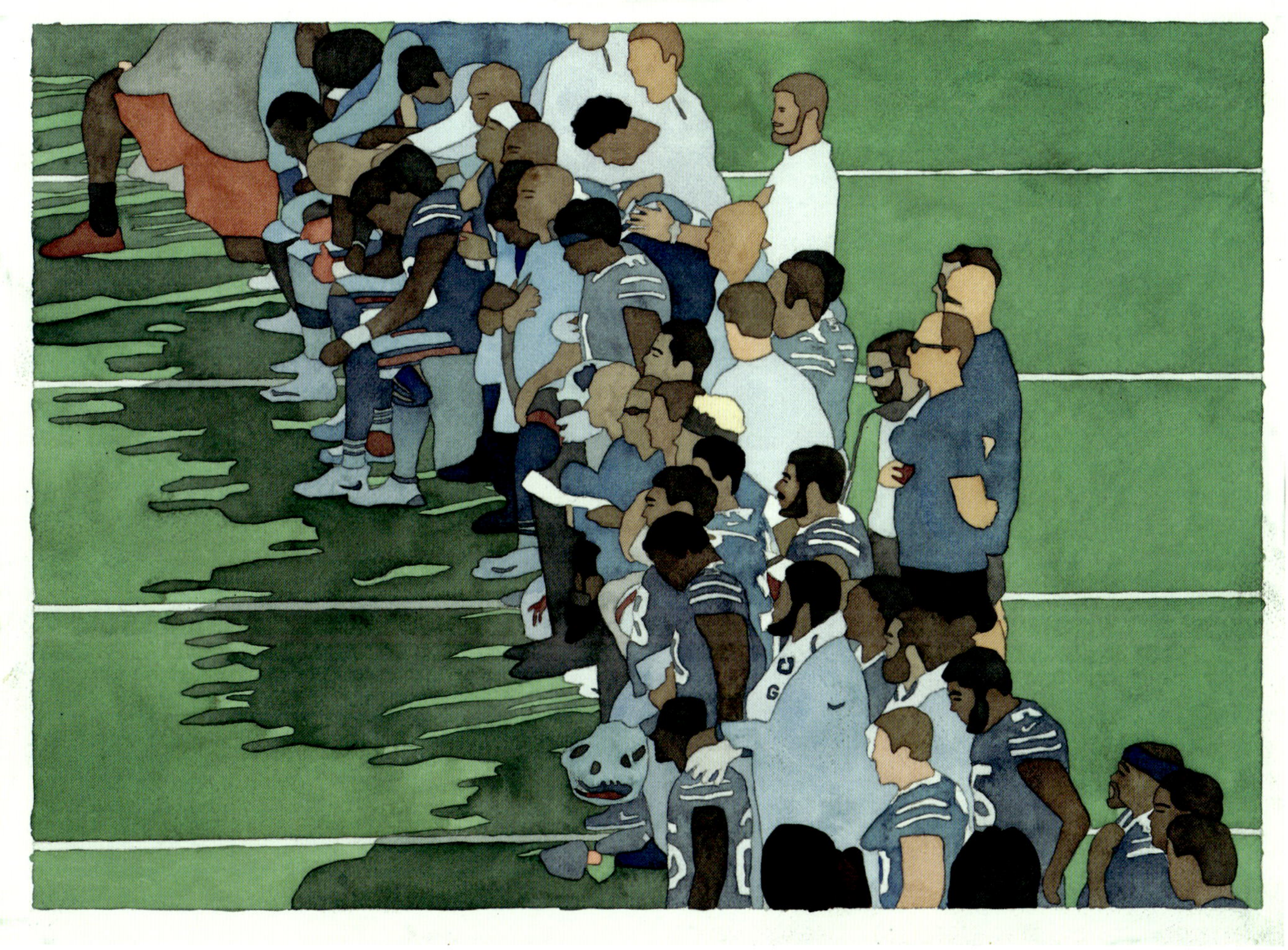

Watercolor for *National Anthem*, 2018

KOTA EZAWA

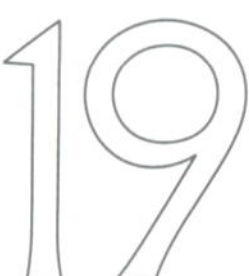

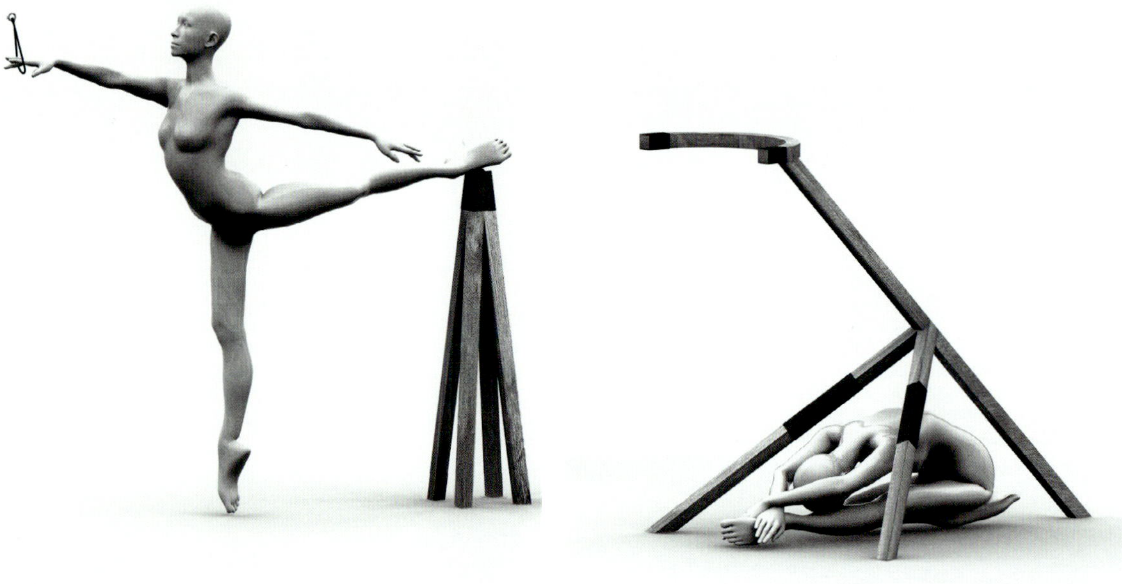

Rendering for *The Master and Form*, 2018

Rendering for *The Master and Form*, 2018

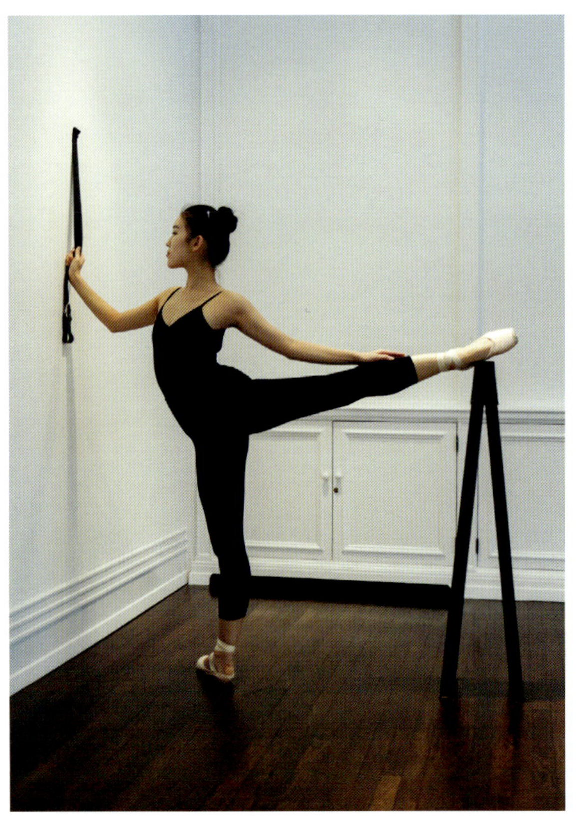

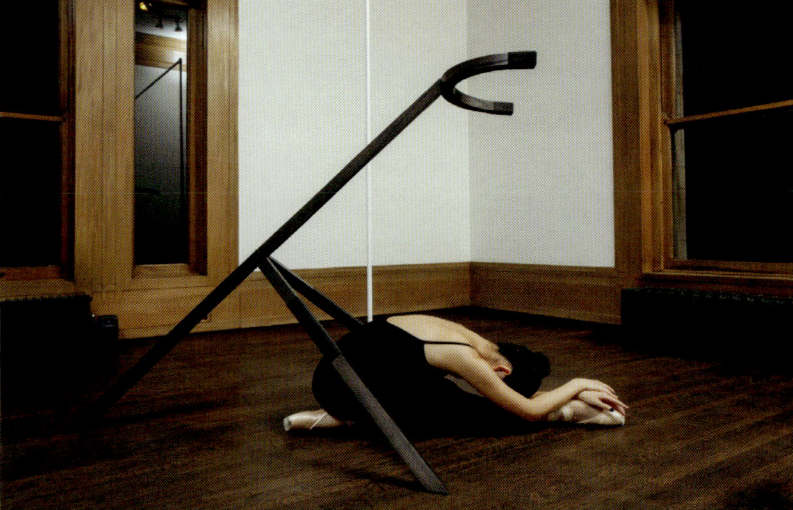

The Master and Form, 2018. Performance view, Graham Foundation, Chicago, IL, 2018

The Master and Form, 2018. Performance view, Graham Foundation, Chicago, IL, 2018

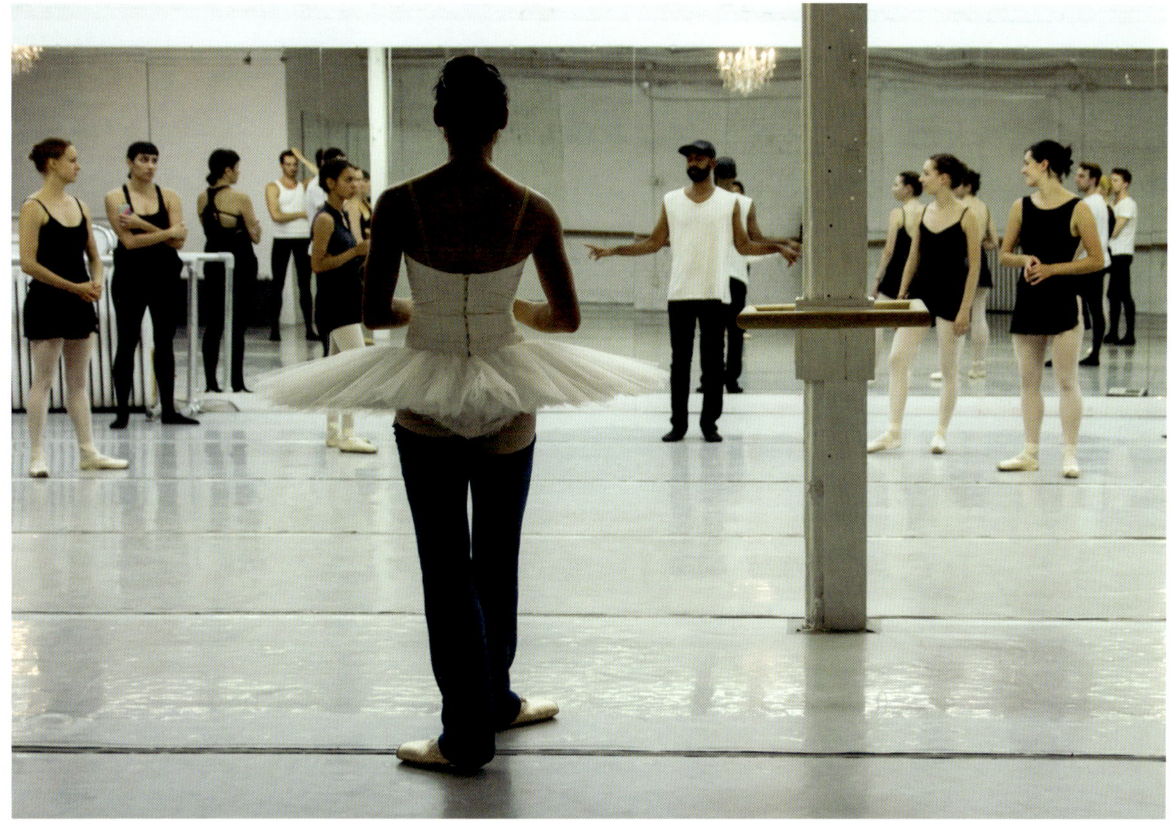

Rehearsal for *Révérence*, 2016

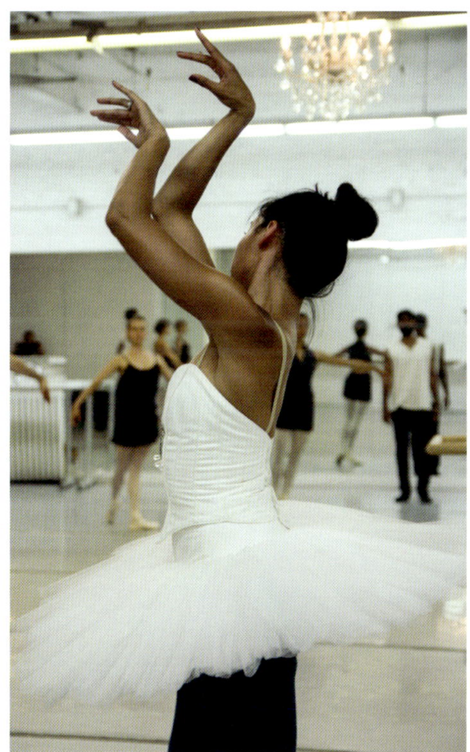

Rehearsal for *Révérence*, 2016

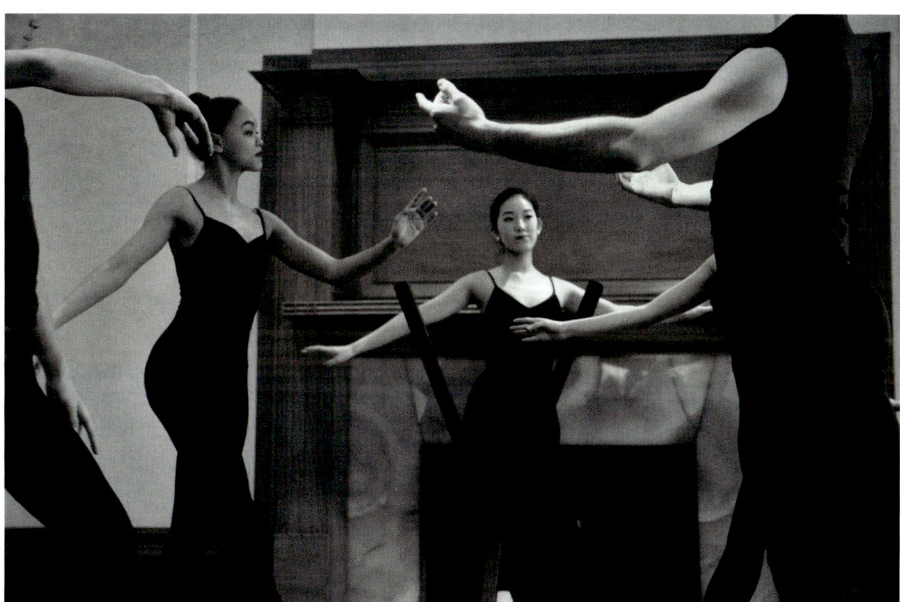

The Master and Form, 2018. Performance view, Graham Foundation, Chicago, IL, 2018

BRENDAN FERNANDES

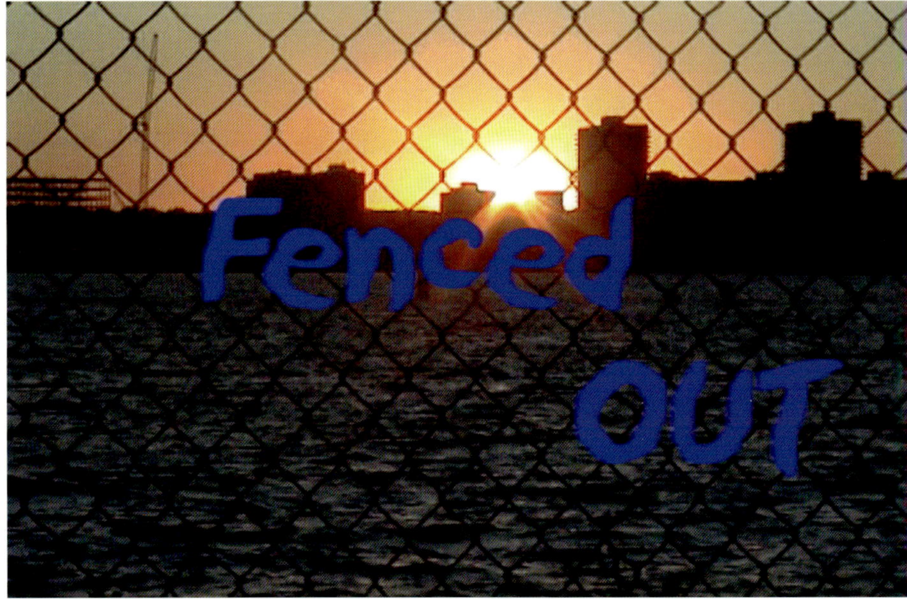

Fenced Out, 2001

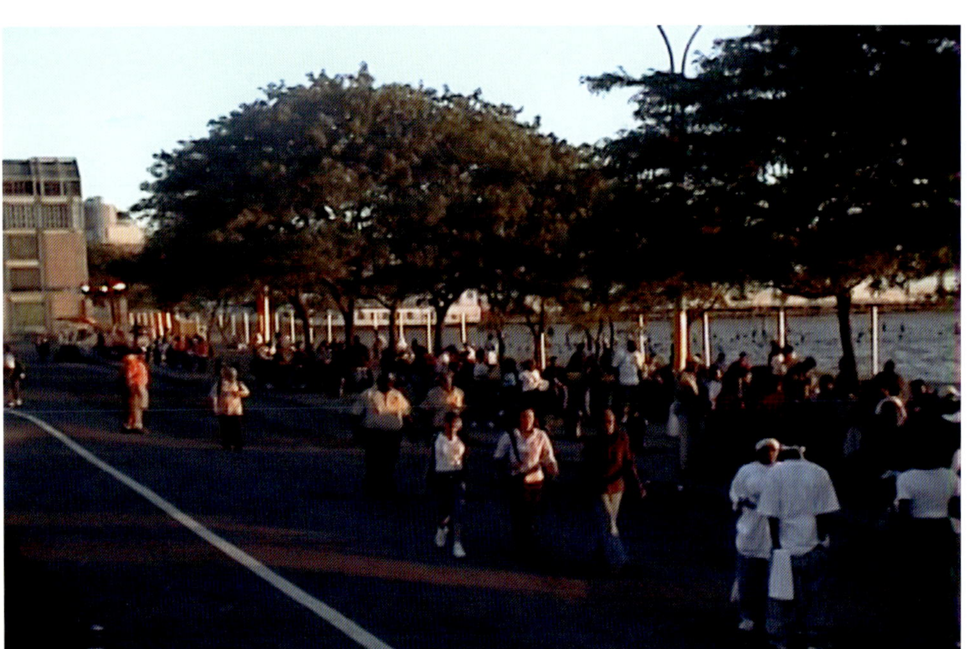

Fenced Out, 2001

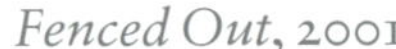

Fenced Out, 2001

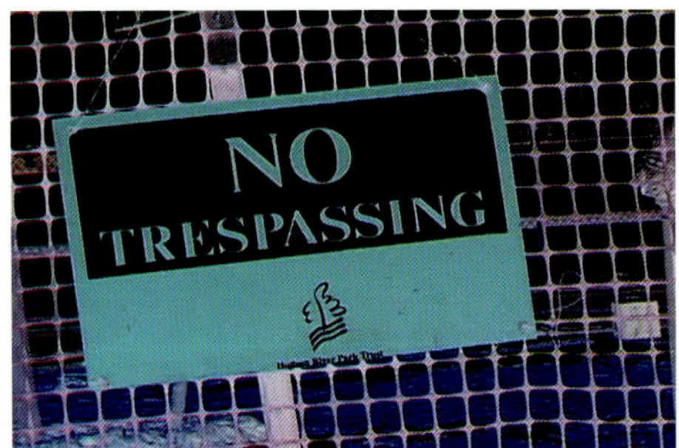

Fenced Out, 2001

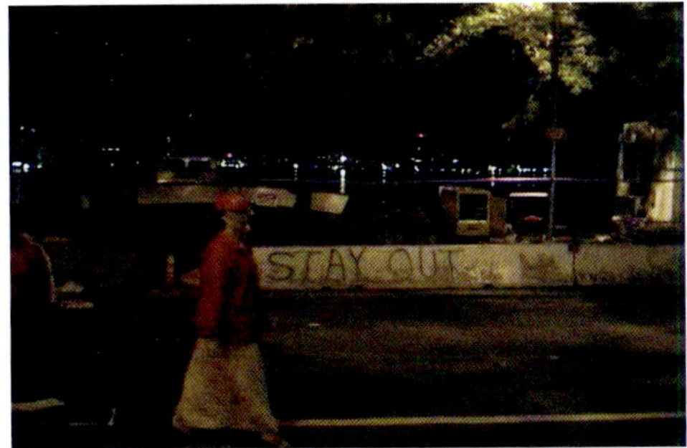

Fenced Out, 2001

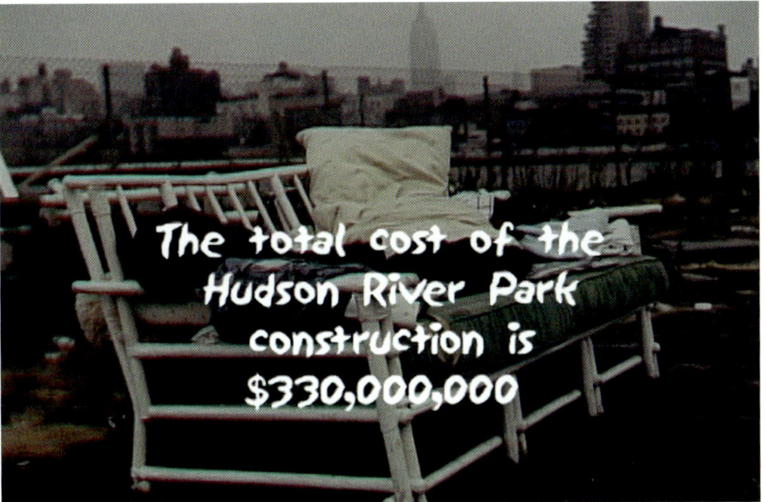

Fenced Out, 2001

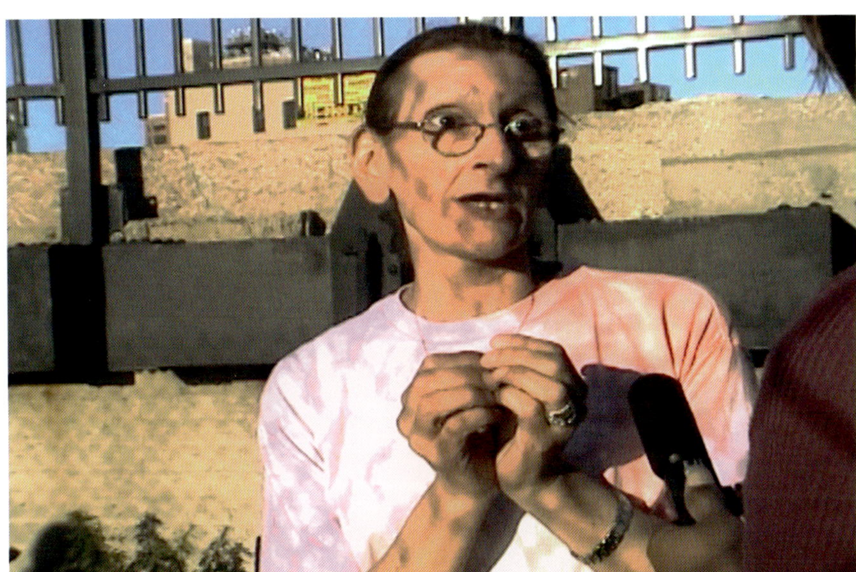

Activist Sylvia Rivera in *Fenced Out*, 2001

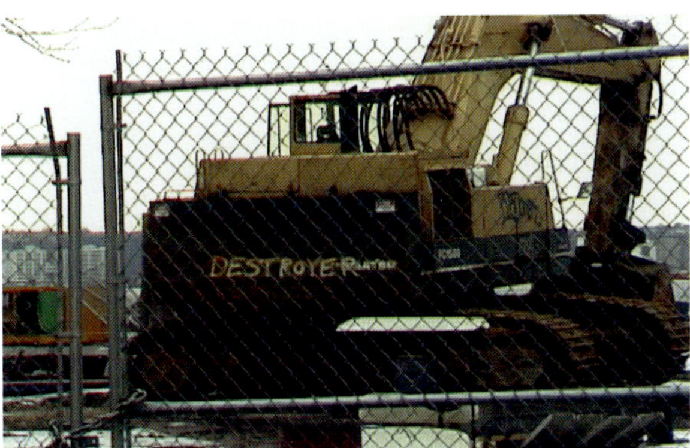

Fenced Out, 2001

Fenced Out, 2001

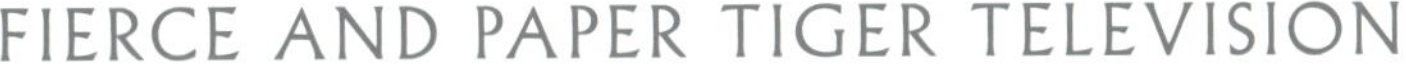

FIERCE AND PAPER TIGER TELEVISION

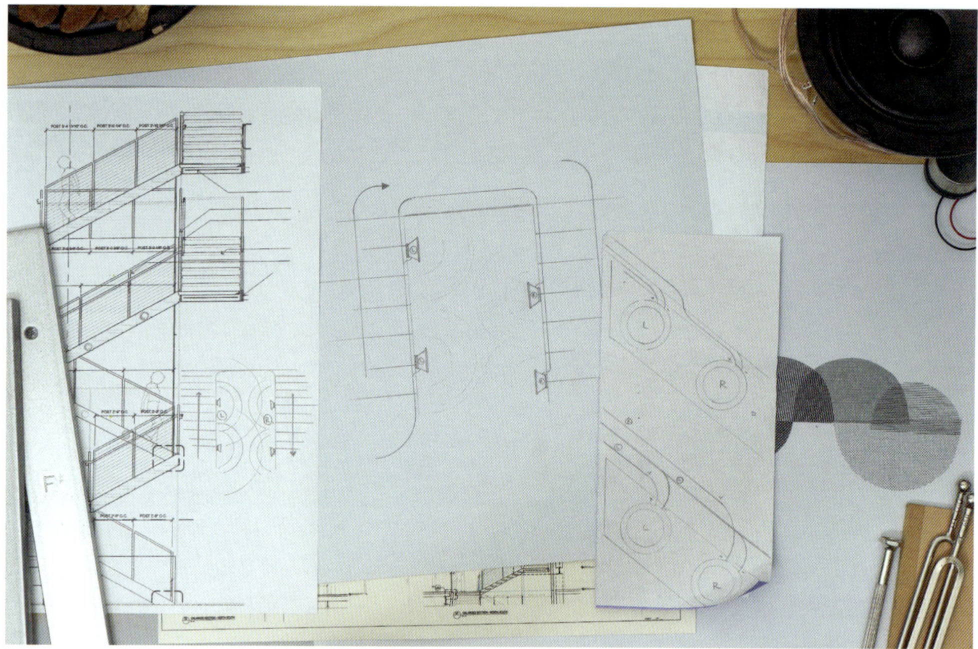

Sketches for installation of untitled work in progress, 2018

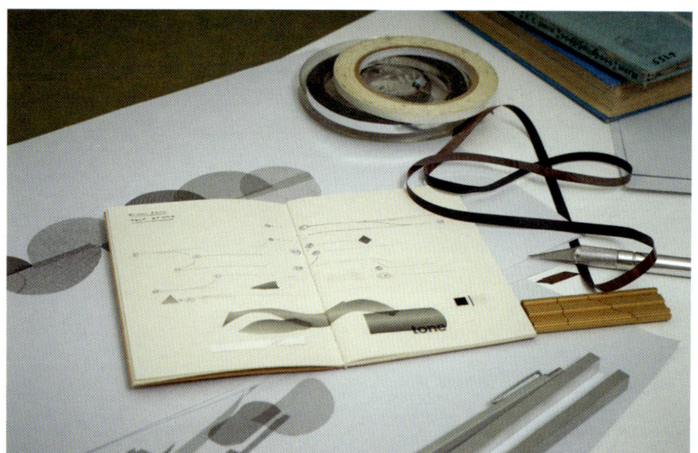

Sketches for installation of untitled work in progress, 2018

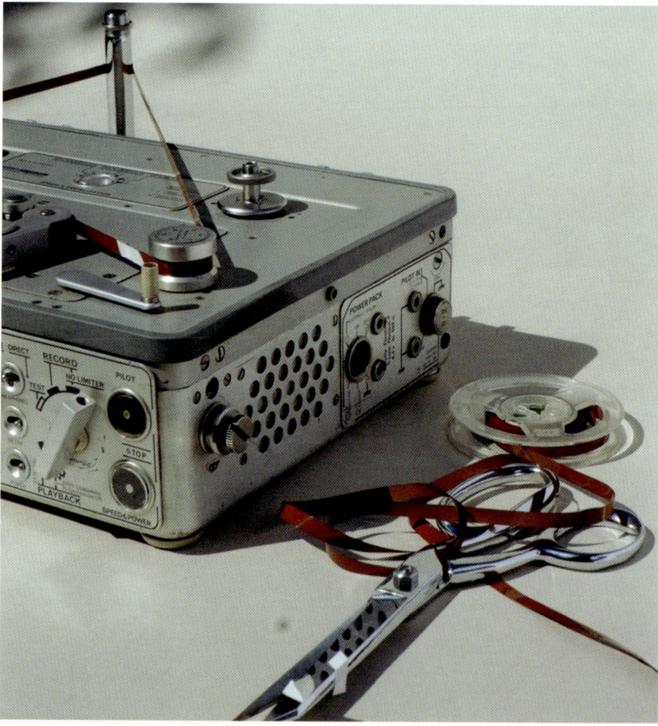

Marcus Fischer and Taylor Deupree, still from the making of *Twine*, 2015

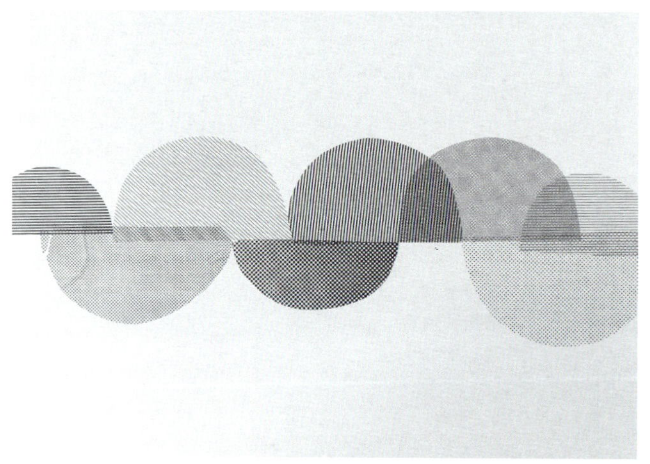

Starting phase of graphic scores based on Letraset texture transfers, 2018

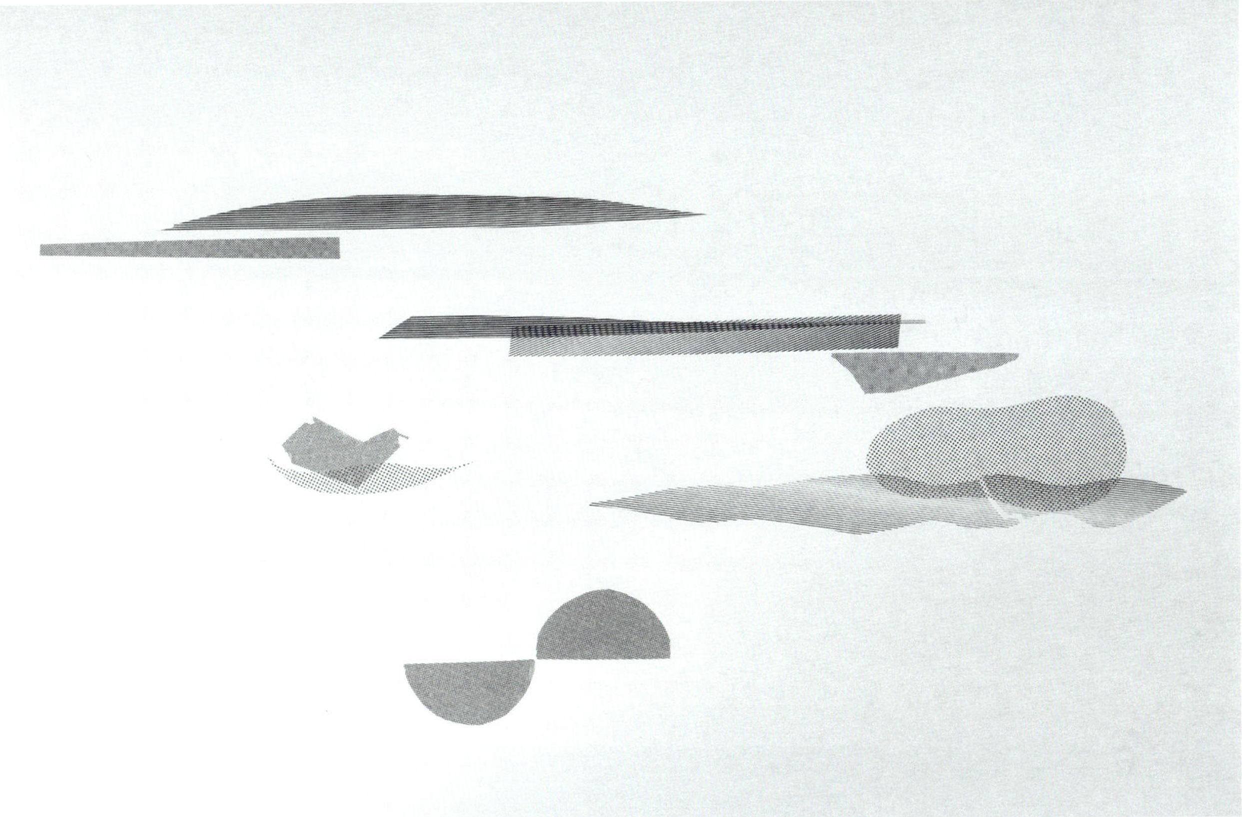

Starting phase of graphic scores based on Letraset texture transfers, 2018

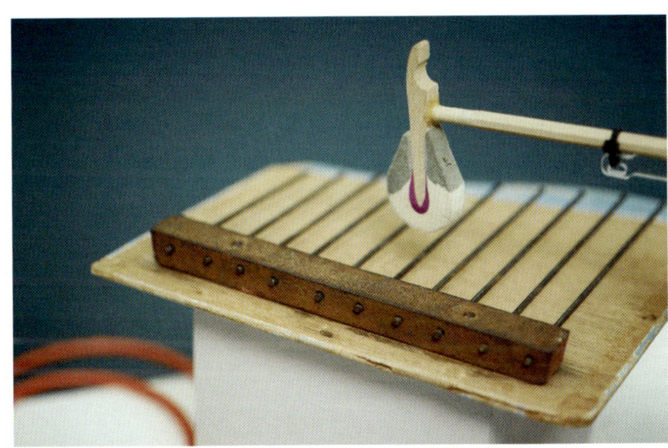

Motion study, 2018

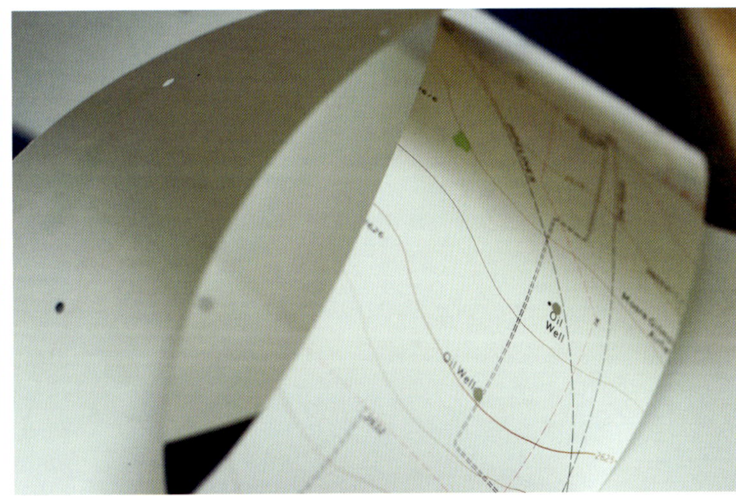

Preparatory diagram for *Well, Well, Well*, 2018

MARCUS FISCHER

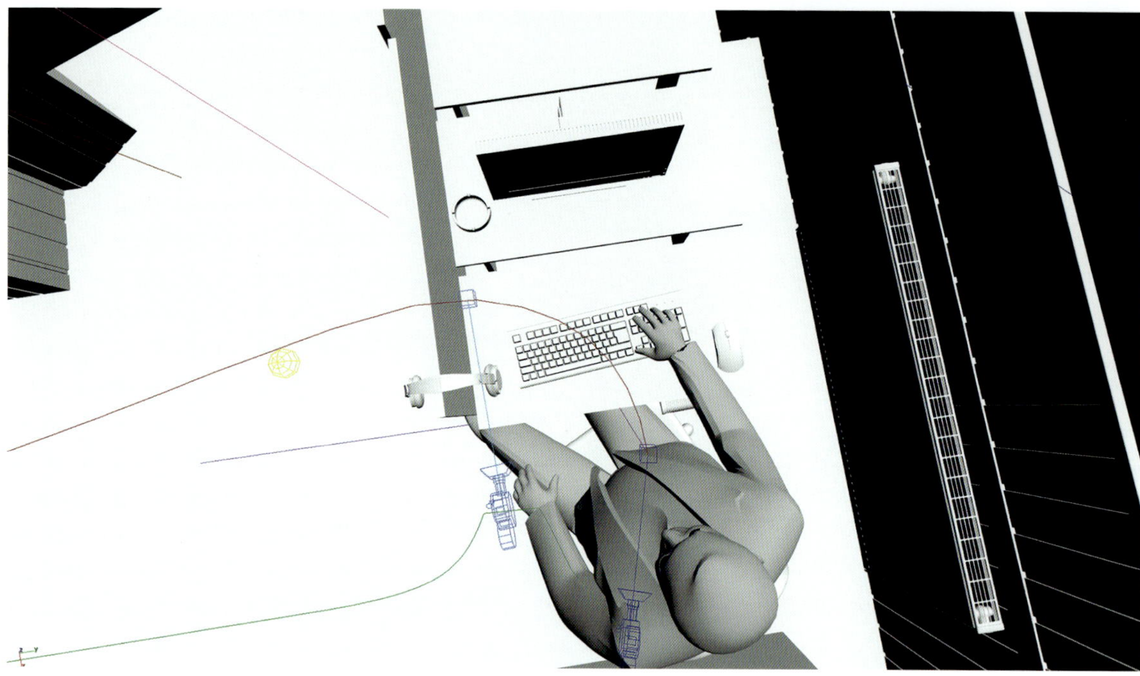

22

Computer simulation of Andreas Temme's line of vision for *77sqm_9:26min*, 2017

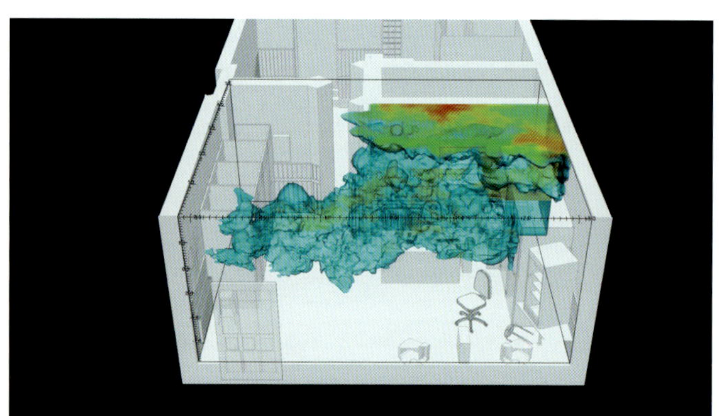

Fluid dynamics simulation of gunpowder residue particles for *77sqm_9:26min*, 2017

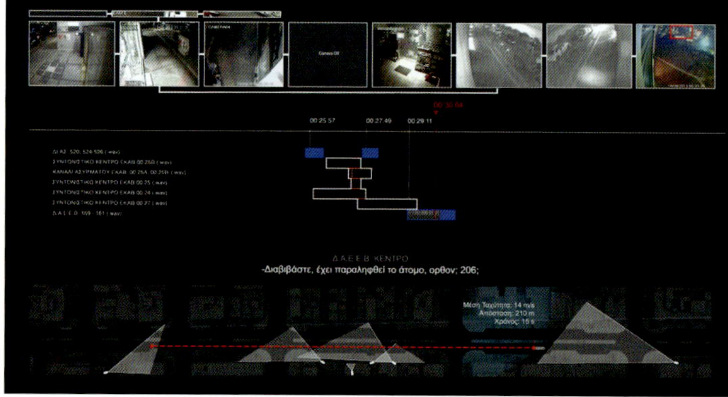

Synchronization of the arrival of the first ambulance for *The Murder of Pavlos Fyssas, 18 September 2013*, 2018

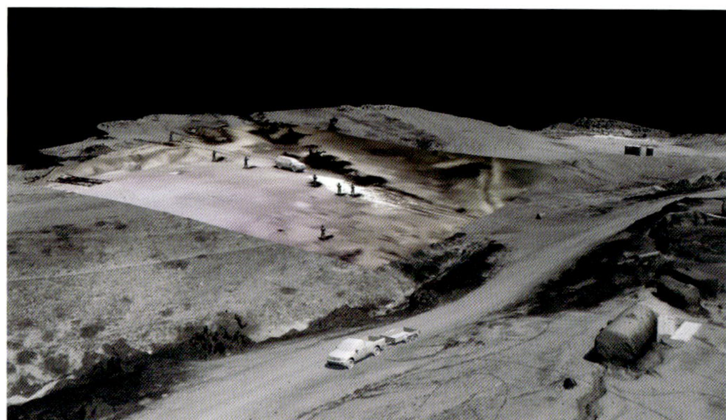

Site model and helicopter footage establishing the locations of actors for *Killing in Umm al-Hiran*, 2018

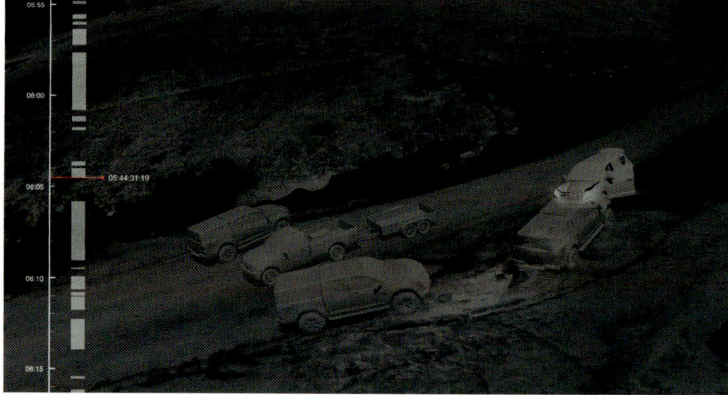

3-D site model depicting locations of vehicles for *Killing in Umm al-Hiran*, 2018

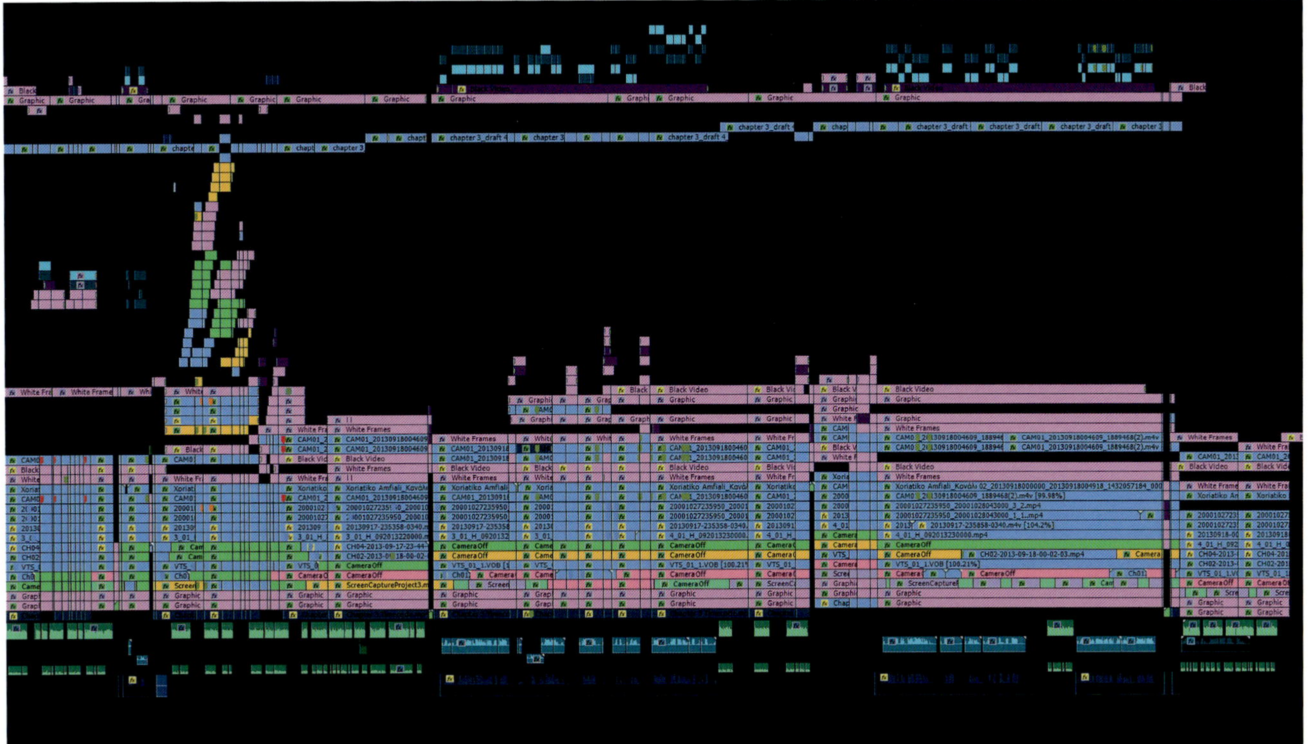

Synchronization of CCTV cameras and video editing process for *The Murder of Pavlos Fyssas, 18 September 2013*, 2018

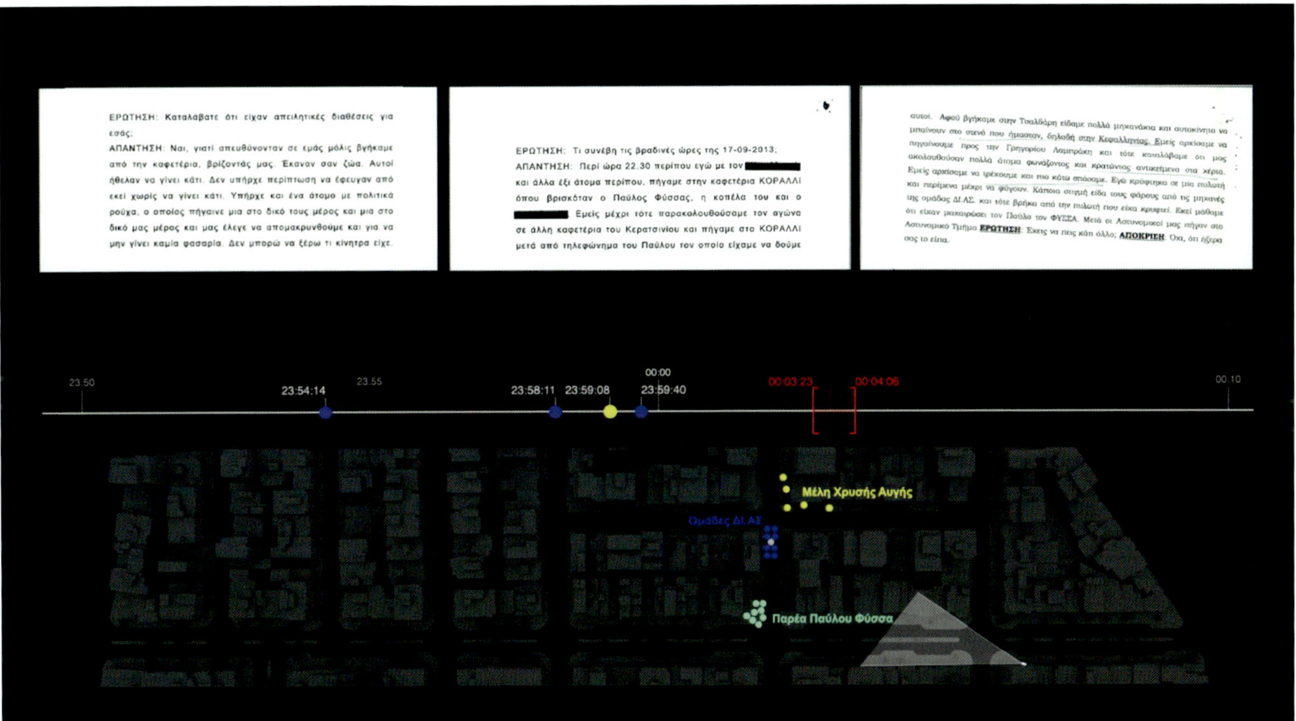

Temporal and spatial analysis for *The Murder of Pavlos Fyssas, 18 September 2013*, 2018

FORENSIC ARCHITECTURE

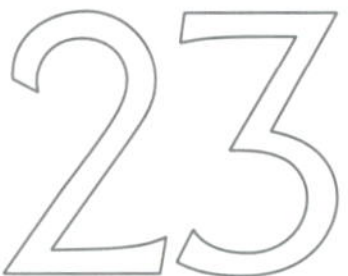

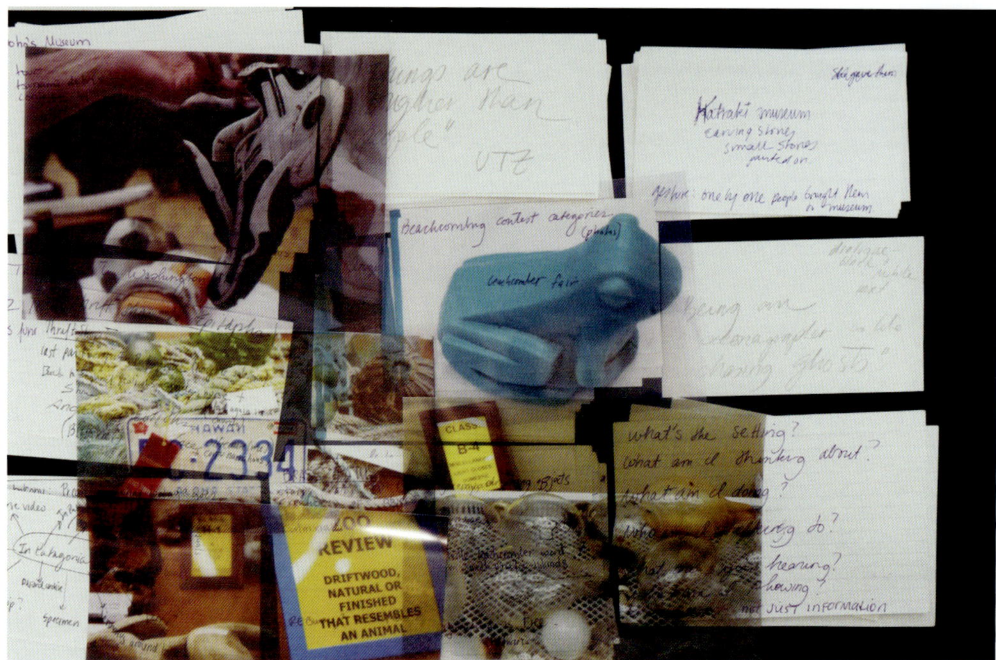

23

Production still from *Gyres*, 2018

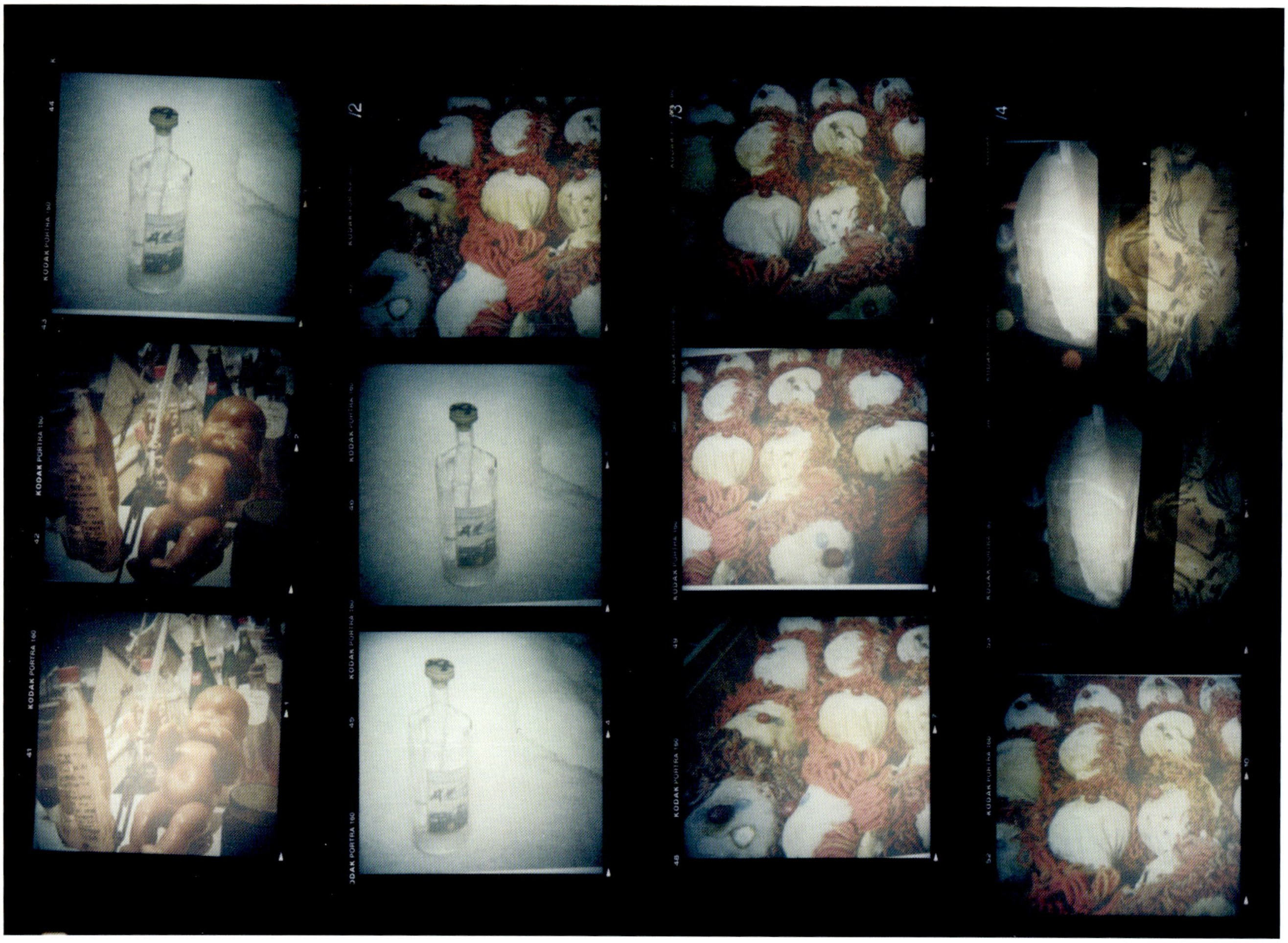

Contact sheet, 2018

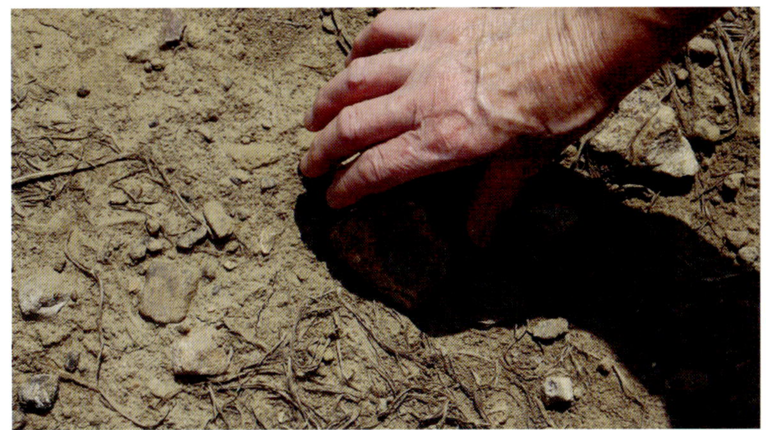

Production still from *Gyres*, 2018

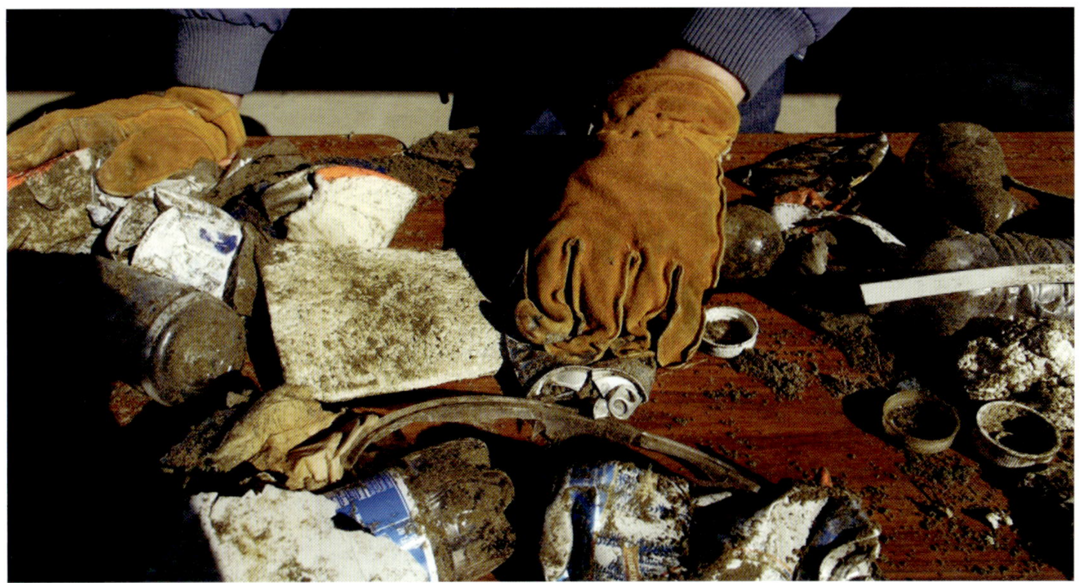

Production still from *Gyres*, 2018

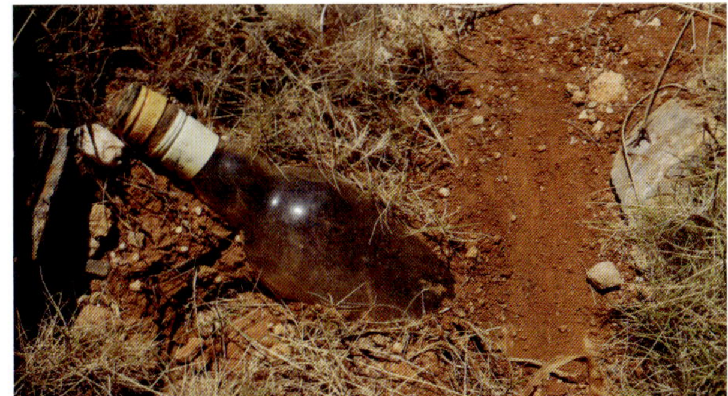

Production still from *Gyres*, 2018

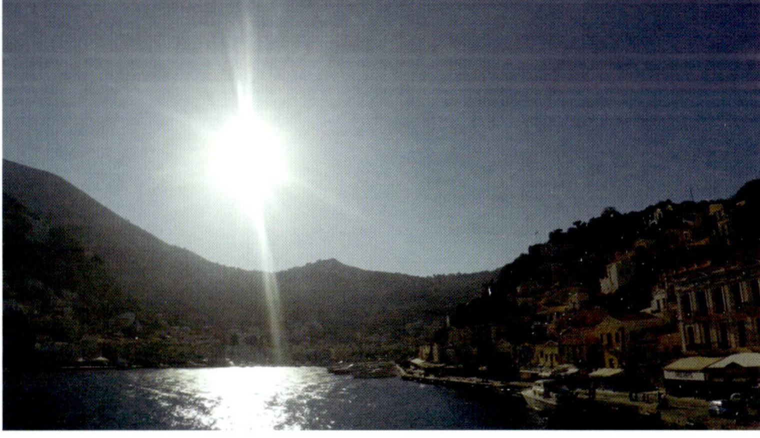

Production still from *Gyres*, 2018

ELLIE GA

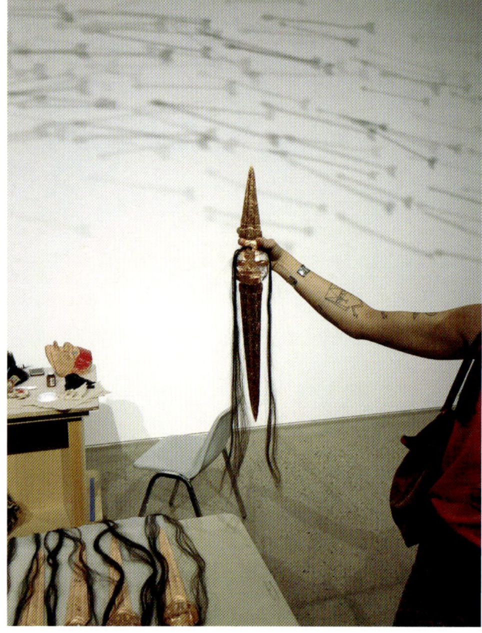

24

Nicholas Galanin and Nep Sidhu, process image for *Axes in Polyrhythm, When My Drums Come Knocking They Watch*, 2018

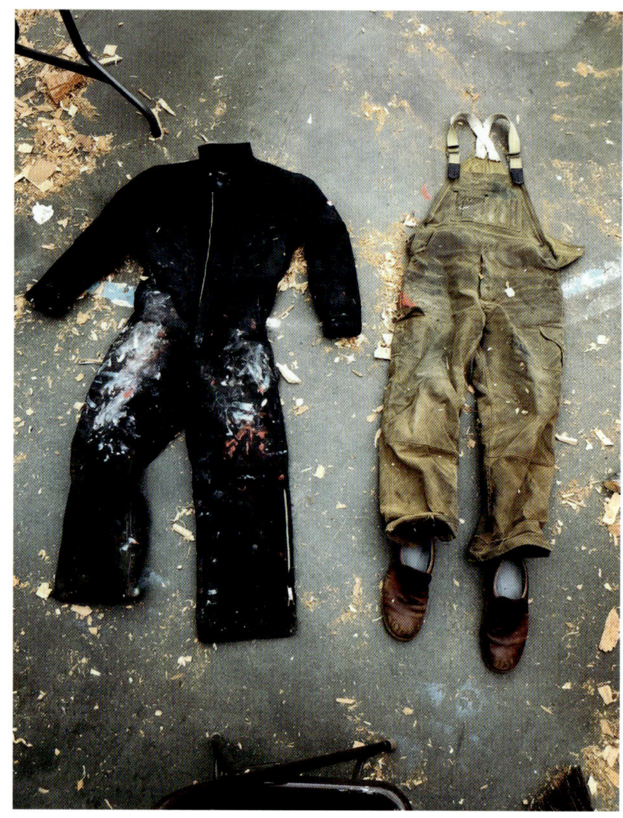

Process image from the carving and painting of *Áa Gaawú ya Yéi Shtoosneixj* (*A Time for Healing*), Yanyeidí totem pole, 2017

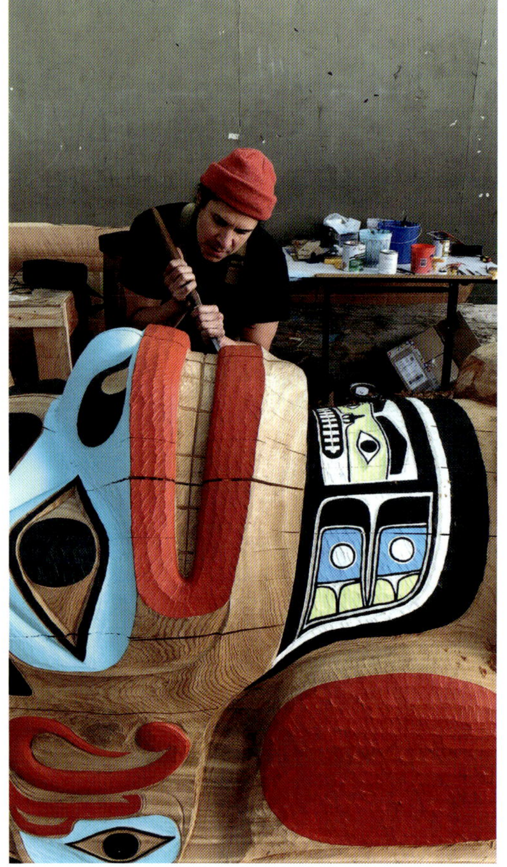

The artist carving *Áa Gaawú ya Yéi Shtoosneixj* (*A Time for Healing*), Yanyeidí totem pole, 2017

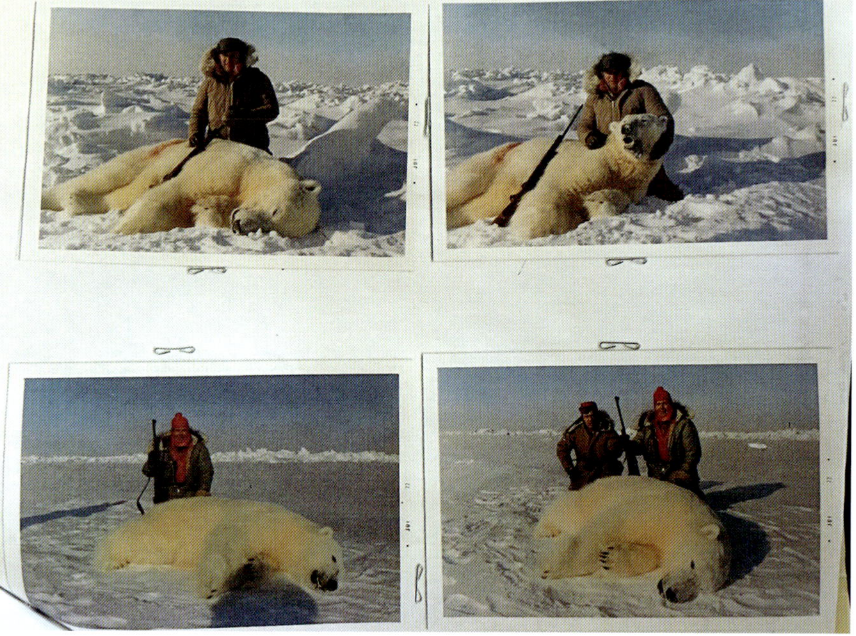

Polar bear shot by white sport hunter, 1960s. Source image for *We Dreamt Deaf*, 2015

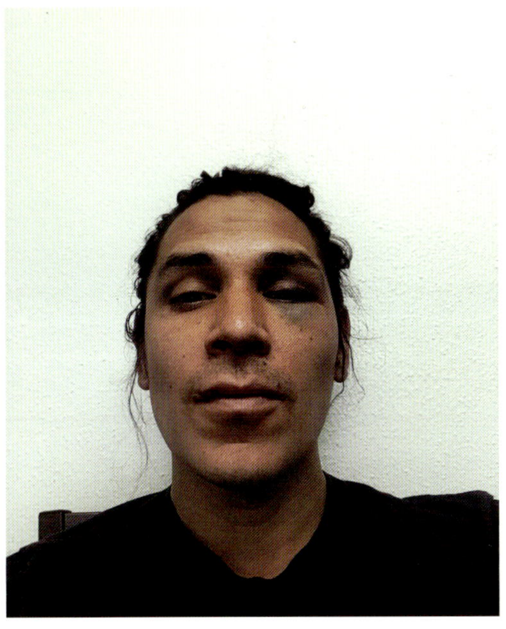

Process image for *The violence of blood quantum, half human (animal), half human (animal) after James Luna*, 2017

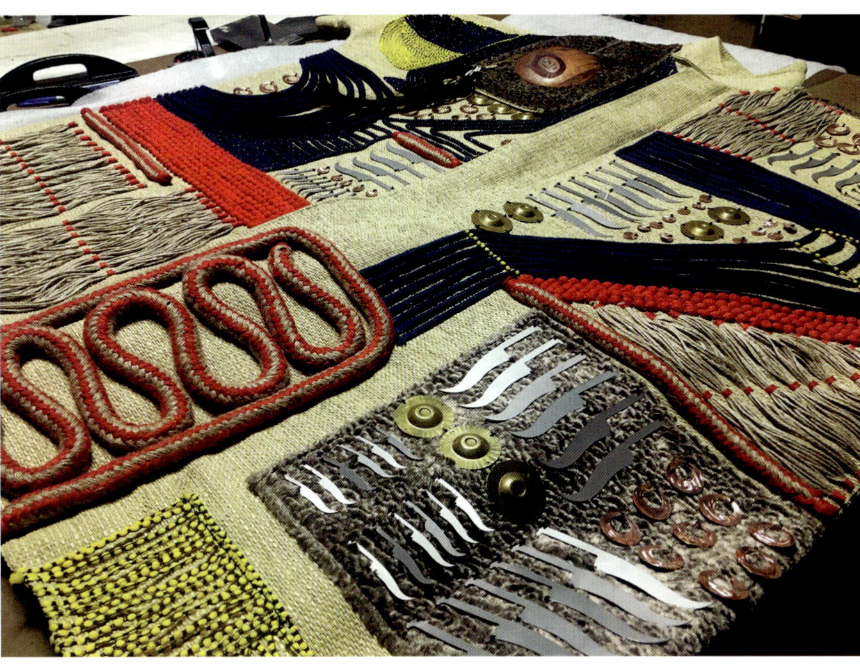

Nicholas Galanin and Nep Sidhu, detail of *No Pigs in Paradise, Series 2*, 2018

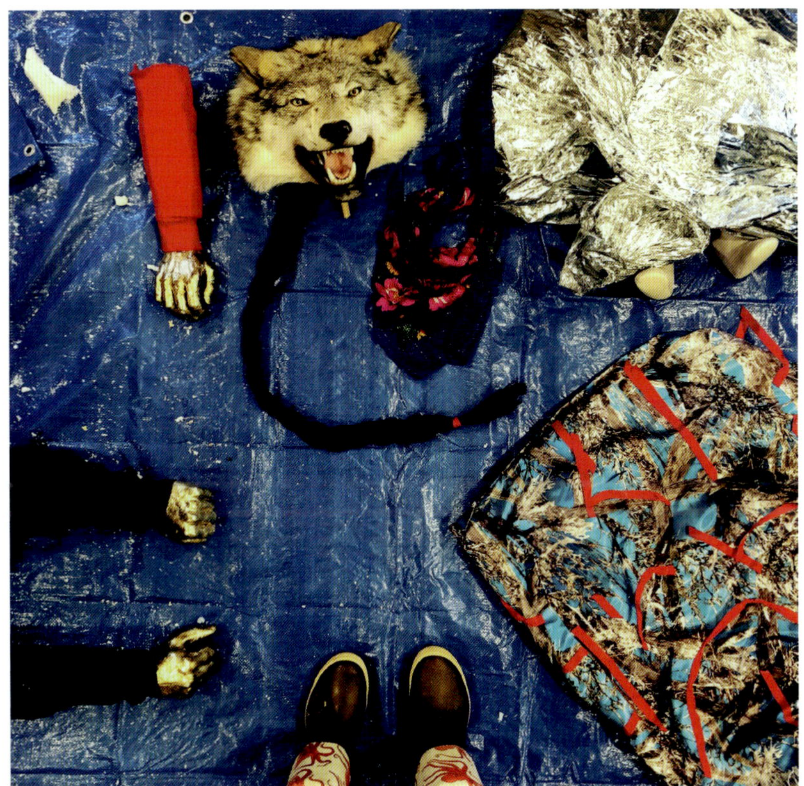

Nicholas Galanin and Merritt Johnson, process image for *Building an eye to better see you*, 2018

NICHOLAS GALANIN

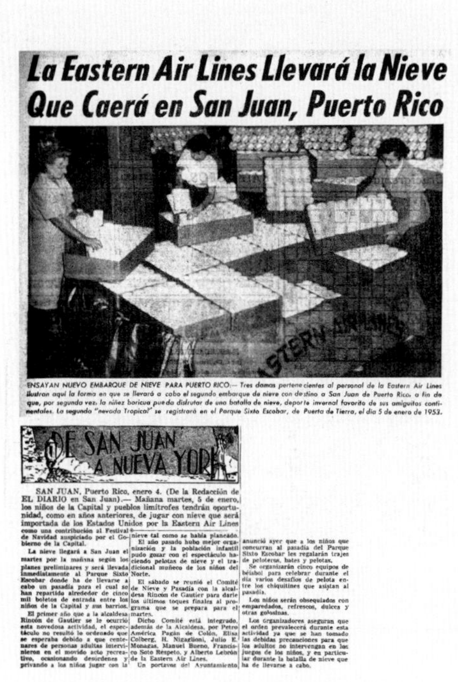

La Eastern Air Lines Llevará la Nieve Que Caerá en San Juan, Puerto Rico

ENSAYAN NUEVO EMBARQUE DE NIEVE PARA PUERTO RICO.— Tres damas pertenecientes al personal de la Eastern Air Lines ilustran aquí la forma en que se llevará a cabo el segundo embarque de nieve con destino a San Juan de Puerto Rico, a fin de que, por segunda vez, la niñez boricua pueda disfrutar de una batalla de nieve, deporte invernal favorito de sus amiguitos continentales. La segunda "nevada Tropical" se registrará en el Parque Sixto Escobar, de Puerta de Tierra, el día 5 de enero de 1953.

DE SAN JUAN A NUEVA YORK

SAN JUAN, Puerto Rico, enero 4. (De la Redacción de EL DIARIO en San Juan).— Mañana martes, 5 de enero, los niños de la Capital y pueblos limítrofes tendrán oportunidad, como en años anteriores, de jugar con nieve que será importada de los Estados Unidos por la Eastern Air Lines como una contribución al Festival de Navidad auspiciado por el Gobierno de la Capital.

La nieve llegará a San Juan el martes por la mañana según los planes preliminares y será llevada inmediatamente al Parque Sixto Escobar donde ha de llevarse a cabo un pasadía para el cual se han repartido alrededor de cinco mil boletos de entrada entre los niños de la Capital y sus barrios.

El primer año que a la alcaldesa Rincón de Gautier se le ocurrió esta novedosa actividad, el espectáculo no resultó lo ordenado que se esperaba debido a que centenares de personas adultas intervinieron en el movido acto recreativo, ocasionando desórdenes y privando a los niños jugar con la nieve tal como se había planeado.

El año pasado hubo mejor organización y la población infantil pudo gozar con el espectáculo haciendo pelotas de nieve y el tradicional muñeco de los niños del Norte.

El sábado se reunió el Comité de Nieve y Pasadía con la alcaldesa Rincón de Gautier para darle los últimos toques finales al programa que se prepara para el martes.

Dicho Comité está integrado, además de la Alcaldesa, por Petro América Pagán de Colón, Elisa Colberg, H. Nigaglioni, Julio E. Monagas, Manuel Bueno, Francisco Soto Respeto, y Alberto Lebrón de la Eastern Air Lines.

Un portavoz del Ayuntamiento anunció ayer que... concurran al pas[eo] Sixto Escobar les... de peloteros, bat[es]...

Se organizarán... béisbol para cele[brar]... día varios desafí[os]... tre los chiquitin[es]... pasadía.

Los niños serán [obsequiados con] emparedados, ref[rescos] y otras golosinas.

Los organizador[es aseguran que] el orden prevalec[erá durante esta] actividad ya que... las debidas preca[uciones para que] los adultos no in[tervengan en los] juegos de los niñ[os, y particu]lar durante la bata[lla de nieve que] ha de llevarse a [cabo].

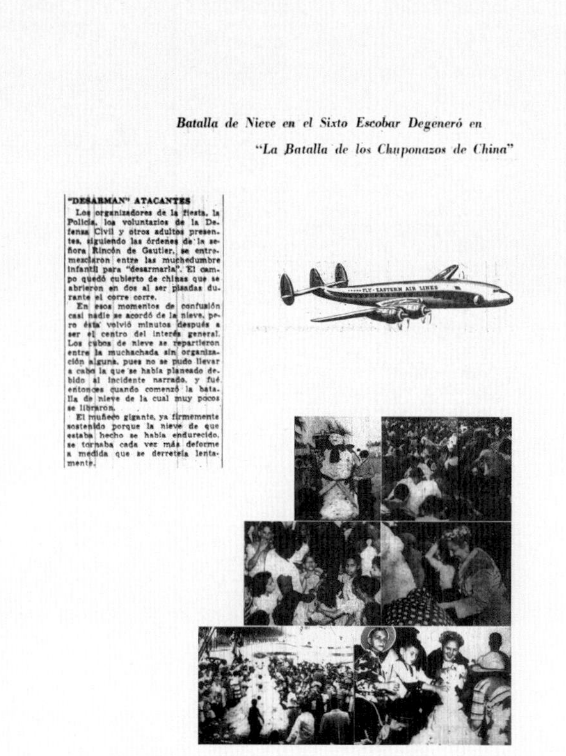

Batalla de Nieve en el Sixto Escobar Degeneró en "La Batalla de los Chuponazos de China"

"DESARMAN" ATACANTES

Los organizadores de la fiesta, la Policía, los voluntarios de la Defensa Civil y otros adultos presentes, siguiendo las órdenes de la señora Rincón de Gautier, se entremezclaron entre las muchedumbre infantil para "desarmarla". El campo quedó cubierto de chinas que se abrieron en dos al ser pisadas durante el corre corre.

En esos momentos de confusión casi nadie se acordó de la nieve, pero ésta volvió minutos después a ser el centro del interés general. Los cubos de nieve se repartieron entre la muchachada sin organización alguna, pues no se pudo llevar a cabo la que se había planeado debido al incidente narrado, y fué entonces cuando comenzó la batalla de nieve de la cual muy pocos se libraron.

El muñeco gigante, ya firmemente sostenido porque la nieve de que estaba hecho se había endurecido, se tornaba cada vez más deforme a medida que se derretía lentamente.

Detail of takeaway publication accompanying *Lluvia con nieve* (*Rain with Snow*), 2014

Detail of takeaway publication accompanying
Lluvia con nieve (*Rain with Snow*), 2014

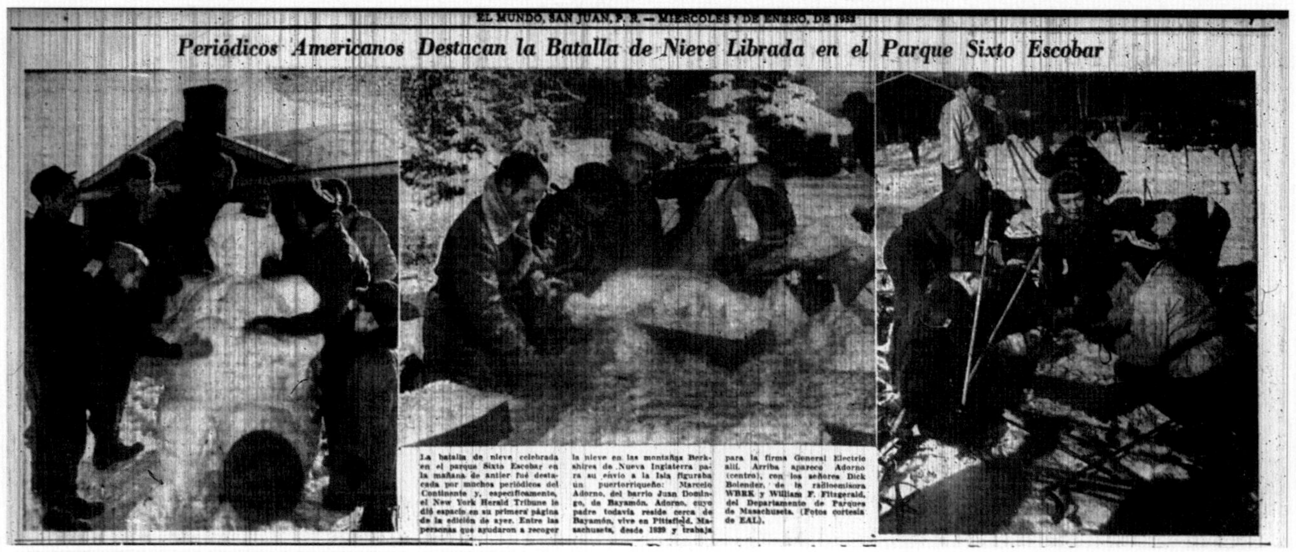

EL MUNDO, SAN JUAN, P. R. — MIÉRCOLES 7 DE ENERO DE 1953

Periódicos Americanos Destacan la Batalla de Nieve Librada en el Parque Sixto Escobar

La batalla de nieve celebrada en el parque Sixto Escobar en la mañana de antier fué destacada por muchos periódicos del Continente y, específicamente, el New York Herald Tribune le dió espacio en su primera página de la edición de ayer. Entre las personas que ayudaron a recoger la nieve en las montañas Berkshires de Nueva Inglaterra para su envío a la Isla figuraba un puertorriqueño: Marcelo Adorno, del barrio Juan Domingo, de Bayamón. Adorno, cuyo padre todavía reside cerca de Bayamón, vive en Pittsfield, Massachusets, desde 1929 y trabaja para la firma General Electric allí. Arriba aparece Adorno (centro), con los señores Dick Bolender, de la radioemisora WBRK y William F. Fitzgerald, del Departamento de Parques de Massachusets. (Fotos cortesía de EAL).

Detail of takeaway publication accompanying *Lluvia con nieve* (*Rain with Snow*), 2014

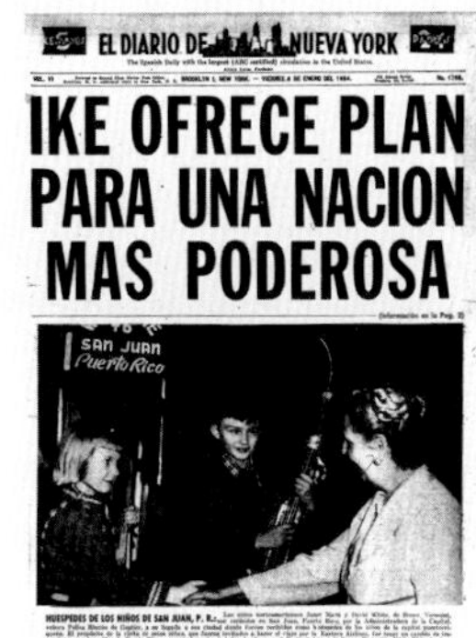

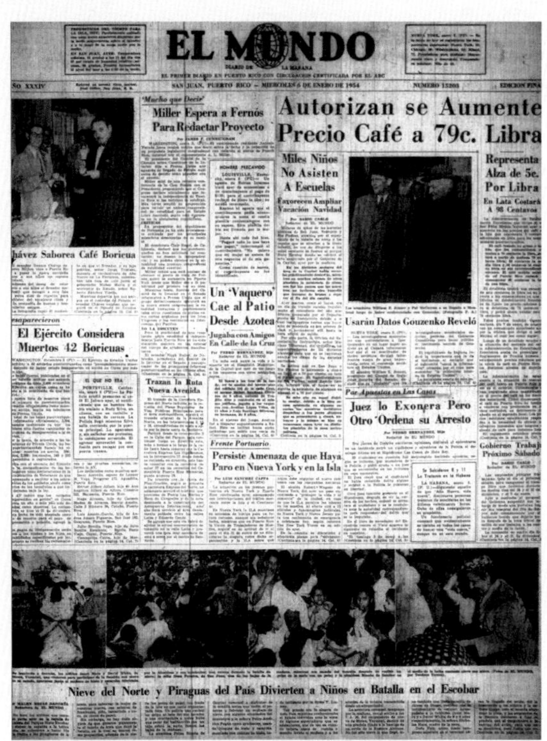

Detail of takeaway publication accompanying *Lluvia con nieve* (*Rain with Snow*), 2014

Detail of takeaway publication accompanying *Lluvia con nieve* (*Rain with Snow*), 2014

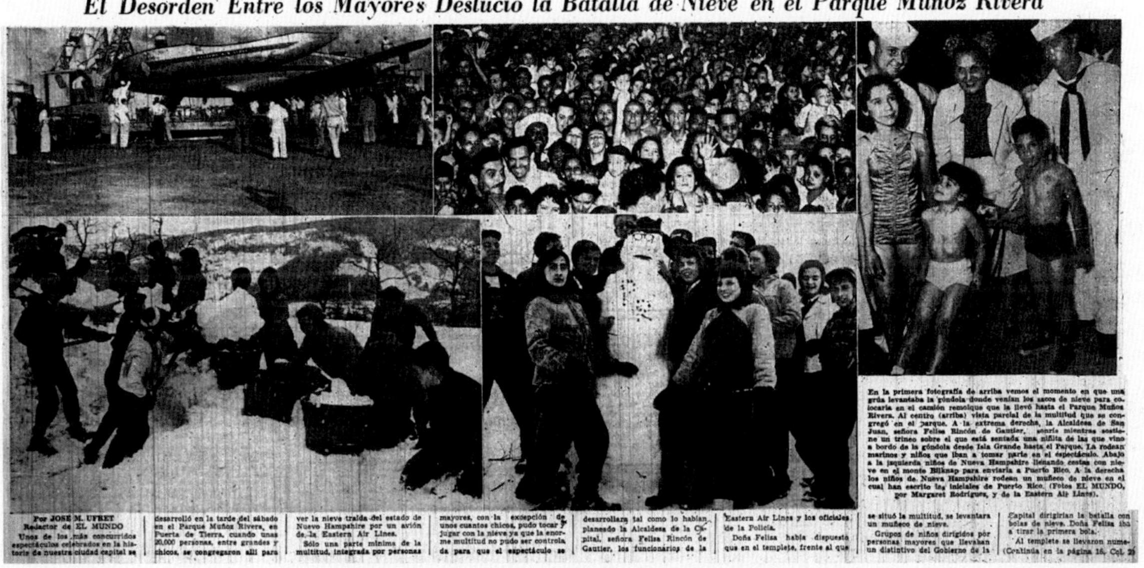

Detail of takeaway publication accompanying *Lluvia con nieve* (*Rain with Snow*), 2014

SOFÍA GALLISÁ MURIENTE

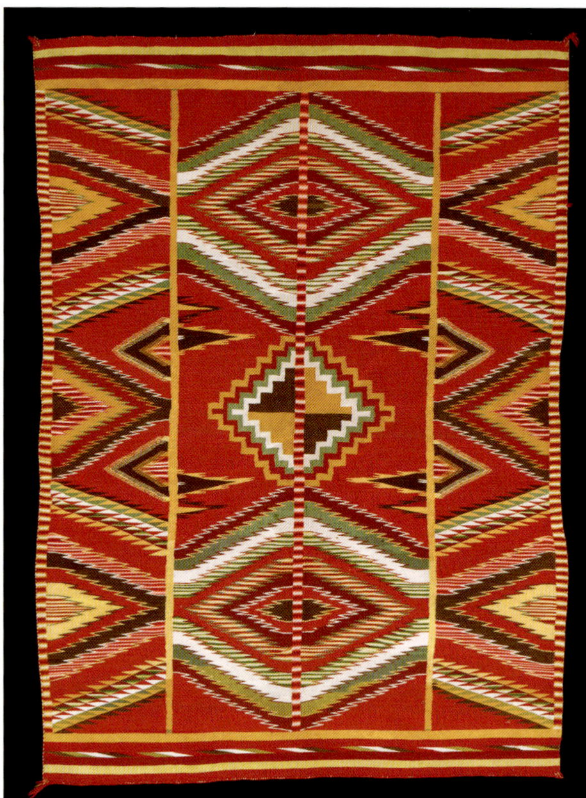

Diné (Navajo) "Eye-dazzler" blanket, c. 1890–95

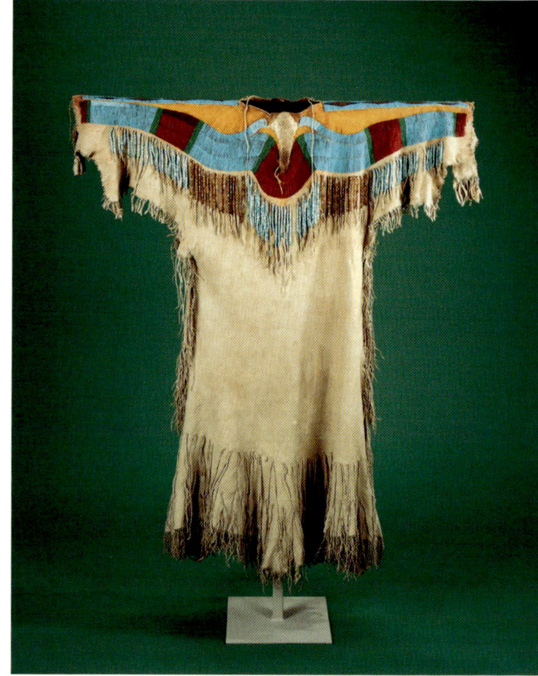

Nez Percé dress, 1890s

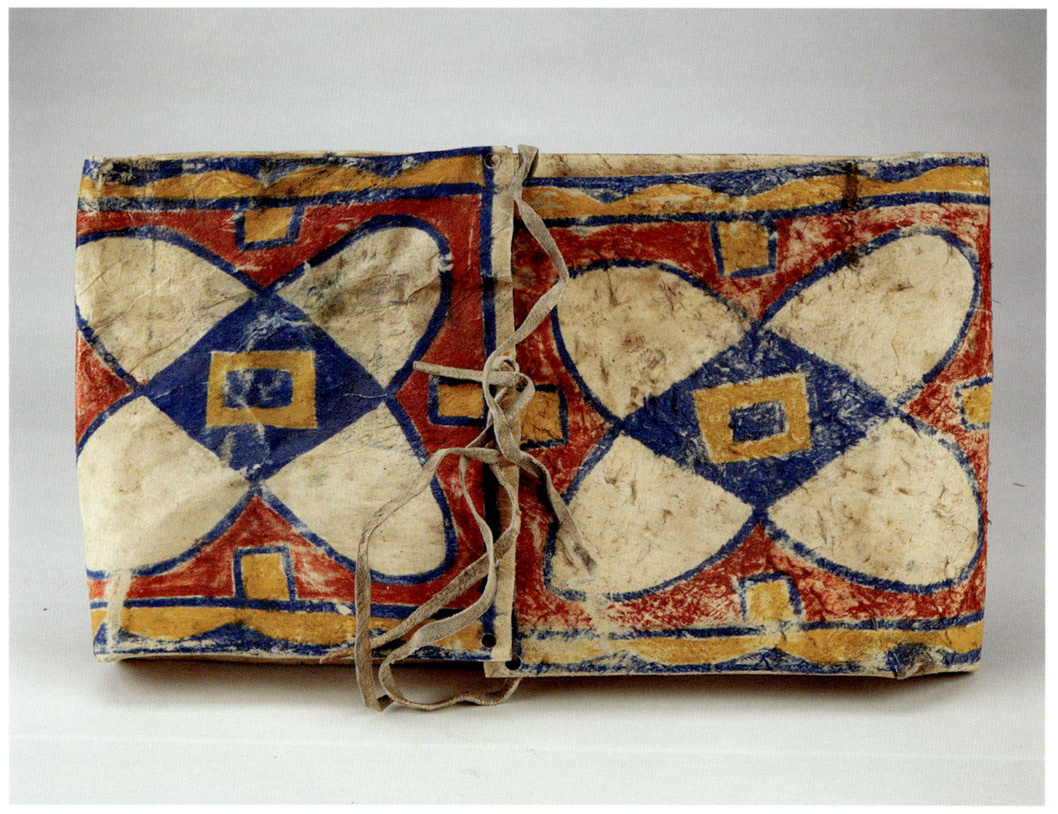

Sioux or Blackfeet parfleche, late 19th century

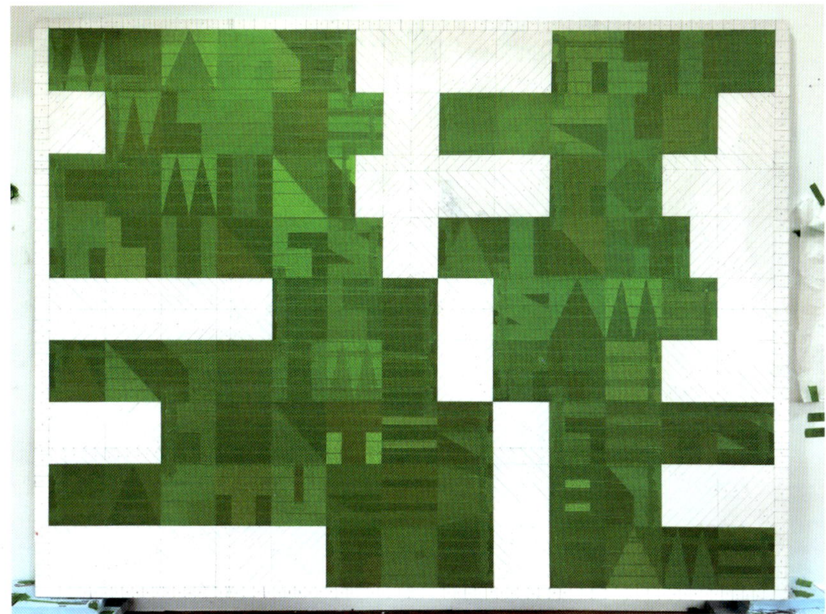

Untitled work in progress, 2018

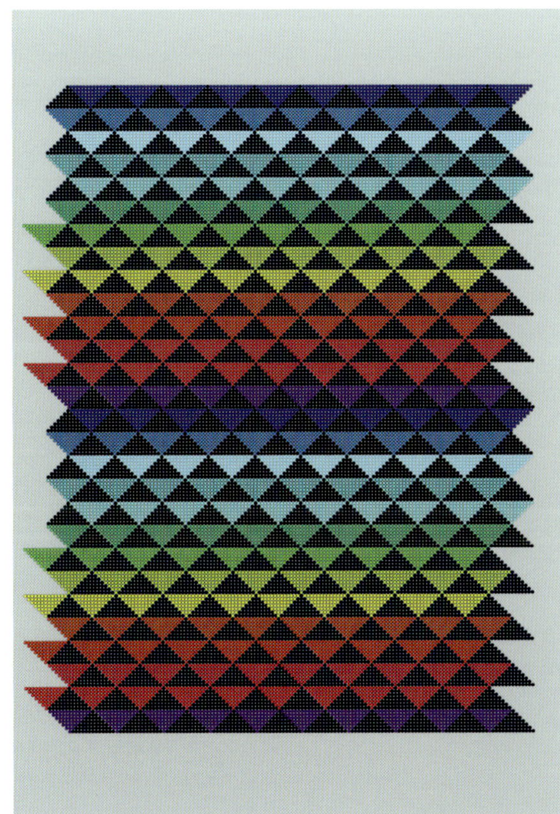

Process image of digital bead patterns, 2018

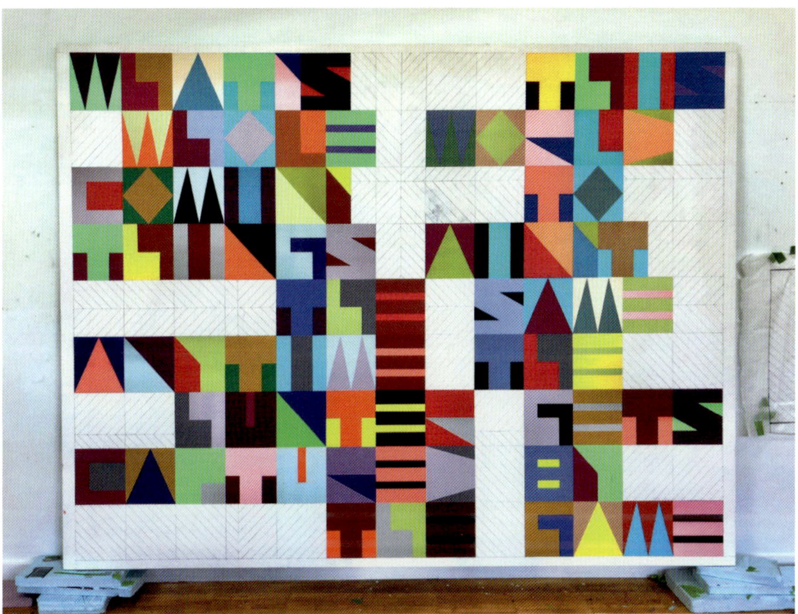

Untitled work in progress, 2018

JEFFREY GIBSON

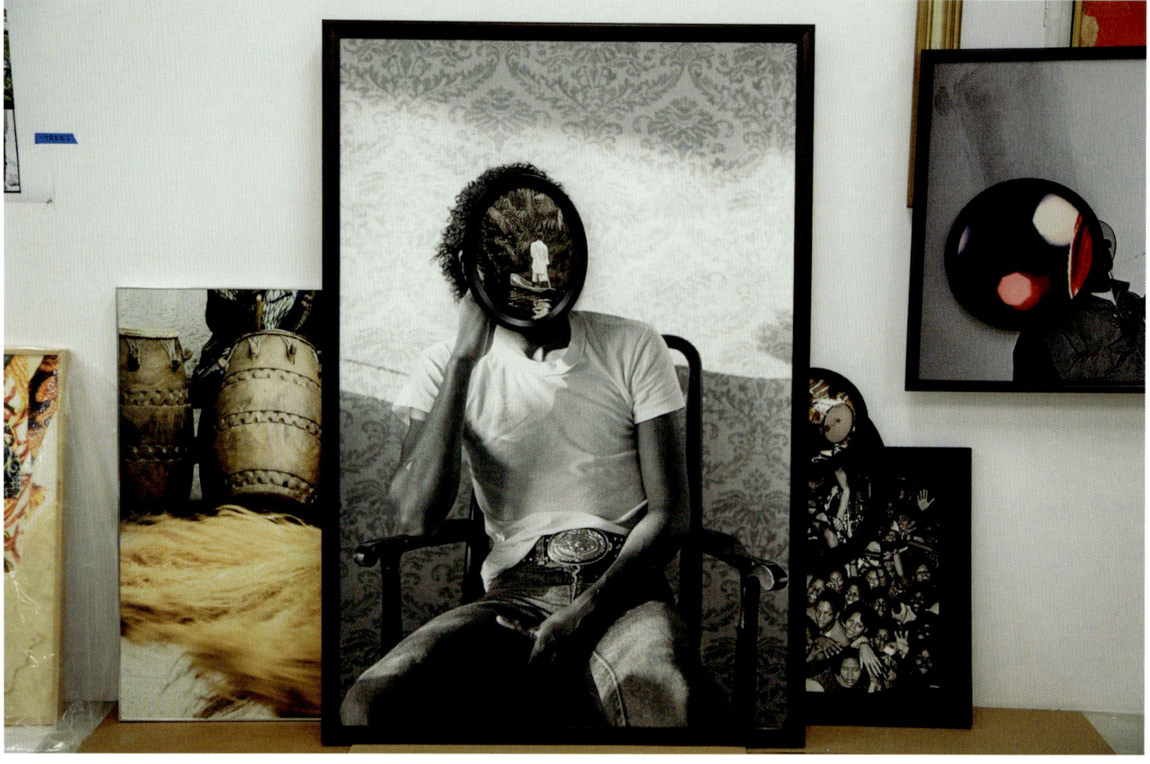

27

Studio, Los Angeles, CA, 2018

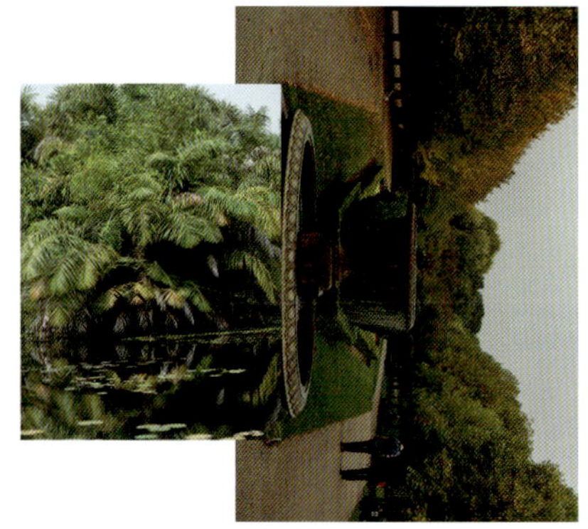

Nzulezo, Ghana, and Regents Park,
London, United Kingdom, 2018.
Source images for untitled work in
progress, 2018

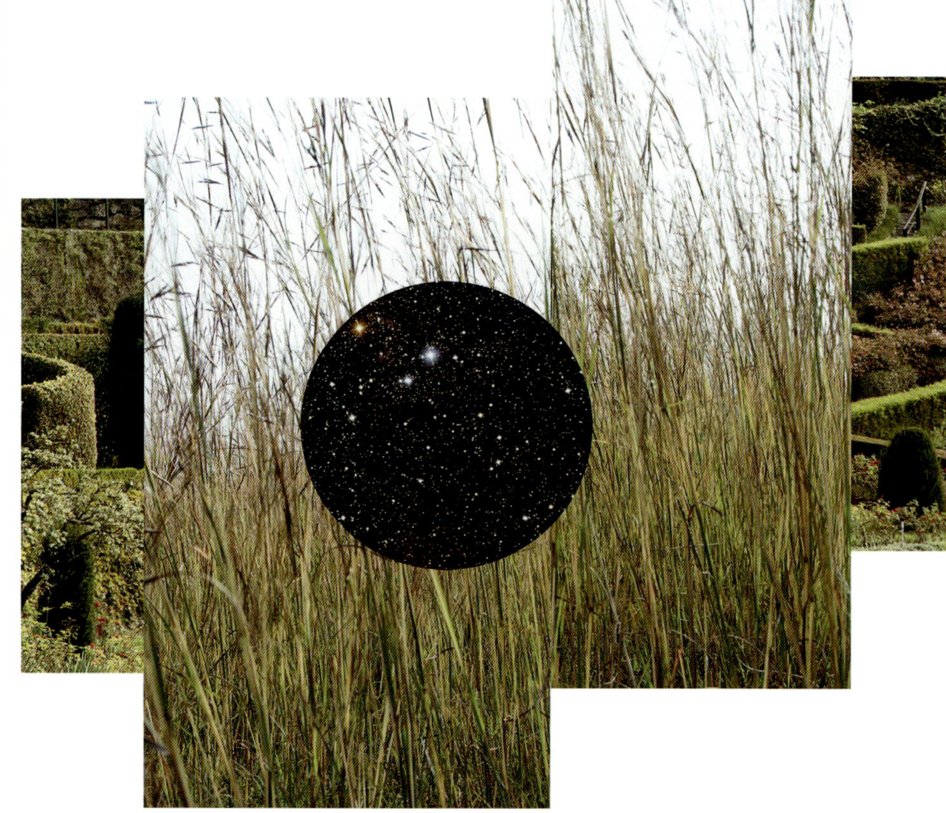

Untitled work in progress, 2018

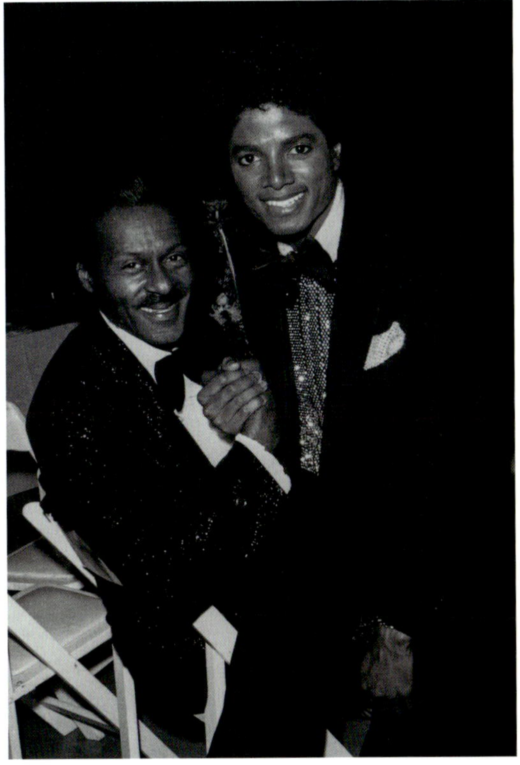

Source image for *Faustian Darkness*, 2014,
and *Pax 3*, 2017

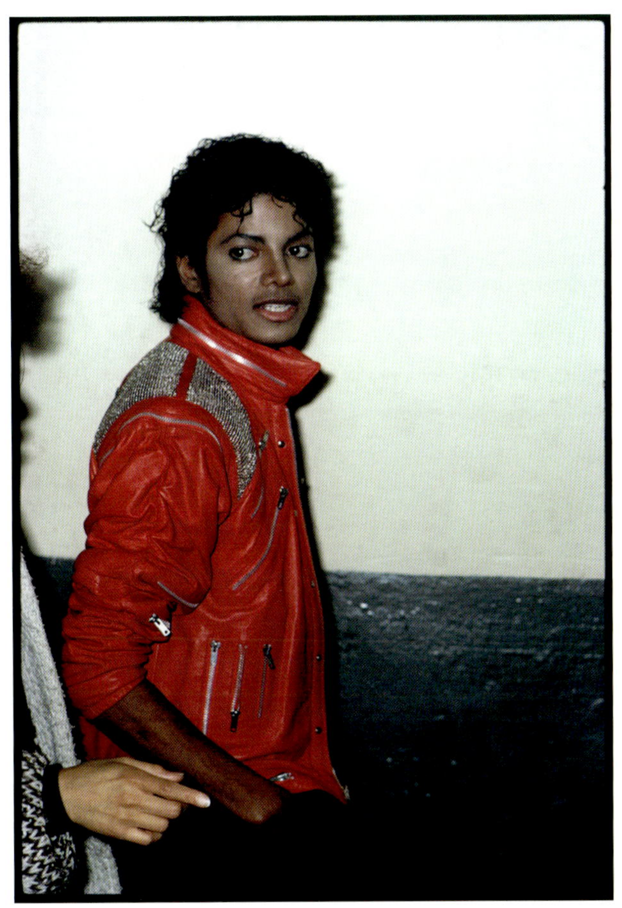

Source image for *Cape Coast* and *Nickel*,
both 2014, and *Euclidean Gris Gris*, 2018

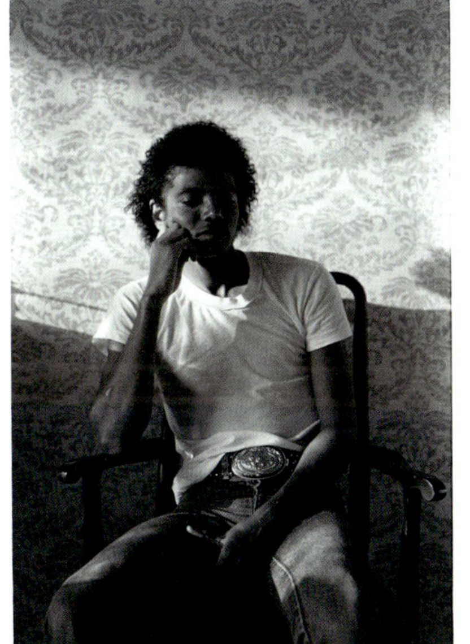

Source image for *Atlanta by
Boat*, 2015

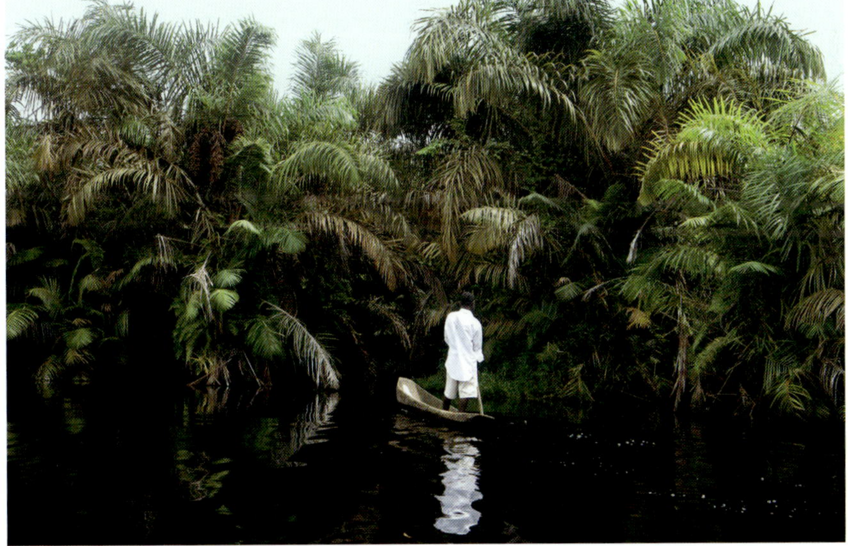

Nzulezo, Ghana, 2007

TODD GRAY

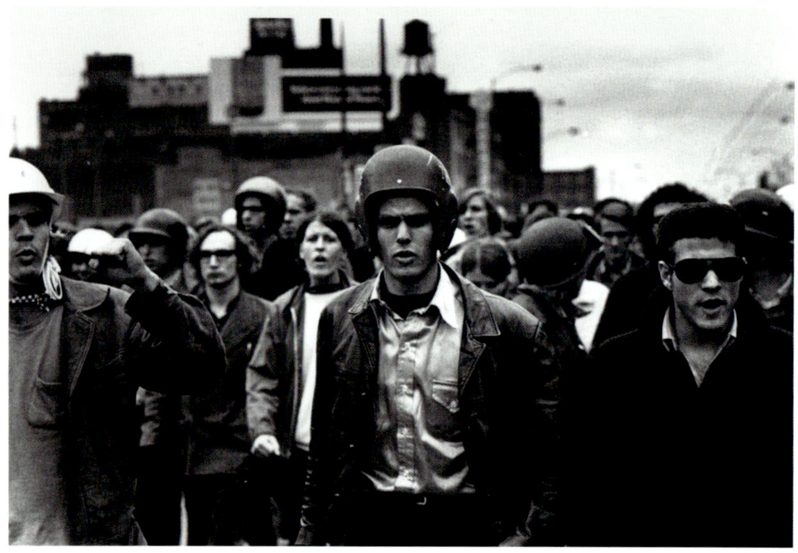

28

Archival material from *The Weather Underground*, 2003

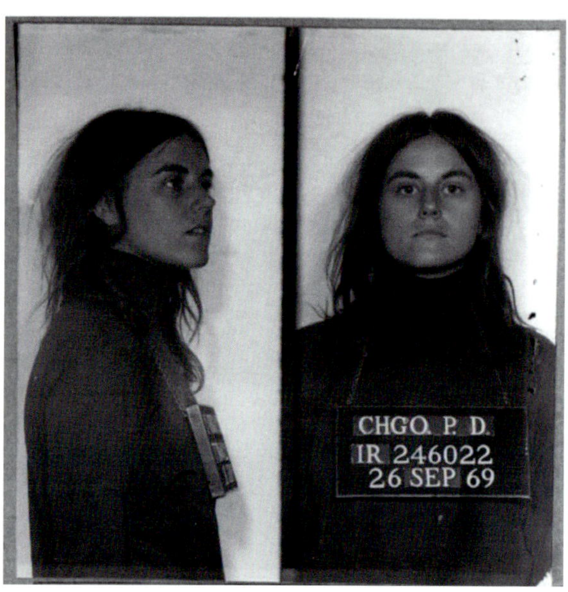

Archival material from *The Weather Underground*, 2003

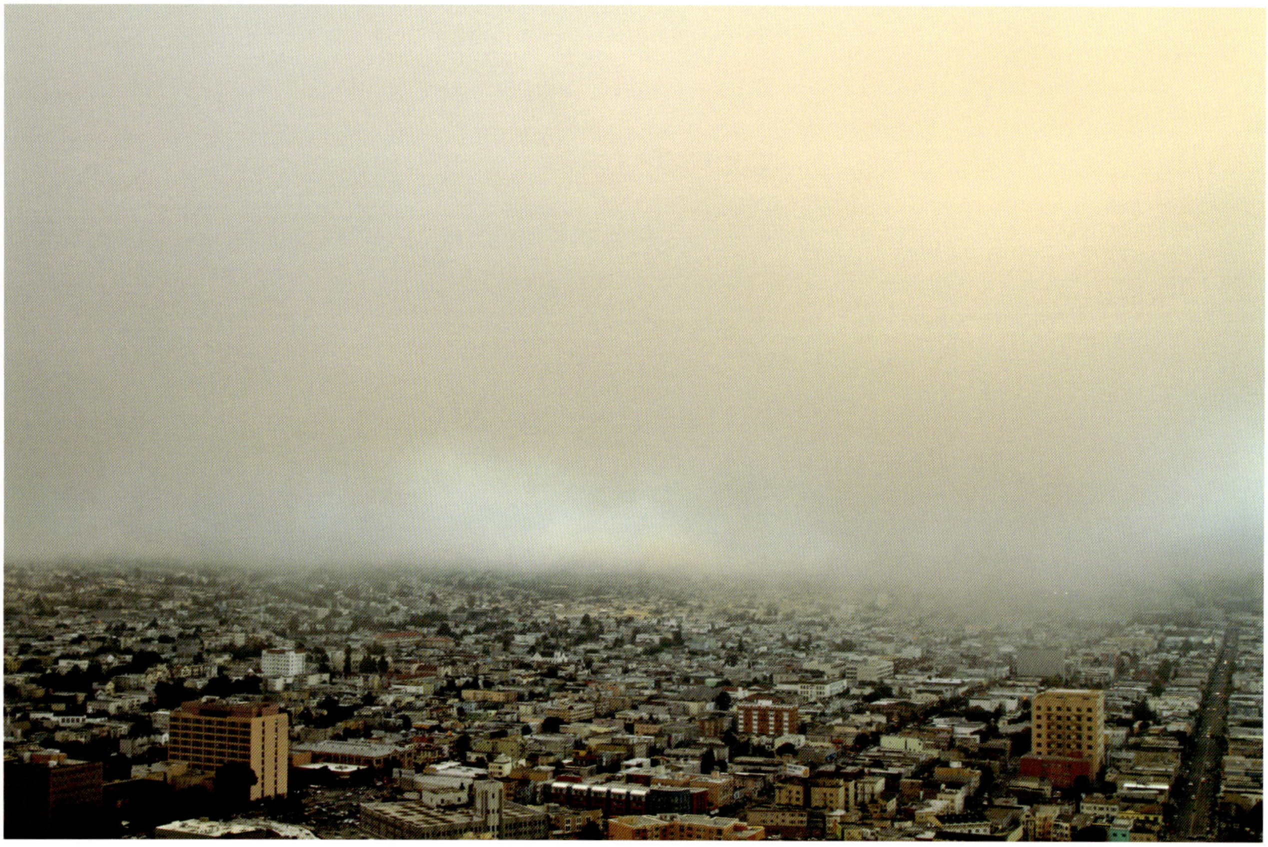

Test for *A Cinematic Study of Fog in San Francisco*, 2011

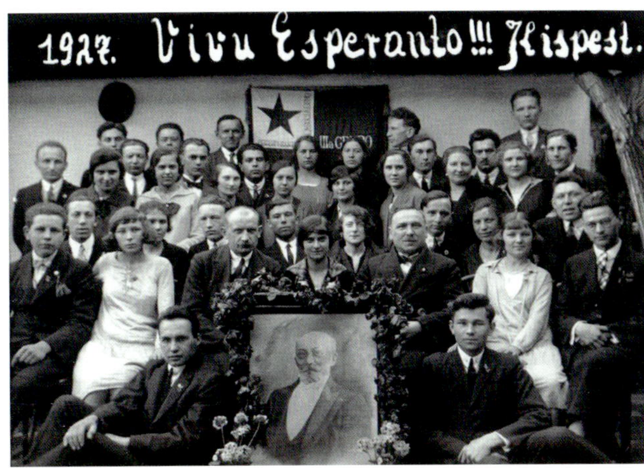

Archival material from *The Universal Language*, 2011

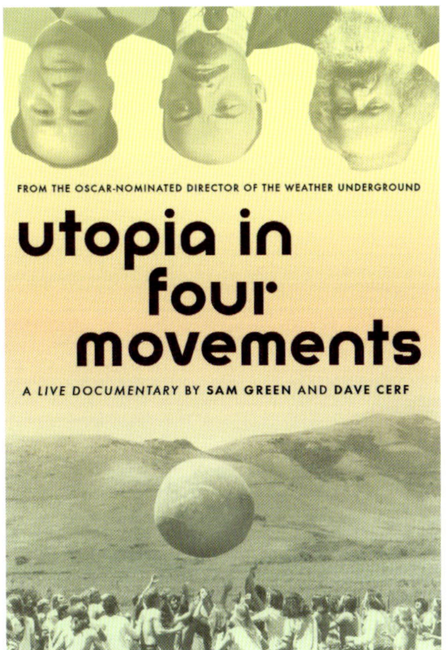

Promotional image for *Utopia in Four Movements*, 2010

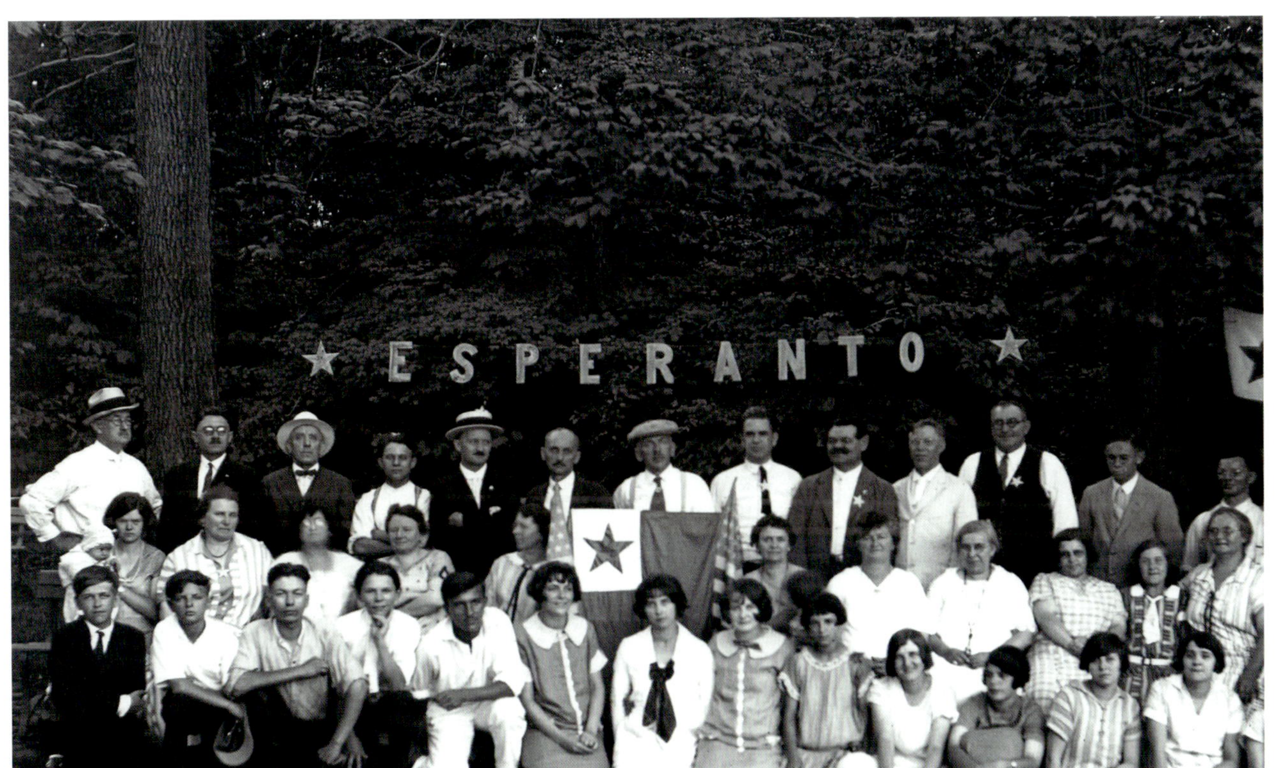

Archival material from *The Universal Language*, 2011

SAM GREEN

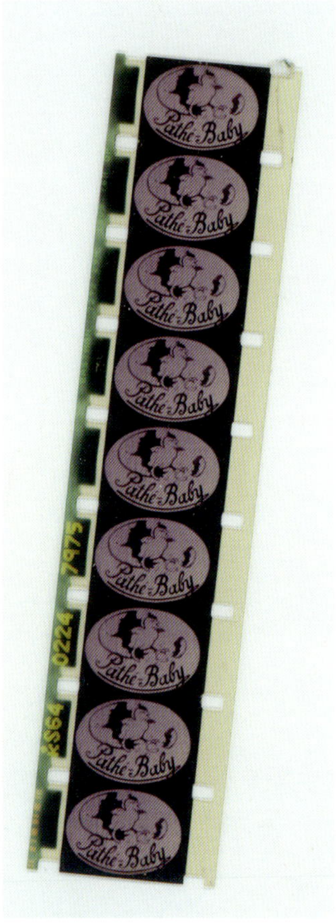

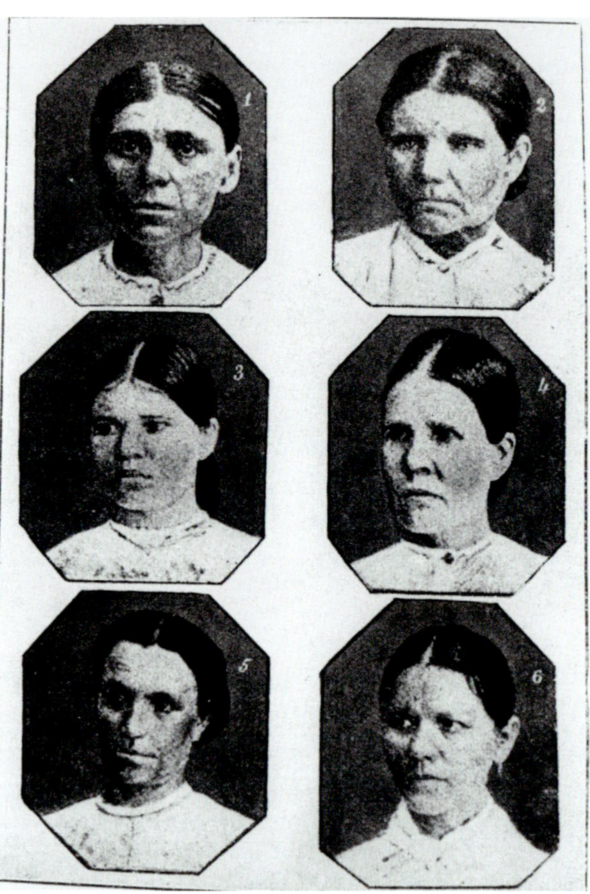

29

Filmstrip outtake from
History Lessons, 2000

Archival material from *History Lessons*, 2000

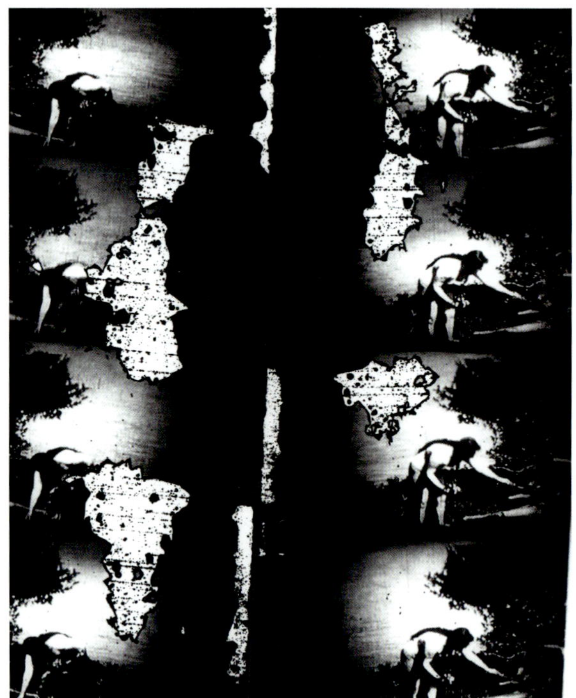

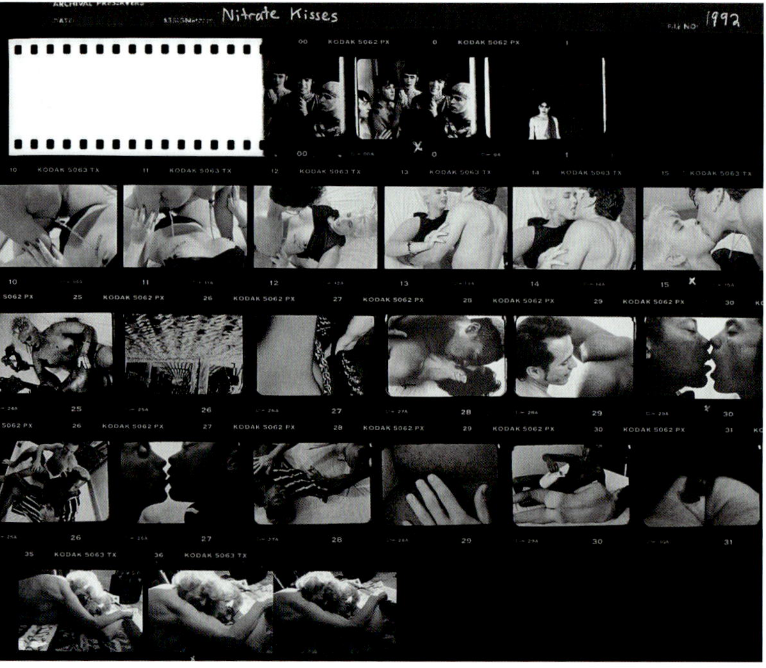

Archival material from *History Lessons*, 2000

Contact sheet for *Nitrate Kisses*, 1992

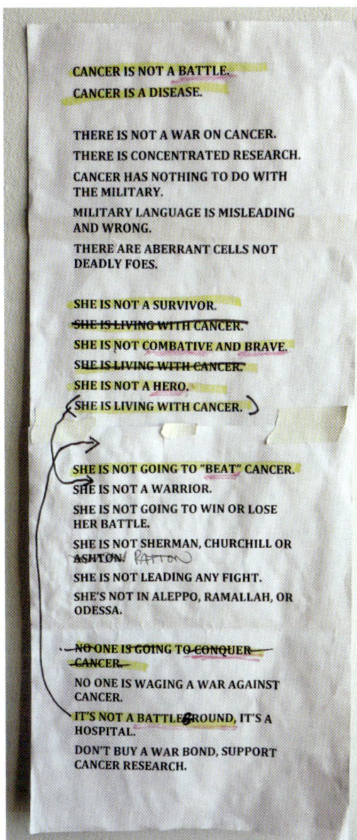

Text for performance of
Evidentiary Bodies, 2017

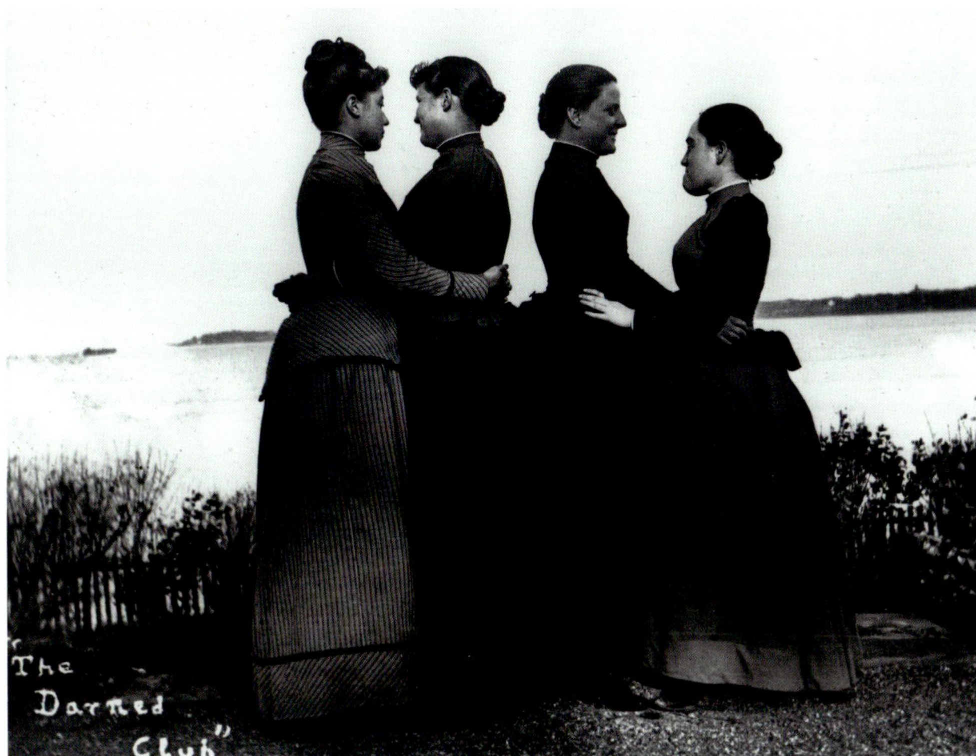

Alice Austen, *The Darned Club*, 1891. Source image for *The Female Closet*, 1998

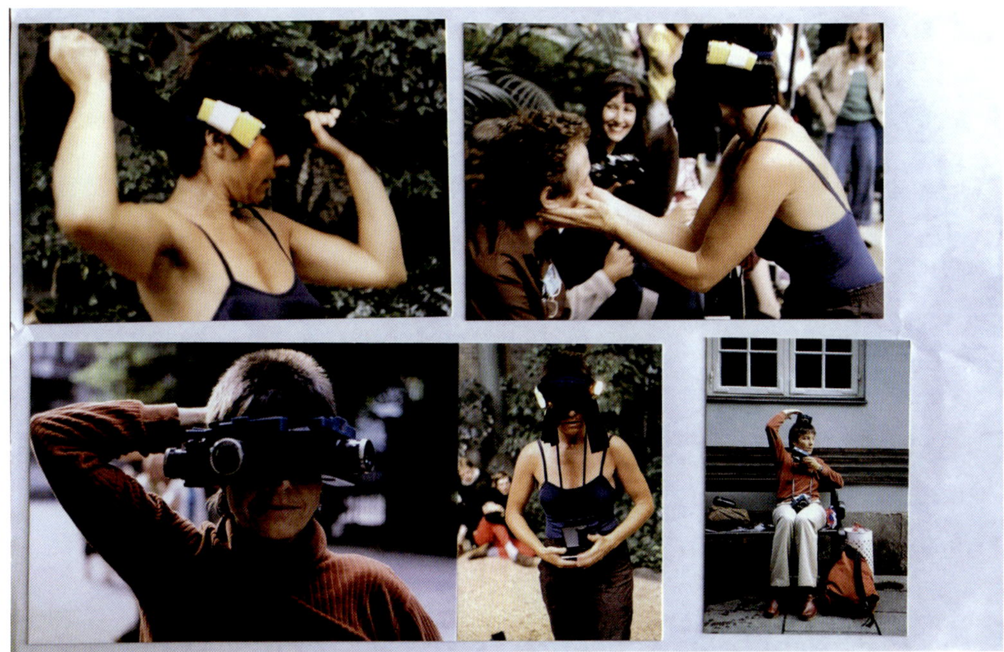

Performance worksheet for *Camerawoman*, 1985

BARBARA HAMMER

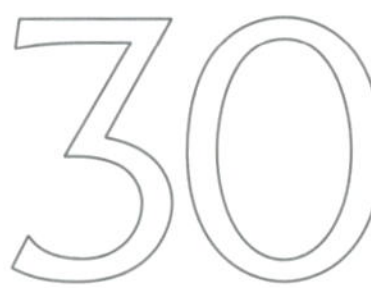

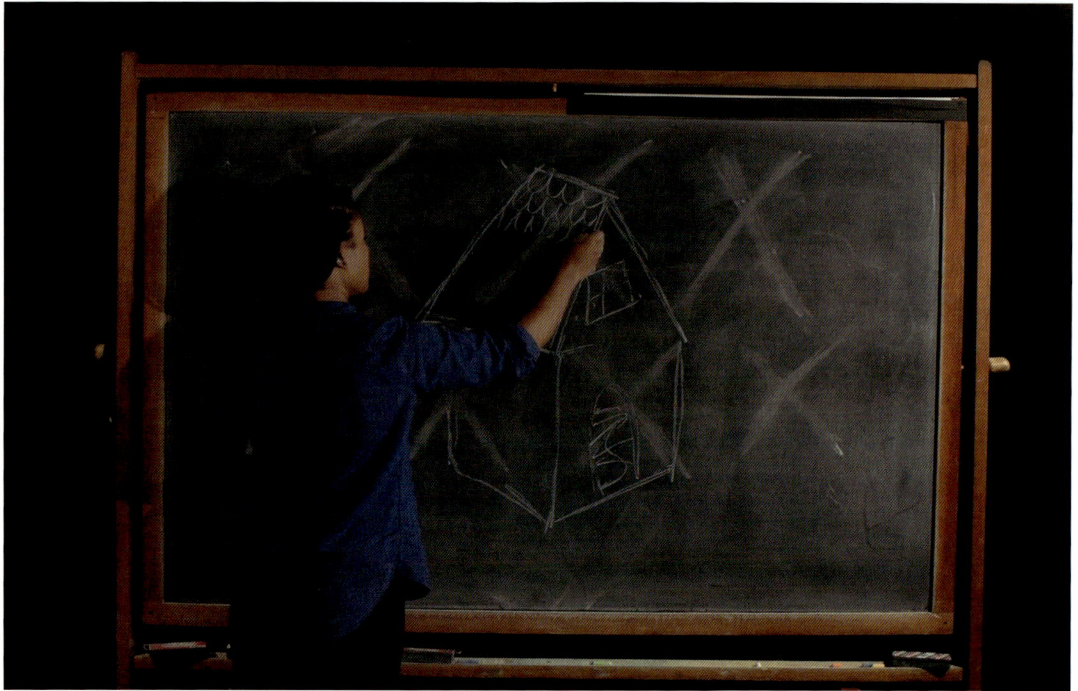

30

Outtake from *Reparation Hardware*, 2018

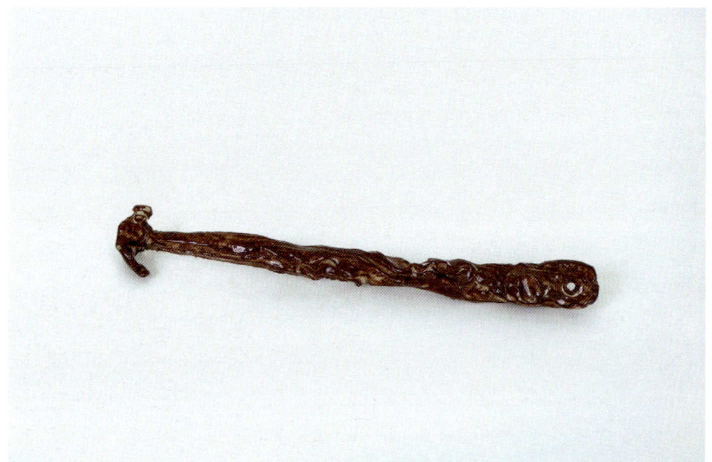

Prop for *Reparation Hardware*, 2018

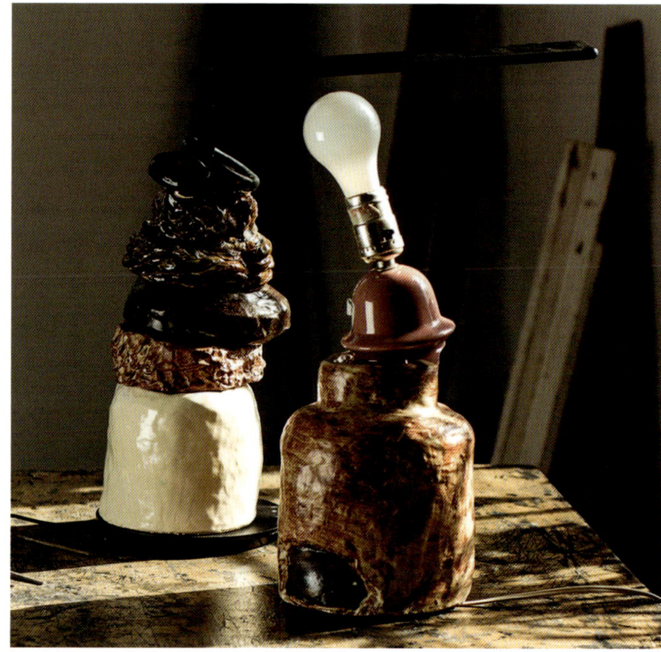

Studio, Williamstown, MA, 2018

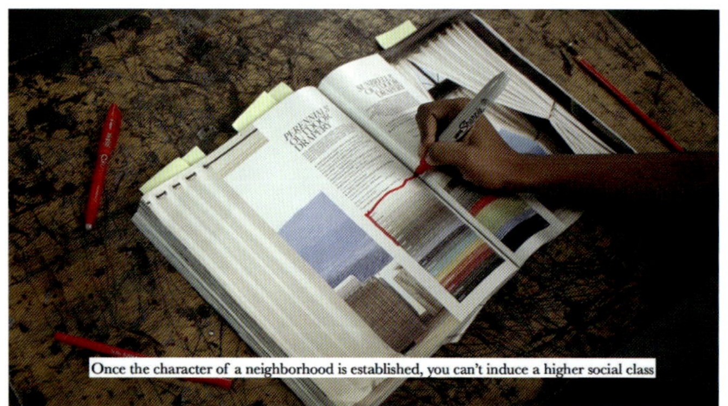

Outtake from *Red Sourcebook*, 2018

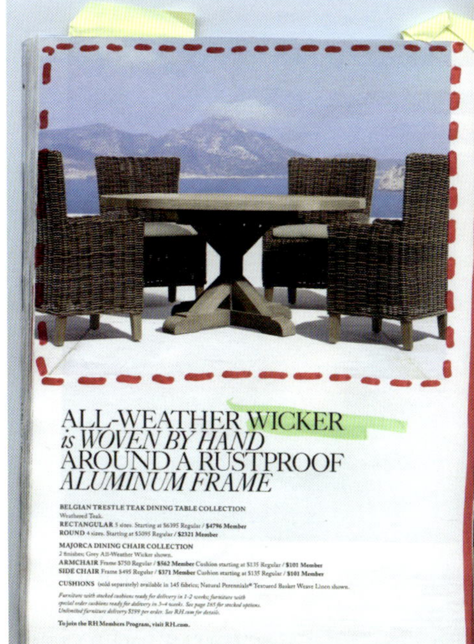

Sketch for *Red Sourcebook* on page from Restoration Hardware catalogue, 2018

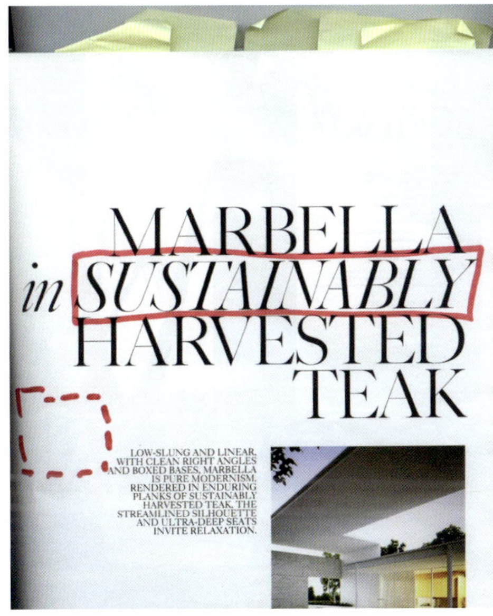

Sketch for *Red Sourcebook* on page from Restoration Hardware catalogue, 2018

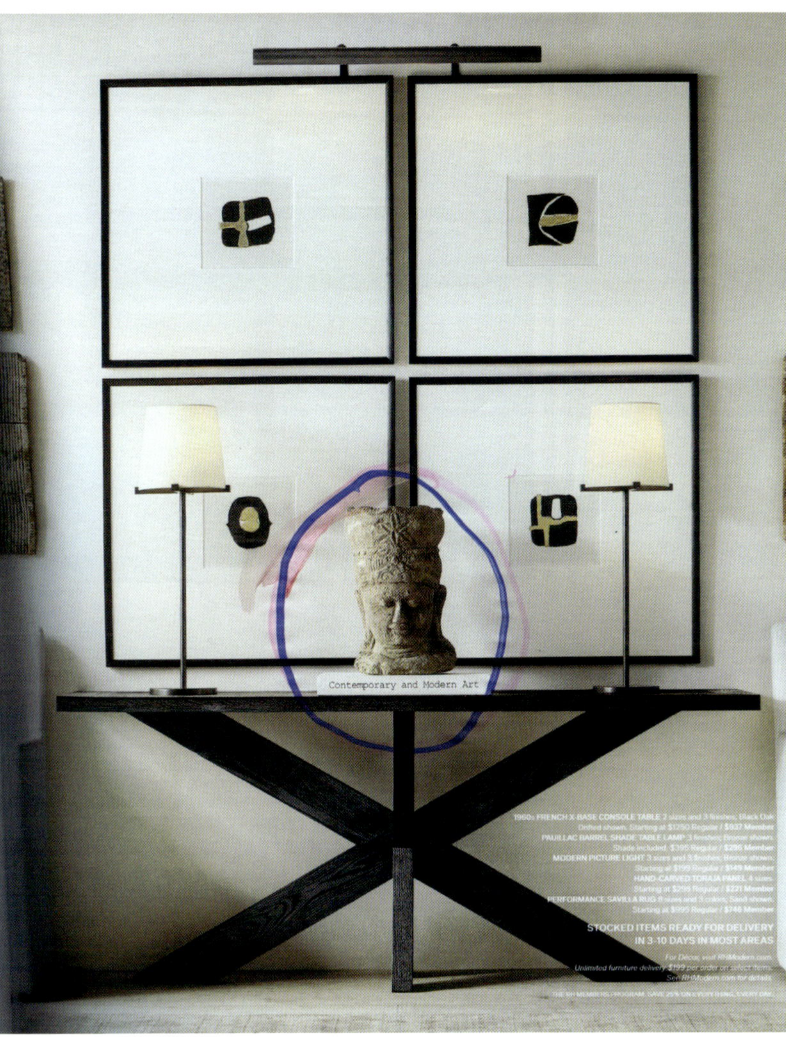

Sketch for *Human Design* on page from Restoration Hardware catalogue, 2018

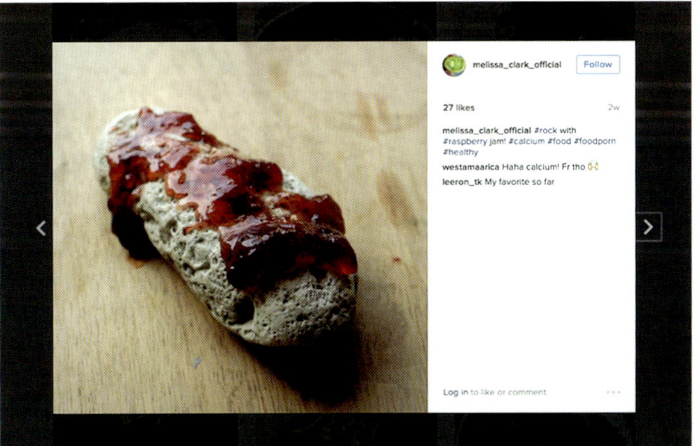

Screenshot of the artist's Instagram account, 2016

ILANA HARRIS-BABOU

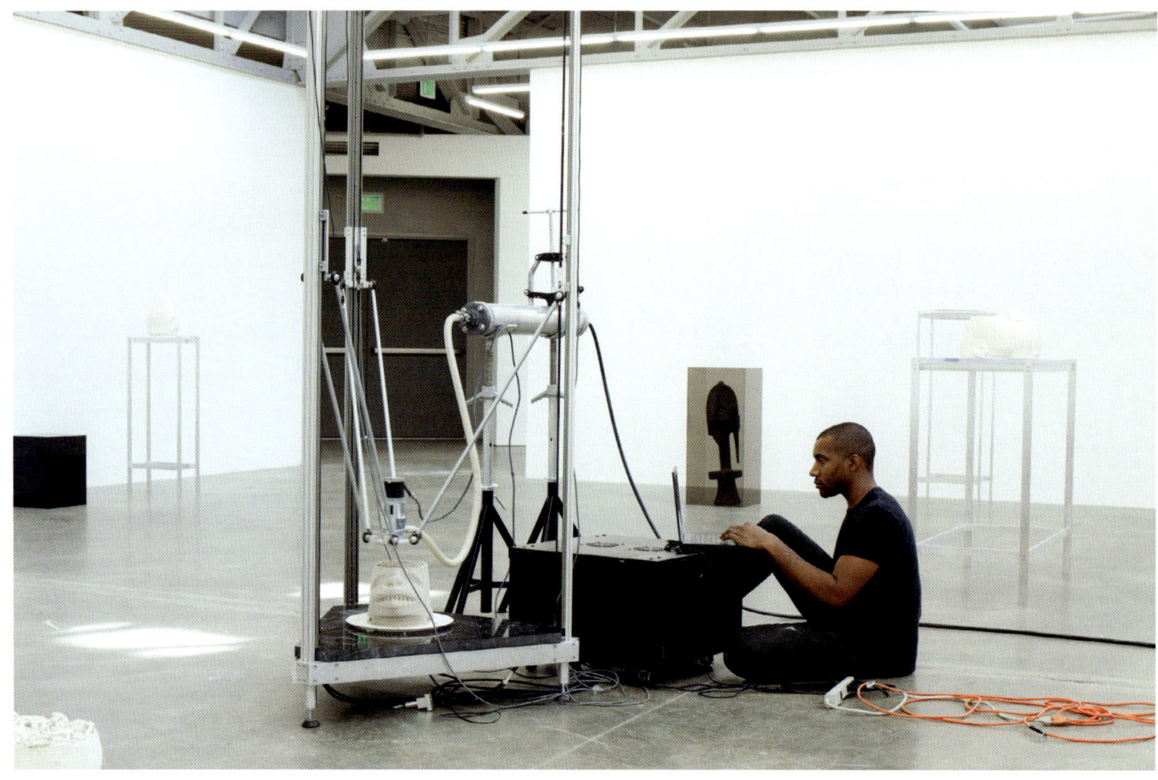

31

The artist 3-D printing for *Dark Povera Part 1*, Atlanta Contemporary, Atlanta, GA, 2017

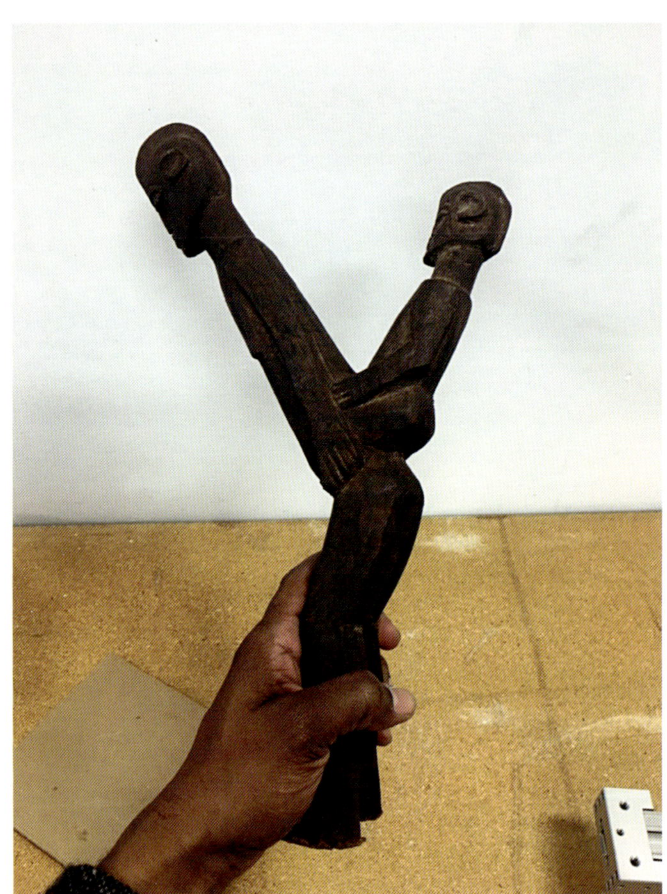

Lobi maternity sculpture, 2018

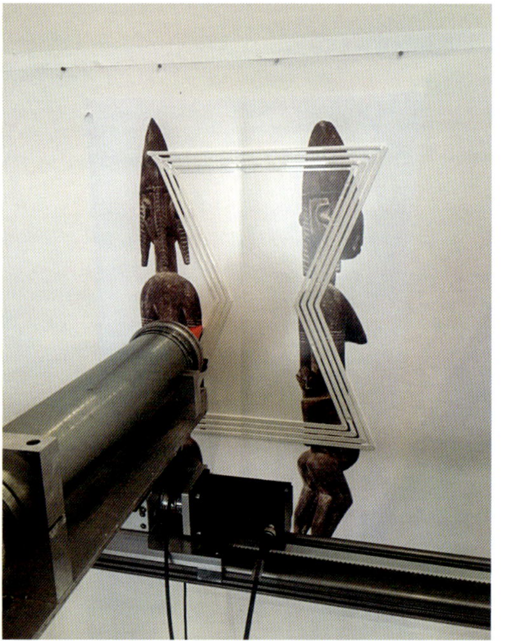

3-D printing for *Abstract Ancestry: Machine Works on Paper*, University of Michigan Institute for the Humanities, Ann Arbor, 2018

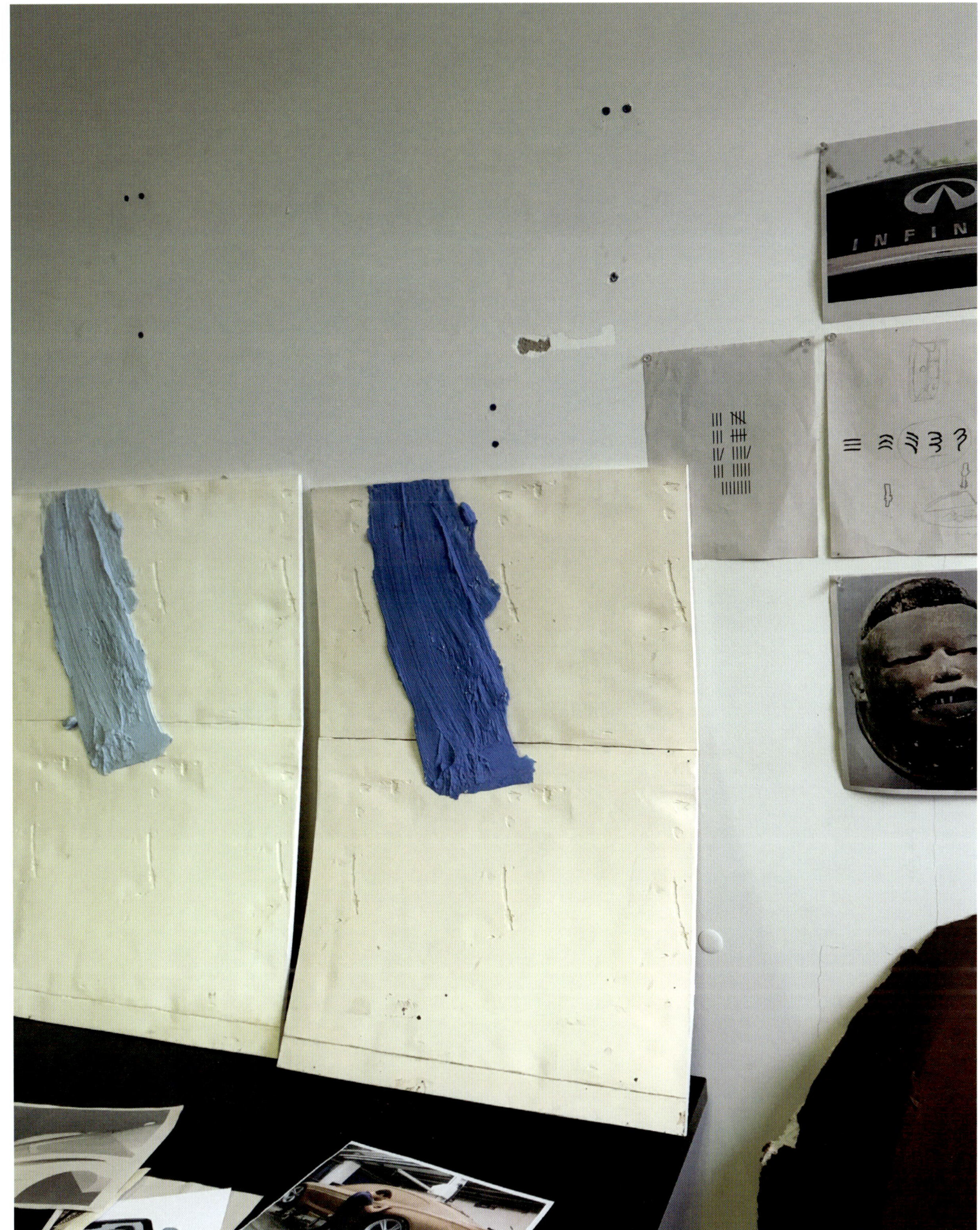

Studio, Detroit, MI, 2018

MATTHEW ANGELO HARRISON

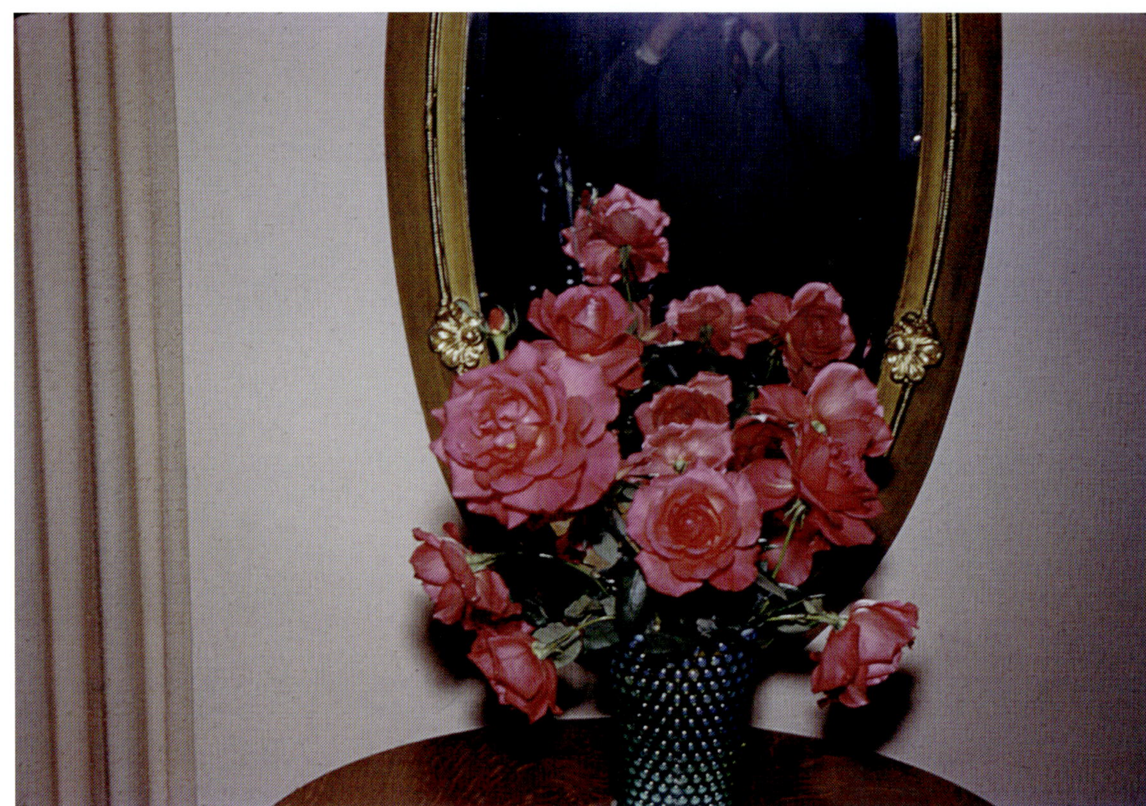

32

Family photograph taken by Martha Hatleberg, date unknown

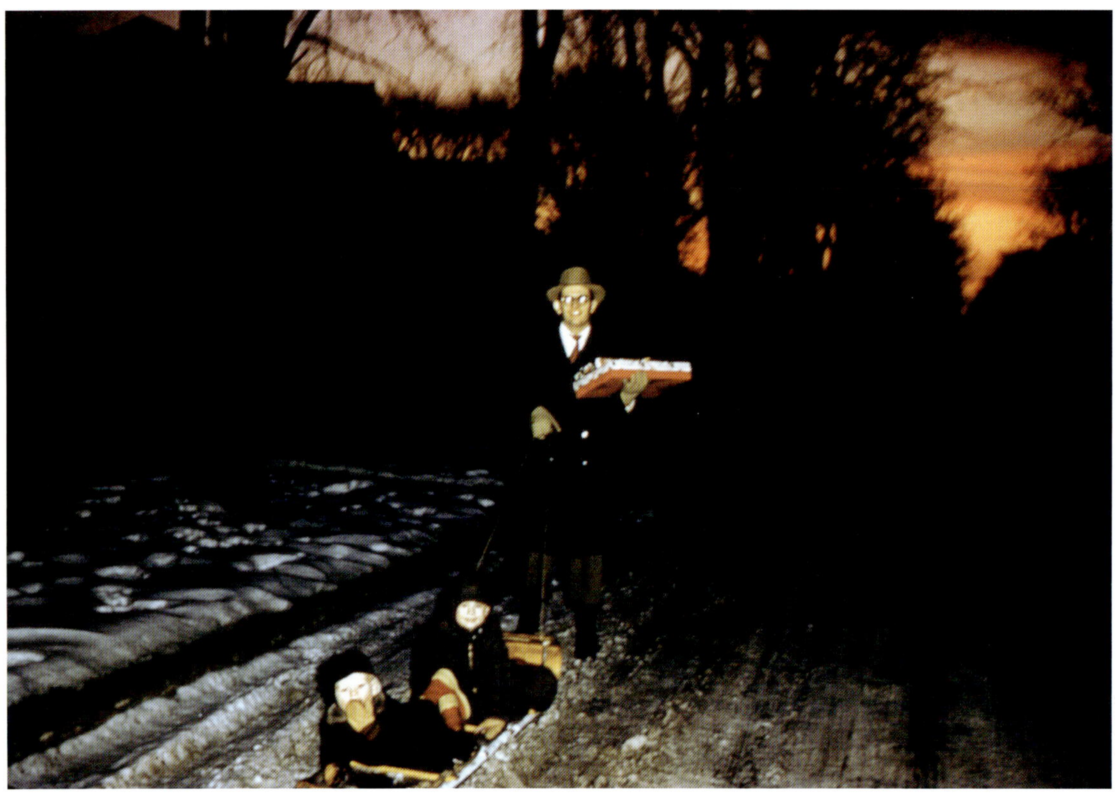

Family photograph taken by Martha Hatleberg, date unknown

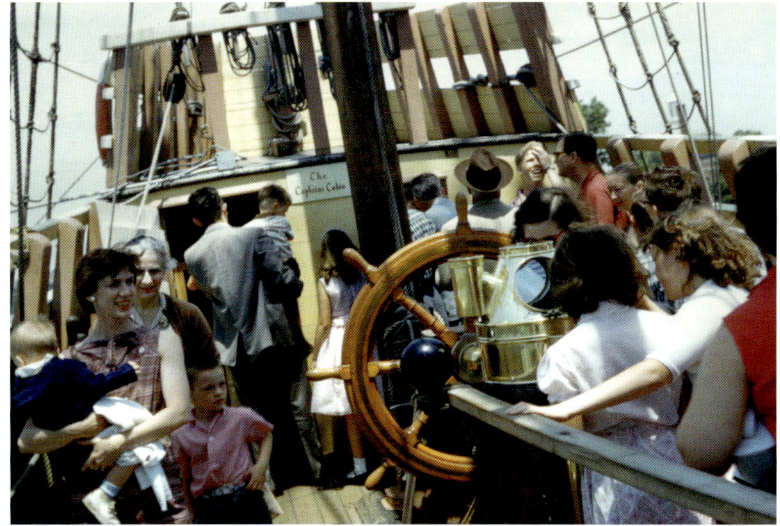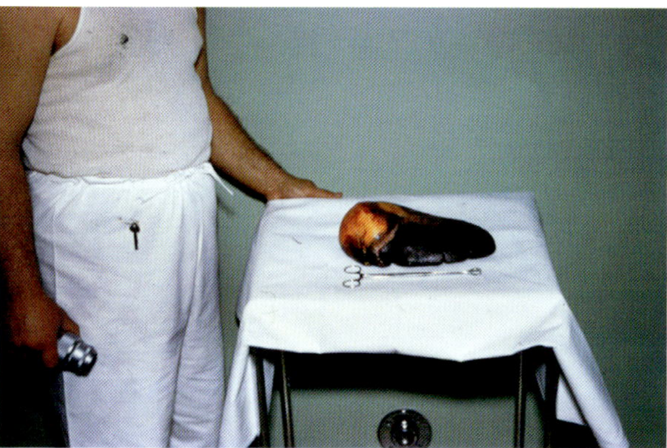

Family photograph taken by Martha Hatleberg, date unknown

Family photograph taken by Martha Hatleberg, date unknown

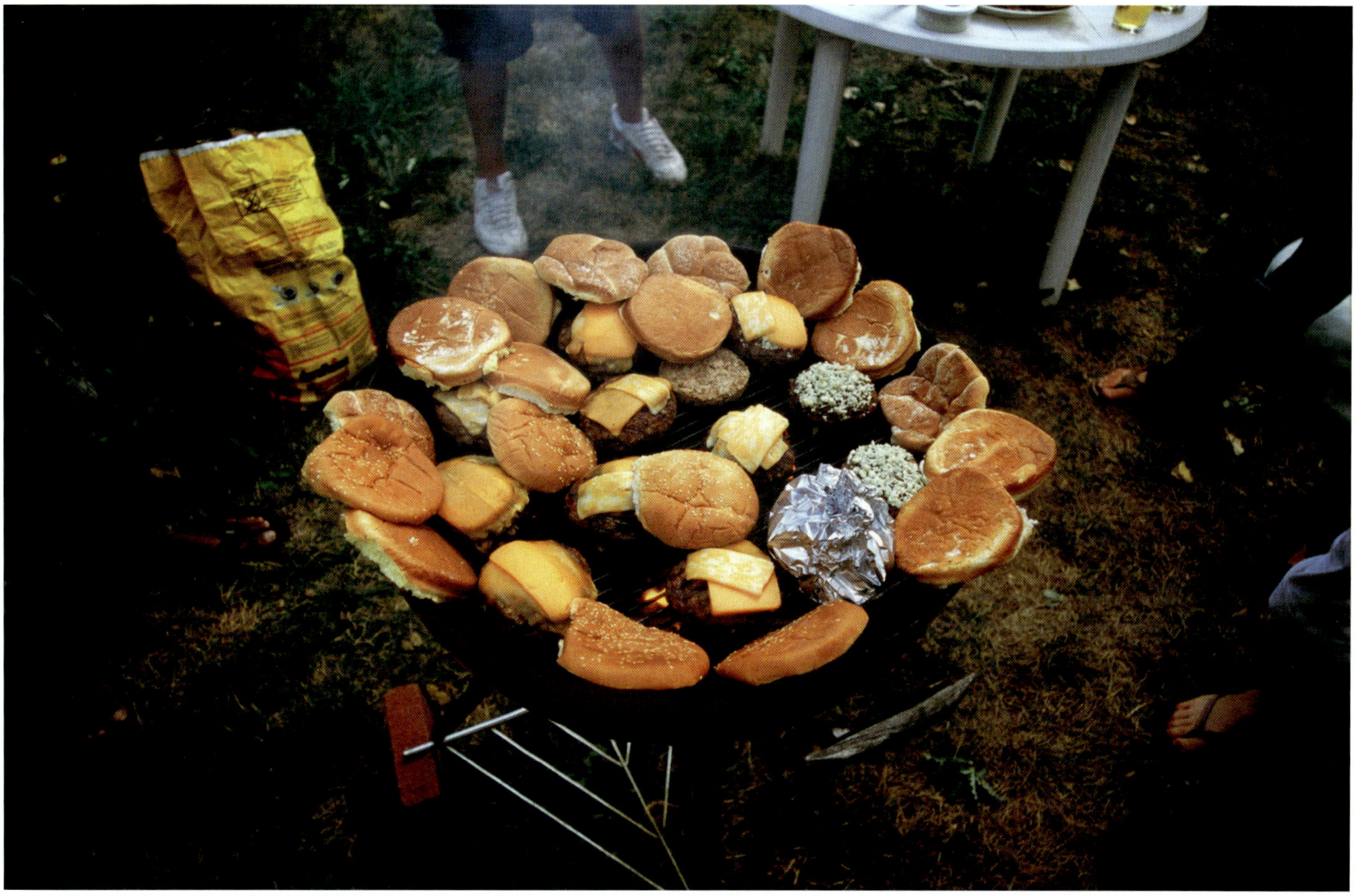

Family photograph taken by Curran Hatleberg, date unknown

CURRAN HATLEBERG

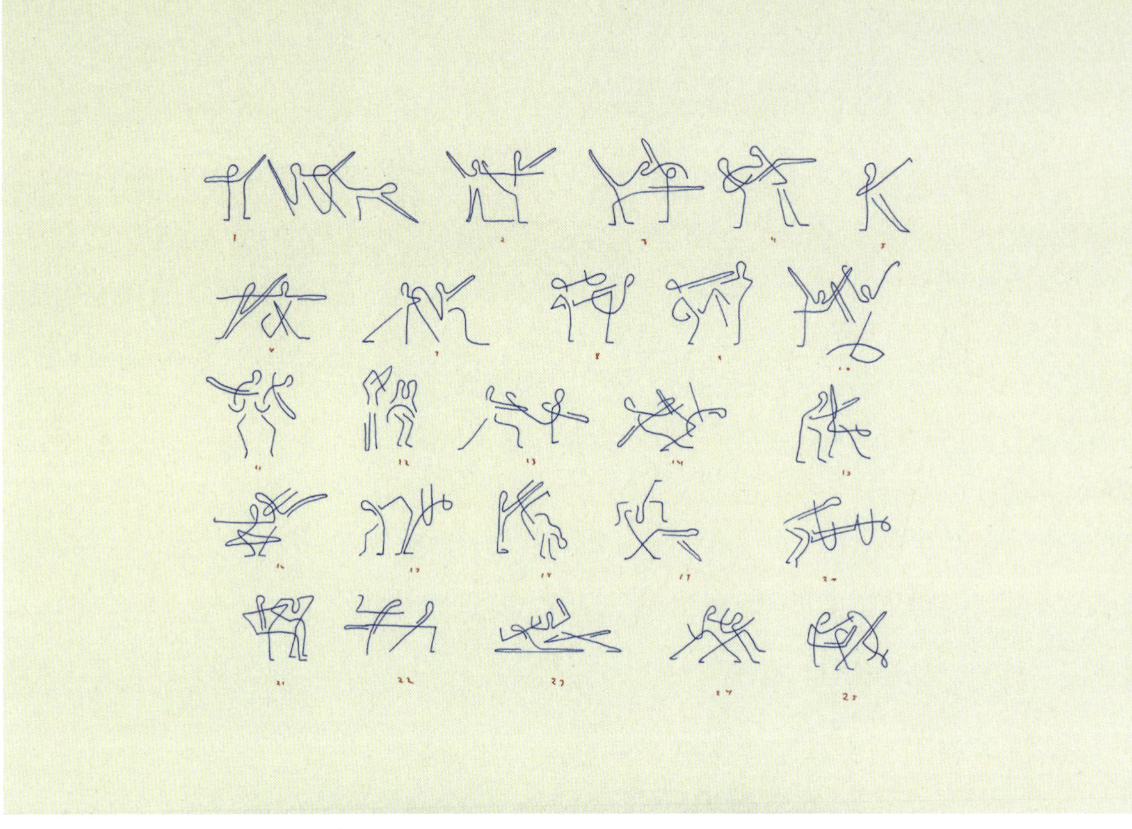

Pas de Deux 2, 2017. Drawing for *Competition*, 2017

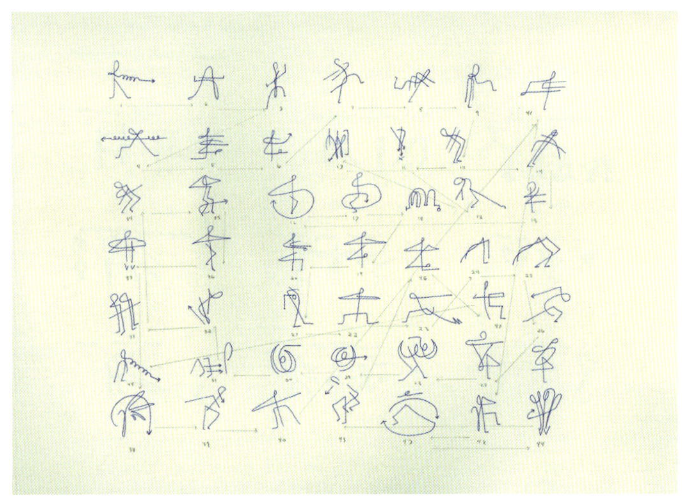

Notation #3, 2017. Drawing for *Competition*, 2017

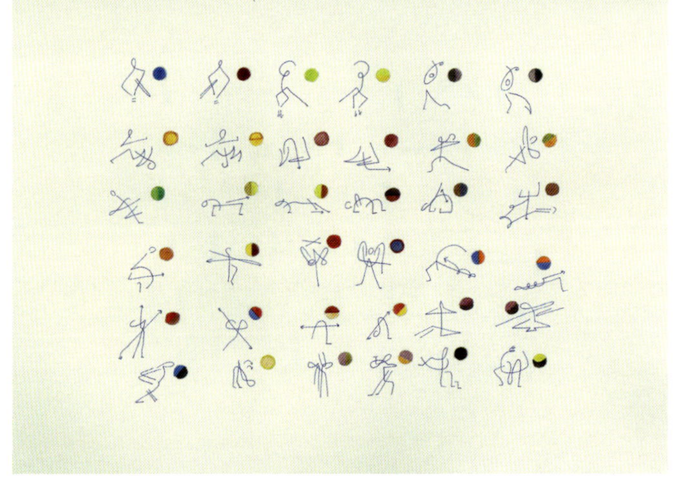

Solo Sequence Notation #1 with Directions, 2017.
Drawing for *Competition*, 2017

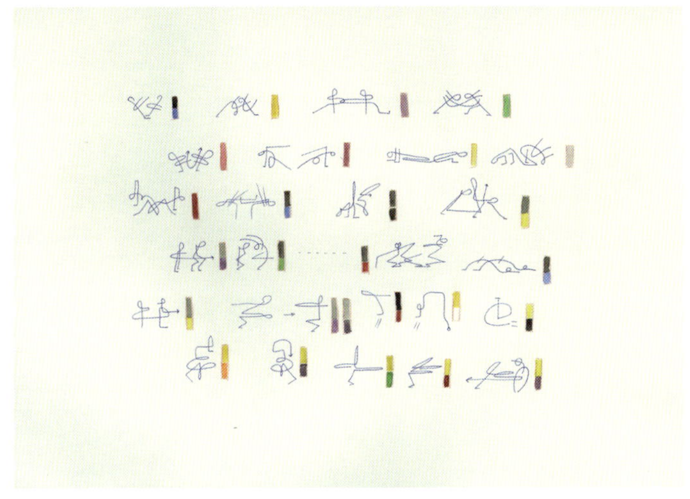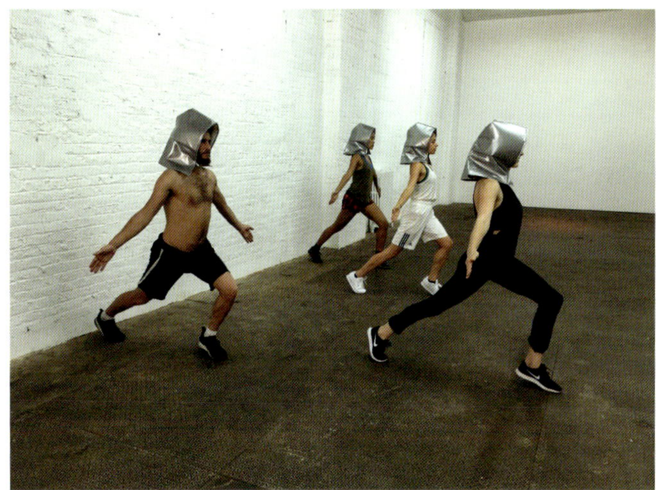

Palindrome Duet, 2017. Drawing for *Competition*, 2017

Drill, 2016. Performance view, Signal, Brooklyn, NY, 2016

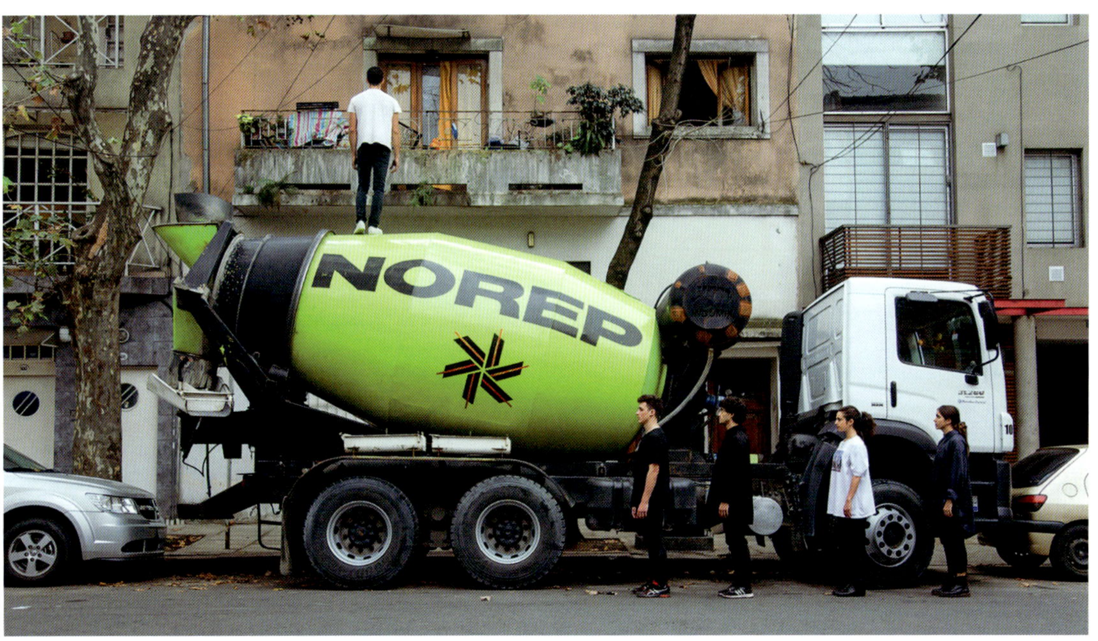

365, 2017. Performance view, Slyzmud, Buenos Aires, Argentina, 2017

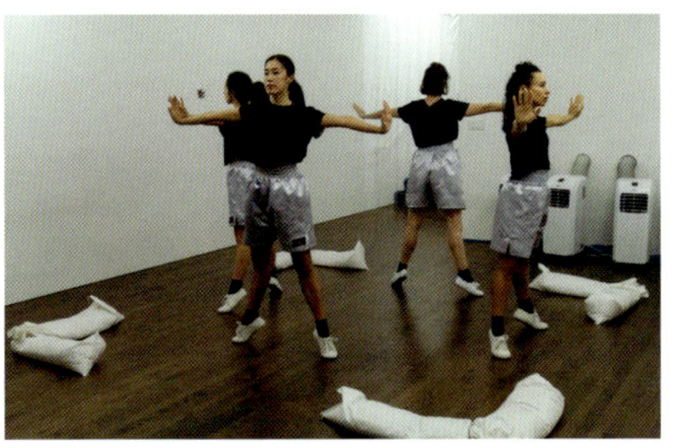

New Max, 2018. Performance view,
Artist's Institute, New York, NY, 2018

MADELINE HOLLANDER

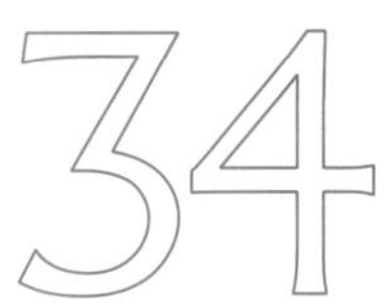

34

HS3
Green Crescent Crowning the Top of a 9th Century Dome
Crescent believed to have been added to the dome upon the city's conquest.
The Regional Museum of Arts and Culture Collection
Marble
69 ⅝ x 66 inches
A.D. 813 (dome) / A.D. 1225 (crescent)

Detail of *Heritage Studies #3, 2015*

HS8
Remains from the Walls of the Second Court
The Second Court was commissioned by the last king of Dynasty XIX to replace
the First Court. It marks the last known addition to the Great Temple.
The International Museum of Ancient Arts and Culture Collection
Limestone
78 x 220 feet
1257 B.C.

Detail of *Heritage Studies #8*, 2015

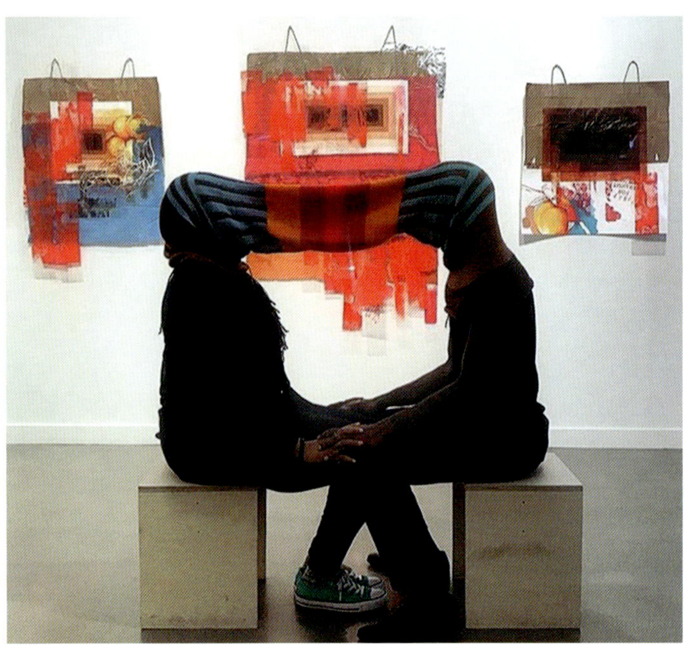

35

Color Study: Two Blues, 2018, worn by the artist and Alteronce Gumby

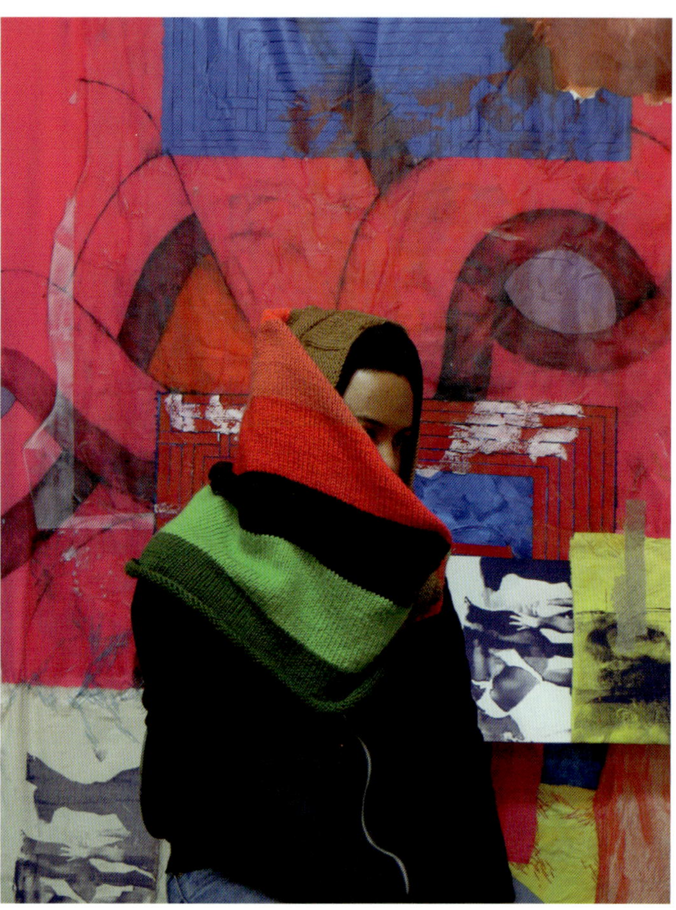

Color Study in 3 Reds, 2 Blacks, 2 Greens, 2016 (worn by Eric N. Mack) in front of *Dajerria All Alone (Bolling v. Sharpe (District of Columbia)) (McKinney Pool Party)*, 2016

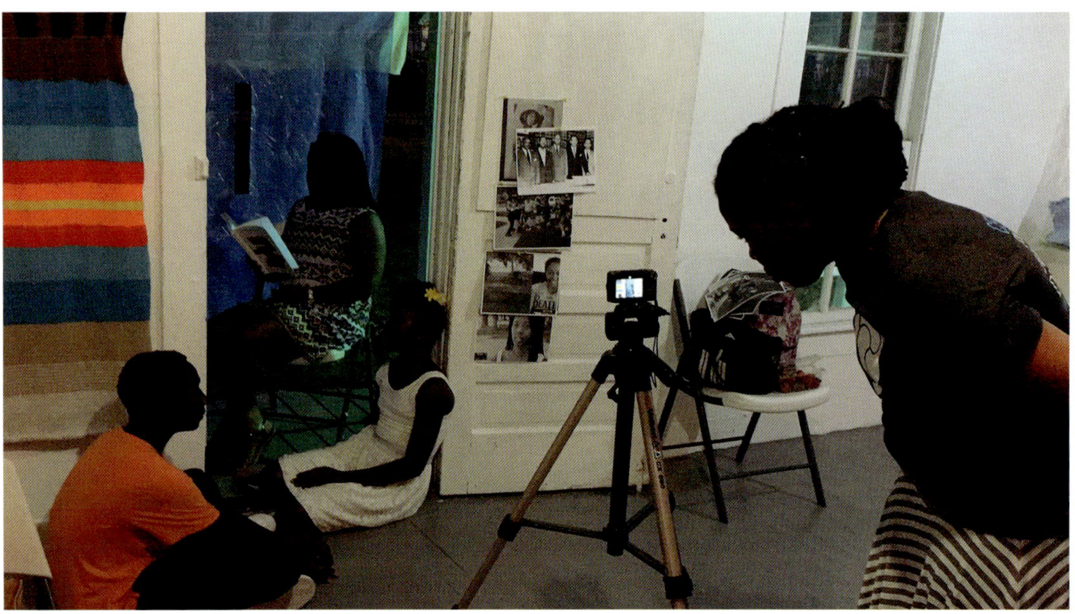

Production still from *Vibrating Boundaries (The Law of the Land)*, 1963–2015, 2015

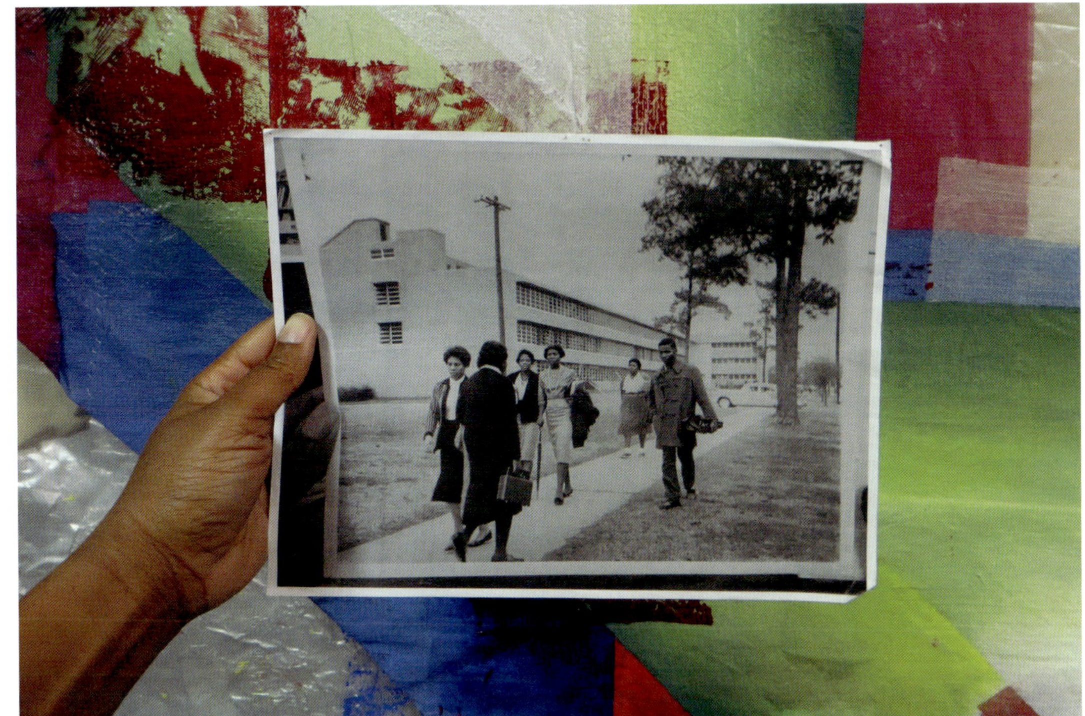

The artist holding a photo of Texas Southern University for Negroes in front of
Avocado Seed Soup (Davis, et al. v. County School Board of Prince Edward County)
(Brown, et al. v. Board of Education of Topeka) (Sweatt v. Painter), 2016

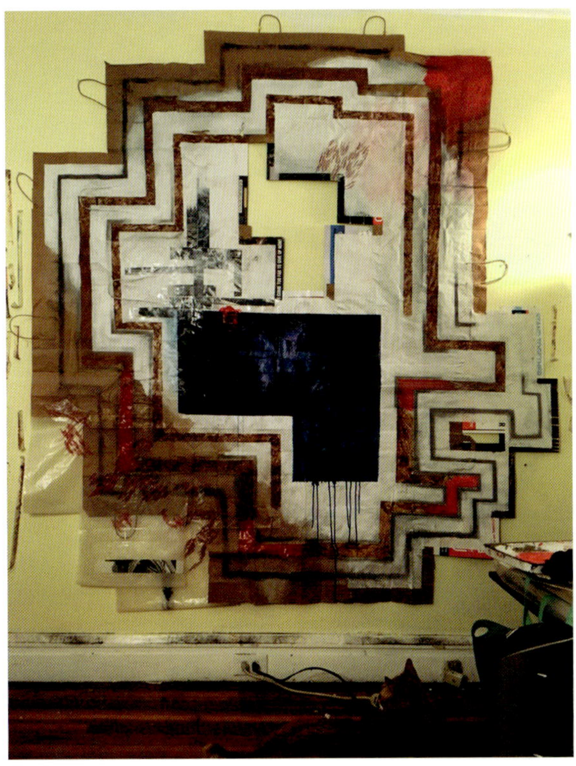

Still Remains (work in progress), studio, New York,
NY, 2017

TOMASHI JACKSON

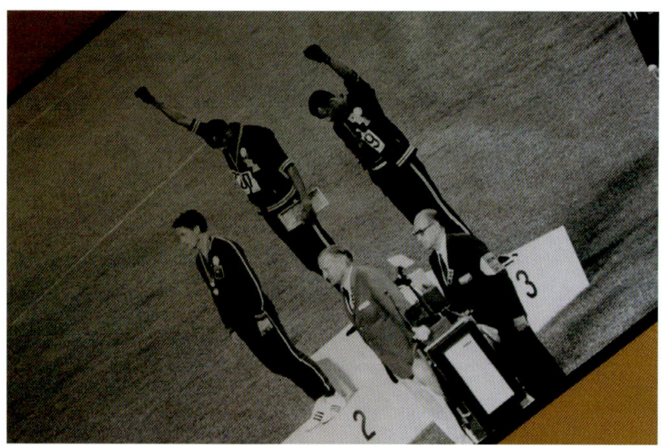

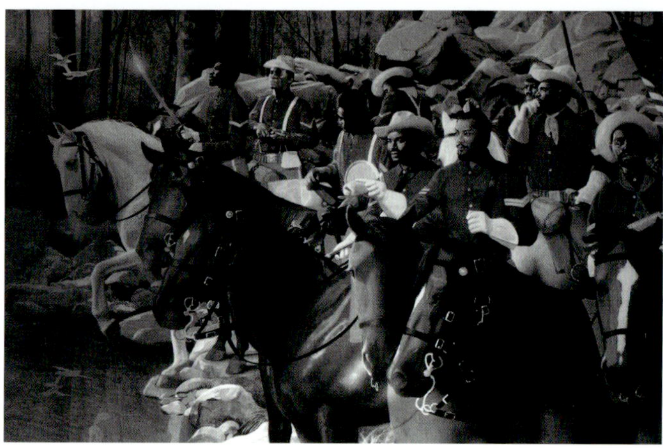

Photograph from home of Reverend Susan Webb, New York, NY, 2017. Process image for *Sensus Plenior*, 2017

Photograph from home of Reverend Susan Webb, New York, NY, 2017. Process image for *Sensus Plenior*, 2017

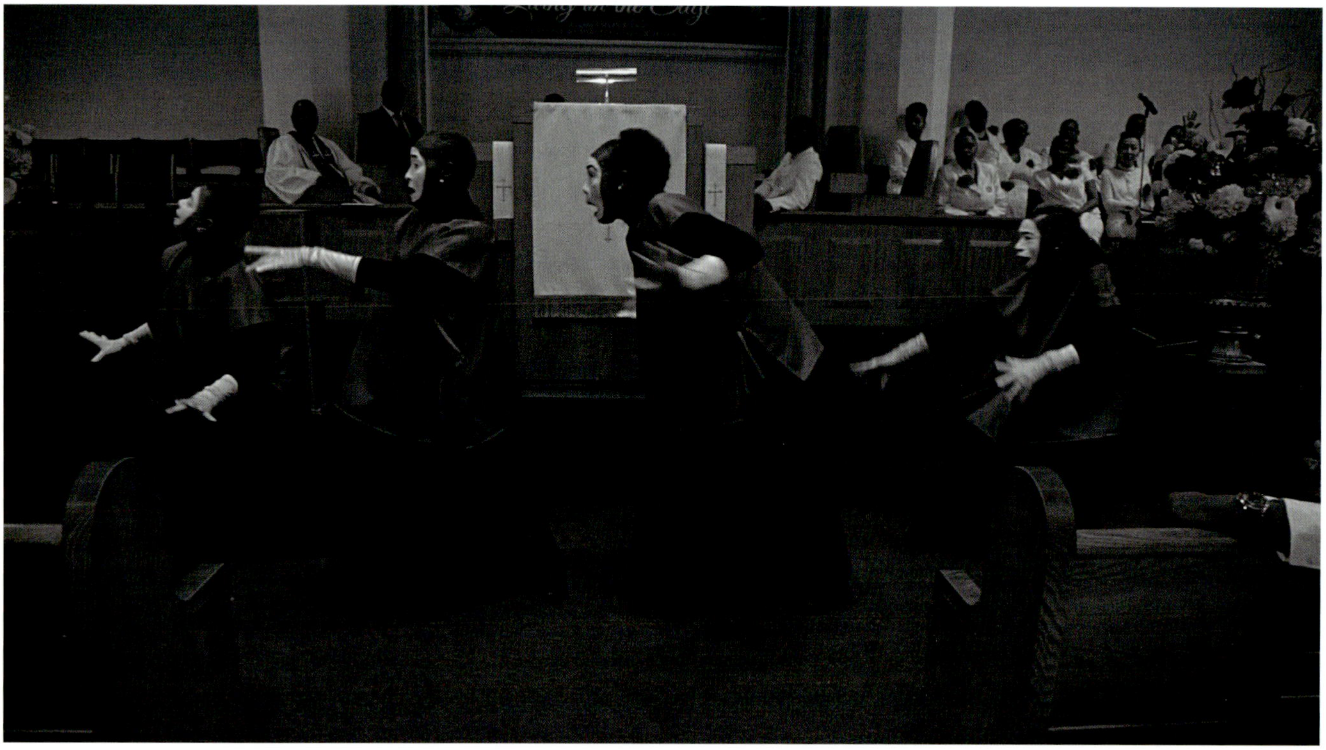

Master Mime Ministry of Harlem at Memorial Baptist Church, New York, NY, 2017. Process image for *Sensus Plenior*, 2017

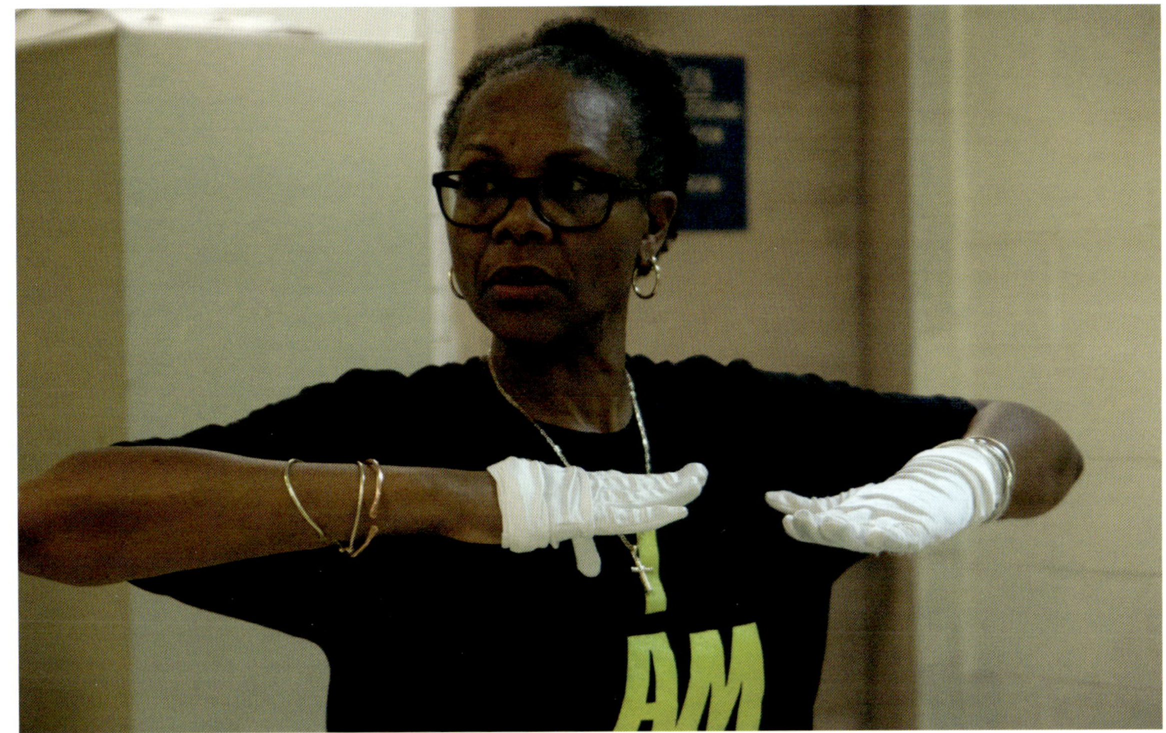

Reverend Susan Webb rehearsing for Master Mime Ministry of Harlem performance, Church of the Master, New York, NY, 2017. Process image for *Sensus Plenior*, 2017

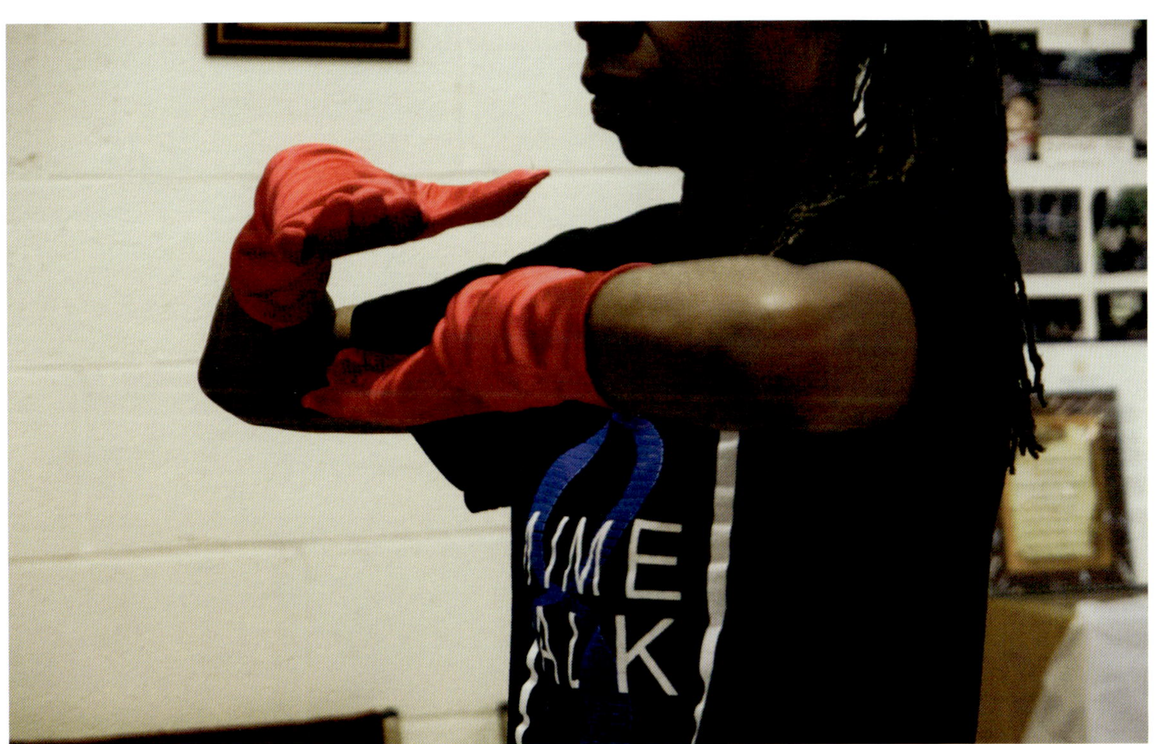

Doris Collins rehearsing for Master Mime Ministry of Harlem performance, Church of the Master, New York, NY, 2017. Process image for *Sensus Plenior*, 2017

STEFFANI JEMISON

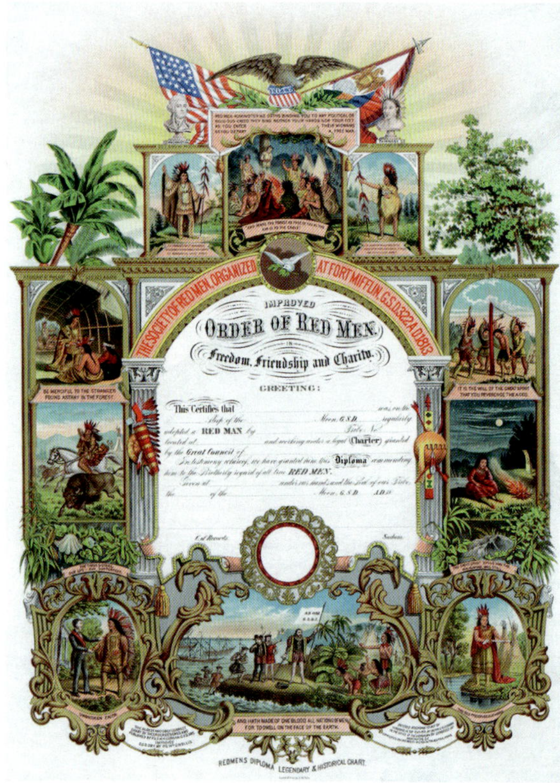

37

Redmens Diploma Legendary & Historical Chart,
Improved Order of Red Men, 1889

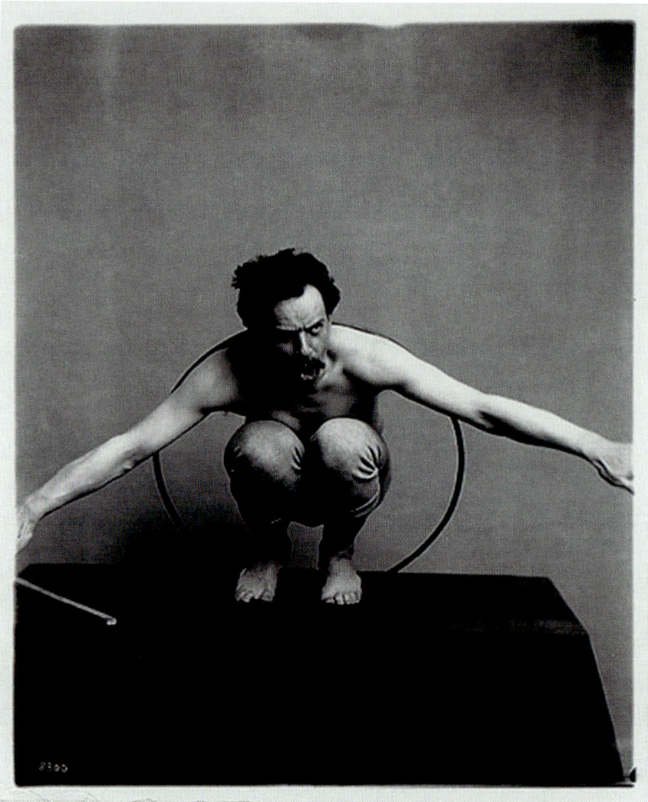

Franz Boas posing for figure in *Hamats'a coming out
of secret room*, National Museum of Natural History,
Washington, DC, 1895 or before

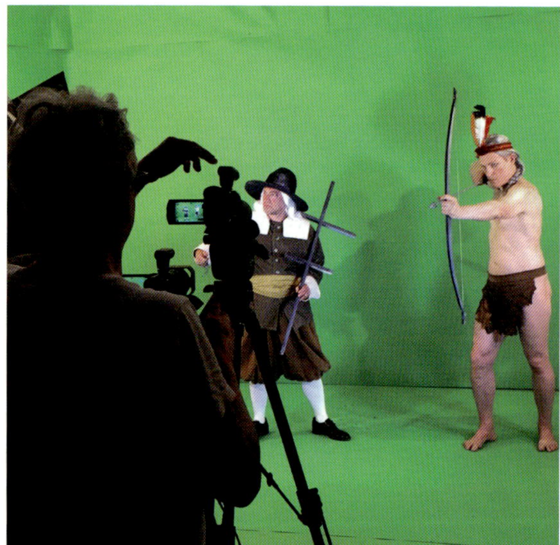

Production still from *City Seal*, 2018

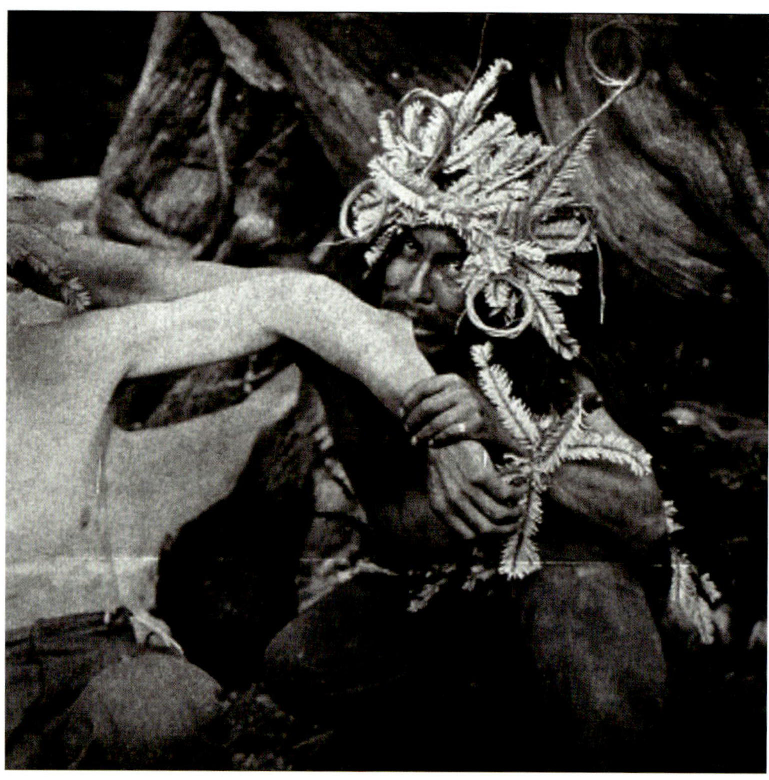

Hamatsa biting Koskimo, c. 1910

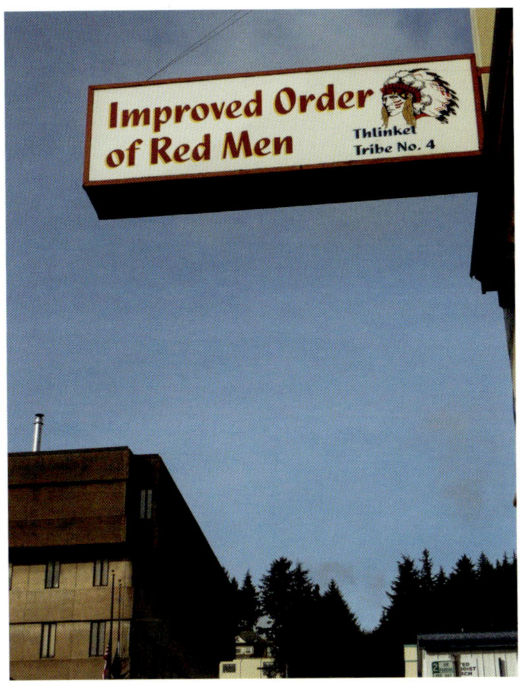

Sign for Improved Order of Red Men,
Ketchikan, AK, 2018

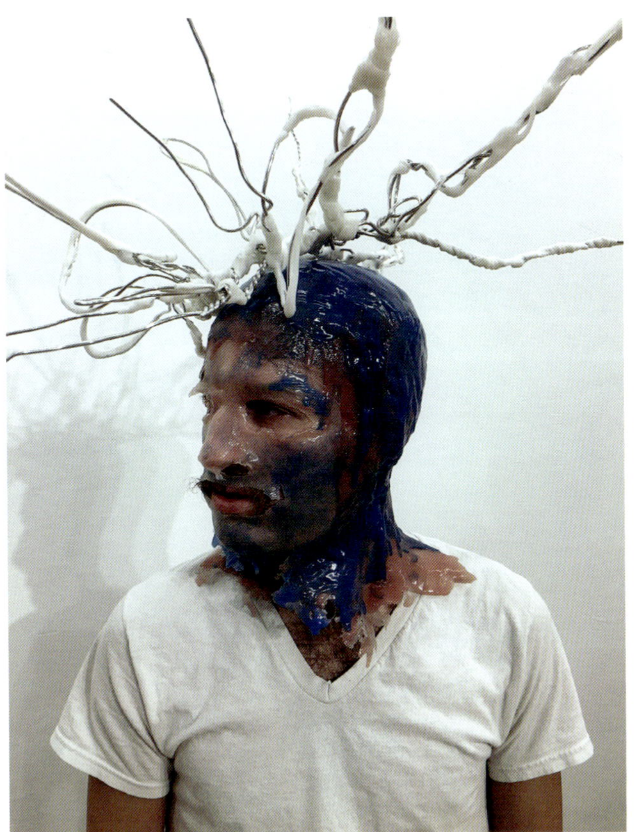

Initiate costume fitting, 2017

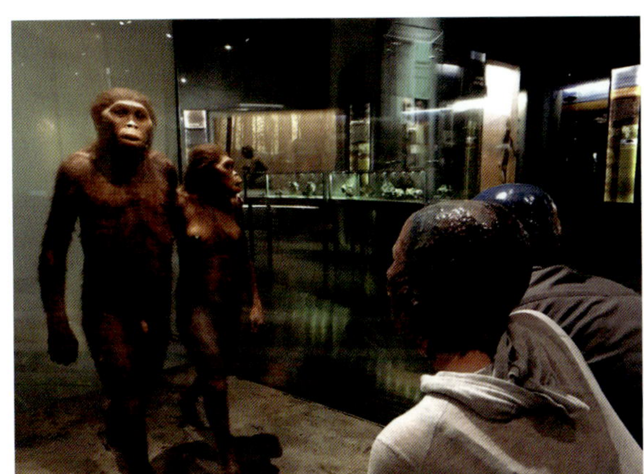

Production still from *The Violence of a Civilization
without Secrets*, 2017

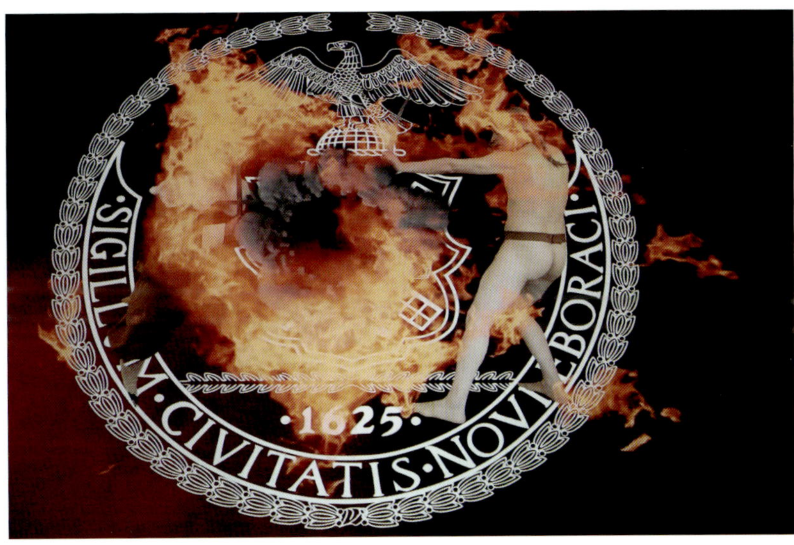

*The New Red Order Presents: The Savage Philosophy of Endless
Acknowledgment*, 2018

ADAM KHALIL, ZACK KHALIL, AND JACKSON POLYS

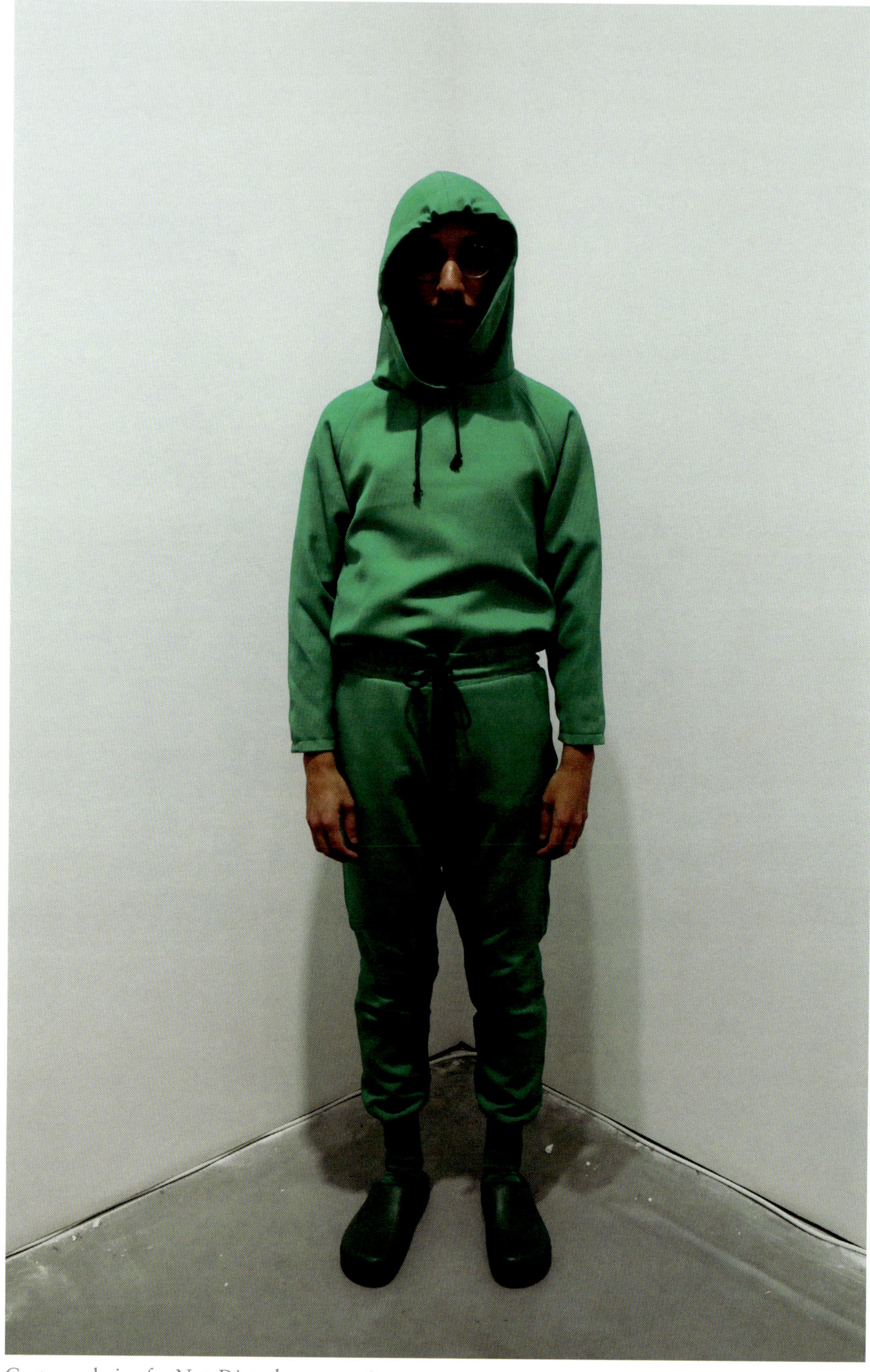

38

Costume design for *Nap Disturbance*, 2018

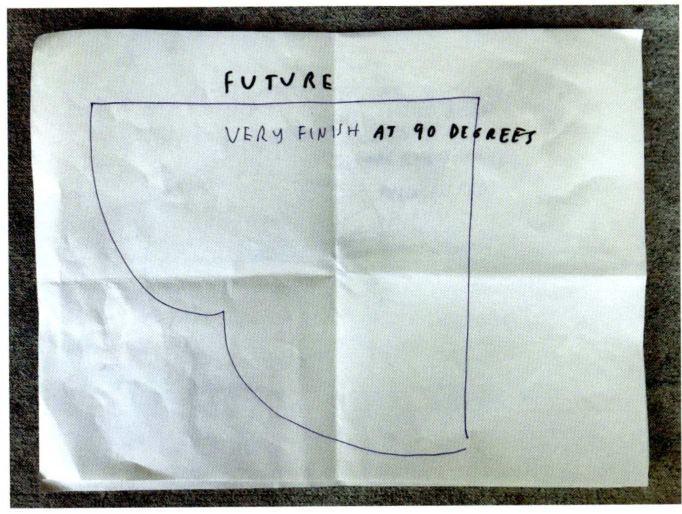

Sketch for *Future Finish*, 2018

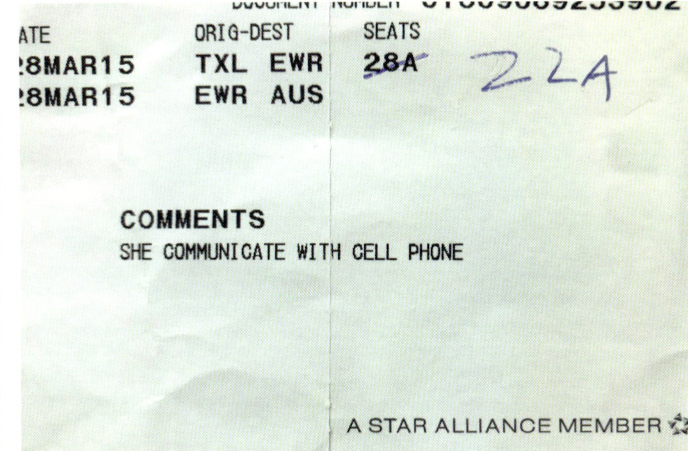

Source image for *Close Readings*, 2016

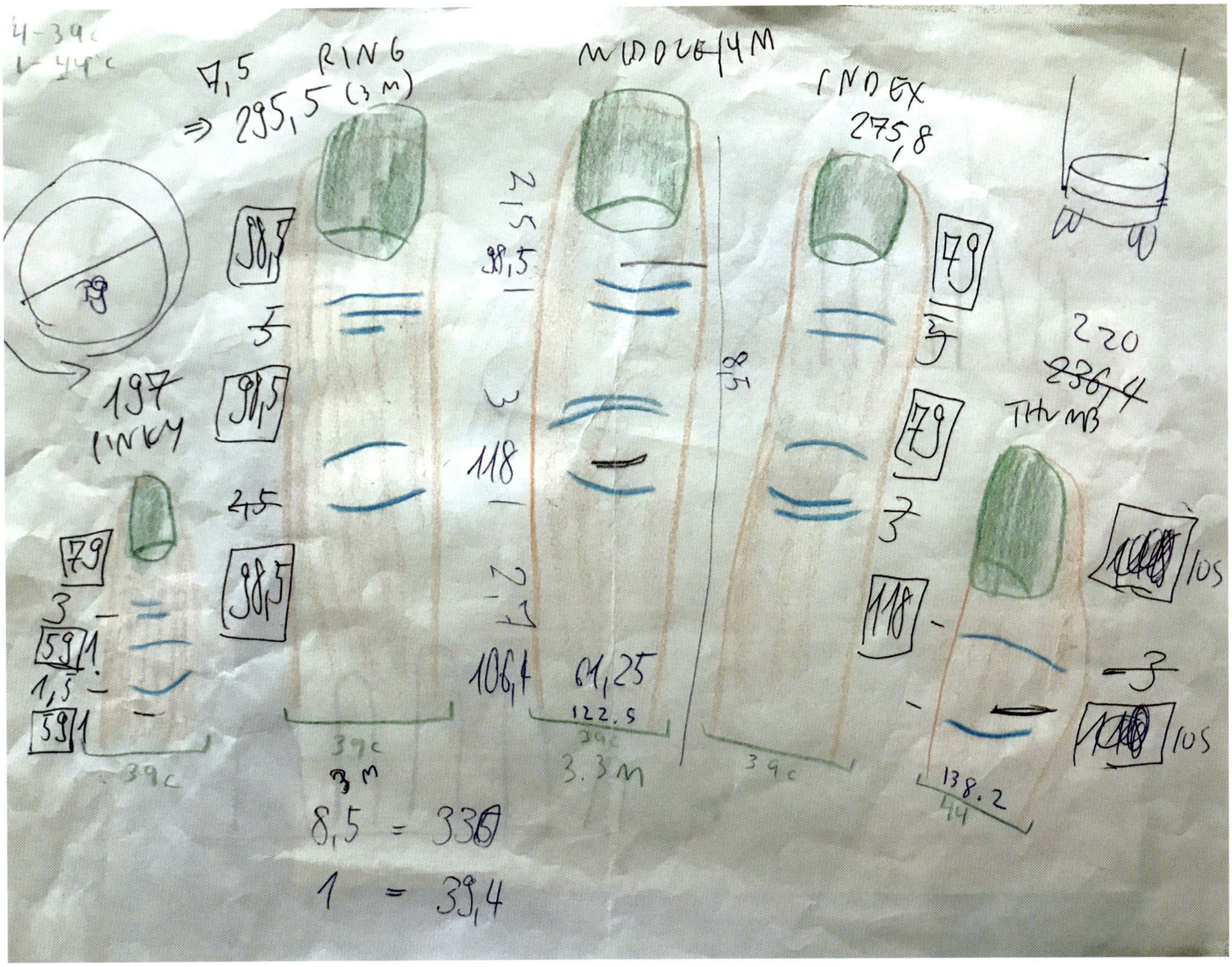

Prop design for *Five Finger Discount History*, 2016

CHRISTINE SUN KIM

189

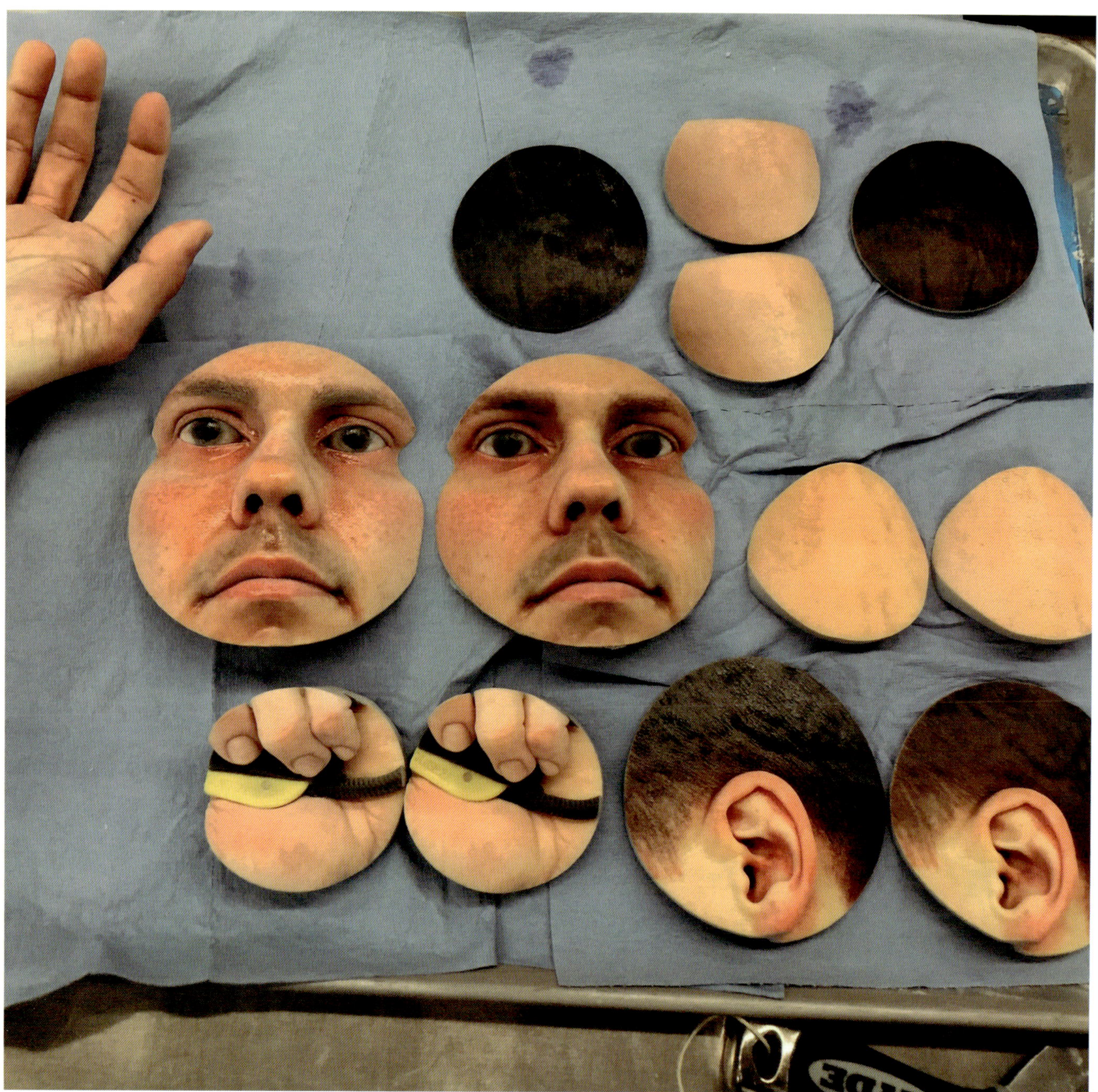

Color tests for 3-D prints, 2018

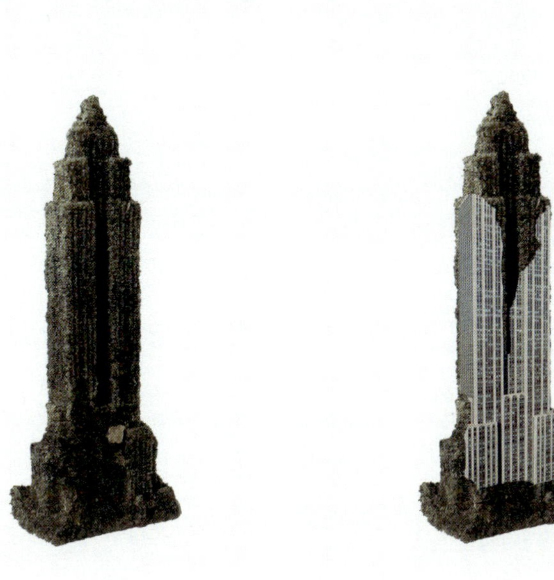

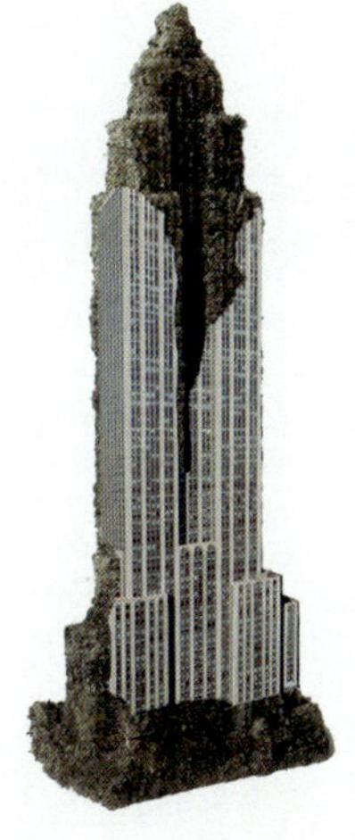

Untitled work in progress, 2018

Untitled work in progress, 2018

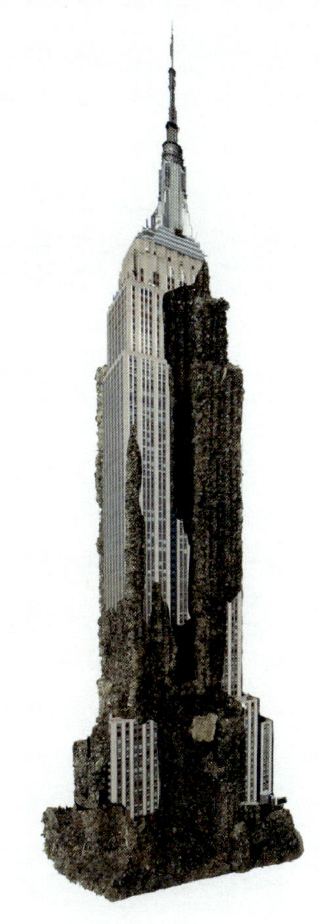

Untitled work in progress, 2018

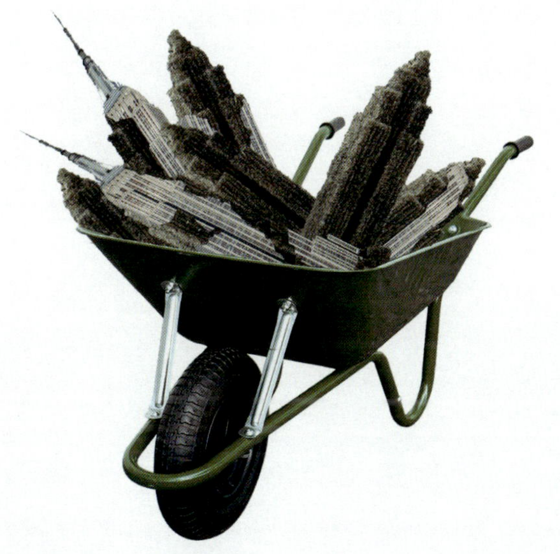

Untitled work in progress, 2018

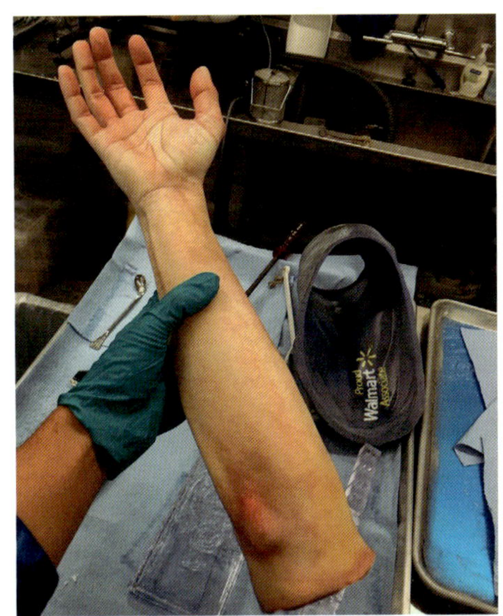

Color tests for 3-D prints, 2018

JOSH KLINE

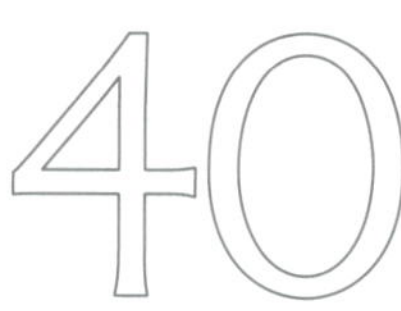

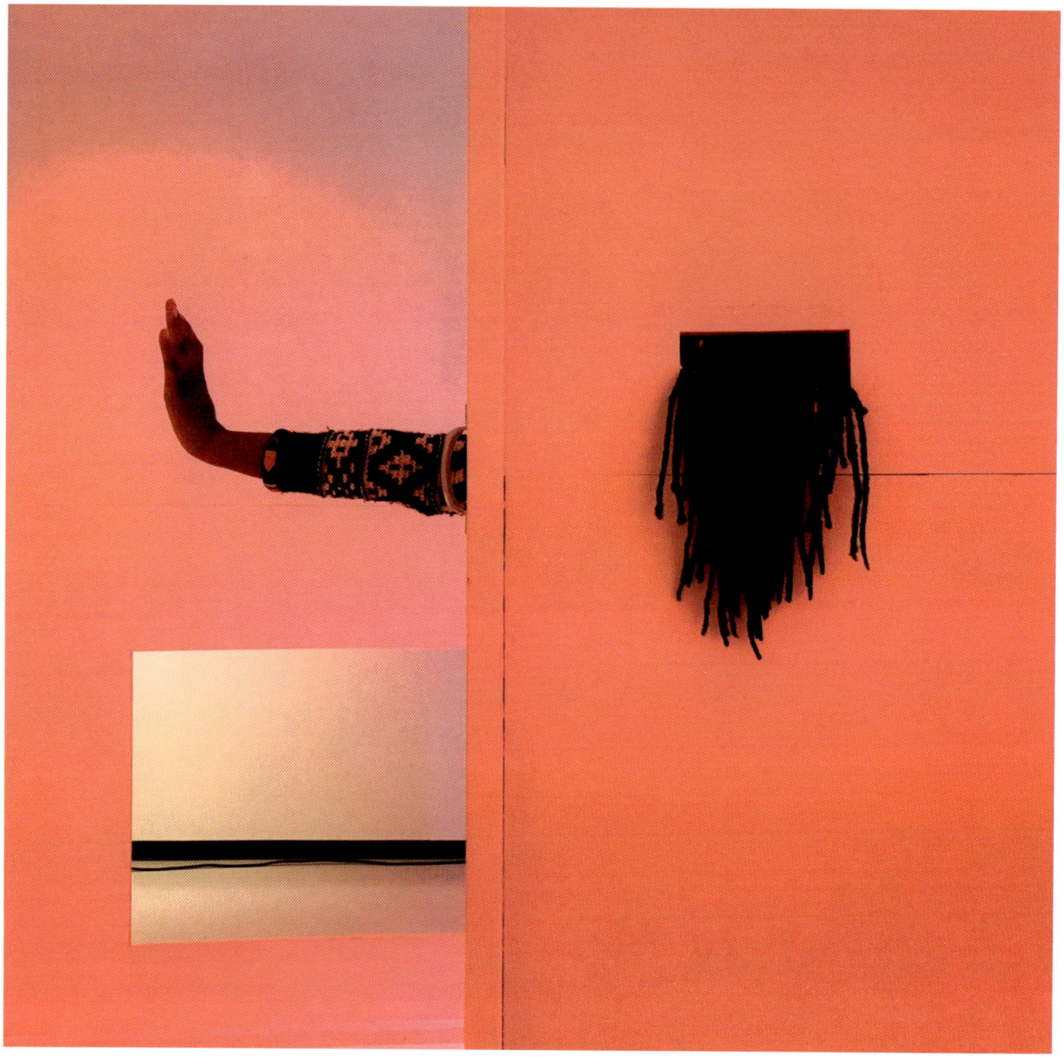

Rehearsal for *In Rehearsal*, 2017

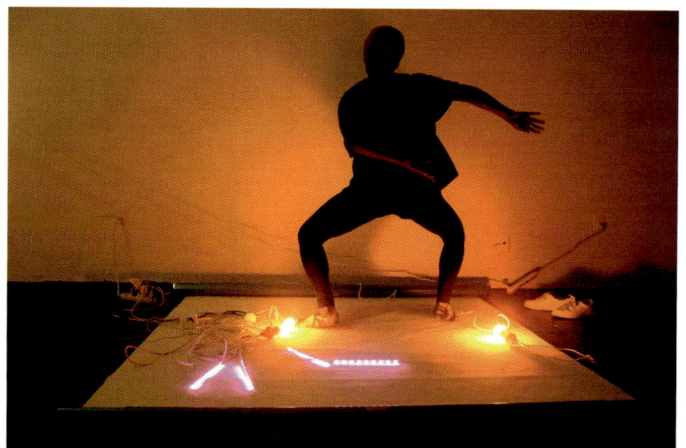

Movement and light tests, 2017

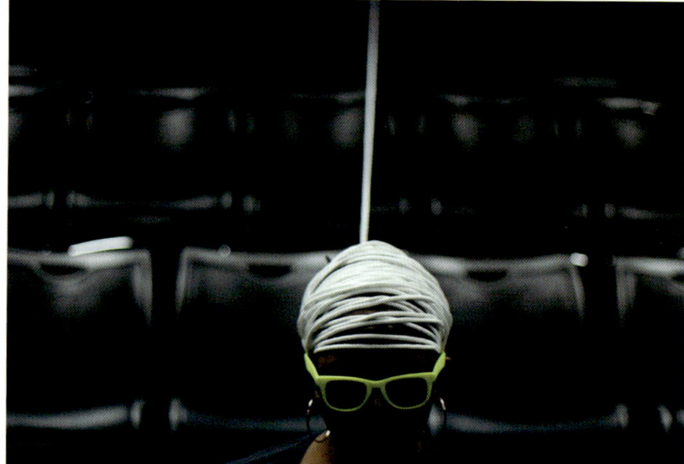

Choreography with object experimentation, 2016

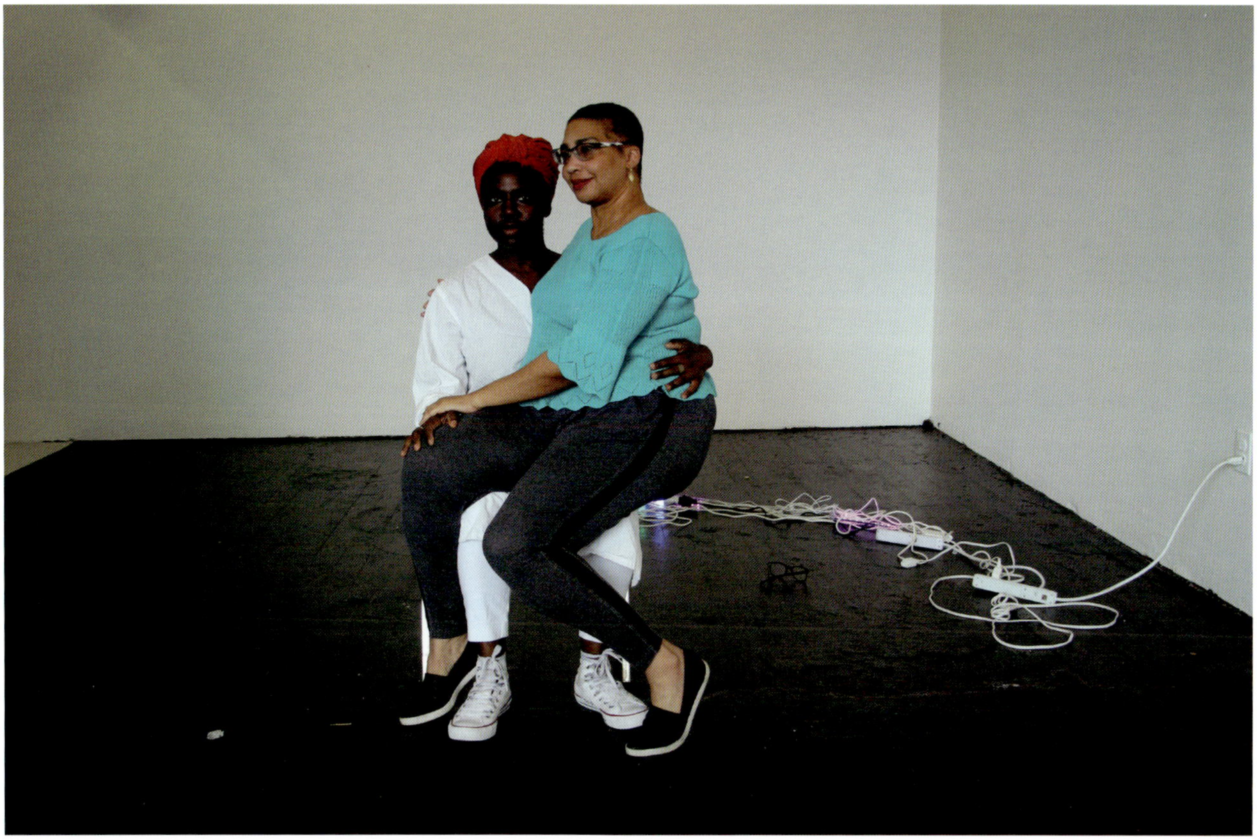

Test for *Lap Series*, 2017

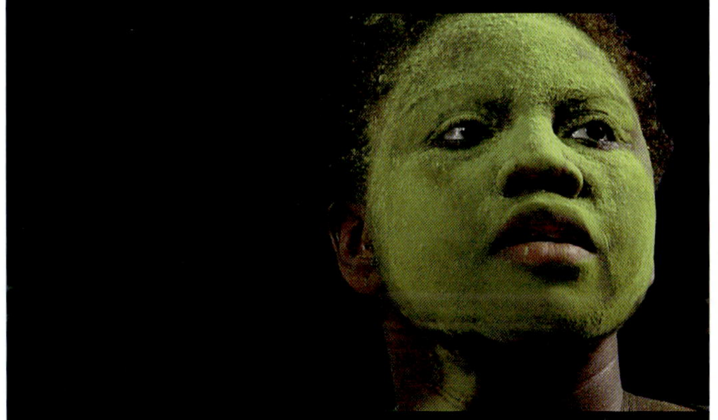

Screen test for *She Think She Kawaii*, 2015

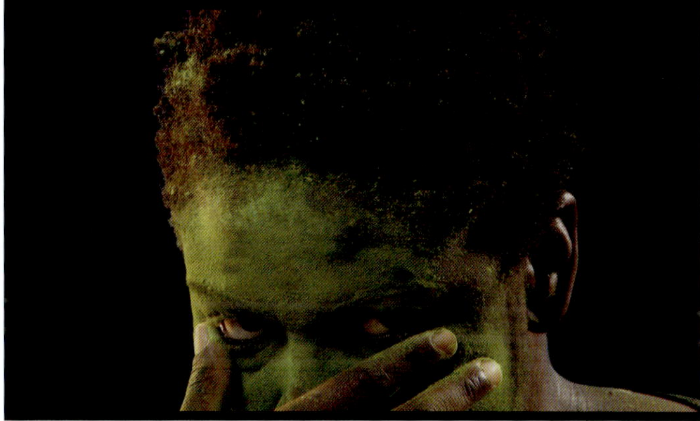

Screen test for *She Think She Kawaii*, 2015

AUTUMN KNIGHT

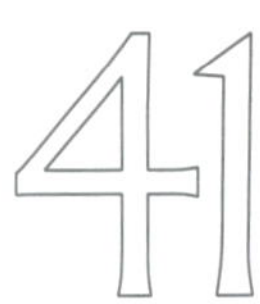

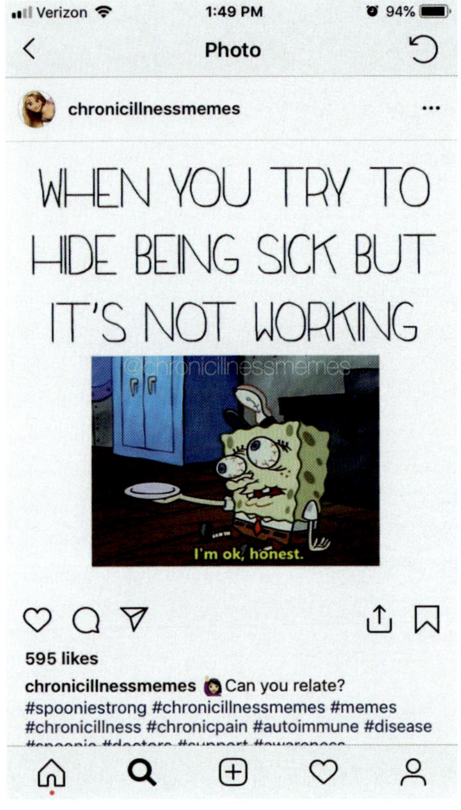

Screenshot of chronicillnessmemes
Instagram account, 2018

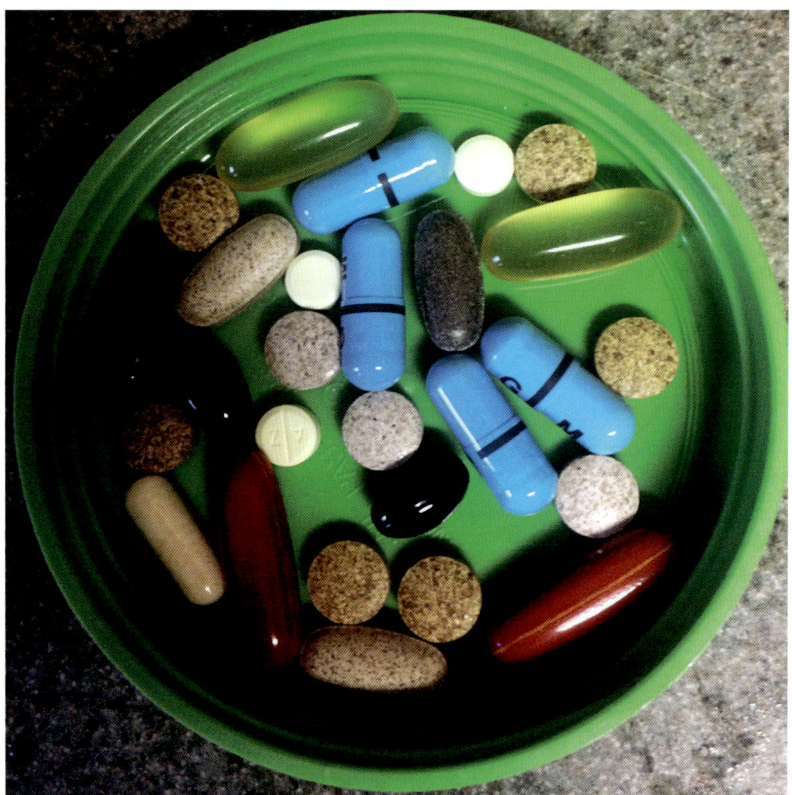

The artist's pills, 2018

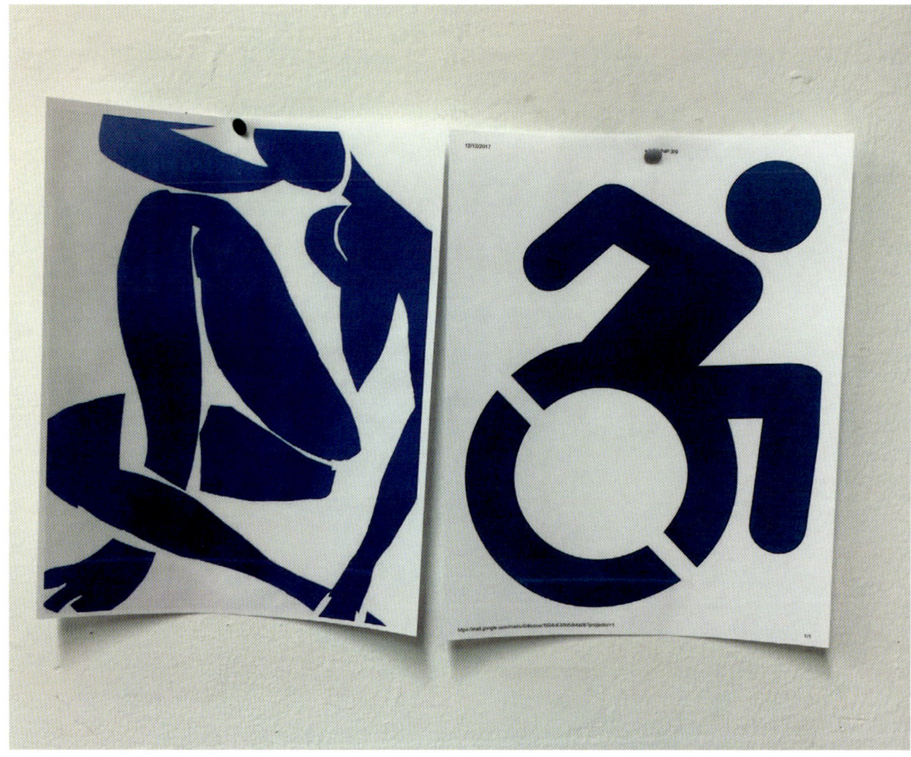

Studio, Philadelphia, PA, 2018

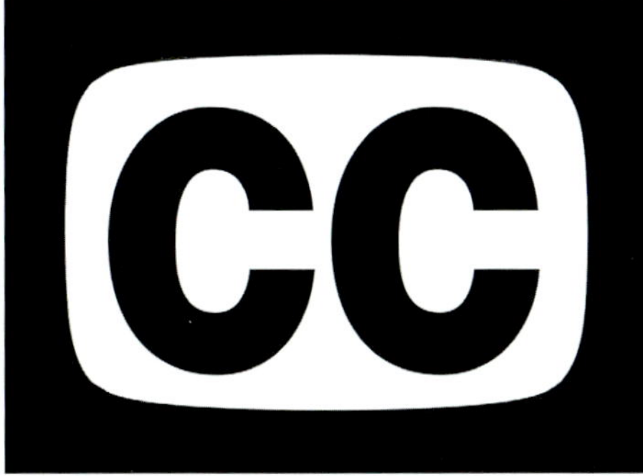

Closed-captioning logo

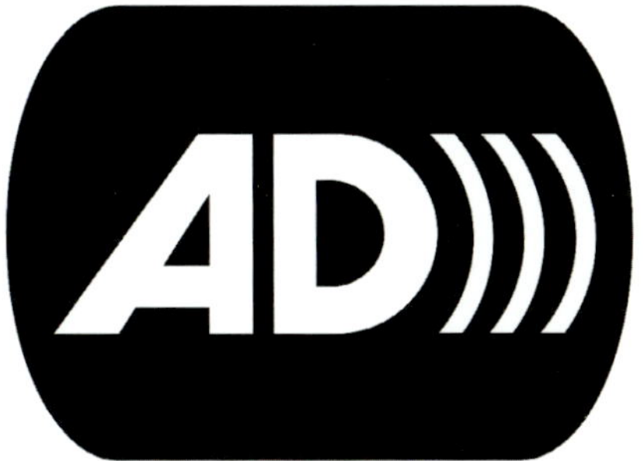

Audio description logo

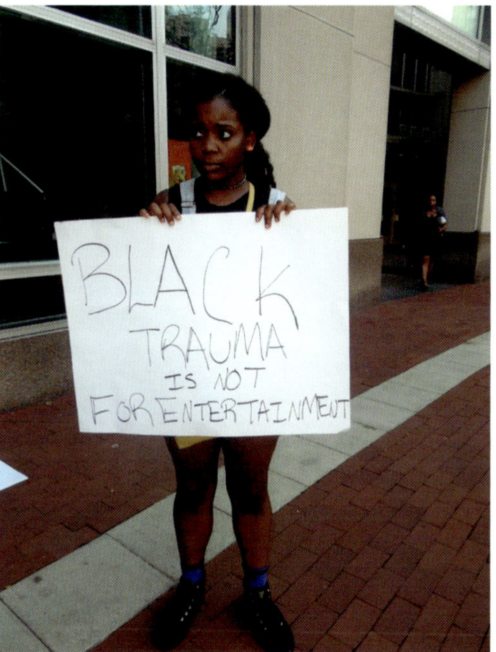

Ariana Beedie/Face A Face Collective, *Black Trauma Is NOT for Entertainment*, 2016

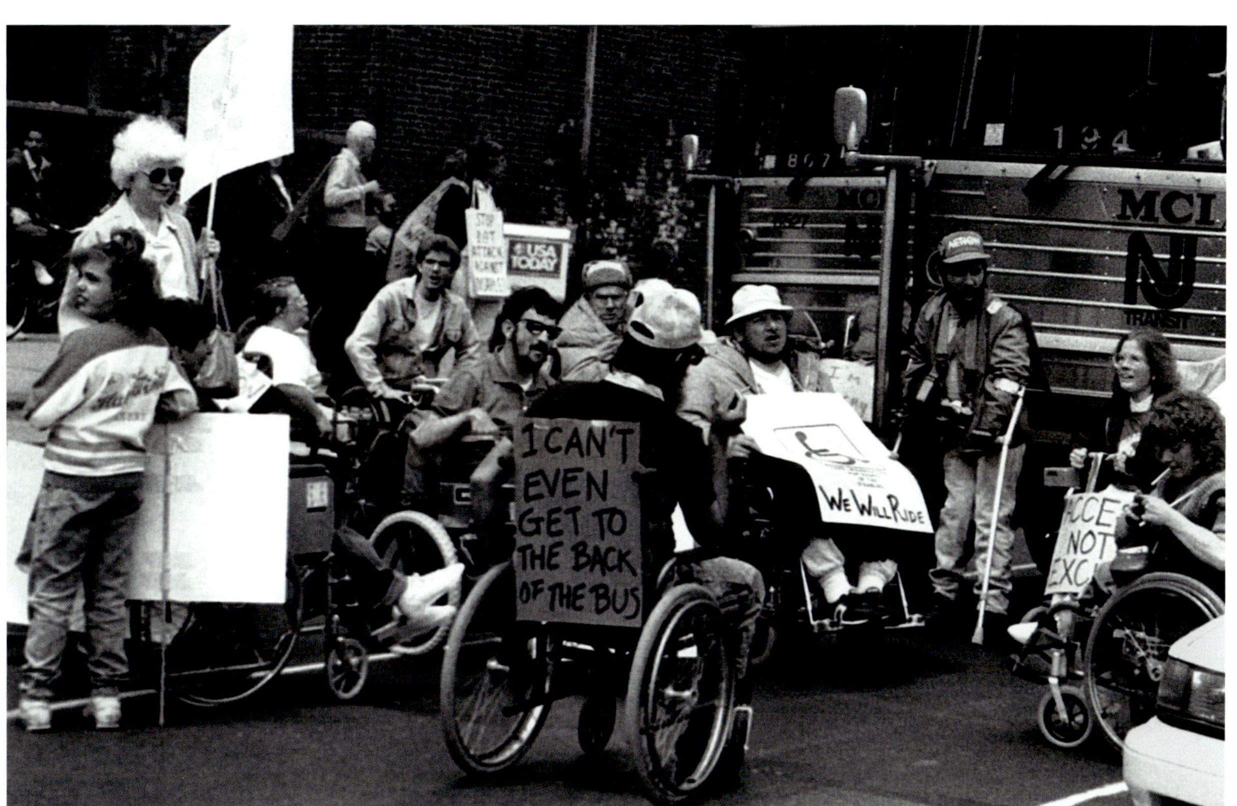

Tim Olin, ADAPT activists protesting for accessible transportation, Philadelphia, PA, 1990

CAROLYN LAZARD

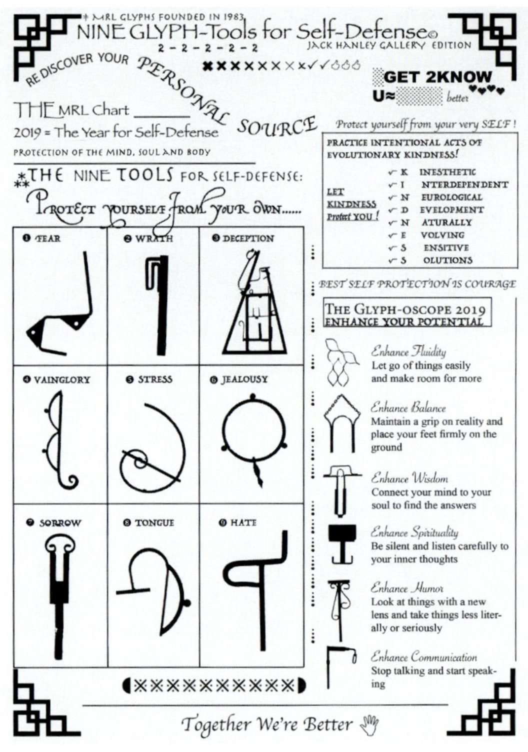

42

Chart for *Access to Tools*, 2018

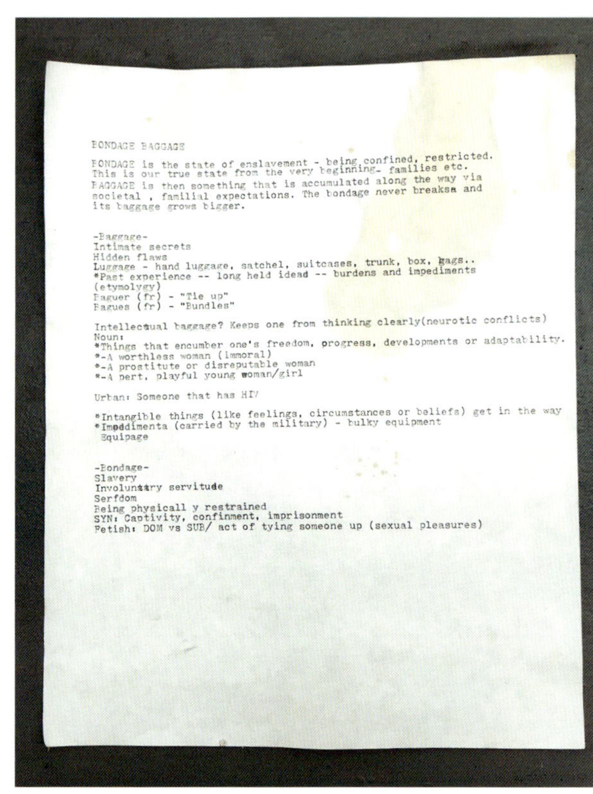

BONDAGE BAGGAGE

BONDAGE is the state of enslavement - being confined, restricted.
This is our true state from the very beginning- families etc.
BAGGAGE is then something that is accumulated along the way via
societal , familial expectations. The bondage never breaksm and
its baggage grows bigger.

-Baggage-
Intimate secrets
Hidden flaws
Luggage - hand luggage, satchel, suitcases, trunk, box, bags..
*Past experience -- long held idead -- burdens and impediments
(etymolygy)
Baguer (fr) - "Tie up"
Bagues (fr) - "Bundles"

Intellectual baggage? Keeps one from thinking clearly(neurotic conflicts)
Noun:
*Things that encumber one's freedom, progress, developments or adaptability.
*-A worthless woman (immoral)
*-A prostitute or disreputable woman
*-A pert, playful young woman/girl

Urban: Someone that has HIV

*Intangible things (like feelings, circumstances or beliefs) get in the way
*Impeddimenta (carried by the military) - bulky equipment
 Equipage

-Bondage-
Slavery
Involuntary servitude
Serfdom
Being physicall y restrained
SYN: Captivity, confinment, imprisonment
Fetish: DOM vs SUB/ act of tying someone up (sexual pleasures)

Notes for *Bondage Baggage*, 2018

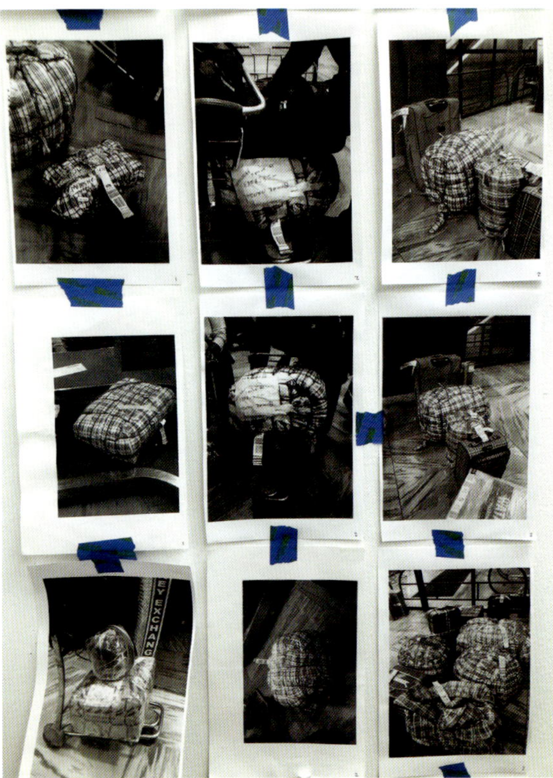

Source images for *Bondage Baggage*, 2018

Source image for *Bondage Baggage*, 2018

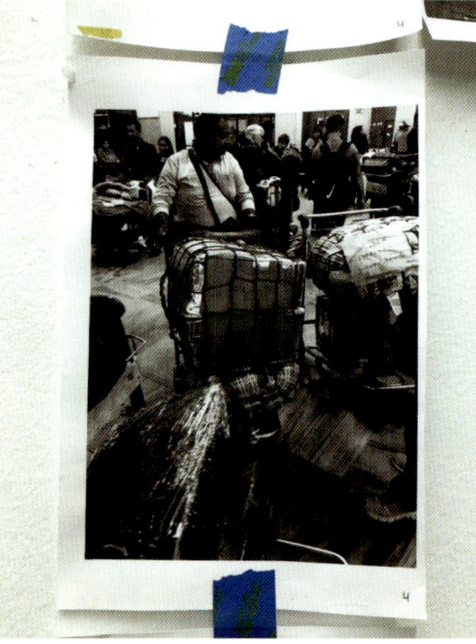

Source image for *Bondage Baggage*, 2018

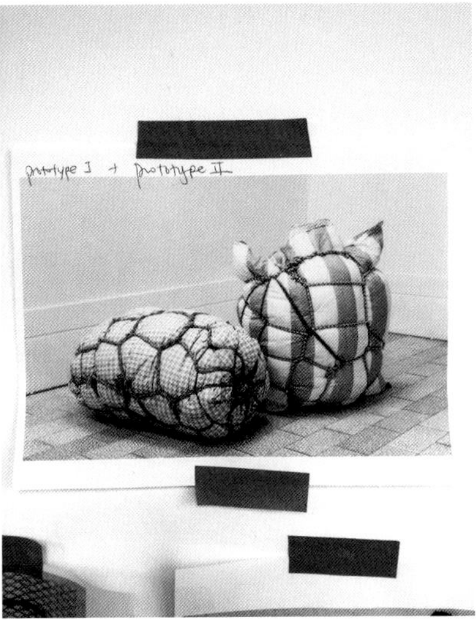

Photo for installation of *Bondage Baggage*, 2018

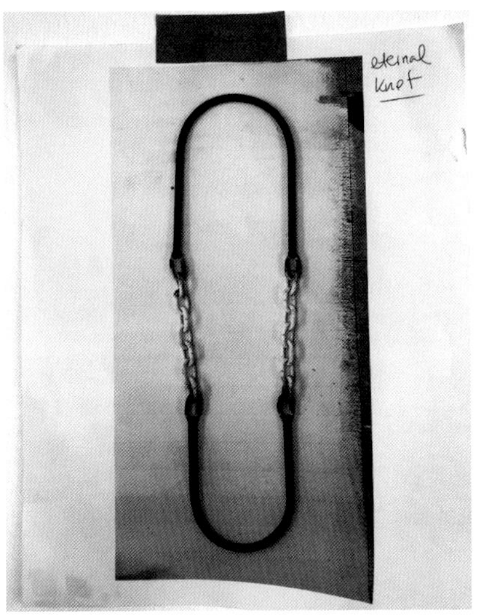

Sketch for *Eternal Knot*, 2017

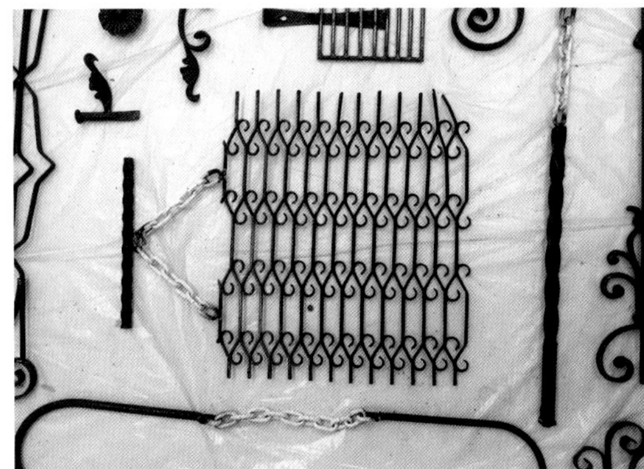

Sketches for glyphs, 2016

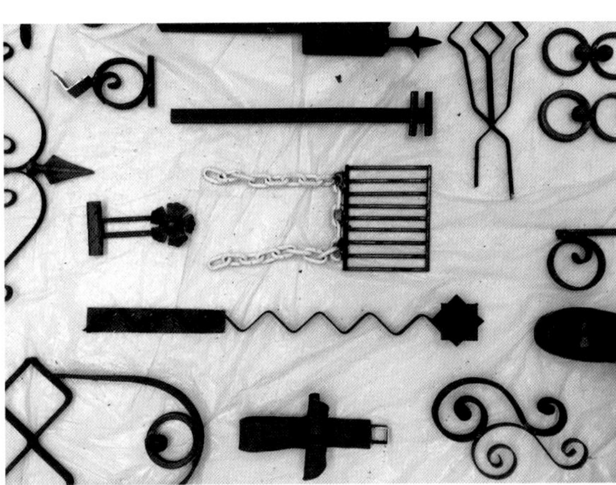

Sketches for glyphs, 2016

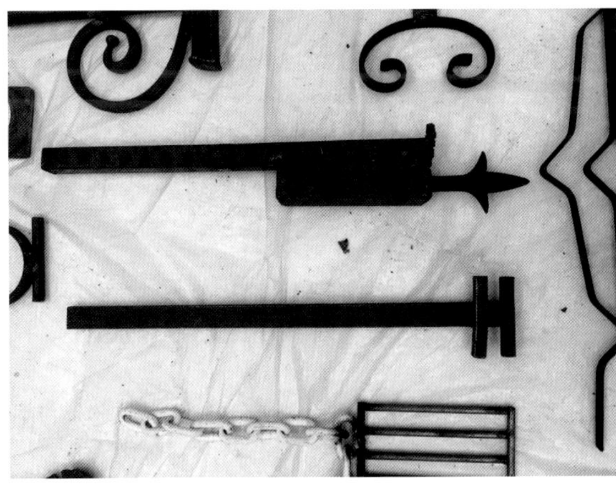

Sketches for glyphs, 2016

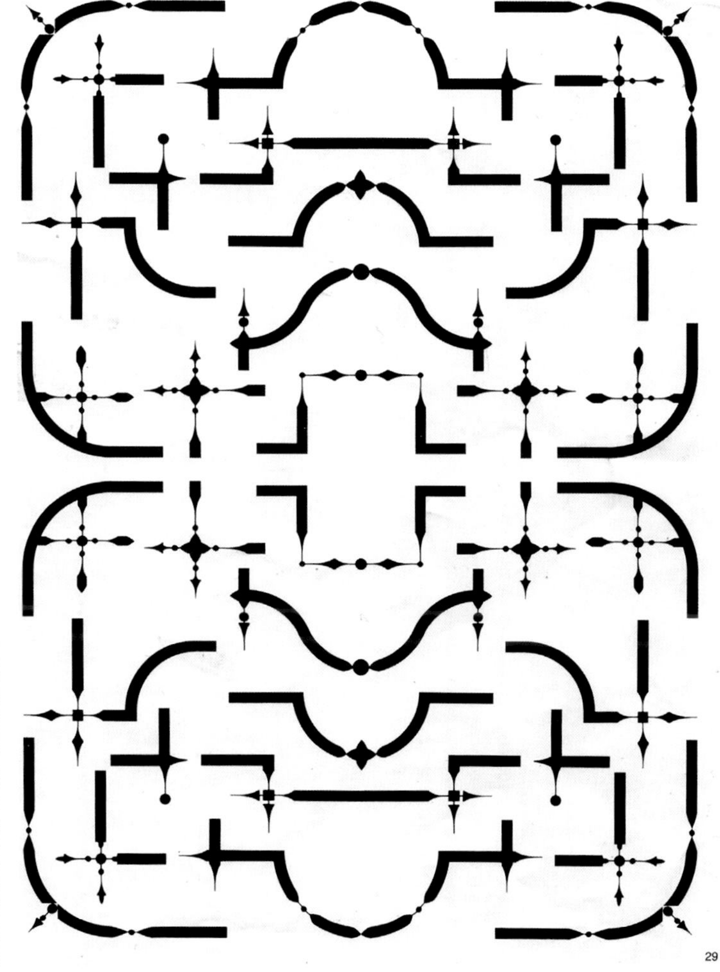

Source image for *Realm* 04, 2016

MAIA RUTH LEE

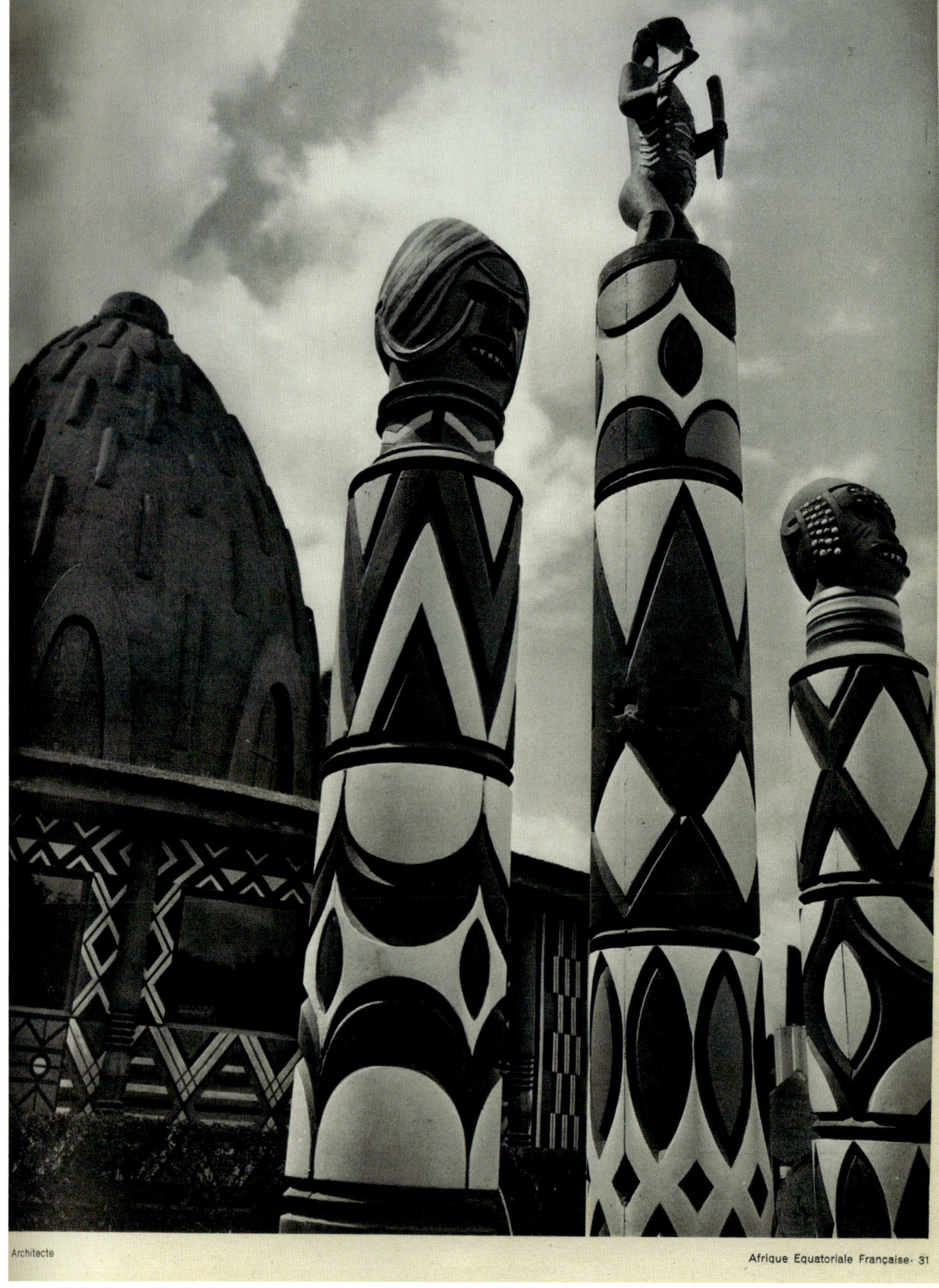

43

Afrique Équatoriale Française page from Studio Deberny Peignot, *Exposition coloniale 1931 Paris: 60 aspects de L'Exposition Coloniale*, 1931

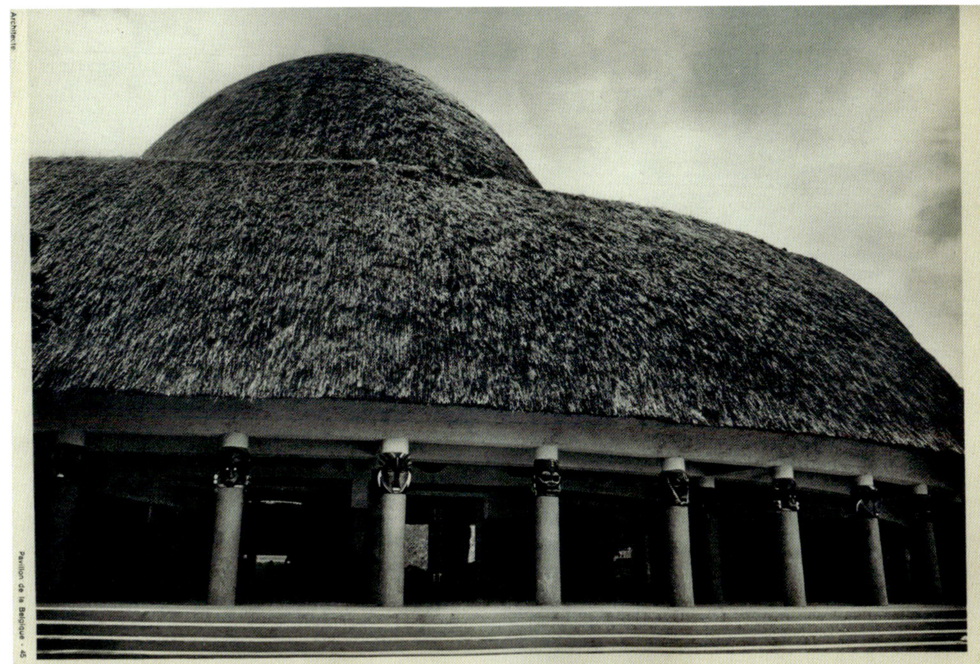

Pavillon de la Belgique page from Studio Deberny Peignot, *Exposition coloniale 1931 Paris: 60 aspects de L'Exposition Coloniale*, 1931

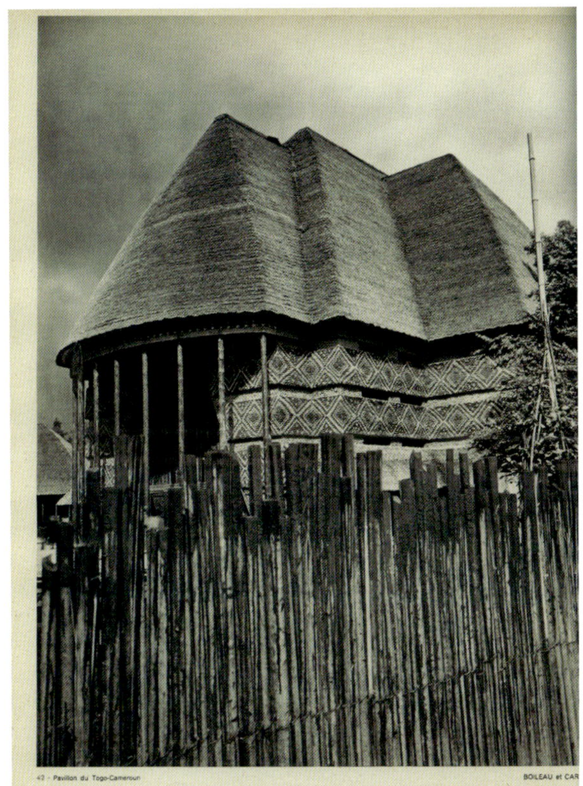

Pavillon du Togo-Cameroun page from Studio Deberny Peignot, *Exposition coloniale 1931 Paris: 60 aspects de L'Exposition Coloniale*, 1931

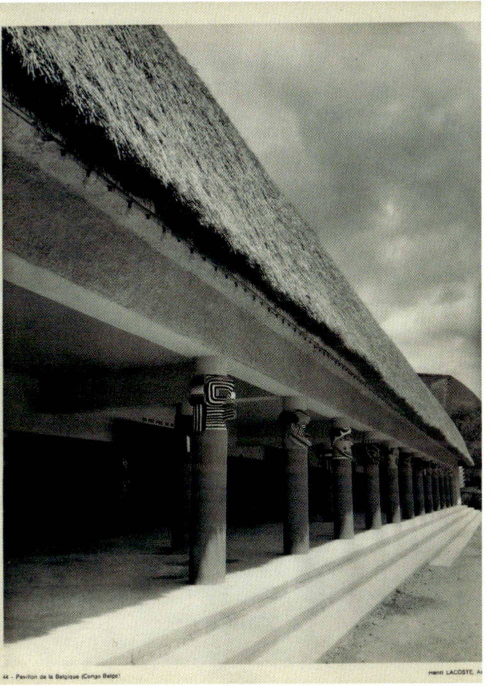

Pavillon de la Belgique page from Studio Deberny Peignot, *Exposition coloniale 1931 Paris: 60 aspects de L'Exposition Coloniale*, 1931

SIMONE LEIGH

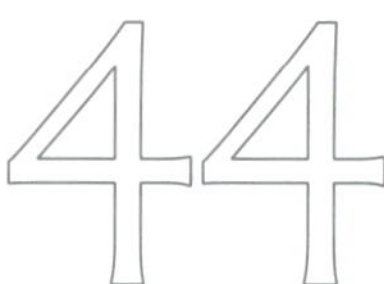

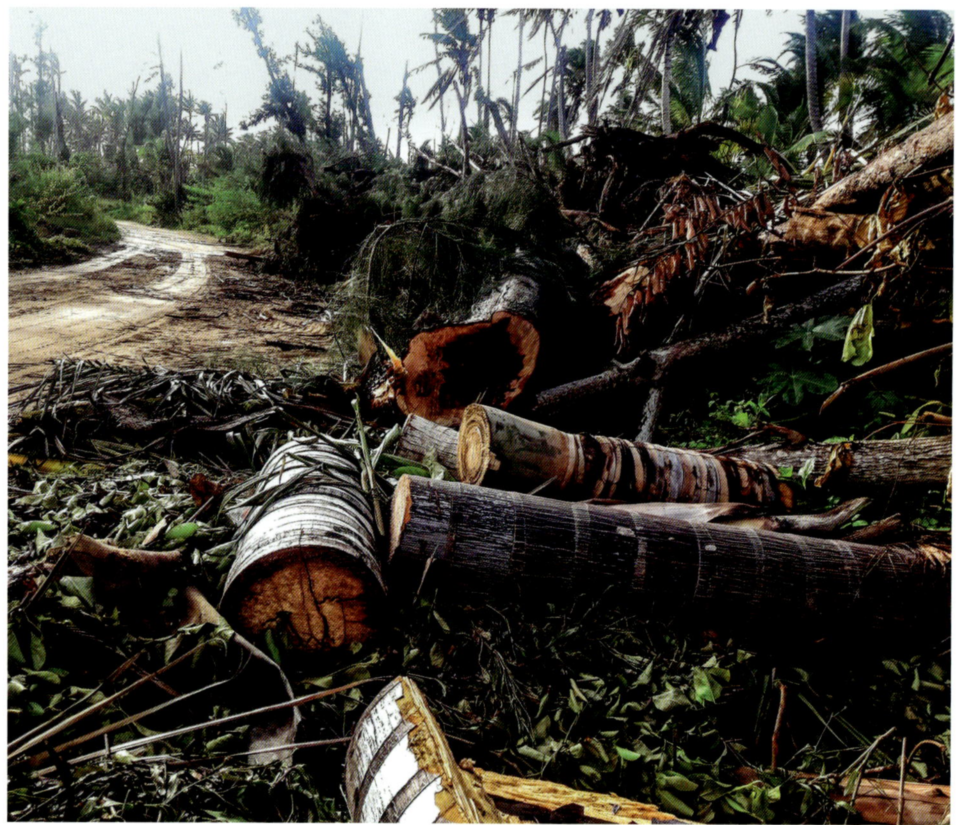

44

Deforestation in a littoral, eastern coast of Puerto Rico, 2018

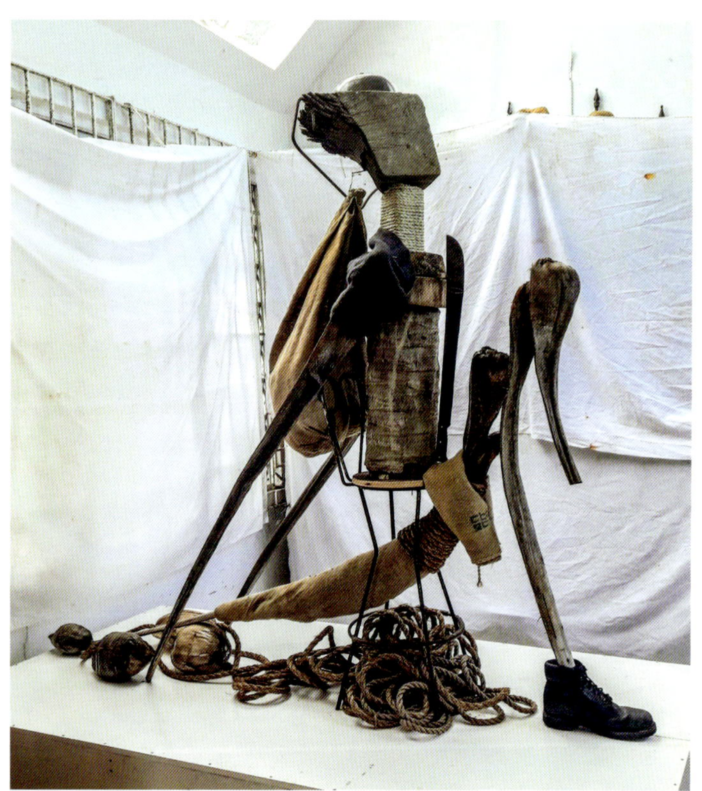

1797: Vencedor #2 (1797: Victorious #2)
(work in progress), 2018

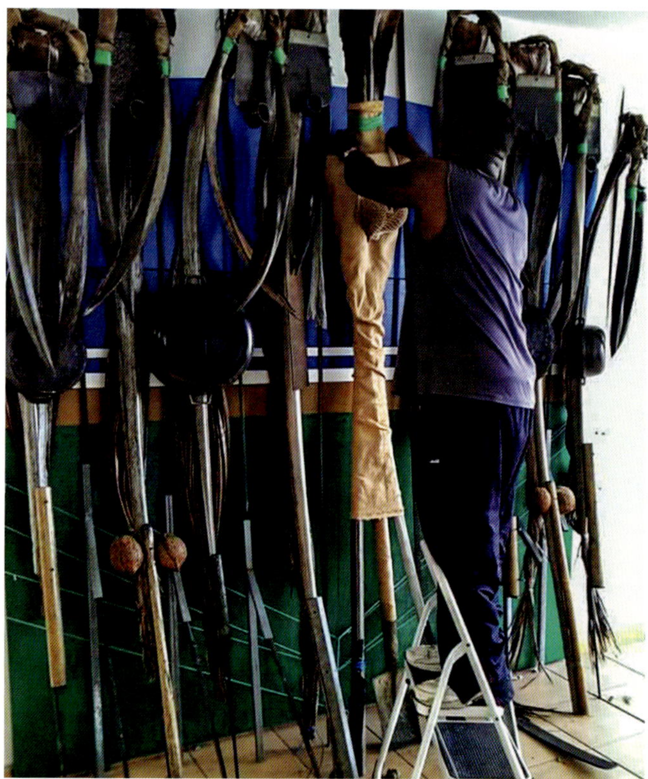

The artist in his studio, Loíza, PR, 2013

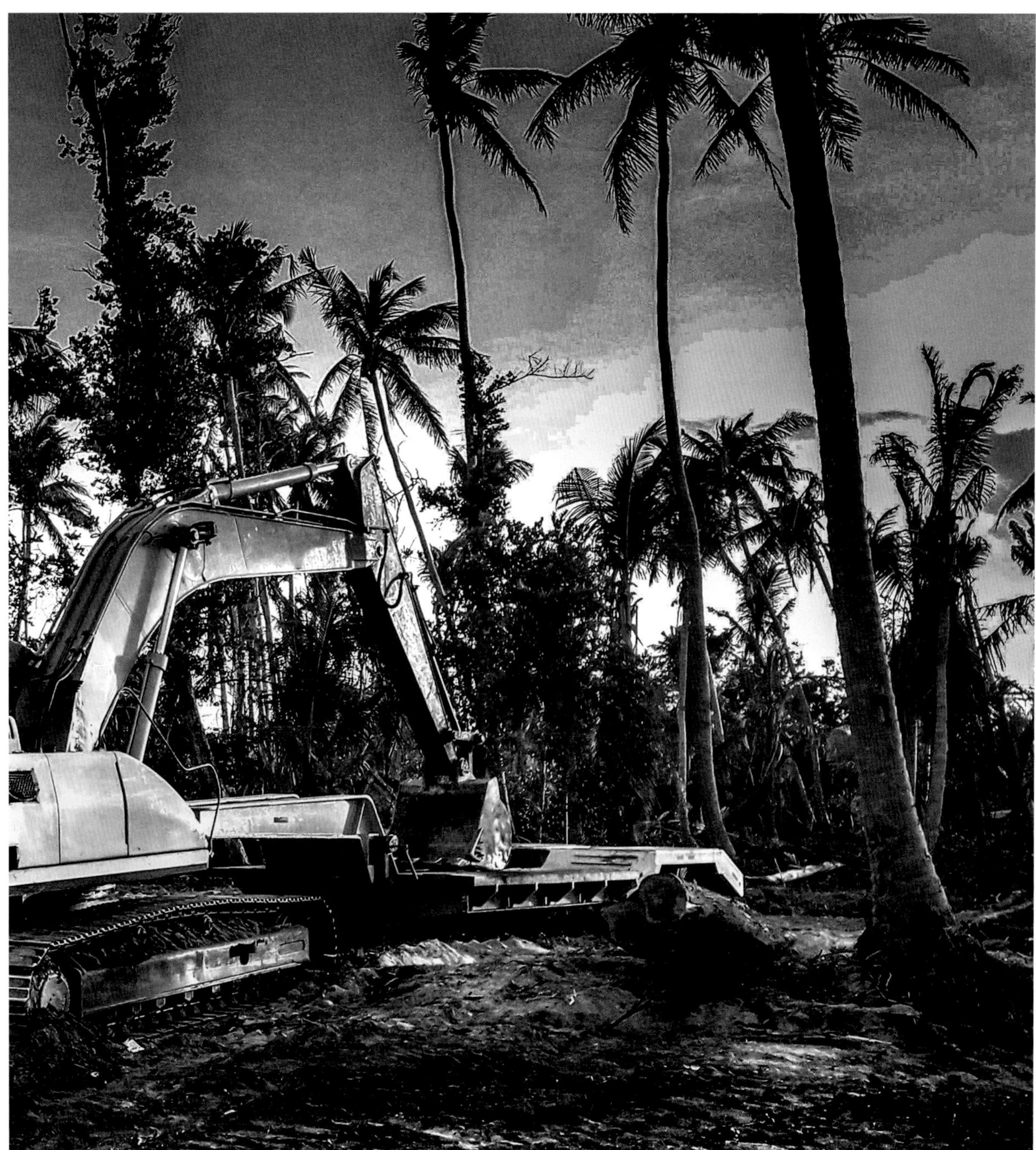

Deforestation in a littoral, eastern coast of Puerto Rico, 2018

DANIEL LIND-RAMOS

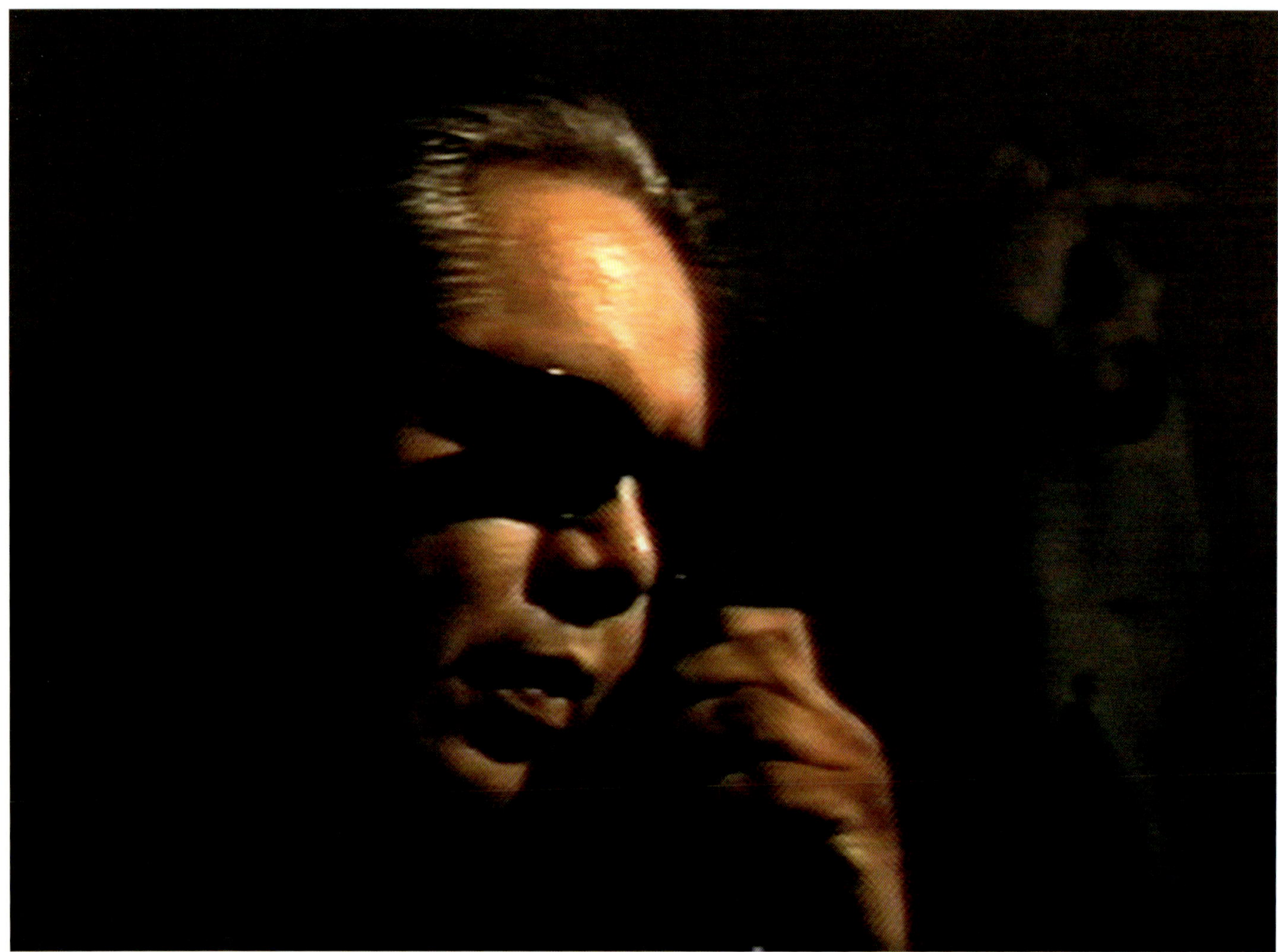

The History of the Luiseño People, 1993

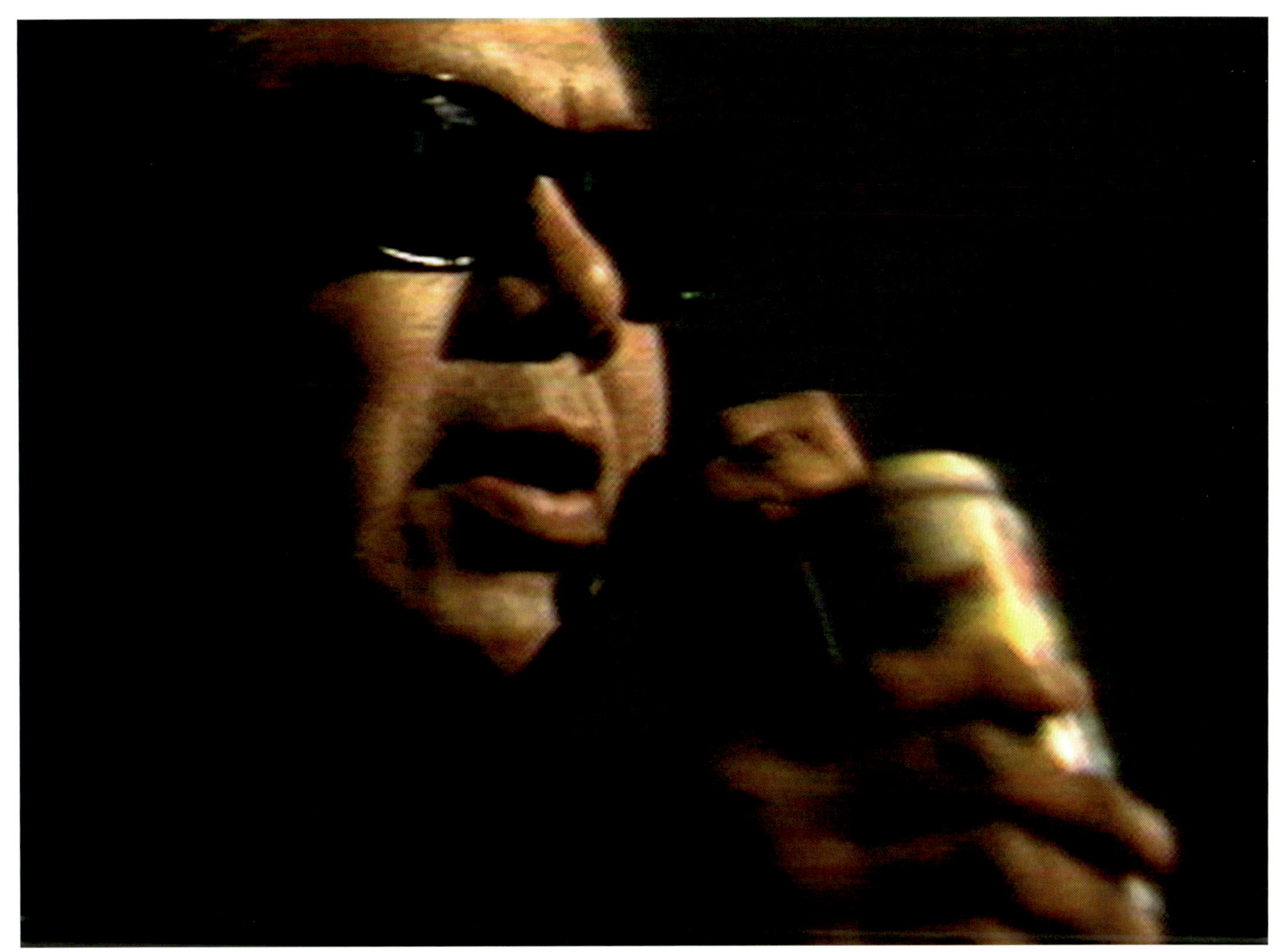

The History of the Luiseño People, 1993

JAMES LUNA

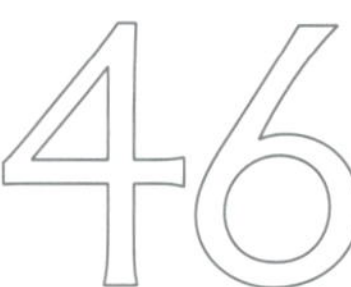

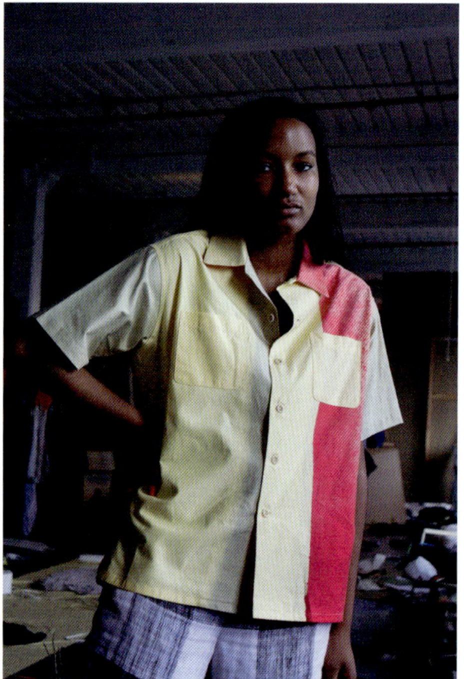

46

Study for *Supreme, Knowledge, Affirmatives*, 2017, worn by Gabrielle Mack

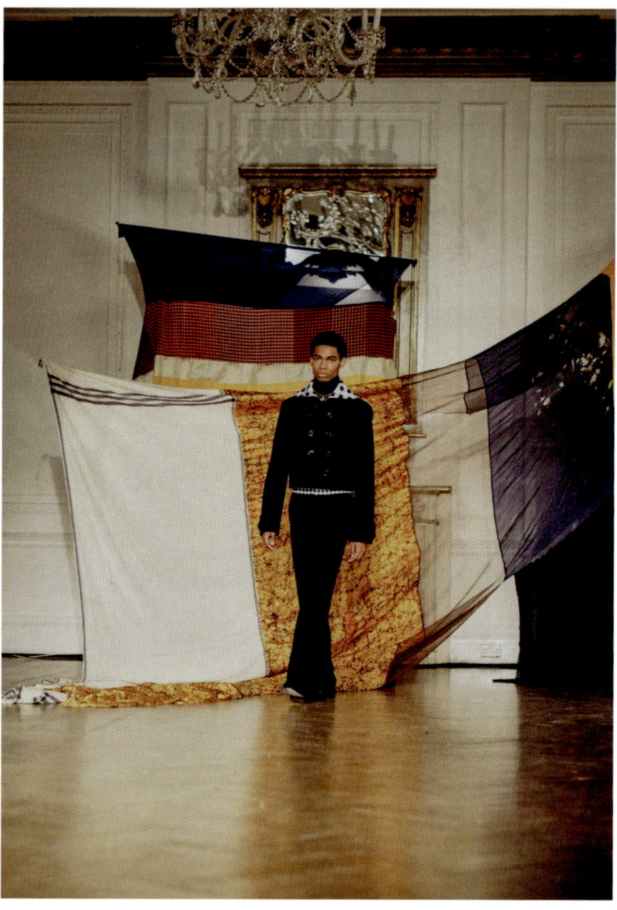

Des Hommes et Des Dieux, 2018. Installation view, Wales Bonner Autumn/Winter runway show, London Fashion Week, United Kingdom, 2018

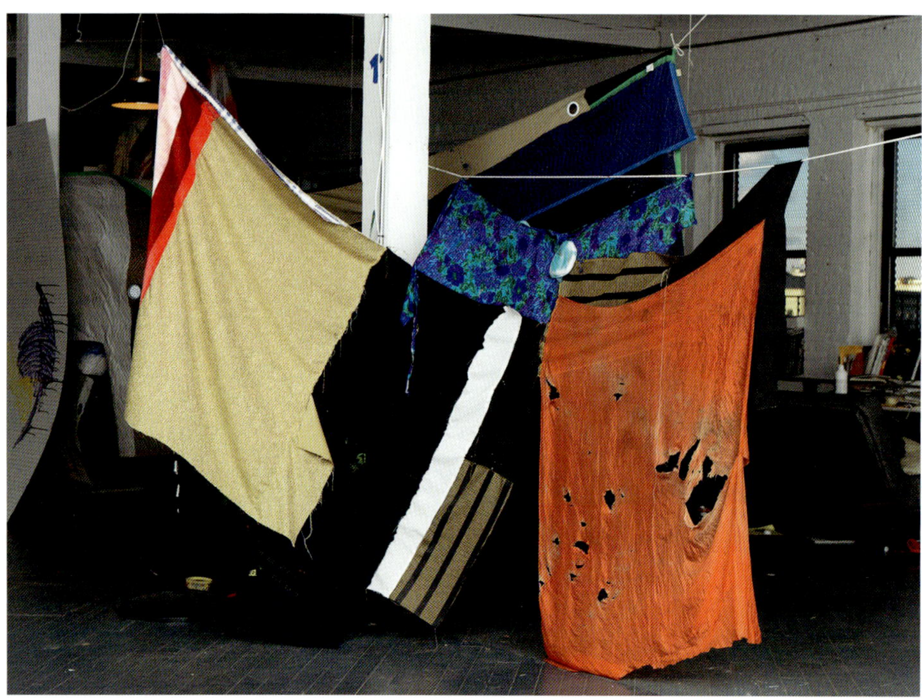

You Forgot to Answer (Errant Map) (work in progress), studio, New York, NY, 2017

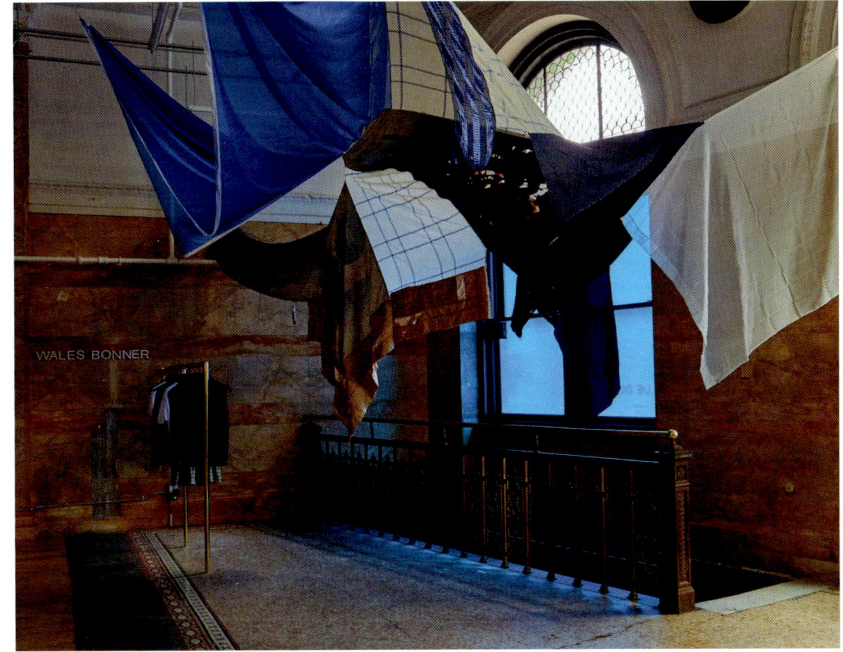

Blue Duets, 2018. Installation view, Wales Bonner Spring/Summer runway show, Totokaelo, New York, NY, 2018

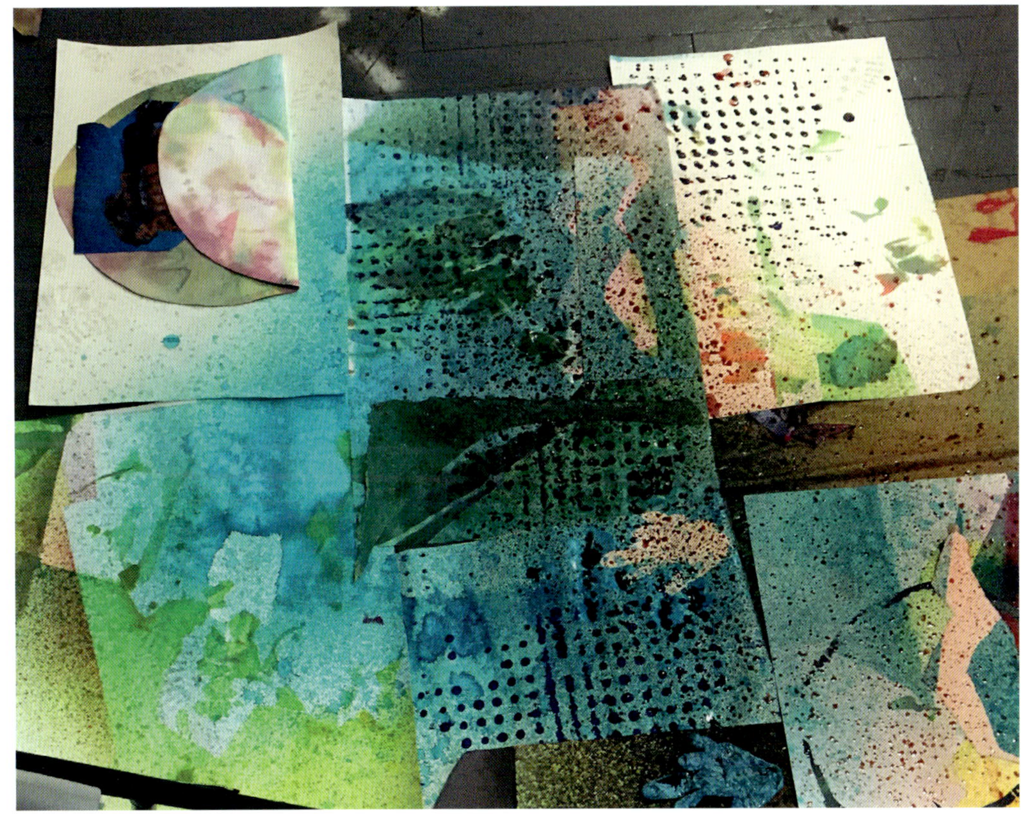

Process image for *She Will Lean with Her Back against the Wall*, 2015

ERIC N. MACK

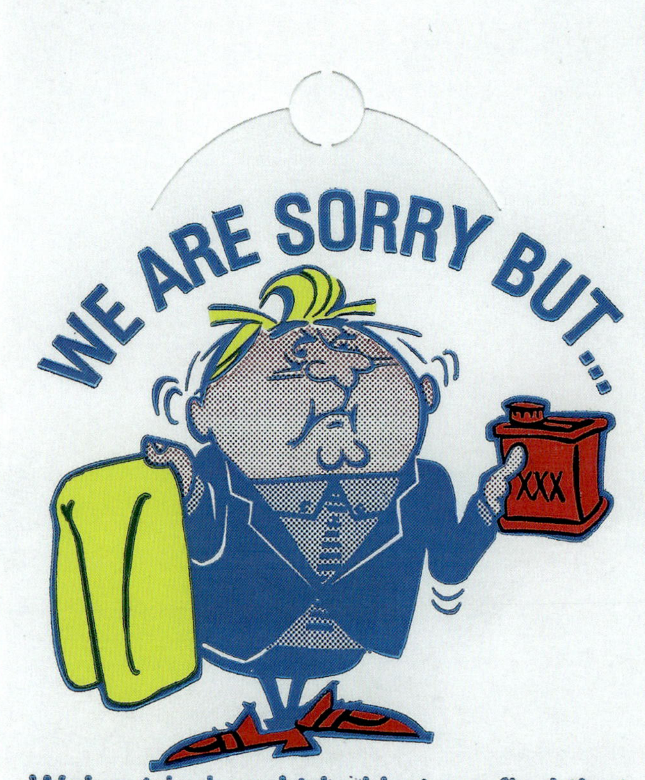

47

Source image for *Dry-Cleaned Shirt*, 2015

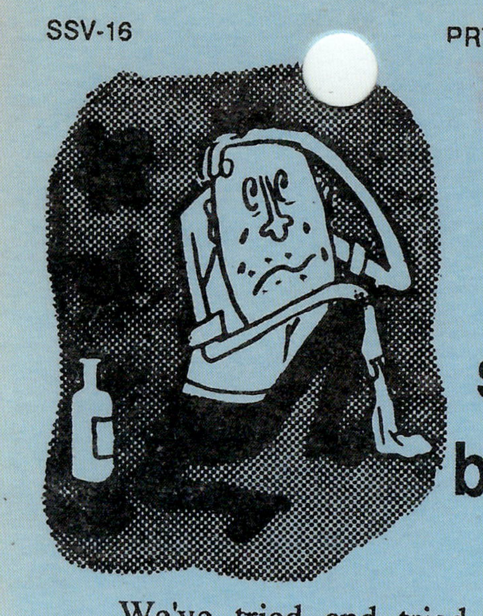

Source image for *Dry-Cleaned Shirt*, 2015

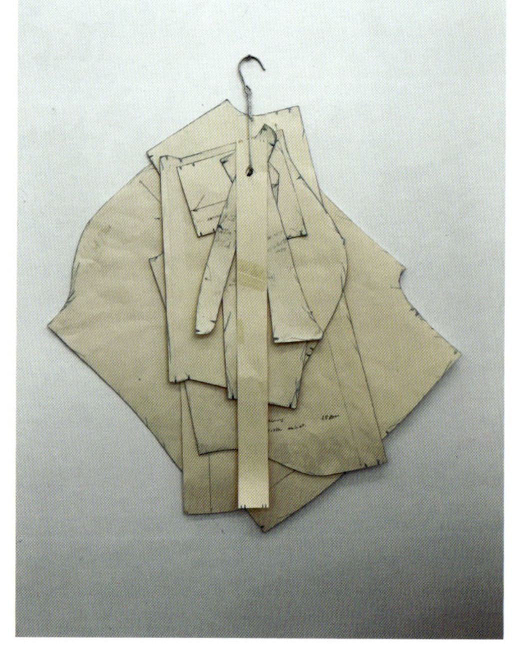

Study for *Dry-Cleaned Shirt*, 2015

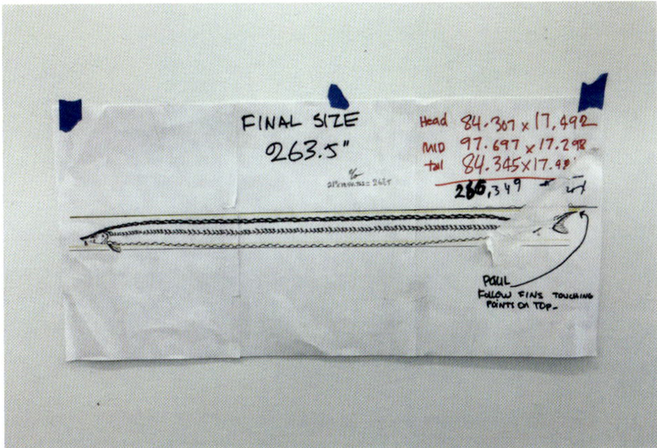

Sketch for *Stretched Sturgeon*, 2015

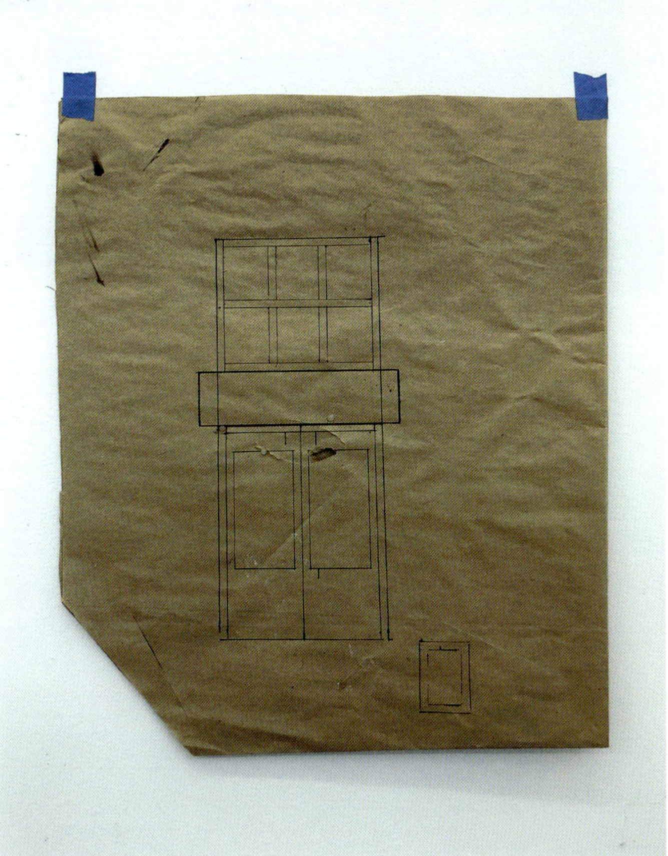

Sketch for *Small Studio*, 2018

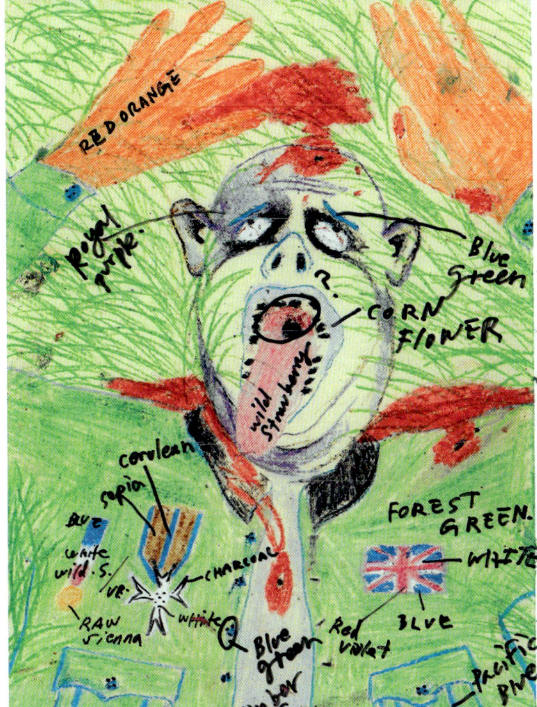

Annotated sketch, 2016

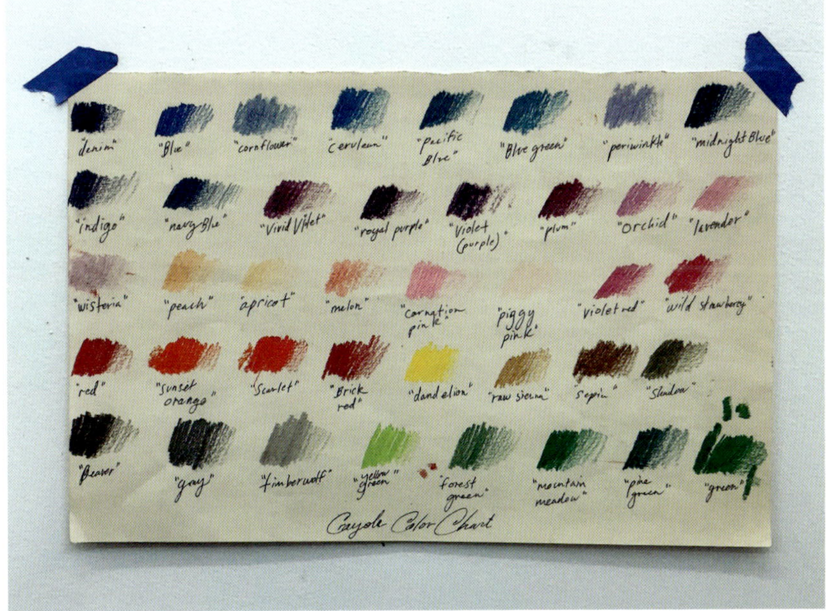

Swatches for *Dead Soldier*, 2016

CALVIN MARCUS

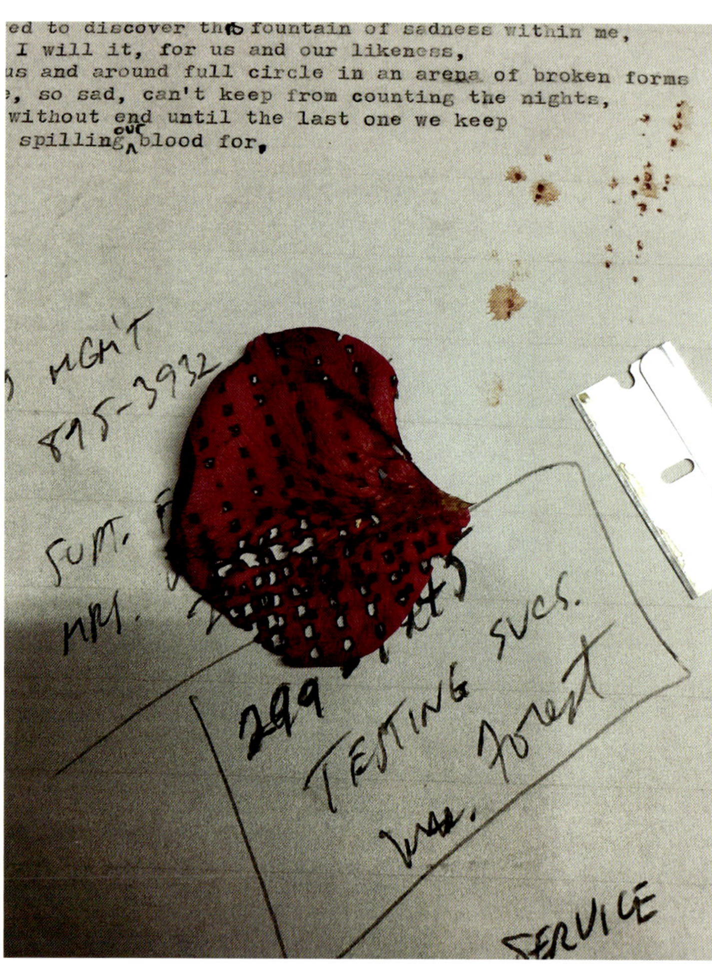

48

Process image for *X—On Subjugation*, 2017

New York Public Library redacted image, 2017

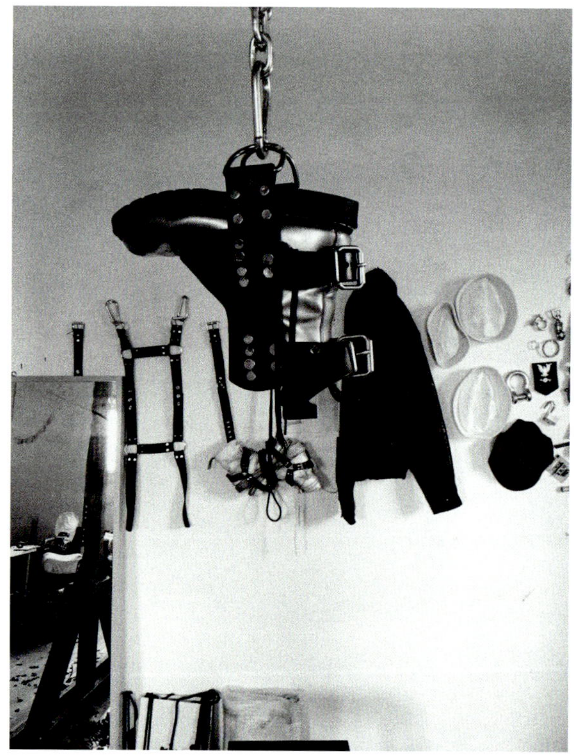

Process image for *X—On Subjugation*, 2017

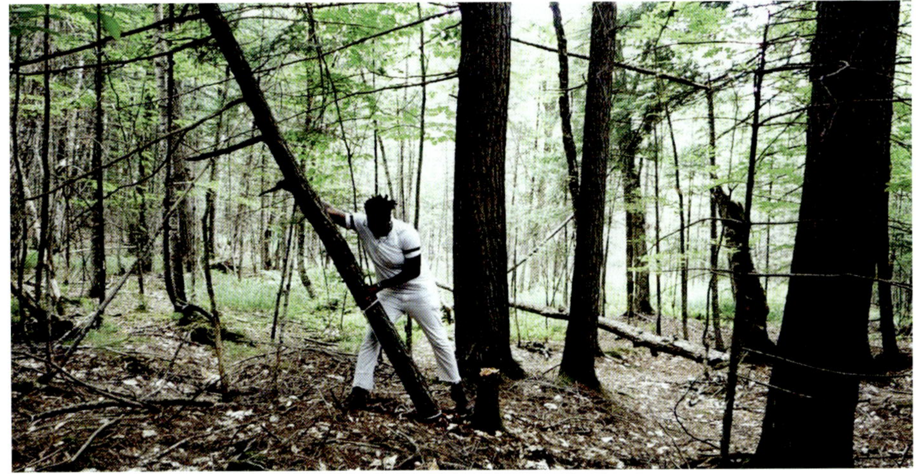

Process image for *I prayed to the wrong god for you*, 2018

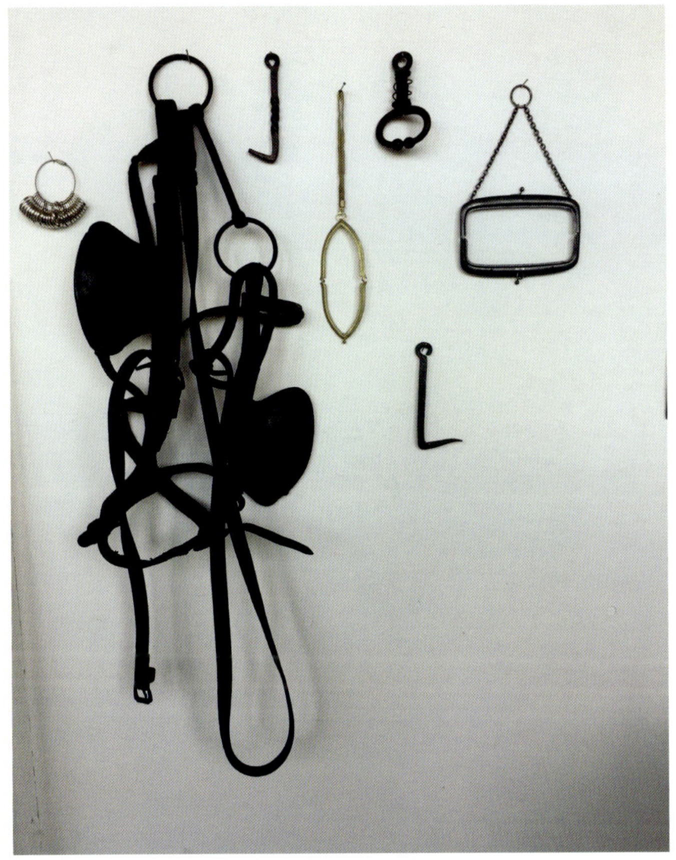

Studio, Philadelphia, PA, 2018

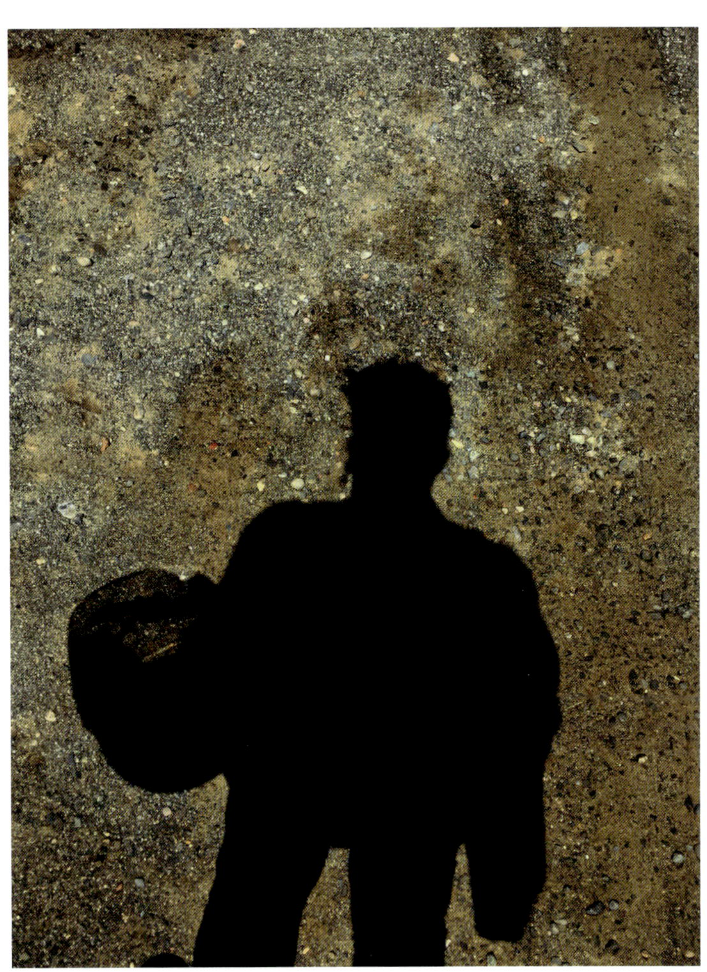

Process image for *I prayed to the wrong god for you*, 2018

TIONA NEKKIA McCLODDEN

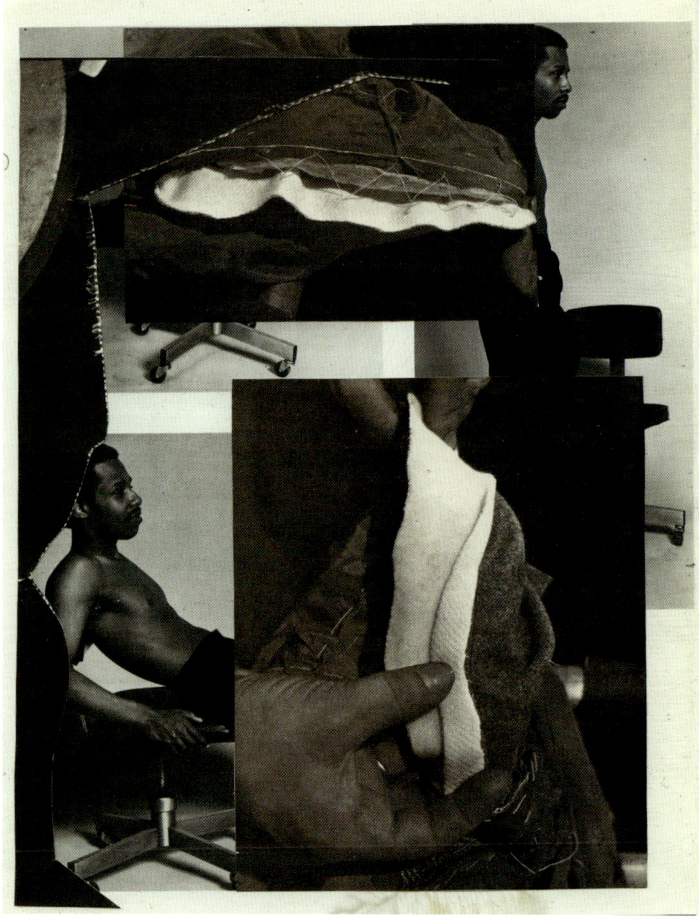

Riots (Disturbios) 5, 2018

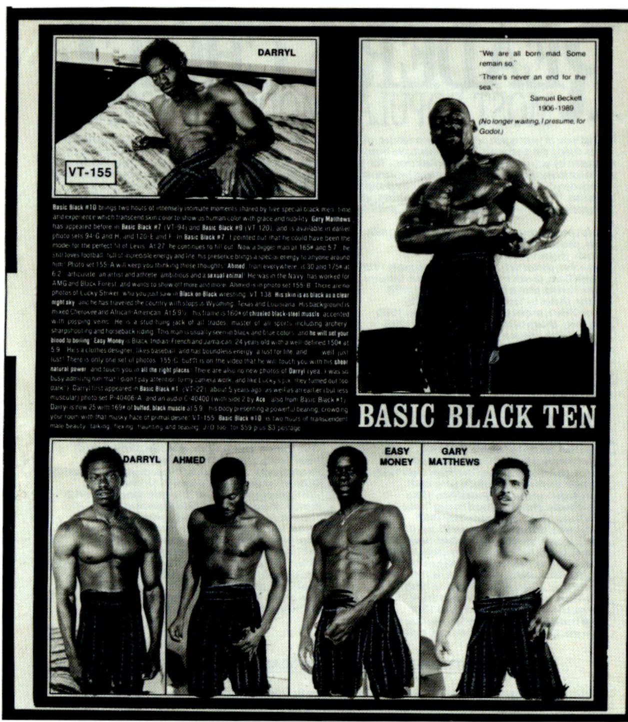

Sketch on magazine page, 2018

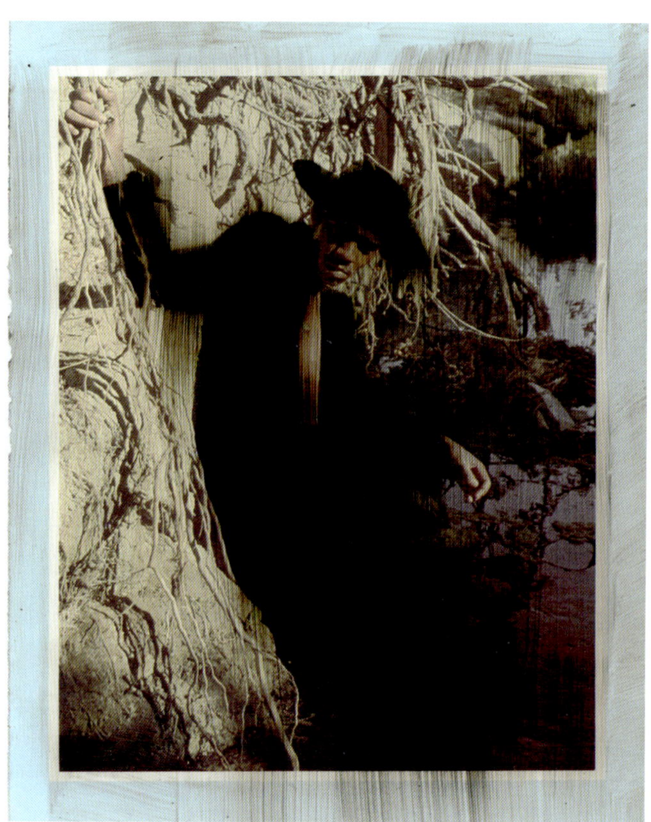

Sketch on magazine page, 2018

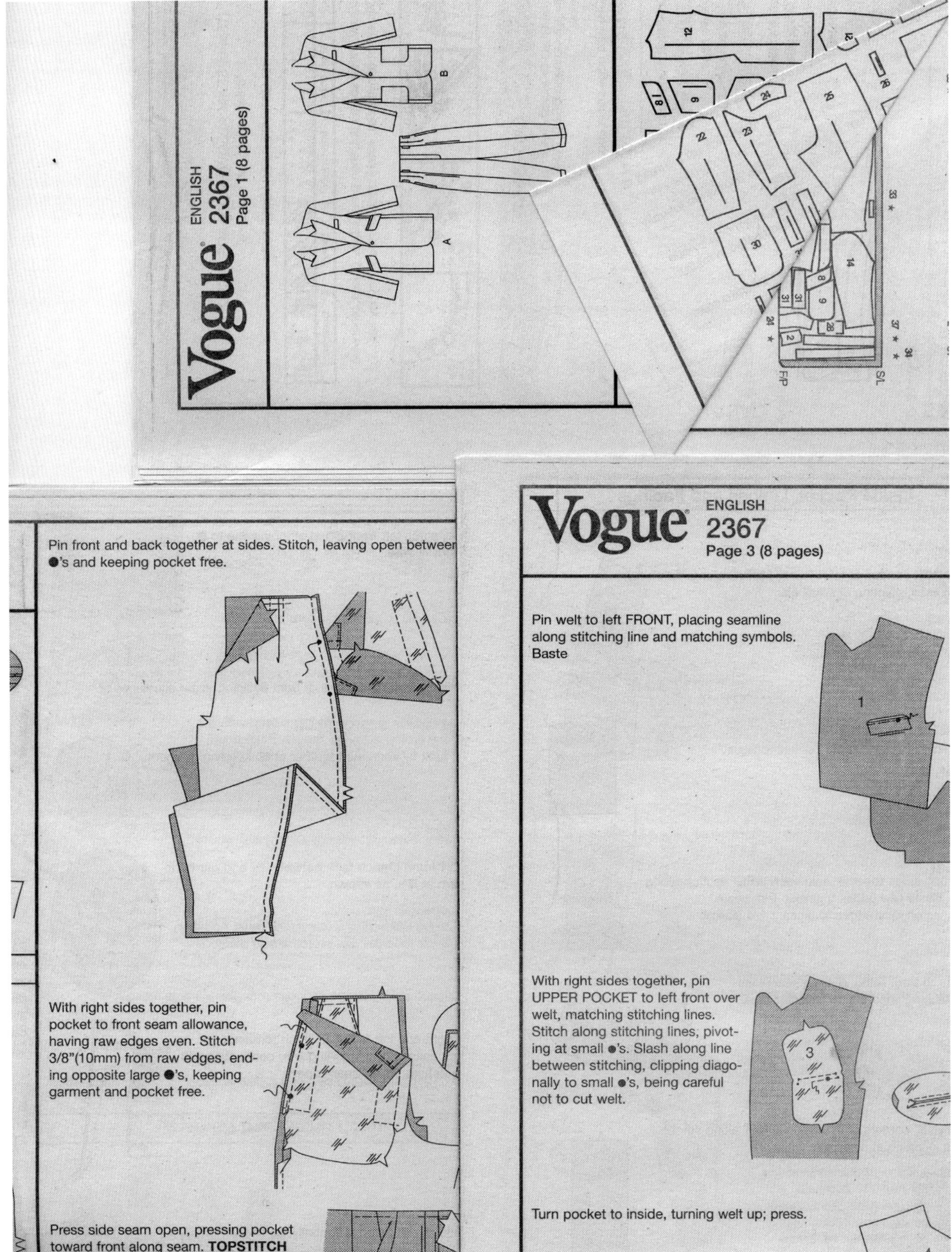

Zoot suit patterns, 1999

TROY MICHIE

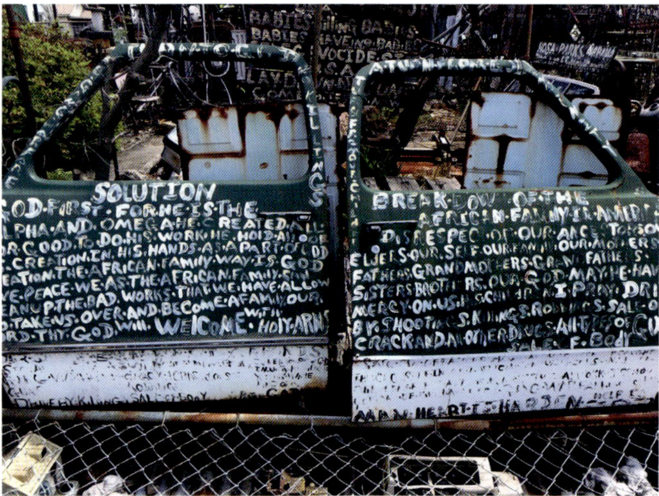

50

Detail of *African Village in America*, 1989–

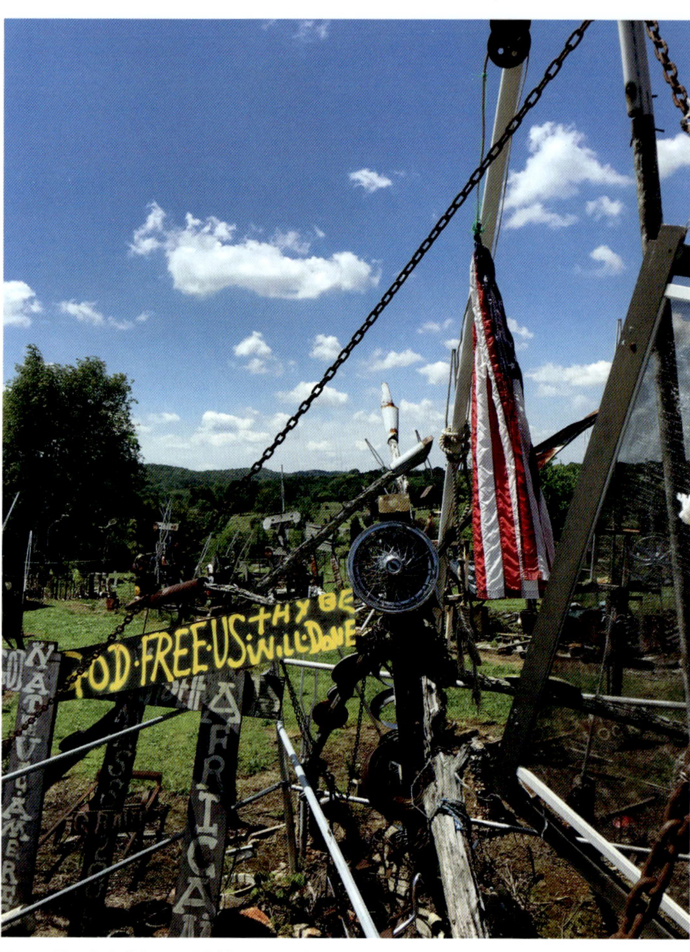

Detail of *African Village in America*, 1989–

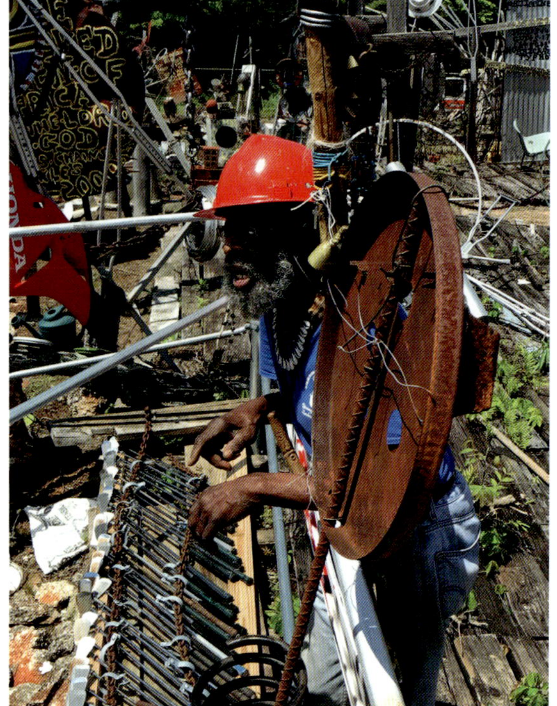

Joe Minter with *African Village in America*, 1989–, Birmingham, AL, 2018

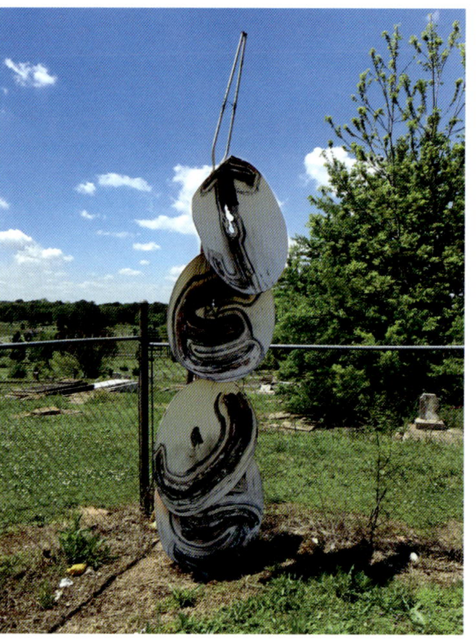

Detail of *African Village in America*, 1989–

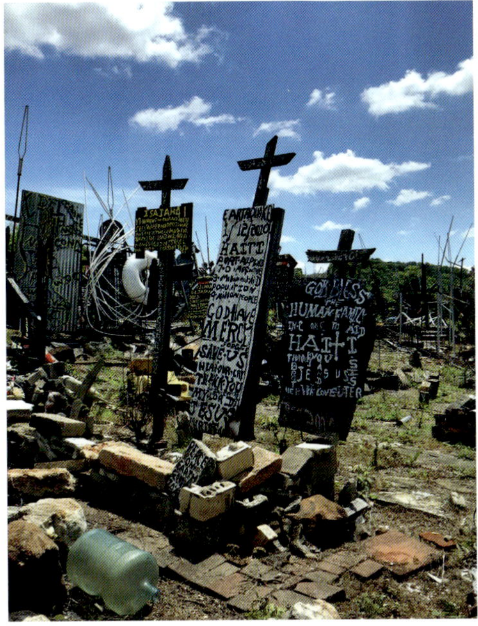

Detail of *African Village in America*, 1989–

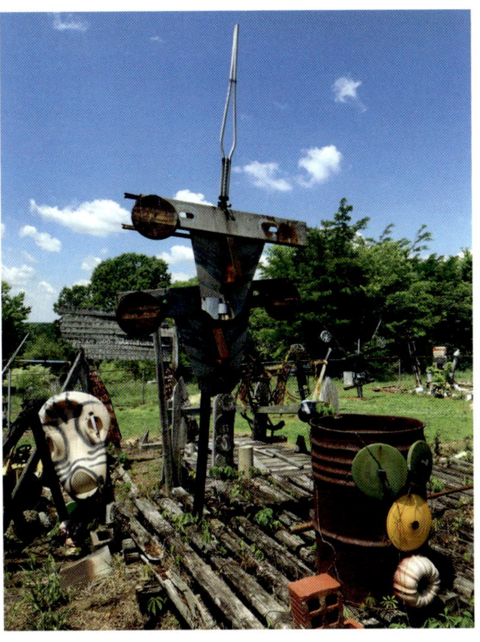

Detail of *African Village in America*, 1989–

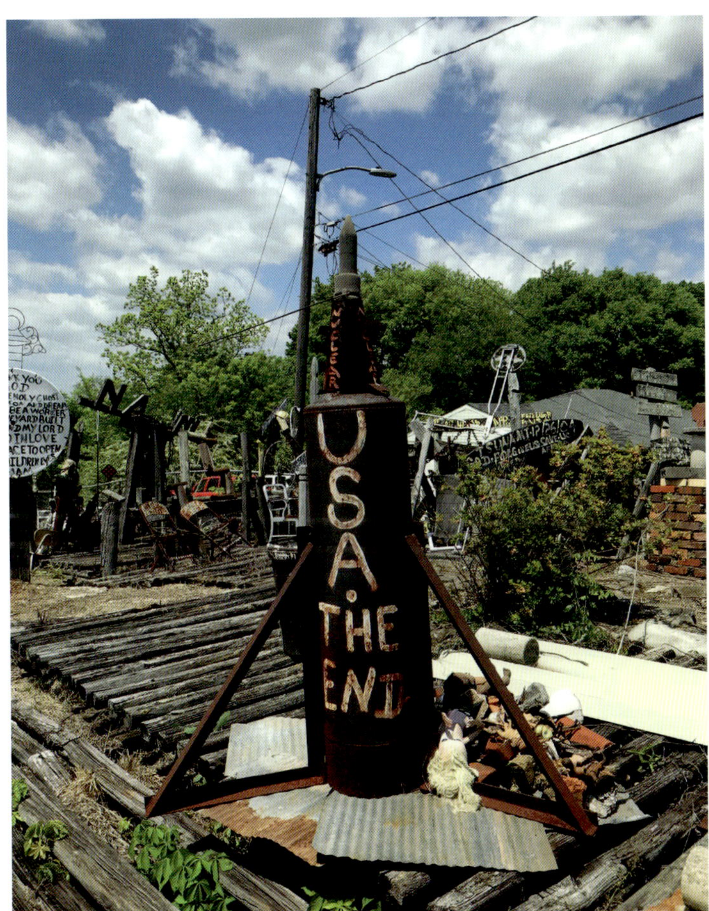

Detail of *African Village in America*, 1989–

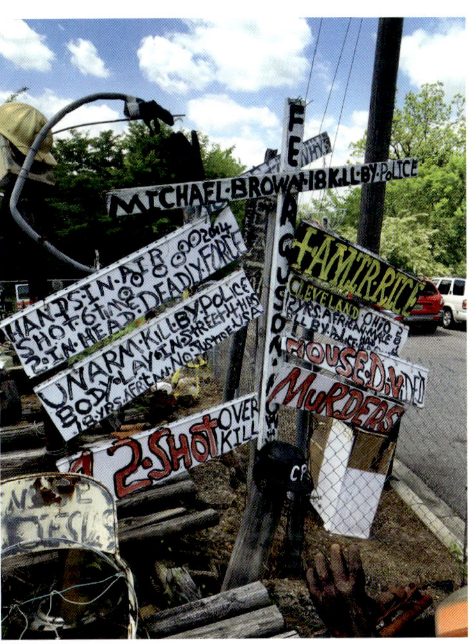

Detail of *African Village in America*, 1989–

JOE MINTER

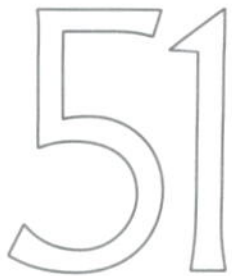

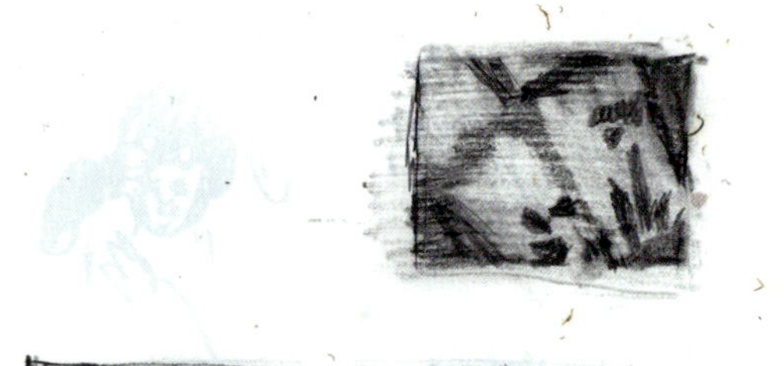

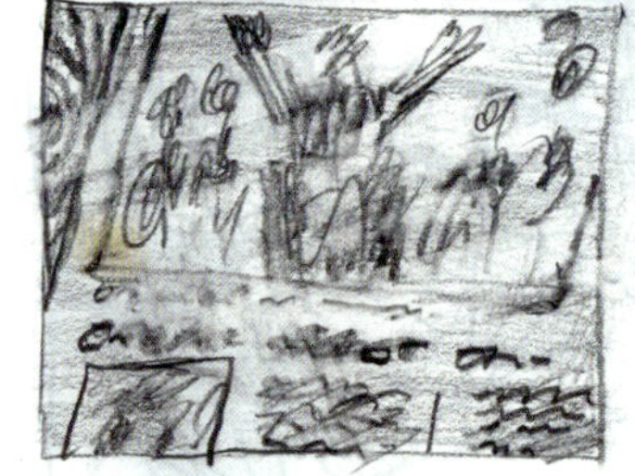

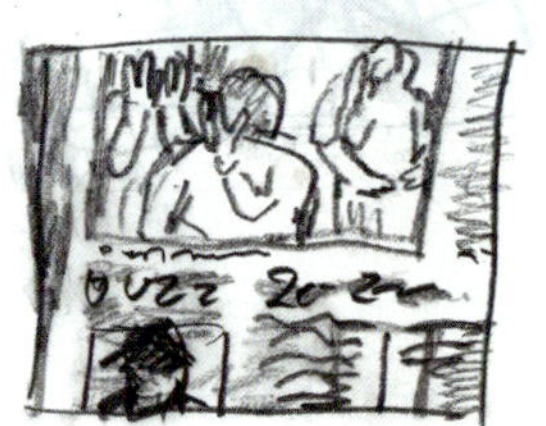

Sketches for *The Paper*, 2016

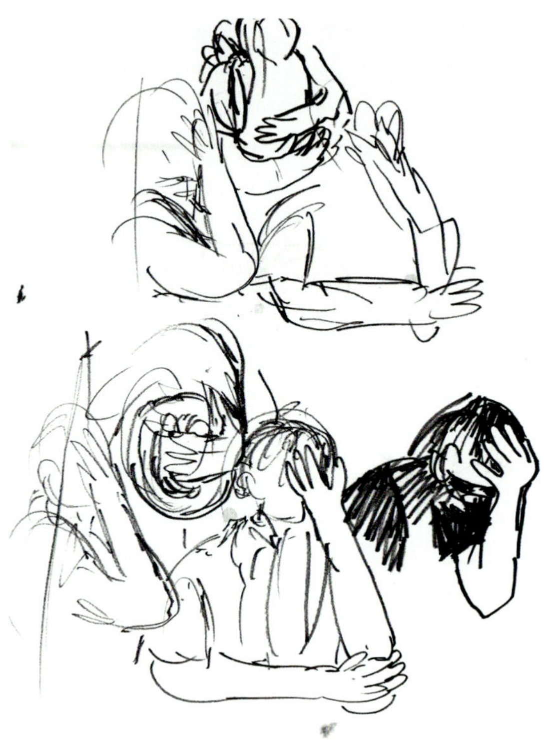

Sketches for *The Paper*, 2016

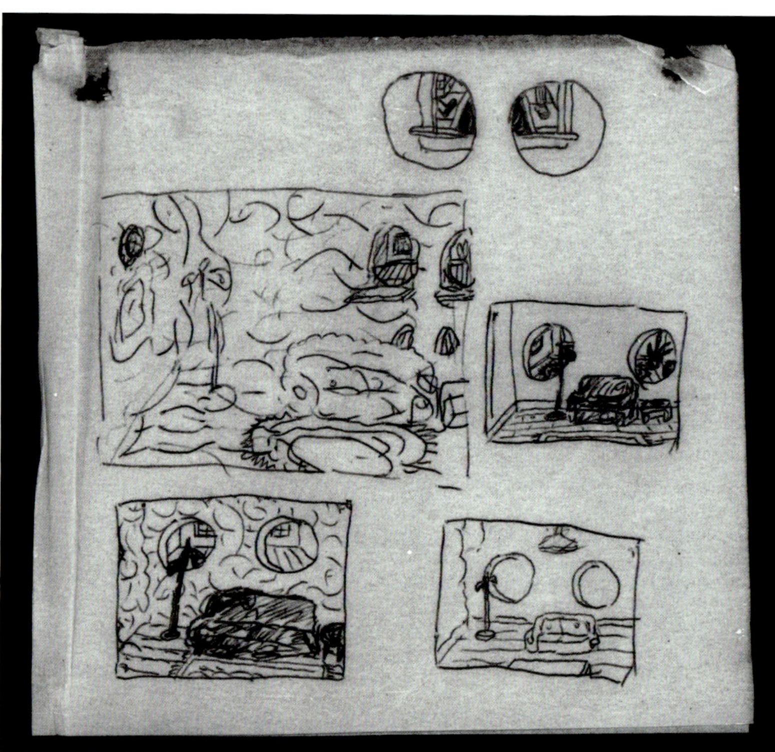

Sketches for *My Place*, 2016

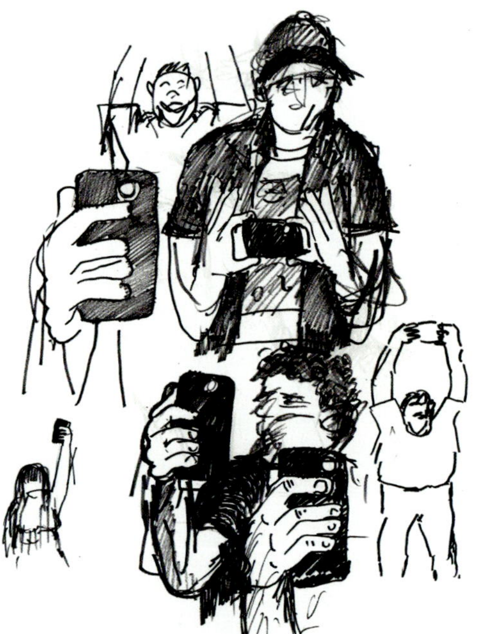

Sketches for *The Screen*, 2016

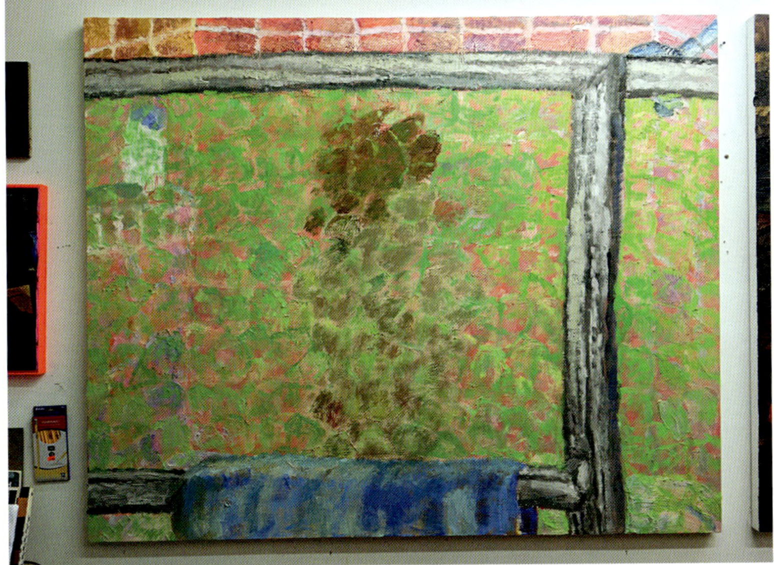

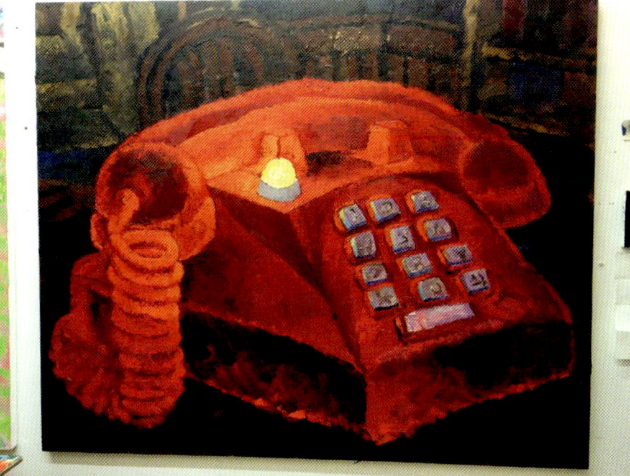

Incoming (work in progress), 2016

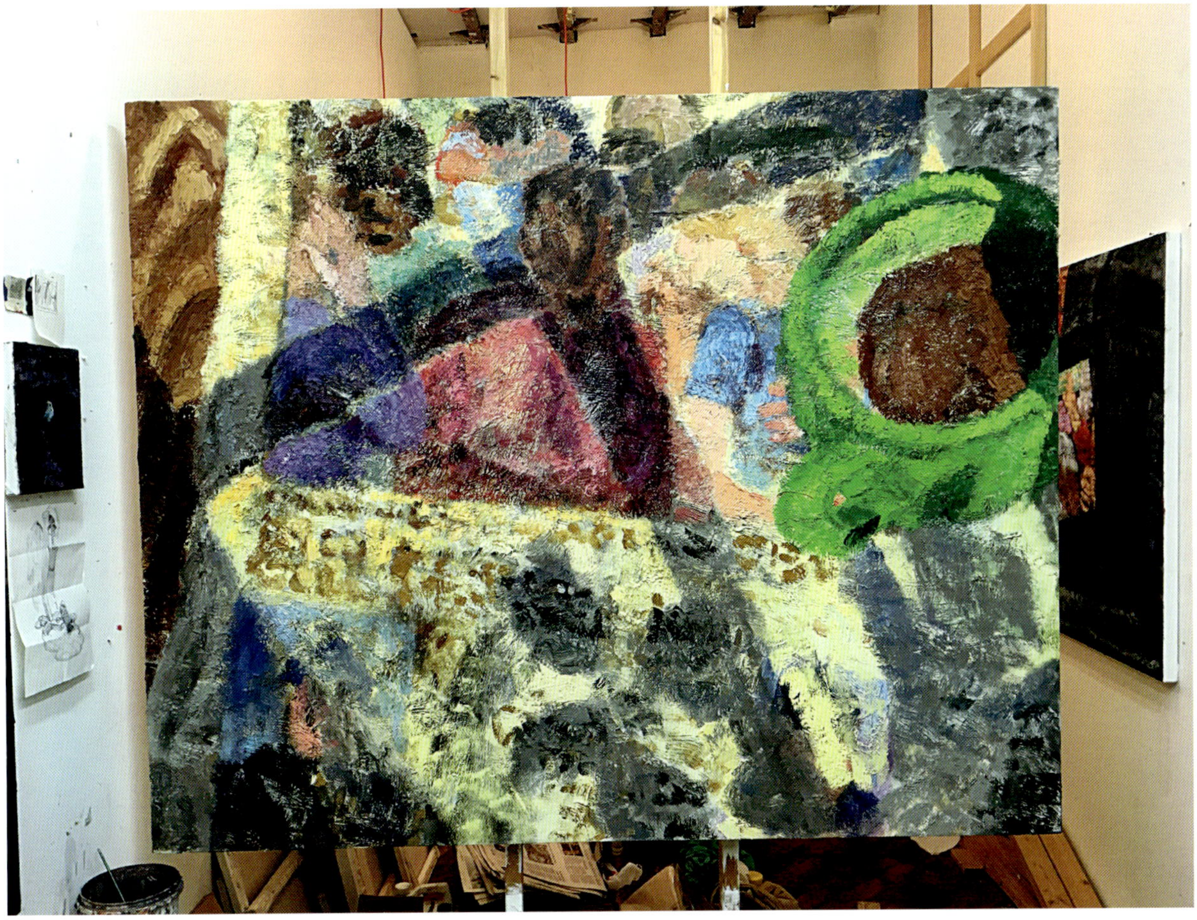

Frosted Glass (work in progress), 2016

The Paper (work in progress), 2016

KEEGAN MONAGHAN

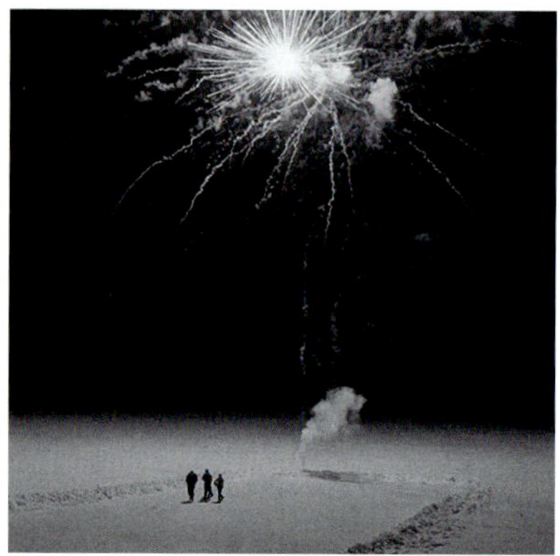

Aleksey Myakishev, *Fireworks in the Kolodozero*, 2015. Source image for *Bootlegger* (work in progress)

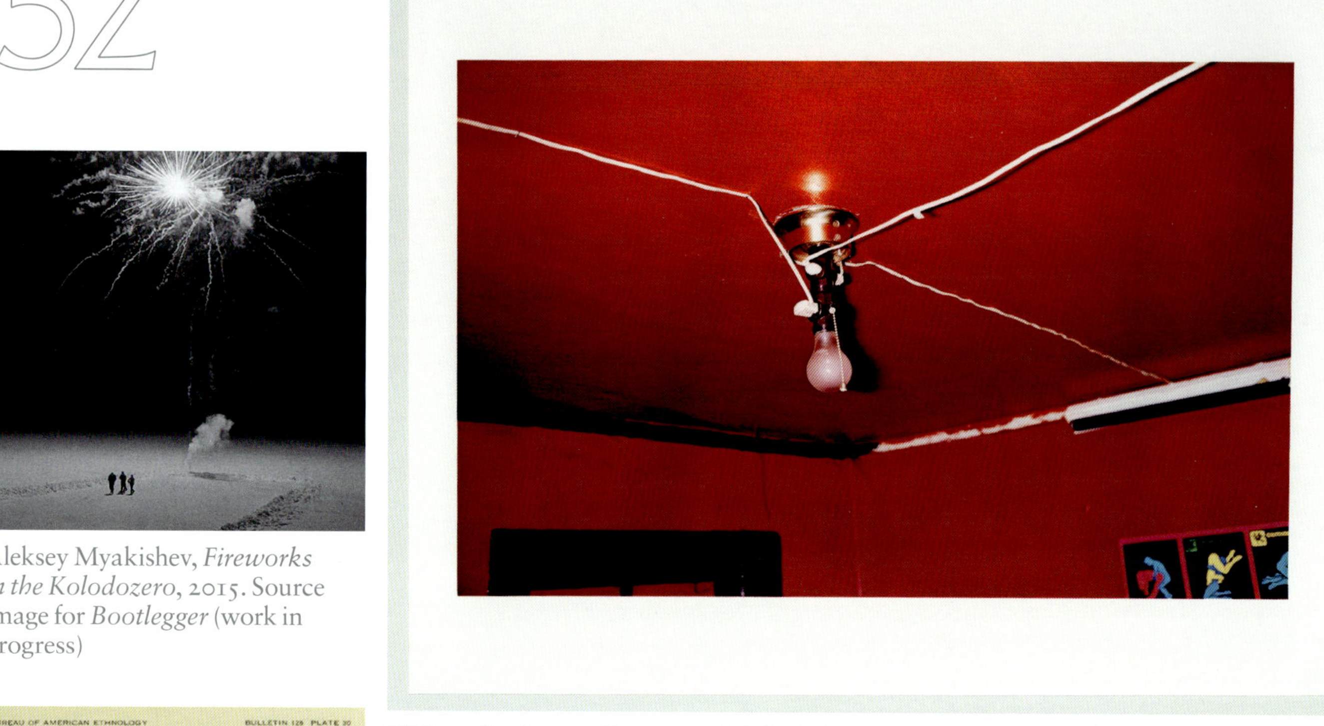

William Eggleston, *Greenwood, Mississippi*, 1973. Source image for *Bootlegger* (work in progress)

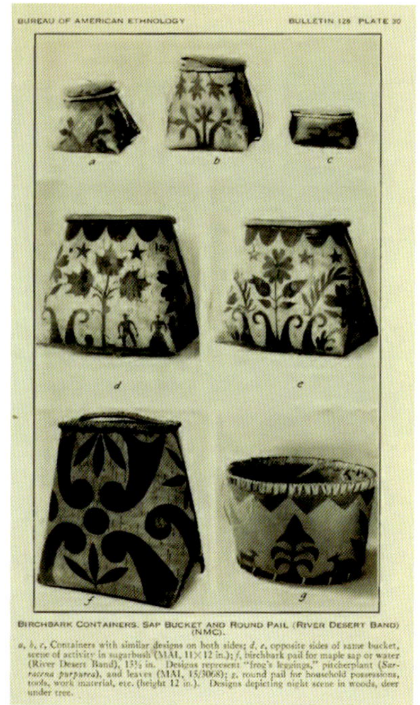

Source image for *In the Name of Progress*, 2018

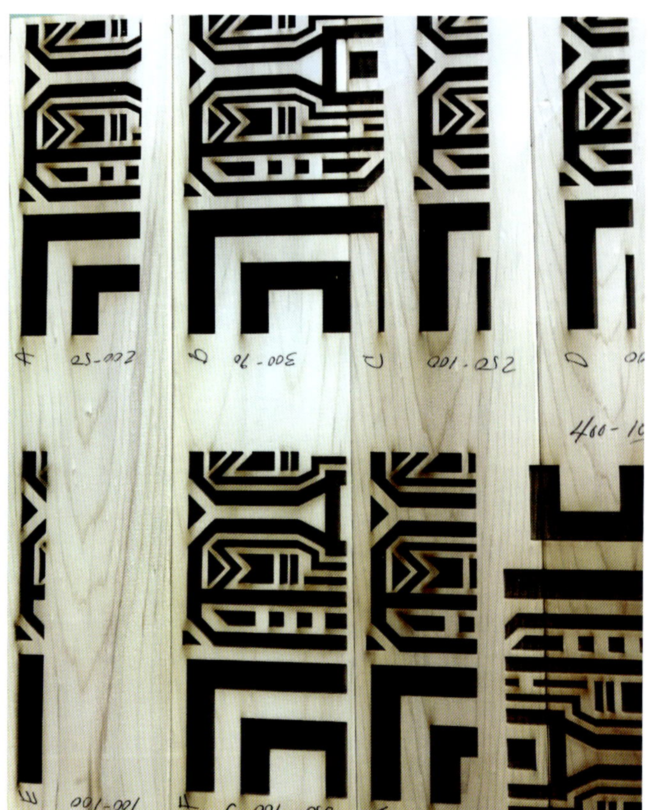

Test plate for pyrography works, 2018

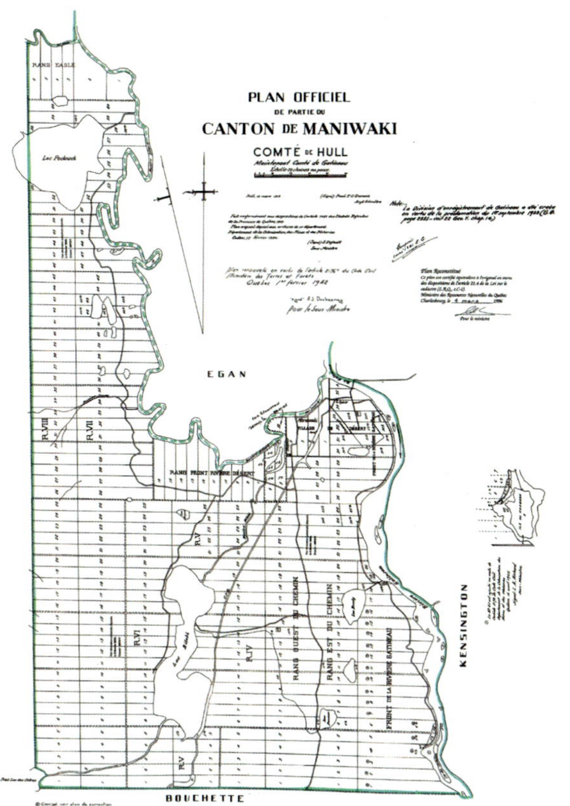

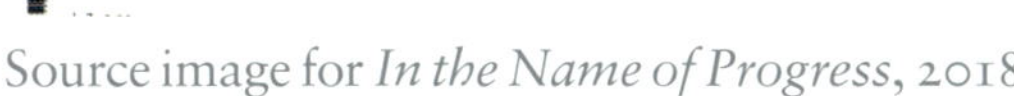

Source image for *In the Name of Progress*, 2018

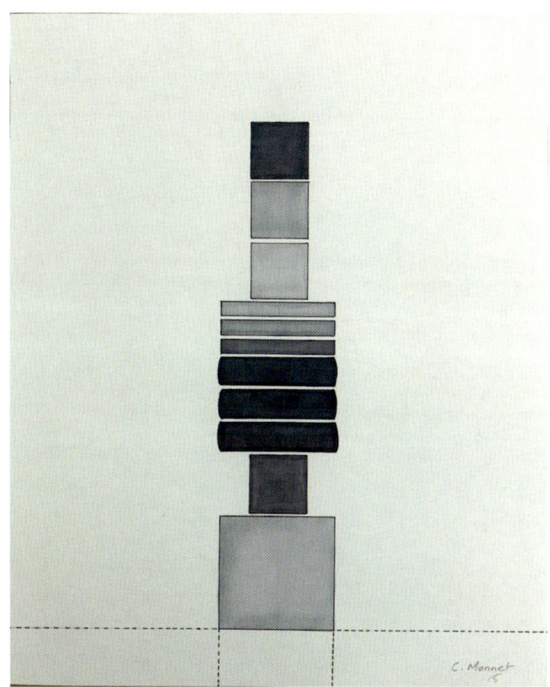

Sketch for *Homo Silvaticus*, 2015

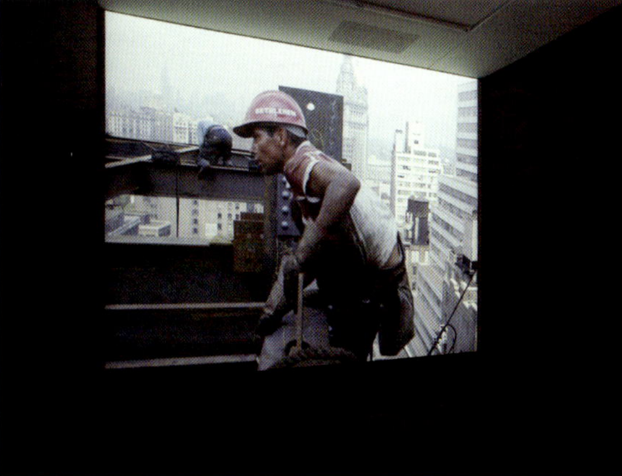

Mobilize, 2015. Installation view, Arsenal
Contemporary NY, New York, NY, 2017

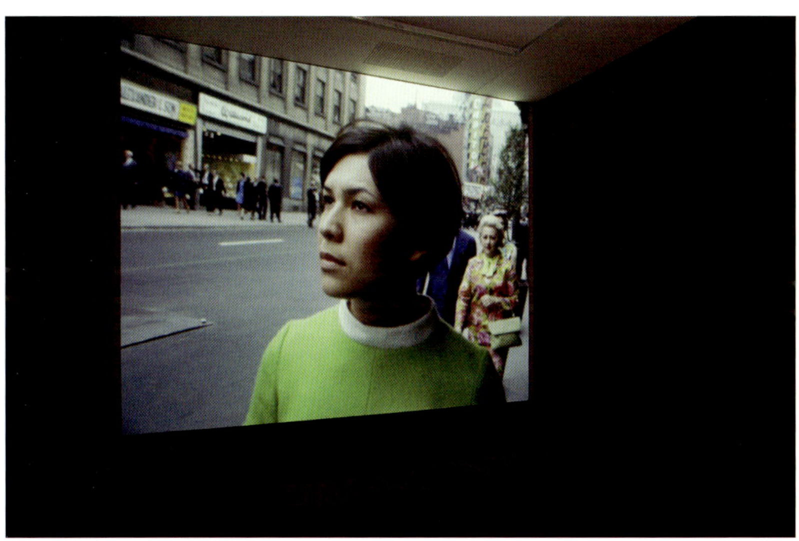

Mobilize, 2015. Installation view, Arsenal Contemporary NY,
New York, NY, 2017

CAROLINE MONNET

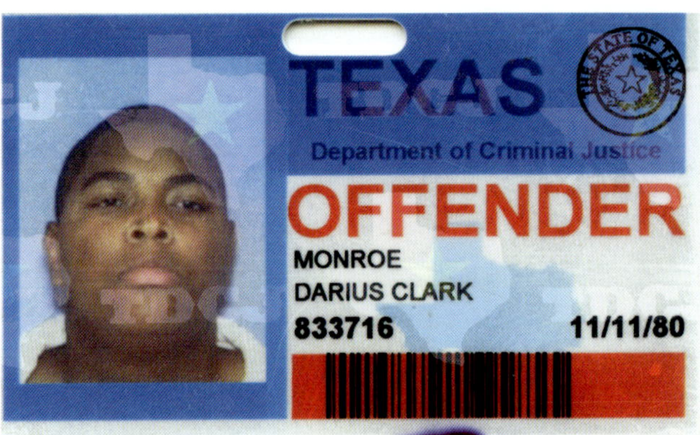

53

The artist's Texas Department of Criminal Justice
prison ID, 1998

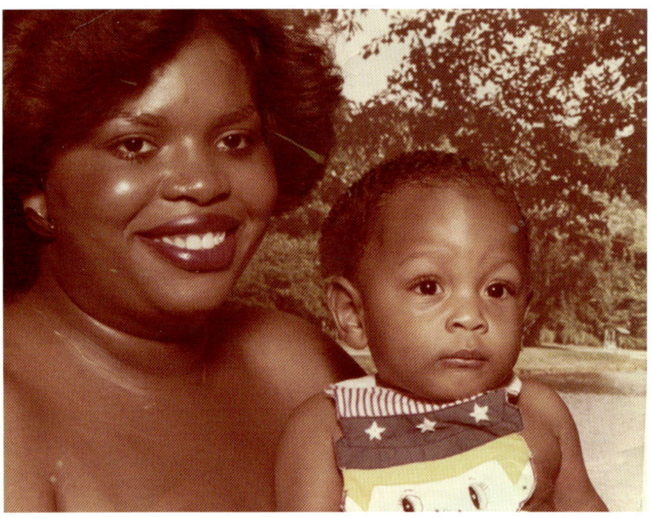

Family photograph of the artist and his mother, 1980.
Source image for *Evolution of a Criminal*, 2014

Family photograph of the artist and his family
after church, 1986

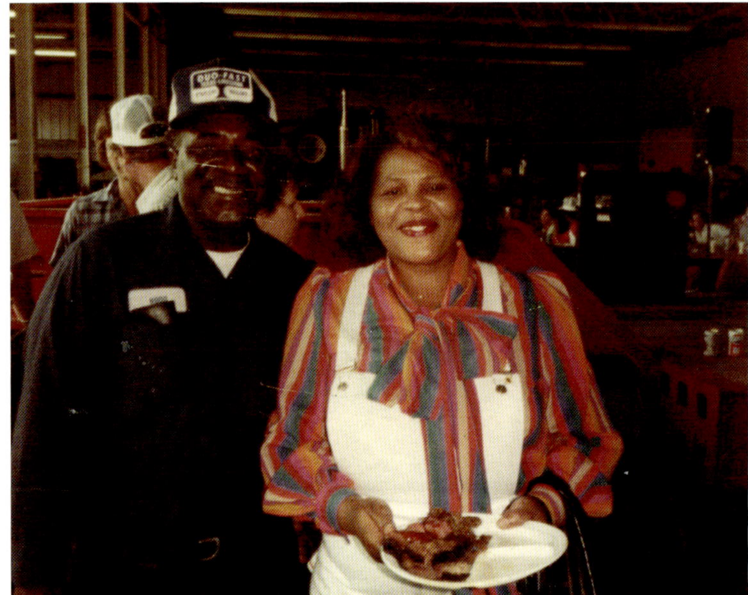

Family photograph of the artist's grandparents, date unknown

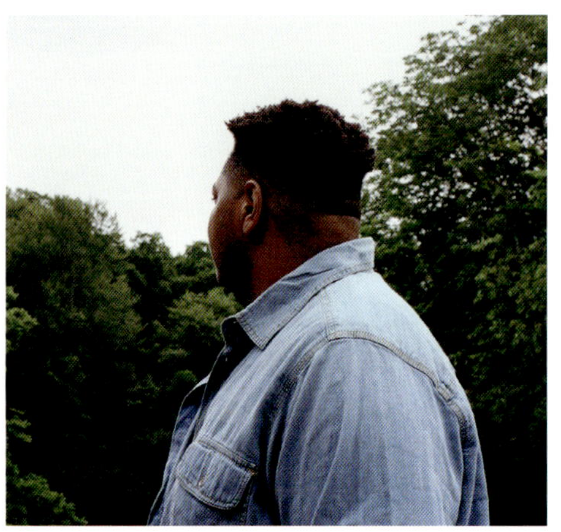

The artist at SPACE on Ryder Farm,
Brewster, NY, 2018

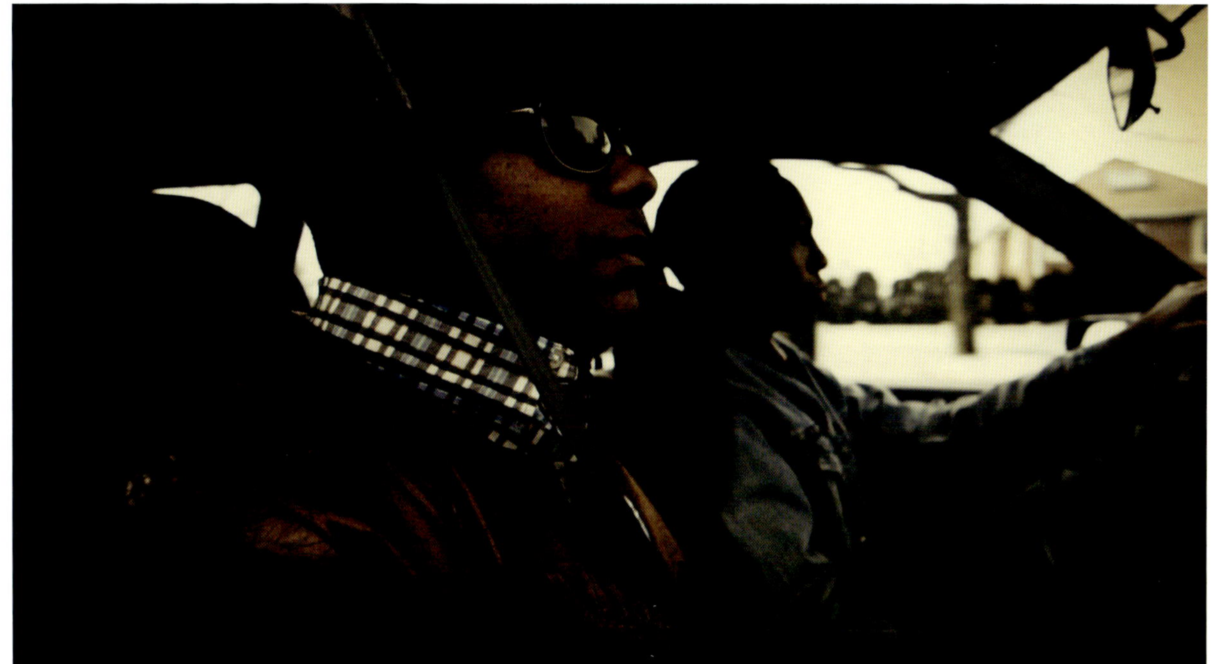

Production still from *Evolution of a Criminal*, 2014

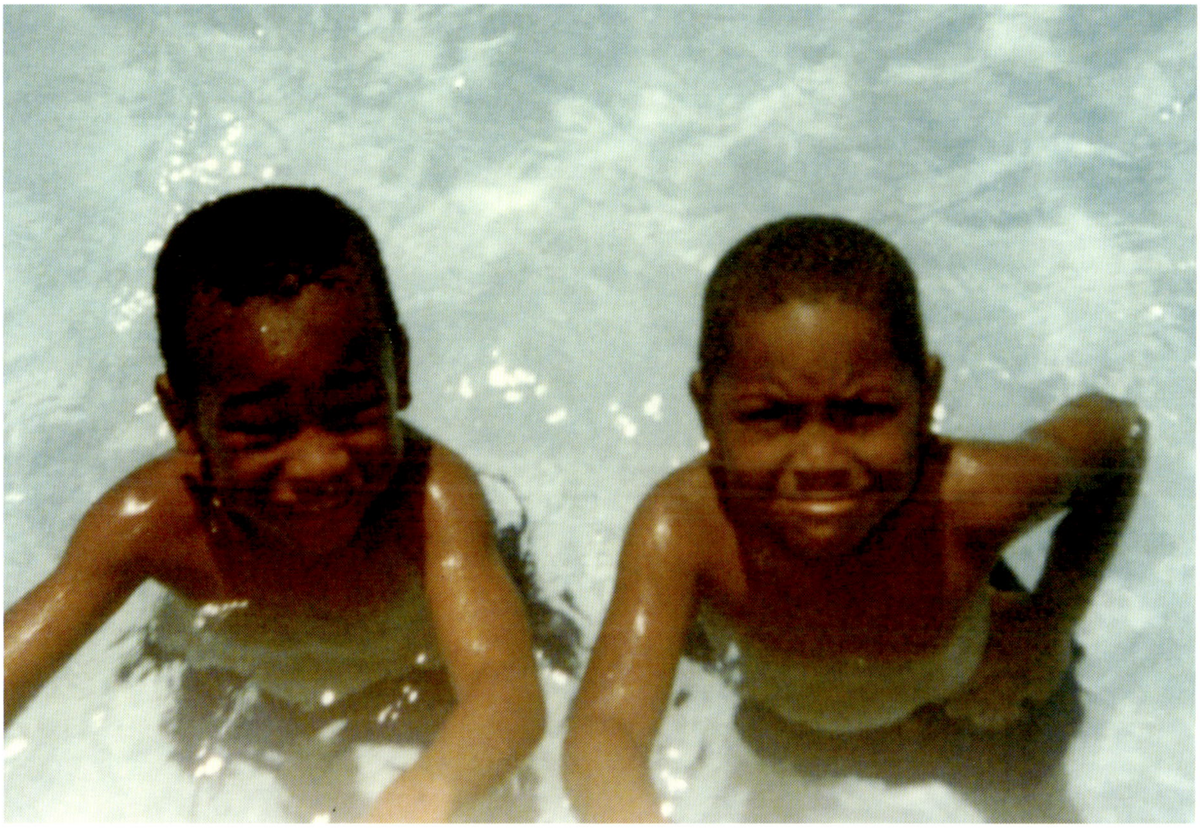

Family photograph, 1985

DARIUS CLARK MONROE

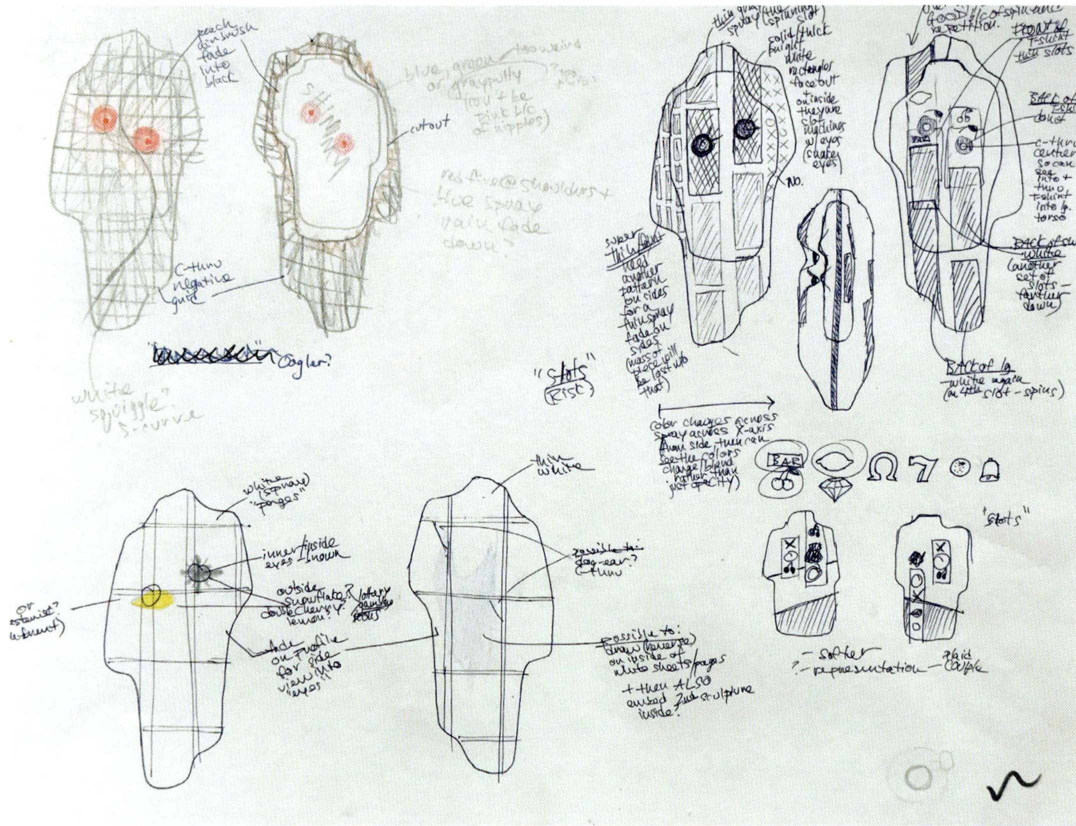

54

Sketches for *Ogler* and *Theoloogian [sic] (with torso)*, 2018

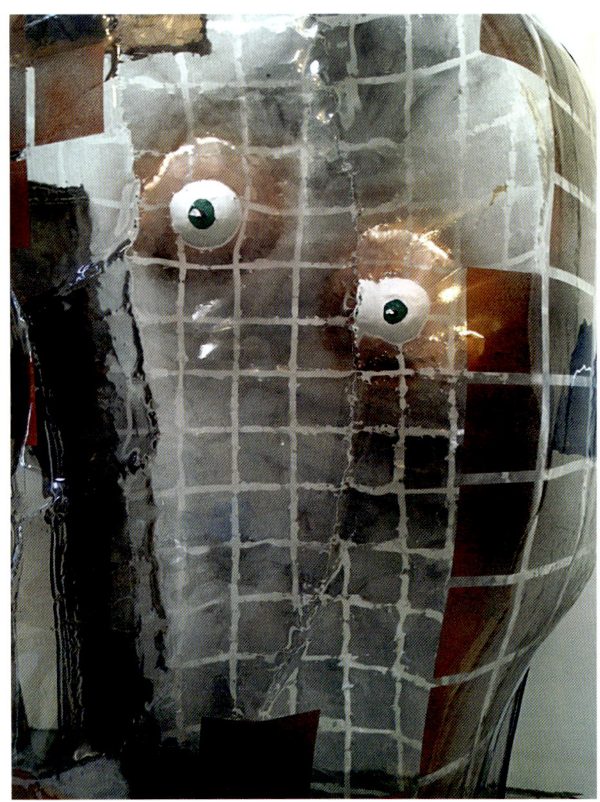

Detail of *Ogler* (work in progress), 2018

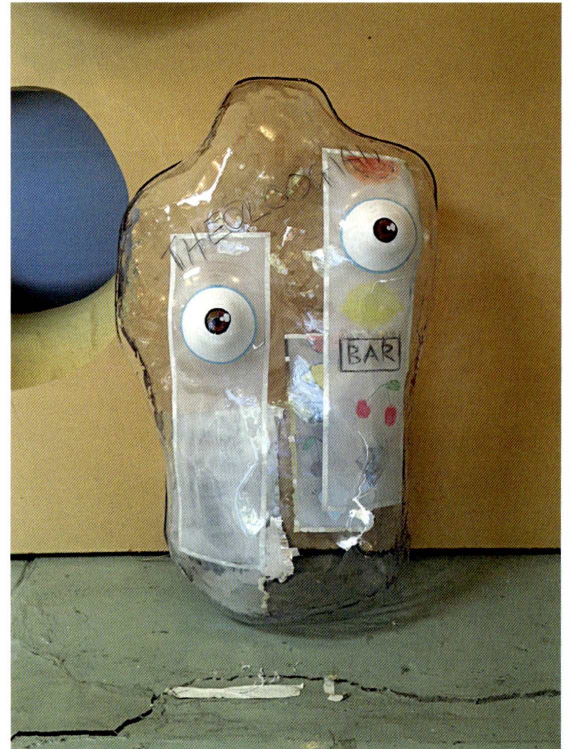

Theoloogian [sic] (with torso) (work in
progress), 2018

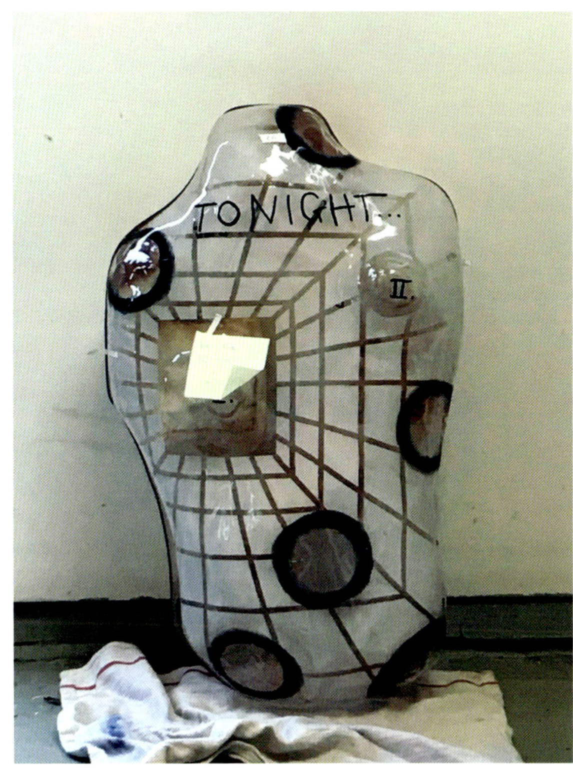

Romanettes (with double heart) (work in progress), 2018

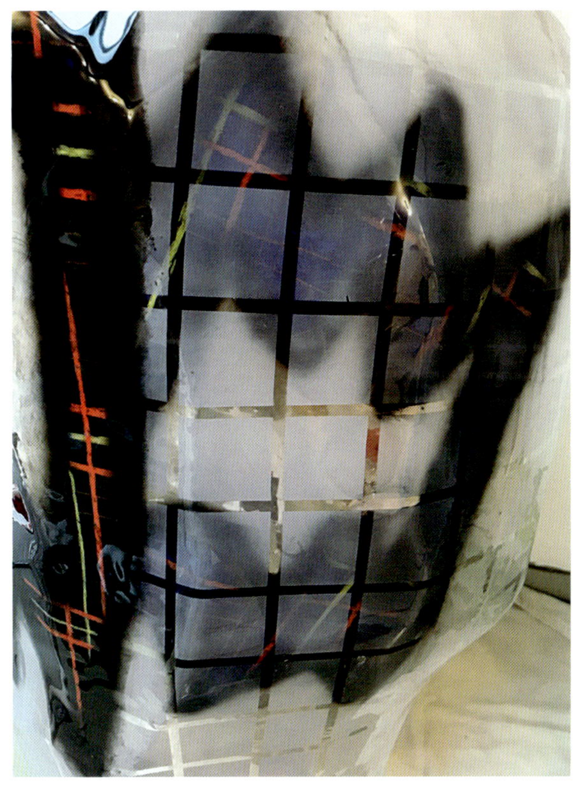

Detail of *Shimmier (with torso, with heart)* (work in progress), 2018

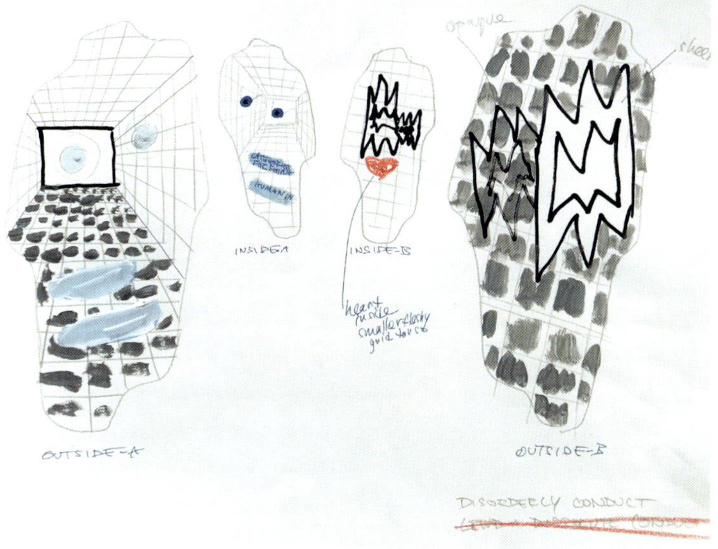

Sketches for *Shimmier (with torso, with heart)*, 2018

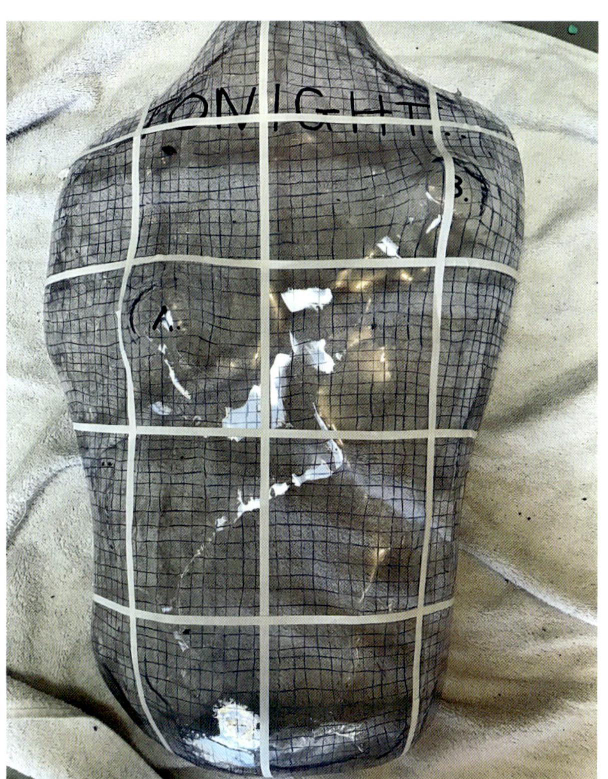

Detail of *Romanettes (with double heart)* (work in progress), 2018

RAGEN MOSS

221

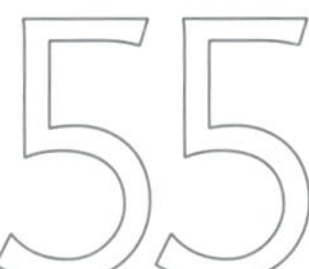

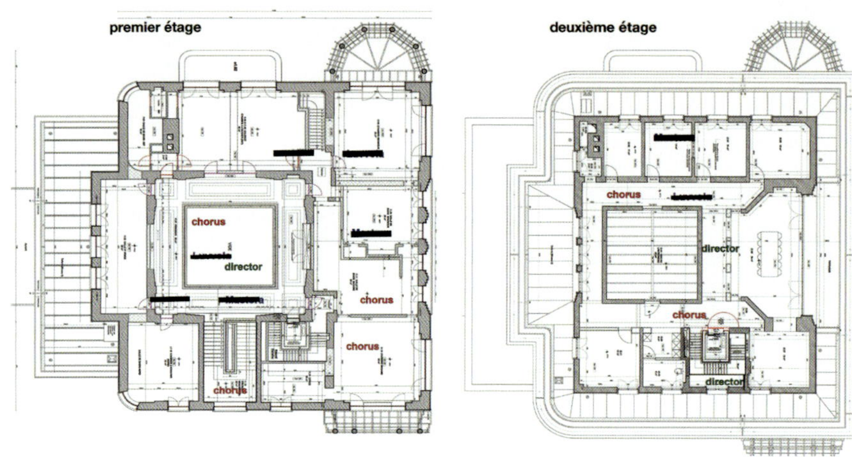

55

Floor plan with dramaturgical notes for *Directory of Portrayals*, Villa Empain, Brussels, Belgium, 2016

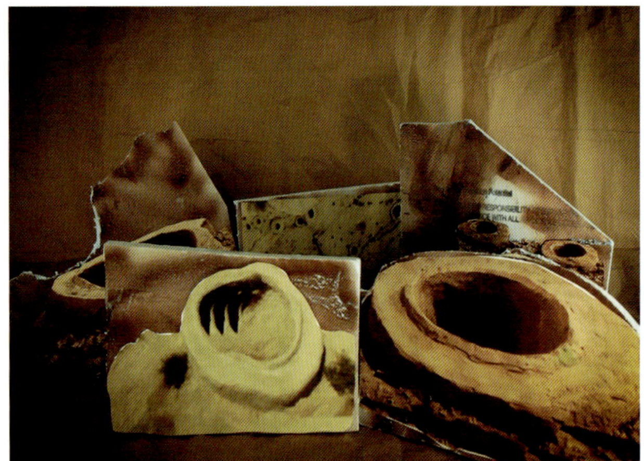

Maquette for *Directory of Portrayals*, 2017

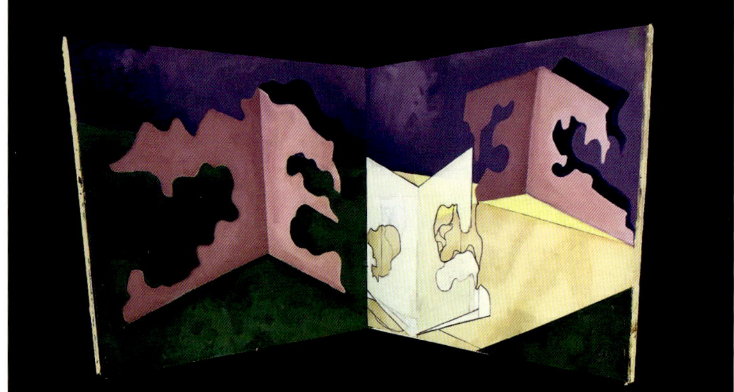

Set painting for *Swamp Study*, 2017

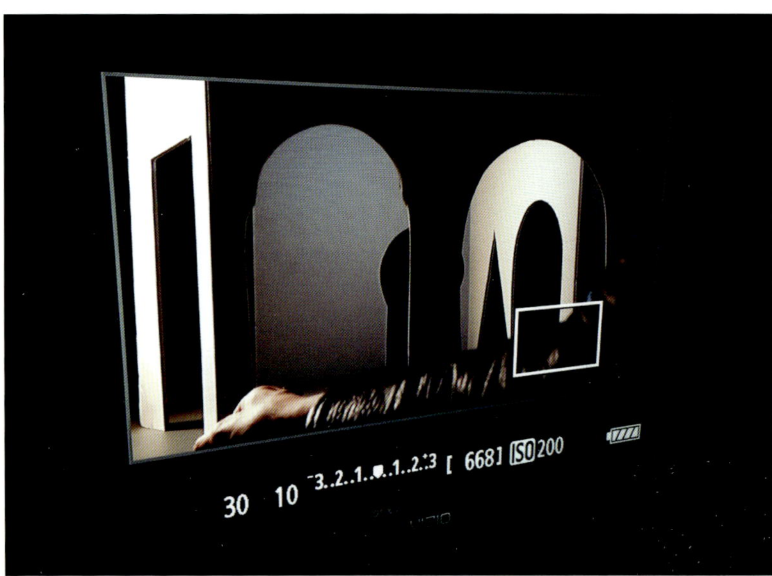

Still from videographic set for *Sounds from Untitled Skies*, 2015

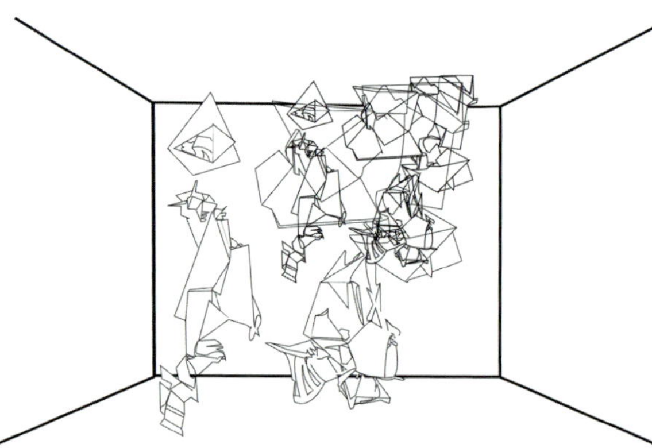

Drawing for set of *Geology Study*, 2010

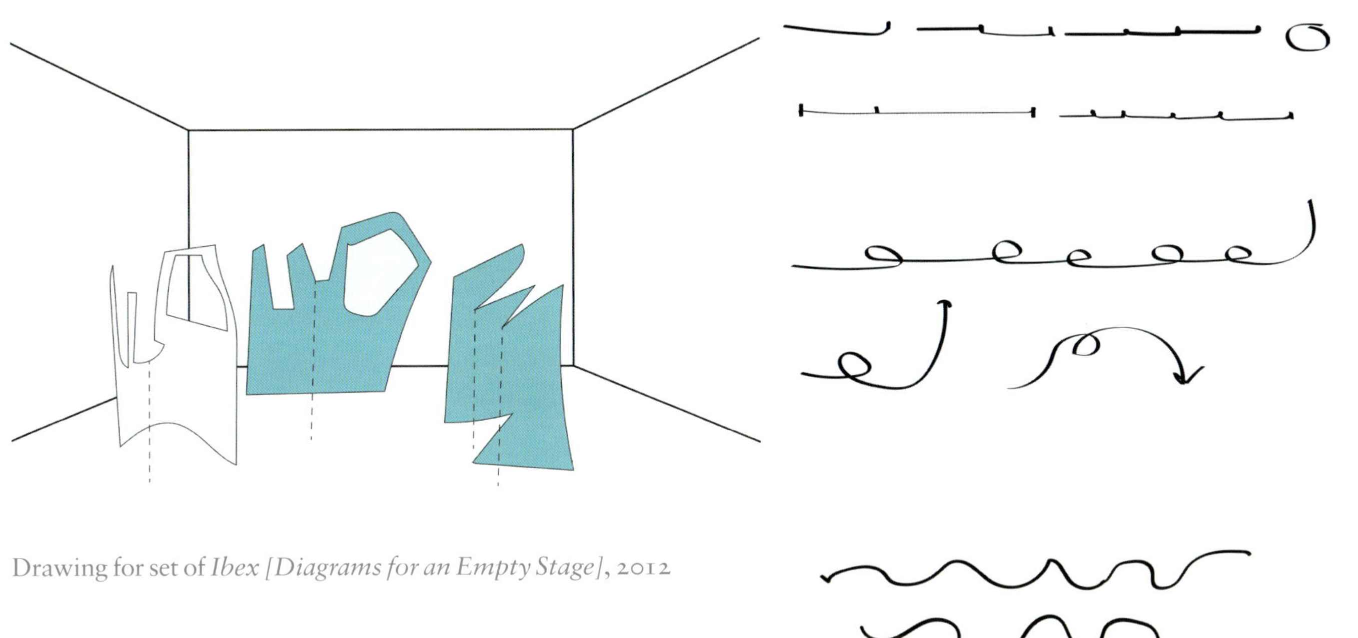

Drawing for set of *Ibex [Diagrams for an Empty Stage]*, 2012

Vocal score diagram for *Inter-Voice*, 2018

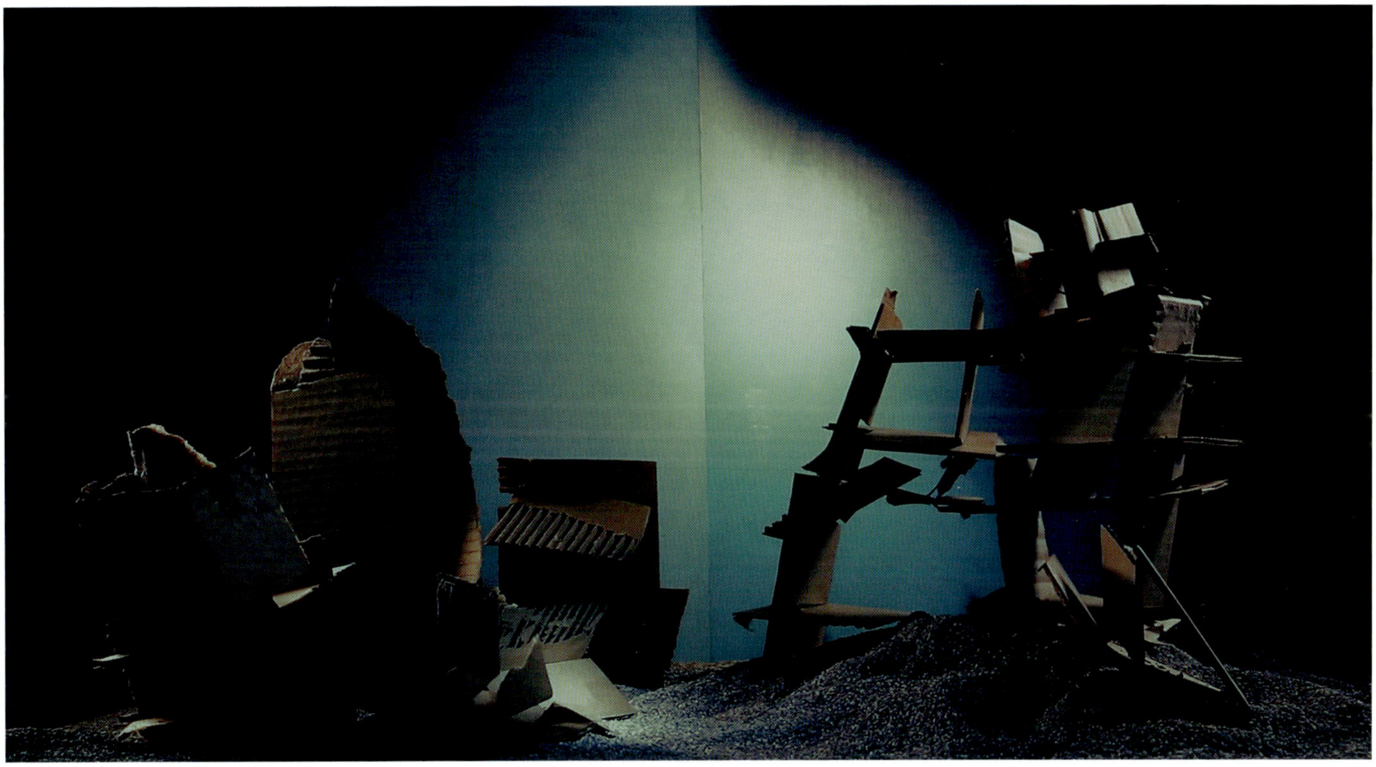

Maquette for video from *Sounds from Untitled Skies*, 2015

SAHRA MOTALEBI

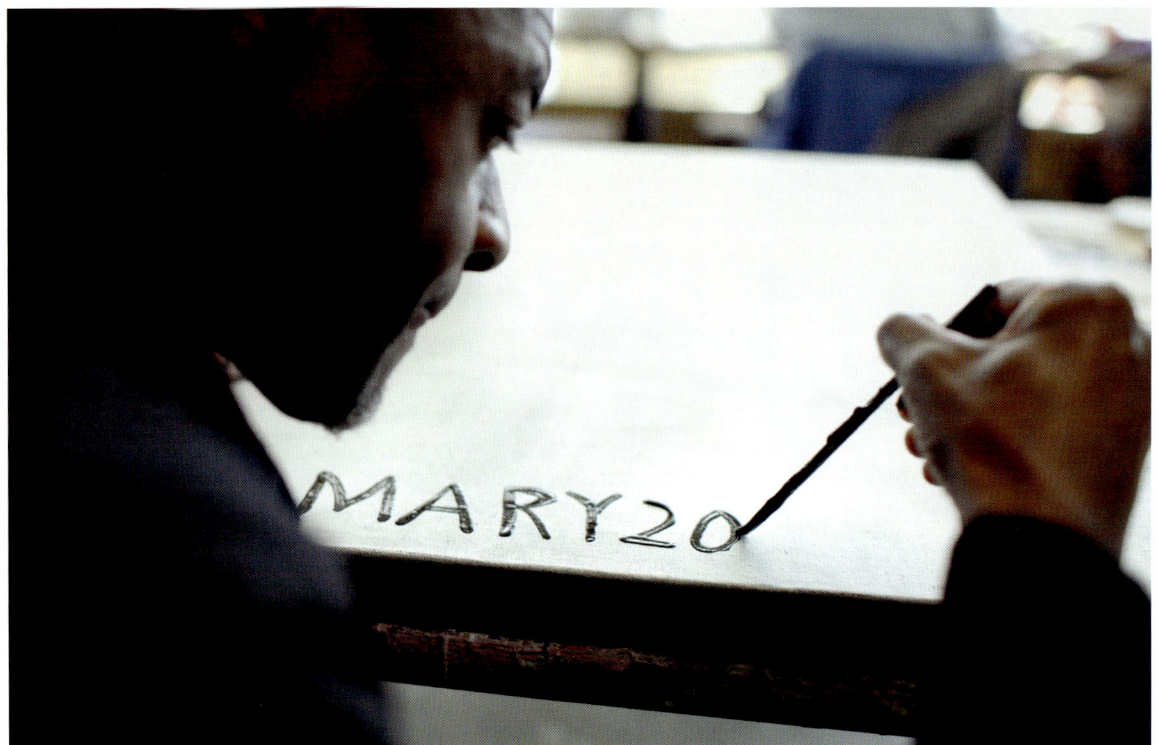

56

The artist in his studio, NIAD Art Center, Richmond, CA, 2018

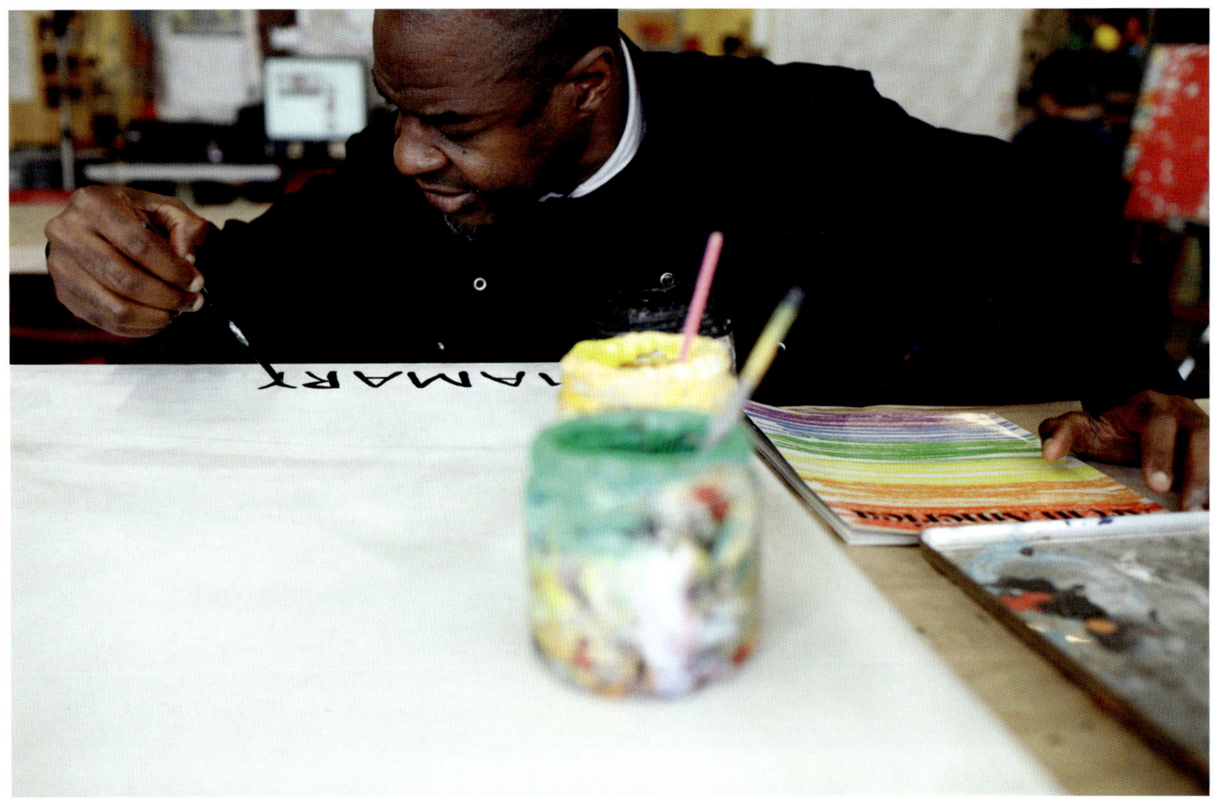

The artist in his studio, NIAD Art Center, Richmond, CA, 2018

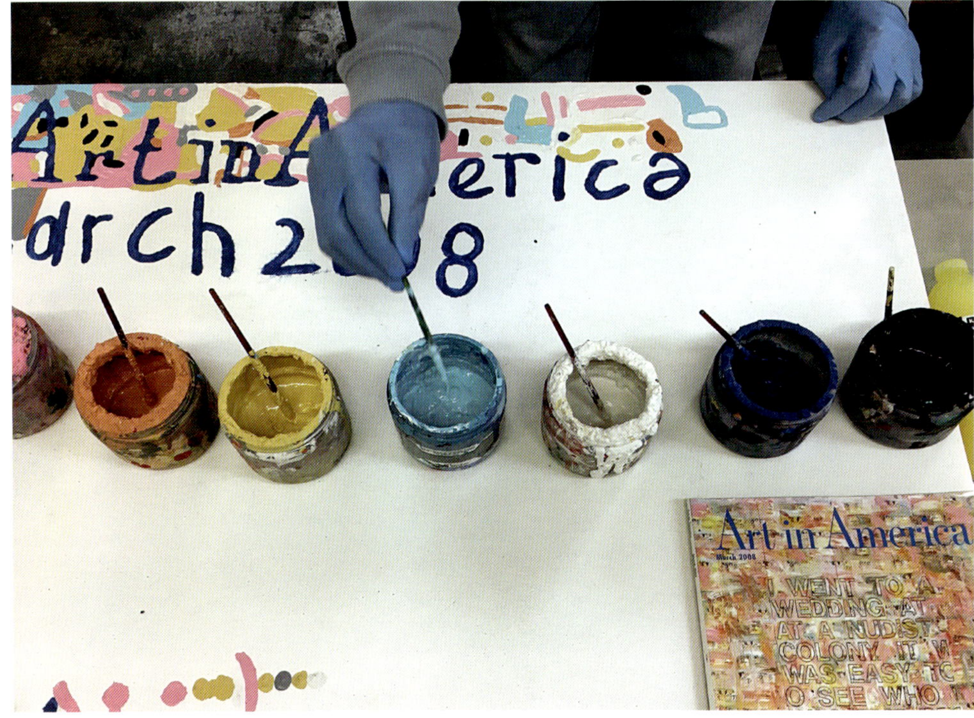

The artist in his studio, NIAD Art Center, Richmond, CA, 2018

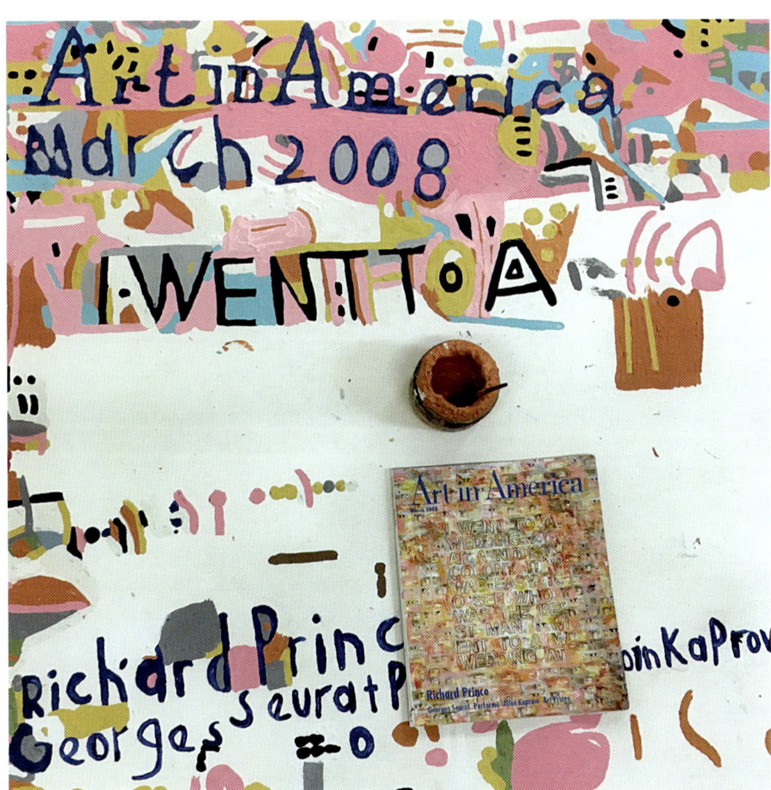

Detail of *untitled* (work in progress), with *Art in America* magazine, 2018

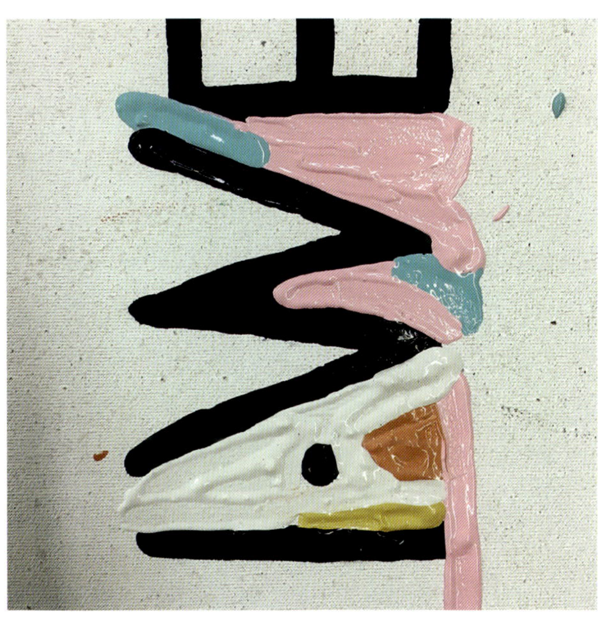

Detail of *untitled* (work in progress), 2018

MARLON MULLEN

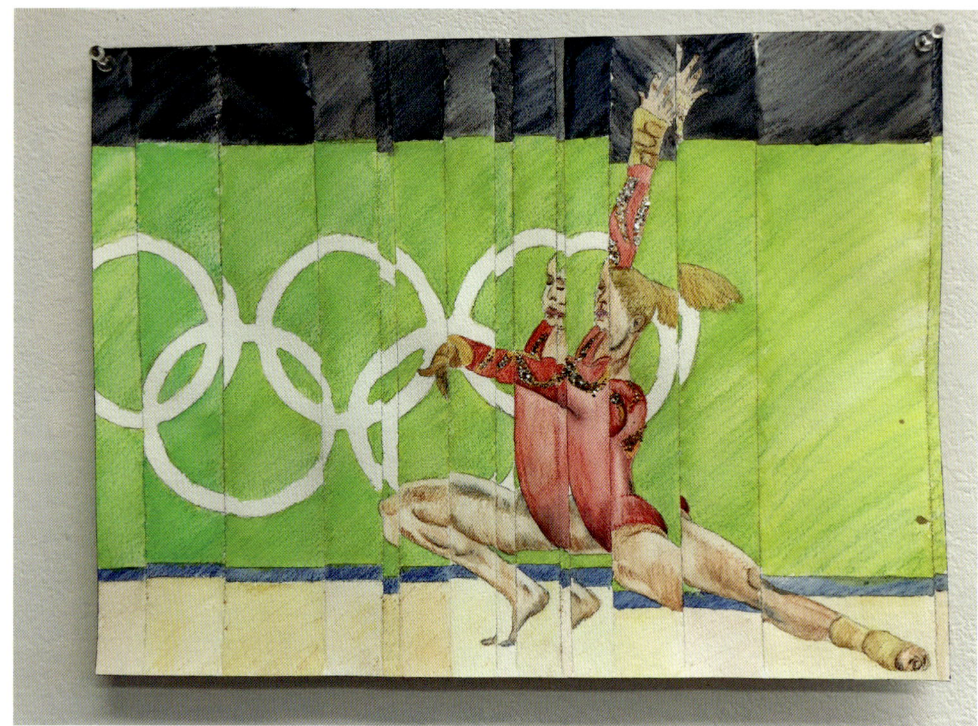

Untitled, 2018

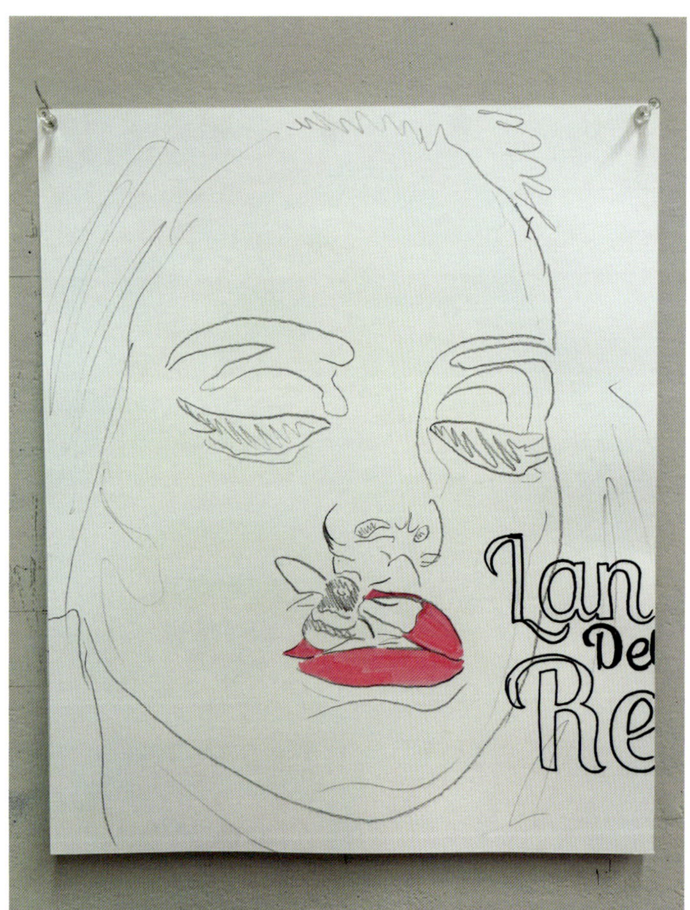

Untitled, 2018

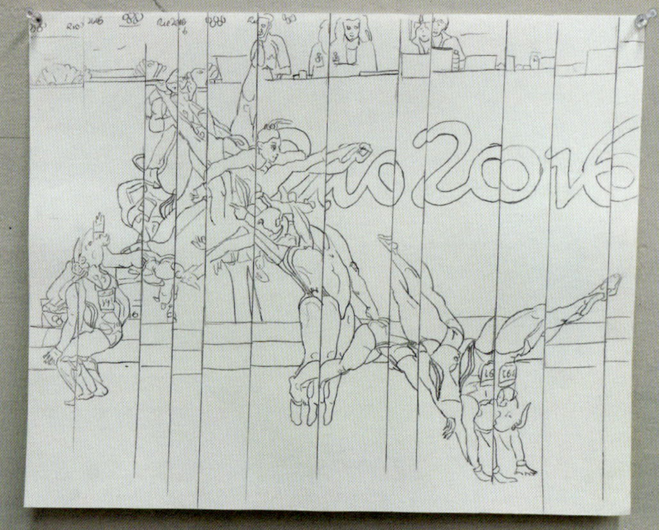

Untitled, 2017

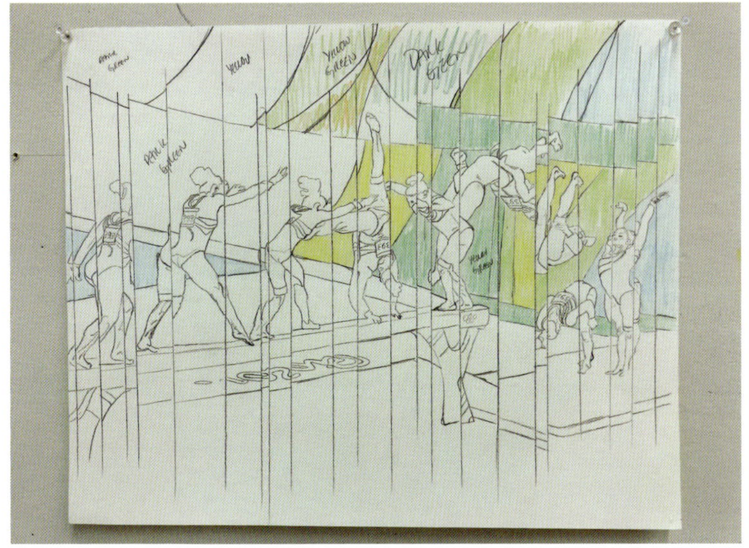

Untitled, 2018

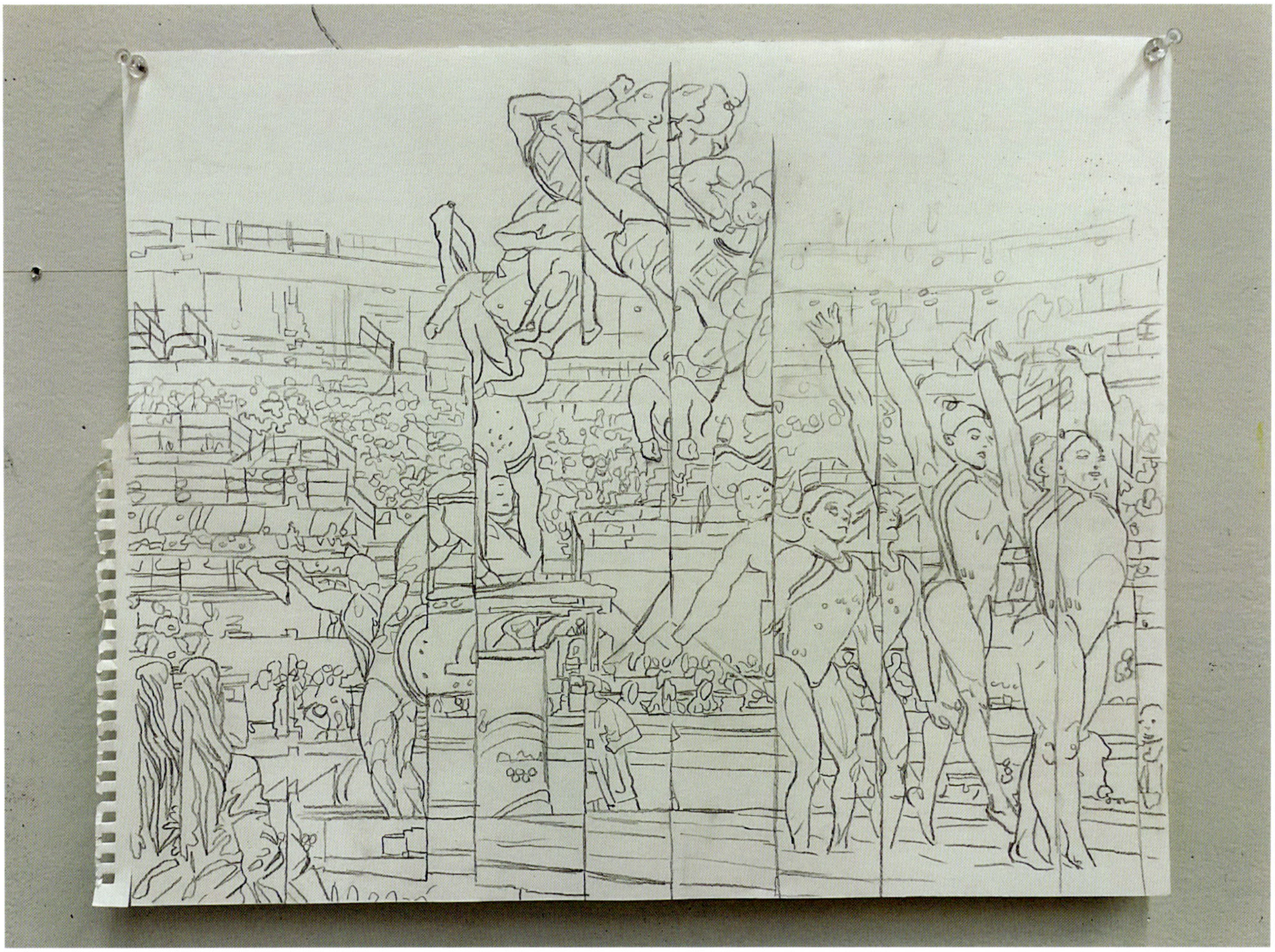

Untitled, 2016

JEANETTE MUNDT

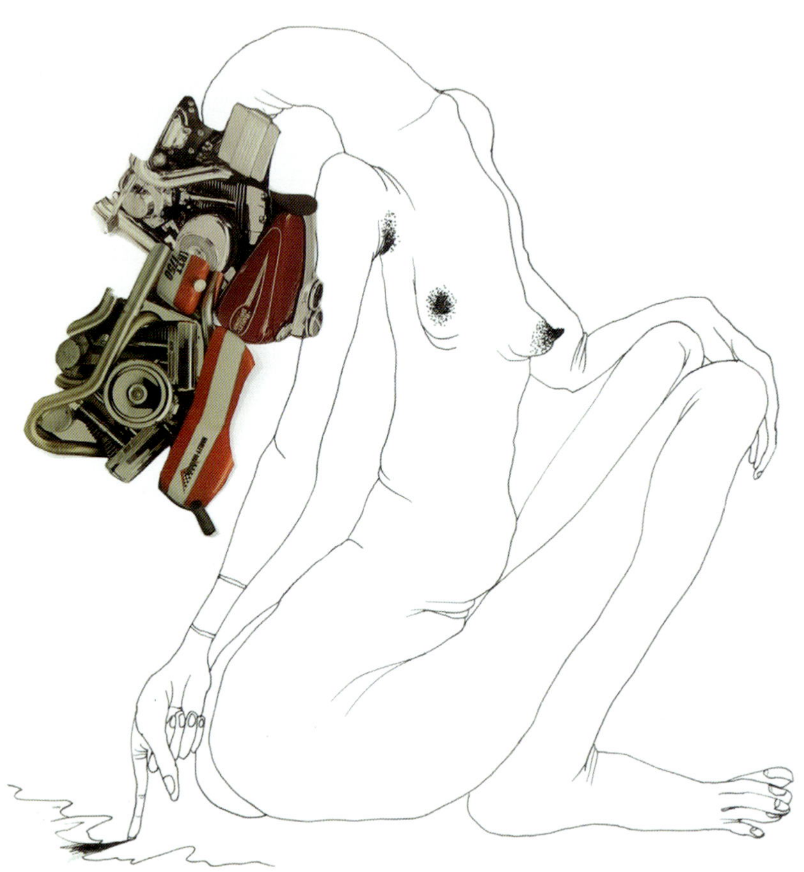

Sketchbook page, 2012–13

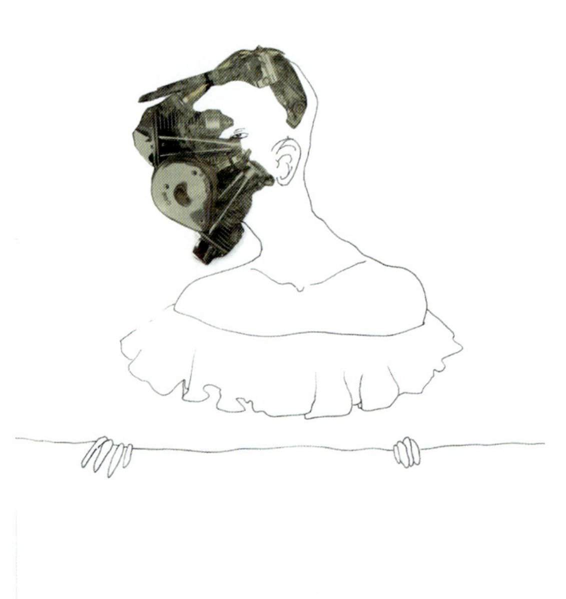

Sketchbook page, 2012–13

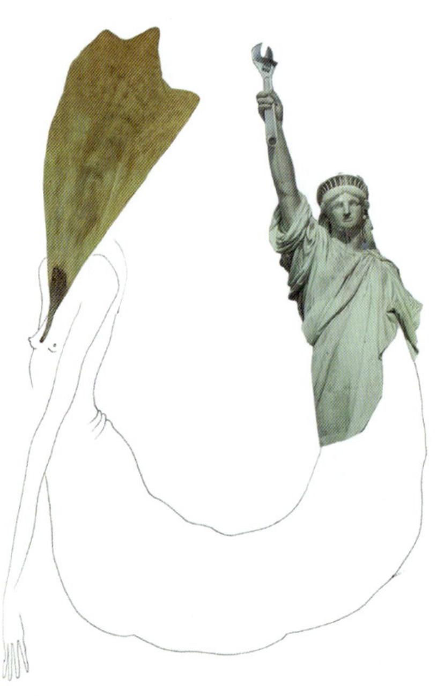

Sketchbook page, 2012–13

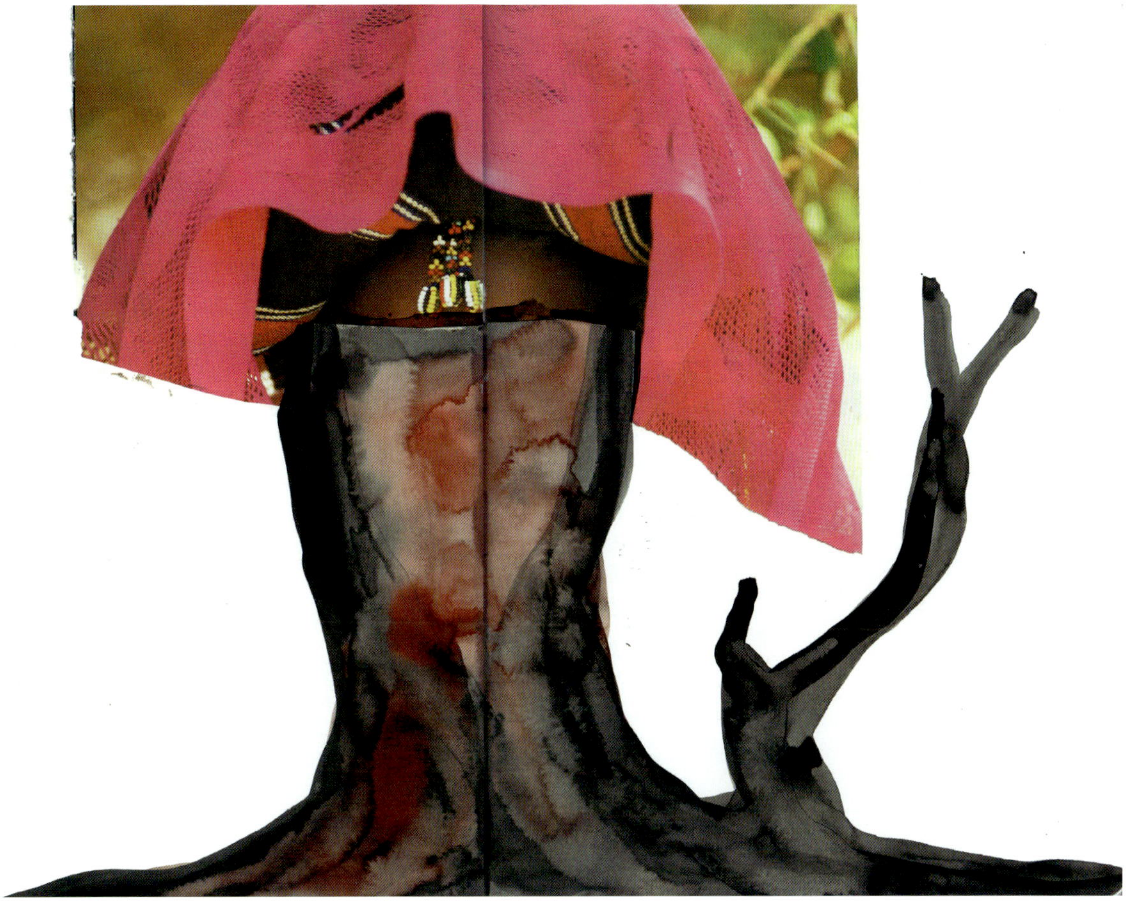

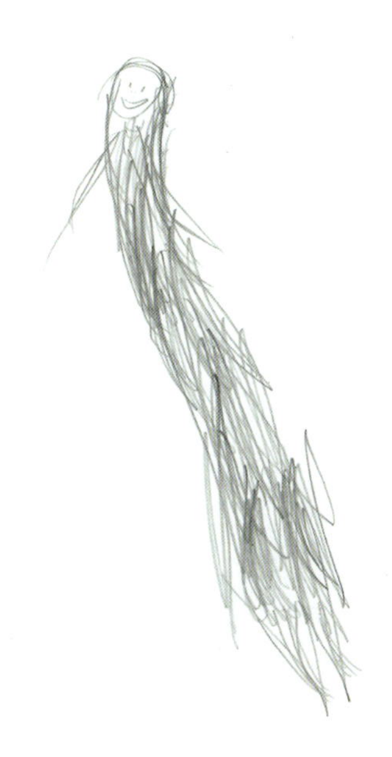

Sketchbook pages, 2017

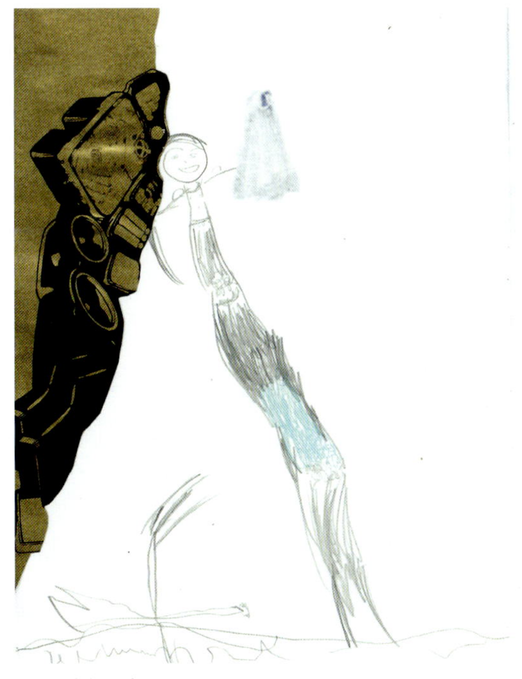

Sketchbook pages, 2013

WANGECHI MUTU

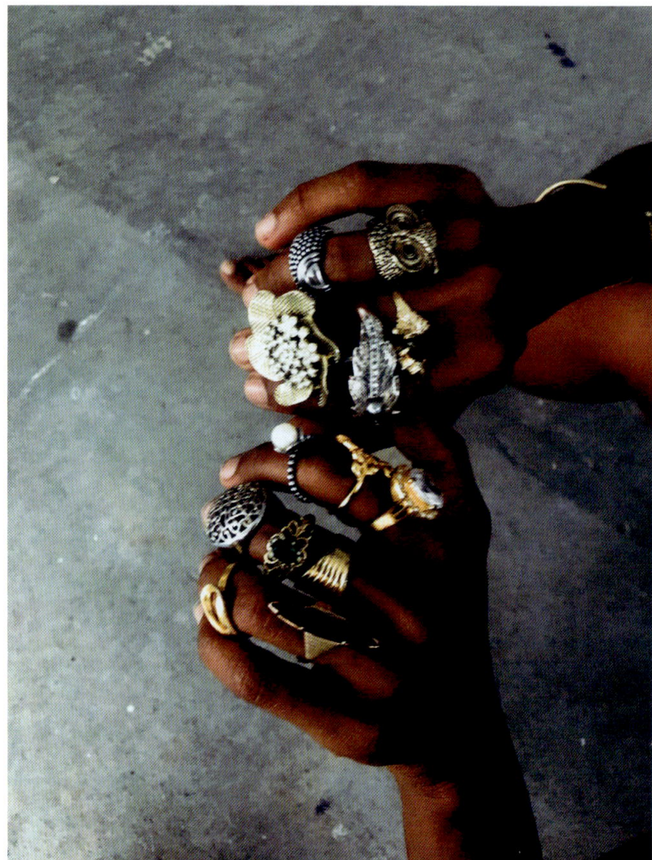

59

Source image for *Ilustraciones de la mecánica
(Illustrations of the Mechanical)*, 2018

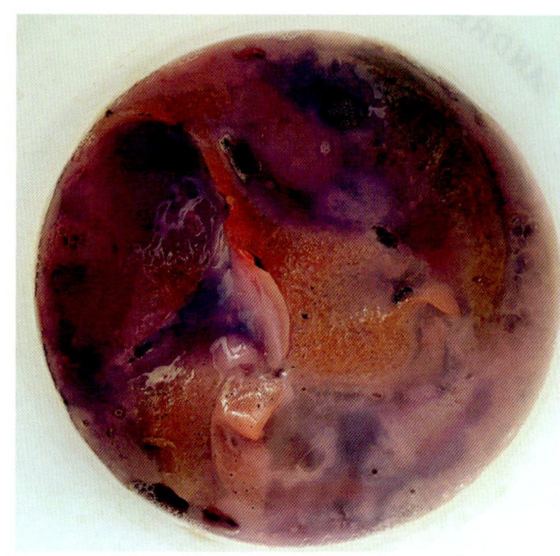

Kombucha mother culture for *Ilustraciones
de la mecánica (Illustrations of the
Mechanical)*, 2018

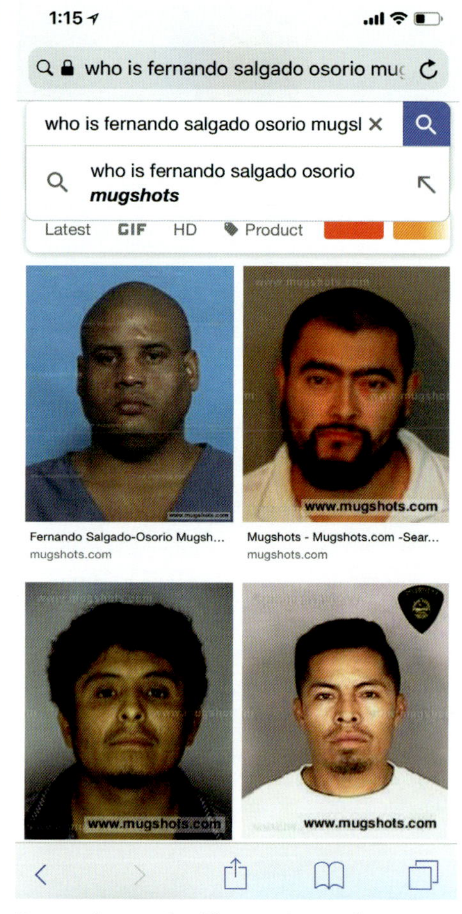

Source image for *Ilustraciones de
la mecánica (Illustrations of the
Mechanical)*, 2017

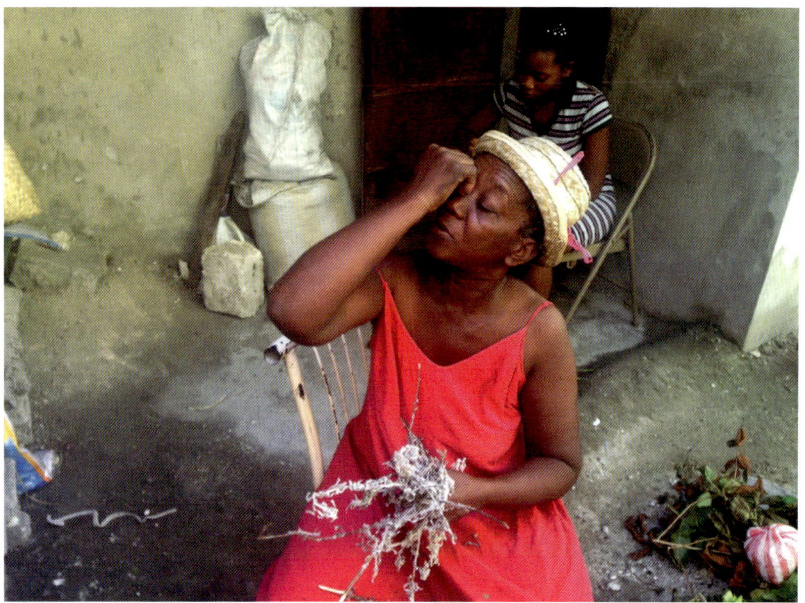

Sonia the healer from Haiti, 2016. Process image for *Ilustraciones de la
mecánica (Illustrations of the Mechanical)*, 2016

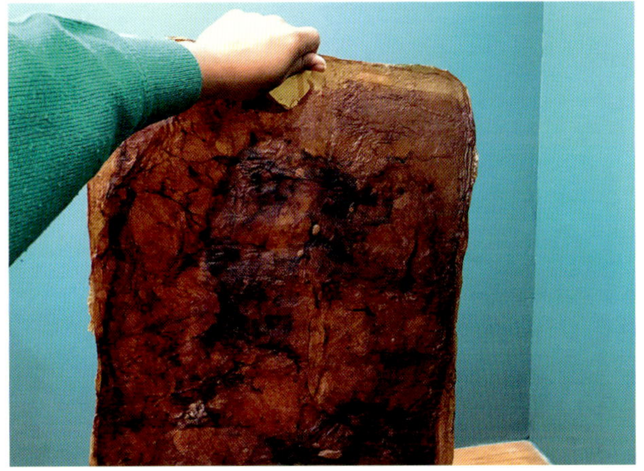

Vegetable leather for *Ilustraciones de la mecánica* (*Illustrations of the Mechanical*), 2017

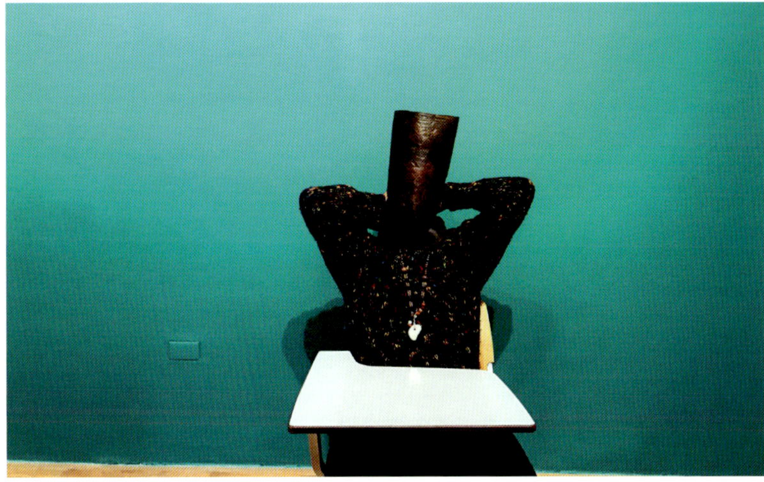

Process image for *Ilustraciones de la mecánica* (*Illustrations of the Mechanical*), 2017

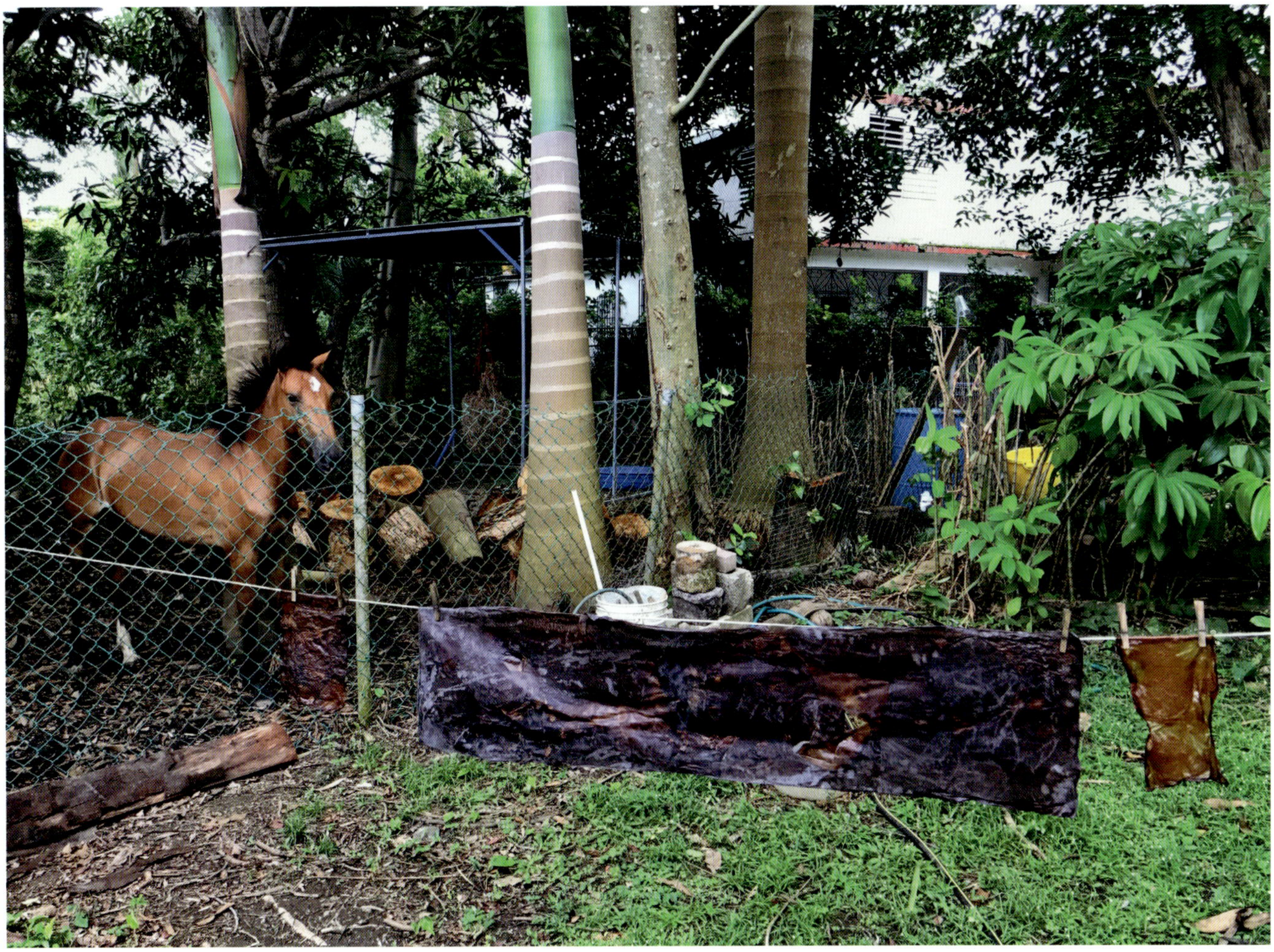

Drying vegetable leather for *Ilustraciones de la mecánica* (*Illustrations of the Mechanical*), 2017

LAS NIETAS DE NONÓ

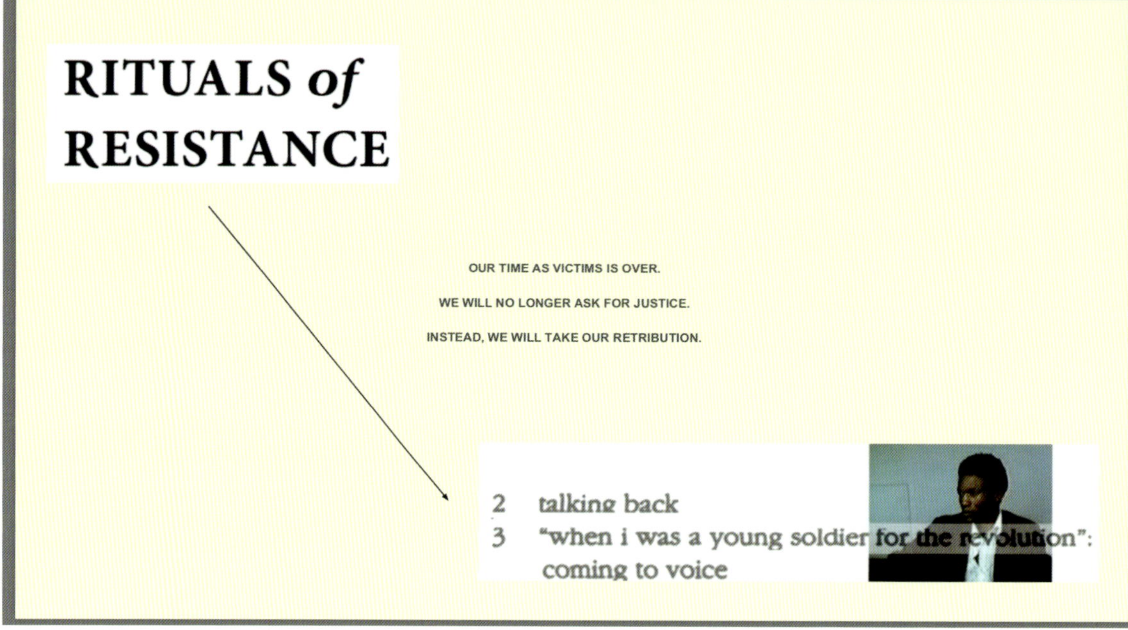

60

Film treatment for Kamasi Washington, *Fists of Fury*, *Hub-Tones*, and *Space Traveler's Lullaby*, 2018

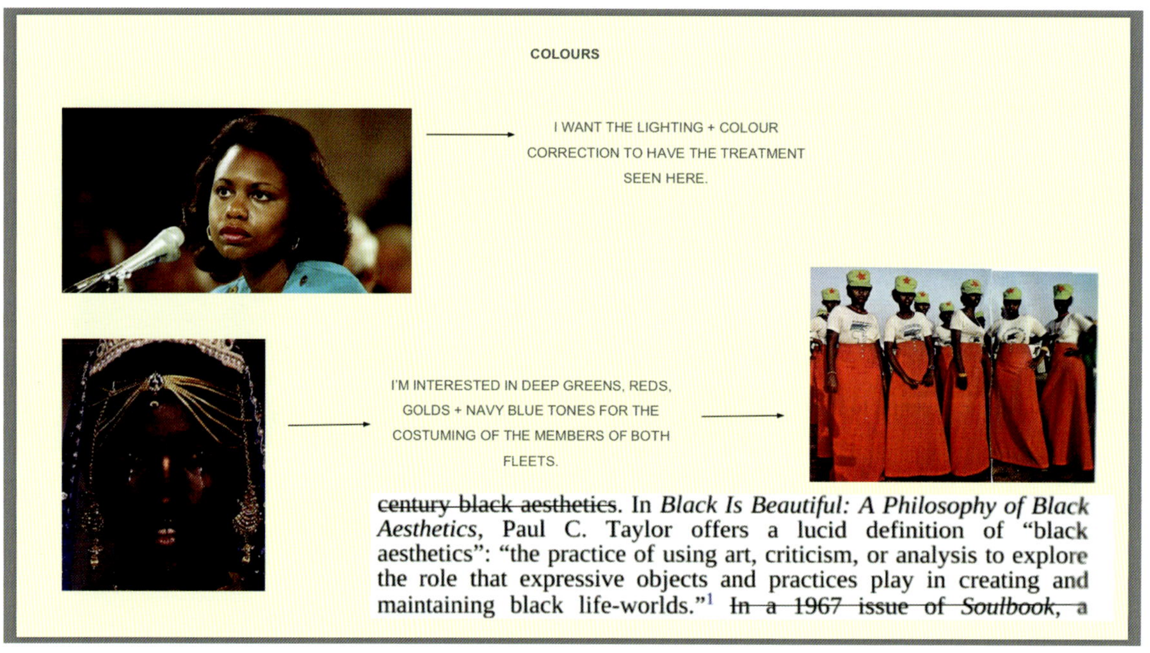

Film treatment for Kamasi Washington, *Fists of Fury*, *Hub-Tones*, and *Space Traveler's Lullaby*, 2018

"Natural Black music projects the myth of Blackness/ And he who is not
Black in spirit will never know/ That these words are true and valid forever"
(Sun Ra 2005, 295). By becoming Black in spirit, one enters the "bottomless pit"
of consciousness, a doorway that leads to advanced laws and rhythms that
span the universe. For Sun Ra, therefore, all of life has a foundation in Blackness,
although this "Blackness in spirit" is often rejected and repressed. Becoming
Black in spirit is what accounts for inner vision, intuition, creative genius,
and spiritual illumination.

WHAT IS IT TO IMAGINE THE SPECTRUM OF BLACKNESS AROUND WALLS THAT CAN GROW EARS?
- Jenn Nkiru

larger dialectic). Fanon (like Brathwaite with his theory of tidalectics)
insists that the most radical black aesthetic movements are always
anticipating the next step "beyond blackness" and actually shaping
whatever blackness is around the impulse to imagine the
unimaginable. When the BAM mobilized the word "black" in the most
radical manner, it was a way of naming the unknown dimensions of
freedom and self-determination. In the most radical BAM usages, the
word "black" always gestures to a profound overturning of the identity
category "Negro" and a desire to reenchant black humanity as much
more than an identity category. "Black" signaled excess, the power of
the *unthought* (that which José Munoz, in *Cruising Utopia*, describes
as the "not yet here").

Film treatment for Kamasi Washington, *Fists of Fury, Hub-Tones,* and *Space Traveler's Lullaby*, 2018

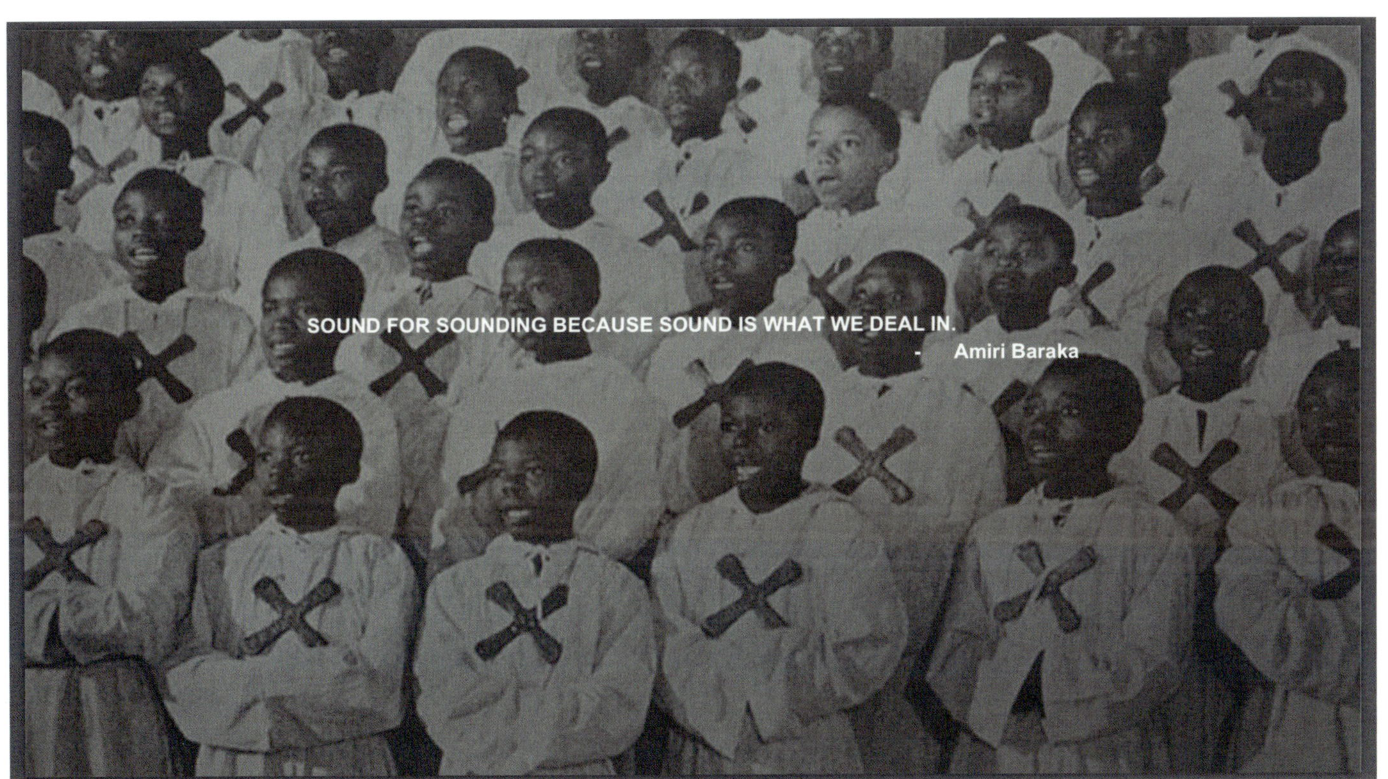

Film treatment for Kamasi Washington, *Fists of Fury, Hub-Tones,* and *Space Traveler's Lullaby*, 2018

JENN NKIRU

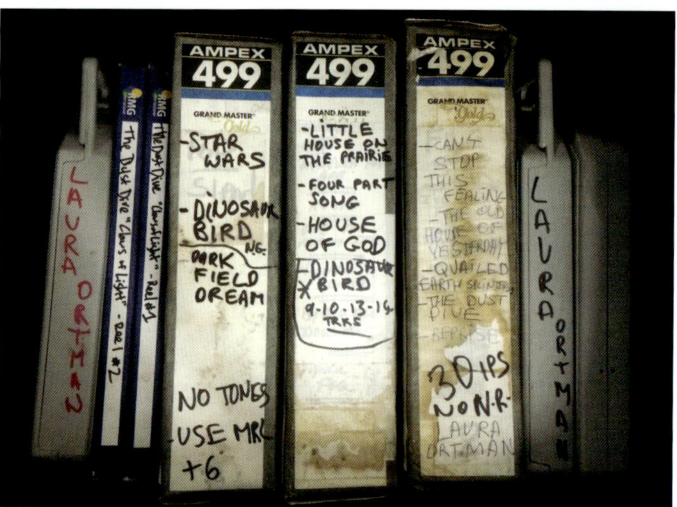

61

Master tapes for the artist's albums, 2018

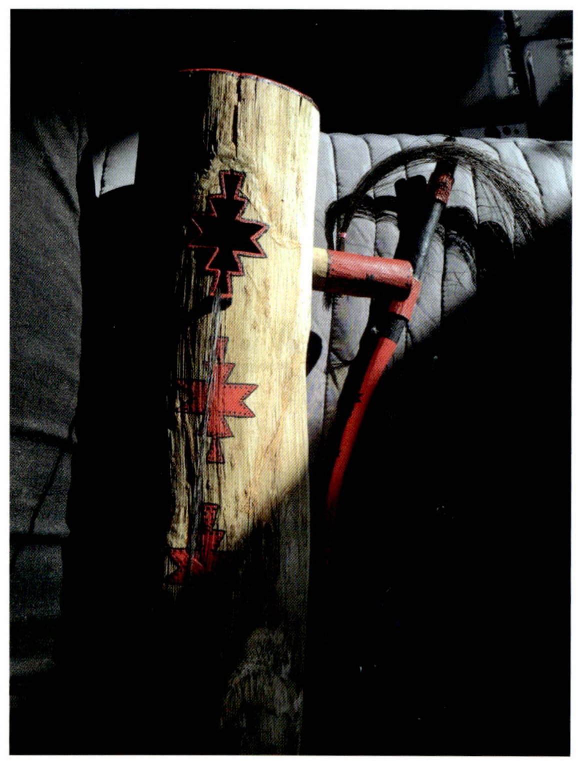

Restringing Apache violin with horse hair, 2018

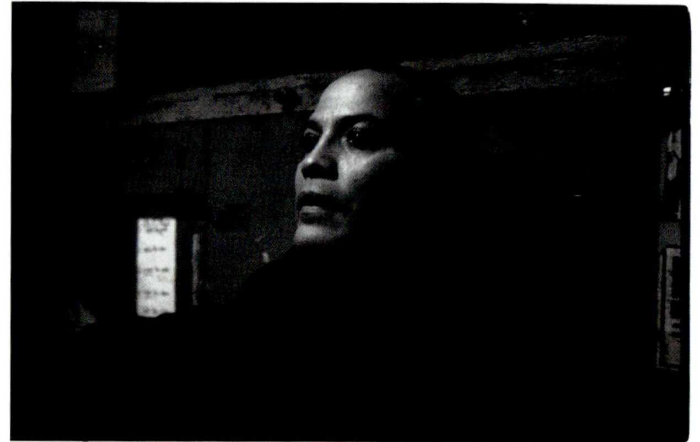

Production still from *I Lost My Shadow*, 2011

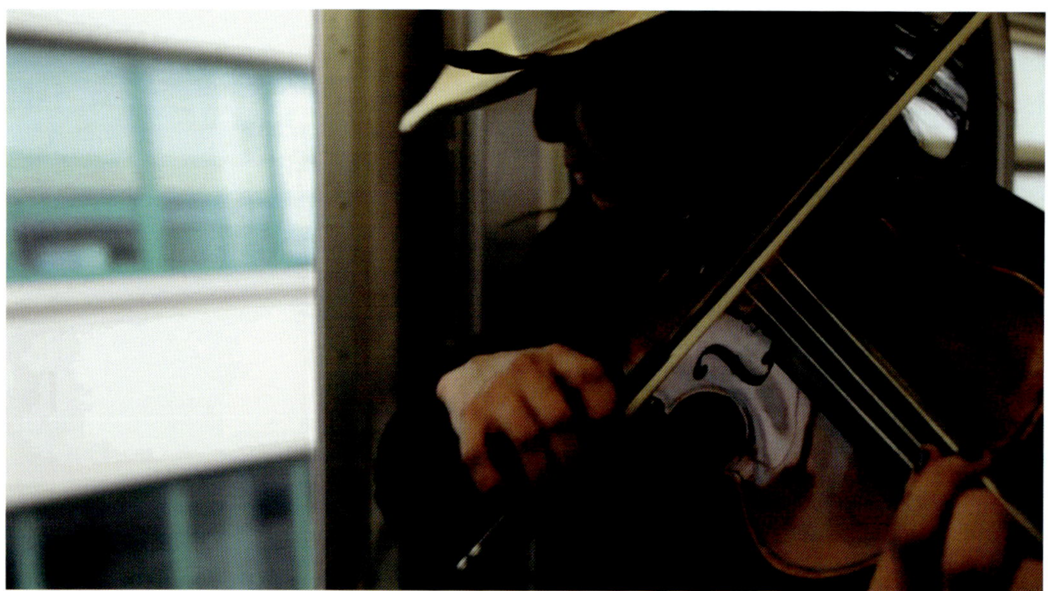

Production still from *I Lost My Shadow*, 2011

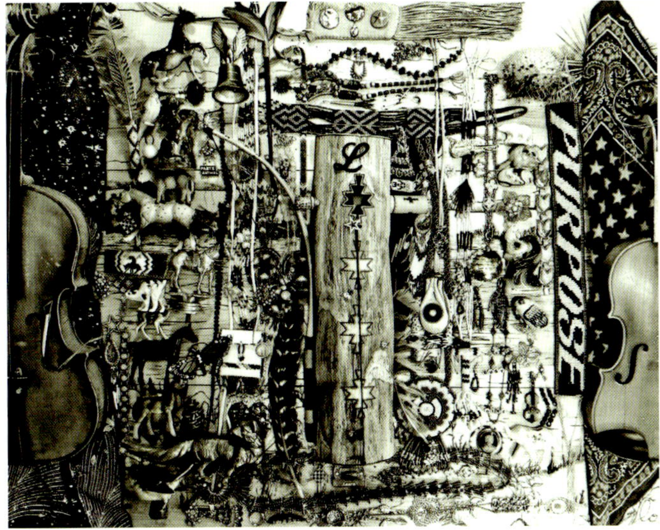

Installation and wood-burned drawing for album cover of
Someday We'll Be Together, 2011

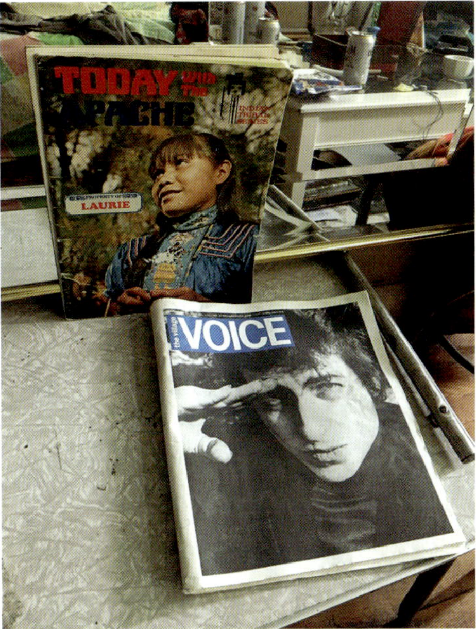

Studio, Brooklyn, NY, 2018

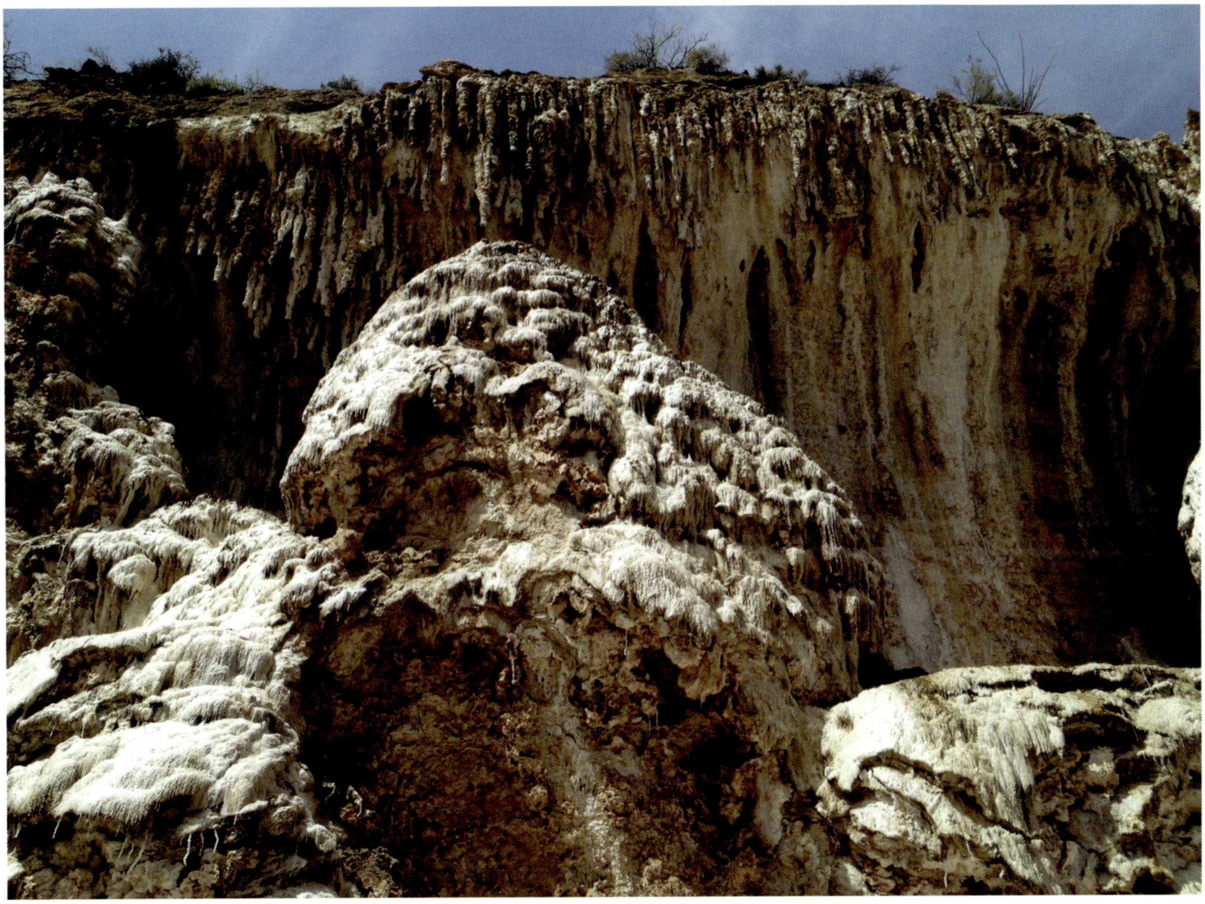

Salt cliffs, White Mountain Apache Tribe Reservation, AZ, 2015

LAURA ORTMAN

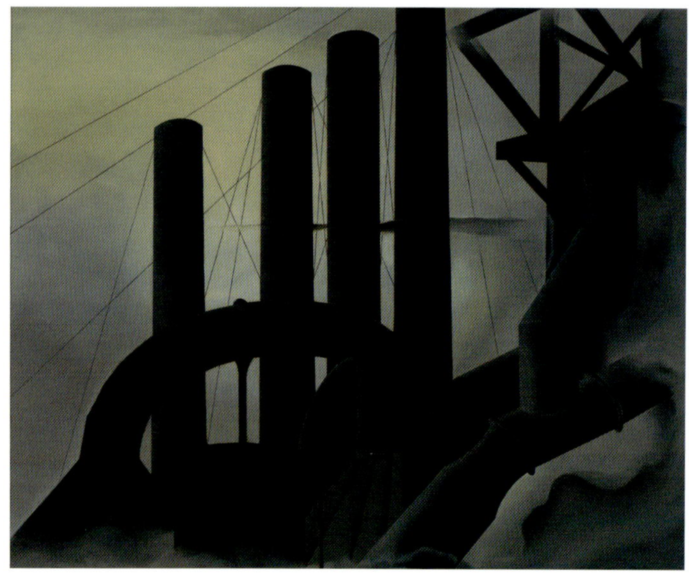

62

Elsie Driggs, *Pittsburgh*, 1927

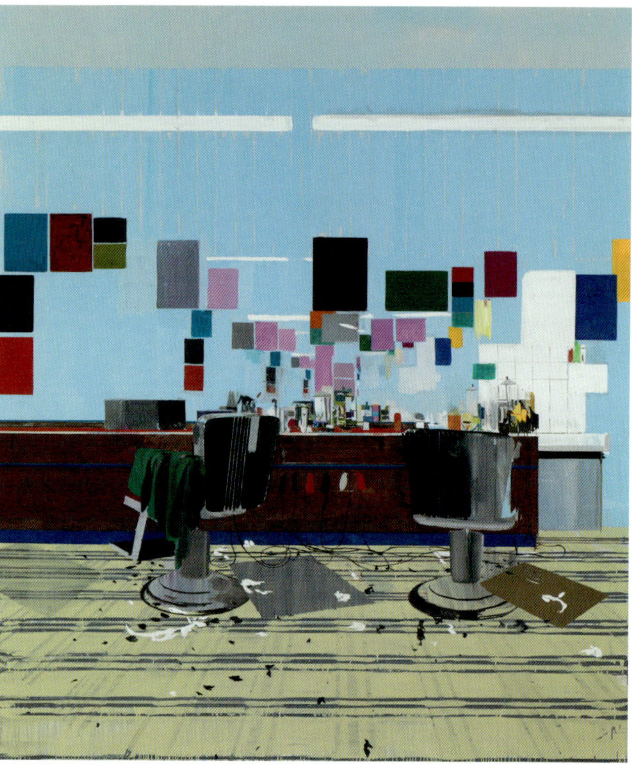

Hurvin Anderson, *Jersey*, 2008

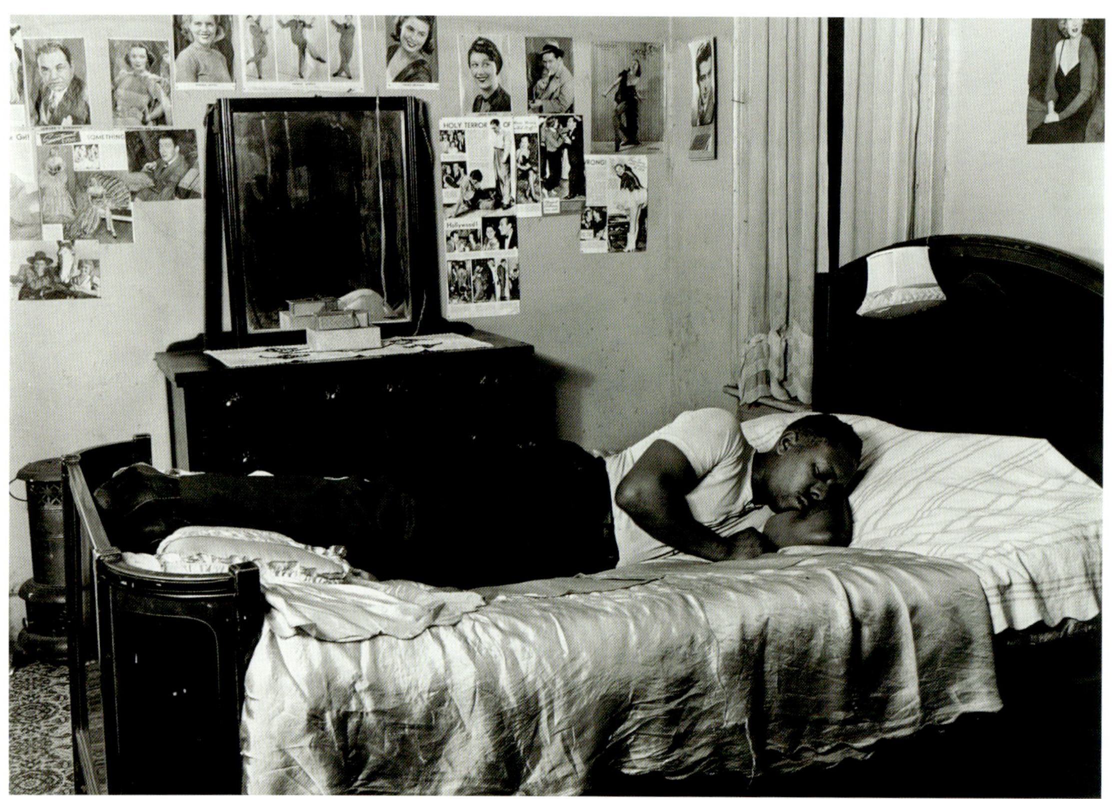

Aaron Siskind, *Harlem Man in Bed*, 1940

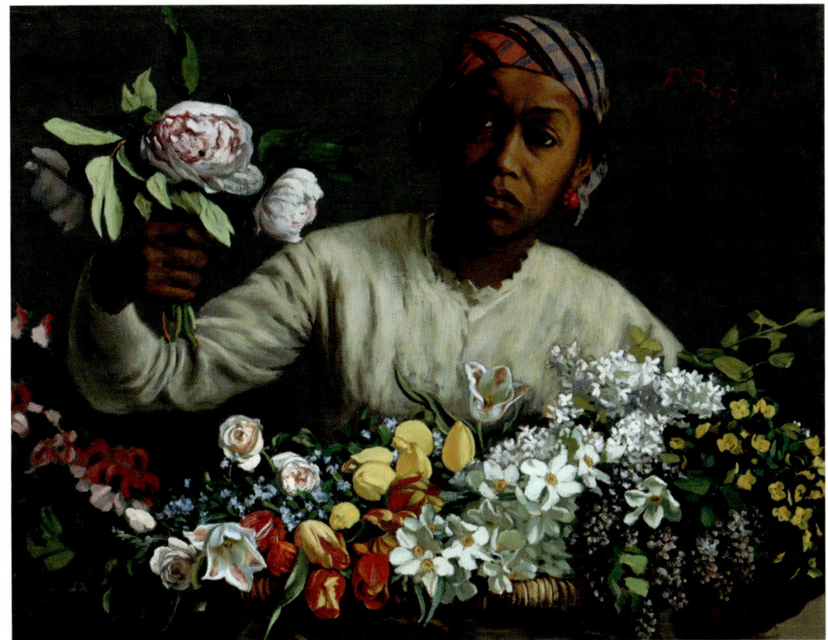

Frédéric Bazille, *Negress with Peonies*, 1870

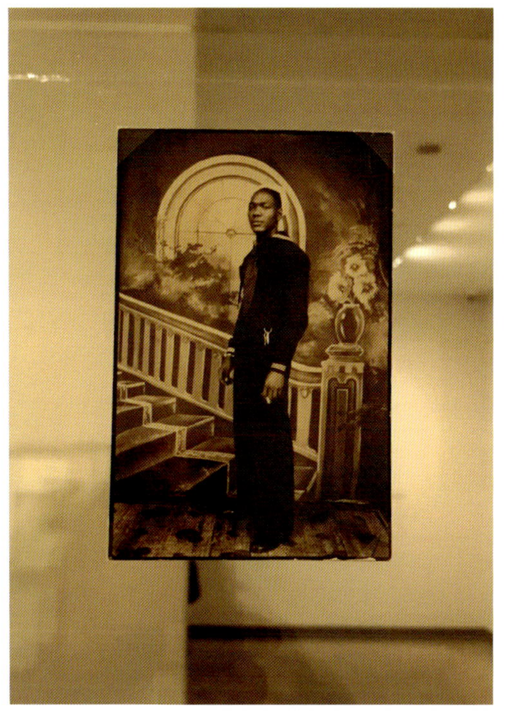

Photograph from *African American Portraits: Photographs from the 1940s and 1950s*, Metropolitan Museum of Art, New York, NY, 2018

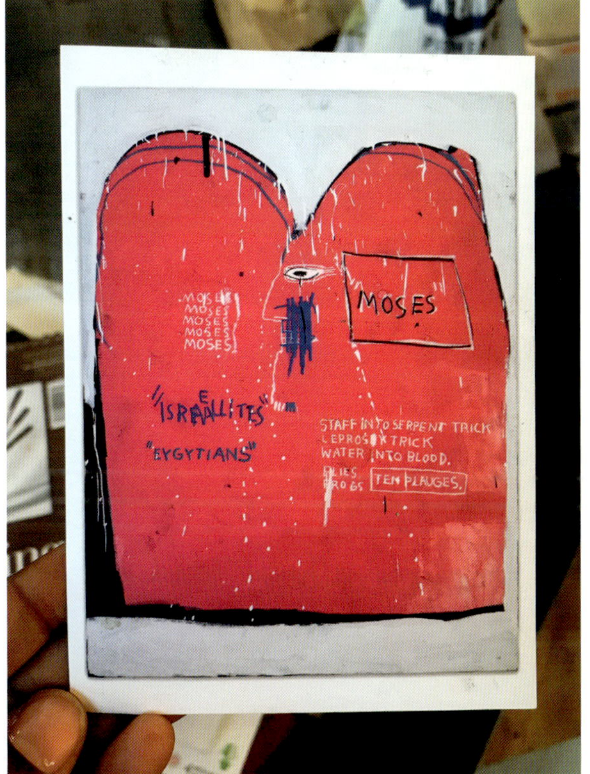

The artist holding a postcard of Jean-Michel Basquiat, *Moses and the Egyptians*, 1982, New York, NY, 2018

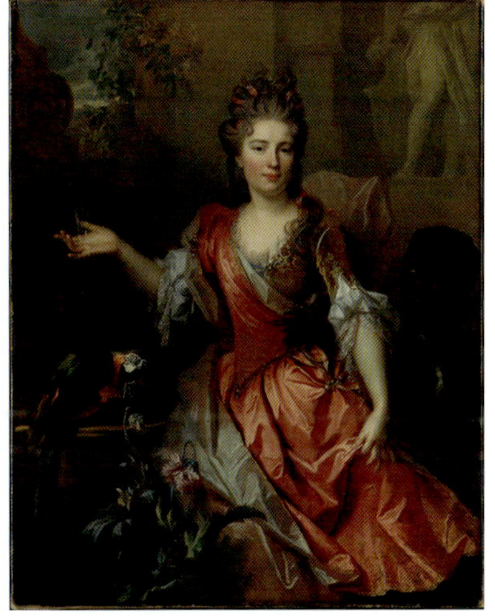

Nicolas de Largillièrre, *Portrait of a Woman, Possibly Madame Claude Lambert de Thorigny (Marie Marguerite Bontemps, 1668–1701), and an Enslaved Servant*, 1696

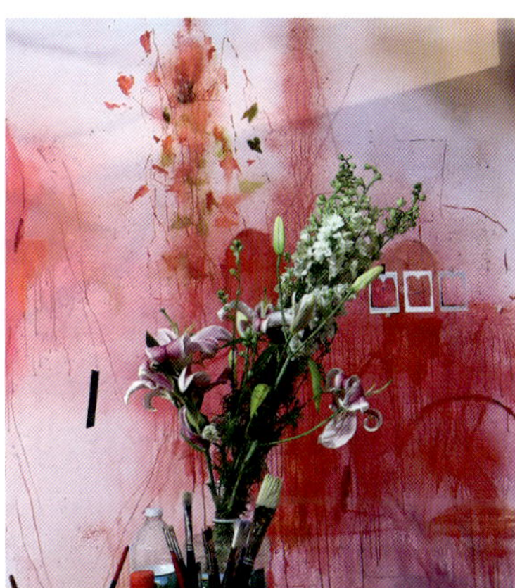

Studio, New York, NY, 2018

JENNIFER PACKER

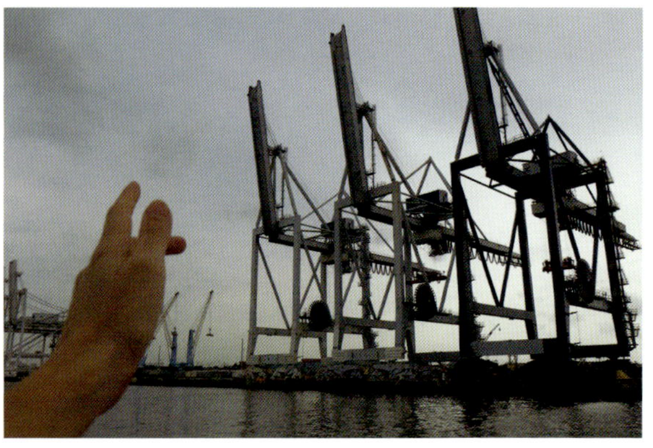

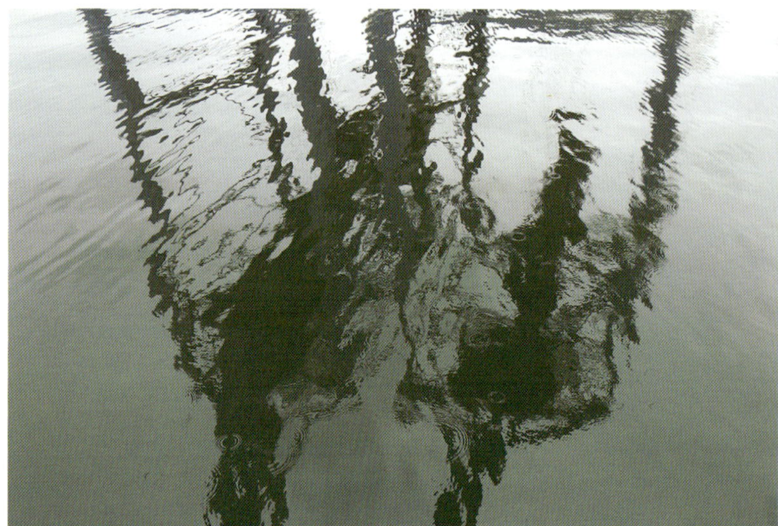

63

Researching reflection on the San Juan Bay, Puerto Rico, 2015

Researching scale on the San Juan Bay, Puerto Rico, 2015

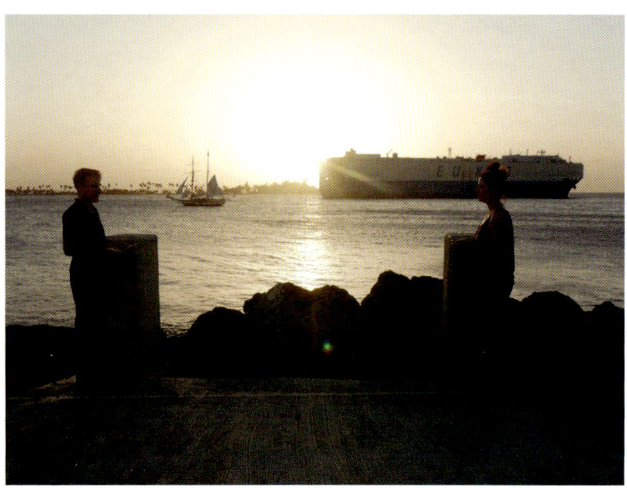

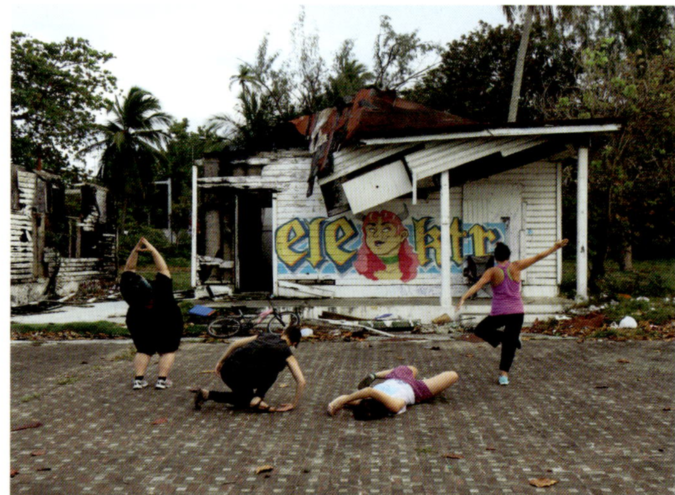

Exercise for *El Weather Bureau*, 2017

David Bergé and nibia pastrana santiago, *Celebrity Eclipse y otros barcos*, 2017

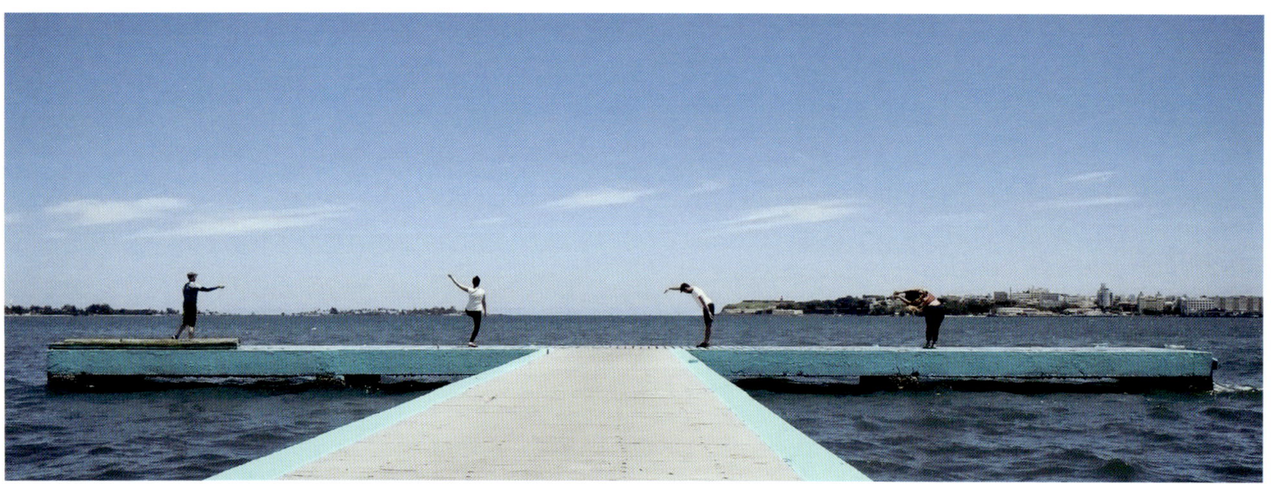

Rehearsal for *fuerzas sutiles (subtle forces)*, 2017

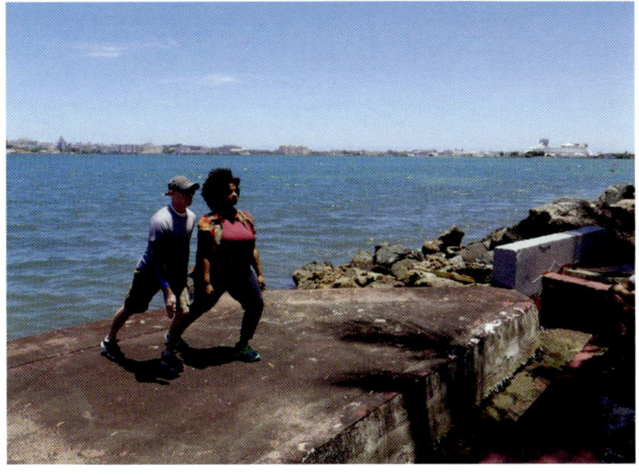

Rehearsal for *fuerzas sutiles* (*subtle forces*), 2017

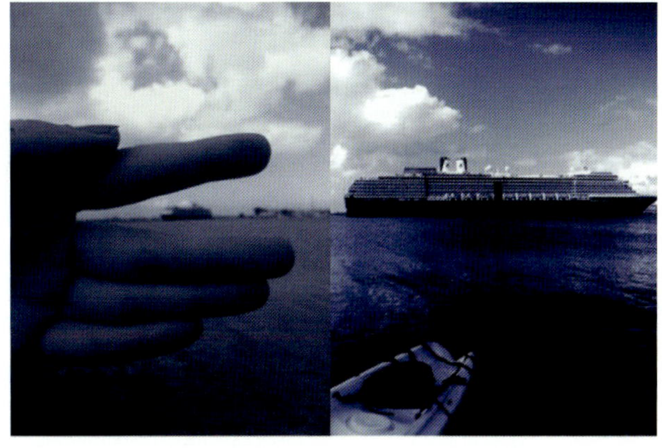

Process image for *maniobra, bahía o el evento coreográfico*
(*maneuver, bay or the choreographic event*), 2015

The body (what?)

1.! The body is a malleable and capable instrument or medium.

2.! The body is an agent for communication that has power over space.

3.! The body's remnants are as important as the body.

4.! The body is a machine aiming to work efficiently.

5.! The body is an organism where the internal experience its externally visible.

6.! The body is vibrating material conductor of sound.

7.! The body is a performer.

8.! The body is a link between events.

9.! The body learns and is domesticated.

10.!The body is a becoming object.

11.!The body is a laboratory for presence and time.

12.!The body is entangled between extensions of itself.

13.!The body is an image.

14.!The body is plural.

15.!The body is contained within styles and relations of authorship.

16.!The body is i.

!

Observations on displacement practice, 2012–13

NIBIA PASTRANA SANTIAGO

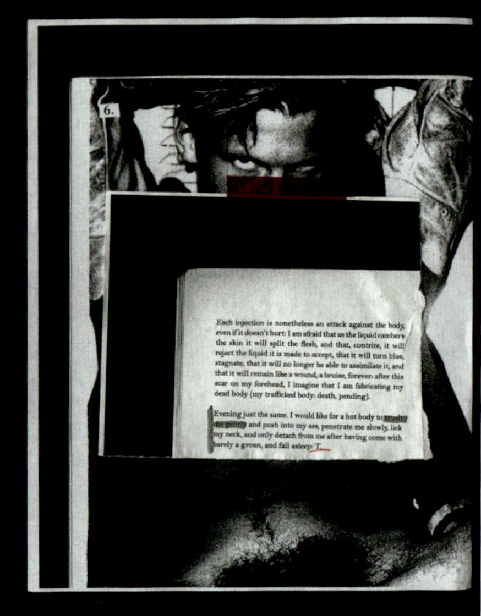

64

Source materials, 2018

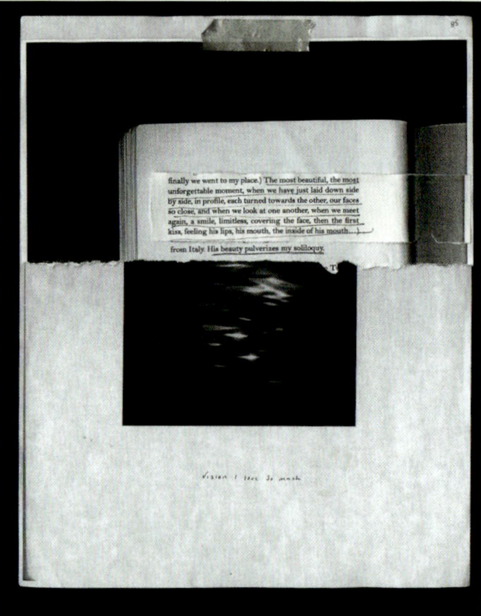

Source materials, 2018

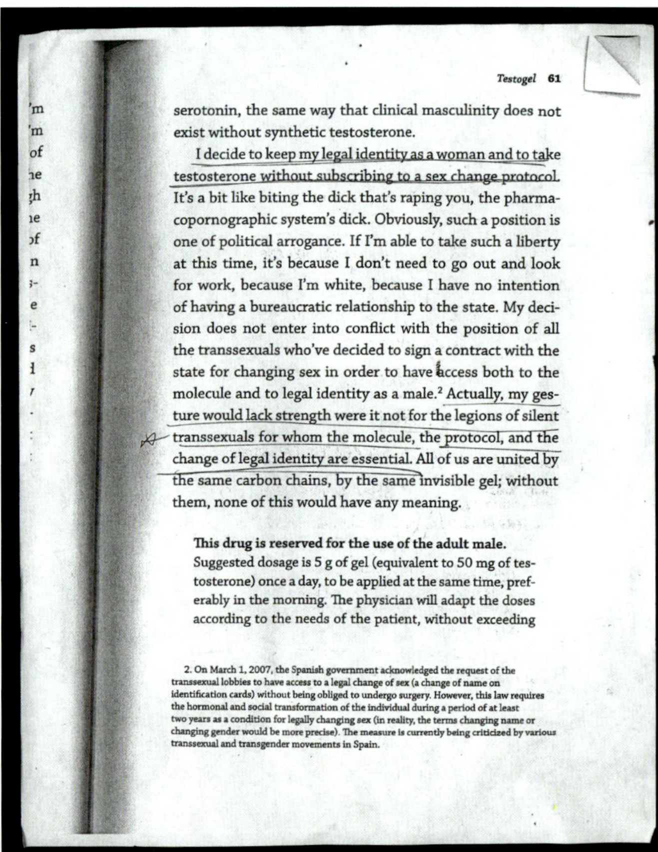

Testogel **61**

serotonin, the same way that clinical masculinity does not exist without synthetic testosterone.

I decide to keep my legal identity as a woman and to take testosterone without subscribing to a sex change protocol. It's a bit like biting the dick that's raping you, the pharma-copornographic system's dick. Obviously, such a position is one of political arrogance. If I'm able to take such a liberty at this time, it's because I don't need to go out and look for work, because I'm white, because I have no intention of having a bureaucratic relationship to the state. My decision does not enter into conflict with the position of all the transsexuals who've decided to sign a contract with the state for changing sex in order to have access both to the molecule and to legal identity as a male.[2] Actually, my gesture would lack strength were it not for the legions of silent transsexuals for whom the molecule, the protocol, and the change of legal identity are essential. All of us are united by the same carbon chains, by the same invisible gel; without them, none of this would have any meaning.

This drug is reserved for the use of the adult male. Suggested dosage is 5 g of gel (equivalent to 50 mg of testosterone) once a day, to be applied at the same time, preferably in the morning. The physician will adapt the doses according to the needs of the patient, without exceeding

2. On March 1, 2007, the Spanish government acknowledged the request of the transsexual lobbies to have access to a legal change of sex (a change of name on identification cards) without being obliged to undergo surgery. However, this law requires the hormonal and social transformation of the individual during a period of at least two years as a condition for legally changing sex (in reality, the terms changing name or changing gender would be more precise). The measure is currently being criticized by various transsexual and transgender movements in Spain.

Source materials, 2018

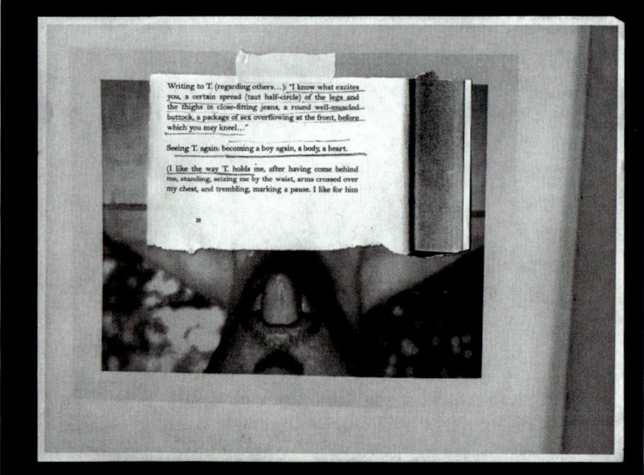

Source materials, 2018

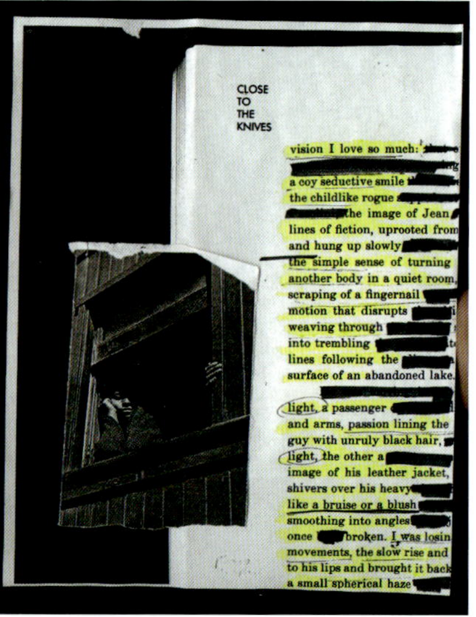

Source materials, 2018

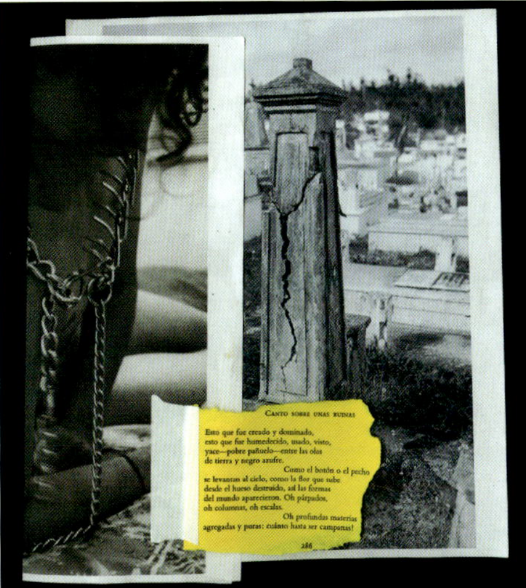

Source materials, 2018

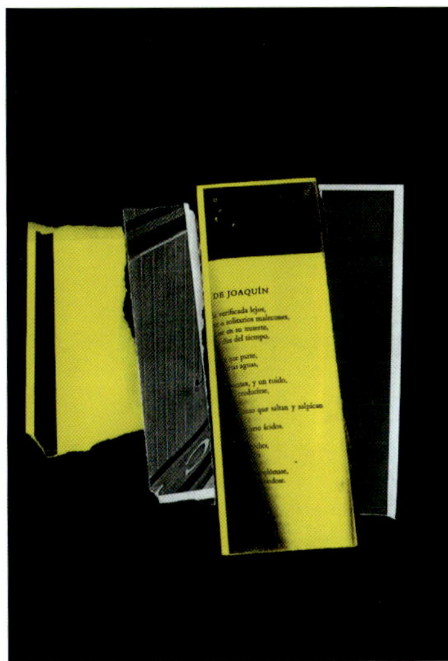

Source materials, 2018

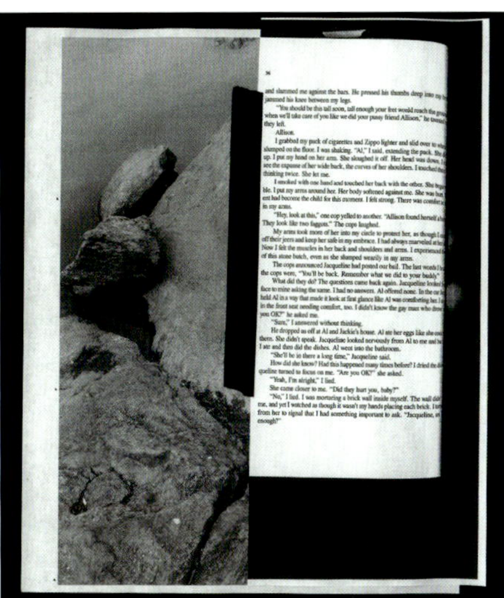

Source materials, 2018

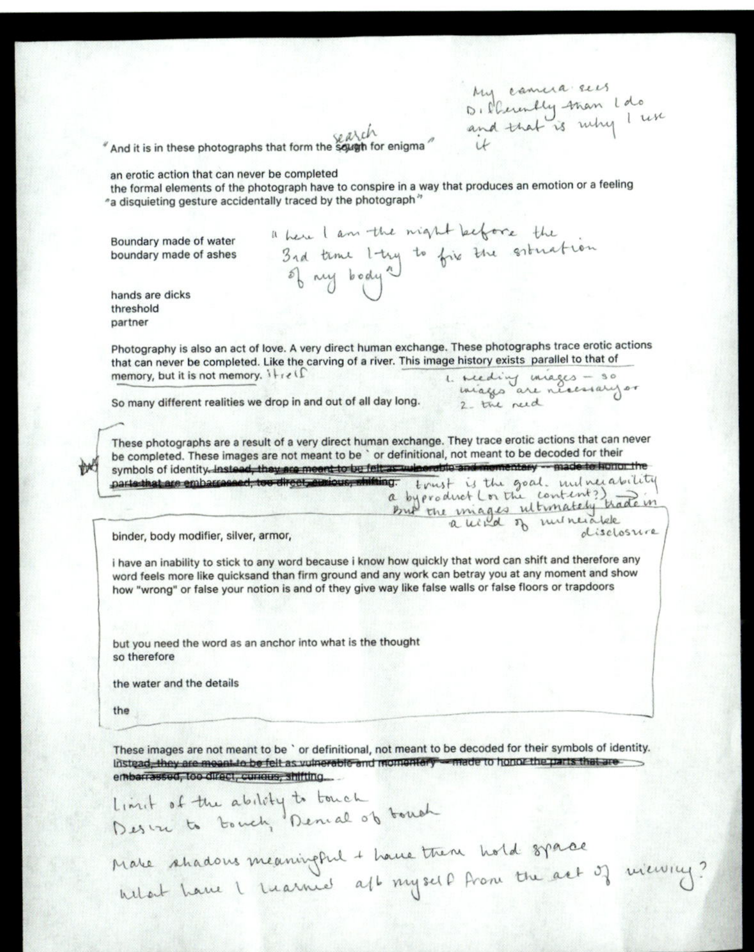

"And it is in these photographs that form the ~~sough~~ search for enigma"

[handwritten: My camera sees Differently than I do and that is why I use it]

an erotic action that can never be completed
the formal elements of the photograph have to conspire in a way that produces an emotion or a feeling
"a disquieting gesture accidentally traced by the photograph"

Boundary made of water
boundary made of ashes

[handwritten: "here I am the night before the 3rd time I try to fix the situation of my body"]

hands are dicks
threshold
partner

Photography is also an act of love. A very direct human exchange. These photographs trace erotic actions that can never be completed. Like the carving of a river. This image history exists parallel to that of memory, but it is not memory. [handwritten: itself]

[handwritten: 1. needing images — so images are necessary or 2. the need]

So many different realities we drop in and out of all day long.

These photographs are a result of a very direct human exchange. They trace erotic actions that can never be completed. These images are not meant to be ` or definitional, not meant to be decoded for their symbols of identity. ~~Instead, they are meant to be felt as vulnerable and momentary -- made to honor the parts that are embarrassed, too direct, anxious, shifting.~~

[handwritten: trust is the goal. vulnerability a byproduct (or the content?) but the images ultimately trade in a kind of vulnerable disclosure]

binder, body modifier, silver, armor,

i have an inability to stick to any word because i know how quickly that word can shift and therefore any word feels more like quicksand than firm ground and any work can betray you at any moment and show how "wrong" or false your notion is and of they give way like false walls or false floors or trapdoors

but you need the word as an anchor into what is the thought
so therefore

the water and the details

the

These images are not meant to be ` or definitional, not meant to be decoded for their symbols of identity. ~~Instead, they are meant to be felt as vulnerable and momentary — made to honor the parts that are embarrassed, too direct, curious, shifting.~~

[handwritten: Limit of the ability to touch
Desire to touch, Denial of touch

Make shadows meaningful + have them hold space
What have I learned ab myself from the act of viewing?]

Source materials, 2018

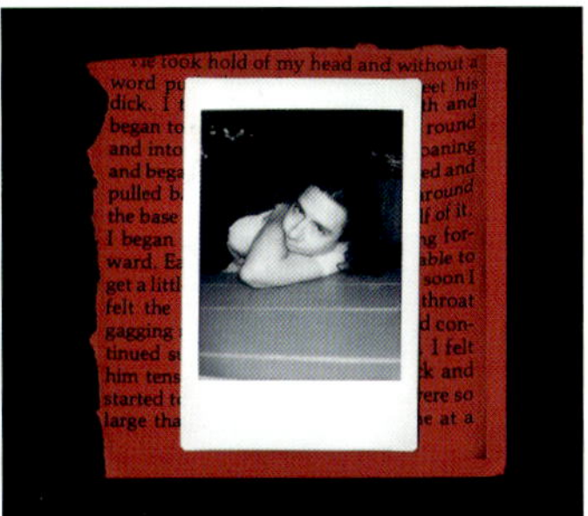

Source materials, 2018

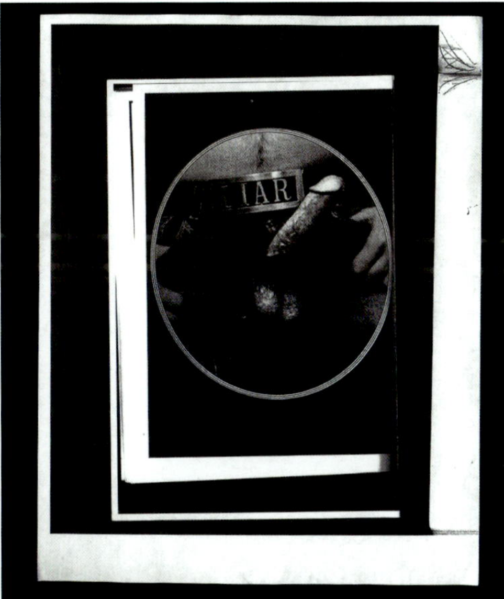

Source materials, 2018

ELLE PÉREZ

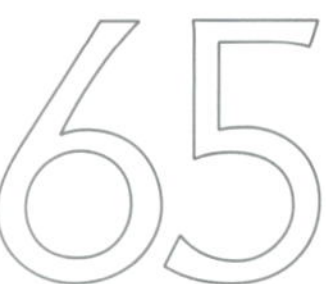

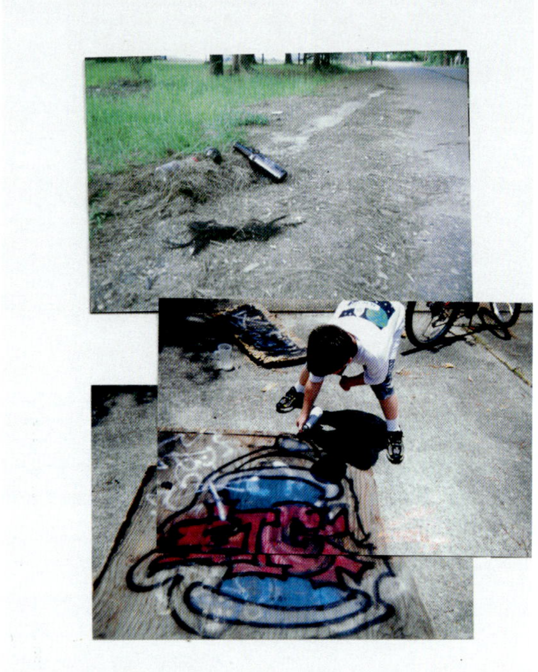

65

Portrait of a friend painting *Slick*, Pineville, LA, c. 1999

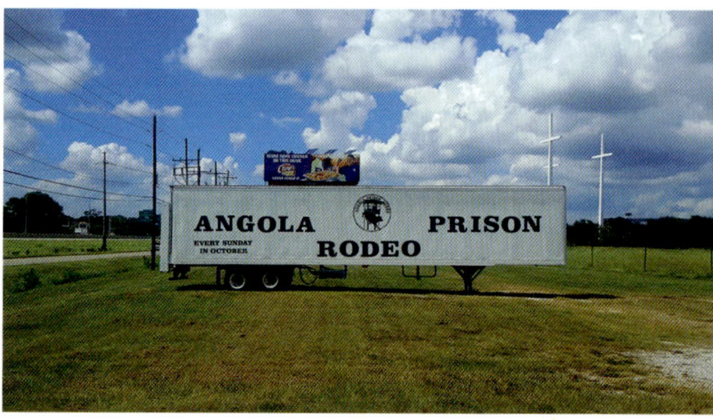

Louisiana State Penitentiary Angola Rodeo advertisement, Baton Rouge, LA, 2018

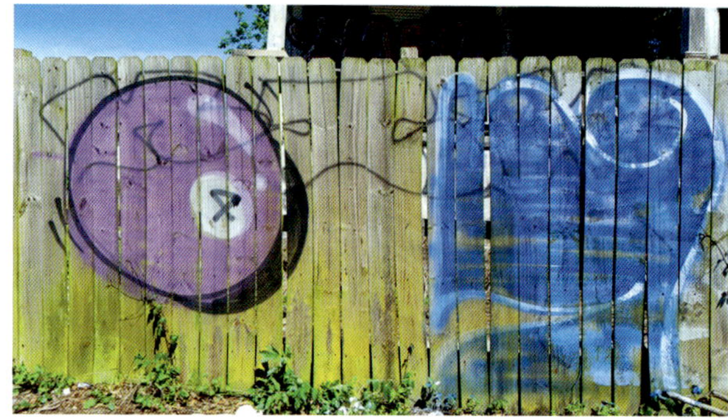

Graffiti on privacy fencing and abandoned house, New Orleans, LA, 2018

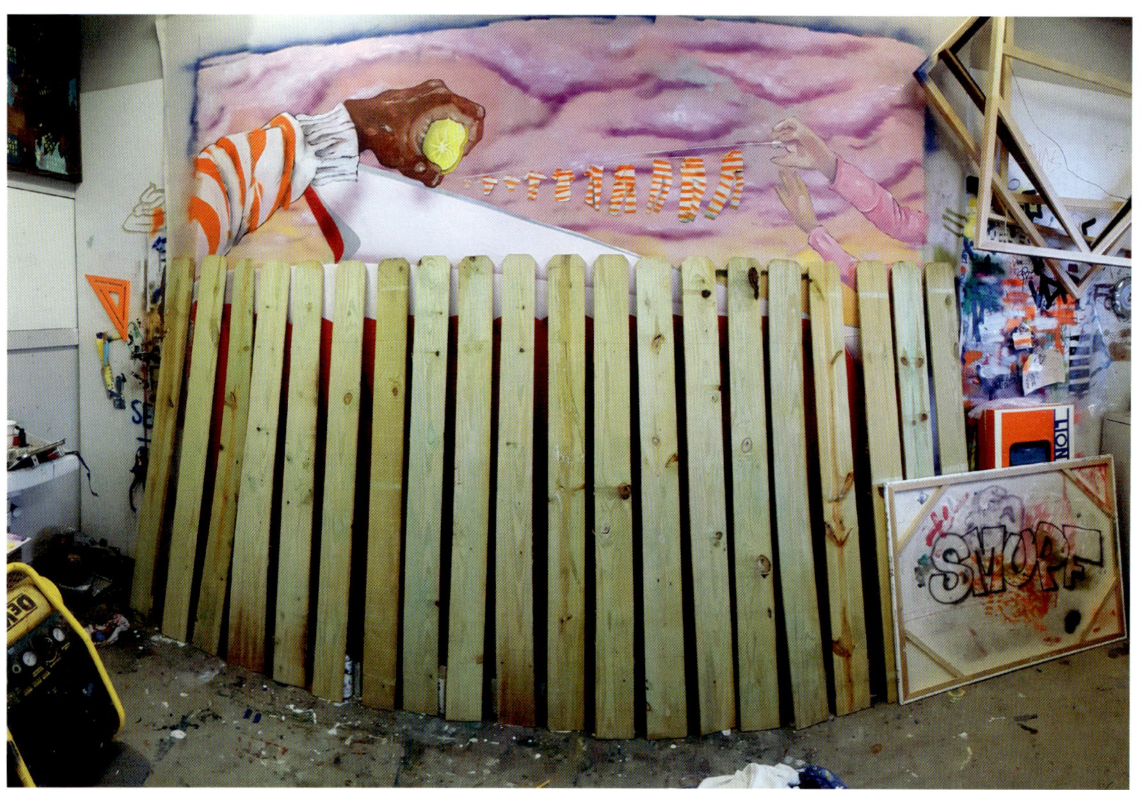

Mock-up of *Lemony Fresh*, studio, Alexandria, VA, 2017

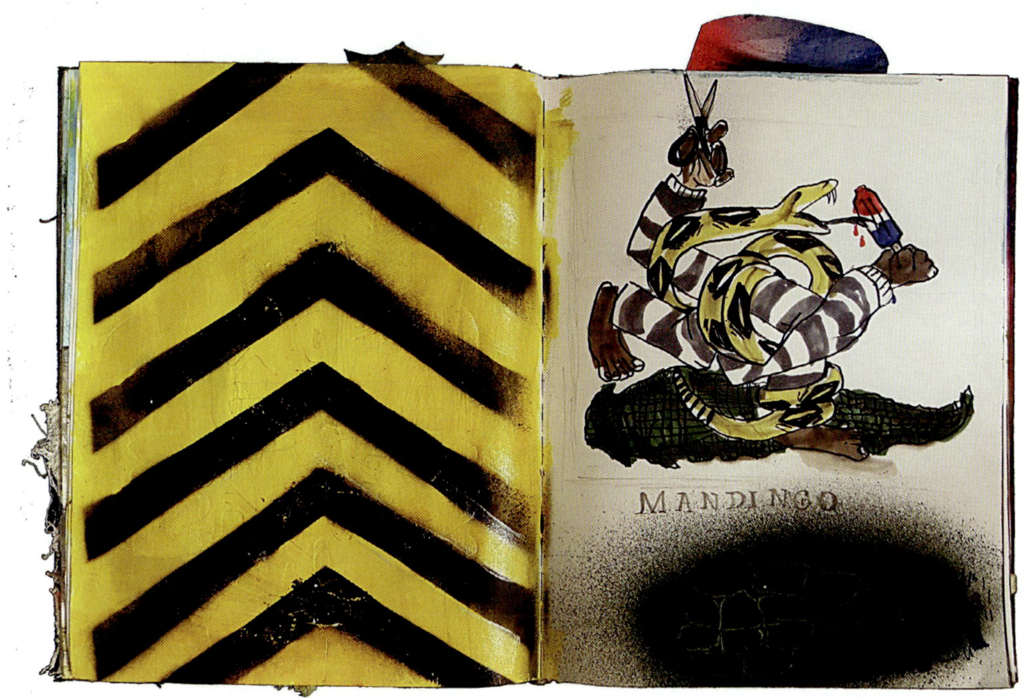

Sketches for *Mandingo/Don't Tread on Me*, 2018

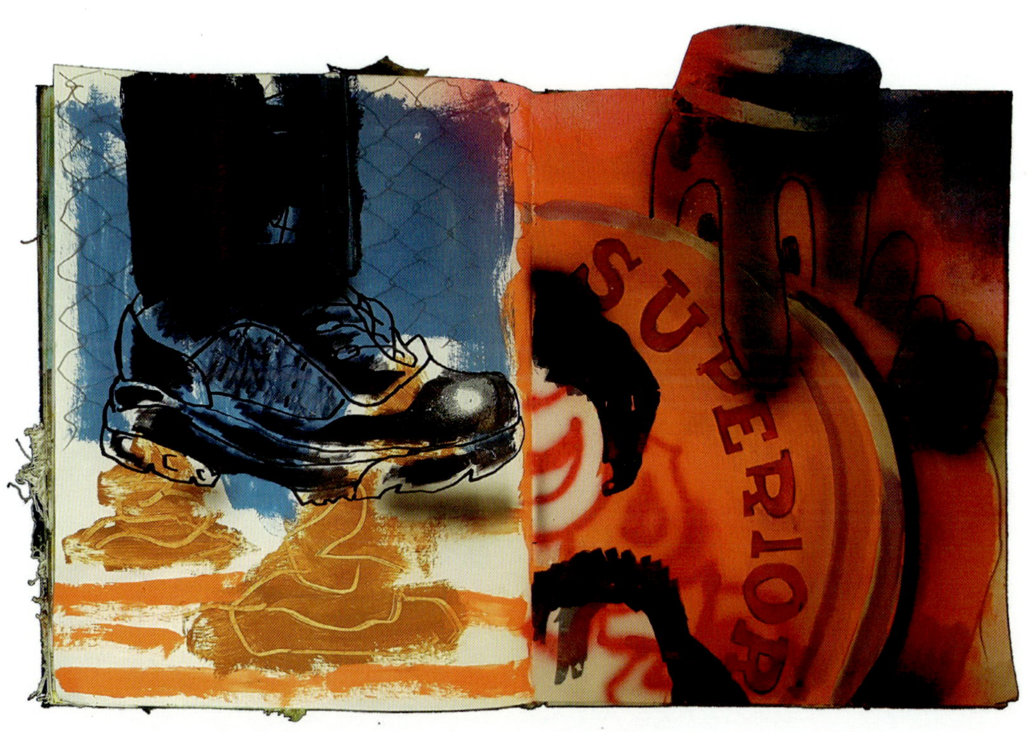

Sketchbook pages, 2018

PAT PHILLIPS

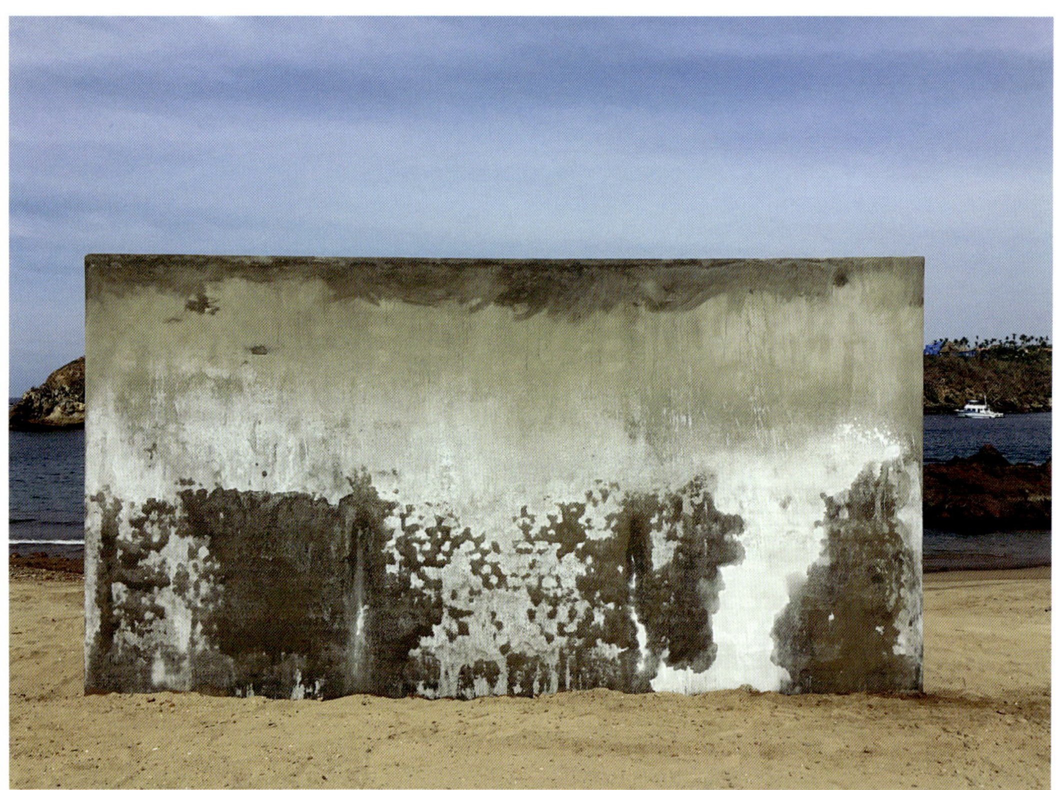

66

Untitled (efflorescence), 2015. Installation view, Costa Careyes, Mexico

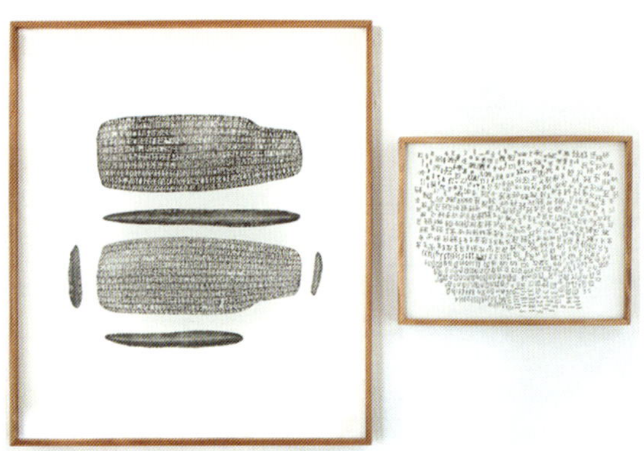

Rongorongo text B (RR4), alien, human, animal, to plant, 2013

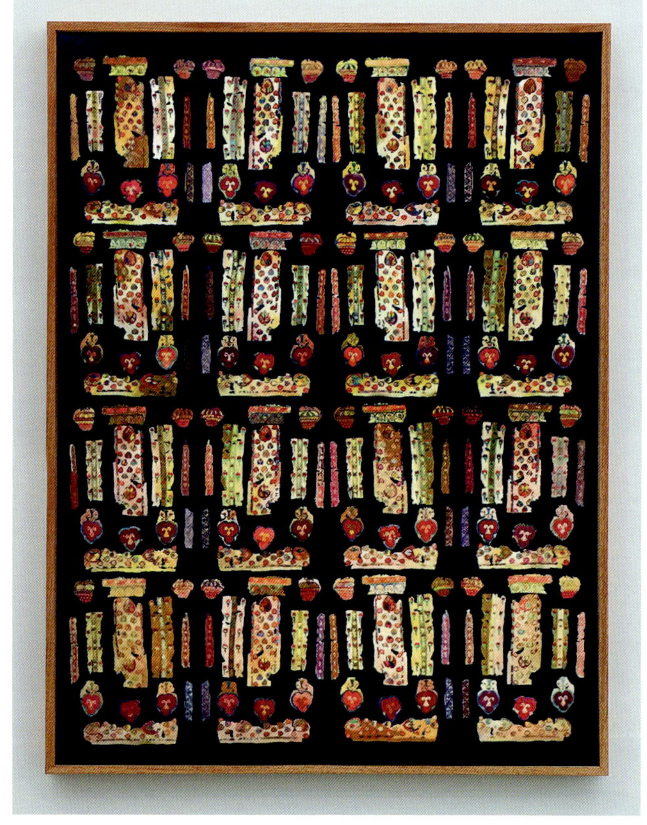

13 fabric fragments from the MET reconstruction, 2016

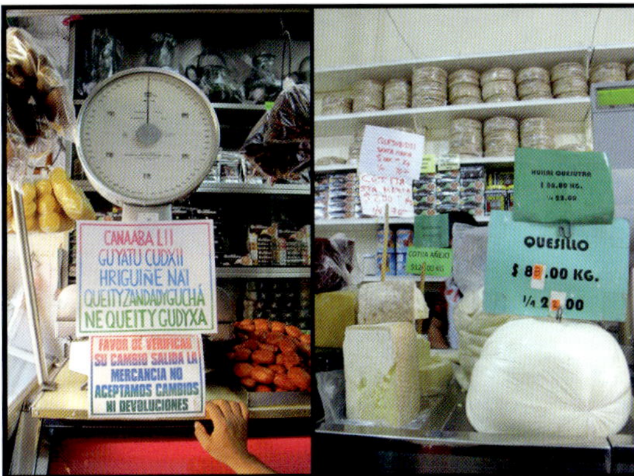

Chatino signs in Oaxacan stores, Soledad Corredor, Centro Histórico, Mexico City, Mexico, 2014

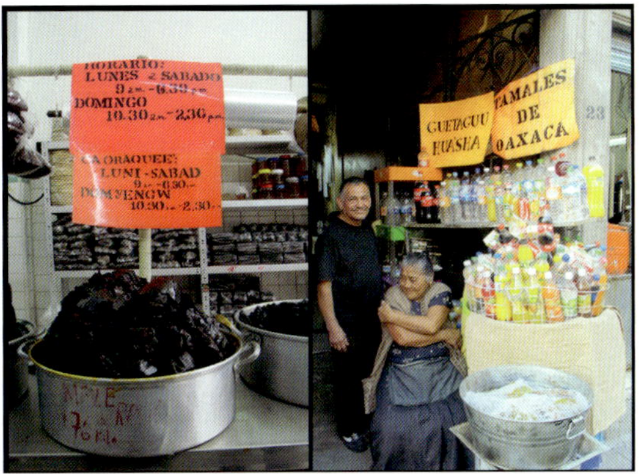

Chatino signs in Oaxacan stores, Soledad Corredor, Centro Histórico, Mexico City, Mexico, 2014

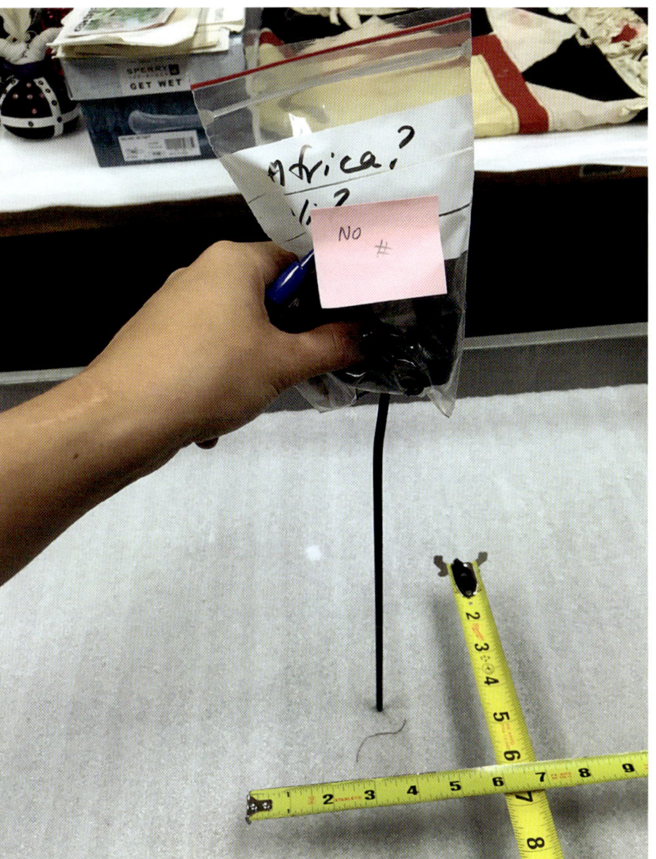

Process image for *One dirt ring reconstruction*, 2016

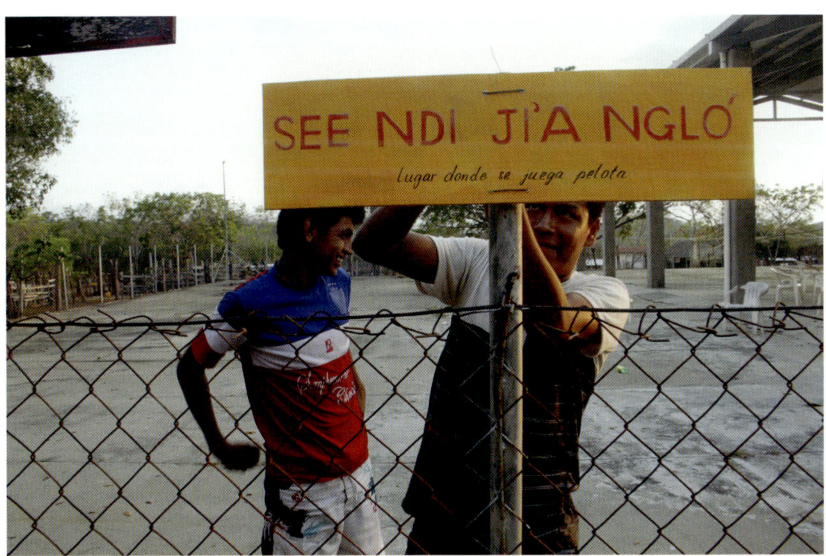

Installing Chatino signage, San Isidro Llano Grande, Oaxaca, Mexico, 2016

GALA PORRAS-KIM

67

Sketchbook pages, 2018

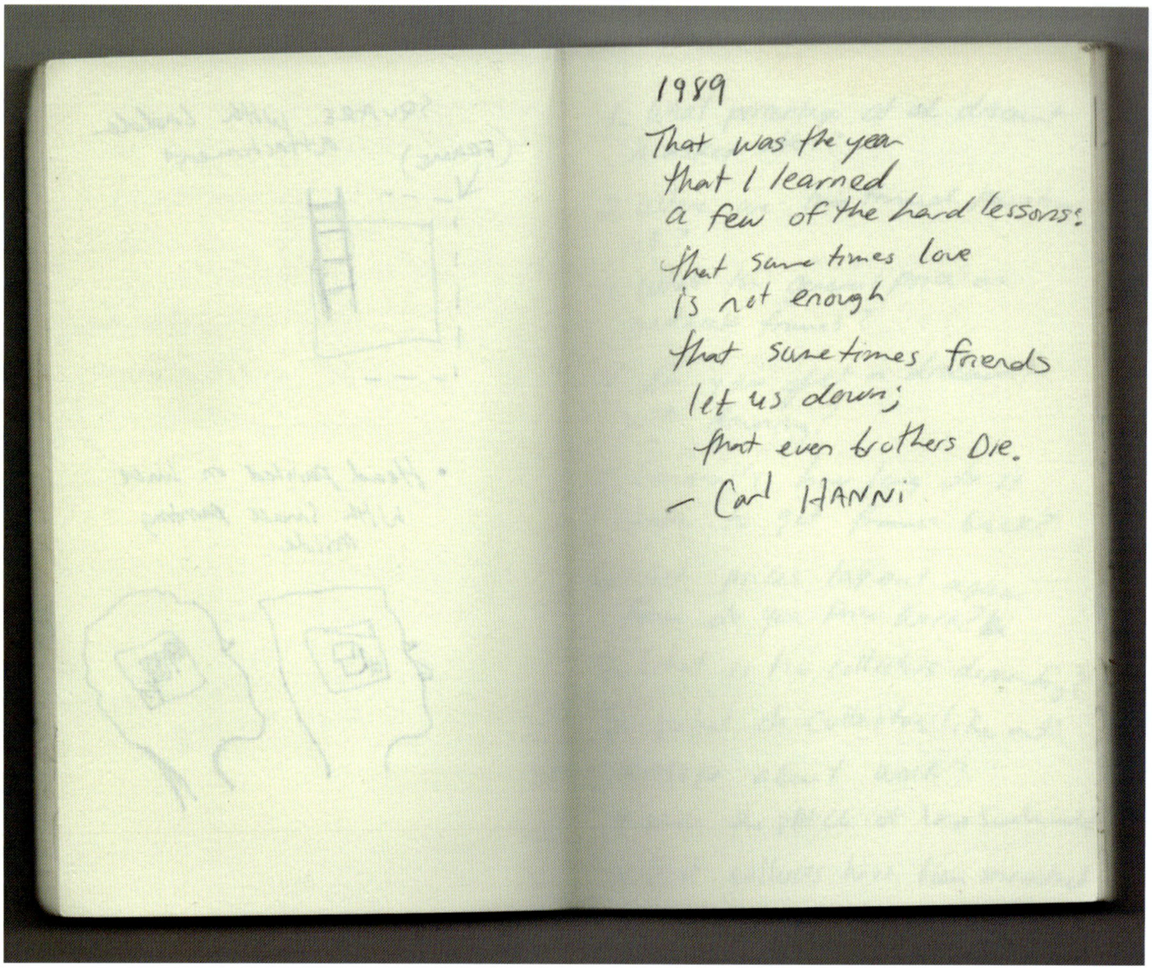

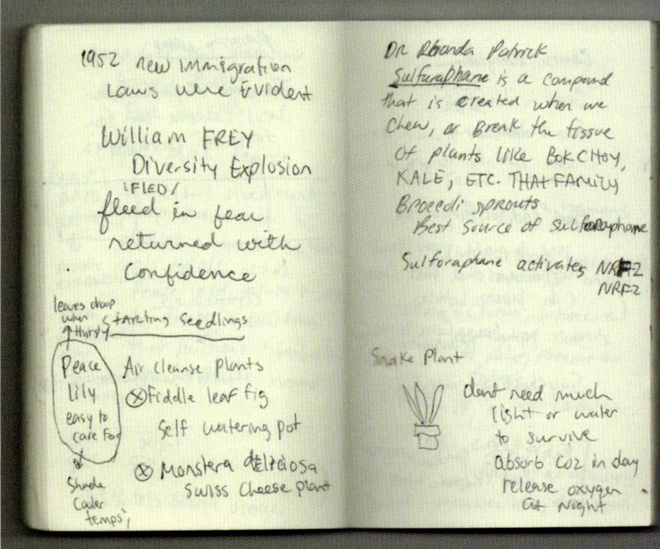

Sketchbook pages, 2018

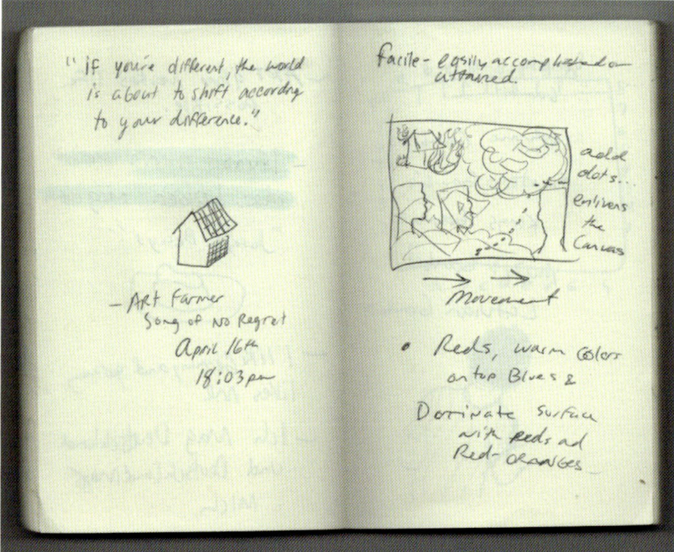

Sketchbook pages, 2018

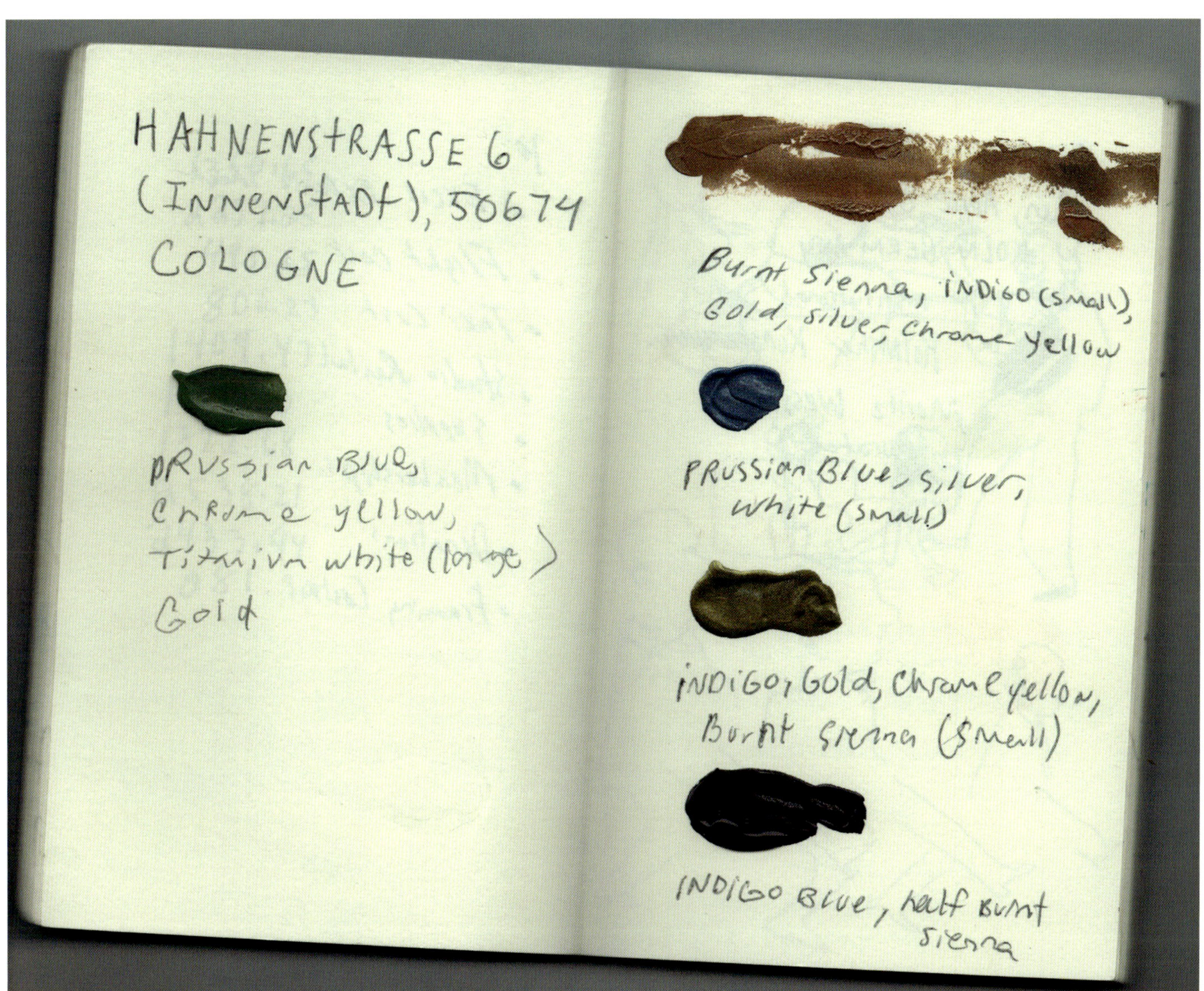

Sketchbook pages, 2018

WALTER PRICE

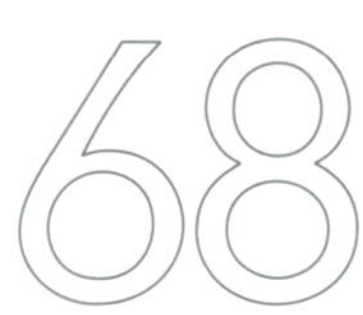

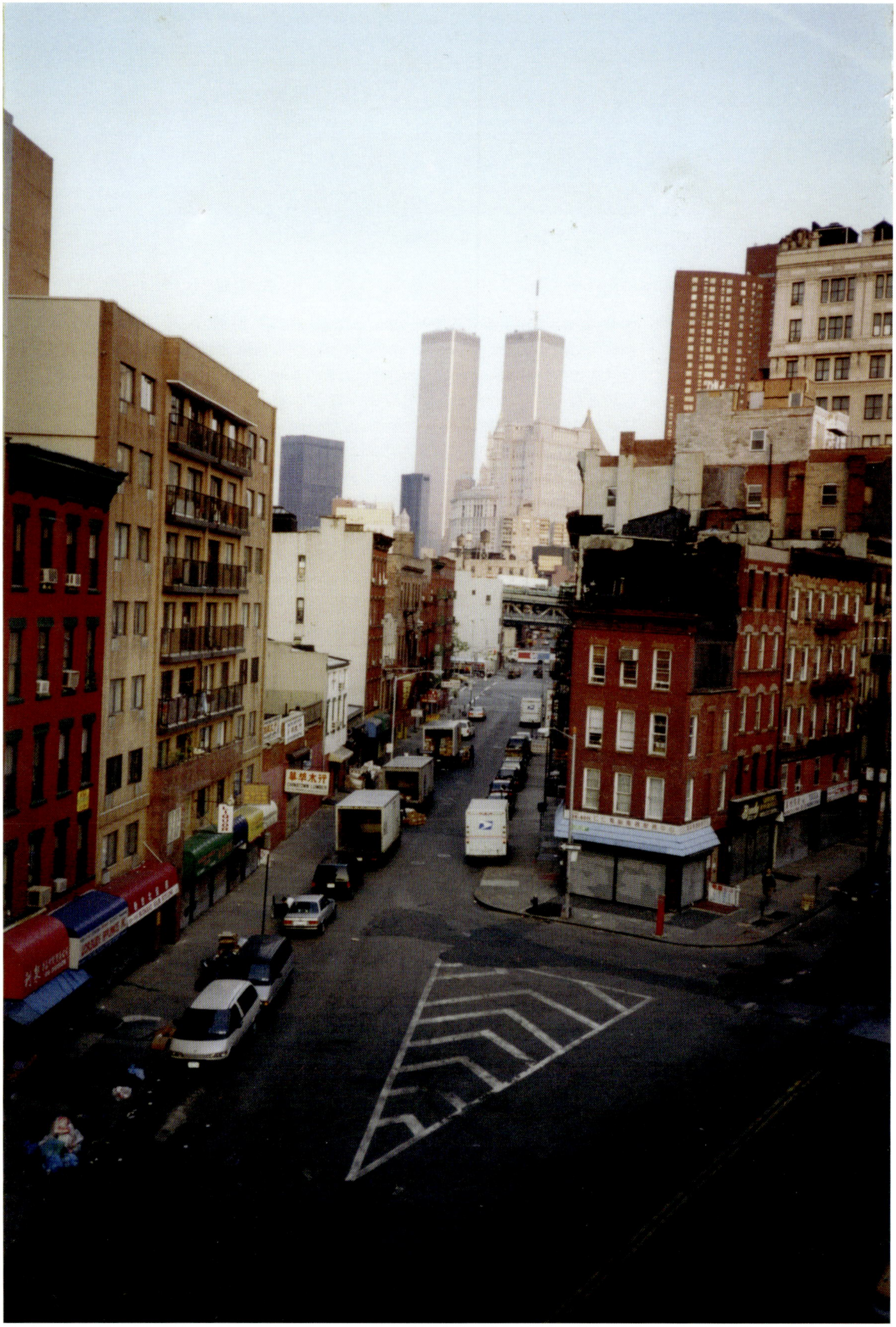

68

Intersection of Canal and Division Streets seen from the artist's window, New York, NY, c. 1990

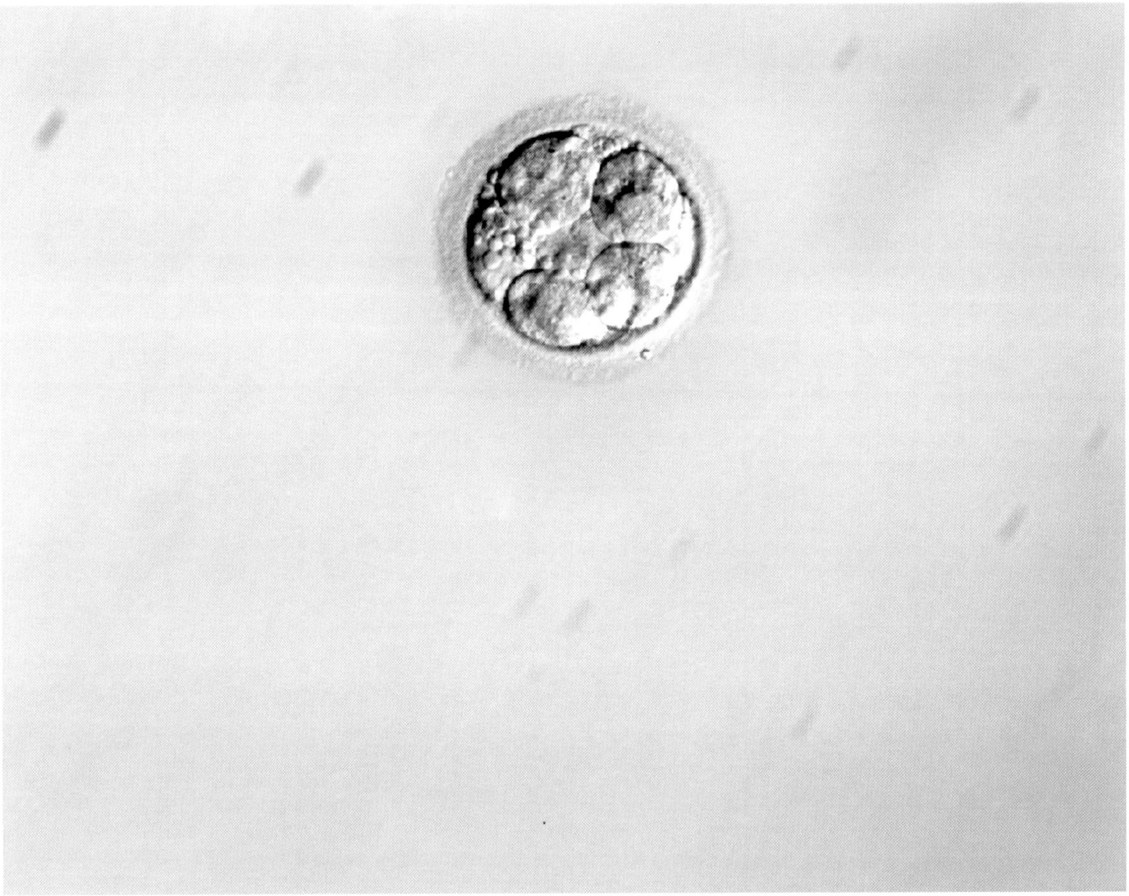

Process image for *All the Best Memories Are Hers*, 2018

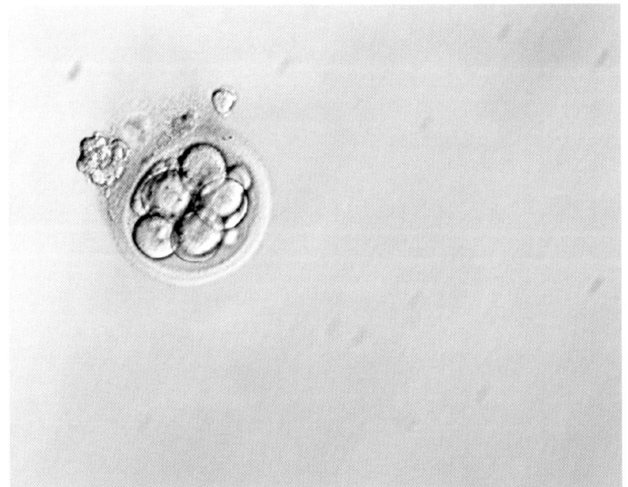

Process image for *All the Best Memories Are Hers*, 2018

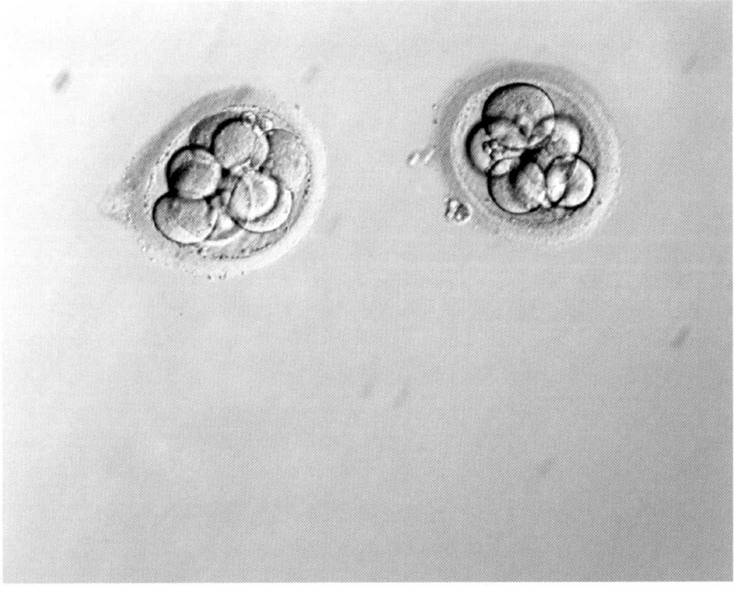

Process image for *All the Best Memories Are Hers*, 2018

CARISSA RODRIGUEZ

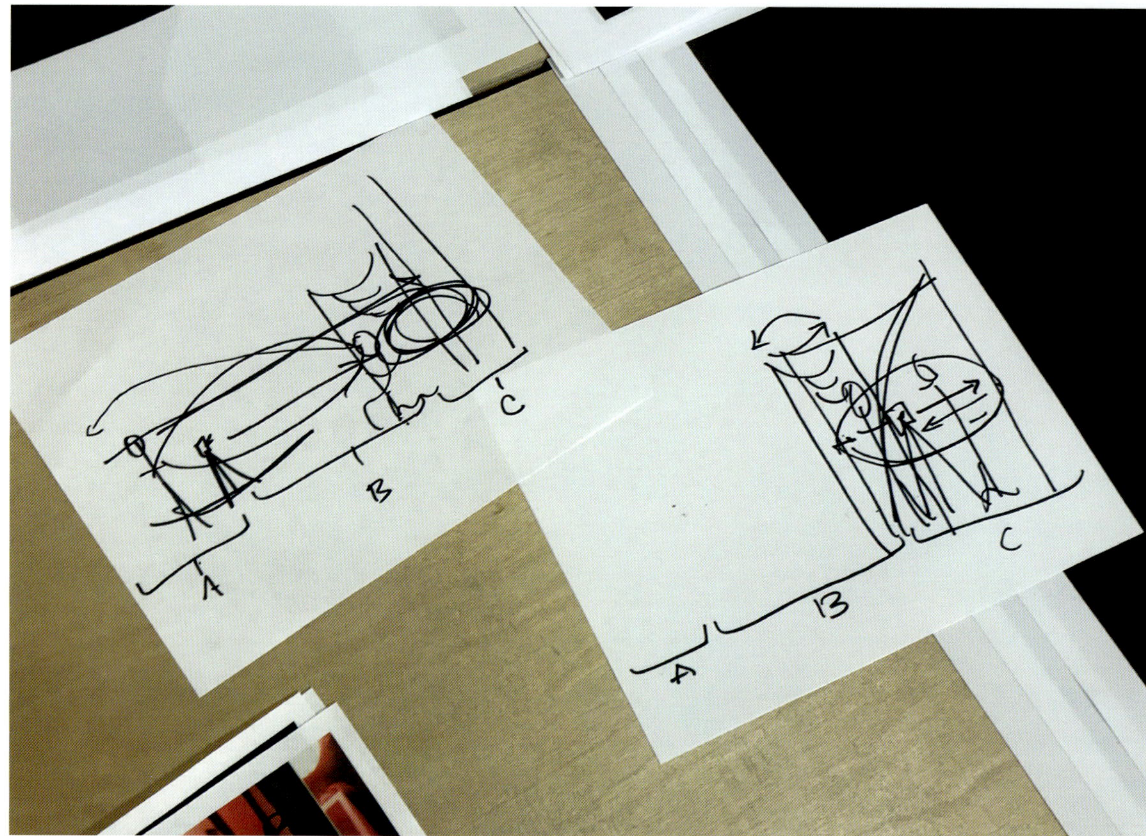

69

Process drawings of photographic constructions including camera, subject, backdrop, and mirror, 2017

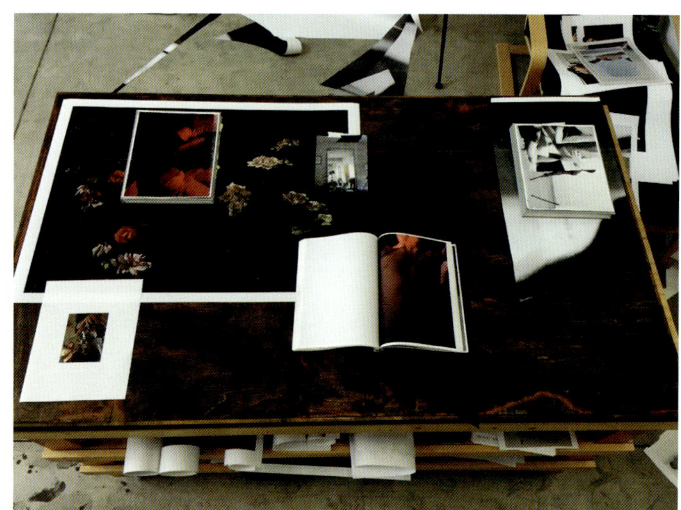

Mock-up for tabletop installation of *Some Recent Pictures*, 2017

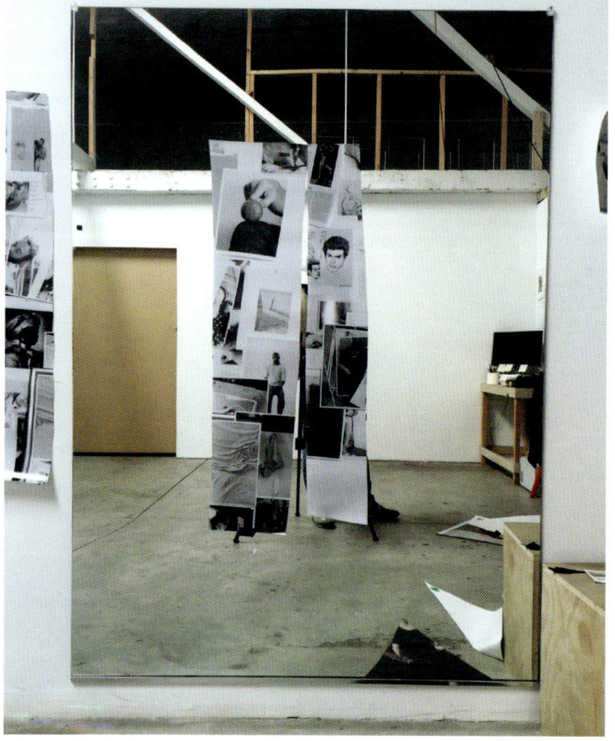

Setup for mirror study, studio, Los Angeles, CA, 2017

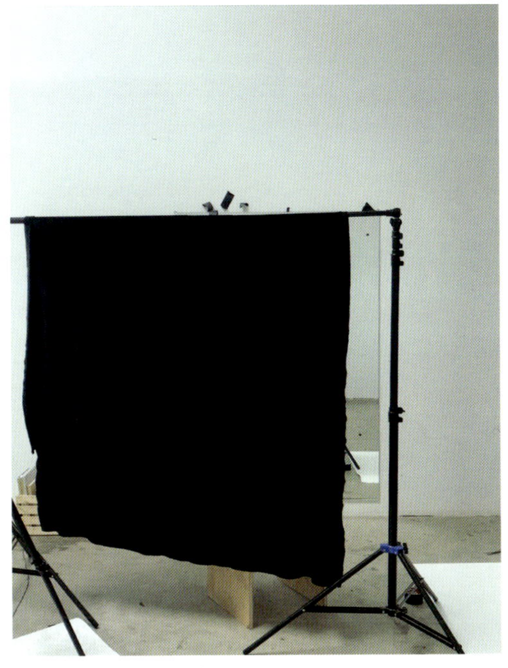
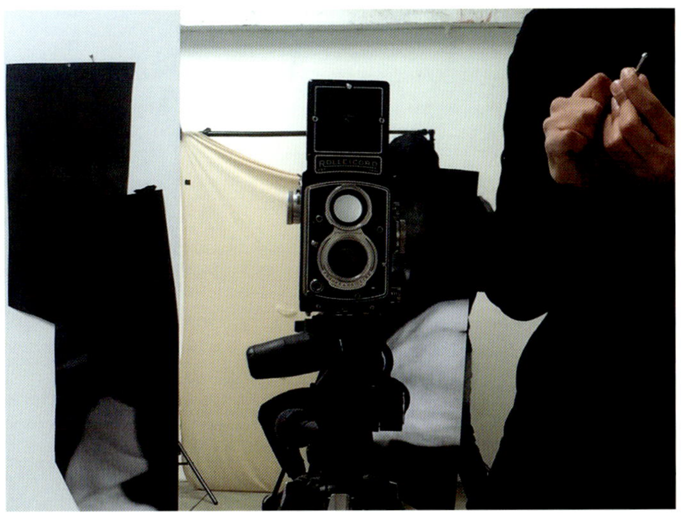

The artist's camera, studio, Los Angeles, CA, 2017

Studio, Los Angeles, CA, 2018

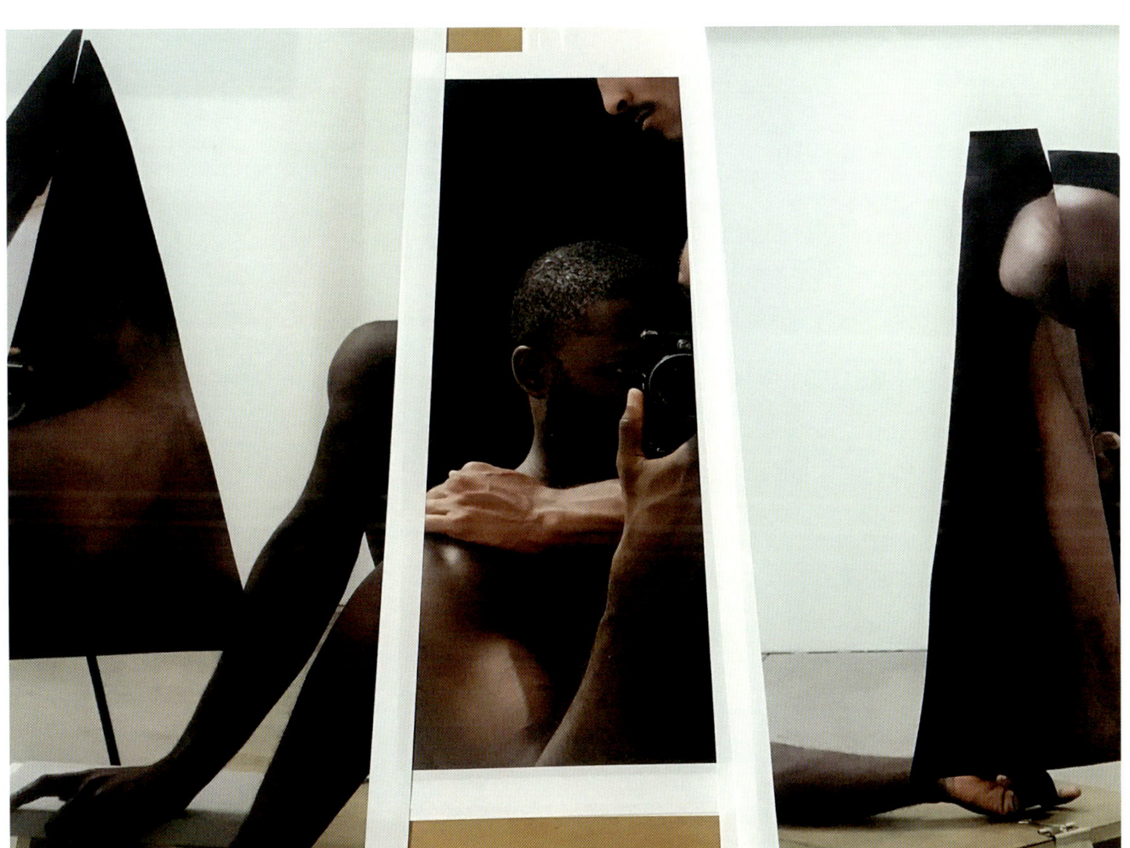

Test prints, studio, Los Angeles, CA, 2018

PAUL MPAGI SEPUYA

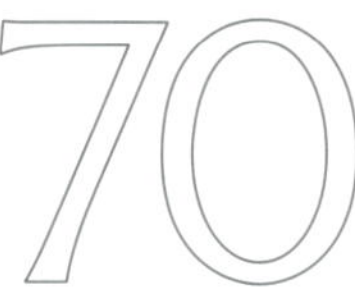

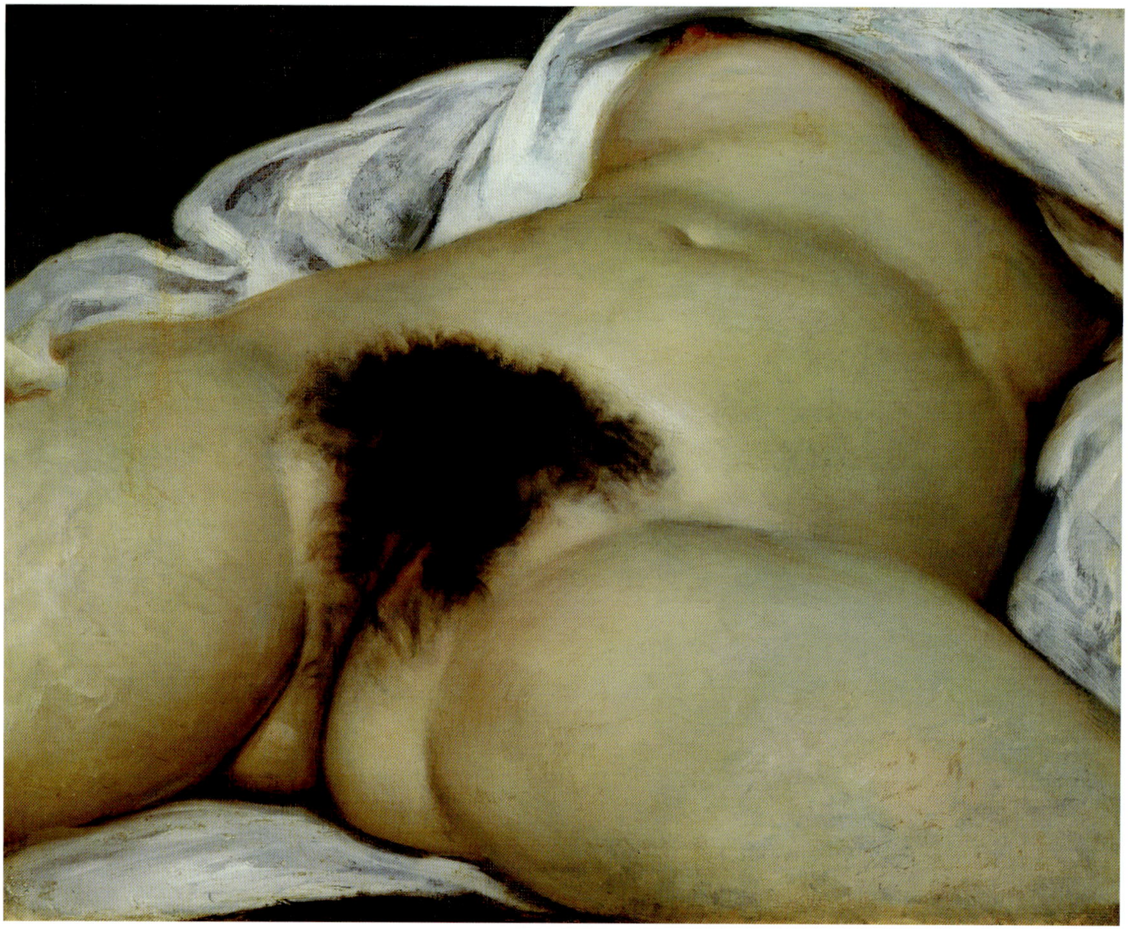

Gustave Courbet, *L'origine du monde*, 1866. Source image for *Baby IV*, 2016

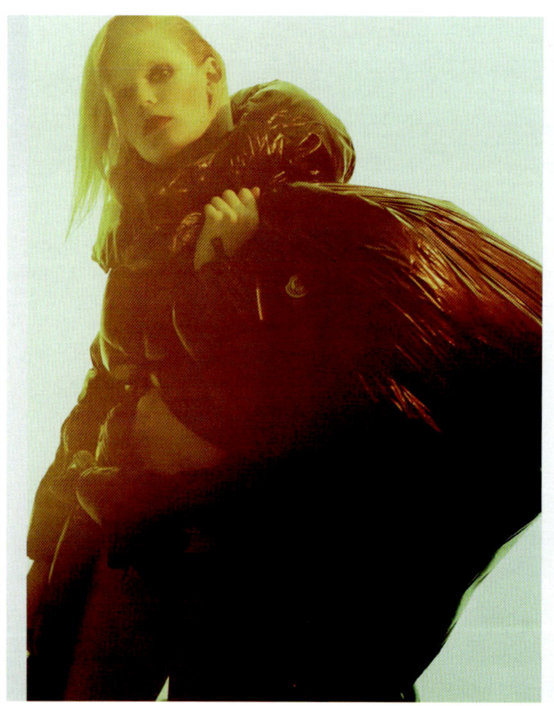

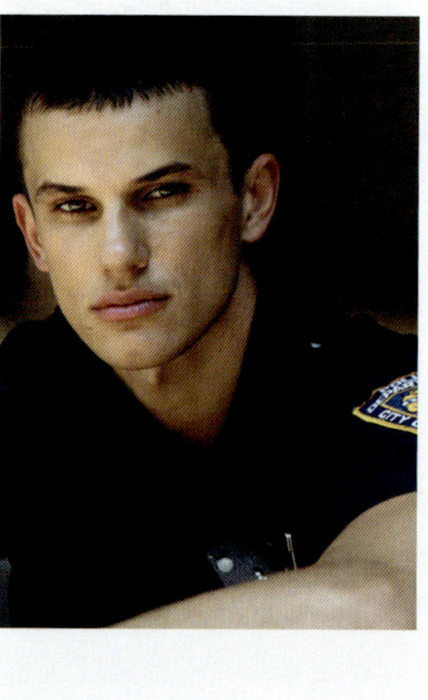

Pages from *Garbagio* editorial feature, *Interview* (Berlin), 2017

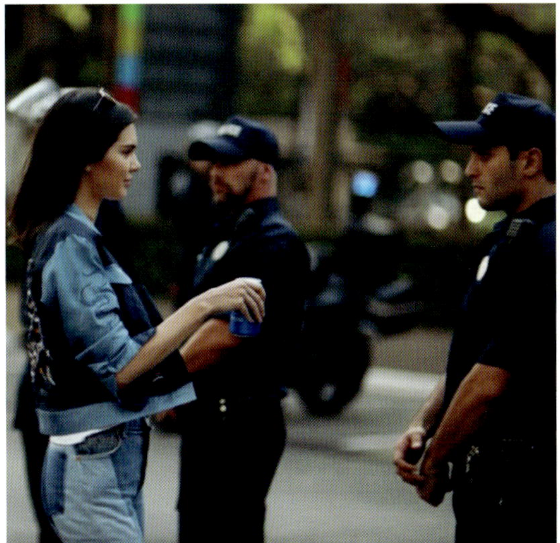

Pepsi commercial featuring Kendall Jenner, 2017. Source image for *Garbagio* editorial feature, *Interview* (Berlin), 2017

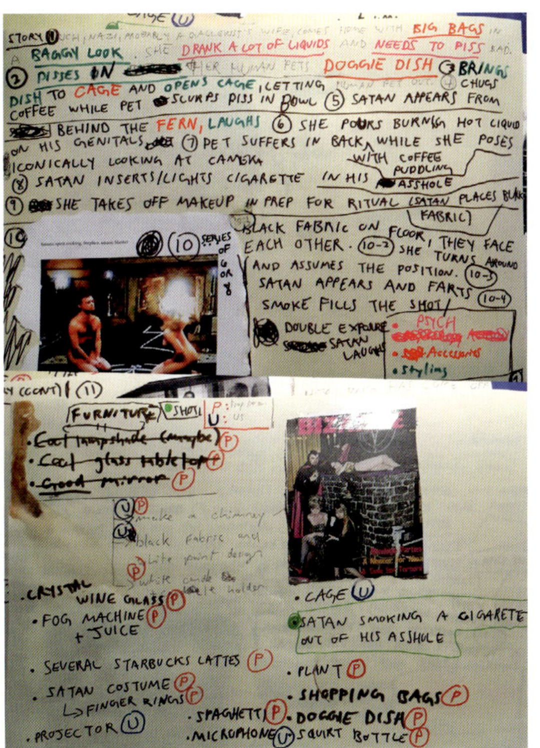

Burke Batelle, Mathieu Malouf, and Heji Shin, sketches for *Fart zur Hölle*, 2018

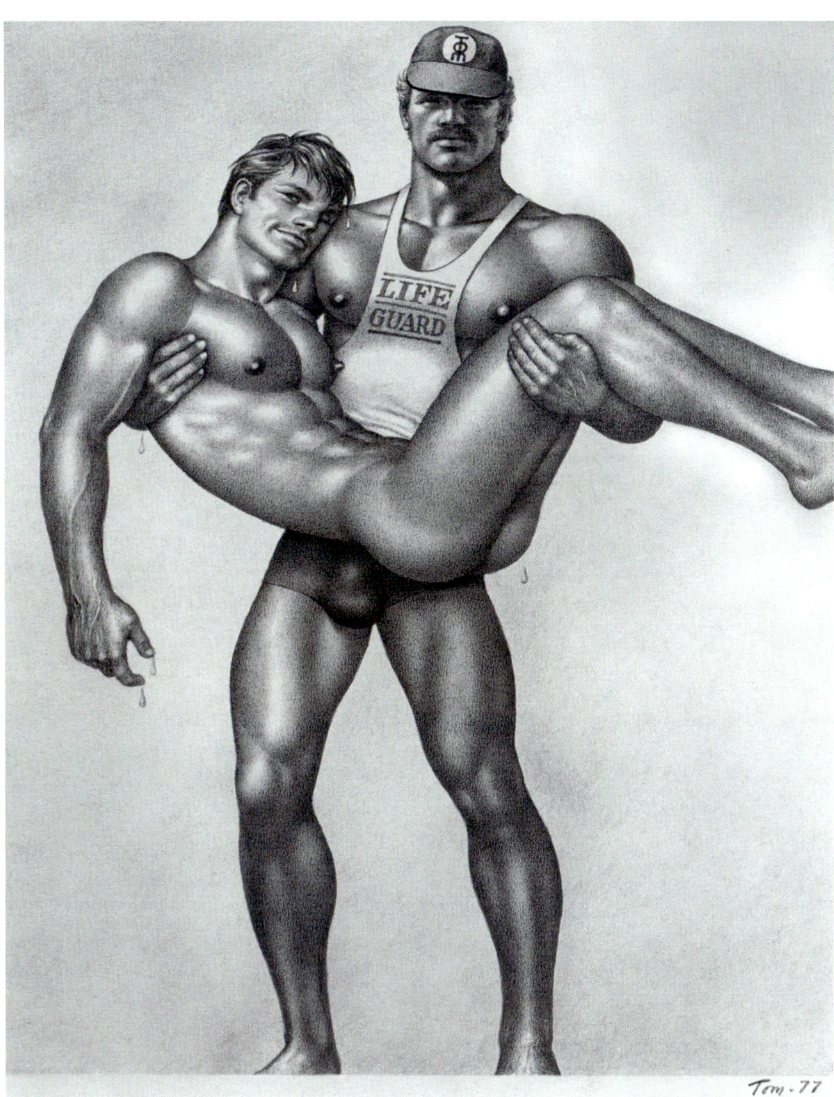

Tom of Finland, *Untitled*, 1977. Source image for *Basic Precinct* and *We Live in a Society*, 2018

HEJI SHIN

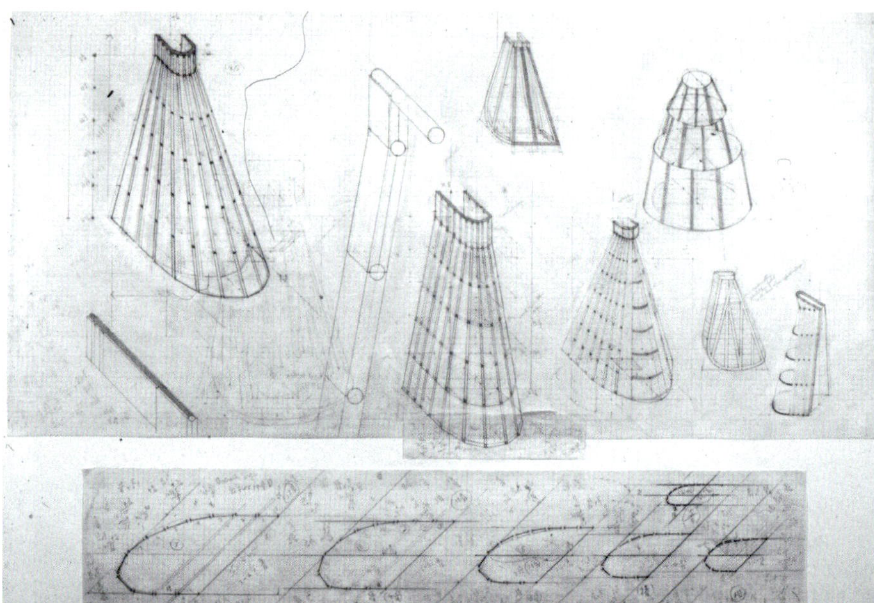

71

Drawing for *Box Pleats*, 1989

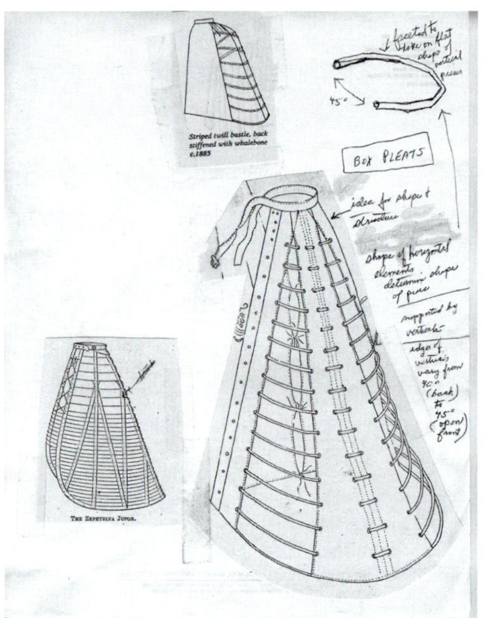

Photocopied source image for *Box Pleats*,
1989

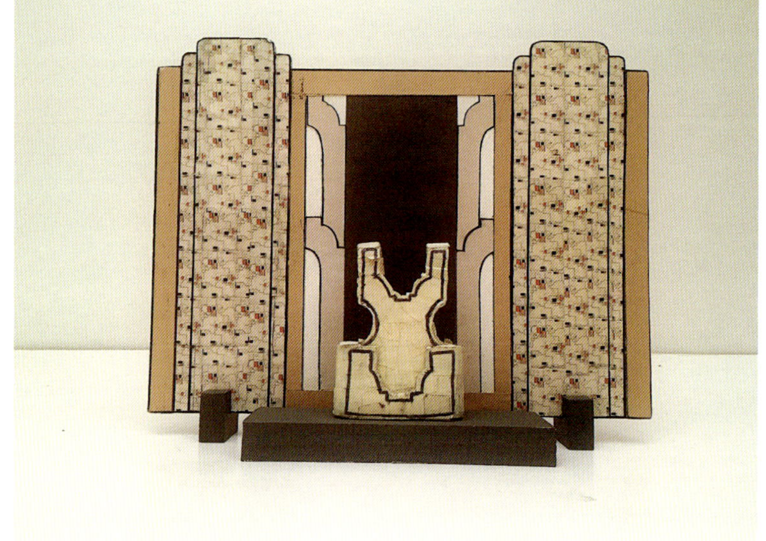

Model for *Window Dressing: Window 3*, 2007

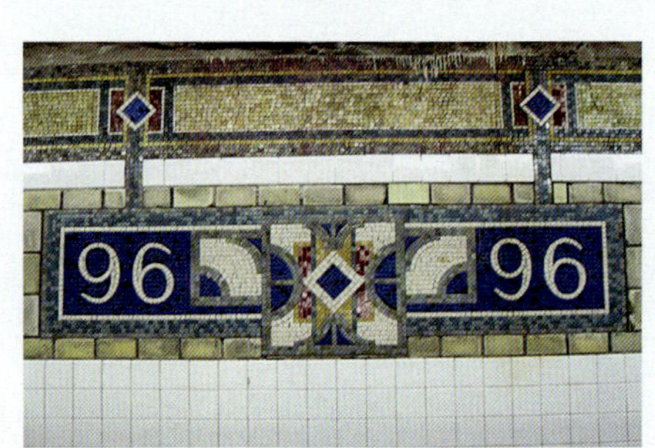

Source images for *Window Dressing: Window 3*, 2007

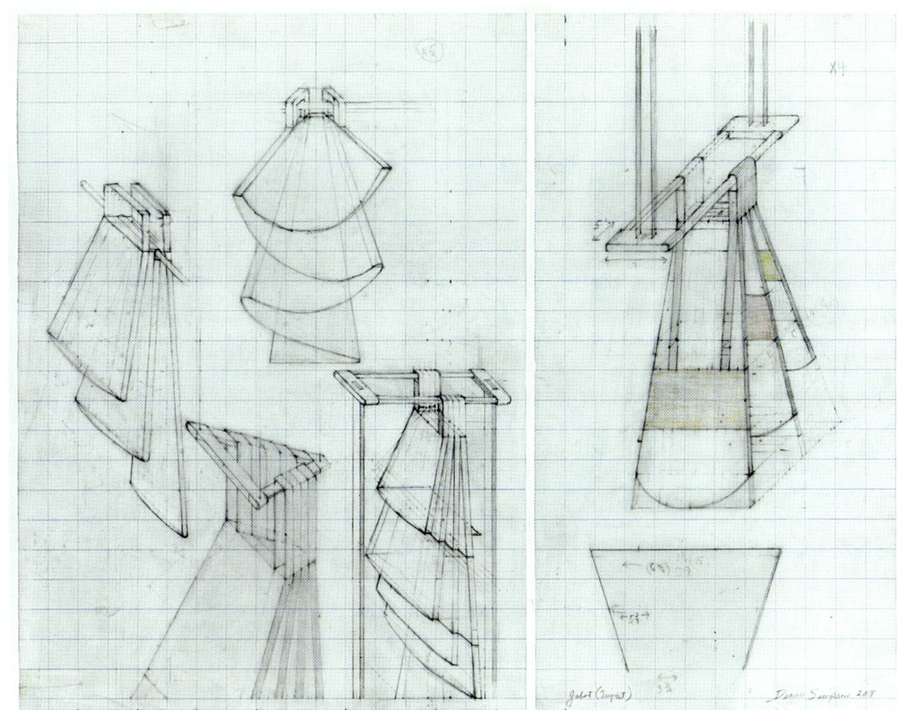

Drawing for *Jabot (triplet)*, 2018

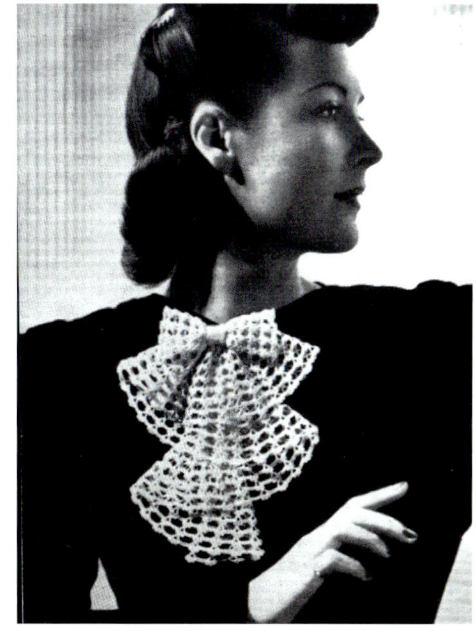

Source image for *Jabot (triplet)*, date unknown

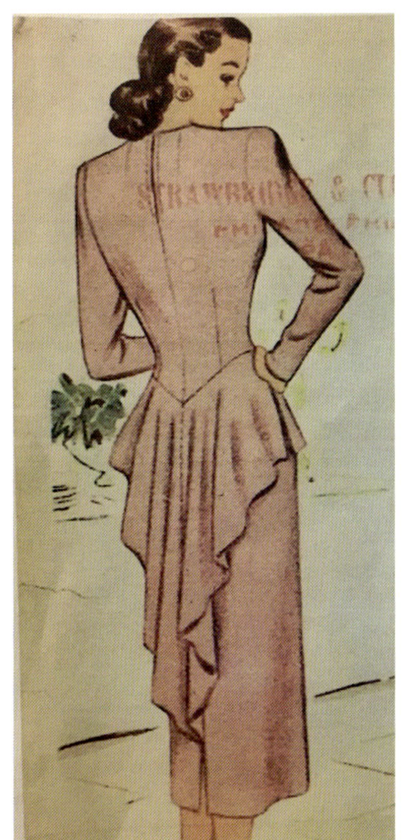

Source image for *Peplum III*, 1940s

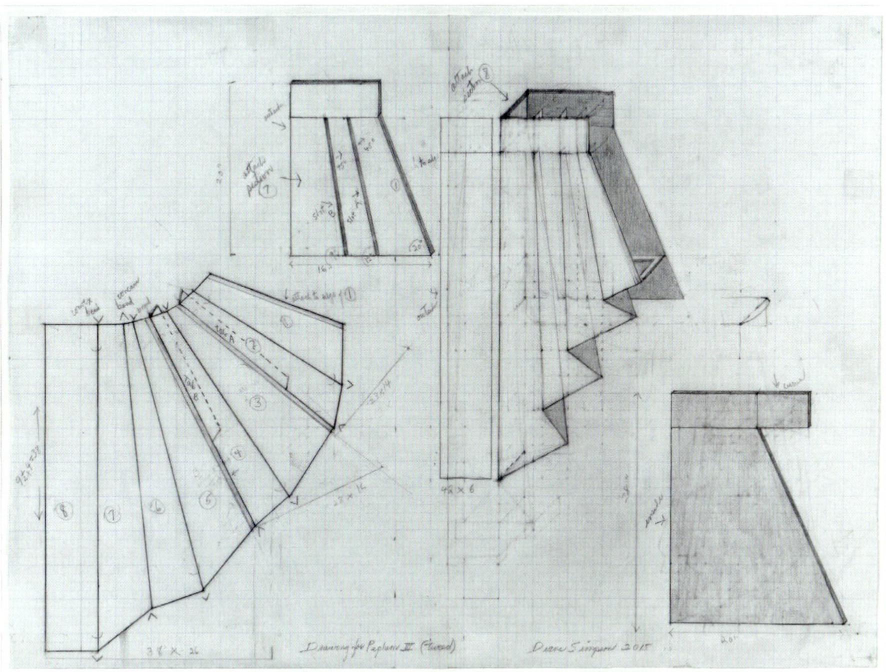

Drawing for *Peplum III*, 2014

DIANE SIMPSON

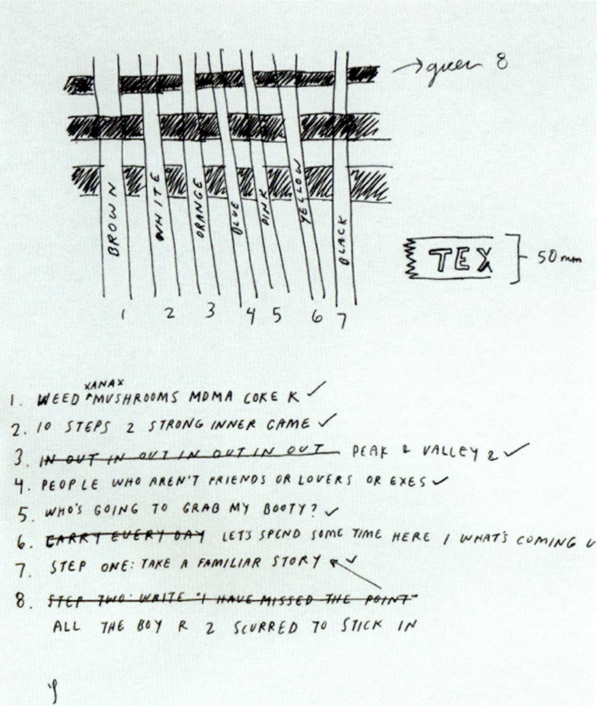

72

Sketchbook page, 2018

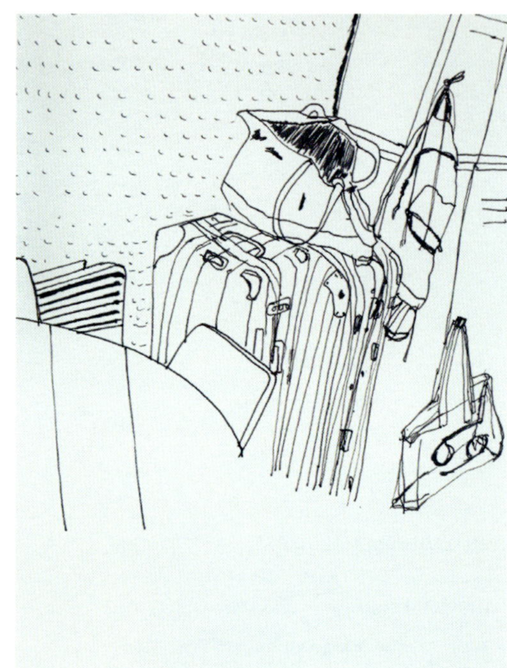

Sketchbook page, 2018

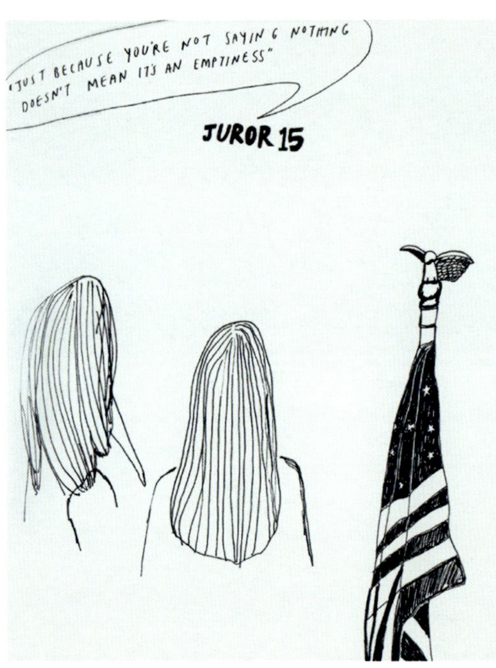

Sketchbook page, 2018

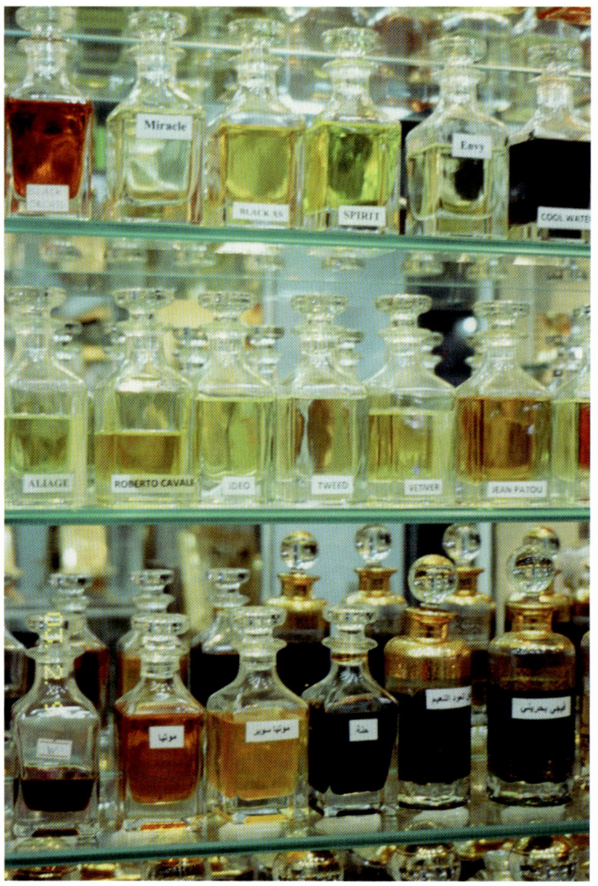

35mm photograph, 2018

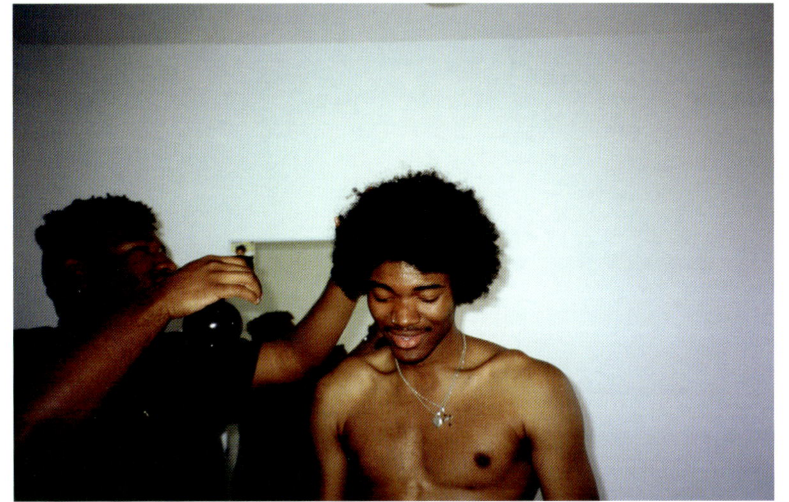

35mm photograph, 2018

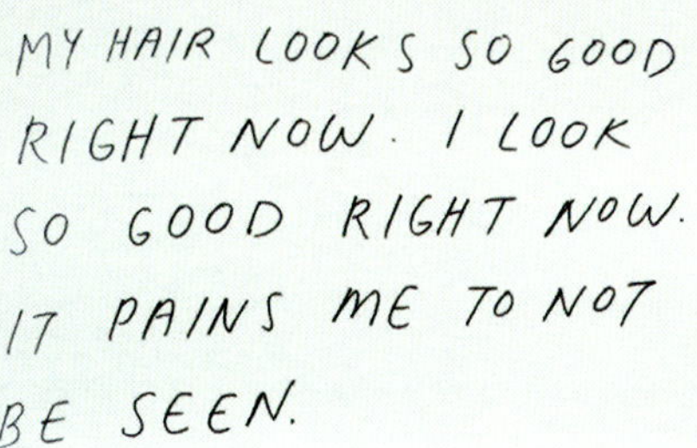

Sketchbook page, 2018

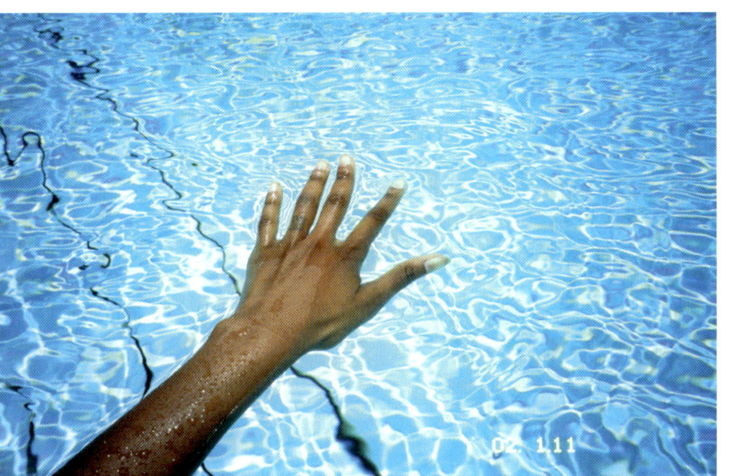

35mm photograph, 2018

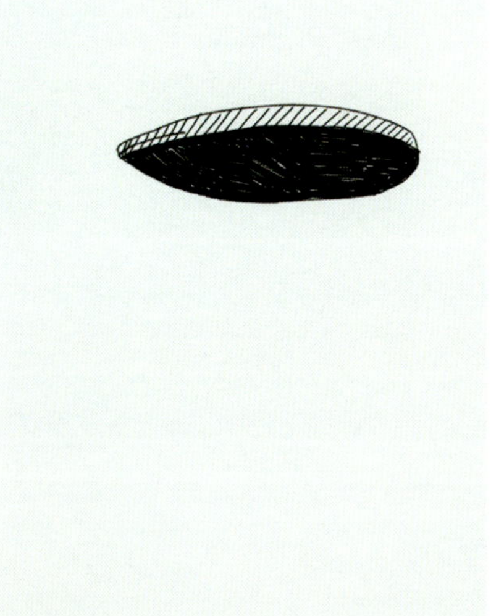

Sketchbook page, 2018

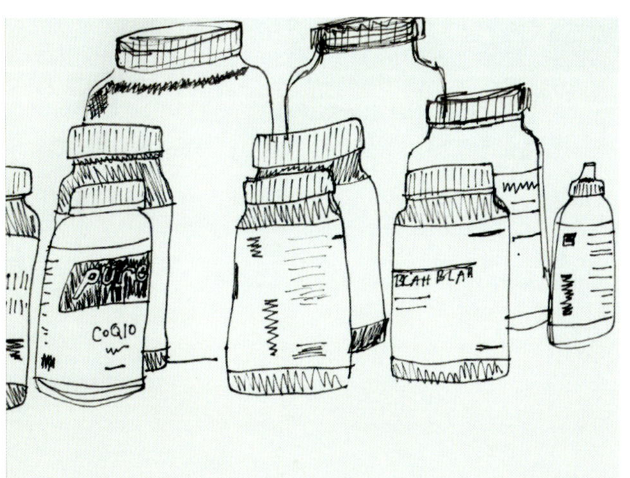

Sketchbook page, 2018

MARTINE SYMS

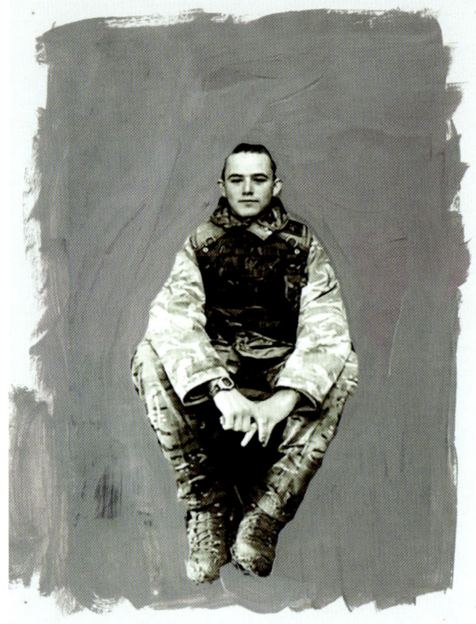

73

Process image for *Suggested Occupation*, 2015–

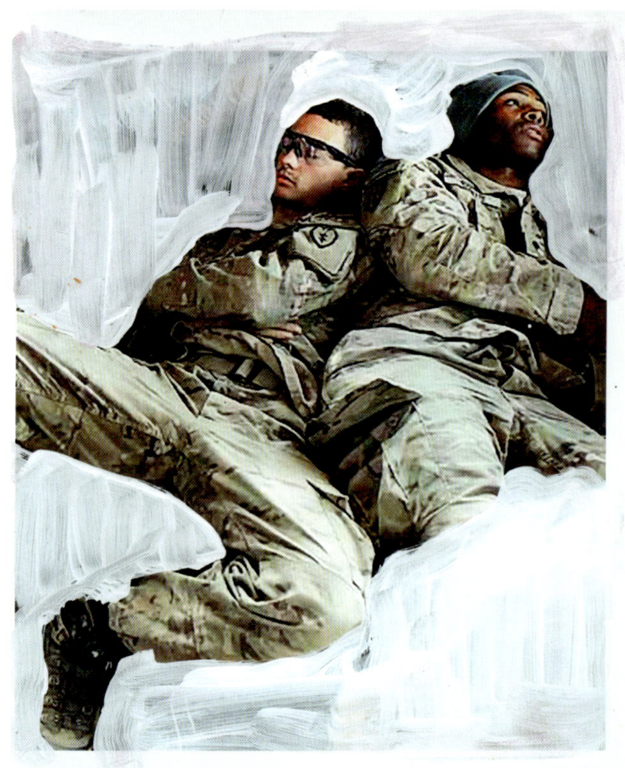

Process image for *Suggested Occupation*, 2016–

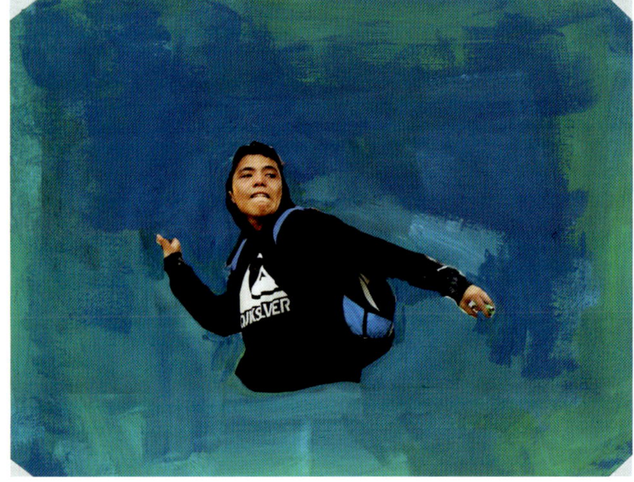

Process image for *Suggested Occupation*, 2018–

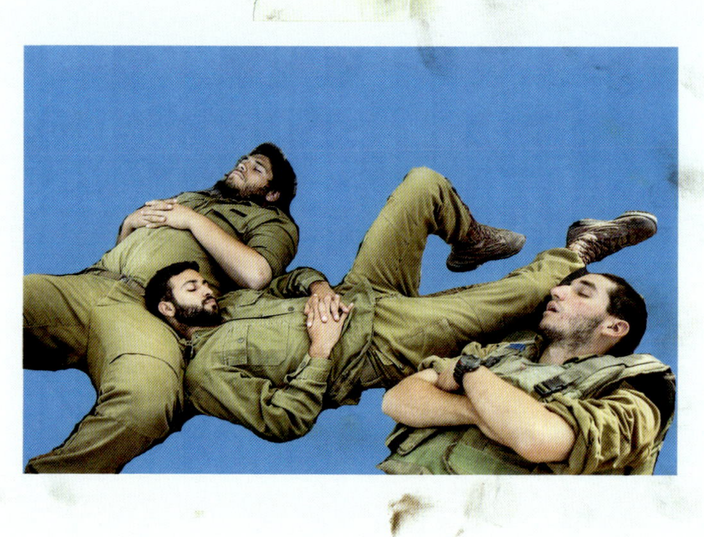

Process image for *Suggested Occupation*, 2017–

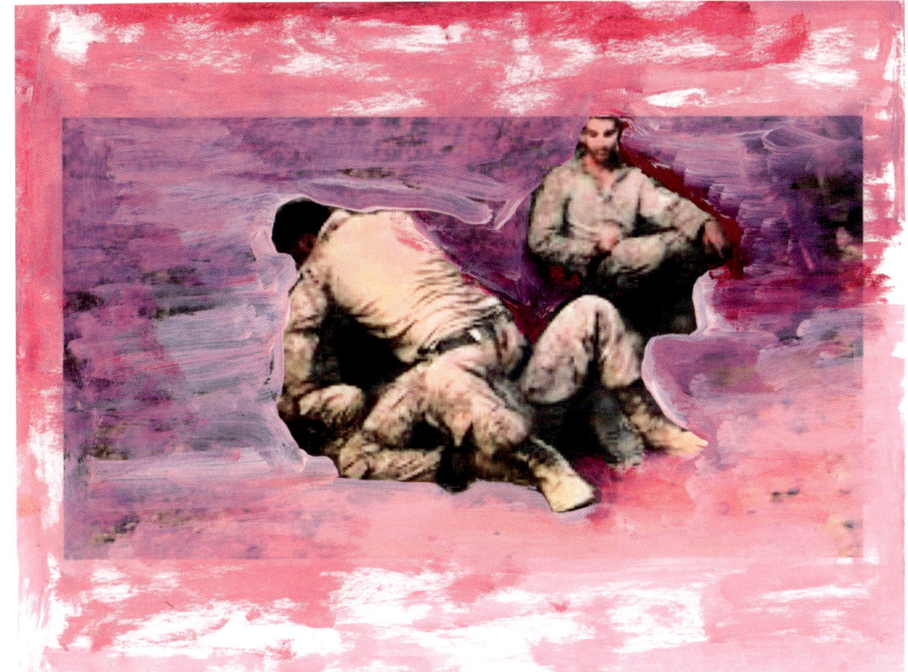

Process image for *Suggested Occupation*, 2019–

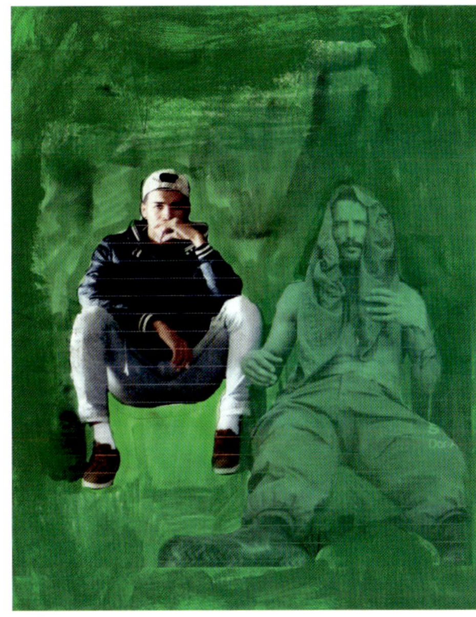

Process image for *Suggested Occupation*, 2018–

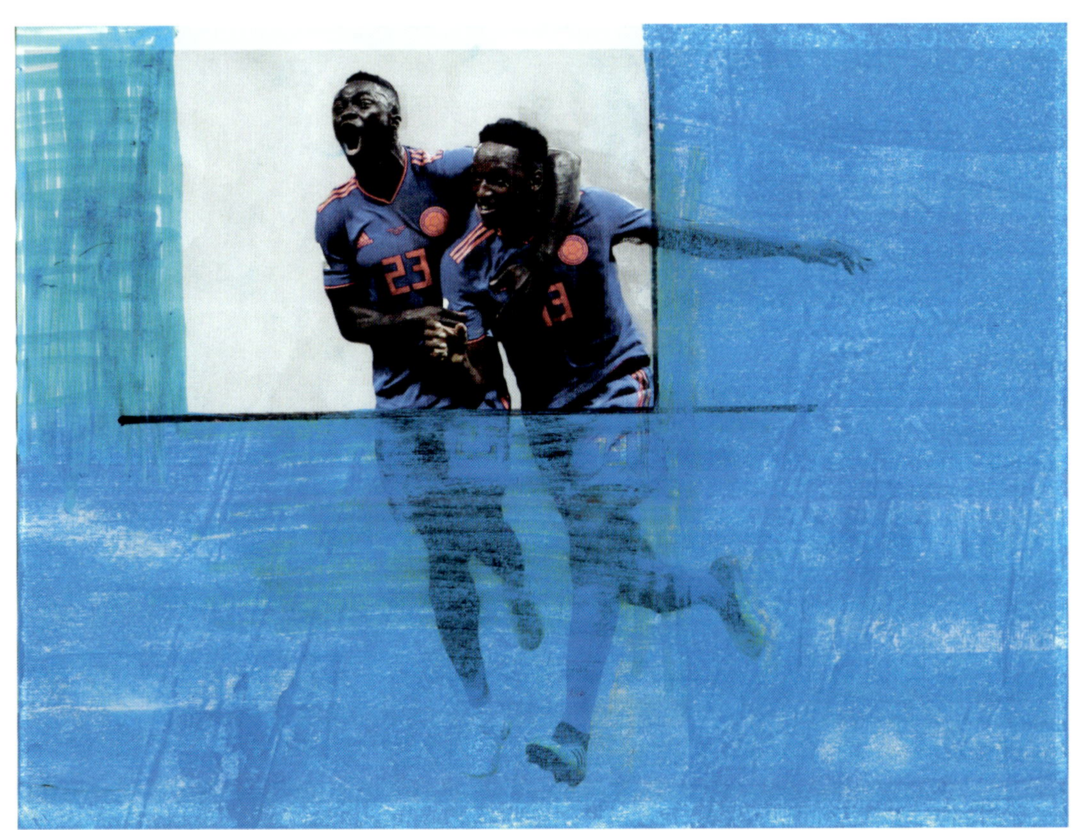

Process image for *Suggested Occupation*, 2018–

KYLE THURMAN

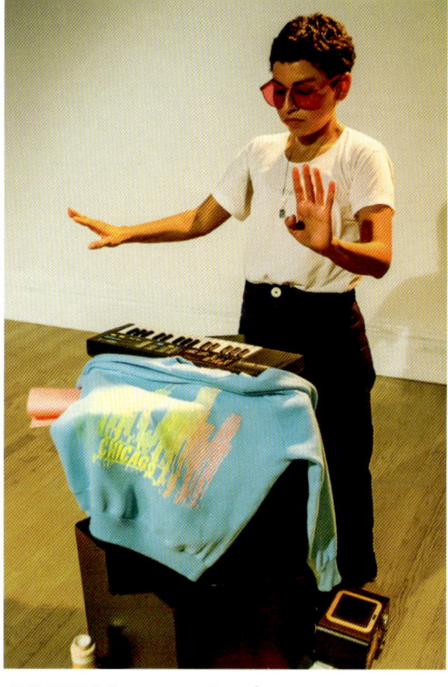

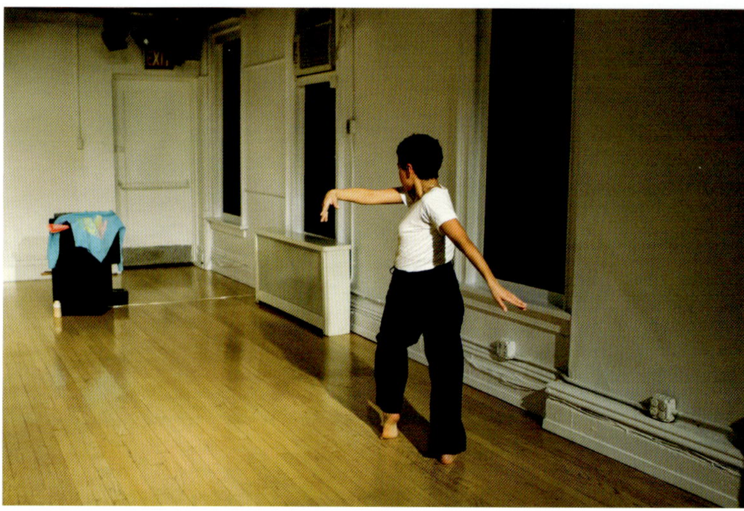

ALBUM, 2017. Performance view (work in progress), Brooklyn Arts Exchange, Brooklyn, NY, 2016

ALBUM, 2017. Performance view (work in progress), Brooklyn Arts Exchange, Brooklyn, NY, 2016

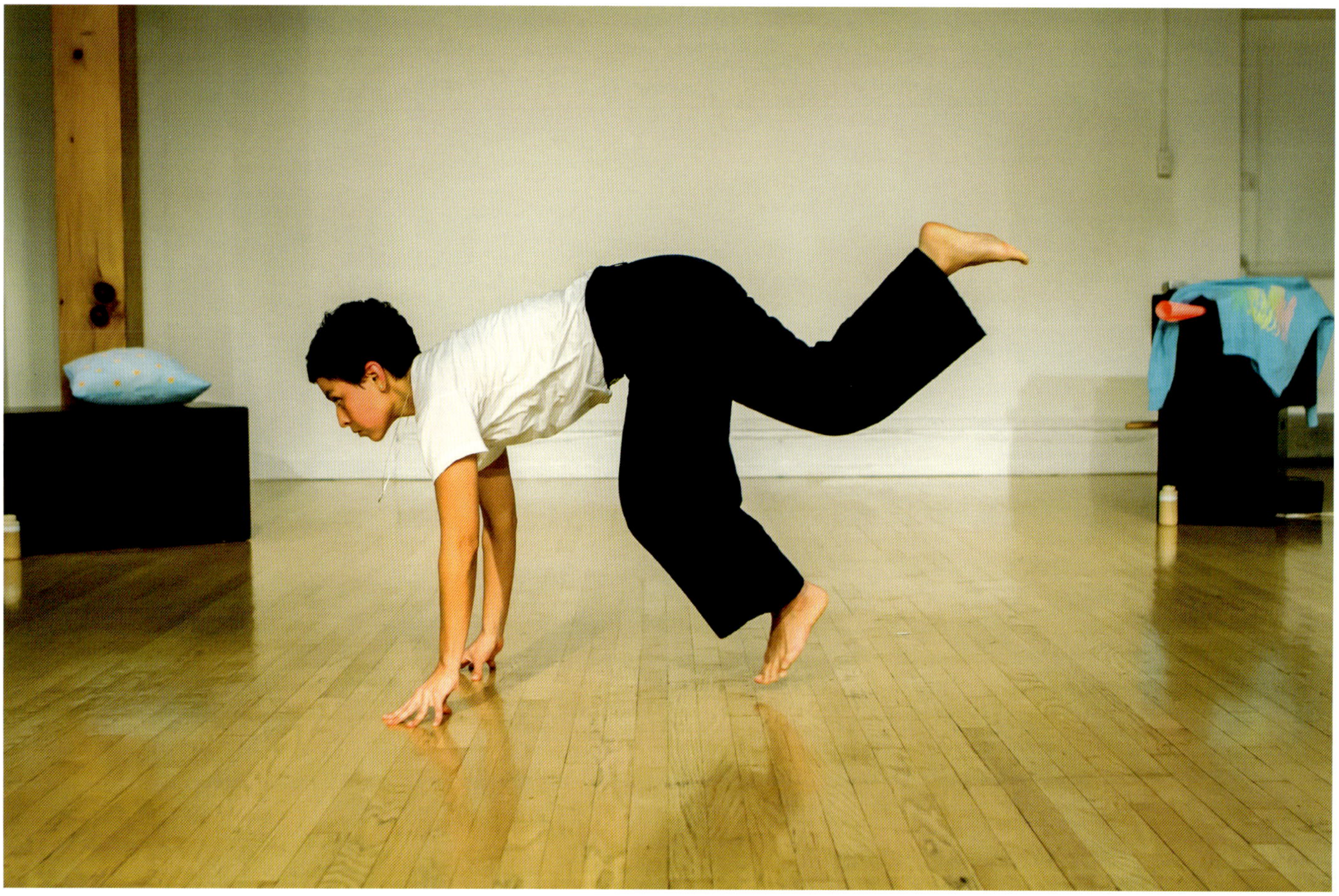

ALBUM, 2017. Performance view (work in progress), Brooklyn Arts Exchange, Brooklyn, NY, 2016

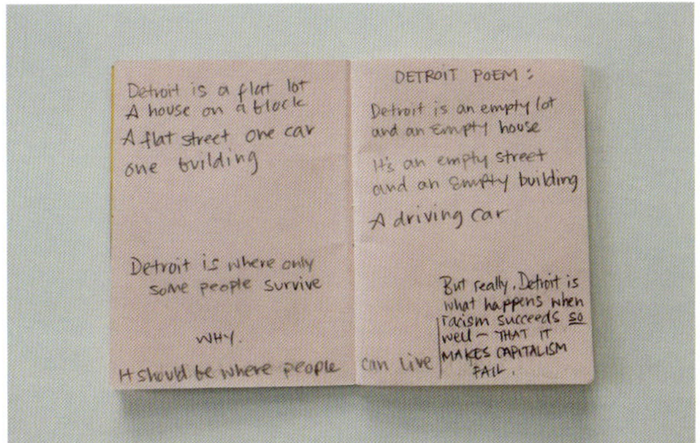

Notes for *Dance Savings*, 2014–18

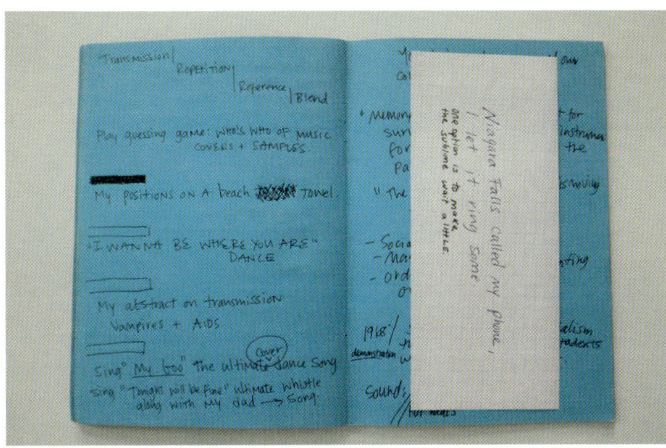

Notes for *Dance Savings*, 2014–18

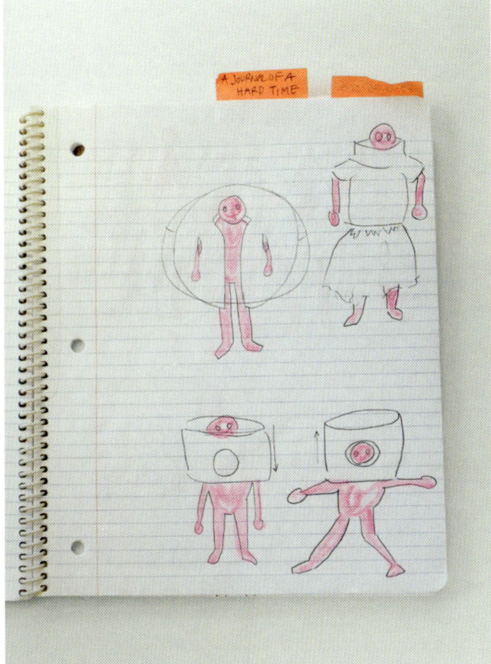

Sketches for *Dance Savings*, 2014–18

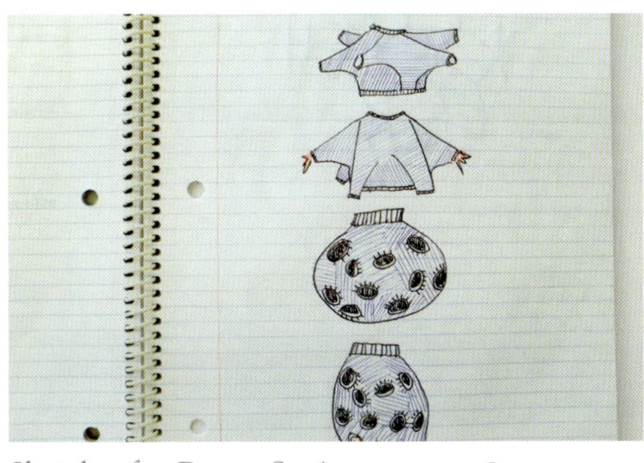

Sketches for *Dance Savings*, 2014–18

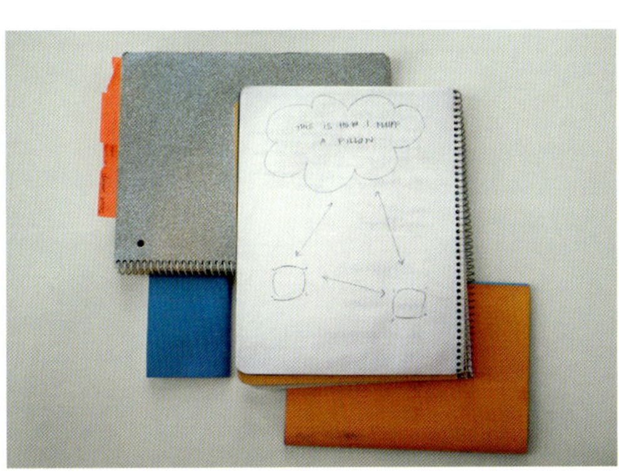

Notebooks and sketchbooks for *Dance Savings*, 2014–18

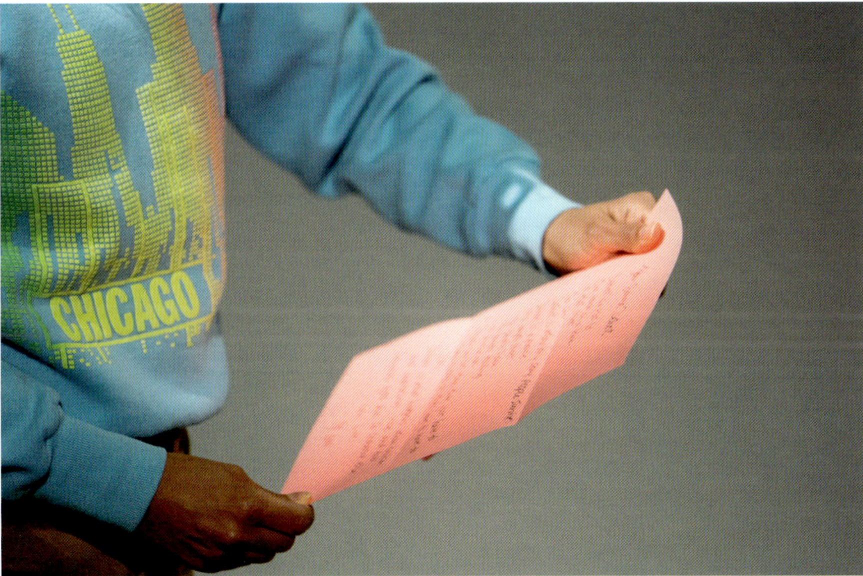

ALBUM, 2017. Performance view, Hirshhorn Museum and Sculpture Garden, Washington, DC, 2018

MARIANA VALENCIA

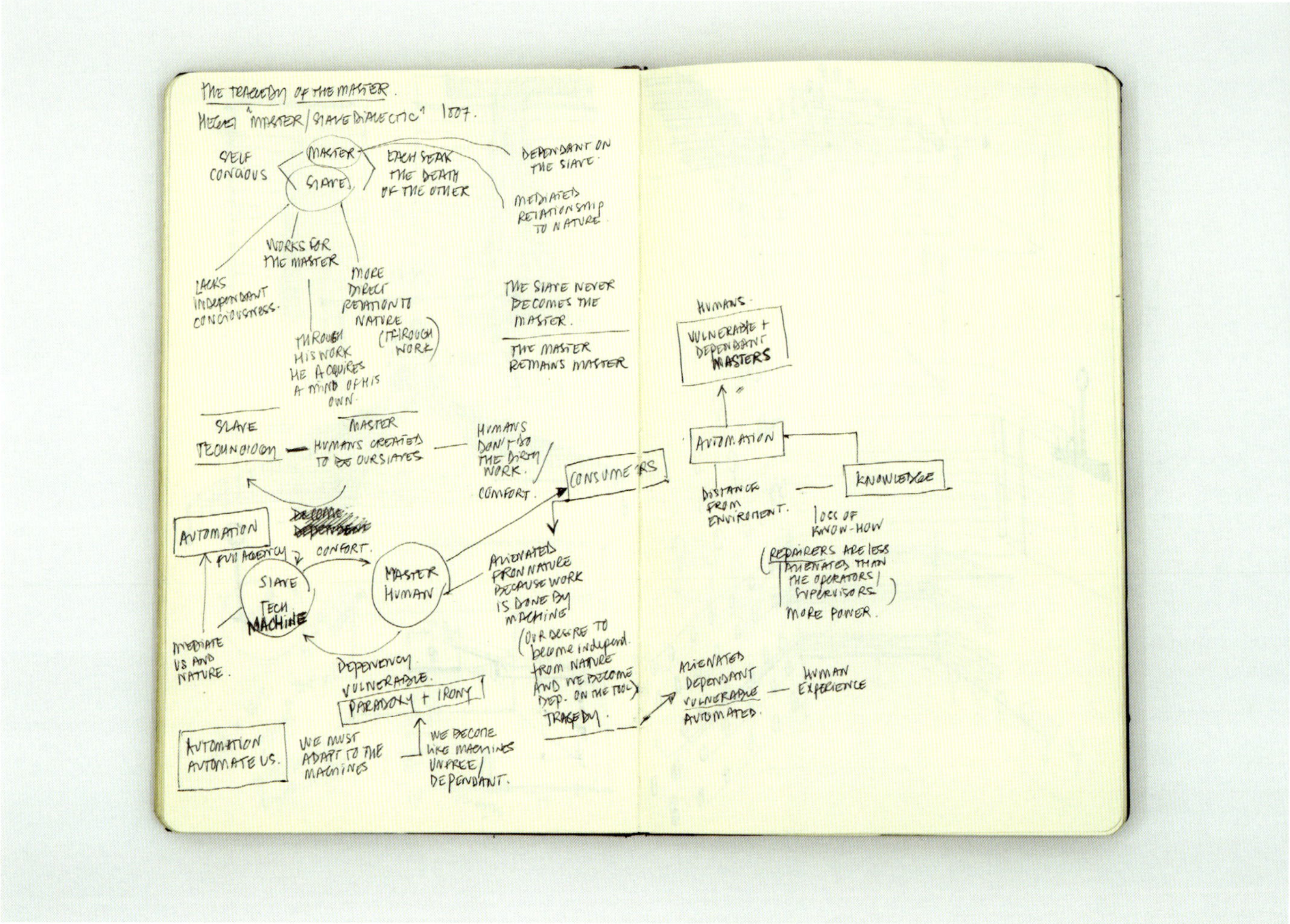

Notes for *National Times*, 2016

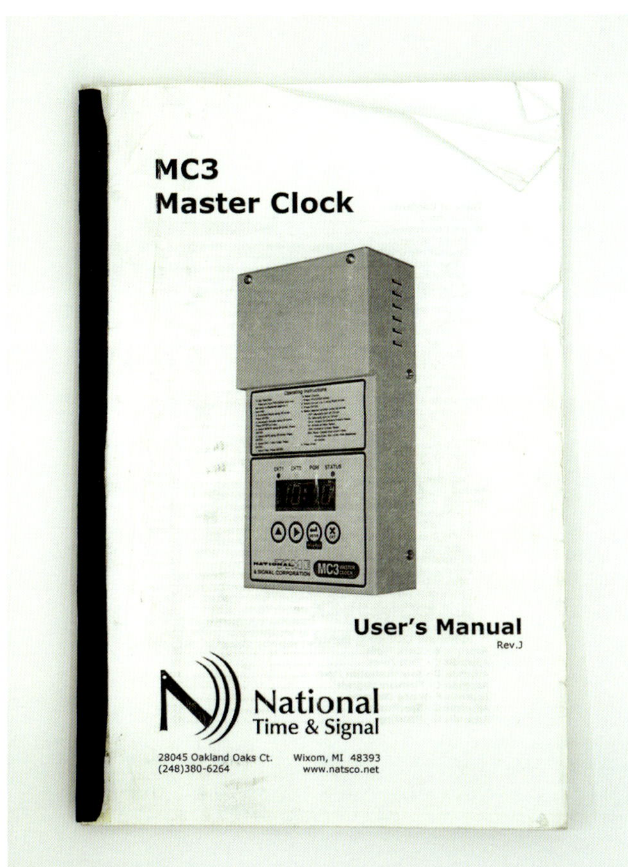

Programming manual for MC3 Master Clock.
Source material for *National Times*, 2016

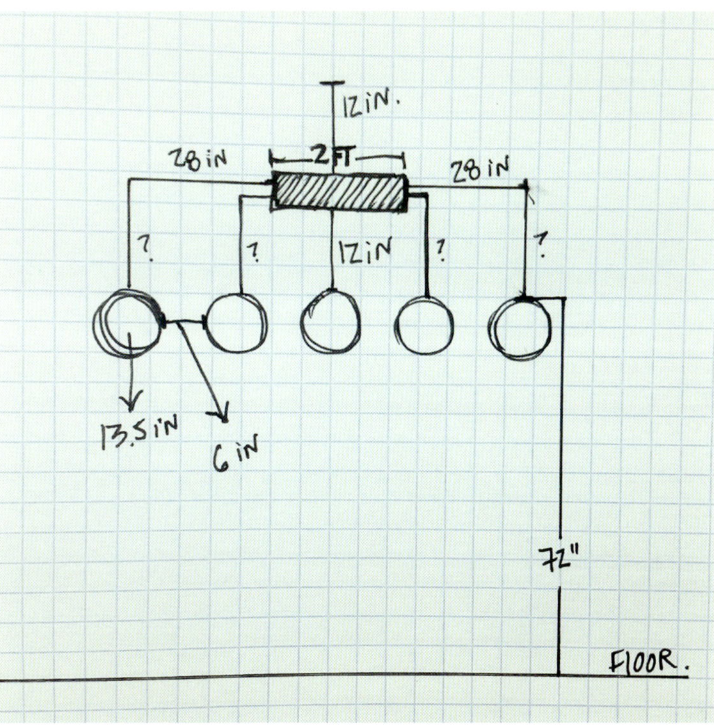

Diagram for *National Times*, 2016

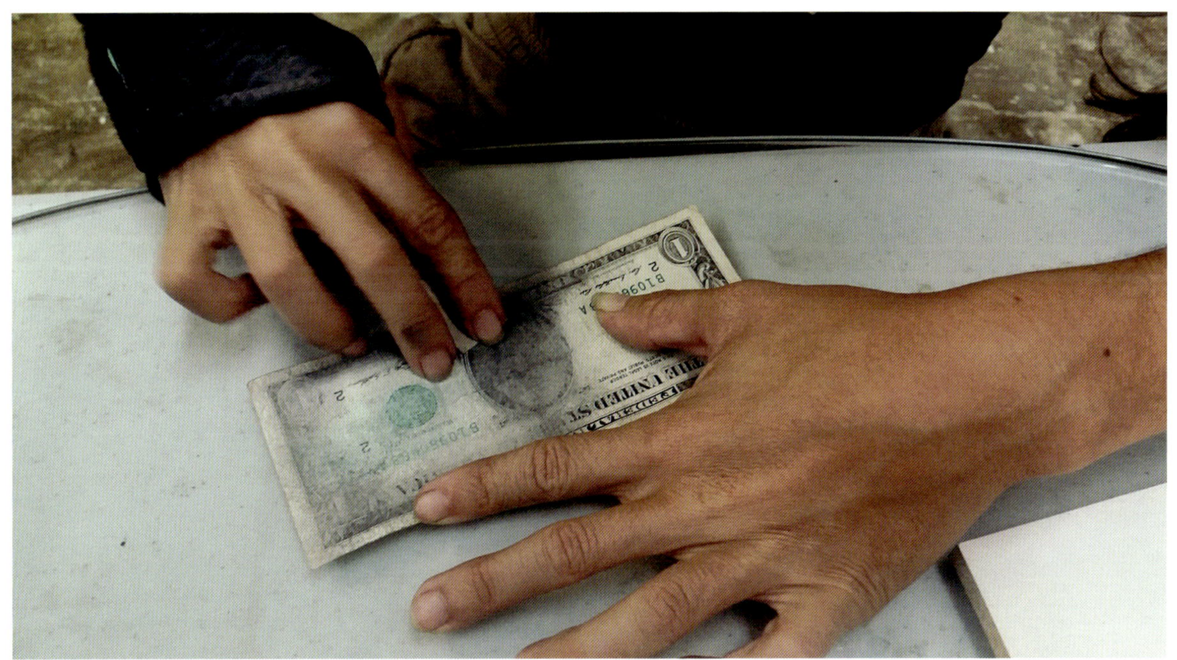

Source image for *National Times*, 2016

AGUSTINA WOODGATE

Entries

2019

1

EDDIE ARROYO

Eddie Arroyo chronicles the effects of displacement in South Florida's Black and Brown neighborhoods, attending closely to urban landscapes where Haitian immigrants and people from other Caribbean nations reside. His present work focuses on depictions of solitary buildings in areas such as Miami's Little Haiti in paintings highlighting today's neoliberal version of colonialism, gentrification, which manifests itself in the eviction of long-time residents and the erasure of local architecture by new developments.

At first glance, Arroyo's paintings might seem like neutral portraits of Little Haiti's environs, the titles disclosing only the addresses of the depicted locations. In his choices of street corners, buildings, and scenes, however, Arroyo addresses the changing face of a neighborhood in transition as well as the communities of people threatened by unscrupulous developers. Low-rise structures are painted in warm hues that would almost function as color fields but for the presence of signage, ads, and graffiti. The cool-toned skies above are frequently overcast—though often, too, they let through a ray of sunshine.

Arroyo is also a local activist, as well as an editor of and active contributor to the regional online art publication *Art Is About*. In his depictions of Little Haiti, he memorializes not just the neighborhood but also the art of Haitian-born mural painter and community leader Serge Toussaint, whose murals grace the facades of many local bodegas, auto-repair shops, and restaurants, as well the vernacular tradition of hand-painted advertisements that cover Miami's local architecture. Arroyo's paintings such as *6041 NE*

2nd Ave., Miami, FL 33137 (2017) and *5825 NE 2nd Ave., Miami, FL 33137* (2016) recall Edward Hopper's masterpieces, with a similar precision of light and the viewer's proximity to low buildings. Extending Hopper's ideas of physical and psychological emptiness, Arroyo does not equivocate in his critique of the forces behind his deserted landscapes: they represent his version of twenty-first century Americana. *MG*

2

KORAKRIT ARUNANONDCHAI

Working across video, painting, performance, and sculpture, Korakrit Arunanondchai wrestles with massive, unrepresentable global systems via autobiographical, phantasmal assemblages of symbolically rich objects and images. Having come of age at a time defined by humans' detrimental impact on the earth, the artist takes entropy as a given. His video works, which reflect this perception of increasing disintegration, are stitched together from densely layered and edited moving images, some dreamlike and others all too real. The ultimate effect is a hallucinatory collage of fragments that emphatically refuses to congeal into a resolved whole.

Arunanondchai's video *with history in a room filled with people with funny names 4* (2017) intertwines a mournful meditation on his aging grandmother's dementia with a kaleidoscopic imagining of the obsolescence of the human species. The complexly cyclical structure of the work, in which images recede and recur over some twenty minutes, contends that time and history are not organized toward a progressivist end point. Rather, the work reflects a reincarnationist system in which past,

present, and future exist continuously. The film flickers between footage of giant crowds mourning the 2016 death of Thai king Bhumibol Adulyadej, protests against the Trump presidency, the deaths of endangered animals, the thousand-acre megatemple Wat Phra Dhammakaya north of Bangkok, and oceans crowded with detritus. There also are appearances by Arunanondchai's invented "drone-spirit" Chantri, frequent collaborator boychild's turn as the snakelike creature Naga from Thai mythology, and a marauding human in a rat suit that nods to Elizabeth Kolbert's 2014 book *The Sixth Extinction*, which ponders the possibility that rats will become a dominant species after humans' demise.

Arunanondchai's video sweeps one along in a flow of decay, but it also points to modes of resistance. The artist draws on Donna Haraway's concept of the Chthulucene, which term she proposes for a past, present, and future epoch in which human and animal refugees pursue "multispecies ecojustice" together. Arunanondchai's multitemporal collages do not simply image the present entanglement of global capital with political, personal, and geologic history but instead imagine new ways of thinking outside of teleological time to recuperate refuges for human, animal, and spirit alike. *AC*

3

OLGA BALEMA

Olga Balema constructs objects and installations from the found, the readymade, and the fabricated, moving fluently through various genres and stylistic points with a material intelligence that encompasses references to art history, cinema, literature, and personal narratives. Consistent throughout, however, is her interest in discomfort. Balema creates a quality of tension evoked by her deliberate misuse of materials, frequently channeled through the structuring and arranging of architectural space.

Geometric shapes, bright colors, and drooping, puffy, or flaccid structures are recurrent protagonists in Balema's work, sometimes making literal reappearances: at her 2015 exhibition *Cannibals* at Croy Nielsen in Berlin, a series of works called *Threat to civilization* (2015)—irregular, tumescent PVC bags filled with water—contained bent steel rods, cannibalized fragments of former sculptures that rusted throughout the course of the show and turned the clear water ruddy and clouded. For her 2017 exhibition at High Art in Paris, *None of the beauty of the landscape can reach her pupils anymore*, Balema covered the delicate plaster flourishes of the gallery's elegant white walls with rows of panels upholstered in quilted or snakeskin pleather and fabric patterned like wood grain, all in a riot of colors that seemed to rebel against the room's decorous ornamentation. The shiny smoothness of the panels, each about the size of a place mat, was rudely ruptured by the occasional tear from which a small dowel poked out, like a cigarette from a pair of lips.

At Art Basel Hong Kong in 2018, Balema channeled her penchant for modulating interiors into a holistic approach to the temporary architecture of the gallery booth by creating a flimsy, unstable-seeming installation of seven paintings and sculptures that sagged and slouched from the impermanent walls. A vertical triptych titled *Visions from a floating world* (2018) appeared to have slid down toward the floor on the ribbons that anchored it high above, its three sections misaligned. Meandering, messy grids ramble across the paintings, a nod to both Balema's inclination to give abstract traditions new material realities and her underlying tendency to manifest the joy, freedom, and psychosis of making art. *JPF*

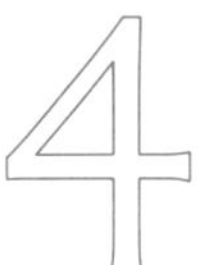

MORGAN BASSICHIS

Morgan Bassichis makes performances that combine stand-up comedy, music, and mysticism into beguiling tales of queer alienation, love, and liberation. The artist's onstage persona skews millennial ingenue, delivering the language of self-care with charmingly entitled obliviousness. This gentle mockery of quintessentially twenty-first-century behaviors nevertheless celebrates the motives behind them. To witness Bassichis at work is a physical experience: you might sing along, cheer, and sigh while also laughing through tears.

Bassichis works with LGBTQ social justice organizations and Jewish Voice for Peace and has written on queer politics and prison abolition. These experiences and concerns infuse recent projects like *The Faggots and Their Friends between Revolutions: The Musical* (2017), an adaptation of an illustrated manifesto–fairy tale published in 1977 for which Bassichis and collaborators transformed the top floor of the New Museum in New York into a psychedelic living room for "new moon potluck musical theater." In *More Protest Songs!* (2018), performed at Danspace Project in New York and released as a live album, Bassichis and a backing band play original cabaret-style ballads that mourn our political present and irreverently summon new possibilities. A playful homage to singer-songwriter and lesbian icon Holly Near's anthem "Singing for Our Lives" descends into the audience singing together, "We're gonna tear down all your prisons . . . / We have debilitating social anxiety . . . / We are on so many pills . . . / And we are singing, singing for our lives."

Citing the playwright Suzan-Lori Parks's proposition that "words are spells," Bassichis uses the transformational power of language to great effect. Over the course of 2017, the artist published *To Do 2017* as part of an online residency with Recess, New York. The project consisted of daily lists comprising wry tasks like "honor gay history by not remembering the names of people I have sex with" and "get over my jealousy stuff before the revolution happens." This transformation of a mundane litany of chores into a comedic, ambitious, perhaps impossible set of directives exemplifies Bassichis's approach to storytelling and the artist's desire to use performance to build collectivity. *MH*

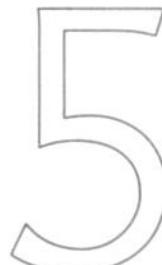

BLITZ BAZAWULE

Samuel "Blitz" Bazawule, aka Blitz the Ambassador, is both a musician and filmmaker, his stage name an embodiment of his aim to bridge perceived divides through a global exchange of hip-hop culture. His diversified approach in that pursuit reflects his multifaceted preoccupation with African and diasporic cultures, ultimately serving as a rebuke of Western perceptions of Africa as a monolith.

Bazawule's musical style and filmic aesthetic are eclectic. He samples from other artists and media, integrating iconic film dialogue and classic hip-hop into his own music, and has developed a unique magical realism in his films born out of African storytelling, asserting in a 2018 interview with *IndieWire* that "African stories are naturally more magical realist than anywhere else in the world." The video he directed for his song "Shine," part of his 2015 *Diasporadical Trilogía*, exemplifies his overlaying of the trials and triumphs of reality with an aspirational imaginary. In it, an African immigrant in New York is coerced by detectives to betray undocumented people in his neighborhood for fear of being deported and losing his young daughter. On her journey home, his daughter is accompanied by an ancestor spirit dressed in a white straw costume inspired by Benin voodoo masquerades, the two of them dancing joyously.

Bazawule's integration of real-world politics and allegorical fantasy is paramount in his most recent project, *The Burial of Kojo* (2018), which is his first feature film. Bazawule began this ambitious cinematic fable by meticulously storyboarding six hundred frames, resulting in a final version with lush Ghanaian landscapes and jewel-toned skies populated by both living family members and their fantastical ancestors. The film centers on a fractured family living amid illegal gold-mining operations in Ghana controlled by Chinese companies. In a radical rebuke of the neocolonialism that he critiques narratively, Bazawule made the film on location in Ghana with an entirely local team using independent financing. The result: the first film of its scale not to be funded by outside interests and yet another example of Bazawule's multifarious approach to representation. *CF*

ALEXANDRA BELL

Alexandra Bell's work examines the narrative systems that construct culture, focusing on how mass media represents those traditionally marginalized in American society. Bell deploys tactics of disruption to reveal how language and the codes of reportage determine the popular perception of official history. The artist suggests that the codified language of race systemically predetermines inequality and enables social hierarchies, and she proposes that in order to undo these racist impulses, one must first know how to identify them.

The news stories Bell examines in *Counternarratives* (2016–) all perpetuate racial and gender stereotypes, which take the forms of false narratives, stereotypical comparatives, false equivalencies, or notable omissions. Bell performs an exacting edit on the articles, with titles, text, layout, and photo placement disrupted to reveal latent failings in journalistic objectivity. For example, the headline in *A Teenager With Promise* (2017) originally read "A Teenager Grappling With Problems and Promise," referring to Michael Brown, whose shooting by police sparked riots in Ferguson, Missouri, and national outrage in 2014. Bell's revisions of the article appear in a triptych format, with one panel bearing her highlighting and annotations, another depicting her redacted alternative, and a third showing Brown's high-school graduation photo.

The articles used to create the works in *Counternarratives*—which includes other titles such as *Olympic Threat, Tulsa Hate Crime,* and *Charlottesville*—all come from the *New York Times,* foregrounding flaws in mainstream journalism. In *No Humans Involved: After Sylvia Wynter* (2018–), Bell explores how the *New York Daily News* portrayed the 1989 Central Park jogger case, a widely publicized crime that resulted in the mistaken conviction of five innocent teenagers of color who went on to serve between six and thirteen years in prison each. The work's title cites an open letter penned by Wynter, a writer and cultural theorist, that points out the underlying "logic of classification" and racial violence manifest in language. The artist's own refusal to accept the "fixed," published form of the news is a powerful means of holding power to account and engages the moral obligation of those who consume media to question what they take in. *LK*

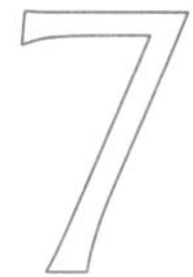

BRIAN BELOTT

A serious commitment to absurdity characterizes the riotous accumulations that make up Brian Belott's work as an artist, performer, and curator. Belott is a voracious collector of overlooked and abject things, many of which appear in his work—found photographs and recordings but also cat food, toothpaste, dollar-store knickknacks, and dirty clothing. Like the Dadaists, he is guided by an interest in transgressing the limits of art and of taste (his own included), and sometimes even of feasibility. For his frozen works (2012–), he suspends various items, including food, in blocks of ice; while frozen, they create a stained-glass effect, but once thawed become a stinking mess.

Belott continues the modernist tradition of borrowing from various realms of folk art. Yet his interest in such sources reads not as ironic provocation but as sincere homage. Long an admirer and collector of children's art, he has staged exhibitions that include his own replicas of found children's drawings and work made by neighborhood kids to create what he has called "a church to children's art." A primary influence is the psychologist and educator Rhoda Kellogg, who starting in the 1940s amassed a vast collection of children's drawings from around the world and developed taxonomies of their common motifs.

Belott's three-dimensional collaged paintings combine various materials and objects into brightly colored, layered compositions that often have a corporeal quality. Socks, often bearing visible traces of wear, appear beneath the Plexiglas surface of his reverse-glass paintings, so called because the image is viewed in reverse through the glass. In the *Puuuuuuuuuufffffs* series (2014–), bulging cotton batting is sandwiched between layers of paper, out of which emerge defunct, adorned calculators and remote controls. Throughout, Belott's use of color and attention to certain recurrent objects has a deliberate, graphic quality that lends a kind of formalist precision to the most mundane materials. *FJP*

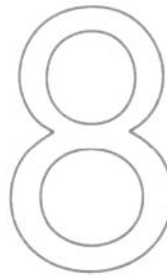

MERIEM BENNANI

Meriem Bennani works in video, installation, sculpture, and drawing, reflecting the social conditioning of lives lived on and with screens and mass media. Inspired by documentary and ethnographic films, reality television, and cartoons, Bennani's videos are suffused with humor that is variously slapstick and acerbic. Most are heightened by postproduction effects that add a layer of surrealism and nod to the current generation's expertise with the animations and add-ons of social media. The works are often presented in multiple channels, projected onto multidimensional surfaces or shown on monitors embedded in custom display structures, propelling the medium to mirror contemporary society's high-volume, close-contact, near-constant relationship with screen culture. For Bennani, expanding the possibilities of how we consume video and time-based work is as important as the content she presents.

Bennani takes as her frequent subjects the lives and experiences of contemporary Muslim women, moving beyond Western media's biased depictions to explore their social roles, fashion, wit, and tight-knit communities. In *Ghariba (Stranger,* 2017), Bennani filmed her female family members in relaxed moments of conversation and commiseration about love, friendship, and aging. Poignant animations of starry skies punctuate stories as unexpected as the work's zany sound effects. Presenting *Ghariba* in colorful sculptures mimicking lounge chairs and hair-salon furniture, the artist requires that the viewer physically inhabit these hyper-contemporary forms—and as only one viewer at a time can see the work, she reinforces the isolation of today's smartphone and personal-screen usage.

One source of tension in Bennani's work is the juxtaposition and coexistence of cultures—religious and secular, high and low, traditional and new, IRL and digital. In *Siham & Hafida* (2017), reality TV tropes vamp up an intergenerational encounter between two Moroccan *chikha* singers, who carry on a form that emerged during French colonial occupation to deliver poetic resistance through popular music. Generations later, younger stars filter this history through the superficiality and accessibility of social media. Bennani projects *Siham & Hafida* onto complex surfaces that distort perspective, with animations lending a cartoonish tone to the drama unfolding between the two protagonists. Here, absurdity conveys a transhistorical examination of the roles of women in Moroccan culture, with the artist using the digital tools of its ostensible corruption to render its continuation into the future. *CH*

ROBERT BITTENBENDER

Robert Bittenbender's assemblages contain so many elements that the eye is initially overwhelmed. The viewer must work patiently to tease apart the found odds and ends—photographs, bits of plastic, shreds of canvas and paper—that the artist has intricately enmeshed. Held together with zip ties, wire, and pushpins, the works hang on the wall and thus retain a relationship to painting. In *Cracked Actress* (2018), the disembodied corner of a golden picture frame struggles to define the work's edge, thrust forward from the wall by eighteen inches of massed material. The grid, which undergirds both Renaissance perspective and 1960s Conceptualism, appears in fragmentary form in many of Bittenbender's works. Strips of black and reflective tape extend out beyond the wooden frame that defines *Electric Thirties* (2018), suggesting a design that unites its scraps of paper, canvas, and transparent blue plastic. In *Rosarie Metropolitan* (2015), metal rods wrapped in aluminum foil run horizontally and vertically, anchoring the composition. Despite their apparently frenetic aspects, the works are rigorously formal. The tondo *Soulful Gardener* (2016) features round and circular forms, such as the oversize links of a discarded necklace, with a looping cable woven throughout providing more irregular curves.

Some elements Bittenbender uses evince unclear origins and thus become abstracted forms; others are easily recognized as castoffs of everyday urban living. Regardless, like portraits, the works inevitably reflect their sources. Bittenbender's titles, meanwhile, layer on a wide range of cultural references. *Broadway Flesh* (2018), an acrylic painting stitched with red thread, recalls a work by Dan Flavin; *Cracked Actress*, a David Bowie song. *Gethsemane* (2018), a group of five painted boards strung together with chains, cites the biblical garden where Jesus spent his last night on earth. Pulling from every register of culture, Bittenbender weaves together the rag ends of the urban fabric. Despite their kinship with painting, his omnivorous objects threaten to propel themselves off the wall and out into the messy world whence they came. *JPF*

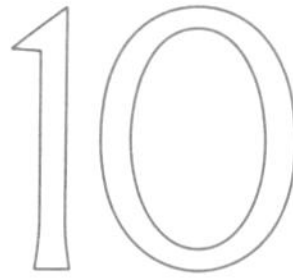

LUCAS BLALOCK

Lucas Blalock's work examines and upends expectations for photography in the digital era. Blalock is known for visually confounding, often humorous photographs in which he makes obvious use of Photoshop, employing tools such as the clone stamp and eraser in a manner that would appear wrong in any other picture. Rather than make the alterations seamless, the usual goal in commercial imagery, he creates bumpy amalgams of digital and analog procedures, including copying and pasting, increasing and decreasing exposure in areas, perspectival shifts, overlaying, and blurring. Yet the artist's works remain visually coherent, even when depicting an object or figure from multiple points of view or when common objects are camouflaged by similar patterns. In one example, *Portrait on the Street (2 men in a donkey suit)* (2016), a man appears to have two right feet. Seemingly composed of images of two different individuals, the figure appears to be simultaneously forming and dissolving, with incongruent limbs overlaid and slivers of his head and torso floating away.

Blalock takes an expansive view of photography, relating it to drawing. The most common tool to describe the world, he argues, is no longer the pen or pencil but instead the camera. With the ubiquity of smartphone and image apps, he argues that we are all mark makers, capturing and sharing the world we inhabit on an everyday basis. For his 2016 artist's book, *Making Memeries*, Blalock applied augmented reality to his photographs. Printed on thick cardboard and resembling a children's book, the publication features boldly colored graphic photographs of ordinary subject matter—a cluster of bricks, a tabletop with a push-button phone. When viewed through a custom smartphone app, the photos take on another life, with new elements popping into view and static ones becoming animated. The telephone shakes as if ringing; musical notes spring from the gray bricks. Throughout his work, Blalock reveals the potential of photography to not only document but actively describe a twenty-first century in which the real and virtual can seem indistinguishable. *CL*

GARRETT BRADLEY

Garrett Bradley's multimedia work draws together broad themes of oppression and conflict with a particular emphasis on place and location. Across a body of moving-image productions that blend elements of documentary and fiction, cinema and video art, Bradley's camera situates wider themes in the minute textures of the everyday, exploring her subjects' struggles and dreams and rooting the sociopolitical in personal and physical experience.

In installations, shorts, and feature-length works, Bradley consistently locates her subjects in particular places—frequently her home city of New Orleans—that become sites of a confrontation between personal narratives and larger historical and political ones. In her nonfiction works, such as *Alone* (2017), a portrait of a single mother in New Orleans whose partner has been incarcerated in a facility that forbids in-person visits, Bradley disrupts the conventional hierarchies of observational documentary, positioning herself as confidant, advocate, and accomplice. Bradley finds echoes of the legacy of American slavery and segregation in the act of separating family members and loved ones, but she grounds these themes through an intimate and detailed rendering of her subjects' feelings of isolation. In her work with performers, such as the docu-fiction *Below Dreams* (2014), New Orleans is not only a backdrop for the characters' movements; it is also integrally bound up in the real and imagined spaces of their lives. In a project forthcoming in 2019, Bradley ambitiously expands this canvas to consider the historical representation of African Americans in early cinema, supplementing and juxtaposing silent-era film footage with her own dreamlike sequences, portraits, and tableaux. *LG*

MILANO CHOW

Milano Chow's practice is an exercise in the construction and disjunction of space in two dimensions. Pulling from the visual language of architecture and design, the artist creates enigmatic environs through careful graphite renderings, photo transfers, and collage. Eerily unassuming, these settings play host to female characters whose autonomous presence subverts the status of paper doll. Part sleight of hand, part trompe l'oeil, Chow's work engages the ways in which representation and observation both mask and display the modern subject, inside the frame and out.

Informed by film sets and architectural renderings, Chow casts her interiors and exteriors as the sites of elusive narratives from which solitary female figures emerge. Transposed from the pages of outmoded fashion magazines, advertisements, and catalogues, they surface from behind curtains, through paned glass, or down flights of stairs, all spaces that feel at once open and opaque. Dressed in disparate styles—an '80s pantsuit, a mod beret, femme florals—the women appear both assertive and aloof, reflections of the buildings they occupy, whether they seem surreal, seductive, or anxiously still.

This tension between public and private perspective, inherent in the exhibitionism of the image, finds its most dramatic form in Chow's recent freestanding double-sided works on paper. In *Recto/Verso II (Open Window)* (2017–18), the viewer first encounters a pale building front pierced by windows, its structural features—pilasters, window moldings, egg-and-dart motifs—informed by Chow's in-depth research into architectural and design history. One window frames the half-silhouette of an androgynous figure, the investigation of whose actions becomes steeped in surveillance, offering both a blockade and a call to entry. Employing the facade as both surface and screen, the drawing's verso acts as a material double bind: rather than the perspectival interior one might expect, the viewer confronts yet another thin, architectural front. A woman in dapper dress balances within this construction, leaning into the window's open frame, a revelation of the former figure disclosed in full. Caught between intimacy and exposure, she plays in the production of voyeuristic viewing, a reality so solid and yet paper thin. *R K*

13

COLECTIVO LOS INGRÁVIDOS

Ingrávido means "weightless," unaffected by the force of gravity. The group of filmmakers known as Colectivo Los Ingrávidos claims a floating, even spectral presence, embracing the malleability and transportability of the moving image to confront the violence and corruption of contemporary Mexico. Their decision to operate anonymously, without the burden of the individual name, stems as much from a spirit of collaboration as from necessity, in a country where many journalists have been disappeared or openly murdered. Theirs is a counter-cinema of elegant rage, a poetics of resistance that contests the unpunished murder of women, the rippling effects of narcocapitalism, and the failures of the state.

Colectivo Los Ingrávidos works across photochemical and digital formats, often in ways that trouble habitual notions of image quality and clarity. Using devices such as the LomoKino 35mm camera (*Itzcóatl*, 2014) and materials such as expired film stock (*Sangre seca* [*Dried Blood*], 2018), they foreground the materiality of the medium, not out of purely formal interest but to amplify the concerns present within the image. In *Sangre seca*, for instance, demonstrations on International Women's Day against gendered violence and misogyny are captured in Kodachrome from 1959 that bathes these scenes in a mottled, crackling bloody red. The filmstrip itself, like those whom it shows and speaks of, is vulnerable and aggressed against yet resilient.

In their embrace of technical imperfection and their insistence that political filmmaking interrogate form as well as content, Colectivo Los Ingrávidos forges an affinity with the militant modernist cinemas of the 1960s and '70s. Yet in describing their work as "infrarealist cinema," they equally assert a link to the Infrarealist movement in poetry, founded in Mexico City in 1975 by a group that included Roberto Bolaño. The artists reimagine the stated aim of those young poets in relation to the emergency of the present: "Blow the brains out of the cultural establishment." *EB*

14

THIRZA CUTHAND

Beginning with her video *Lessons in Baby Dyke Theory* (1995), made when she was a teenager, Thirza Cuthand has adapted a punk aesthetic and goofy humor into a highly personal, layered body of work marked by biting sarcasm and a confessional on-screen presence. While her fondness for pop genres like sci-fi, horror, and fairy tales is evidenced by such titles as *Colonization: The Second Coming* (1996), *Through the Looking Glass* (1999), and *You Are a Lesbian Vampire* (2008), she uses their tropes to rigorously explore issues of sexuality, queer and Indigenous identities, and mental health.

Throughout her work, Cuthand addresses these subjects with an often deceptively DIY aesthetic and sardonic mode of address. *2 Spirit Introductory Special $19.99* (2015) uses the format of a cheesy QVC-style infomercial to address nonbinary notions of gender that existed in First Nations tribes before contact with white settlers. Against a green-screen backdrop of an idyllic knoll, the artist wryly delivers her sales pitch for a 2 Spirit Support Network, complete with complimentary swag including dental dams and a kitchen whisk ("perfect for light-impact play and making eggs and pancakes the next morning"). In *Just Dandy* (2013), another digitally dropped-in backdrop simulates Cuthand's impromptu presentation at an Indigenous Revolutionary Meeting where she recounts a dangerous sexual liaison with a so-called Evil Queen—a character "played" by a Playmobil action figure that resembles the diabolical monarch from *Snow White and the Seven Dwarfs* but obviously indexes Elizabeth II. As Cuthand's monologue details her raunchy royal dalliance and then laments having to see her former fling everywhere—on coins and stamps and television—she interweaves a dense network of metaphors about sexual and white-settler domination and dandelions as invasive colonial species and eco-venereal disease. *LG*

15

JOHN EDMONDS

In a photograph titled *The Villain*, John Edmonds portrays a lean figure with piercing eyes, ones that are unafraid to stare back at the camera. Fuzzy Bantu knots rest atop their head, and a bloodred bandana covers their nose, cheekbones, and jawline. But it is the eyes that beckon, haunt, and seduce. *The Villain* is part of Edmonds's body of work *Tribe: Act One* (2018), which reenacts the tensions arising from modernism's entanglements with blackness while presenting queer and gender-nonconforming subjects as archetypal characters. In another example from the series, *Face as Mask II* (2018), Edmonds playfully quotes Man Ray's storied drag photograph *Marcel Duchamp as Rrose Selavy* (c. 1920–21). In *Modernity* (2018), his subject sits erect, almost sculptural, before a sheer violet curtain that echoes

the drama of Carl Van Vechten's Harlem Renaissance studio portraits, and presents an intricately carved wooden mask that rests on a table. Calling to mind the use of African power objects as Surrealist "inspiration" or ethnographic source material by European artists in the early twentieth century, the mask here performs a vital role, both actor and prop.

Making Black interiority and queer collectivity central to his work, Edmonds probes the aesthetic possibilities of deconstructing desire through costuming, posturing, and role play. He choreographs garments, objects, and bodies through strategies of veiling and unveiling. His *Du-Rags* series (2017) features Black men donning the familiar headdress in bedroom scenes, nearly always facing away from the camera, at times exuding a regal glow. These works draw inspiration from the tale of Saint Veronica, who offered the cross-bearing Christ a cloth on which to wipe his face, leaving an imprint that would become a Christian relic. Edmonds prompts his Black male models, often friends and loved ones, to inhabit the space of divine sacredness elsewhere as well; in *American Gods* (2017), three men don the triad of pan-African colors, black, red, and green, with their faces softly illuminated and their bodies arranged in a pyramid. Edmonds's pictures interrogate the possibilities of Black iconicity, conjuring a divinity that is emphatically queer and unrelentingly beautiful. *JBB*

16

NICOLE EISENMAN

Known primarily for paintings that resist categorization, Nicole Eisenman has increasingly incorporated sculpture into a practice that renders

everyday life with both tenderness and absurdity. Refusing to conform to a single style, Eisenman combines a variety of art-historical traditions, including classicism, Fauvism, and Expressionism, but her perspective is decidedly queer. She tackles universal themes through an autobiographical lens, often portraying Brooklyn bar scenes, raucous parties, and close friends as allegories of human folly in droll, figurative works.

Since 2012, Eisenman has increasingly embraced the tactile potential of sculpture. Her presentation in the 2013 Carnegie International in Pittsburgh included a selection of paintings along with seven plaster works. Interspersed among idealized classical statuary on the balcony of the Carnegie Museum of Art's Hall of Sculpture, Eisenman's lounging, kissing, slouching forms depicted the human body as an awkward vessel of abjection and embarrassment. The figures, at once introspective and unruly, suggested antiheroes drawn from contemporary myth and metaphor.

Continuing her study of the human body as a site of simultaneous desire and discomfort, Eisenman's contribution to the 2017 iteration of Skulptur Projekte Münster in Germany consisted of a fountain with five larger-than-life plaster and bronze figures located in a central public promenade. Reinterpreting one of the oldest forms of public art, Eisenman created a constellation of lumpy, gender-ambiguous bodies that deteriorated over time, a wry contrast to the permanence and perfection of classical figurative water features. The bloated figures were scattered around a shallow basin and appeared placid, even lackadaisical, as water bubbled from an open beverage can and sprinkled and squirted from various body parts. A low-grade sense of melancholy permeated the scene, the psychological space between the figures creating a narrative in which boundaries between individual and group, object and audience became blurred. In her latest works, Eisenman continues to push such tableaux into the monumental, with figures locked in somber procession perhaps alluding to the current political landscape as a dire slog. *LO*

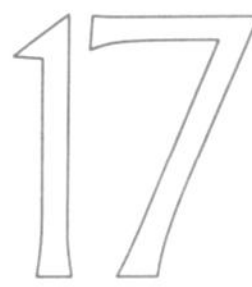

JANIVA ELLIS

In her oil paintings, Janiva Ellis blends elements of comic formalism and figuration to playfully approach the task of translating pain, tension, and empathy into an expansive dialogue. Making pointed use of humor, Ellis repurposes imagery from Western art history and popular culture, appropriating and transforming animated characters and compositions that illuminate an exploitative cultural history checkered with oppressive modes of caricature. At once anguished and playful, wry and disconcerting, her figures bear the weight of externally fueled doubts and fears as well as that of allegorical violence. Their exaggerated gestures and masklike grimaces are a response to uninformed assumptions, a visual indication of the slippage between self-perception and apprehended difference.

Incorporating the familiar visual language of cartoons, Ellis's bright scenes are punctured by brutality; she pairs the tension of trauma with the release of the sardonic and absurd. Borrowing its composition from a scene in the 1997 anime fantasy *Perfect Blue*, Ellis's *Curb Check Regular, Black Chick* (2017) depicts a pastoral landscape and farmers market in muted tones using sketchlike brushwork. In contrast, a graphically rendered woman in the foreground is portrayed as a cacophony of bold color and form: pulpy viscera erupt from her chest while her doe eyes tear. Oblivious pink-toned women and children recede into the background,

and the viewer is left to imagine what emotional assault may have transpired. In *Co-Panicing* (2017), Ellis uses loose strokes to depict a woman's ponytailed head, wide eyes blank and mouth gaping, severed from her body and dissolving into a blue void. Her abandoned body is painted an unmodulated shade of black with exaggerated outlining, while a cartoonish, morphing critter rattles at the bottom of the composition, almost a grotesque extension of the woman's severed form. In these works, Ellis throws the physical manifestations of psychological violence into sharp relief. She captures the comic inanity of human suffering met with indifference and doubt. *LO*

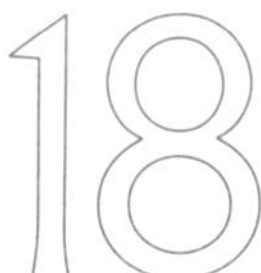

KOTA EZAWA

Kota Ezawa translates psychologically charged moments embedded in the public consciousness into drawings and digital animations made up entirely of flat shapes. He pares scenes down to their essentials, removing details in favor of swaths of color, in turning cultural icons into iconography. His interests span a broad scope of cultural arenas and their intersections, perhaps best exemplified by his 2002 *The Simpson Verdict*. This animation of the resolution of the 1995 murder trial of O. J. Simpson mobilizes the tangle of issues that preoccupy Ezawa—film, sports, celebrity, art history, race, violence, politics. The key figures of the courtroom drama appear in forms like paper cutouts, identifiable to viewers already familiar with them, while the actual audio of the verdict plays in the background, animating and contextualizing their stilted gestures and expressions. Evoking stop-motion

aesthetics, his works seem to shudder from frame to frame, reminding the viewer that, while they are based on videos, the animations are in fact assembled from the artist's still approximations of these culturally resonant moments.

Ezawa's most recent work, *National Anthem* (2018), is an animation that depicts NFL players kneeling during "The Star-Spangled Banner" to protest police violence against unarmed Black men—a highly contested practice popularized by since-blackballed quarterback Colin Kaepernick in 2016. Repurposing footage of multiple teams, the work adapts the familiar pan of the sports-broadcast camera over statuesque athletes on their respective sidelines. Using watercolor paintings as frames, Ezawa achieves a grainy quality akin to archival news footage; the textured, pooling color is richer in some places than others. A somber, orchestral string arrangement of the national anthem plays, the timeless audio creating a cohesive narrative despite the visibly disparate teams and the disjunctions between one frame and the next. Without commentary from pundits or scrolling chyrons, the players appear united, stoic, and overcome by both reverie and boredom, no matter whether they are standing or kneeling. As in all of his work, in removing the extraneous, Ezawa draws attention to the subtle gestures—the flick of an eye or clench of a fist—that mark shifts in emotion for his hyperexposed subjects. *CF*

BRENDAN FERNANDES

Trained as a ballet dancer, Brendan Fernandes uses dance to foreground queer embodiment, considerations of labor, and critiques of colonialism in his practice. Existing at the intersections of movement, performance, and sculpture, his work explores the mutability of identity and the systems of power that produce social meaning. Critiques of colonial collecting strategies and the display of African art in Western museums are common subjects in his practice, for example in *Authority Inside* (2016), a ballet performance staged in the archival vault of the African art collection at the Agnes Etherington Art Centre in Kingston, Ontario. A number of Fernandes's recent projects explore queer community, precarity, and resilience in the wake of the 2016 terrorist attack at Pulse, a gay club in Orlando, Florida. Treating the nightclub both as a space for queer world making and a site of loss, *Free Fall* (2016), *Free Fall 49* (2017), and works from Fernandes's 2017 residency *Steady Pulse* at Recess in New York pay homage to those who died during the attack via sculptures and performances centered on the fallen body.

At the Graham Foundation's Madlener House in Chicago in 2018, Fernandes showed *The Master and Form*. Equal parts performance and sculptural environment, the work focuses on the dynamics of discipline to consider how the culture of ballet is intrinsically tied up with questions of agency and control, pain and pleasure, and labor. Fernandes worked with the design and architecture firm Norman Kelley to create minimal sculptures involving scaffolding, ropes, and supports that enable dancers to achieve and sustain more perfect ballet positions while also allowing for rest and recovery. In purpose and form, these structures evoke both medieval torture and BDSM devices. Dancers from the Joffrey Academy of Dance interacted with the works in rehearsals and performances, moving through iconic ballet positions in pursuit of the mastery of these highly idealized forms. *The Master and Form* raises questions of how, and to what end, bodies are controlled and

manipulated while positing that labor entailing pain and sacrifice is a site of both potential oppression and potential pleasure. *AR*

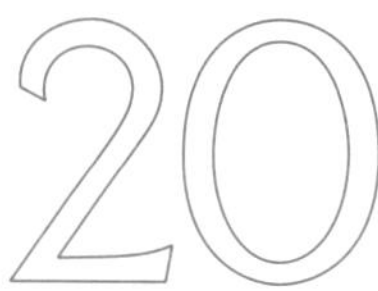

FIERCE AND PAPER TIGER TELEVISION

Beginning in the 1980s, New York City's Christopher Street Pier provided a safe gathering space for LGBTQ youth of color, who were—then as now—often highly vulnerable to acts of violence, oppression, and police harassment. There, these communities of young people, many of whom are low income, homeless, or marginally housed, found a sense of security and freedom of expression. In the summer of 2000, however, they were displaced as the pier was fenced off to begin development on what would eventually become Hudson River Park.

FIERCE, an organization focused on empowering LGBTQ youth of color in New York, was founded around the time of the pier's temporary shuttering, centered on the principle that queer youth must themselves influence social and political dialogues in order to create change and protections for their communities. In 2001, the group collaborated with media collective Paper Tiger Television (PTTV) and queer youth drop-in center New Neutral Zone to produce *Fenced Out*, a short documentary examining the conflict over the Christopher Street Pier, gentrification, and the erasure of queer histories and spaces. Founded in 1981, PTTV is committed to the promotion of media literacy and the belief that freedom of speech comes through open access to channels of communication, in contrast to the corporate-controlled mainstream.

Fenced Out reflects this activist approach. A product of the "youth media" movement of the time, its formal, conceptual, and narrative aspects speak directly to the medium's concerns surrounding access, self-representation, and visibility. A diaristic look at the importance of the pier develops into an intergenerational dialogue between the film's young producers and LGBTQ activists from the 1960s to the 1980s, touching on the neighborhood's historic relationship to the gay liberation movement. In the end, the film transforms into a call to action for the preservation of the pier as a site for these communities, despite acts of aggression by local residents, law enforcement, and local governments. Gentrification around Hudson River Park and in the surrounding neighborhoods persists today, while FIERCE and PTTV continue to provide platforms for media activism, community building, and youth empowerment. *RK*

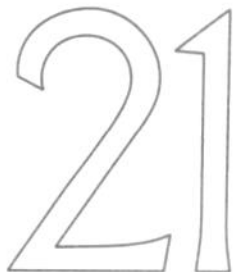

MARCUS FISCHER

Marcus Fischer's recordings are riddled with the residue of obscured encounters or found sound: the soft vibration of a steam pipe, a pine cone rolled across a manipulated microphone, tape loops stretched to exaggerated lengths. These sounds surface in stand-alone music, audio installations, and scores for mesmeric video pieces that often depict natural or quiet environs, from waving fields of dry grass to empty skate parks. When paired, sound and image slowly expand, taking on the texture of a space, atmosphere, or emotion.

Fischer's works often unfold as an interpretation and transformation of his environment through the collection and layering of sensory material. He often defines a situation within which to focus attention and make space for contingent connections to occur, similar to a Cagean score. *Circular Ruins*, a 2018 sound installation, presents one such framework. Returning to an album he released in 1998, Fischer installed six identical LPs to play in surround sound, amplifying and altering the variations and repetitions produced by each album's run-out groove, creating a layered auditory environment from a perceived void.

This interest in defining a space for chance, transference, and improvisation assumes a sociopolitical bent in *Words of Concern* (2017). The work emerged from an open call Fischer extended to his peer artists and the residency staff at the Robert Rauschenberg Foundation in Captiva, Florida, on the day before Donald Trump's inauguration, allowing them to voice their concerns regarding the incoming administration. Over the course of a three-minute loop, their voices unfold in measured rhythm, each an audible part of a larger chorus of collective unease. The tension and tenuousness of their words is echoed in the work's minimal presentation: extending from a vintage tape recorder on the ground, a tape loop cycles from floor to ceiling as it plays, precariously cradling a reel suspended over the machine below. Part archive, part atmosphere, Fischer's practice attends to the soft tissue of our surrounding world. Whether through the ambient intention of aggregate sounds or distinctly framed concerns, Fischer creates spaces in which to listen, reflect, and, perhaps, heal. *RK*

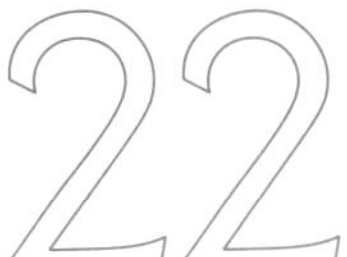

FORENSIC ARCHITECTURE

Founded in 2010 by Israeli-British architect Eyal Weizman, Forensic Architecture (FA) is an independent research agency that investigates contemporary conflict, police violence, and human-rights violations within the urban landscape. Employing architects, researchers, software developers, and artists, FA collects, reorganizes, and interprets public-domain data as a way to access and address abuses of power and their physical traces. Its investigations have spanned research into U.S. drone warfare in the Middle East, the Grenfell Tower fire, ecocide in Indonesia, and the death of migrants off the coast of Libya. Using satellite photos, civilian camera footage, audio recordings, and eyewitness testimony, FA adapts architectural analysis to confront state crime, offering alternative forms of evidence and new opportunities for accountability.

In 2017, FA partnered with the activist group the People's Tribunal "Unraveling the NSU Complex" to investigate one of a series of murders carried out by the National Socialist Underground (NSU), a German neo-Nazi cell targeting predominantly immigrant communities. Together, they focused on the shooting of internet-café proprietor Halit Yozgat in Kassel, Germany, in 2006, the ninth in a string of ten NSU killings. Suspiciously, a Hessian state intelligence agent, Andreas Temme, was present at the scene at the time of the murder but claimed neither to have heard gunshots nor seen the dying Yozgat lying on the ground as he exited the shop. Using leaked photographs and computer logins from the crime scene, FA created a to-scale reconstruction of the site as well as a digital 3-D model, then used these to carry out a series of reenactments and experiments to determine whether Temme could truly have failed to witness the crime. Using these tools, along with the testimonies of others present at the café and related audio recordings, the group produced *77sqm_9:26min* (2017), a video installation and report presented at Documenta 14 in Kassel and at two German parliamentary inquiries. Their findings increased doubt surrounding both Temme's testimony and the veracity of German intelligence agencies involved in the investigation. The case demonstrates the operative principles of what Weizman calls "counter forensics"—the inversion of the state's institutionalized gaze and the mobilization of microanalysis to unravel longer-term and larger-scale structural forms of violence. *RK*

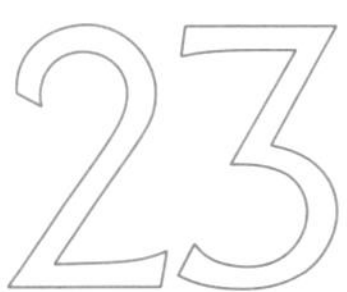

ELLIE GA

The ocean is an archive: lurking in its depths are stories of drift and death, survival and wonder. Its watery expanses recur across Ellie Ga's research-based performances, videos, installations, and photography, providing a fitting metaphor for the artist's fluid approach, which folds together history, politics, and narrative. Ga turns to lighthouses, driftwood, rescue boats, and marine mythology, using the fragmentary energies of the essayistic impulse to join personal experience with public memory and forge correspondences across space and time.

Ga spent five months as artist in residence aboard a research vessel locked in ice near the North Pole. This experience resulted in *The*

Fortunetellers (2009–11), a series of works that includes a multimedia performance in which she recalls this frozen time, willfully wandering across an array of seemingly disconnected topics, including palmistry, plankton, and wristwatch advertisements. When the boat finally broke free, its crew members threw messages in bottles overboard, destined for addressees the currents would choose. In her double-projection installation *Strophe, a Turning* (2017), Ga returns to this gesture of hope and abandon, connecting it to the ongoing humanitarian crisis of asylum seekers in Greece. On the island of Lesbos, heaps of life jackets lie piled on the shore, obliquely figuring the mass grave that the Mediterranean has become for many seeking to reach the shores of Fortress Europe; in a monastery on the island of Symi, Ga encounters the image of Michael Panormitis, the archangel associated with messages in bottles, an icon of aspirations for a future that may or may not arrive. Abandoning oneself to the currents can be a kind of freedom, but so too can it be a matter of perilous uncertainty. The installation's title echoes this double resonance, referring at once to the literal back-and-forth of the alternating video channels, to the uncertain liberties of artistic creation invoked by the stanza, or strophe, of a poem, and to the "downward turning" found within the Greek word καταστροφή, catastrophe. *EB*

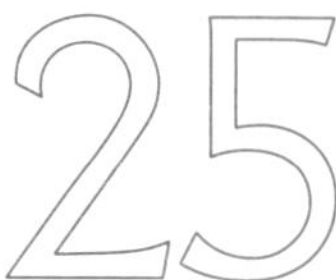

24

NICHOLAS GALANIN

Nicholas Galanin dismantles settler-imposed categorizations and legislations of indigeneity by imaging an Indigenous culture that cannot be romanticized or contained. Drawing on his experiences as a Tlingit and Unangax̂ man, Galanin's practice dramatizes the evolution of violence inflicted on Indigenous people by settler states, from forced assimilation to demands for performance of cultural otherness deemed authentic by the non-Indigenous. Galanin skewers these expectations using myriad materials and processes.

Galanin often confronts viewers with their own assumptions about what Native art should look like. To this end, he juxtaposes forms — ceramic arrowheads with European delftware patterning, or non-Native carved totems with William Morris floral designs. In a two-channel video titled *Tsu Heidei Shugaxtutaan 1 and 2* (2006), Galanin presents a Raven Dance performed to electronic music and a hip-hop performance improvised to a customary Tlingit song. To create the photo series *Kill the Indian, Save the Man* (2016) and the sculpture *The Saved Man* (2016), Galanin recarved Indonesian-made imitations of Tlingit masks, leaving the commodified symbols of Indianness as piles of wood chips. The artist formed the debris into new masks embodying their apocalyptic creation story and reflecting the violence inflicted on Indigenous communities and the difficulty of rebuilding what has been destroyed. The works insist on the resilience of culture in community rather than form, which carries over to the video *Unceremonial Dance Mask, 21st Century* (2017), where Galanin animates another remade mask through dance by a dancer without any other regalia. This guising of ceremony as unceremonial is protective and assertive of the perseverance, creativity, and continuation of Indigenous culture in the face of settler desire for collection and control.

"The attempt to control and erase us is based on grading and categorizing how closely we match the characters written into settler accounts of our ancestors," Galanin wrote in the Walker Art Center's digital magazine in 2018. His work celebrates and contributes to the vital continuum of Indigenous creation, past, present and future. *AC*

25

SOFÍA GALLISÁ MURIENTE

Sofía Gallisá Muriente interrogates the colonial relationship between Puerto Rico and the mainland United States in works that span photography, video, and installation. Gallisá Muriente's artwork often reframes found texts and images to highlight the ideological underpinnings of narratives that perpetuate and market Caribbean cultural difference. Deeply committed to Puerto Rican self-sufficiency in the face of ever-harsher austerity measures imposed under the aegis of the U.S. government meant to address the island's $123 billion debt, Gallisá Muriente also codirects the San Juan art space Beta-Local, which offers free classes, hosts important residencies and public programming, and, following Hurricane Maria, distributed significant emergency aid.

The raw material for Gallisá Muriente's video *Lluvia con nieve (Rain with Snow*, 2014) is forty seconds of newsreel footage reporting a 1955 publicity stunt, organized by the American company Eastern Airlines and the mayor of San Juan, for which two tons of snow were flown from Vermont and dropped onto a baseball field for a snowball fight in celebration of Three Kings Day (Epiphany). Although the event remains well known in Puerto Rico, Gallisá Muriente had to go to great lengths to find this brief documentation, ultimately coming across it by chance at the National Archives near Washington, DC — a fact that speaks to the lack of infrastructural support for Puerto Rico to maintain its own history. Gallisá Muriente stretches the clip over nearly fourteen minutes, accompanying it with a slowed-down version of the titular mambo by Puerto Rican musician Mon Rivera. As the percussion gradually slows, the video footage moves at a snail's pace so that the snow becomes recognizable as a fraught symbol of reconciliation between the island and the rest of the United States not long after the commonwealth adopted its 1952 constitution.

Elsewhere too, Gallisá Muriente's practice requires slow looking and contemplation of seemingly trivial images and events. In *B-roll* (2017), the artist coopts extra footage from promotional videos used by the island's government to entice investors. By emphasizing the insidiousness of the repetitive drone's-eye views of a purchasable paradise, Gallisá Muriente contests sanitized images of U.S.–Puerto Rico relations and repudiates the privileging of a visitor economy that frames the territory as an exotic Eden for tourist and investor consumption. *AC*

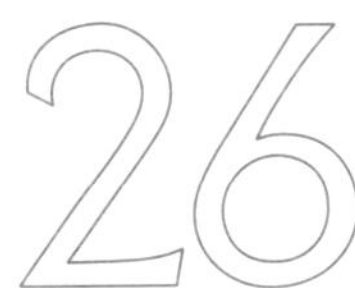

JEFFREY GIBSON

In paintings, sculptures, videos, and performances, Jeffrey Gibson calls attention to overlooked histories that complicate the dominant narrative of Eurocentric modernism, in particular that of abstraction. Gibson asks what American art history would look like if the work of modernist Indigenous American artists, such as Oscar Howe or George Morrison, had been canonized alongside that of Frank Stella, Dan Flavin, and Agnes Martin.

Gibson's approach incorporates the colors and geometric patterns associated with modern and "traditional" objects such as Native jewelry, weavings, and clothing, as well as quilts made by his grandmothers. Colorful fringe and copper jingles on the head, shoulders, and legs of *BIRDS OF A FEATHER* (2017) may appear playful but also imbue the figure with confrontational potency. The geometry and repetition of the monochrome beadwork reflect both modernist and Indigenous art histories while covering the figure in a protective layer, augmented with text on the stomach displaying the titular phrase. Gibson often uses lines from pop songs or protest slogans in his work, with a lyric like "Burn baby burn" in an eponymous piece from 2015 adding another dimension to the patterning and speaking directly to audiences that may lack experience with the Indigenous references.

Gibson cites the importance of his early experience with dance—from time spent as a youth both in nightclubs and with relatives at powwows—which he sees as a space for self-exploration and celebration of individuality. Recent garmentlike works refer to the shirts associated with the Ghost Dance movement, a cultural phenomenon in Native American cultures in the late 1800s that, in part, encouraged peaceful resistance to white expansion. In *WITHOUT YOU I'M NOTHING* and *STAND BY ME* (both 2018), Gibson exaggerates the scale and weight of the garments, combining beadwork and fringe with found quilts and neon satins and silks printed with imagery from his own previous work. Through these layered references to histories of conflict, adornment, and his own life, Gibson offers a way to represent the complexity and subjectivity of identity while reinvigorating ceremonial forms as tools for yielding individual power. *LP*

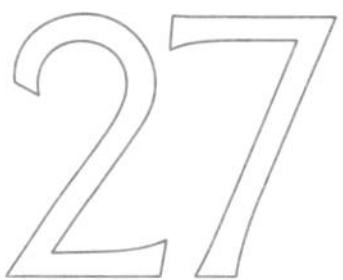

TODD GRAY

Todd Gray mines his experience as a subject in the African diaspora to create photographs, performances, and sculptures that comment broadly on the polymorphous nature of identity. Like Carrie Mae Weems and Lorna Simpson, Gray uses the tenets of conceptual photography to draw attention to the ideologically constructed nature of the image and address issues around representation and race.

In his ongoing *Exquisite Terribleness* series (2013–), Gray mounts photographs in visibly used frames from thrift stores in South Los Angeles and Johannesburg and overlaps them in assemblages that hang on the wall. This act of layering results in a kind of sculptural photography and allows Gray to carefully conceal certain aspects of the images he uses; faces, for example, are often completely obscured. The photos include South African and Ghanaian landscapes that may carry personal or historical meaning, portraits of unidentifiable figures, and, notably, pictures of Michael Jackson from Gray's own archive, taken when the artist worked as the singer's personal photographer in the 1970s and early 1980s. Gray uses images of Jackson, who figures prominently in the artist's work, to interrogate the mental colonization of the diasporic subject and the results of white-supremacist thinking. This deployment dovetails with Gray's method of fragmented assemblage, which disallows representations of diasporic identity from appearing cohesive or easily comprehensible. Gray draws inspiration from cultural theorist Stuart Hall's 1996 essay "Cultural Identity and Diaspora," which contends that cultural identity is a constantly transforming entity that is "not an essence but a positioning" by and within narratives of the past.

Gray often reuses and repositions the same image across multiple works. For example, the clasped Black and white hands in *Pax 3* (2017) appear again in *Maya Venus* (2018), and the river landscape appearing there also structures the compositions of *Pax 3* and *Pax* (2016–17). Like any presumed "essence," the particular image thus has multifarious potential meanings across many contexts. In highlighting this principle of reconfigurability, Gray avoids explicitly coding a particular meaning of blackness or the diasporic experience. Rather, he confronts the viewer with indeterminate artworks that reflect his conviction that subjectivity is composed of a continuously shifting plurality of identifications. *AC*

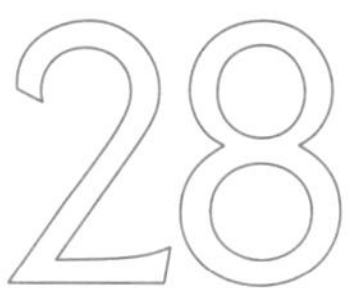

28

SAM GREEN

Sam Green's documentaries are characterized by gentleness and humor, even as they fearlessly probe complex ideas and fraught historical events. His films humanize subjects that are often dismissed as trivial, such as Esperanto (*The Universal Language*, 2011) and *The Guinness Book of World Records* (*The Measure of All Things*, 2014). 2003's *The Weather Underground*, nominated for an Academy Award, finds meaning and even beauty in the titular subject, an extremist group of the 1960s and '70s most remembered for a bombing campaign.

With *Utopia in Four Movements* (2010), an exploration of the meaning of utopia and the attenuation of its power in the twentieth century, Green

expanded into what he calls "live documentary," a performance that combines live music and narration with projected still and moving images. The live elements add an intimacy and vitality generally absent from documentary film, building a relationship with the audience and including them in the story. Editing takes place not only in the cutting room but also in the theater as performers respond to the mood of the crowd. Live documentary also lends a unique flexibility to Green's narratives: no story is ever final and no performance repeatable.

This format exquisitely suits the content of *A Thousand Thoughts* (2018), which features a live score performed by the documentary's subject, the experimental-music ensemble Kronos Quartet, an adventurous group of string players who have taken on myriad forms including Renaissance motets, contemporary composition, and pop songs. Onstage, Green narrates the story and the quartet performs while filmed interviews and archival footage are projected behind them. The project uniquely captures the magic of live music, turning cinema into a singular, fugitive moment shared by performer and audience. In an era in which films are most frequently experienced on small, private screens, Green both forges a new immanence for the medium and restores the enveloping, communal experience that once defined it. *JPF*

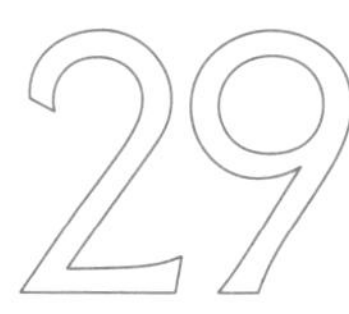

29

BARBARA HAMMER

Since the early 1970s, prolific filmmaker Barbara Hammer has created experimental cinema that is formally inventive, passionately embodied, and politically aware. Hammer has worked in 8mm, Super 8, and 16mm

film, and analog as well as in HD video, often mixing archival or found scenes with scripted sequences and spontaneous footage of friends and lovers. She has also used technologies such as optical printing and computer-generated imagery, and in addition to film produces installations, collages, photographs, and writing. At times she transforms film into a spatial medium; in *Available Space* (1979) she projected moving images onto walls, objects, snow, and even herself. "My work deconstructs a cinema that often objectifies or limits women," she has said in a statement on her website, and "makes these invisible bodies and histories visible. As a lesbian artist, I found little existing representation, so I put lesbian life on this blank screen."

Hammer has spoken of being powerfully influenced by Maya Deren, in particular her *Meshes of the Afternoon* (1943)—the only work by a woman shown in film school at a time when Hammer was one of few female students. *History Lessons* (2000) expresses Hammer's desire to present the bodies, relationships, and narratives of queer women that are missing from both cinema and history. In the film, she reinserts lesbians into historical events while reclaiming negative portrayals of them. A series of scenes in New York's Meatpacking District features women in dandyish, masculine garb reenacting lurid newspaper photos by crime photojournalist Weegee.

Hammer's recent works also take up personal confrontations with disease and treatment. *A Horse Is Not a Metaphor* (2008) and *Evidentiary Bodies* (2018) seek to communicate her own experience with chemotherapy, while also testifying to the artist's ceaseless fascination with the visual world. Despite the astonishing range of Hammer's techniques and interests, she has consistently pursued the transmission of subjective, corporeal experience—especially of being a woman and a lesbian—through both content and technique, exploiting the limits of film's possibilities to inspire new sensations in the viewer. *JPF*

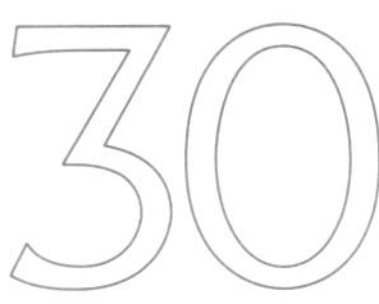

ILANA HARRIS-BABOU

Working in video, performance, and sculpture, Ilana Harris-Babou interrogates the painful histories and uncomfortable realities of racism and disenfranchisement with the ever-smiling, can-do attitude of aspirational home-improvement television. Her videos, shot in sharp high-definition and populated by fragile, antifunctional ceramic tools that also form their own showroomlike installations, imitate the instructional systems of idealized living manifest in home-buying and cooking shows in ironic, critical takes on both the format and the culture that produced it.

Harris-Babou's video *Reparation Hardware* (2018) skewers the "rustic chic" marketed by retailers that inverts the cultural status of upcycled luxuries. Though found wood and other previously used materials are presented by their peddlers as neutral and nostalgic, the artist points out the histories of labor, use, and value that they carry. Giving herself the title of "Reparator," she calls for restitution to be made to the descendants of enslaved African Americans in the dreamy, even-keeled tone of an interior designer as she reveals how generations of white economic stability have been sustained by a denial of fair remuneration and human rights for those who performed the labor to build the United States. The film concludes by showcasing a product line of useless assemblages of ceramic sculptures and found objects, whose namesakes include Reconstruction-era thinkers and later advocates of reparations, including Thaddeus Stevens, Mary McLeod Bethune, and Ta-Nehisi Coates.

Similarly dysfunctional tools punctuate *Finishing a Raw Basement* (2017), a video starring a pair of upbeat interior decorators portrayed by Harris-Babou and her mother, Sheila Harris. (The artist has often collaborated with Harris in an acknowledgment of the value of the intergenerational transmission of knowledge.) The women perform an absurdist renovation on a cellar, using nail polish as wall paint and indirectly referencing the dilapidated foundations of American society. Their language juxtaposes modern American markers of taste and class—"open concept, vaulted ceilings"; "midcentury"—with the radical words of Black lesbian poet Audre Lorde, who responded to the ideal of the American dream by saying, "Deep down, I know that dream was never mine." *CH*

MATTHEW ANGELO HARRISON

Matthew Angelo Harrison subjects cultural artifacts to industrial and digital technologies, creating hybrid forms that address issues of labor, identity, and cultural inheritance. In the 2018 *Dark Silhouettes* series, Harrison embedded wooden sculptures from West Africa in blocks of polyurethane resin, then carved abstract patterns of holes and debossings into the resin using a CNC router, visually fragmenting the objects within. For a 2016 exhibition at the Museum of Contemporary Art, Detroit, he collected and scanned African masks, digitally combined and manipulated the scans, and then rendered them using 3-D printers that emit ribbons of clay. Notably, Harrison built these printers himself, drawing on his experience making clay prototypes for Ford Motors in Detroit. These machines have appeared at work alongside the artist as part of his performances, but they also exist independently as sculptures titled *The Consequence of Platforms* (2016–). This multipronged collaboration between the artist and his 3-D printers makes his labor visible and debunks the notion of digital technology as immaterial and autonomous.

Harrison selects objects, materials, and technologies that, when combined, address the relation and distance between African American and African culture and identity—a concept he calls "abstracted ancestry." That some of the "African" artifacts he uses are authentic antiquities from specific tribes, others are mass produced for markets in Detroit, and still others are of unknown origin speaks both to the objects' continued cultural currency and to the erasures enacted by colonialist collecting practices. Other materials used by Harrison are also freighted with associations: pedestals that resemble midcentury design or Minimalist sculpture are made from aluminum and bulletproof glass, referencing windows protecting liquor stores in Detroit. Like the arte povera artists of postwar Italy (an influence he cites), Harrison uses materials that challenge standards of value and authenticity. For Harrison, the idea of the "prototype" is key—that thing that is at once real and a proposal for the future. *FJP*

CURRAN HATLEBERG

Curran Hatleberg takes photographs on drives around the United States, following his intuition to find subjects and locations that exist in the margins of popular imagination. When arriving in a new place, Hatleberg takes time to get to know those who live there, sometimes seeing them briefly, other times meeting them over days, weeks, or months. The resulting portraits issue from a collaboration between photographer and subject where those depicted are actively involved in their own self-representations.

While the settings of these photos' subjects are evocative in their own right, portraiture is at the center of Hatleberg's practice. He puts individual faces to untold stories, specifying in all their complexity American lives that are too often reduced to superficial narratives of race, class, or politics. In *Untitled (Girl with Snake)* (2016), a young white girl sits amid the rubble of a building, holding a snake and covering her mouth, looking off into the distance. Behind her, a Black woman stands, gazing either at the ruins that also surround her, at the girl, or at the photographer, or possibly at all three. The relationship of the people to the place they inhabit, each other, and Hatleberg fails to resolve into an easily legible narrative about natural disaster, race relations, or poverty. Rather, the ambiguity Hatleberg cultivates prevents viewers from easily reducing the scene to a news headline, leaving them instead with curiosity about his subjects' lives.

It is this sense of the life of an individual that Hatleberg seeks. His portraits endeavor to show that the unpredictable and unexpected live within each of us, challenging stereotypes that limit the complicated reality of any one person. Working in the lineage of photographers such as William Gedney, Katy Grannan, and Justine Kurland, Hatleberg uses his camera to get to know strangers and share something of them with others, in an attempt to undermine bias and forge a connection across distance and difference. *ES*

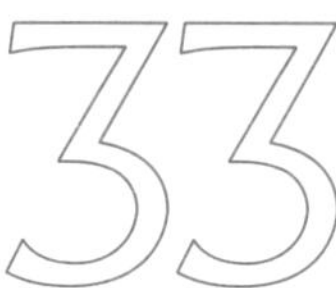

MADELINE HOLLANDER

What are the boundaries between our bodies and the environments we inhabit? How exactly do we define the nuances that govern our interactions with the systems, man-made or naturally occuring, that surround us? For Madeline Hollander, performance is employed as a tool for such an examination, targeting the choreography of contemporary infrastructures—the quotidian, the rote, and the invisible. On Hollander's terms, dancers, viewers, architectures, and machines are equally and intelligently entangled, resulting in work that traverses received notions of visual art, installation, and performance.

In Hollander's 2018 work *New Max* at the Artist's Institute in New York, four dancers clad in boxing shorts and black mesh T-shirts gathered in the institute's sunroom with four air-conditioning units set at 65 degrees Fahrenheit. The performers' task: raise the temperature of the gallery to 85 degrees via their own body heat by going through a repertoire of motions, including choreography inspired by warm-up routines, tropical-storm patterns, frostbite-prevention techniques, and windmills and other energy-harnessing technologies. In *New Max*, Hollander constructs a microecology, a self-contained symbiotic system to regulate and drive temperatures in which viewers are also implicated. At the same time, she grapples with the process of and conditions for thermal-energy transfer—and, consequently, human complicity in global warming.

Hollander also probes the limits of documentation, for example in *ARENA* (2017), which paired seven dancers on a New York City beach and a Queens Parks and Sanitation sand-rake truck to focus on the ephemerality of performance art. In choreography designed specifically for creating markings in the sand, the dancers and the rake become enmeshed in a score that refuses a linear reading. As the dancers leave their traces, so does the rake. Are the dancers leading, or is the truck? The score is made visible and then erased. Once again, Hollander points to the ecological: sand is disappearing from shorelines, beaches are disappearing, and with them the jobs and social systems formed around them. Hollander asks us to rethink our negotiations with the technologized agents that surround us and the systems in which we are knowingly and unknowingly embedded. *JL*

IMAN ISSA

At first sight, it can be difficult to determine where a work of art by Iman Issa begins and where it ends. Text panels and plinths, usually part of the apparatus of the institution, turn out to be made by the artist, and to play more than a framing role. Issa refers to these creations as "displays," a term signaling the importance of the site of presentation and experience of viewing. Often composed of multiple, disparate elements, Issa's works prompt dialogue rather than offering finished statements.

As a student in Cairo, Issa initially focused on political science and philosophy, with a particular interest in phenomenology. Art offered a way to more actively address the political and historical dimensions of individual perception and memory, an interest she honed during a year spent as a museum guard in Seattle. In projects ranging from multipart displays to films to collections of short stories, Issa stages evocative encounters with objects, architecture, and public space. The *Material* series (2010–12), which presents alternative forms to existing monuments, subverts the heroic logic of monumental sculpture by pairing small groupings of objects with titles that refer obliquely to history. Two spherical lamps on a table, for example, are suggestively called *Material for a sculpture recalling the destruction of a prominent public monument in the name of national resistance* (2010).

In *Heritage Studies* (2015–), a series of spare geometric constructions of painted wood, copper, brass, and other materials, Issa revisits historical artifacts from museum collections in order to probe their contemporary resonance. While a label may refer to a specific historical object, the accompanying sculpture bears little physical or material resemblance to its designation. A large stick-figure form balanced atop two small plinths relates dialogically, rather than equivalently, to the label that reads "Twelve Pointed Star from a 13th Century Building Façade." The use of the word *studies* in the series title suggests a provisional status, inviting revision, personal association, and even dissent. *FJP*

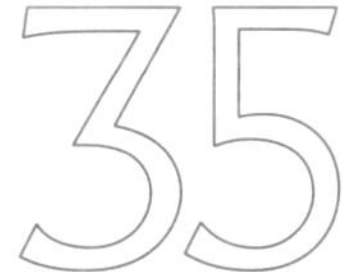

TOMASHI JACKSON

In her paintings, sculptures, videos, and works on paper, Tomashi Jackson uses abstraction to examine systemic racial injustice in the United States. Jackson works with traditional fine-art techniques such as painting and printmaking as well as craft-based practices like knitting and embroidery. Within these forms, Jackson collages found materials that often have specific autobiographical references—food wrappers from children she cared for as a nanny—or historical references—avocado seeds, inspired by stories of people using them for soup during the Civil War. She often uses gauze, taking up its association with the treatment of bodily injuries.

Jackson's densely layered, vividly colored works, such as 2016's *Dajerria All Alone (Bolling v. Sharpe (District of Columbia)) (McKinney Pool Party)*, are largely abstract. She embeds within them screenprinted photographs, taken both from civil rights–era documentation and current events, that highlight police brutality, racial profiling, and advocacy against these injustices. Her layering of transparencies and opacities, expanses of color, and documentary images creates complex, often disorienting surfaces that complicate background and foreground, subject and support. Her videos, such as *Self-Portrait: Tale of Two Michaels* (2014), extend this approach, digitally combining news footage, color fields, staged performances, and still lifes.

Jackson's wide-ranging material interests are fed by art-historical, legal, and social histories. Most recently, she has focused on housing displacement in the United States, in particular in New York City; voting, segregation, and transportation in and around Atlanta; and the five court cases that Thurgood Marshall argued leading to the 1954 Supreme Court decision *Brown v. Board of Education of Topeka* that struck down school segregation as unconstitutional. In this last project, Jackson highlights the remarkable similarity between Marshall's approach to color theory and that of Josef Albers in his *Interaction of Color* (1963). Both men described color as relative, explaining that a viewer's perception of any given color is understood only in relation to the colors around it. Color is, therefore, not fixed and definite but constantly changing. The resulting multifaceted, vibrant works are built around this resonance, using the comparison to critique racist thinking and policy in visual form. *ES*

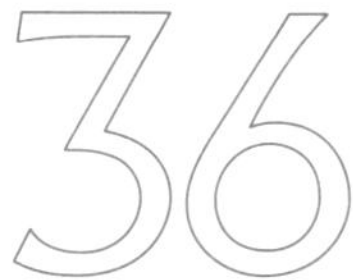

STEFFANI JEMISON

Solresol is an artificial language developed in the early nineteenth century by François Sudre that allows speaking via pitch. Created to be a universal system, the language is based on the familiar seven syllabized notes, *do re mi fa sol la ti*. In various works, Steffani Jemison experiments with solresol by giving its utopianism new political possibilities, combining it with the codes invented to subvert the strictures of slavery in America. Jemison's audio installation *Recitatif (What if we need new words?)* (2017) manifests how words and phrases such as "freedom" and "opposite of power" can become melodies while also attending to the alternative literacies present in African American culture. In configuring language to become a universal tune, Jemison extends the liberatory potential of Black secrecy into the contemporary moment.

Jemison's moving-image work explores various aspects of the technological and narrative possibilities of video, including the absence and arrival of sound, the emergence of the chase scene, narrative expectations for racialized characters, and depictions of Black vernacular culture. It also furthers her interest in code. The title of her 2017 video *Sensus Plenior* is Latin for "fuller meaning," a concept used in religious interpretations to describe divine intent that goes beyond human language. The black-and-white video opens with the leader of the Master Mime Ministry of Harlem, ordained minister Susan Webb, in a living room practicing gestures ranging from intricate hand and arm movements to variegated facial expressions, then follows her from the application of her makeup to a performance in a church. Standing before a cross, Webb begins miming to the song "Anointing" by gospel artist J Moss. It begins with the words "Eyes have never seen," but the lyrics quickly become indecipherable, and the images begin to move in slow motion. In keeping with the title, the result explores the range of the music's metaphysicality and spirituality through Webb's rhapsodic choreography. Such a deep engagement with artistic invention and politics, which runs throughout Jemison's films, drawings, and performances, offers audiences the opportunity to engage with forms yet unimagined, signaling the possibilities for a radically innovatory aesthetics. *EK*

37

ADAM KHALIL, ZACK KHALIL, AND JACKSON POLYS

In their video *The Violence of a Civilization without Secrets* (2017), Adam Khalil and Zack Khalil, both of Ojibway descent, and Jackson Polys, of Tlingit heritage, challenge the settler consumption of Native American culture by unfolding the story of "Kennewick Man," a nine-thousand-year-old skeleton found in Washington State in 1996. The tribes of the Columbia River Basin recognized him as an ancestor and demanded the repatriation of his remains; the scientific apparatus challenged their claims, asserting the right to study the bones. Using archival footage, CGI, and newly shot material, the artists'

dynamic exploration of this episode opens onto expansive, urgent concerns: what it means to live on stolen land within the ongoing violence of settler colonialism; what is at stake in white fantasies of indigeneity; and how one might challenge racist logics of archaism, erasure, and assimilation to assert the vitality of Indigenous cultures in the present and future. In the video's closing minutes, a man and woman wearing grotesque silicone masks walk through a museum displaying Indigenous artifacts and anthropological dioramas. Baring their teeth in aggressive fascination, they literalize the monstrous encounter with expropriation and domination that still so often passes as edification, as leisure.

The New Red Order Presents: The Savage Philosophy of Endless Acknowledgment (2018) explodes these essayistic strategies into a multimedia performance. With the participation of collaborators whom the artists identify as "informants"—raising questions of complicity and knowledge production—the work marshals frequent shifts of tone and topic to sound a polyvocal call for decolonization. At turns humorous, contemplative, and confrontational, the performance uses non-Indigenous actors Jim Fletcher and Kate Valk as proxies for the artists, ushering the viewer through the practice of land acknowledgment, the history of "playing Indian," the contradictions of the noble-savage archetype, and what it would mean to trade the role of ally for the role of accomplice. *EB*

38

CHRISTINE SUN KIM

Christine Sun Kim's works examine a full repertoire of aural experience,

from church bells to silence to gestures that denaturalize how we communicate and listen to one other. In exploring the nature of sound, she creates operas, installations, drawings, and objects. Her oeuvre, which emerges from the perspective of a culturally Deaf artist whose first language is a signed one, steadily inquires into the possibilities of what has been overlooked, offering us new ways of exploring the relationship between sonic expression and intimate forms of communication.

Kim resituates the musical score as a drawing full of visual, sonic, and political possibilities. In *Suggested Amounts* (2018), she reimagines the score as a "sound diet," a visionary landscape that charts how different forms of communication, particularly those from deaf culture such as American Sign Language (ASL), might receive equal space and significance, thereby subverting the sensorial prioritization spoken languages receive. The four-part series includes the charcoal-on-paper work *Suggested Amount of Allowing Friends to Sing Songs to a Baby*, which elongates and reimagines decrescendos by interweaving whole, half, and quarter notes with extended sections of *p*, the notation for *piano*, which instructs the musician to play softly. Like other works in the group, the piece familiarizes the viewer with the tempos of listening and near silences required in moving from spoken to nonspoken languages.

Kim's works draw on her experience of communicating in ASL, which employs the body, mouth, eyes, and hands. The installation *Game of Skill 2.0* (2015), for example, asks audiences to move agilely in tracing the path of a blue rope suspended across the gallery space, keeping the lead of an audio device in contact with the cord in order to hear a text by the artist about the complexities of making a future. In order to access Kim's language, the audience, much like ASL speakers, must move physically. This method, with audience members becoming performers, is a common one in Kim's work, which in turn requires us to critically enact the creativity required to transform our approach to not othering difference. *EK*

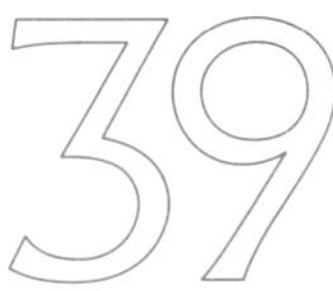

JOSH KLINE

Josh Kline explores the conditions of technology, politics, and labor, employing new tools and materials to transform and comment on cultural touchstones. One of Kline's series, *Blue Collars* (2014–), is created from 3-D scans of workers such as janitorial staff and delivery persons, merging their 3-D-printed body parts with objects indicative of the jobs they perform. These tableaux, such as *Cost of Living (Aleyda)* (2015), with the eerily lifelike head, feet, and hands of a housekeeper from a Manhattan luxury hotel placed on a cleaning cart alongside sponges and sanitizing spray, examine the objectification, consumption, and exploitation of laborers in contemporary capitalism. Kline's process mimics the conflation of their bodies and humanity with the corporate and class identities imposed on them while they are in uniform, on the job.

Kline also takes up technology as a tool of speculation, sampling figures and forms from mass media to envision realities just slightly removed from the everyday. In the 2015 video *Crying Games*, he uses face-substitution software to create a political fantasy in which the architects of the American invasion of Iraq—George W. Bush, Donald Rumsfeld, and others—have been brought to justice and make tear-filled apologies for their actions instead of offering the egregious

rationalizations to which we are accustomed. Kline's uncanny fiction proposes the possibility of contrition and atonement for the United States' ongoing history of military aggression.

Since 2014, Kline has been working on a science-fiction cycle of installations about the politics and economics of the twenty-first century. The most recent chapter, *Civil War* (2017), featured a radical utopian film shot on 16mm titled *Another America Is Possible* (2017). In it, a family cookout in the year 2043 concludes with the burning of Confederate flags, a vision of an America at peace attempting to overcome its dark history of white nationalism. The installation's sculptural components, on the other hand, included an austere landscape of grayscale debris comprising concrete casts of middle-class furniture, gardening tools, and children's toys. This ambivalent juxtaposition is emblematic of Kline's practice, as he simultaneously imagines both the possibility and the ruin embedded in our contemporary moment. *AF*

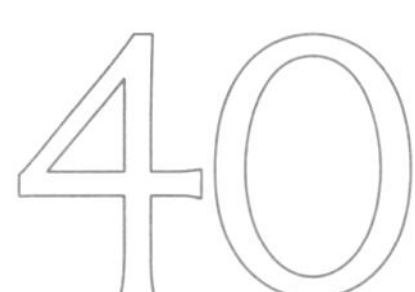

AUTUMN KNIGHT

Absurdity runs amok in the work of Autumn Knight, becoming an avenue via which we may navigate societal crises of identity. Her performance-interventions demonstrate how these crises have high stakes for those on the margins, and specifically for Black women. Drawing on her background in theater, Knight plays with and preys on popular audiences' failure to grasp and discuss the ways in which social structures define, shape, and enact power on bodies based on race, gender, class, and geography.

In her performance series *Sanity*

TV (2016–), Knight stages a fictional talk show in which her guests are in fact the audience whom she observes, prods, and cajoles. Those who attempt to compete with the host's antics are always outmatched. The gradual breakdown of logic that occurs reveals the ineptitude of public discourse when it comes to critical issues concerning identity. As emcee, Knight refuses to pacify the crowd as we might expect; rather, she dives into the discomfort and makes us sit with our failure to communicate. In the installment titled *On Location in Berlin* (2018), she tells the audience, "It's okay for someone to immediately challenge your authority. Be down with that, come close to that. Lean in to it."

Knight grounds her seemingly whimsical works in real-life events. Her short video *Directions to Prairie View* (2017) meditates on the ways in which mundane activities can carry a steep cost for Black women. The piece uses e-mails from the artist's time as an adjunct at Prairie View A&M University in Texas, the same university where Sandra Bland was to begin working when she was arrested during a traffic stop in 2015. Bland was found dead in her jail cell three days later. In the video *Roaches Aren't the Easiest Creatures to Milk* (2017), Knight muses on the would-be trend of consuming cockroach secretions for their protein value in alternation with naming structures that produce systemic racism and injustice. The idea of consuming the maternal ooze of cockroaches, the presence of which in homes and apartment complexes is so readily racialized, typifies the absurdity around injustice based on race, class, and gender that Knight's work confronts. *AD*

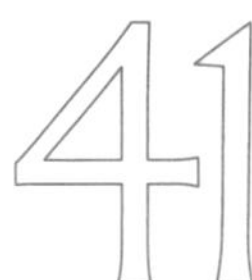

CAROLYN LAZARD

Carolyn Lazard's multidisciplinary practice addresses the politics and sociality of disability and dependency. In videos, sculptures, performances, and texts that advocate a turn away from the exploitations of capitalism and toward a reliance on one another, they are committed to creating work that acts as personal catharsis and enunciates networks of care by and for people identifying with disability. Lazard is a cofounder of the Canaries, a collective of artists living with autoimmune and other chronic conditions, and writes on issues engaging with queer and crip theory. Texts such as "How to Be a Person in the Age of Autoimmunity" (2013) and "Colostomy Fannypack" (2017) use wry humor and frank disclosure to question the sickness/health dichotomy and the ableist inscription of abjection onto disability.

Focusing attention on the work of recovery, Lazard's recent video *Consensual Healing* (2018) mimics the conventions of Eye Movement Desensitization and Reprocessing (EMDR) therapy, which is used to treat posttraumatic stress disorder. Combining a script that takes inspiration from Octavia Butler's trans-species sci-fi love story *Bloodchild* (1984) with the pendulous swinging orb used in EMDR to trigger a lucid state akin to REM sleep, the work explores fiction as a means to ethically represent trauma and healing. *A Recipe for Disaster* (2018) explores questions of accessibility by layering multiple audio narrations and a scrolling text onto an episode of Julia Child's cooking show *The French Chef* (1963–73), the first television program in the United States to employ subtitles.

Lazard's interventions ultimately render the episode illegible for all, proposing, perhaps, that a commitment to access necessitates a willingness to sit in discomfort with others. *CRIP TIME* (2018) shows the artist's hands as they apportion a week's supply of various medications into plastic pill containers, performing a routine task that takes a full ten minutes to complete. By focusing on the temporality of disability, Lazard positions its slowness as a means to disrupt expectations of able-bodied productivity and open up different modes of liveliness and creation. *AR*

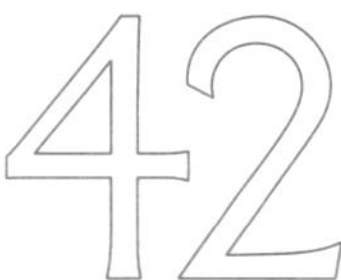

MAIA RUTH LEE

In her paintings and sculptures, multidisciplinary artist Maia Ruth Lee uses a glossary of appropriated decorative motifs to consider the transposition of meaning and the nature of signs and symbols. Lee grew up in Kathmandu, Nepal, where her parents were Bible translators and linguists working to establish an alphabet for the predominantly oral Sherpa language. She moved to New York in 2011 and, drawing from her experiences in the Himalayas, began incorporating glyphs, alphabets, and lexicons into her art practice, in which she develops personal archives based on decontextualized found fragments as a method to create instinctive structures for communication.

In a multipart series of wrought-iron wall sculptures titled *Auspicious Glyphs* (2016), Lee appropriates and isolates the decorative elements that ornament fences and window bars throughout New York City, reassembling the shapes to create a new symbolic vocabulary. Originally parts of fixtures that establish boundaries,

Lee's architectural fragments are transformed into beguiling ciphers that the artist intends to express moods, values, and worldviews with intuitive clarity. The simplified, linear forms, resembling ancient hieroglyphs or zodiac symbols, convey notions of harmony and perspective through a visceral economy of language.

Lee's paintings executed in India ink on raw canvas also draw on found source material. In a series of works titled *Realm* (2016), the artist creates compositions based on single pages of a catalogue compiling various decorative borders that range from art-historical motifs to banal clip-art designs. The stark black-and-white works are rendered in painstaking detail, taking on the appearance of printed textiles. Initially giving the impression of a strict, conceptual act of appropriation and transfer, Lee's invisible labor instead shows reverence for the original designs and the intellectual labor of their makers. *LO*

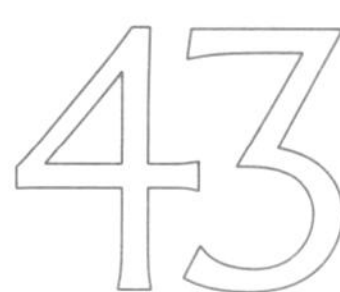

SIMONE LEIGH

Working primarily in sculpture but also across video, performance, installation, and social practice, Simone Leigh examines the propensity of objects to embody and communicate fields of knowledge. Focused on forms rooted in African and African American cultural traditions, Leigh considers notions of Black female subjectivity and its potential to explore questions of labor, beauty, pleasure, utility, and agency.

Leigh's ceramic works problematize space and its relationship to the body through a close study of modernist and vernacular art and architecture. Her references have included West African adobe architecture;

the 1931 Paris Colonial Exposition, which comprised pavilions of hybrid architectural modes and emergent modernism; a Mississippi café called Mammy's Cupboard housed in the figure of an enormous woman's skirt; and face jugs produced by enslaved African American potters in South Carolina. Realized on scales varying from the intimate to that of public-art installations, Leigh's work coalesces the body with architecture, exploring the anthropomorphic features of objects and their functions, interrogating narratives of modernism and subjectivity.

Leigh has also long been interested in amplifying histories and strategies of radical care and community, specifically those of the Black Panther Party's People's Free Medical Clinics and the United Order of Tents, a clandestine society of Black nurses and physicians founded during the Civil War. In 2014, Leigh created *Free People's Medical Clinic*, which provided free treatments and workshops in the former home of Dr. Josephine English, the first Black ob-gyn in New York state. Her 2016 exhibition *The Waiting Room* further expanded on these and other historical examples, positing different forms of Black female knowledge, action, and resistance as medicine. Leigh's latest video, *Untitled (M*A*S*H*)* (2018), amalgamates her performative projects and her sculpture. Framed as an episode of the eponymous TV show, it features an entirely Black female cast of artists, writers, performers, and scholars, all of whom have previously collaborated with Leigh. The video is emblematic of the interdisciplinary nature of Leigh's practice, and her commitment to privileging the labor and experiences of Black women and femmes while gesturing toward traditions of radical generosity and providing models for equitable pathways that benefit us all. *DRK*

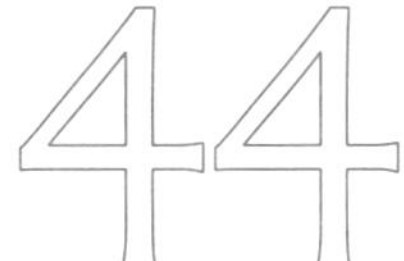

DANIEL LIND-RAMOS

A native of the coastal town of Loíza, Puerto Rico, Daniel Lind-Ramos has developed a body of work concerned with the role of Black Puerto Ricans in the island's colonial history. Lind-Ramos first gained acclaim in the 1980s and '90s with luminous figurative oil paintings. Works such as *La elegida* (*The Chosen One*, 1985–86) and *Tránsito* (*Transit*, 1988–89) take the form of rituals marking the passage of life and death. During the 1990s, Lind-Ramos began working on painting-assemblages in which the painting became an object to which other significant items from his local surroundings and culture could be added. In *Santiago o la transformación de la memoria* (*Santiago, or The Transformation of Memory*, 1998), he uses an aesthetic syncretism to deconstruct the Catholic, European, and racialist hierarchies implicit in Loíza's annual Fiestas de Santiago Apóstol.

To confront the local community with its own history, Lind-Ramos frequently returns to the subject of the 1797 British invasion of Puerto Rico, in which the English colonial power was defeated due to the efforts of the Black residents of Loíza and San Mateo de Cangrejos along with the island's creoles and Spaniards. Many of his assemblages, such as *Guardacostas* (*Coast Guards*, 2012), include items that could be read as masks and instruments of self-defense to suggest the presence of a Black militia. In his drawings, such as *Victoria en Costa Serena* (*Victory in Costa Serena*, 2010), Lind-Ramos takes up the concept of the carnival as theorized by Mikhail Bakhtin, which construes festival times as not only a

respite from social structures but also an instrument of criticism of the dominant social and political order. In a work related to a victory in the struggle against unscrupulous developers, the diversity of masks reveals the complexity of Puerto Rican identity and that of the Caribbean in general. Lind-Ramos decenters Puerto Rican art, making the focus of his practice not San Juan but Loíza, and the core of his thematic an Afro-Antillean discourse emerging from his aesthetic experience. *MG*

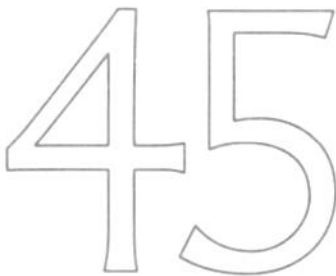

JAMES LUNA

Over a more than thirty-year career, James Luna rigorously interrogated America's iconography of Indigenous experience and settler-colonialist mythologies through a wide array of practices, including multimedia installation, video, and performance. Frequently using his own body as an object alongside commonplace materials and situations, Luna foregrounded his multifarious identity as an artist of Payómkawichum, Ipi, and Mexican American descent to incisively analyze the complexities at the heart of Native culture, from its transcendent spiritual associations to its history of genocide and disenfranchisement to the challenges and mundanities of everyday reservation life. Aiming to "transform the gallery space into a battlefield," per a phase he used often in biographical statements, Luna confronted white spectatorship through witty but rigorous performances such as *Artifact Piece* (1987), in which he lay in a museum display case surrounded by ephemera from his daily life, or *Take a Picture with an Indian* (2011), in which he stood outside Washington, DC's Union Station inviting passersby to pose for a photograph with him.

Luna's 1993 video *The History of the Luiseño People* belies the grandiose sweep of its title. Instead, it depicts simply Luna himself, spending a lonesome Christmas on his couch in California's La Jolla Indian Reservation. Chain-smoking while drinking his way through a six-pack of beer, Luna mounts a thirty-minute solo performance in which he calls friends, relatives, and exes on the phone, taking on the various roles of drinking buddy, cool uncle, exasperated son, and deadbeat dad, while holiday-movie classics play on the television in the background. Oscillating between the tragic and the comic, the shocking and the banal, Luna's performance is a penetrating exploration of the intersection of Native and white American cultures in miniature, peeling back layers of enforced holiday cheer to reveal its everyday manifestations in all of their bittersweetness and black comedy. *LG*

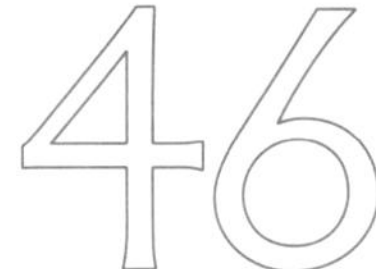

ERIC N. MACK

Eric N. Mack sews and drapes garments and textiles that he then paints on, dyes, or collages with what he calls "everyday fragments"—materials sourced from newspapers, magazines, and art-world ephemera, as well as his own drawings and to-do lists, or objects like pegboard, rope, and fans. Simultaneously painting and soft sculpture, and often displayed in expansive, site-specific installations, his works collapse the distinctions and hierarchies between the two mediums—and interrogate the gap between art and fashion—in evoking an expanded history of American abstraction. Mack builds artworks that vary in form, translucence, and density, seeking to locate personal associations in the viewer who may relate their colors, textures, and references to clothing and cultural markers in their own lives and closets.

For Mack, fabrics carry an accessible material symbolism, whether that of utilitarian everyday wear, well-worn favorite garments, or high fashion. *Supreme, Knowledge, Affirmatives* (2017), for example, uses the familiar display tactic of a clothing rack to explore color through repetition and difference on dyed cotton shirts. These resonances allow for entry into the artist's abstract works as both constructions and surfaces, just as fashion itself is as much about composing surfaces on ourselves as it is about regarding compositions on others. In *Palms on Cotton* (2017), found fabric, a blanket, a dyed bedsheet, and a parasol are adjoined and suspended together, to be viewed in the round. Mack's exploration of the space between fashion and fine art includes titles in tribute to the looks of designer and stylist Misa Hylton-Brim, known for creating unmistakable outfits for 1990s hip-hop stars like Missy Elliot and Sean "Diddy" Combs, and collaborations with London-based designer Grace Wales Bonner that touch on Afro-Caribbean writing, nautical clothing, and the histories of jazz and queer Black literature. Mack frequently makes use of the packing blanket, playing on its industrial firmness, its evocation of warmth, and its readymade border as frame. Despite the visual constraints inherent in that frame, these works share the artist's broader attention to gesture, collage, and space as he seeks to emphasize the charged exchange between artwork, environment, and viewer. *CH*

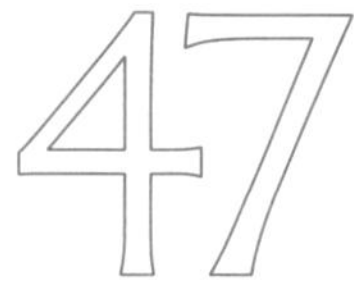

CALVIN MARCUS

Toggling between sculpture and painting, Calvin Marcus has a penchant for heterogeneity. His output traverses putrid green monochromatic paintings with sculptures of chicken carcasses secured at their centers, molded as self-portraits; childlike sketches of sinister heads; and sculptural readymades consisting of martini-glass-emblazoned resort shirts wrapped in plastic dry-cleaning sleeves. Sea animals appear both as teeny, anthropomorphized poolside loungers in roughly crafted bowls that show the indentations of the artist's fingers and as platters of deboned fish sculpted in clay alongside unappetizing noodles. Marcus pushes concrete ideas and themes to points of exhaustion, executing them with modest material means: "I don't want to become a master of anything," he remarked to *Mousse* magazine in 2015.

For the series *Were Good Men* (2016), the artist made a set of drawings of soldiers fallen in leaves of grass, then projected the sketches onto linen in order to blow them up to lifelike scale. Marcus crops the bloodied bodies, with bulging eyes, rotting black teeth, and tongues outstretched, with a filmic sensibility. Viewers seem to witness the millisecond after a bullet's violent impact, the moment at which each man takes his last breath. Not only has Marcus created a panoramic scene of the grotesqueries of war, he manages to capture the psychic charge of fear and the inevitability of death. Evoking George Grosz, Otto Dix, and Marsden Hartley's expressionist "portraits" of officers, as well as the Buddhist-informed Japanese tradition of *kusōzu* (the depiction of bodies in successive stages of decomposition), Marcus's soldiers are a site for both Whitmanesque contemplation and recoil. The men also offer proxies for the ghastly faces Marcus has created in his self-portraits, suggesting how the devilish actually resides in warped versions of our own perspectives. *JBB*

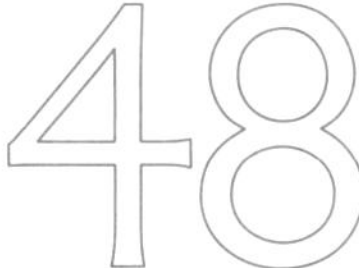

TIONA NEKKIA McCLODDEN

Artist and filmmaker Tiona Nekkia McClodden has embedded herself within the archives of a Black, queer genealogy in order to render it visible, even as her own practice extends it. In an oeuvre that includes film, installation, and sculpture, McClodden trains her attention on both her own biography and the histories of other figures in an exploration of blackness, the fluidity of time, and re-memory.

The artist's most recent examinations have focused on the lives of three gay Black men: poet Essex Hemphill, composer Julius Eastman, and writer Brad Johnson. McClodden's studies allow her subjects an opacity that neither flattens nor dilutes their legacies. In her efforts to care for and respond to these fragmented, fragile archives, McClodden undertakes a process that is at once spiritual and analytical. *Affixing Ceremony: Four Movements for Essex* (2015), for example, is an online project that functions both as a meditative space of remembrance for the late Hemphill and a medium through which McClodden visualizes a digital presence for him, using his writings on myth, death, queerness, and cyberspace, audio and video footage, and interviews with Hemphill's collaborators and loved ones.

In her study of Johnson, who died of complications from AIDS in 2011, McClodden prioritizes the physical, in some cases implicating her own body in pursuit of a kind of *jouissance*, the Lacanian embrace of pleasure almost to the point of pain. In response to Johnson's writings, McClodden created *The Brad Johnson Tape* (2017), a ten-part video recorded on a single VHS cassette in which she performs ten exercises related to BDSM play. In one chapter, *X— On Subjugation*, the artist is suspended by her feet from a rig recalling the obstacle-course structures she saw as a child on her father's military bases as she recites Johnson's poem "On Subjugation."

McClodden holds the corporeal and incorporeal as data necessary in order to see, to respond to, and to be in conversation with. Ever methodical and precise, she affirms that the archive is never static, suggesting that we all can be implicated in its making and remaking in order to see histories anew. *JL*

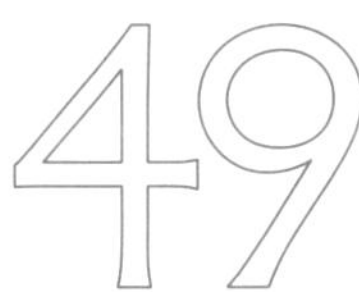

TROY MICHIE

Growing up in the cross-cultural, bilingual border city of El Paso, Texas, gave Troy Michie what he calls a "collage mentality," a sensibility he mobilizes in his collages and assemblages. Michie repurposes found photographs and clothing to explore the interplay between self-presentation and the construction of identity, especially in relation to histories of queer and minority masculinity, and often appropriates images of men of color from vintage gay-porn magazines, most of which were marketed to white men. In combining and overlaying the bodies of the models, his works intervene in a voyeuristic regime that fetishized and silenced them, with photomontage both serving to represent the complexity of identity and operating as a tool to critique existing stereotypes.

Michie seeks out clothing and accessories that are emblematic of larger histories. Two recent shows in New York, at Recess (2017) and Company gallery (2017–18), centered on a particularly charged item: the zoot suit. First popularized by African American and Latino men in the 1940s, the flamboyant garments became the flash point for the 1943 Zoot Suit Riots in Los Angeles, in which white military personnel and civilians attacked their wearers. While the style's excessive use of fabric was condemned by some as unpatriotic amid wartime rationing, the violence reflected the city's racial tensions and widespread racism toward Latino men. In the works, Michie collaged images of the suits, treated the garments themselves as the basis for assemblages, and invited other artists to contribute their own versions (perhaps nodding to the fact that zoot suits historically were custom made). Michie also draws on theories of camouflage to address the use of style as a form of protection, especially by marginalized individuals. His work demonstrates how fashion can be a powerful expression of identity, a strategy for survival, and at times a dangerous liability. *FJP*

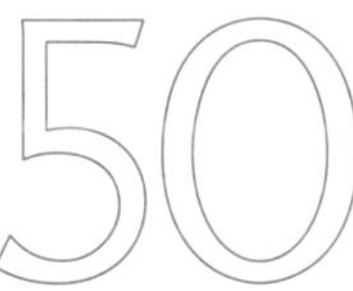

JOE MINTER

Joe Minter uses found materials to create allegorical mixed-media critiques of the history of race and class inequities in the United States. Utilizing his training in construction and welding, he repurposes the detritus of rural life to create dense, geometrically complex, often anthropomorphic totems that mine African American history and the rich tradition of Southern yard art. A deeply religious man, Minter was called to art by what he describes in an oral history (1998–2001) for the Souls Grown Deep Foundation as an "idea handed down . . . by God . . . to use that which has been discarded, just as we as a people have been discarded [and] made invisible."

Minter is best known for the immersive sculptural environment *African Village in America* (1989–), which he created in his native Birmingham, Alabama, on his half-acre property abutting two historically Black cemeteries. His discrete sculptures—abstract assemblages of rusted chains, agricultural tools, household furniture, inexpensively made garments, license plates, wood fragments on which he occasionally paints text—employ the same techniques, aesthetics, and materials as those installed on his land to pay homage to African Americans like those buried in the nearby graves, and to the events and icons that exemplify the ongoing struggle for a just democracy in the United States. The imagined lives of past owners and mechanical uses animate the materials, invoking the history of labor that is so closely tied to the enslavement of African peoples in the American South and its lasting legacy of inequity.

Minter's sculptures loom like skeletal reminders of this ongoing struggle, with evocative titles such as *Earth Movers* (1993–94), a reference both to tools the work comprises (shovels, grab hooks, chains) and to unpaid and otherwise exploited laborers; *The Dreamer* (2005), an allusion to the mystical dream-catcher form implied by a spoked wheel; and *'63 Foot Soldiers* (1999), which conjures those who marched in the historic campaign led by Dr. Martin Luther King Jr. in Birmingham, the work's form representing two allies with arms linked in defiance. In each case, Minter's poetic titles compound the complexity with which he imbues commonplace objects. *CF*

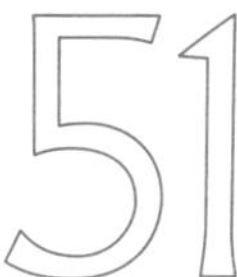

51

KEEGAN MONAGHAN

Keegan Monaghan's paintings of everyday scenes—with their tactile and heavily worked surfaces, glowing light sources, and subjective sensibility—seem to channel aspects of Impressionist painting, but they are very much of today's image world. Like social-media snapshots, they emphasize a first-person perspective. In *Introspection* (2016), the viewer looks down through a transparent plate and table onto a pair of legs—perhaps the artist's own. In *Basement View* (2016–17), we watch through a grate set into a brick wall as unsuspecting feet stroll down the street outside. Is the gaze that of a voyeur preying on pedestrians, a prisoner longing for the world outside, or simply a tenant picking up something from storage? In Monaghan's paintings, everyday life is at once magical, threatening, and banal. The sense of being inside the artist's head is taken to an extreme in *My Place* (2016), in which the viewer peers out through a pair of cartoonish eyeholes from inside a cushiony orange brain furnished with couch, end table, and so on, much like the living room visible in the world beyond.

In Monaghan's works, every object vibrates with life—which renders both unsurprising and unsettling the appearance of some of these objects in three dimensions as sculptures. The sculpture *Telephone* (2017) depicts a melting red rotary handset seemingly pulled from a painting titled *Incoming* (2016–17), adding weight and reality to Monaghan's vision of the world even as its hand-formed character announces it as pure fiction. Monaghan, who was born just outside of Chicago, shares his loopy

surrealism, both silly and sinister, with Chicago Imagists like Jim Nutt and Ed Paschke; his favored palette—luminous brights against black-light violets—recalls the night scenes of Archibald Motley, a Chicago painter of an earlier era. Like these artists, Monaghan transforms the familiar real into personalized fantasy. *JPF*

52

CAROLINE MONNET

Caroline Monnet's moving-image works and mixed-media installations combine a precise, formalist approach and a deep affective engagement with the contradictions of Indigenous life and identity in Canada. Drawing on her French and Algonquin heritage, Monnet seeks a middle ground between Indigenous and non-Indigenous spaces. Her video *Transatlantic* and accompanying collage *Bridging Distance* (both 2018) literalize this space in images that document an oceanic journey from Europe to North America via the Saint Lawrence River, succinctly exemplifying the fluid nature of intercultural exchange.

Dismantling ossified notions of cultural identity, Monnet's works instead accentuate qualities of mobility and change. *Mobilize* (2015) utilizes 1960s-era footage from the National Film Board of Canada's archives depicting Native life and work from the snowy forests and rivers of the north to southern Canada's urban centers. Set to the song "Uja" by the celebrated Inuk composer and throat singer Tanya Tagaq, Monnet's percussive intercutting isolates and juxtaposes examples of Indigenous expertise, on display in tasks ranging from threading snowshoes to making canoes from a felled birch to positioning steel girders at the top of a skyscraper. In this way, the film devises a continuity between traditional and modern labor practices, mapping the trajectories of Native life in the twentieth century. In *Creatura Dada* (2016), a formidable sextet of Native women—among them the great Abenaki documentary film director Alanis Obomsawin—gorge themselves on a banquet of champagne, lobsters, and oysters. Monnet's close framing forcefully upends conventional representations of Indigenous women by placing them amid splendor and finery, festooned in jewelry and luxury fashion, enjoying haute cuisine with an almost erotic fervor. Through jagged fragmentary montage, Monnet's video generates an explosive discourse that runs counter to portrayals of Native victimhood and poverty, mobilizing in its place subversive and decadent celebration. *LG*

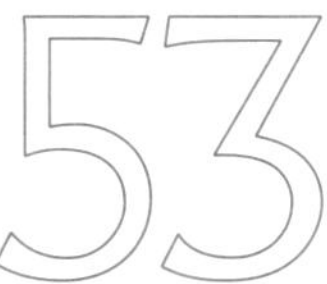

DARIUS CLARK MONROE

Working in fiction film, documentary, and television, Darius Clark Monroe creates intimate portraits that tease out the dense inner lives of his subjects. Focused on the lived experiences of Black people—and in particular, Black men—Monroe's work asserts the right of his subjects to contain contradictions still rarely explored onscreen.

Monroe's debut feature, *Evolution of a Criminal* (2014), insists on this interiority in the context of his own life. Almost jarring in its honesty, the documentary traces the ripple effects of poverty and systemic racism in his hometown, and the devastating consequences of his decision to rob a bank at sixteen. Through reenactments and painstaking interviews with his family and others who were directly affected, *Evolution of a Criminal* yields a compelling portrait of what it means to come of age in a society that never afforded you the innocence of youth in the first place. Diving deep into what Black men think and feel, rather than just how they are perceived, is characteristic of Monroe's work. As part of the team behind the HBO series *Random Acts of Flyness* (2018–), created by filmmaker Terence Nance, Monroe helped envision a singular take on contemporary blackness through skits concerning myriad topics, such as a reparations app called "Bitch Better Have My Money" and a biting but humorous segment on Hollywood's insidious archetypes.

In his latest works, Monroe revisits the subject of sports, a domain he explored with his 2018 short *Black 14*, which uses archival footage to chronicle the experiences of fourteen Black football players facing racist policies at the University of Wyoming in 1969. In his currently underway new series, Monroe traces the outsize role of sports in American culture, this time focusing on tennis and handball. Shot entirely on film (a first for his documentary output), the series examines the lives of players and club owners, and the communities they have built around each sport. Probing broader issues of grief, displacement, and the process of aging, Monroe subverts the sports-doc form, filtering our fixation on the game through the consequences of what happens off the court. *DLC*

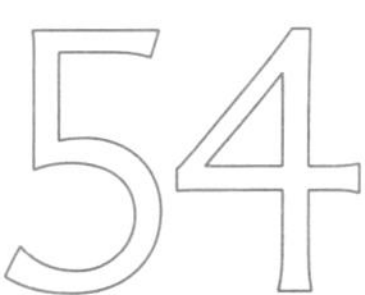

RAGEN MOSS

Ragen Moss creates objects out of polychromed plastic, paint, and other materials, with the works' biological intimations underscored by the way that the clear or translucent surfaces suggest skin. In Moss's *Vigilante (with Apple, with Pear)* (2017), an oblong peach-colored object that resembles a truncated torso hangs suspended from a thin filament. Two blurry, jagged black lines outline clear areas through which two inner sculpted forms painted in blues and reds—perhaps an apple and pear—appear. Moss makes bodily references explicit through drawn allusions to organs or appendages, for example the breasts that appear on *Consumptive Reader, 1st Degree (with Lemon)* (2017). Because most of their gestures are contained on the interior of the work, Moss's objects upset the manner in which we expect to operate as a viewer. Words, when they appear, are only awkwardly legible because they are abridged or rendered on the works' insides.

Moss's works require a constant sifting through layers in order to perceive, reflecting the artist's long-held interest in spatiality. Her most recent solo exhibition, in 2017 at New York gallery Ramiken, literalized a related interest in excavation by taking place in a basement, giving viewers the physical experience of approaching artwork outside the white cube. With all the sculptures hanging from long metal bars, the experience was akin to entering a meat locker. The resonance emphasized Moss's affinity with Paul Thek. But instead of, like Thek, staging the tension between rot and preservation, Moss's pristinely encased floating gestures entice the viewer. Upon inspection, the hanging forms, some with relatively rigid geometries, others more biomorphic, engage the viewer in a push-pull between their glossy exteriors and the possibility of peering within. If we think of these sacs as cocoons, having all of the nutrients to support life, then these works nourish the viewer by providing an endless array of what is possible. *AC*

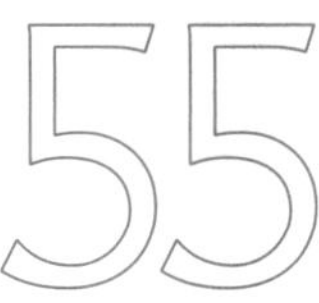

SAHRA MOTALEBI

Sahra Motalebi is an artist, composer, and vocalist who works at the intersection of performance and installation. Drawing on her training in classical voice and architecture, her work combines recordings, paintings, sculptures, video, text, and song. The shadow play *Intangible Heritages, Belief's Demise* (2014) follows the transformations of an archetypal character over three life stages, each played by a different actor. *Sounds from Untitled Skies* (2015) presents "landscape portraits" composed of poems drawn from notes and fragments of journal entries sung against a projection of otherworldly architectural maquettes made from paper and other disposable materials. In these performances, Motalebi draws on a variety of historical and cultural forms and textual research—including classical art songs, traditional Persian music, ancient theatrical and religious texts, experimental theater of the early twentieth century, eighteenth-century European paper architecture, and the scenography of 1960s and '70s dance—to examine the nature of subjective experience and the construction of identity.

Since 2016, Motalebi has presented iterations of *Directory of Portrayals*, an ongoing, open-form opera (or anti-opera) comprising exhibitions, texts, and staged events. Structuring these components is a libretto drawn from the artist's exchanges with her sister, a conservative Muslim English teacher who lives in Iran. When Motalebi began the project, the two had never met in person—they did so for the first time only in 2018. Thus their relationship has played out almost entirely via digital forms of communication, often encrypted because of concerns about surveillance. The opera, which evolves alongside their relationship, appropriates the text messages, voice recordings, photos, and gifs exchanged by the sisters, both played by Motalebi. Its staging changes with each performance, incorporating elements that include multichannel video, spoken text, music, sculptural sets, and AI language-translation software. As in her previous work, Motalebi embraces the disjunction produced by multiple, irreconcilable elements, preferring that a performance show rather than hide its seams. In conveying the sisters' relationship through and across shifting multimedia platforms, the opera reflects on the role of technology in shaping our relation to subjectivity, intimacy, cultural difference, and narration itself. *FJP*

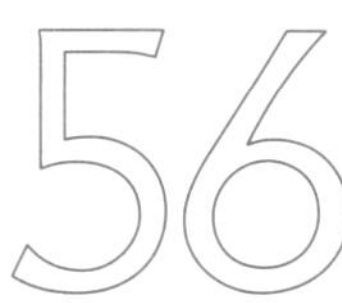

MARLON MULLEN

Marlon Mullen's approach to painting is as materially sumptuous as it is formally astute. Working primarily with acrylic on canvas, the artist begins with a source image typically taken from the cover or interior page of a magazine, often one from the ranks of art periodicals and auction catalogues. He then lays down the key elements of his composition with a generous application of paint—the title script from publications like *Artforum*, or shapes reinterpreted from another artist's work, be it Paul Strand or Kerry James Marshall. Once these details are defined, Mullen swathes the forms in yet more acrylic, creating a balanced surface in which his original schema and the surrounding visual field carry equal significance.

Painting as an interpretative practice takes on added weight for Mullen, an artist with autism spectrum disorder who communicates mostly nonverbally. While the painterly medium has often been referred to as a form of visual language, Mullen's specific use of color, gesture, and abstraction creates an embodied conversation between the artist, his source material, and the viewer. All of Mullen's works are untitled, but text is often embedded in his impasto-rich surfaces, undulating across the visual field. One canvas from 2015, thickly coated in fleshy beige acrylic, is punctuated by the words *ANCIENT EMPIRES* in free-floating, chrome-yellow capitals, while another from the same year is seemingly signed "Robert Moth" below a collection of heavily rendered shapes in blue, orange, black, and peach—seemingly a wry distillation of Motherwell's approach to Abstract Expressionism.

In its frequent adapting of imagery from current and historical arts publications, Mullen's work invokes aspects of representation, interpretation, and taste. The artist pulls most of his sources from art and design subscriptions at NIAD (Nurturing Independence through Artistic Development) Art Center, a progressive art studio that supports the endeavors of artists with disabilities based in Richmond, California. Through NIAD, Mullen has been able to maintain an autonomous practice and participate in the contemporary art world. The result is a body of work that operates both within and in conversation with its institutionalized frameworks. *RK*

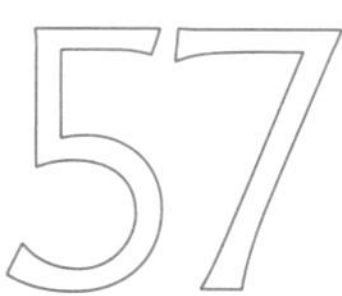

JEANETTE MUNDT

Drawing from a seemingly disparate array of repurposed film stills, idyllic landscapes, and art-historical references, Jeanette Mundt's paintings probe societal constructs and the fissures they create. Her diverse approaches are reflected in the material slippage of her surfaces, which form a varied dialogue between saturated linen, electric color, and black permanent marker. While each of her strategies is distinct, all explore the replication, fracture, and circulation of popular images, as well as the identities those images have historically produced, perpetuated, and capitalized on.

Often developing various themes simultaneously, Mundt examines the perception and representation of gender, sexuality, history, and celebrity. In *Born Athlete American*, a series from 2017–19, the artist presents scenes of the U.S. Women's Olympic Gymnastic Team at the 2016 games in Rio de Janeiro. Rendered in oil and glitter, each painting portrays one gymnast midroutine. Whether focused on Simone Biles, Madison Kocian, or Aly Raisman, each canvas portrays a stream of still photos from the New York Times to create a syncopated clash of individual frames and a dynamic continuous narrative. By complicating the composition, Mundt accentuates the physical strain on each woman's body as well as the societal scrutiny the sport draws. Palpably tense, each image makes visible the ways in which gender stereotypes and national identities are projected and picked apart via mass media.

This interest in the ways women's bodies are framed, circulated, and surveyed becomes self-reflexive in Mundt's abstracted selfie paintings. In her 2018 show *Lana Del Rey*, named for the American singer-siren, the artist included a suite of knowingly kitsch canvases—garish mashes of bubble-gum pink, camouflage, and loose line work—each revealing a seminude caricature of the artist. A wry recasting of the traditional self-portrait, Mundt's appropriation and reinterpretation of the bathroom-mirror selfie questions the status of voyeurism and contemporary image consumption. Whether treating identities performed in public or in private, Mundt draws attention to the implications of images and the assumptions they codify. *R K*

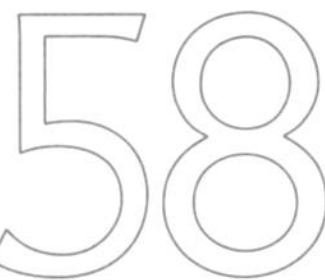

WANGECHI MUTU

Representations of empowered women of color and their relationship to nature unites Wangechi Mutu's diverse practices of collage, watercolor, video, sculpture, and performance. Since moving part-time to Nairobi, Mutu has reintroduced sculpture to her work. As in her collage paintings, notable for their motile female forms composed of appropriated images from fashion and ethnographic magazines as well as her own watercolors, photographs, and embellishments such as glitter and pearls, she creates sculptural amalgams of manufactured and natural found materials. She builds soil, mud, petrified trees, and stones onto preexisting frameworks so that they appear to grow and emerge from one another to form larger-than-life hybrid female bodies that she calls *Sentinels* (2017–).

By embedding into her sculptures organic matter found outside her Nairobi studio, Mutu anthropomorphizes the land she inhabits. The *Sentinels* probe historically demeaning, hypersexualized fallacies surrounding the relationships between female bodies, African bodies, labor, and nature in an effort to expose widespread biases; or, as she described in a 2018 interview conducted for Anderson Ranch Arts Center, to "vandalize the original narrative and make something dignified." In her view, the survival of both the human race and the earth depends on a nuanced coexistence—a truth of which she has become keenly aware in Nairobi as technology increasingly encroaches on the familiar landscape of her youth. The *Sentinels* stand as an almost gothic invocation of our need to honor a planet made increasingly unstable and uninhabitable by the effects of climate change.

Her depiction of female bodies in this pursuit is not incidental. Women are traditionally associated with the land—the concept of Mother Earth comes to mind—and, like the earth, they have historically been victimized by patriarchal forces. In the face of those realities, Mutu casts women as the saviors and the sustainers of the human race through the bounty of the land. Her figures wield that combination of myth and reality as they stand to fiercely protect the earth from which they emerged. *CF*

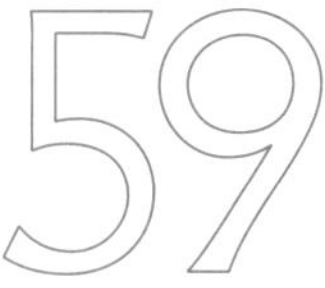

LAS NIETAS DE NONÓ

Las Nietas de Nonó comprises two sisters, Lydela and Michel Nonó, whose joint practice encompasses performance, theater, dance, and visual art, combined with activism and education. The themes of struggle, marginalization, and family that drive their event making are rooted in their home neighborhood, Barrio San Antón in Carolina, Puerto Rico, where rural life has been despoiled by industrialization. The sisters' performances explore both the historical and contemporary conditions of Black communities in cultures where racism exacerbates hierarchies among impoverished people and perpetuates colonial social mechanisms such as mass incarceration and displacement. Las Nietas seek identification with their audiences, many of whom have lived the very oppressions and traumas the duo depicts.

Las Nietas de Nonó established Patio Taller (Patio Workshop) in 2011 in the former home of their grandparents (*nietas* means "granddaughters"). The intimate space for theater, art workshops, and community activities incorporates Afro-diasporic practices of honoring ancestral knowledge, using and reusing found materials, and communing around meals. It also serves as a site of creative exchange within the Caribbean, hosting arts residencies. At Patio Taller, Las Nietas have debuted works such as *Manual del bestiario doméstico* (*Manual of the Domestic Bestiary*, 2014), which explores the dissolution of families due to overincarceration as seen from the perspective of the women left behind. In it, actors from the community circulate throughout the house and garden, its spaces and the performed situations evoking a small apartment, a jail, and a school. Another performance, *Illustraciones de la mecánica* (*Illustrations of the Mechanical*, 2016), uses video, props, and masks, as well as a laboratory set with an operating table and a mirror hung high to reflect simulated surgery, to examine the demonization of ancestral healing practices and violence against the bodies of Black women, who have been subject to mass sterilizations and unwanted caesarean births in Puerto Rico. The work's integration of organic materials and processes, including fermentation that produces a vegetable "leather" and the dissection of iguana skin (the animal is an invasive, crop-devouring species on the island), invoke applied ecology, material transmutation, and other methods Las Nietas explore as ways to cure their land. *CH*

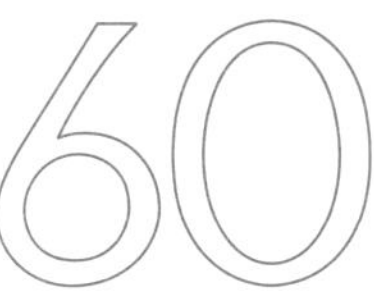

JENN NKIRU

Sound and image are of equal importance in Jenn Nkiru's viscerally kinetic videos, which map the global proliferations of Black music, fashion, and visual culture. Her works blend the audiovisual dynamism of the music video form with the sensitivity and attention of documentary cinema. Shot on location in New York, *En Vogue* (2017) reclaims voguing as a dance originating in Black queer club culture through rhythmic montage and vibrant cinematography by acclaimed visual artists Bradford Young and Arthur Jafa. Her video *REBIRTH IS NECESSARY* (2017) reconstructs a vivid tapestry of Black diasporic culture, taking up a welter of sources including Sun Ra's Afrofuturist xeno-mythologies, Alice Coltrane's cosmic-spiritualist public-access television show, and the writings of Fred Moten, Audre Lorde, and James Baldwin. The work gracefully intercuts iconic images and figures with sensitively rendered microportraits of individuals displaying a vivid assortment of styles, situating them physically, formally, and historically within Black cultural traditions and iconographies.

Nkiru's works frequently take the shape of music videos and collaborations with musical artists—including videos made in 2018 for songs by Neneh Cherry ("Kong") and Kamasi Washington ("Hub-Tones") and second-unit direction for Beyoncé and Jay-Z's "Apeshit"—as well as documentaries that explore the wealth of Black sonic forms. Her new project, *BLACK TO TECHNO* (2019), focuses on the expansive cultural geography of techno music, mapping the exchange of styles and techniques between Detroit, the genre's birthplace, and Berlin, where it exploded as a highly malleable global style. In a statement on this project, the artist asserts that "techno is not just a musical gesture but a philosophical, sonic and anthropological one." In Nkiru's retelling, techno is an expansive cultural technology that crosses oceans, decades, and cultural boundaries to form industries and infrastructures, subcultures and affective spaces—"an othered sound created by groups of othered people." *LG*

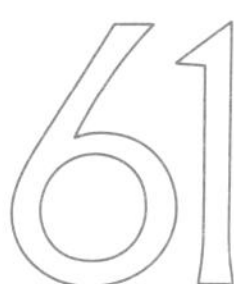

LAURA ORTMAN

A musician who blurs the lines between the avant-garde and tradition, Laura Ortman creates sonic landscapes. While her signature instrument is the violin, she also plays Apache violin, amplified piano, electric guitar, keyboards, and pedal-steel guitar. When she sings, Ortman often distorts her voice through a megaphone, and she makes extensive field recordings of her surroundings, including traffic near her home in Brooklyn. Both in live performance and on recorded albums and soundtracks, these sounds are layered and mixed into dense and dreamy environments.

Ortman learned to play the violin as a child, but she studied visual art in college. After graduation, she moved to New York to pursue the latter, initially working in installation and performance. She soon returned to the violin, however, and began making four-track home recordings that combined her singing and playing with a multitude of other sounds both composed and improvised. Ortman, who often cites New York City as her muse, took up with its downtown experimental music scene, working with artists such as Martin Bisi, Tony Conrad, and Okkyung Lee.

A White Mountain Apache, Ortman is deeply involved in the Native American community in New York and across the United States. She frequently collaborates with Indigenous musicians, visual artists, poets, and filmmakers, performing and recording with Raven Chacon, Demian Diné Yahzi', Caroline Monnet, and Jock Soto, among others. Together with bassist Carlos Santistevan and percussionist Marshall Trammell, Ortman is a member of In Defense of Memory, a performance-based political-education practicum for Black, mestizo, and Native musicians that debuted at SITE Santa Fe in 2018. The group uses improvisation to build solidarity, citing the history and organizing strategies of the Pueblo Revolt of 1680. Recently, Ortman has been producing an audio map of Native New York, collecting recordings of sounds, songs, stories, and voices of Native Americans who live in the city and surrounding areas in a reflection on the deep roots of Native peoples in New York as well as the life and work of the contemporary diasporic community of Indigenous people, especially artists, who reside there today. *MH*

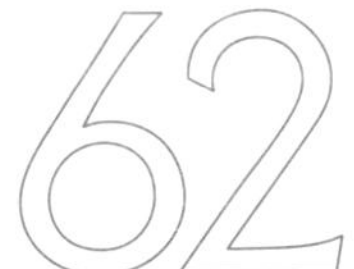

JENNIFER PACKER

Jennifer Packer describes her impetus to paint portraits as the desire to "present or protect humans in the work." Her depictions, usually of close friends and family members, declare her emotional connection to her subjects. First we are struck by the intimacy of the titles, which bear first names: Tia, Jerriod, James. The painting *For James III* (2013) shows the artist's father lying prone, shirtless, curled on a mattress, returning our gaze. Packer renders his body in splotches of browns, oranges, and burnt sienna, warm tones that contrast with the cool greens and blues of the bedding, the tender treatment capturing her protective impulses. It is no surprise that the artist titled her 2017 exhibition at the Renaissance Society in Chicago *Tenderheaded*.

Packer's approach to her subjects is to depict them up close. *April, Restless* (2017) portrays a woman, seated and facing us, with a typewriter and other accoutrements of a desk behind her. The figure emerges from a field of yellow, which swells outside Packer's jaunty line work. April's restlessness may reside not only in her rendering but also in the collection of objects behind her, suggestive of so many other things to do in a day.

Packer paints floral arrangements as well, at times dedicated to particular individuals. She dedicated one such painting of a funerary bouquet, *Say Her Name* (2017), to Sandra Bland, a young Black woman who died in police custody in 2015 in Texas. Lush greenery with pink and blue florets rises out of a divided background of black and luminous yellow-white. Drawing on the still lifes of artists such as Juan Sánchez Cotán, Edouard Manet, Henri Fantin-Latour, and Giorgio Morandi, the work creates a complex relationship to mortality, desire, and family. And as in her portraits, Packer brings to bear a formal line and sophistication with color that indexes not only what she represents but also her own emotional state. Her reflections on the care of self and others allude to complicated, dire issues, such as the violence that Black and Brown people face in their everyday lives. *AC*

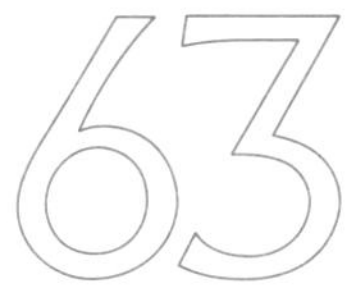

NIBIA PASTRANA SANTIAGO

Choreography concerns itself with the demarcation of space, an inherently territorial act. Dance artist nibia pastrana santiago understands the resulting relationships between choreographer, performer, and audience to be enmeshed in a complex power dynamic—one that, in her work, she relates to the colonial force enacted on Puerto Rico by the United States. Instead of occupying a traditional stage, her "choreographic events" unfold in charged spaces, often outdoors, and implicate both the gaze and the body of the viewer.

In her manifesto *La bailarina vaga* (*The Lazy Dancer*, 2013), pastrana santiago describes the titular figure as possessing a key attribute: "The lazy dancer has no duty to dance." She thus overturns the typical notion that work is worthy and should be rewarded. In a Puerto Rican context, where local labor has often served distant powers, laziness can be a form of resistance. For *taller de nada* (*workshop on nothing*, 2015), the artist invited a diverse group of artists and performers to "do nothing" together. A sign on the wall declared, "*Nada es posible*"—the phrase not a declaration of despair but rather an optimistic rallying cry that recalls John Cage's assertion "I have nothing to say, and I am saying it."

Like Cage, pastrana santiago also embraces indeterminacy. *Fuerzas sutiles* (*subtle forces*, 2017) took place in a hangar at San Juan's Isla Grande Airport. Its enormous doors opened like a proscenium curtain behind four dancers whose repeated, simple movements evoked the work of Yvonne Rainer, while the airplanes taxiing in the background provided another choreography. This piece emerged from the artist's ongoing historical and physical investigation of San Juan Bay, which in addition to the airport hosts an abandoned U.S. Navy base. Since Hurricane Maria, ruins play an increased role in this research: much of the port was affected, and the hangar where *fuerzas sutiles* took place was destroyed, layering fresh cataclysm on the location's past projection of military force and its subsequent neglect. Embedding her works in such pregnant sites, pastrana santiago seeks to chart a new relationship between the body, space, and history. *JPF*

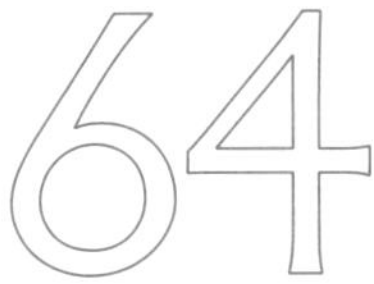

64

ELLE PÉREZ

Elle Pérez's early work explores the intertwining of aspiration and illusion in composed photographs of people transfiguring the aesthetics of their lives. Their images traverse the church basements of the Bronx's punk circles, the rings and locker rooms of its underground wrestling scene, the LGBTQ nightclubs of New York, Baltimore, and New Haven, and the *fiestas patronales* of Puerto Rico. Using documentary photography's visual language of monochrome realism and activated compositions, Pérez's depictions of insular worlds are, crucially, rooted in fantasy. Staged, lit, and sequenced, these works coalesce in the slippage between fiction and reality, underscoring art and identity's shared paradox wherein illusion can construct truth.

In the 2018 exhibition *In Bloom*, at 47 Canal gallery in New York, Pérez turned to their own life. The nine works presented glimpses of the everyday—friends, sex, nature, bathrooms—reverberating with desire

and a tension drawn out across the sequenced photographs. At first glance, crisp details and dreamy light seem to accentuate a kind of confessional or diary of the artist's queerness, in images of a bloody fist (*Dick*, 2018), their partner's top surgery scars (*Warm Curve*, 2018), or their stained binder hanging to dry (*Binder*, 2015). Beyond and in addition to their emotional resonance, however, the works are formal studies. In *Dick*, the bloody traces of fisting and a tangle of limbs become color and lines: the body can be read as both content and form. Rather than create a deadpan image of sexual intimacy as a way to illuminate an act or identity, Pérez demonstrates how easily bodies can be transfigured and reimagined by fragmenting, framing, lighting, and manipulating their images.

Pérez's photographs remain deliberately elusive while evincing hints of personal history and identity, or intimacy and tenderness. The images exist as captures of surfaces and forms and as conceptual objects, resisting interpretation and assumptions made on appearance alone; per the artist, they are "neither reflections of reality nor imprints of personhood." Instead, they are reflections upon the failure of appearances to align with identity, imaging the beauty and truth found in those gaps and tensions. *CH*

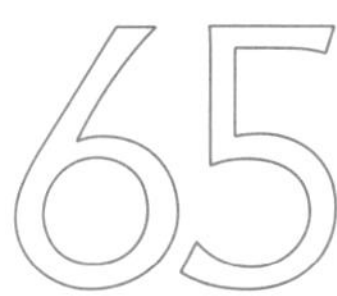

65

PAT PHILLIPS

Pat Phillips uses elements of graffiti, folk art, and landscape painting to create large, color-rich, reference-dense works full of satire and humor. In so doing, he advances a commentary on race in America from the perspective of a young Black man living

in the South. *Brown v. Blue* (2015), for example, offers a searing critique of police brutality and the extrajudicial killings of Black people in a macabre riff on the children's story of Humpty Dumpty. A brown egg in schoolboy uniform has fallen from a wall and cracked its shell while a rainbow drips bloodred rain in the background. The hand holding a toy gun in the foreground evokes the killing of Tamir Rice, the twelve-year-old shot and killed by a Cleveland police officer while playing with a toy gun on a playground, while a poster plastered to Dumpty's wall drawn in the style of a Newport cigarettes advertisement featuring the header "Loosey!" alludes to the death of Eric Garner, the Staten Island man who died after being placed in a chokehold by an NYPD officer.

Phillips works with varied materials and grounds, all reminiscent of his earlier years painting on dilapidated surfaces. Graffiti infuses his work for gallery spaces, including references to iconic train painters such as Fab 5 Freddy, J.son, and Seen from New York as well as the Louisianians Ken82 and Goose SFR. In *Cheech Imperial Wizard* (2017), we see Phillips's bent for the satiric and the absurd further at play. Spray-painted onto the rear doors of a blue and white church bus is an orange, cartoonish figure wearing a Ku Klux Klan hood and nothing else. The figure is a cheeky nod to the titular character of artist Vaughn Bodé's popular underground comic of the '60s and '70s, who quickly became a quintessential figure in New York City subway art. So too is Phillips defining his own legacy in responding to the blights of Americana with a deftness aligned with the ongoing traditions of humorists across mediums and disciplines. *JL*

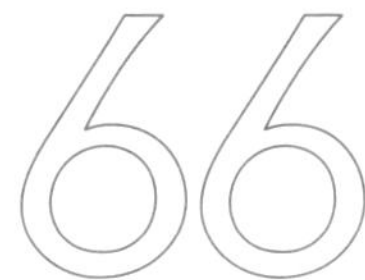

GALA PORRAS-KIM

While Gala Porras-Kim's investigative creative process is rigorous and anthropologically rooted, her work also retains the experimental spirit of an artist looking in from the outside. It responds rather than merely describes, reflecting a liberty unavailable with more academic approaches. In 2016, for example, Porras-Kim's term at a residency in Oaxaca, Mexico, led her to work with a Chatino community in the town of San Isidro Llano Grande. Porras-Kim initiated a collaboration with the group's eldest members to develop an orthography for the oral Chatino language, who created an alphabet based on the roman one that could be used on municipal signage in the area. With the project, titled *Chatino spelling of public places* (2016), 105 new spellings were created for the town's public spaces and installed throughout.

Porras-Kim's unconventional avenues often result in hybrid reconstructions of traditional forms that are both aesthetic and functional. Another exploration of Zapotec language variants resulted in the LP *Whistling and Language Transfiguration* (2012). Focusing on the language and culture of the Zapotec people, the album translates their spoken words into their equivalents in whistling, a form of communication used by the Zapotec as a means of resistance during periods of colonization. Porras-Kim also explores similar themes within the institutions that steward ethnographic objects. *78 west Mexico ceramics from the LACMA collection: Nayarit Index* (2017) is a large-scale, photorealistic drawing taking the form of a visual index that addresses the limits of its own observation and scientistic description in general. As an "index" whose only apparent organizational principle is scale, the work asks to what extent we can truly understand a people or value a heritage through the objects and information that outlive it. Porras-Kim's works remind us that the dynamic process of translation is the only means we have to access the knowledge and history of other cultures. *LK*

WALTER PRICE

Walter Price's paintings invite us to dwell in the liminal space between abstraction and figuration. His keen attention to color, line, and texture frames his work as he traverses real and imagined landscapes. His canvases, often intimate in scale, draw on the artist's personal experiences as well as on cultural iconography in resistant, polysemic ways. In Price's *hyperthermic conditioning 2* (2017), for example, three ambiguous forms stippled in blue lean into the painting's foreground. Meanwhile, three brown figures clad in pink shirts are positioned nearby on what appears to be a tiled floor, while on the painting's horizon another of the group faces away toward a blue expanse. From the painting's title, we can imagine a setting that is generating immense levels of heat: a sweltering summer afternoon down South, a night of sweaty dancing, or perhaps, an allusion to the artist's stint as a firefighter in the United States Navy.

Price's paintings energetically render together narratives that seem to compete with each other, combining domestic interiors and exterior montages in deeply saturated hues. At times these internal tensions result in carefully framed visual combustions, such as in *Not an Attack Vessel (Pedestal Lady)* (2018), where the body of a woman who appears to be dancing transubstantiates into a mottled blue translucent cloud, leaving only her high-kicking legs behind. The work shares a brick-wall patterning with *merge sort* (2017), where a green couch resting against a green brick wall is engulfed in green flames that flicker with red tendrils. Above, the blue sky is streaked by a thick gray line—a cloud promising some sort of incoming reprieve for the flames, or a purely abstract element?—and at the left edge of the painting, illegible and seemingly bisected letters align. From Price's work we can glean one central argument: a painting's true story lives in the architecture of its color. *JL*

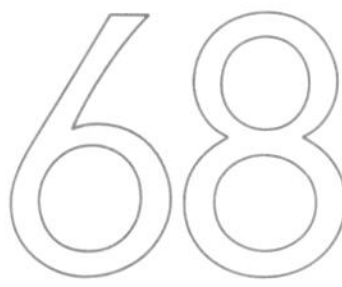

CARISSA RODRIGUEZ

"The child was as delicate as a moonbeam, pure as freshly fallen snow, and as lovable as the sun." In Robert Walser's paragraph-long story "The Maid," this child, perfect as nature itself, goes missing, plunging the titular caretaker into a search across continents and decades. When at last she is found, the girl is a woman: the lost one has metamorphosed, invalidating the terms of the initial relationship by taking a path marked out all along.

This parable offers insight into the dynamics of natality and transformation that mark Carissa Rodriguez's *The Maid* (2018), a video following the iterations of Sherrie Levine's sculpture *Newborn* (1993–94) through collectors' homes, a museum, and an auction house. A copy of Constantin Brancusi's orb of latent potential *Le nouveau-né* (1915), *Newborn* was fabricated in two versions, one crystal and one black glass. The work is as exemplary of Levine's critique of originality and authorship as it is of how swiftly that challenge to the governing principles of the art system would be recuperated. Rodriguez's camera buoyantly moves around the organic, ovular form, drawing out the tension between Levine's conceptual gesture and the object's sensuousness, lingering on a wall plaque listing its estimated price. This infant leaves the artist's care to circulate through economies of money and desire, becoming something else even as it remains itself.

The Maid resonates with Rodriguez's activities over the years as part of the artist collective Reena Spaulings, which has used collaboration and anonymity to question value and the cult of genius. It also ties the temporality of the art object to the potentiality of life—something found, too, in *All the Best Memories Are Hers* (2018), a series of gelatin silver prints of embryos cryogenically frozen at a fertility clinic and thus suspended in time. Art and assisted reproductive technology, as forms of (re)production, might seem the purest, most innate inauguration of the new. Yet both, Rodriguez suggests, are profoundly alienated from nature, bound to technology, tethered to market forces—and no less wondrous for it. *EB*

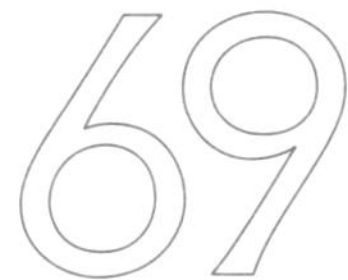

PAUL MPAGI SEPUYA

Through myriad experiments and formal adaptations, Paul Mpagi Sepuya's photography has consistently been grounded in studio and domestic portraiture. Documenting and describing the queer and artistic communities to which he belongs, he unravels notions of a subject's singular identity and a work's singular author while maintaining a commitment to technically precise and formally acute photographic processes.

Like much of his work, Sepuya's recent series *Figures, Grounds & Studies* (2015–17), in particular its subgroup *Mirror Studies*, fragments and multiplies the genre of portraiture. Whether depicting one body or two, himself or intimate others, he uses torn and abstracted sections of old prints, mirrors, and found images to depict bodies that appear in shards even as they retain a state of elusive, multifaceted wholeness. At the same time that he explores the possibilities for describing a person, Sepuya takes up the studio as a second, central subject of his art. It serves as the landscape in which his portraits are set, a place for testing new approaches, and a site of communion, both with the friends that come through and the influences that he conjures in dialogue.

Many of Sepuya's images emphasize the relationship between artist, camera, and image by depicting the camera itself, and often the artist's own body—for example Sepuya's latest work, the series *Dark Room* (2017–), which does so while further emphasizing collaboration. Traditionally, the act of making a photograph—representing the world through a viewfinder and lens—privileges the artist's gaze. In order to challenge the dominance of his own perspective, Sepuya invites friends and fellow artists to bring their own cameras into his home or studio and shoot alongside him. In *Darkroom Mirror (_2100135)* (2017), the result is a double portrait/self-portrait, Sepuya and his collaborator's camera nearly overlapping in the center of the image as their bodies frame them photographing each other. This work, like so many of Sepuya's inquires, uses a moment captured in the studio to highlight the multiplicity of perspective and the entangled nature of conversation that complicates past and present, author and observer. *ES*

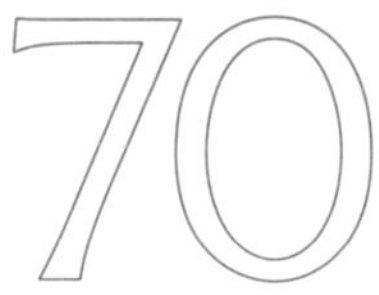

HEJI SHIN

Heji Shin's practice questions the slippage between social mechanisms of morality, intimacy, and consumption. Employing provocation and humor, her photographs situate the viewer in close proximity to her subjects, who range from infants midbirth to couples having sex to suggestively homoerotic encounters with and between male police officers. Raw and immediate, Shin's work moves fluidly between commercial and fine-art photography, her images often flirting with taboo while remaining intentionally ambiguous. Engaging these various social and cultural contexts, the artist's unapologetic presentation of actual events creates an open space for dialogue, engaging a diverse range of responses from discomfort to desire.

For her 2016 show at Real Fine Arts gallery in New York, Shin exhibited a series of large-scale birthing photographs titled *Baby 1–7* (2016). Each presents an infant's head just after crowning, with the remainder of the body still unborn. By documenting actual labor, Shin upsets the art-historical trope of the mother and child as well as the quaintness of baby photography. Centered on the brutal reality of childbirth, the closely cropped images pervert portraiture by rendering these half-born entities as alien, bloodied, and grotesque, aggressively exhibiting the dissociation and violence of becoming.

While Shin moves freely between art and advertising, she adheres to the conceptual implications of her subject matter regardless of milieu. In her 2017 campaign for the fashion-design team Eckhaus Latta, Shin photographed straight and queer couples during intercourse. By refocusing the relationship between eroticism, fashion, and advertising, the artist challenges the traditional attraction of voyeuristic viewing as well as public perceptions associated with gender, sexuality, and desire—an interest echoed in Shin's 2018 exhibition at Reena Spaulings Fine Art, *Men Photographing Men*. Depicting suggestive portraits of policemen alongside images of explicit gay sex, Shin called on viewers to construct personal narratives through an intimate encounter with these works and their evocation of beefcake magazines, film noir, and security monitors. Witness or spectator, intimacy or pornography: Shin posits the space between passive and active forms of engagement as both open and testing. In a society oversaturated with images of sex and violence, we must choose the ways we see. *R K*

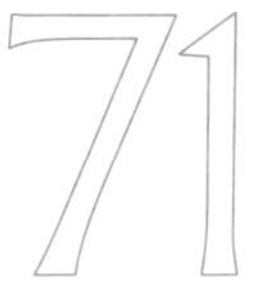

71

DIANE SIMPSON

Since the 1970s, Diane Simpson's practice has explored the translation and dissonance effects that result when two-dimensional forms are rendered in three-dimensional space. Working across drawing and sculpture, Simpson takes her source material from in-depth research into the conception and construction of clothing, design objects, and architecture.

Simpson begins her process by focusing on one element—an armor skirt, Art Deco detailing, antique wallpaper—from which she creates a precise axonometric drawing using her own system involving parallel 45-degree angles. In this method, the front and rear planes of the object appear as exact correlates of their source, while the angled planes between them are foreshortened and distorted. Meticulously executed by

hand, the resulting image becomes both an abstraction of the original object as well as a schematic blueprint for its reimagining. Beginning in the late 1970s, Simpson began to use these drawings like architectonic plans to construct sculptural models. First made using corrugated cardboard, the sculptures have evolved to incorporate a variety of materials including fiberboard and perforated aluminum. Simpson's attention to the fabrication of her works, expertly crafted by the artist herself through a rigorous amalgamation of sawing, joinery, and hand-coloring, speaks to the individual parts having the same importance as the unified whole, an echo of bespoke design and aggregate building.

Through their material references, specific construction, and human scale, Simpson's sculptures evoke not only architecture but also the body, often through their resemblance to structured garments. Transforming the flexibility of fabric into abstract engineering, collars and capes become both firm and fantastic conjunctions of soft touches and hard lines. Works such as *Peplum VI* (2016) and *Jabot (starched and hinged)* (2018) directly address elements of Elizabethan or feminine dress, while the artist's *Samurai* (1980–83) and *Window Dressing* (2007–) series speak to aspects of theatrics, staging, and display. Reflective of Simpson's keen, careerlong focus on the relationship between function and form, her work articulates the ways in which perspective become tailored to the literal and metaphoric space one occupies, be it that of gender, class, or station. *R K*

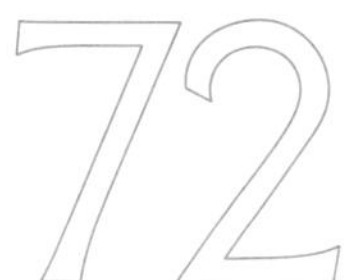

MARTINE SYMS

Martine Syms explores pervasive archetypes and mundane depictions of Black experience and femininity in America. Mining literature, the internet, film, and television, she considers how these representations gain power through circulation. Her work posits that ceaselessly consuming and sharing images forms a kind of surveillance—a sense we are always being watched—and that our identities are a performance.

Facetiously self-identifying as a "conceptual entrepreneur," Syms intervenes directly in the ubiquitous platforms we use for communication and identity production. Her practice is multifaceted, spanning film, performance, sculpture, graphic and web design, writing, and publishing. Whether in a PowerPoint presentation for her live, improvisational lecture *Misdirected Kiss* (2015) or in her augmented-reality app, *wyd rn* (2017, made in collaboration with digital strategy and design studio Special—Offer), which expands an installation of photographs into the digital space of a viewer's smartphone, Syms operates in the very infrastructures where images and their associations are disseminated. The strategy of layering in Syms's works—collaged images, overlaid narratives and personae, overlapping digital and analog modalities—underscores her position that identities are constructed and that the images we encounter mediate and politicize the personal and private. She weaves together tropes from entertainment and everyday life, from TED Talks and Tyra Banks "power poses" to a *Basketball Wives* gif to her own SMS messages.

Syms's addresses themes of

decorum and discipline in her recent film *Incense Sweaters & Ice* (2017), which centers around Girl, a liar who collects photographs. As in much of the artist's work, the film reaches beyond personal experience to the historical, drawing on Jacqueline Najuma Stewart's *Migrating to the Movies* (2005), which tracks the relationship between the Great Migration and the rise of urban moviegoing as a source of not only entertainment but also stereotypes and self-representations. In searing critiques tempered with humor and sincerity, Syms reflects on the way Black women are brought up to anticipate and react against racism in their self-presentation and challenges the archetype of struggle often imposed on women, especially women of color. *MK*

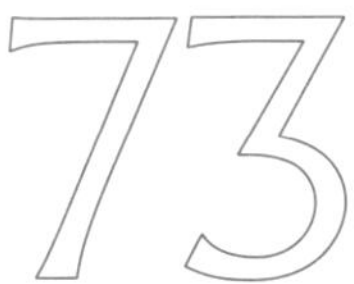

KYLE THURMAN

Kyle Thurman consumes, manipulates, and reproduces found objects and appropriated images, enacting a sequence of transformations that disrupts their original significations and allows new stories to emerge. In a group of paintings begun in 2010, Thurman boiled artificially dyed flowers found at urban markets in order to extract the synthetic pigments, which were then sprayed over the dried petals scattered on canvas to create random, allover patterns reminiscent of industrially fabricated textiles. Such a blurring of utility and form also characterizes the 2016 sculpture *matches*, which collides more deliberately with history. For this work, Thurman acquired an early-twentieth-century Tramp Art picture frame in the shape of a heart with two holes for photographs. The original

was scanned and digitally enlarged so that a new version could be 3-D printed and ultimately cast to become a cobalt blue glass wall hanging supported by a rusted nail. These transformative gestures convert a historical craft object into an industrially fabricated signifier of contemporary technological capability and its residual complications.

Since 2015, Thurman has engaged in a daily drawing practice that uses appropriated images from various news outlets as sources. He has assembled an ongoing archive of photographs focusing on the mass-media's proliferation of archetypal male figures, such as soldiers, athletes, and priests. Thurman removes the backgrounds from the originals, reducing the images to figures. Using these documents as references, he then creates sparse, near-life-size drawings with charcoal, pastel, pencil, and marker on seamless colored paper that offer hints of context through details such as watches, tattoos, combat boots, and earbuds. Titled chronologically, the framed *Suggested Occupation* drawings, like cells of a graphic novel, construct a slowly unfolding narrative taking up themes of social anxiety, conflict, biography, and psychology. The human scale of the works confronts both the viewer and the architecture in which they are presented and helps register the presence of the artist's body, with smudges and fingerprints creating an unusual physical encounter with media imagery. As the desensitizing cycle of digital consumption is slowed, the identities of the sleeping, stretching, fighting men are obscured and disjointed scenes of masculinity and sexuality unfold. *LO*

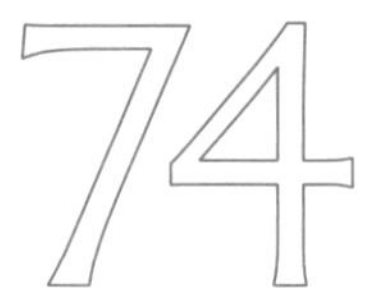

MARIANA VALENCIA

Mariana Valencia works in dance and choreography, her pratice intermingled with storytelling, object theater, and humor. She charismatically draws in audiences through layers of personal memory, sharing her reflections with an intense intimacy as if she were speaking to her closest friends. Valencia might deftly croon a popular song to provide an associative link from one flashback to another—the Fugees' "Killing Me Softly," for example, used in her recent solo work *ALBUM* (2017) to recall her early teens in Chicago. In the piece, she stitches together fragments of her childhood and family life—even an homage to her love of rice—and ends the performance by dancing a duet with her sweatshirt to Gloria Estefan's "Conga."

Valencia is also influenced by her family's history: her parents immigrated to the United States from Guatemala, shaping her investigation of culture, transmission of knowledge, and family in its myriad forms. Ethnographic research also provides a guide, with each new work beginning through a study of how societies share and merge traditions and beliefs. In her lecture-monologue *Originators* (2016), she combines a travelogue of observations compiled while researching the sonidero dance tradition in Mexico with personal anecdotes of her identity as a queer Latina. Valencia also takes inspiration from an ongoing writing practice that she refers to as "dance savings": an accumulation of journal entries, letters to collaborators, questions, observations, and drawings. Language is as central to her work as movement, with the artist creating juxtapositions between narrative content and physical form, for example tracing of a two-dimensional geometric representation of the universe on the floor while discussing Assotto Saint, a poet and performer who died during the AIDS crisis, as a way of recuperating his work and spirit. *GH*

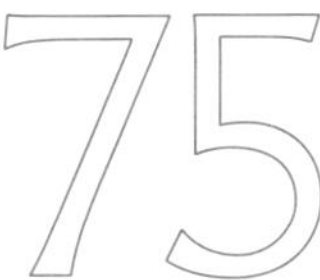

AGUSTINA WOODGATE

Agustina Woodgate's artwork mobilizes the symbolic resonances of familiar things through processes of material transformation. In *National Times* (2016), clock hands rigged with sandpaper slowly erase their own numbers; for *$8.05* (2016), currency equaling the artist's home state of Florida's minimum hourly wage is ground into a pile of dust; in *Cosmética* (*Cosmetic*, 2017), particles produced by erasing obsolete classroom maps are compressed into a cosmetics palette. In 2016, Woodgate installed *El palacio de las aguas corrientes* (*The Palace of the Running Waters*), a sculpture consisting of twelve functional drinking fountains, in a gallery located in a neighborhood of Buenos Aires in which clean water is often scarce. While these acts of iconoclasm have a playful, even humorous quality, they take as raw material the objects that structure our access to land, time, and resources. Woodgate is also a cofounder of TVGOV, a think tank for public finance reform that uses data to measure land depletion and in consequence encourages a sustainable use of natural resources. Whether reconfiguring objects, municipal infrastructure, or the tax code, Woodgate's projects creatively upend economic and political systems.

In 2011, Woodgate started Radioee.net (Radio Espacio Estación), a roving, translingual radio station that addresses issues of mobility, migration, and movement. Each broadcast lasts for twenty-four hours and takes place in a different location, from Berlin to Buenos Aires to the Amazon to Washington, DC, constructing through interviews, audio clips, and performances what the station calls an "audio portrait of a place in time." Often made while literally in transit—on board a boat in Miami, or walking the streets of Istanbul—recent episodes have addressed topics ranging from rising sea levels to slang and language learning. In connecting local communities to globally dispersed listeners, Radioee.net marshals networked audio space to intervene in and reshape political geographies. *FJP*

Contributors

Erika Balsom (EB)
Jessica Bell Brown (JBB)
Andrianna Campbell (AC)
Dessane Lopez Cassell (DLC)
Ashton Cooper (ASC)
Ayanna Dozier (AD)
Julia Pelta Feldman (JPF)
Alex Fialho (AF)
Carly Fischer (CF)
Leo Goldsmith (LG)
Marcela Guerrero (MG)
Greta Hartenstein (GH)
Carmen Hermo (CH)
Megan Heuer (MH)
Frances Jacobus-Parker (FJP)
Eunsong Kim (EK)
Danielle Rose King (DRK)
Ramsay Kolber (RK)
Lola Kramer (LK)
Margaret Kross (MK)
Christopher Y. Lew (CL)
Jessica Lynne (JL)
Lindsey O'Connor (LO)
Laura Phipps (LP)
Allie Rickard (AR)
Elisabeth Sherman (ES)

1 EDDIE ARROYO

5825 NE 2nd Ave., Miami, FL 33137, 2016. Acrylic on canvas, 36 × 48 in. (91.4 × 115.2 cm). Collection of the artist; courtesy the artist and Spinello Projects, Miami

5825 NE 2nd Ave., Miami, FL 33137, 2017. Acrylic on canvas, 28 × 36 in. (71.1 × 91.4 cm). Collection of the artist; courtesy the artist and Spinello Projects, Miami

5825 NE 2nd Ave., Miami, FL 33137, 2018. Acrylic on canvas, 27 × 39 in. (68.6 × 99.1 cm). Collection of Dr. Ernesto and Malena Erdmann

5901 NW 2nd Ave., Miami, FL 33127, 2018. Acrylic on canvas, 30 × 28 in. (76.2 × 71.1 cm). Collection the artist; courtesy the artist and Spinello Projects, Miami

Speak Early, Speak Proud, Speak Loud, 2018. Acrylic on canvas, 30 × 24 in. (76.2 × 60 cm). Collection of the artist; courtesy the artist and Spinello Projects, Miami

2 KORAKRIT ARUNANONDCHAI

with history in a room filled with people with funny names 4, 2017. High-definition video, color, sound; 23:32 min. Collection of the artist; courtesy the artist; Clearing, New York and Brussels; and Carlos/Ishikawa, London

3 OLGA BALEMA

A selection of sculptures, 2016–19. Mixed media, various dimensions. Collection of the artist; courtesy the artist; High Art, New York; and Hannah Hoffman, Los Angeles

4 MORGAN BASSICHIS

Nibbling the Hand That Feeds Me, 2019. Performance. Courtesy the artist

5 BLITZ BAZAWULE

The Burial of Kojo, 2018. High-definition video, color, sound; 80 min. Courtesy the artist

6 ALEXANDRA BELL

A selection of works from *No Humans Involved: After Sylvia Wynter*, 2018–19. Photolithography and screenprint on paper, 22 ½ × 17 in. (57.2 × 43.2 cm) each. Collection of the artist

7 BRIAN BELOTT

Untitled, 2018. Mixed media in ice in freezer, 79 × 27 × 32 in. (200.7 × 68.8 × 81.3 cm). Collection of the artist; courtesy the artist and Gavin Brown's enterprise, New York and Rome

Untitled, 2018. Mixed media in ice in freezer, 79 × 27 × 32 in. (200.7 × 68.8 × 81.3 cm). Collection of the artist; courtesy the artist and Gavin Brown's enterprise, New York and Rome

Untitled, 2018. Mixed media in ice in freezer, 79 ×

27 × 32 in. (200.7 × 68.8 × 81.3 cm). Collection of the artist; courtesy the artist and Gavin Brown's enterprise, New York and Rome

Untitled (Fan Puff), 2016. Mixed media, 83 × 73 × 8 ½ in. (210.8 × 185.4 × 21.6 cm). Collection of the artist; courtesy the artist and Gavin Brown's enterprise, New York and Rome

8 MERIEM BENNANI

A selection of as-yet-untitled viewing stations, 2019. Mixed media, dimensions unknown. Collection of the artist

9 ROBERT BITTENBENDER

Broadway Nights, 2015. Mixed media, dimensions variable. Private collection

Sister Carrie, 2017. Mixed media, 32 × 24 × 18 in. (81.3 × 61 × 45.7 cm). Collection of the artist; courtesy the artist and Lomex, New York

Untitled, 2017. Acrylic and graphite on foam board with found objects, 23 ⅝ × 20 ⅞ in. (60 × 75 cm). Collection of the artist; courtesy the artist and Lomex, New York

A sculpture, date unknown. Mixed media, dimensions unknown. Collection of the artist; courtesy the artist and Lomex, New York

10 LUCAS BLALOCK

Bananas, 2018. Inkjet print mounted on aluminum,

16 × 20 in. (40.6 × 50.8 cm). Collection of the artist; courtesy the artist; Galerie Eva Presenhuber, New York and Zurich; and Rodolphe Janssen, Brussels

Donkeys Crossing the Desert, 2019. Inkjet print on vinyl and app, 17 × 29 ft. (5.2 × 8.8 m). Collection of the artist; courtesy the artist; Galerie Eva Presenhuber, New York and Zurich; and Rodolphe Janssen, Brussels

The Nonconformist, 2017–19. Inkjet print mounted on aluminum, 85 × 60 in. (215.9 × 152.4 cm). Collection of the artist; courtesy the artist; Galerie Eva Presenhuber, New York and Zurich; and Rodolphe Janssen, Brussels

Some Eggs, 2018. Inkjet print mounted on aluminum, 36 × 42 in. (91.4 × 106.7 cm). Collection of the artist; courtesy the artist; Galerie Eva Presenhuber, New York and Zurich; and Rodolphe Janssen, Brussels

11 GARRETT BRADLEY

A.K.A., 2019. High-definition video, color, sound; run time unknown. Courtesy the artist

12 MILANO CHOW

Floor Plan I, 2019. Graphite, ink, vinyl paint, and photo transfer on paper, 30 ½ × 26 ¾ in. (77.5 × 67.9 cm). Collection of the artist; courtesy the artist; Chapter NY, New York; and Mary Mary, Glasgow

Floor Plan II, 2019. Graphite, ink, vinyl paint, and photo transfer on paper, 30 ½ × 26 ¾ in. (77.5 × 67.9 cm). Collection of the artist; courtesy the artist; Chapter NY, New York; and Mary Mary, Glasgow

Night Exterior I, 2019. Graphite, ink, vinyl paint, and photo transfer on paper, 23 × 43 ¾ in. (58.42 × 111.1 cm). Collection of the artist; courtesy the artist; Chapter NY, New York; and Mary Mary, Glasgow

Night Exterior II, 2019. Graphite, ink, vinyl paint, and photo transfer on paper, 23 × 40 in. (58.42 × 101.6 cm). Collection of the artist; courtesy the artist; Chapter NY, New York; and Mary Mary, Glasgow

Night Exterior III, 2019. Graphite, ink, vinyl paint, and photo transfer on paper, 23 × 40 in. (58.42 × 101.6 cm). Collection of the artist; courtesy the artist; Chapter NY, New York; and Mary Mary, Glasgow

13 COLECTIVO LOS INGRÁVIDOS

Impresiones para una máquina de luz y sonido (*Impressions of a Sound and Light Machine*), 2014. 16mm film, black-and-white, sound; 7 min. Courtesy the artists

Itzcóatl, 2014. 16mm film, color, sound; 5 min. Courtesy the artists

14 THIRZA CUTHAND

Just Dandy, 2013. High-definition video, color, sound; 7:37 min. Courtesy the artist

2 Spirit Introductory Special $19.99, 2015. High-definition video, color, sound; 4:27 min. Courtesy the artist

15 JOHN EDMONDS

A selection of photographs from *Tribe*, 2018. Inkjet prints, various dimensions. Collection of the artist; courtesy the artist and Company Gallery, New York

Five black-and-white photographs, 2019. Inkjet prints, various dimensions. Collection of the artist; courtesy the artist and Company Gallery, New York

16 NICOLE EISENMAN

Procession, 2019. Bronze, plaster, steel, cloth, fiberglass, fog machine, aluminum, silicone, paint, leather, video, and mixed media. Works include:

The General, 2018
Head with Demon, 2018
Insubstantial Subjects, 2019
Man at the Center of Men, 2019
Museum Piece con Gas, 2019
Perpetual Motion Machine, 2019
Pole Bearer, 2019
Sherpson, 2018
Three Walkers, 2019

The General: Collection of Eric Green. Other works: Collection of the artist; courtesy the artist; Susanne Vielmetter Los Angeles Projects; and Anton Kern, New York

17 JANIVA ELLIS

As-yet-untitled painting, 2019. Oil on canvas, 9 × 21 ½ ft. (2.74 × 6.55 m). Collection of the artist; courtesy the artist and 47 Canal, New York

18 KOTA EZAWA

National Anthem, 2018. High-definition video projection, sound, color; 2:07 min. Collection of the artist; courtesy the artist and Haines Gallery, San Francisco

National Anthem (Buffalo Bills), 2018. Watercolor on paper, 11 × 16 in. (26.4 × 40.6 cm). Collection of the artist; courtesy the artist and Haines Gallery, San Francisco

National Anthem (Denver Broncos), 2018. Watercolor on paper, 9 × 19 in. (21.6 × 48.3 cm). Collection of the artist; courtesy the artist and Haines Gallery, San Francisco

National Anthem (Jacksonville Jaguars), 2018. Watercolor on paper, 8 × 23 in. (20.3 × 58.4 cm). Collection of the artist; courtesy the artist and Haines Gallery, San Francisco

National Anthem (The Roar of the Jaguars), 2018. Watercolor on paper, 13 × 23 in. (33 × 58.4 cm). Collection of the artist; courtesy the artist and Haines Gallery, San Francisco

19 BRENDAN FERNANDES

The Master and Form, 2018. Steel scaffolding, ropes, audio recording, and performance. Works include:

In Arabesque, 2018. Ash wood with leather and carpet, 43 ¾ × 10 ¼ × 10 ¼ in. (111.1 × 26 × 26 cm)

In Cambré à Terre, 2018. Stained ash wood, leather, and carpet, 50 ¾ × 62 ½ × 3–8 ¼ in. (128.9 × 6.4 × 8.3–21 cm)

In First, in Fifth, 2018. Ash wood, leather, and carpet, 48 ¾ × 21 ¾ × 24 ¼ in. (123.8 × 55.2 × 61.6 cm)

In Passé, in Fourth, 2018. Stained ash wood, leather, and carpet, 80 × 42 ¼ × 2–4 ¼ in. (203.2 × 61.6 × 5.1–10.8 cm). Joyner/ Giuffrida Collection

In Second, 2018. Ash wood, leather, and carpet, 6 × 1 ¾ × 71 in. (15.2 × 4.4 × 180.3 cm). Rennie Collection, Vancouver

Collection of the artist; courtesy the artist and Monique Meloche Gallery, Chicago, unless otherwise noted. Originally commissioned by the Graham Foundation for Advanced Studies in the Fine Arts, Chicago. Design: Norman Kelley

20 FIERCE AND PAPER TIGER TELEVISION

Fenced Out, 2001. Video, color, sound; 20 min. Courtesy FIERCE, New Neutral Zone, and Paper Tiger Television

21 MARCUS FISCHER

Ascent/Dissent, 2019. Sound installation; run time unknown. Collection of the artist

Untitled (Words of Concern), 2017. Tape recorder, tape loop, spindle, sound; 3 min., overall dimensions variable. Collection of the artist

22 FORENSIC ARCHITECTURE

77sqm_9:26min, 2017. High-definition video, color, sound; run time unknown. Collection of the artists; commissioned by the People's Tribunal "Unraveling the NSU Complex"; Haus der Kulturen der Welt, Berlin; and Documenta 14

23 ELLIE GA

Gyres 1–5, 2019. Multichannel video, color, sound; run time unknown, overall dimensions variable. Collection of the artist; courtesy the artist and Bureau, New York

24 NICHOLAS GALANIN

A selection of photographs from *Kill the Indian, Save the Man*, 2016. Inkjet prints, 14 × 19 in. (35.6 × 48.3 cm) each. Collection of the artist

As-yet-untitled installation, 2019. Medium unknown, dimensions unknown. Collection of the artist

25 SOFÍA GALLISÁ MURIENTE

Lluvia con nieve (Rain with Snow), 2014. Video, black-and-white, sound; 13:32 min. Collection of the artist

26 JEFFREY GIBSON

PEOPLE LIKE US, 2019. Canvas, cotton, linen, brass grommets, nylon thread, cotton thread, artificial sinew, glass, stone, and plastic beads, nylon fringe, grosgrain ribbon, tin jingles, wooden tipi poles, and deer hide; garment: 120 × 74 × 8 in. (304.8 × 188 × 20.3 cm), pole: 4 × 120 × 4 in. (10.2 × 304.8 × 10.2 cm). Collection of the artist; courtesy of the artist; Sikkema Jenkins & Co., New York; Kavi Gupta, Chicago; and Roberts Projects, Los Angeles

STAND YOUR GROUND, 2019. Canvas, cotton, linen, polyester, nylon, vinyl, sequins, brass grommets, nylon thread, cotton thread, artificial sinew, glass beads, nylon fringe, grosgrain ribbon, copper jingles, wooden tipi poles, and deer hide; garments: 108 × 74 × 8 in. (274.3 × 188 × 20.3 cm) each, pole: 4 × 120 × 4 in. (10.2 × 304.8 × 10.2 cm) pole. Collection of the artist; courtesy of the artist; Sikkema Jenkins & Co., New York; Kavi Gupta, Chicago; and Roberts Projects, Los Angeles

As yet untitled, 2019. Fabric, glass and plastic beads, brass grommets, nylon ribbon, polyester laces, acrylic on canvas, and artificial sinew, approximately 5 ½ × 18 ft. (1.7 × 5.5 m). Collection of the artist; courtesy the artist; Sikkema Jenkins & Co., New York; Kavi Gupta, Chicago; and Roberts Projects, Los Angeles

27 TODD GRAY

Euclidean Gris Gris 2, 2018. Four inkjet prints in artist's and found frames, 74 × 47 × 5 ½ in. (188 × 119.4 × 14 cm). Collection of the artist; courtesy the artist and David Lewis, New York

Pax 3, 2017. Three inkjet prints in artist's and found frames, 48 ¾ × 38 ½ × 3 ½ in. (123.8 × 97.8 × 8.9 cm). Private collection

Slipping into Darkness, All the Honey Gone, 2018. Three inkjet prints in artist's frames and found frames, 51 ½ × 60 ½ × 4 ½ in. (130.8 × 153.7 × 11.4 cm). Collection of the artist; courtesy the artist and Meliksetian | Briggs, West Hollywood, CA

28 SAM GREEN

As-yet-untitled video performance, 2019. Video, color, sound, run time unknown, and live performance. Courtesy the artist

29 BARBARA HAMMER

History Lessons Redux, 2000/2019. Live slideshow, 16mm film transferred to video, color, sound. Courtesy the artist

30 ILANA
   HARRIS-BABOU

Human Design, 2019.
High-definition video, color,
sound; run time unknown.
Collection of the artist

Red Sourcebook, 2018.
High-definition video,
color, sound; 4:11 min.
Collection of the artist

Reparation Hardware,
2018. High-definition
video, color, sound; 4:05
min. Collection of the artist

31 MATTHEW ANGELO
   HARRISON

Bodily Study: Binary Rest,
2019. Zebra skulls and
resin, 29 × 15 × 15 in. (73.7 ×
38.1 × 38.1 cm). Collection
of the artist; courtesy the
artist and Jessica Silverman
Gallery, San Francisco

*Dark Silhouette: Remnant
for Disruption*, 2019.
Malian spears and tinted
resin, 96 × 6 × 6 in. (243.8 ×
15.2 × 15.2 cm). Collection
of the artist; courtesy the
artist and Jessica Silverman
Gallery, San Francisco

*Dark Silhouette: Remnant
for Disruption*, 2019.
Malian spears and tinted
resin, 96 × 6 × 6 in. (243.8 ×
15.2 × 15.2 cm). Collection
of the artist; courtesy the
artist and Jessica Silverman
Gallery, San Francisco

*Dark Silhouette: Remnant
for Disruption*, 2019.
Malian spears and tinted
resin, 96 × 6 × 6 in. (243.8 ×
15.2 × 15.2 cm). Collection
of the artist; courtesy the
artist and Jessica Silverman
Gallery, San Francisco

*Dark Silhouette: Suku
Adaptation*, 2019. African
masks and resin, 72 × 12 ×
13 in. (182.9 × 30.5 × 33 cm).
Collection of the artist;
courtesy the artist and
Jessica Silverman Gallery,
San Francisco

*Dark Silhouette: Suku
Adaptation*, 2019. African
masks and resin, 72 × 12 ×
13 in. (182.9 × 30.5 × 33 cm).
Collection of the artist;
courtesy the artist and
Jessica Silverman Gallery,
San Francisco

*Template for Vagrant
Biographies*, 2019.
Clothing, African sculp-
tures, and resin, 54 ×
36 × 16 in. (137.2 × 91.4 ×
40.6 cm). Collection of the
artist; courtesy the artist
and Jessica Silverman
Gallery, San Francisco

32 CURRAN HATLEBERG

Riverfront, 2013. Inkjet
print, image: 21 × 26 ⅛ in.
(53.3 × 66.4 cm). Collection
of the artist; courtesy the
artist and Higher Pictures,
New York

Untitled (Afternoon), 2018.
Inkjet print, image: 16 ½ ×
20 ½ in. (41.9 × 52.1 cm).
Collection of the artist;
courtesy the artist and
Higher Pictures, New York

Untitled (Blue Truck),
2016. Inkjet print, image:
26 × 32 ½ in. (66 × 82.6 cm).
Collection of the artist;
courtesy the artist and
Higher Pictures, New York

Untitled (Camaro), 2017.
Inkjet print, image: 19 ×
23 ½ in. (48.3 × 59.7 cm).
Collection of the artist;

courtesy the artist and
Higher Pictures, New York

Untitled (Dominoes), 2016.
Inkjet print, image: 26 ¼ ×
21 in. (66.7 × 53.3 cm).
Collection of the artist;
courtesy the artist and
Higher Pictures, New York

Untitled (Front Porch),
2013. Inkjet print, image:
14 × 17 ½ in. (35.6 ×
44.5 cm). Collection of the
artist; courtesy the artist
and Higher Pictures,
New York

Untitled (Girl with Snake),
2016. Inkjet print, image:
23 ¼ × 29 ¼ in. (59.1 ×
74.3 cm). Collection of the
artist; courtesy the artist
and Higher Pictures,
New York

Untitled (Hole), 2016.
Inkjet print, image: 23 ¼ ×
29 ¼ in. (59.1 × 74.3 cm).
Collection of the artist;
courtesy the artist and
Higher Pictures, New York

Untitled (Mantis), 2018.
Inkjet print, image: 20 ×
25 in. (50.8 × 63.5 cm).
Collection of the artist;
courtesy the artist and
Higher Pictures, New York

*Untitled (Man with
Bees)*, 2017. Inkjet print,
image: 17 × 21 ⅛ in. (43.2 ×
53.7 cm). Collection of the
artist; courtesy the artist
and Higher Pictures,
New York

Untitled (Picnic), 2017.
Inkjet print, image: 14 ×
17 ½ in. (35.6 × 44.5 cm).
Collection of the artist;
courtesy the artist
and Higher Pictures,
New York

Untitled (Stoop), 2015.
Inkjet print, image: 17 ½ ×
14 in. (44.5 × 35.6 cm).
Collection of the artist;
courtesy the artist and
Higher Pictures, New York

*Untitled (Watermelon
with Bees)*, 2017. Inkjet
print, image: 23 ¼ × 29 ¼ in.
(59.1 × 74.3 cm). Collection
of the artist; courtesy the
artist and Higher Pictures,
New York

33 MADELINE
   HOLLANDER

As-yet-untitled perfor-
mance, 2019. Courtesy
the artist

34 IMAN ISSA

A selection of sculptures
from *Heritage Studies*,
2016–19. Mixed media,
various dimensions.
Collection of the artist;
courtesy the artist and
Rodeo, London and
Piraeus, Greece

35 TOMASHI JACKSON

Home Taste Like Home,
2019. Acrylic, oil, reflective
paper, and sand on
paper, gauze, and canvas,
dimensions unknown.
Collection of the artist;
courtesy the artist and
Tilton Gallery, New York

As-yet-untitled work, 2019.
Mixed media, 40 ¼ × 111 ½ ×
42 ¼ in. (102.2 × 283.2 ×
107.3 cm). Collection of the
artist; courtesy the artist
and Tilton Gallery,
New York

As-yet-untitled work, 2019.
Acrylic, oil, reflective paper,
and sand on paper, gauze,

and canvas, dimensions unknown. Collection of the artist; courtesy the artist and Tilton Gallery, New York

36 STEFFANI JEMISON

Sensus Plenior, 2017. High-definition video, black-and-white, sound; 34:36 min. Courtesy the artist. Coproduction: Jeu de Paume; Fondation Nationale des Arts Graphiques et Plastiques, Paris; and CAPC Musée d'Art Contemporain de Bordeaux

37 ADAM KHALIL, ZACK KHALIL, AND JACKSON POLYS

The Violence of a Civilization without Secrets, 2017. High-definition video, color, sound; 10 min. Courtesy the artists. Produced by inhabitants.tv, Mariana Silva, and Pedro Neves Marques

As-yet-untitled video, 2019. High-definition video, color, sound; run time unknown. Courtesy the artists

38 CHRISTINE SUN KIM

Degrees of Deaf Rage Concerning Interpreters (terps), 2018. Charcoal and oil pastel on paper, 49 ¼ × 49 ¼ in. (125 × 125 cm). Collection of Du Yan

Degrees of Deaf Rage in Everyday Situations, 2018. Charcoal and oil pastel on paper, 49 ¼ × 49 ¼ in. (125 × 125 cm). Collection of Du Yan

Degrees of Deaf Rage While Traveling, 2018. Charcoal and oil pastel on paper, 49 ¼ × 49 ¼ in. (125 × 125 cm). Collection of Du Yan

Degrees of Deaf Rage within Educational Settings, 2018. Charcoal and oil pastel on paper, 49 ¼ × 49 ¼ in. (125 × 125 cm). Collection of Du Yan

Degrees of Institutional Deaf Rage, 2018. Charcoal and oil pastel on paper, 49 ¼ × 49 ¼ in. (125 × 125 cm). Collection of Du Yan

Degrees of My Deaf Rage in the Art World, 2018. Charcoal and oil pastel on paper, 49 ¼ × 49 ¼ in. (125 × 125 cm). Collection of Du Yan

39 JOSH KLINE

Six as-yet-untitled works, 2019. Mixed media, 24 × 20 in. (61 × 50.8 cm) each. Collection of the artist; courtesy the artist; 47 Canal, New York; and Modern Art, London

40 AUTUMN KNIGHT

Roaches Aren't the Easiest Creatures to Milk, 2017. Video, color, sound; 5:20 min. Courtesy the artist

Sanity TV, 2016–. Performance in three parts. Courtesy the artist

41 CAROLYN LAZARD

As-yet-untitled installation, 2019. Wall-arm medical mounts, monitors, and high-definition video; color, sound, run time unknown, overall dimensions variable. Collection of the artist

42 MAIA RUTH LEE

Bondage Baggage 4, 2018. Tarp, rope, tape, luggage, bedding, and used clothing, 67 × 35 × 21 in. (170.2 × 88.9 × 53.3 cm). Collection of the artist

Bondage Baggage 5, 2018. Tarp, rope, tape, luggage, and burlap, 44 × 19 ½ × 21 ½ in. (111.8 × 49.5 × 54.6 cm). Collection of the artist

As-yet-untitled installation, 2019. Steel, dimensions variable. Collection of the artist

43 SIMONE LEIGH

#8 Village Series, 2019. Ceramic, 5 × 4 × 4 ft. (1.5 × 1.2 × 1.2 m). Collection of the artist; courtesy the artist and Luhring Augustine, New York

Sphinx, 2019. Bronze and raffia, 73 × 73 × 43 in. (185.4 × 185.4 × 109.2 cm). Collection of the artist; courtesy the artist and Luhring Augustine, New York

Stick, 2019. Bronze, 85 × 63 × 63 in. (215.9 × 160 × 160 cm). Collection of the artist; courtesy the artist and Luhring Augustine, New York

44 DANIEL LIND-RAMOS

Centinelas (Sentinels), 2013. Steel bars, palm-tree trunk, burlap, plywood, rope, spoons, mirrors, earth, steel tubes, tools, cauldron, palm-tree branches, and wire, 120 × 114 × 48 in. (304.8 × 289.6 × 121.9 cm). Collection of the artist

Maria-Maria, 2019. Metal basin, wooden seat, lamp, tarp, coconuts, palm-tree trunk, steel sheet, rope, beads, fabric, tacks, wood, plastic tubing, steel bars, scissors, and wooden box, dimensions unknown. Collection of the artist

1797: Vencedor (1797: Victorious), 2017–18. Burlap, fabric, palm-tree trunks, wooden seat, steel sheet, boot, tacks, bells, rope, plastic bags, baseball glove, coconut, tools, masking tape, shovel, machete, mirror, ribbon, pins, and wire, 67 × 33 × 70 in. (170.2 × 83.8 × 177.8 cm). Collection of the artist

45 JAMES LUNA

History of the Luiseño People, 1993. Video, color, sound; 27 min. Courtesy the artist's estate and Video Data Bank, School of the Art Institute of Chicago

46 ERIC N. MACK

A selection of as-yet-untitled works, 2019. Fabric, dye, acrylic, pins, and thread, dimensions unknown. Collection of the artist; courtesy the artist; Morán Morán, Los Angeles; and Simon Lee, London

47 CALVIN MARCUS

Conspiracy of Asses, 2019.
Watercolor and vinyl paint
on linen, 79 × 101 ⅝ in.
(22.9 × 258 cm). Collection
of the artist; courtesy the
artist; Clearing, New York
and Brussels; and David
Kordansky Gallery,
Los Angeles

As-yet-untitled painting,
2018–19. Watercolor
and vinyl paint on linen,
79 × 101 ⅝ in. (22.9 ×
258 cm). Collection of
the artist; courtesy the
artist; Clearing, New York
and Brussels; and David
Kordansky Gallery,
Los Angeles

As-yet-untitled painting,
2018–19. Watercolor
and vinyl paint on linen,
101 ⅝ × 79 in. (258 ×
22.9 cm). Collection of
the artist; courtesy the
artist; Clearing, New York
and Brussels; and David
Kordansky Gallery,
Los Angeles

As-yet-untitled painting,
2018–19. Watercolor
and vinyl paint on linen,
101 ⅝ × 79 in. (258 ×
22.9 cm). Collection of
the artist; courtesy the
artist; Clearing, New York
and Brussels; and David
Kordansky Gallery,
Los Angeles

48 TIONA NEKKIA
McCLODDEN

*I prayed to the wrong
god for you*, 2019. Multichannel video installation,
color, sound; running
time unknown, and six
hand-carved tools in
vitrine, overall dimensions
unknown. Collection of the
artist; courtesy the artist
and Company Gallery,
New York

49 TROY MICHIE

*Borderwalk / This Thin
Edge of Barbed Wire*,
2019. Found photograph,
paper, tape, papier-mâché,
cardboard, clothing, belt,
ink, graphite, wax pencil,
and acrylic on woven
magazine pages, 51 ×
40 in. (129.5 × 101.6 cm).
Collection of the artist;
courtesy the artist and
Company Gallery,
New York

*Hung Out to Dry / This
Land Was Mexican Once*,
2019. Found photograph,
paper, tape, papier-mâché,
garment bag, towel,
rope, clothing, belt, ink,
graphite, wax pencil, and
acrylic on woven magazine
pages, 51 × 40 in. (129.5 ×
101.6 cm). Collection of the
artist; courtesy the artist
and Company Gallery,
New York

*Los atravesados / The Skin
of the Earth Is Seamless*,
2019. Found photograph,
paper, tape, papier-mâché,
canvas, clothing, belt, ink,
graphite, wax pencil, and
acrylic on woven magazine
pages, 51 × 40 in. (129.5 ×
101.6 cm). Collection of the
artist; courtesy the artist

and Company Gallery,
New York

*Yo soy un puente tendido /
This Is My Home*, 2019.
Paper, tape, canvas, papier-
mâché, towel, clothing, ink,
graphite, wax pencil, and
acrylic on woven magazine
pages, 51 × 40 in. (129.5 ×
101.6 cm). Collection of the
artist; courtesy the artist
and Company Gallery,
New York

50 JOE MINTER

The First Fireplace, 1998.
Mixed media, 55 × 36 ×
13.5 in. (139.7 × 91.4 ×
34.3 cm). Arnett Collection

Lightening the Load,
2004. Mixed media, 56 ×
18 × 18 in. (142.3 × 45.7 ×
45.7 cm). Arnett Collection

'63 Foot Soldiers, 1999.
License plates, shoes, toys,
chains, metal grate, paint,
plastic, and clothes, 59 ×
81 × 31 in. (149.9 × 205.7 ×
78.7 cm). Birmingham
Museum of Art, AL,
Museum purchase with
funds provided by Mr. and
Mrs. James Outland

Three Flying Saucers,
2000. Mixed media, 58 ×
41 × 23 in. (147.3 × 104.1 ×
58.4 cm). Arnett Collection

51 KEEGAN
MONAGHAN

Blue Door, 2019. Oil on
canvas, 78 ⅛ × 60 ⅛ in.
(198.4 × 152.7 cm).
Collection of the artist;
courtesy the artist and James
Fuentes Gallery, New York

Incoming, 2016–17.
Oil on canvas, 60 ⅜ ×

72 in. (153.4 × 182.9 cm).
Collection of Ninah and
Michael Lynne

Puddle, 2019. Oil on
canvas, 60 ¼ × 72 ⅛ in.
(153 × 183.2 cm). Collection
of the artist; courtesy the
artist and James Fuentes
Gallery, New York

52 CAROLINE MONNET

Creatura Dada, 2016.
16mm film, color, sound;
4 min. Courtesy the artist

Gephyrophobia, 2012.
16mm film, black-and-
white, sound; 3 min.
Courtesy the artist

Mobilize, 2015. Video,
color, sound; 3 min.
Courtesy the artist

53 DARIUS CLARK
MONROE

*All Iowa Lawn Tennis
Club*, 2019. 16mm film
transferred to high-
definition video, color,
sound; 15 min. Collection
of the artist; courtesy the
artist and Topic Studios,
New York

Maravilla, 2019. Archival
films transferred to high-
definition video, color and
black-and-white, sound;
8 min. Collection of the
artist; courtesy the artist
and Topic Studios,
New York

Serve, 2019. 16mm film
transferred to high-
definition video, color and
black-and-white, sound;
15 min. Collection of the
artist; courtesy the artist
and Topic Studios,
New York

South Oxford, 2019.
16mm film transferred to
high-definition video, color,
sound; 11 min. Collection
of the artist; courtesy the
artist and Topic Studios,
New York

54 RAGEN MOSS

Author (with Arm), 2018.
Acrylic, polyethylene,
copper, and steel hardware,
51 × 38 ½ × 12 in. (129.5 ×
97.8 × 30.5 cm). Collection
of the artist

*Bullfighter (with 2 other
Bullfighters)*, 2019. Acrylic,
polyethylene, aluminum,
and steel hardware, 52 ×
36 × 25 in. (132.1 × 91.4 ×
63.5 cm). Collection of the
artist

Driver (with Passenger),
November 2018. Acrylic,
polyethylene, aluminum,
and steel hardware, 53 ×
30 × 22 in. (134.6 × 76.2 ×
55.9 cm). Collection of the
artist

Figure (with Arm), 2018.
Acrylic, polyethylene,
copper, and steel hardware,
51 × 38 ½ × 12 in. (129.5 ×
97.8 × 30.5 cm). Collection
of the artist

Miner, 2019. Acrylic,
polyethylene, cotton,
charcoal, copper, and steel
hardware, 43 × 35 × 12 in.
(109.2 × 88.9 × 30.5 cm).
Collection of the artist

Ogler, 2018. Acrylic,
polyethylene, copper, and
steel hardware, 43 ½ × 22 ×
15 ½ in. (110.5 × 55.9 ×
39.4 cm). Collection of the
artist

*Romanettes (with double
Hearts)*, 2018. Acrylic,
polyethylene, aluminum,
and steel hardware; two
components, 24 ½ × 15 ×
8 ½ in. (62.2 × 38.1 ×
21.6 cm) each. Collection
of the artist

*Shimmier (with Torso,
with Heart)*, 2018. Acrylic,
polyethylene, copper, and
steel hardware, 43 ½ × 22 ×
15 ½ in. (110.5 × 55.9 ×
39.4 cm). Collection of
the artist

*Theoloogian [sic] (with
Torso)*, 2018. Acrylic,
polyethylene, aluminum,
and steel hardware, 43 ½ ×
22 × 15 ½ in. (110.5 × 55.9 ×
39.4 cm). Collection of the
artist

55 SAHRA MOTALEBI

Directory of Portrayals,
2019. Performance and
installation, dimensions
variable. Courtesy the
artist

56 MARLON MULLEN

untitled, 2017. Acrylic on
canvas, 36 × 36 in. (91.4 ×
91.4 cm). Collection of the
artist; courtesy the artist;
JTT, New York; and Adams
and Ollman, Portland, OR

untitled, 2018. Acrylic on
canvas, 24 × 16 in. (61 ×
40.6 cm). Collection of the
artist; courtesy the artist;
JTT, New York; and Adams
and Ollman, Portland, OR

untitled, 2018. Acrylic on
canvas, 36 × 26 in. (91.4 ×
66 cm). Collection of the
artist; courtesy the artist;
JTT, New York; and Adams
and Ollman, Portland, OR

untitled, 2018. Acrylic on
canvas, 36 × 36 in. (91.4 ×
91.4 cm). Collection of the
artist; courtesy the artist;
JTT, New York; and Adams
and Ollman, Portland, OR

untitled, 2018. Acrylic on
canvas, 40 × 52 in. (101.6 ×
132.1 cm). Collection of
the artist; courtesy the
artist; JTT, New York;
and Adams and Ollman,
Portland, OR

57 JEANETTE MUNDT

*Born Athlete American: Aly
Raisman II*, 2018. Oil and
glitter on canvas, 40 × 76 in.
(101.6 × 193 cm). Collection
of Andrew Black

*Born Athlete American:
Laurie Hernandez I*, 2018.
Oil and glitter on canvas,
50 × 60 in. (127 × 152.4 cm).
Collection of the artist;
courtesy the artist and
Société, Berlin

*Born Athlete American:
Simone Biles I*, 2017. Oil on
canvas, 42 × 50 in. (106.7 ×
127 cm). Jansen Collection,
Germany

*Born Athlete American:
Simone Biles III*, 2019. Oil
and glitter on canvas, 50 ×
60 in. (127 × 152.4 cm).
Collection of the artist;
courtesy the artist and
Société, Berlin

58 WANGECHI MUTU

*Poems by my great
grandmother I*, 2017.
Mixed media including
red soil, cow horn, wood,
paper pulp, aluminum
pots, metal rods, and
graphite, dimensions
variable. Collection of the

artist; courtesy the artist;
Gladstone Gallery, New
York; and Victoria Miro,
London

Sentinel I, 2018. Paper pulp,
wood glue, concrete, wood,
glass beads, stone, rose
quartz, gourd, and jewelry,
87 ¾ × 17 ¾ × 22 in. (222.9 ×
45.1 × 55.9 cm). Collection
of the artist; courtesy the
artist; Gladstone Gallery,
New York; and Victoria
Miro, London

Sentinel II, 2018. Paper
pulp, wood glue, concrete,
wood, beads, stones, rose
quartz, and bone, 78 ¾ ×
25 ½ × 22 ½ in. (200 × 64.8 ×
57.2 cm). Collection of the
artist; courtesy the artist;
Gladstone Gallery, New
York; and Victoria Miro,
London

59 LAS NIETAS DE
NONÓ

*Ilustraciones de la
mecánica (Illustrations
of the Mechanical)*, 2016.
Performance. Courtesy
the artists

60 JENN NKIRU

As-yet-untitled video,
2019. High-definition
video, color, sound; run
time unknown. Courtesy
the artist. Produced by
Iconoclast

61 LAURA ORTMAN

My Soul Remainer, 2017.
High-definition video,
color, sound; 5:44 min.
Directed by Nanobah
Becker (Diné). Shot by
Blackhorse Lowe (Diné).
Recorded by Martin Bisio.
Courtesy the artist

62 JENNIFER PACKER

The Body Has Memory, 2018. Oil on canvas, 60 × 48 in. (152.4 × 121.9 cm). Collection of Miyoung Lee and Neil Simpkins

Cheyenne, 2018. Oil on canvas, 40 × 40 in. (101.6 × 101.6 cm). Collection of the artist; courtesy the artist; Corvi-Mora, London; and Sikkema Jenkins & Co., New York

An Exercise in Tenderness, 2017. Oil on canvas, 9 ½ × 7 in. (24 × 18 cm). Private collection

A Lesson in Longing, 2019. Oil on canvas, 102 × 105 in. (259.1 × 266.7 cm). Courtesy the artist, Corvi-Mora, London; and Sikkema Jenkins & Co., New York

As-yet-untitled painting, 2019. Oil on canvas, dimensions unknown. Courtesy the artist, Corvi-Mora, London; and Sikkema Jenkins & Co., New York

63 NIBIA PASTRANA SANTIAGO

objetos indispuestos o inauguraciones suspendidas o finales inevitables para un casi-baile (*indisposed objects or suspended inaugurations or inevitable endings for an almost dance*), 2019. Performance. Courtesy the artist

64 ELLE PÉREZ

Eight as-yet-untitled photographs, 2019. Inkjet prints, approximately

52 × 36 ⅝ in. (132.1 × 93 cm) each. Collection of the artist; courtesy the artist and 47 Canal, New York

65 PAT PHILLIPS

The Farm, 2018. Acrylic, oil pastel, airbrush, and aerosol paint on canvas, 79 × 54 in. (200.7 × 137.2 cm). Courtesy the artist

Mandingo / DON'T TREAD ON ME, 2018. Acrylic, oil pastel, airbrush, and aerosol paint on canvas, 52 × 60 in. (132.1 × 152.4 cm). Courtesy the artist

As-yet-untitled site-specific mural, 2019. Acrylic, oil pastel, airbrush, wood, and aerosol paint, dimensions unknown. Courtesy the artist

66 GALA PORRAS-KIM

A work on paper, 2019. Graphite on paper, Plexiglas, and felt-tip pen, dimensions unknown. Collection of the artist; courtesy the artist; Commonwealth and Council, Los Angeles; and Labor, Mexico City

A selection of as-yet-untitled sculptures, 2019. Medium unknown, dimensions unknown. Collection of the artist; courtesy the artist; Commonwealth and Council, Los Angeles; and Labor, Mexico City

67 WALTER PRICE

Everything's connected, 2018. Acrylic on wood, 16 × 60 in. (40.6 × 152.4 cm).

Collection of the artist; courtesy the artist; Karma, New York; and Modern Institute, Glasgow

Sit some to the side for the shell end, 2018. Acrylic and collage on wood, 16 × 20 in. (40.6 × 50.8 cm). Collection of the artist; courtesy the artist; Karma, New York; and Modern Institute, Glasgow

The things that horse ourselves for uncertainty, 2018. Acrylic, gesso, and vinyl paint on canvas, 58 × 58 in. (147.3 × 147.3 cm). Collection of the artist; courtesy the artist; Karma, New York; and Modern Institute, Glasgow

Upgrayyed, 2018. Acrylic on wood, 20 × 16 in. (50.8 × 40.6 cm). Collection of the artist; courtesy the artist; Karma, New York; and Modern Institute, Glasgow

With the tranquility of cows lying in the meadows, 2018. Acrylic on wood, 16 × 20 in. (40.6 × 50.8 cm). Collection of the artist; courtesy the artist; Karma, New York; and Modern Institute, Glasgow

68 CARISSA RODRIGUEZ

The Maid, 2018. High-definition video, color, sound; 12:22 min. Collection of the artist; courtesy the artist and Karma International, Zurich and Los Angeles

69 PAUL MPAGI SEPUYA

Studio, 2017–18. With additional works by

Dicko Chan, James Garcia, Ariel Goldberg, Clay Kerrigan, Clifford Prince King, Giancarlo Montes Santangelo, Emerson Ricard, A. L. Steiner, Peter Tomka, and Derrick Woods-Morrow. Inkjet prints, various dimensions. Collection of the artist; courtesy the artist; Document, Chicago; Susanne Vielmetter Los Angeles Projects; and Team Gallery, New York

70 HEJI SHIN

Baby 1, 2016. Inkjet print, 23 ¼ × 30 ¹¹⁄₁₆ in. (59 × 78 cm). Collection of the artist; courtesy the artist; Reena Spaulings Fine Art, New York; and Galerie Bernhard, Zurich

Baby 6, 2016. Inkjet print, 30 ¹¹⁄₁₆ × 23 ¼ in. (78 × 59 cm). Collection of the artist; courtesy the artist; Reena Spaulings Fine Art, New York; and Galerie Bernhard, Zurich

Baby 7, 2016. Inkjet print, 30 ¹¹⁄₁₆ × 23 ¼ in. (78 × 59 cm). Collection of the artist; courtesy the artist; Reena Spaulings Fine Art, New York; and Galerie Bernhard, Zurich

Baby 10, 2016. Inkjet print, 23 ¼ × 30 ¹¹⁄₁₆ in. (59 × 78 cm). Collection of the artist; courtesy the artist; Reena Spaulings Fine Art, New York; and Galerie Bernhard, Zurich

Baby 16, 2017. Inkjet print, 30 ¹¹⁄₁₆ × 23 ¼ in. (78 × 59 cm). Collection of the artist; courtesy the artist;

Reena Spaulings Fine Art, New York; and Galerie Bernhard, Zurich

K W1, 2018. Inkjet print, dimensions unknown. Collection of the artist; courtesy the artist; Reena Spaulings Fine Art, New York; and Galerie Bernhard, Zurich

71 DIANE SIMPSON

Jabot (triplet), 2018. Fiberboard, colored pencil, linen, steel, oil stain, wood, and fabric, 43 × 33 × 21 in. (109.2 × 83.8 × 5.1 cm), fabric lengths variable. Collection of the artist; courtesy the artist; Corbett vs. Dempsey, Chicago; JTT, New York; and Herald St, London

Jabot (with pauldrons), 2018. Aluminum tube, iron pipe fittings, foam board, linen, crayon, mahogany, and screws, 51 × 39 × 20 in. (129.5 × 99.1 × 50.8 cm). Collection of the artist; courtesy the artist; Corbett vs. Dempsey, Chicago; JTT, New York; and Herald St, London

Lambrequin and Peplum, 2017. Painted fiberboard, crayon on polyester, and copper tacks, 109 × 50 × 31 in. (276.9 × 127 × 78.7 cm). Collection of the artist; courtesy the artist; Corbett vs. Dempsey, Chicago; JTT, New York; and Herald St, London

Peplum III, 2014. Fiberboard, wood stain, polyester, gessoed linen, colored pencil, and crayon, 42 × 19 × 11 in. (106.7 × 48.3 × 27.9 cm). Private collection

Peplum IV, 2015. Aluminum, steel, rivets, and enamel, 48 × 29 × 18 in. (121.9 × 73.7 × 45.7 cm). Collection of the artist; courtesy the artist; Corbett vs. Dempsey, Chicago; JTT, New York; and Herald St, London

Robe, 1986. Wood stain and colored pencil on fiberboard, 80 × 86 × 42 in. (203.2 × 218.4 × 106.7 cm). Collection of the artist; courtesy the artist; Corbett vs. Dempsey, Chicago; JTT, New York; and Herald St, London

Valance and Peplum, 2017. Enamel on fiberboard and wood, vintage ceiling tin, and steel, 89 × 96 × 5 ¾ in. (226.1 × 243.8 × 14.6 cm). Collection of the artist; courtesy the artist; Corbett vs. Dempsey, Chicago; JTT, New York; and Herald St, London

Window Dressing: Background 4, Apron VI, 2003/2007. Foam board, wood, enamel, wallpaper, marker, spunbond polyester, aluminum, and mylar fabric, 104 × 120 × 28 in. (264.2 × 304.8 × 71.1 cm). Collection of the artist; courtesy the artist; Corbett vs. Dempsey, Chicago; JTT, New York; and Herald St, London

72 MARTINE SYMS

She Mad: Comfort Zone, 2019. Multichannel video installation, color, sound; run time unknown, overall dimensions variable. Collection of the artist; courtesy the artist;

Bridget Donahue, New York; and Sadie Coles, London

73 KYLE THURMAN

Suggested Occupation 3, 2016. Charcoal and pastel on paper in artist's frame, 40 ⅝ × 43 ⅝ in. (103.2 × 110.8 cm). Whitney Museum of American Art, New York, Gift of Alex Glauber

Suggested Occupation 4, 2016. Charcoal and pastel on paper, 41 ⅜ × 27 ⅞ in. (105.1 × 70.8 cm). Whitney Museum of American Art, New York, Gift of Alex Glauber

Suggested Occupation 9, 2017–18. Acrylic, charcoal, encaustic, and pastel on seamless paper in artist's frame, 23 ⅝ × 28 ¼ in. (60 × 71.8 cm). Collection of the artist

Suggested Occupation 22, 2018. Charcoal, colored pencil, marker, oil, and pastel on seamless paper in artist's frame, 42 ⁷⁄₁₆ × 44 ½ in. (107.8 × 113 cm). Collection of Sascha S. Bauer

Suggested Occupation 29 (Career Day), 2019. Acrylic, charcoal, glass, oil, pastel, and vinyl paint on seamless paper in artist's frame, 35 ¾ × 33 in. (90.8 × 83.8 cm). Collection of the artist

Suggested Occupation 30, 2019. Charcoal, ink, and pastel on seamless paper in artist's frame, 75 × 48 in. (190.5 × 121.9 cm). Collection of the artist

Suggested Occupation 31 (trying to remember a voice), 2019. Acrylic, charcoal, colored pencil, oil, and pastel on seamless paper in artist's frame, 40 × 69 ½ in. (101.6 × 176.5 cm). Collection of the artist

74 MARIANA VALENCIA

Futurity, 2019. Performance. Courtesy the artist

75 AGUSTINA WOODGATE

National Times, 2016. Clocks, hardware, and sanding twigs, dimensions variable. Collection of the artist; courtesy the artist and Spinello Projects, Miami

As of January 31, 2019

Whitney Museum
of American Art
Staff

Hakimah Abdul-Fattah
Jay Abu-Hamda
Hunter Adams
Stephanie Adams
Liz Afre
Aqsa Ahmad
Haley Allen
Justin Allen
Adrienne Alston
Casey Amspacher
Sofie Andersen
Dwayne Anderson
Karly Anderson
Sofa Answar
Jason Anzovino
Marilou Aquino
Morgan Arenson
David Armacost
Moboluwaji Arogbo
I. D. Aruede
Joshua Ascherman
Josue Avendano
Wendy Barbee-Lowell
Bernadette Beauchamp
Teo Beauchamp
Charles Beck Jr.
Michael Beiser
Deja Belardo
Harry Benjamin
Karen Bergman
Caitlin Bermingham
Christina Bernstein
Danielle Bias
Isabella Biberaj
Stephanie Birmingham
Ivy Blackman
Hillary Blass
Andes Blitz-Torres
Brian Block
Richard Bloes
Alexandra Bono
Eric Bouldin
Rebecca Boxbaum
Robert Brackett
Holly Brennan
David Breslin
Michael Brogan
Colin Brooks
Lisa Brown
Veronica Brown

Algernon Brown
Douglas Burnham
Rosalee Burns
Shavonne Burns
Ronald Burrell
Garfield Burton
Anne Byrd
Heddy Cabanas
Elizabeth Cabot
Natali Cabrera
Pablo Caines
Savannah Campbell
Margaret Cannie
Jane Carey
Amanda Carrasco
Leslie Castaneda
Sunil Chaddha
Samuel Chang
David Chapman
Derrick Charles
Jose Chavez
Andrew Chee
Inde Cheong
Max Chester
Margaret Katherine
   Cheyne
Claire Cheyney-Henry
Virginia Chow
Kai Chuan
Jennifer Ciarleglio
Ramon Cintron
Mariam Cisse
Randy Clark
Ron Clark
Andrew Cone
Terrel Cooper
Errol Coore
Brenna Cothran
Heather Cox
Kimberly Craig
David Crane
David Critides
Caroline David
Amanda Davis
Lawrence DeBlasio
Monserrate DeLeon
Amalia Delgado Hodges
Margo Delidow
Donna De Salvo
Hilary Devaney
Masseny Diakite
Jasmine Diggs
Nicholas DiLeonardi
Lauren DiLoreto
John Donovan

Marisa Donovan
Louis DosReis
Isabelle Dow
Kate Dowd
Lisa Dowd
Anita Duquette
Kasim Earl
Adrienne Edwards
Joanna Epstein
Cesar Espinoza
Alvin Eubanks
Reid Farrington
Joel Fear
Natasha Fearon
Carly Fischer
Seth Fogelman
Jackie Foster
Karissa Francis
Samuel Franks
Denis Frederick
Murlin Frederick
Lauri Freedman
Kyle Freeman
Annie French
Levi Friedman
Dante Fumagalli
Madaline Gardner
Donald Garlington
Anthony Gennari
Ronnie George
Jennie Goldstein
Daniela Gomez
Ellen Gompers
Saleem Gondal
Amber Gonzalez
Jeanette Gonzalez
Lucas Gonzalez
Alex Goodship
Hilary Greenbaum
Steven Grimaldi
Marcela Guerrero
Mark Guinto
Peter Guss
Stewart Hacker
Rita Hall
Adrian Hardwicke
Tara Hart
Greta Hartenstein
Barbara Haskell
Andrew Hawkes
Maura Heffner
Todd Heim
Dina Helal
Elizabeth Henschen
Alana Hernandez

Lawrence Hernandez
Jennifer Heslin
Megan Heuer
Albert Hicks IV
Rujeko Hockley
Ann Holcomb
Kimberly Hollely
Nicholas S. Holmes
Michael Honigsberg
Abigail Hoover
Jacob Horn
David Huerta
Sarah Humphreville
Beth Huseman
Chrissie Iles
Gina Im
Malcolm Jackson
Zoe Jackson
Carlos Jacobo
Patricia James
Armando Garcia Jaramillo
Spivey Jean
Darnell Jenkins
Jesse Jenkins
Michael Jensen
Nancy Joyce
Delaney Jungers
Rory Keeley
Caroline Kelley
Joshua Kessler
Chris Ketchie
Elena Gonzalez Ketelsen
Safwan Khan
David Kiehl
Patricia Kilbride
Thomas Killie
Elizabeth Knowlton
Ramsay Kolber
Tom Kraft
Margaret Kross
Summer Krounbi
Melinda Lang
Amanda Langworthy
Martha LaRose
Erin Law
Cathy Lebowitz
Sang Soo Lee
Joseph Leib
Dani Lencioni
Jen Leventhal
Danielle Levy
Christopher Lew
Benjamin Lipnick
Ruth Lizardi
Kelley Loftus

Maude Loggin
Mark Loiacono
Robert Lomblad
Kelly Long
Brianna Lowndes
Ryan Macon
Doug Madill
Hector Maldonado
Claire Malloy
Jessica Man
Carol Mancusi-Ungaro
Louis Manners
Gregory Marcus
Rachel Marino
Anna Martin
Madison Martin
Miguel Martinez
Heather Maxson
Caitlin McKee
James McKnight
Alexander Mejia
Bridget Mendoza
Mathieu Menten
Ariel Mercado
Graham Miles
David Miller
Christie Mitchell
Matthew Moon
Lorryn Moore
Nicole Morales
John Moran
Michael Moriah
Michael Morrissey
Victor Moscoso
Lara Moynagh
Maggie Mugharbel
Seamus Mullin
Elaine Muniz
Amelia Murcott
Meer Musa
Micah Musheno
Zabie Mustafa
Eleonora Nagy
Vishal Narang
Daniel Nascimento
David Neary
Ruben Negron
Robert Neitzer
Randy Nelson
Tracey Newsome
Katy Newton
Jonathan Nicholson
Rachel Ninomiya
Carlos Noboa
Jaison O'Blenis

Nicolas Ochart
Lindsey O'Connor
Dennis Orlov
Nelson Ortiz
Ahmed Osman
Xiomara Ossorio
Eloise Owens
Nicky Ozir
Luis Padilla
Kimie Page
Jessica Palinski
Jane Panetta
Joseph Parise
Max Parry-McDonell
Christiane Paul
Jessica Pepe
Natasha Pereira
Roberto Perez
Kara Pernicano
Jason Phillips
Laura Phipps
Angelo Pikoulas
Elizabeth Plahn
Raymond Podulka
Lindsay Pollock
Carla Posner
Kathryn Potts
Eric Preiss
Eliza Proctor
Laura Protzel
Andrea Provvido
Melissa Pujols
Eric Pullett
Vincent Punch
Christy Putnam
Emma Quaytman
Lauren Quesada
Dylan Radcliff
Alina Ramirez
Julie Rega
Amanda Reichert
Andrea Gomez Resendiz
Gregory Reynolds
Omari Richards
Yevgeniy Riftin
Felix Rivera
Gabriella Robles
Melissa Robles
Enrique Rocha
Manuel Rodriguez
Yosmerilyn Rodriguez
Gina Rogak
Clara Rojas-Sebesta
Justin Romeo
Sara Romo

Antonio Rosa
Joshua Rosenblatt
Amy Roth
Ricki Rothchild
Scott Rothkopf
Dominick Roumo
Janet Rucker
Emily Russell
Angelina Salerno
Laura Salomon
Leo Sanchez
Awa Sanogo
Ximena Santiago
Galina Sapozhnikova
Lynn Schatz
Meryl Schwartz
Peter Scott
David Selimoski
Aliza Sena
Jason Senquiz
Dumitru Sersea
Stephen Sewell
Joseph Shepherd
Leslie Sheridan
Elisabeth Sherman
Molly Shimko
Sadia Shirazi
Adelina Simmonds
Dyeemah Simmons
Rachel Sipser
Matt Skopek
Eileen Skyers
George Smith
Roxanne Smith
Joel Snyder
Karl Snyder
Michele Snyder
Stephen Soba
Elizabeth Soland
Barbi Spieler
Carrie Springer
Mark Steigelman
Minerva Stella
Jennifer MacNair Stitt
Betty Stolpen
Emilie Sullivan
Jeeyoung Sung
Denis Suspitsyn
Elisabeth Sussman
Haley Tanenbaum
Jocelyn Tarbox
Melanie Taylor
Joseph Teliha
Ellen Tepfer
Ashley Thimm

Latasha Thomas
Ariana Thrasher
Zoe Tippl
Rebekah Torres
Ana Torres-Hurtado
Ambika Trasi
Stacey Traunfeld
Beth Turk
Lauren Turner
Matthew Vega
Eric Vermilion
Nancy Viglione
Billie Rae Vinson
Igor Vroublevsky
Farris Wahbeh
Rebecca Walsh
Beatrix Walter
Jenyu Wang
Adam D. Weinberg
Alexandra Wheeler
Anne Wheeler
Clemence White
Ashanti White-Wallace
Olivia Wilcox
Andrew Wojtek
Sasha Wortzel
Lori Wright-Huertas
Ally Xing
Christy Yanis
Hilary Yeh
Lauren Young
Madison Zalopany
Sefkia Zekiroski
Jessica Zhao
Lily Zhou
Alex Zylka

As of November 30, 2018

Photography and Reproduction Credits

2 Images courtesy the artist and Spinello Projects, Miami; photographs by Eddie Arroyo. **3** Image courtesy the artist; boychild; Clearing, New York and Brussels; and Carlos/Ishikawa, London; photograph by Alexander Addington-White. **4** Image courtesy the artist and High Art, New York. **5** (top) Image courtesy MoMA PS1, Queens, NY; photograph by Charles Roussel; (bottom) Photograph by Andrew Kist. **6** © Africa Film Society. **8** Image courtesy the artist and Gavin Brown's enterprise, New York and Rome; photograph by Thomas Müller. **9** (top) Photographs by Jason Mandella; © The Kitchen; (bottom left) Photograph by Pablo Enriquez; © MoMA PS1; (bottom right) Photograph by Photo Solutions; © Art Dubai 2017. **10** Image courtesy the artist and Lomex, New York. **11** Images courtesy the artist; Galerie Eva Presenhuber, New York and Zurich; and Rodolphe Janssen, Brussels. **12** Photographs by Akasha Rabut; © America 2018. **13** Image courtesy the artist and Chapter NY, New York. **16** Photographs by Lance Brewer. **17** Image courtesy the artist and Susanne Vielmetter Los Angeles Projects. **18** Image courtesy the artist and 47 Canal, New York; photograph by Joerg Lohse. **19** Image courtesy the artist and Haines Gallery, San Francisco. **20** (top) Image courtesy the artist and Monique Meloche Gallery, Chicago; photograph by Brendan Leo Merea; (bottom) Image courtesy the artist and Monique Meloche Gallery, Chicago; photograph by Wendy Ploger. **21** Images courtesy FIERCE, New Neutral Zone, and Paper Tiger Television. **22** Photograph by Marcus Fischer. **24** Image courtesy the artist and Bureau, New York. **27** Image courtesy Sikkema Jenkins & Co., New York; Kavi Gupta, Chicago; and Roberts Projects, Los Angeles; photograph by Jason Wyche. **28** Image courtesy the artist; Meliksetian | Briggs, West Hollywood, CA; and David Lewis, New York; © the artist and Meliksetian | Briggs, 2018. **29** Photograph by Reed Hutchinson. **32** Image courtesy the artist and Jessica Silverman Gallery, San Francisco; photograph by John Wilson White. **34** Images courtesy the artist and Beach Sessions Dance Series; (top) Photograph by Grant Slater; (bottom) photograph by Justin Chao. **35** Image courtesy the artist; Rodeo, London and Piraeus, Greece; and Carlier | Gebauer, Berlin; photograph by Gunter Lepkowski. **36** Image courtesy the artist and Tilton Gallery, New York; photograph by Adam Reich. **39** Images courtesy the artist and White Space, Beijing; photographs by Christian Liebermann. **40** Images

courtesy the artist; **47** Canal, New York; and Modern Art, London. **41** Photograph by Walter Wlodarczyk. **42** (top) Image courtesy the artist and Essex Street, New York; photograph by Ben Tran; (bottom) Image courtesy the artist and Essex Street, New York; photograph by Jason Mandella. **43** Image courtesy the artist and Jack Hanley Gallery, New York; photograph by Brad Farwell. **44** Image courtesy the artist and Luhring Augustine, New York; photograph by Farzad Owrang; © Simone Leigh. **45** Photograph by Daniel Lind-Ramos. **46** Image courtesy the Denver Art Museum. **47** Images courtesy the artist; Baltic Center for Contemporary Art, Gateshead; and Simon Lee Gallery, London. **48** Image courtesy the artist; Clearing, New York and Brussels; and David Kordansky Gallery, Los Angeles; photograph by Marten Elder. **49** (top) Image courtesy the artist and Company Gallery, New York; photograph by Constance Mensh; (bottom) Image courtesy the artist and Company Gallery, New York. **50** Image courtesy the artist and Company Gallery, New York. **51** Photograph by Stephen Pitkin/Pitkin Studio; © 2018 Joe Minter/Artists Rights Society (ARS), New York. **52** Image courtesy the artist and James Fuentes Gallery, New York; photograph by Jason Mandella. **53** Photograph by Rita Taylor. **54** Image courtesy the artist and Topic Studios, New York. **55** Photograph by Dario Lasagni. **56** Image courtesy the Kitchen, New York; photograph by Paula Court; © Paula Court. **57** Image courtesy NIAD Art Center, Richmond, CA; Adams and Ollman, Portland, OR; and JTT, New York. **58** Images courtesy the artist and Société, Berlin; photographs by Gustavo Murillo. **59** Image courtesy the artist and Gladstone Gallery, New York and Brussels. **60** Photographs by Timo Ohler. **63** Image courtesy the artist; Corvi-Mora, London; and Sikkema Jenkins & Co, New York; photograph by Matt Grubb. **64** Photograph by Rolando Meléndez. **65** Images courtesy the artist and 47 Canal, New York. **66** (bottom) Photograph by Elliott Racca. **67** Image courtesy the artist and Commonwealth and Council, Los Angeles. **68** Image courtesy the artist and Karma, New York; photograph by Thomas Mueller. **70** Image courtesy the artist; Team Gallery, New York; Document Gallery, Chicago; and Susan Vielmetter Los Angeles Projects. **72** Image courtesy the artist; Corbett vs. Dempsey, Chicago; JTT, New York; and Herald St, London; photograph by Tom Van Eynde.

73 (top) Image courtesy the artist;
Bridget Donahue, New York; and
Sadie Coles, London; photograph by
Mark Blower; (bottom) Image
courtesy the artist; Bridget Donahue,
New York; and Sadie Coles, London;
photograph by Brian Forrest.
74 Photograph by Joerg Lohse.
75 (top) Photograph by Ian Douglass;
(bottom) Image courtesy the artist
and the Hirshhorn Museum and
Sculpture Garden, Washington,
DC. 76 Image courtesy the artist
and Spinello Projects, Miami;
photograph by Jesus Petroccini. (top
left, middle, bottom) Photographs by
Eddie Arroyo; (top right) Photographs by MeccaAKAGrimo.
116 (top right) Image courtesy the
artist and Nick Sethi; photograph
by Nick Sethi. 117 (top) Photographs
by Phillip Huang; (bottom left)
Photograph by Rory Mulhere.
121 (top left) Photograph by Ian
Douglas; (top right) Photograph
by Drew Kaufman; (bottom)
Photograph by Sam Richardson.
126–27 Images courtesy Golden
Gate Kindergarten Association.
136 (top right) RIBA Collections;
image courtesy the Royal Institute
of British Architects. 142 (top left)
Collection of National Portrait
Gallery, Smithsonian Institution,
Washington, DC; image courtesy
National Portrait Gallery,
Smithsonian Institution; (top right)
Collection of the Metropolitan
Museum of Art, New York.
147 Photograph by Francesco
Cavallari. 150 (top) Images courtesy
the artist and Monique Meloche
Gallery, Chicago; renderings by
Norman Kelley Architects; (bottom)
Images courtesy the artist and
Monique Meloche Gallery, Chicago;
photographs by RCH. 151 (top,
bottom left) Images courtesy the
artist and Monique Meloche Gallery,
Chicago; photographs by Erato
Tzavara; (right) Images courtesy the
artist and Monique Meloche Gallery,
Chicago; photograph by Milo Bosh.
152–53 Images courtesy FIERCE,
New Neutral Zone, and Paper Tiger
Television. 154–55 Photographs by
Marcus Fischer. 156 (middle left)
Image courtesy Forensic Architec-
ture and Dr. Salvador Navarro-
Martinez. 158–59 Images courtesy
the artist and Bureau, New York.
161 (top right) Photograph by Nep
Sidhu; (bottom) Photograph by
Merritt Johnson. 164 (top left)
Collection of the Minneapolis
Institute of Art; (top right, bottom)
Collection of the Denver Art
Museum; © Denver Art Museum.
167 Photographs by Todd Gray.
168 (top left) Photograph by David
Fenton; (bottom) Photograph
by Andy Black. 171 (top right)
Collection of Historic Richmond
Town, Staten Island, NY. 174 (top)

Courtesy the artist and Jessica
Silverman Gallery; photograph by
Corine Vermeulen. 179 (top right)
Image courtesy the artist and Signal,
Brooklyn; photograph by Kyle
Clairmont Jacques; (middle)
Photograph by Daniela Amdan;
(bottom) Image courtesy the artist
and the Artist's Institute, New York;
photograph by Christopher Aque.
182 (top left) Photograph by Davida
Nemeroff; (top right) Photograph by
Tomashi Jackson; (bottom)
Photograph by Omar Jackson Sr.
183 (bottom) Photograph by Tomashi
Jackson. 186 (top left) Image courtesy
Wikimedia Commons; (top right)
Image courtesy National Anthropol-
ogy Archives, Washington, DC;
© Smithsonian Institution; (bottom
right) Photograph by Edward Curtis.
187 (top left) Photograph by Jackson
Polys. 192–93 Photographs by
Autumn Knight. 194 Image courtesy
@chronicillnessmemes. 195 (top
right) Photograph by Ariana Beedie,
Face A Face Collective; (bottom)
Collection of Tom Olin; Image
used by permission; © Tom Olin.
200 (top, bottom left) Photographs
by Daniel Lind-Ramos; (bottom
right) Photograph by Dennis Mario
Rivera. 201 Photograph by Daniel
Lind-Ramos. 202–03 Images
courtesy Video Data Bank, www
.vdb.org, School of the Art Institute
of Chicago; © James Luna. 204 (top
left) Photograph by Eric N. Mack;
(top right) Photograph by Jamie
Stoker; (bottom) Image courtesy
the artist and Morán Morán, Los
Angeles; photograph by Matt
Grubb. 205 (top) Image courtesy the
artist and Totokaelo. 206 (top right)
Collection of the Whitney Museum
of American Art, New York.
218 (top) Photograph by the Texas
Department of Criminal Justice;
(bottom) Photograph by Chioke
Nassor. 219 (top) Photograph by
Daniel Patterson. 222 (bottom left)
Photograph by Minsun Sohn.
224 Images courtesy NIAD Art
Center, Richmond, CA; Adams and
Ollman, Portland, OR; and JTT,
New York. 225 Images courtesy
NIAD Art Center, Richmond, CA;
Adams and Ollman, Portland, OR;
and JTT, New York; (bottom)
Photographs by R. J. Mickelson.
234 (middle right) Photograph by
Aran Tharp. 236 (top left) Collection
of the Whitney Museum of American
Art, New York; (top right) © Tate,
London 2018; (bottom) Image
courtesy of the George Eastman
Museum. 237 (top left) Collection
of the National Gallery of Art,
Washington DC; (bottom middle)
Collection of the Metropolitan
Museum of Art, New York. 238 (top
left) Photograph by nibia pastrana
santiago; (middle left) Photograph
by Andrea Canepa; (middle right)

Photography by El Weather Bureau
participant; (bottom) Photograph
by David Bergé. 239 (top left)
Photograph by David Bergé; (top
right) Photograph by nibia pastrana
santiago. 244 (bottom left)
Collection of the Los Angeles
County Museum of Art; image
courtesy Commonwealth and
Council, Los Angeles; photograph
by Nephew Garnett; (bottom right)
Collection of Beate and Christopher
Chee; image courtesy Commonwealth and Council, Los Angeles;
photograph by Nephew Garnett.
245 Photographs by Gala Porras-
Kim. 252 (top) Collection of Musée
d'Orsay, Paris. 253 (top right)
© Tom of Finland Foundation/
Artists Rights Society (ARS), New
York. 255 (bottom left) Image
courtesy SoVintagePatterns.com.
260 Photographs by Alex Escalante.
261 (bottom right) Image courtesy
the Hirshhorn Museum and Sculpture Garden, Washington, DC.

This catalogue was produced on the occasion of the 2019 Whitney Biennial, held at the Whitney Museum of American Art, New York, May 17–September 22, 2019, and organized by Jane Panetta and Rujeko Hockley, with Ramsay Kolber.

The film program was organized by Maori Karmael Holmes, Sky Hopinka, and Matt Wolf.

The performance program was organized by Jane Panetta, Rujeko Hockley, and Greta Hartenstein.

The exhibition was coordinated by Maura Heffner and Lindsey O'Connor.

Whitney Biennial 2019 is presented by

TIFFANY & CO.

Major support is provided by The Rosenkranz Foundation and the Whitney's National Committee.

Generous support is provided by Lise and Michael Evans; and the John R. Eckel, Jr. Foundation.

Significant support is provided by 2019 Biennial Committee Co-Chairs: Beth Rudin DeWoody, Bob Gersh, Miyoung Lee, and Fred Wilson; and 2019 Biennial Committee members: Ashley Leeds and Christopher Harland, Diane and Adam E. Max, Annette and Paul Smith, Bill Block, the Debra and Jeffrey Geller Family Foundation, Rebecca and Martin Eisenberg, Amanda and Glenn Fuhrman, Barbara and Michael Gamson, Marjorie and James D. Kuhn, Kourosh Larizadeh and Luis Pardo, Melanie Shorin and Greg S. Feldman, and Dora and Cranford Stoudemire; Further Forward Foundation, the Kapadia Equity Fund, The Keith Haring Foundation Exhibition Fund, Katie and Amnon Rodan, and Sotheby's.

Additional support is provided by the Consulate General of the Federal Republic of Germany and the Consulate General of Sweden in New York.

Funding is also provided by special Biennial endowments created by Melva Bucksbaum, Emily Fisher Landau, Leonard A. Lauder, and Fern and Lenard Tessler.

Curatorial research and travel for this exhibition were funded by an endowment established by Rosina Lee Yue and Bert A. Lies, Jr., MD.

Whitney Museum of American Art
99 Gansevoort Street
New York, NY 10014
whitney.org

Distributed by
Yale University Press
302 Temple Street
P.O. Box 209040
New Haven, CT 06520-9040
yalebooks.com/art

Printed and bound
in the United States
10 9 8 7 6 5 4 3 2 1

ISBN 978-0-300-24275-1
ISSN 1043-3260

This publication was produced by the publications department at the Whitney Museum of American Art, New York: Beth A. Huseman, director of publications; Jennifer MacNair Stitt, editor; Beth Turk, editor; and Jacob Horn, editorial coordinator.

Project manager
Elizabeth Levy

Editor
Domenick Ammirati

Design
Common Name

Production
Nerissa Dominguez Vales
and Sue Medlicott,
The Production Department

Typesetting
Julie Allred,
BW&A Books, Inc.

Proofreader
Polly Watson

Printing and binding
Meridian Printing,
East Greenwich, RI

Separations
Altaimage, New York